MINNESOTA

SOUTHERN COVERAGE

COVERED IN THE NORTHEASTERN ALL-OUTDOORS ATLAS

COVERED IN THE CENTRAL & NORTHWEST ALL-OUTDOORS ATLAS

N

Minnesota Southern Coverage

Southern Minnesota all-outdoors ATLAS
by Sportsman's Connection

Editor and Publisher *Jim Billig*
Managing Editor *Todd Whitesel*
Senior Editor *Joe Shead*
Editorial Assistant/Writer *Cody Gilbert*
Creative & Production Director *Kurt Mazurek*
Production Coordinator *Shelly Wisniewski*
Page Design/Layout *Julie Mazurek*
Senior Cartographers/GIS Specialists *Eric McPhee, Dave Yapel*
Cartographers/GIS Specialists *Paul Howard, Joe Verdegan*
Senior Cartographer *Linda Crandall*
Information Systems Manager *Jon Fiskness*
Information Specialists *Sean Billig, Daine Billmark*
Research *Scott Mickelson*

SPORTSMAN'S® connection

ISBN 1-885010-43-5

Sportsman's Connection
1423 N. Eighth St., Superior, Wisconsin 54880
800-777-7461
www.scmaps.com

READER'S GUIDE -Getting the most from your All-outdoors Atlas

We are pleased to present the first edition of the *Sportsman's Connection All-outdoors Atlas*. Take a few minutes to thumb through the pages and you'll see that this is no ordinary book of maps. The *All-Outdoors Atlas* is a complete guide to southern Minnesota's great outdoors, presenting helpful and useful information on your favorite activities, places, and facilities. But it's much more.

Unlike general road atlases or even back road state atlases, the *Sportsman's Connection All-outdoors Atlas* series are comprehensive, highly detailed, map books revealing the extraordinarily diverse and numerous opportunities for outdoor enthusiasts across the state. Presented within is activity-specific information, including maps, tables, charts, and more, to plan everything from an afternoon bike ride to an extended camping trip.

Each map page presents a highly detailed view of individual sections (quadrants) of southern Minnesota in rich, full color. Easy-to-read symbols and informative tables make it a snap to find the locations and facilities to enjoy your favorite outdoor activities including fishing, hunting, camping, golfing, wildlife watching, snowmobiling, cross-country and downhill skiing, and places such as state parks, state forests, wildlife management areas, wildlife refuges, and more.

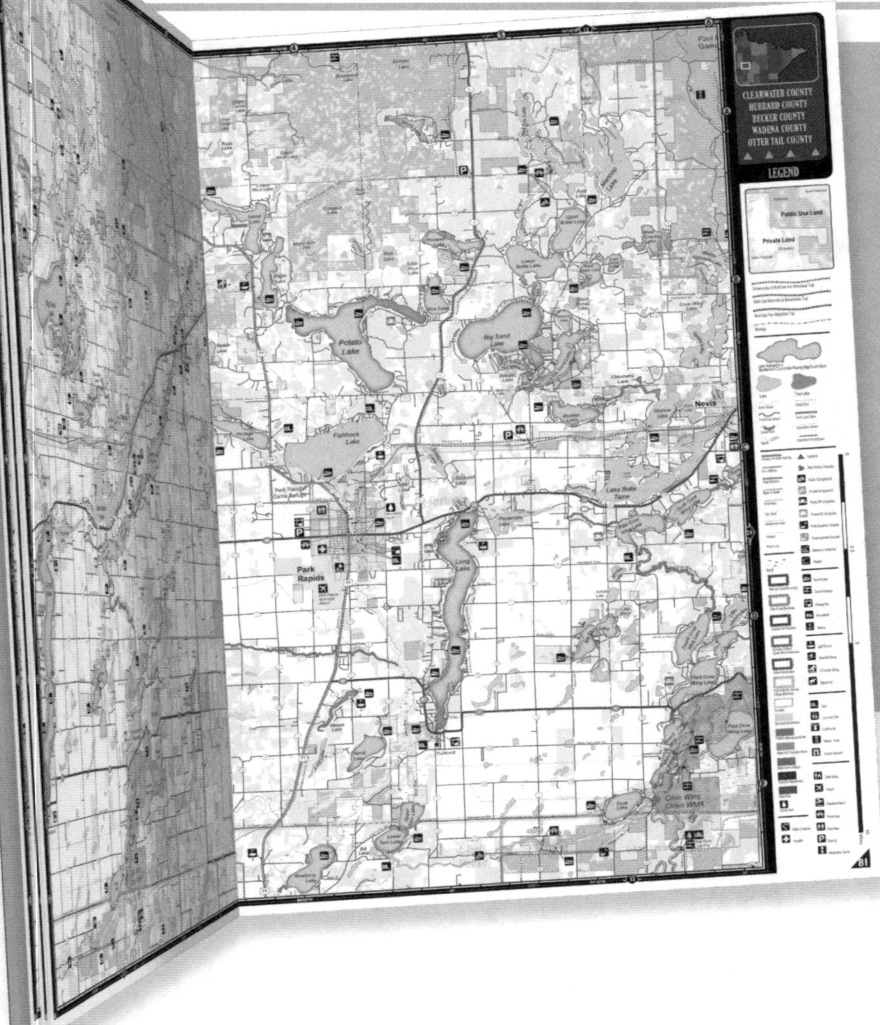

- **Handy legend** on every map page
- **Public vs. private** land
- **Forested vs. non-forested** land cover
- **Highlighted lakes** indicate fishing waters featured in Sportsman's Connection® Fishing Map Guides
- **Fishing streams and lakes** featured in fishing section tables
- **Wildlife Management Areas** with details included in hunting section tables
- **Waterfowl Production Areas** with location index
- **State Parks** with details and accommodations included in tables
- **State Forests** with details on trails and camping
- **Campgrounds and campsites**, both public and private
- **Forest and other service roads** not shown in even the most detailed back roads atlases
- **ALL Snowmobile trails** including state, local & spurs
- **ATV/Multi-use motorized trails**
- **Multi-use, non-motorized trails** for hiking & biking
- **Cross-country ski trails** cross referenced to tables
- **State canoe routes** including rapids classes
- **Golf Courses** with information table
- **Scientific Natural Areas** cross referenced to tables
- **Wildlife Viewing** and identification guide

The *Sportsman's Connection All-outdoors Atlas* offers excellent detail and refinement in a portable, information-filled guide utilizing a "lay-flat" binding to ensure pages stay open for ease of use.

Planning a trip to a state park? We've made it easy. An overview map on page 134 displays all the state parks within southern Minnesota. In addition, a comprehensive table is provided, presenting details such as park acreages, amenities, campsites, facilities, trails and much more. From the overview, one can navigate to specific Atlas pages, where each park and surrounding region is revealed in greater detail. It's the fun and easy way to plan your trip!

Atlas Design

Your *Sportsman's Connection Southern Minnesota All-outdoors Atlas* covers 29,242 square miles in Minnesota (34,192.5 total) at a detail of 1:100,000, the equivalent scale of 30- by 60-minute USGS quadrangle maps. A wall map mosaic of the region approximately 14¾ feet tall by 7½ feet wide can be created by joining the 94 pages of maps together from two books.

Map Grids & Coordinates

The beginning of the Atlas consists of map pages that include coordinates on the edges (1-6 on the top and A-E on the sides) that are referred to in the editorial tables and indexes as a location aid. Convenient page grids are included on Page 1 and on the back cover.

Latitude and longitude coordinates are fully labeled on the outside edges of each page at 10-minute intervals with mid-point minute labels every 5 minutes and tick marks for each minute in between. These coordinates can be input into a Global Positioning System (GPS) unit to determine one's exact location.

In addition, the Universal Transverse Mercator (UTM) grid is displayed at intervals of 10,000 meters on the outside edges of each map page. UTM is a coordinate system based on the meter that makes it possible to locate one's position anywhere, as every point on Earth now has a unique two-number address expressed in meters. To use the UTM grid, you can place a transparent grid overlay on the map to sub divide the grid, or you can draw lines on the map connecting corresponding ticks on opposite edges. The distances can be measured in meters at the map scale between any map point and the nearest grid lines to the south and west. The northing of the point is the value of the nearest grid line south of it plus its distance north of that line; its easting is the value of the nearest grid line west of it plus its distance east of that line (see sportsmansconnection.com/utm for further information).

Overview Maps, Editorial, Tables & Charts

Each editorial section begins with an overview map with page grids illustrating locations of opportunities for a given activity within the region. Each numbered location is tied to an adjacent information table that includes page numbers and coordinates for its location on the Atlas pages. For example, the overview map for the cross-country skiing section includes numbered locations of trail heads, which are referenced in the accompanying table that includes information on trail type, length, whether lighted, etc., along with map and grid coordinates to the location in the Atlas section. Conversely, these trail head locations are indicated on the map pages in the Atlas section by number, which allows the reader to cross-reference any given point back to the overview map and table in the editorial section. Alphabetical lists are included in the index beginning on the next page and continued in the back of the Atlas.

Public Lands

Federal, state and county lands that are open to the public depicted in this atlas are based upon information provided by various sources including government agencies. While Minnesota is blessed with a wealth of public land, portions of it may have restricted access and may occur adjacent to or partially within private land. Only a few areas are completely open to public use. Although state parks and county parks are composed almost entirely of public land, in many cases, private parcels also lie within those boundaries. State forests include significant tracts of private land. Parcels of at least 40 acres within those forests and county lands are illustrated as publicly accessible IF the majority of a parcel is indeed publicly owned. As such, there may be cases where as much as half of that land is actually in private hands. Verify access and/or restrictions with the local managing land agency as necessary. Please be careful to obey trespassing laws and ALWAYS respect the rights of private-property owners when venturing into areas with mixed ownership. Because private landholdings are constantly changing, as land parcels are bought and sold, we recommend consulting county plat books for the most current information on private land ownership, particularly those parcels too small to be meaningfully represented within these pages.

And though we have made substantial efforts to provide users with accurate and current information, we cannot guarantee that all sources and source materials are error-free. As such, this Atlas should be used in that spirit and, of course, that of the great outdoors.

INDEX OF PLACE NAMES

City, pg, coordinates

OTHER INDEXES

Other Alphabetical Indexes Beginning on Page 157

- Golf Courses
- Private Campgrounds
- Lakes
- Rivers & Streams
- Cross-Country Ski Trails
- Waterfowl Production Areas

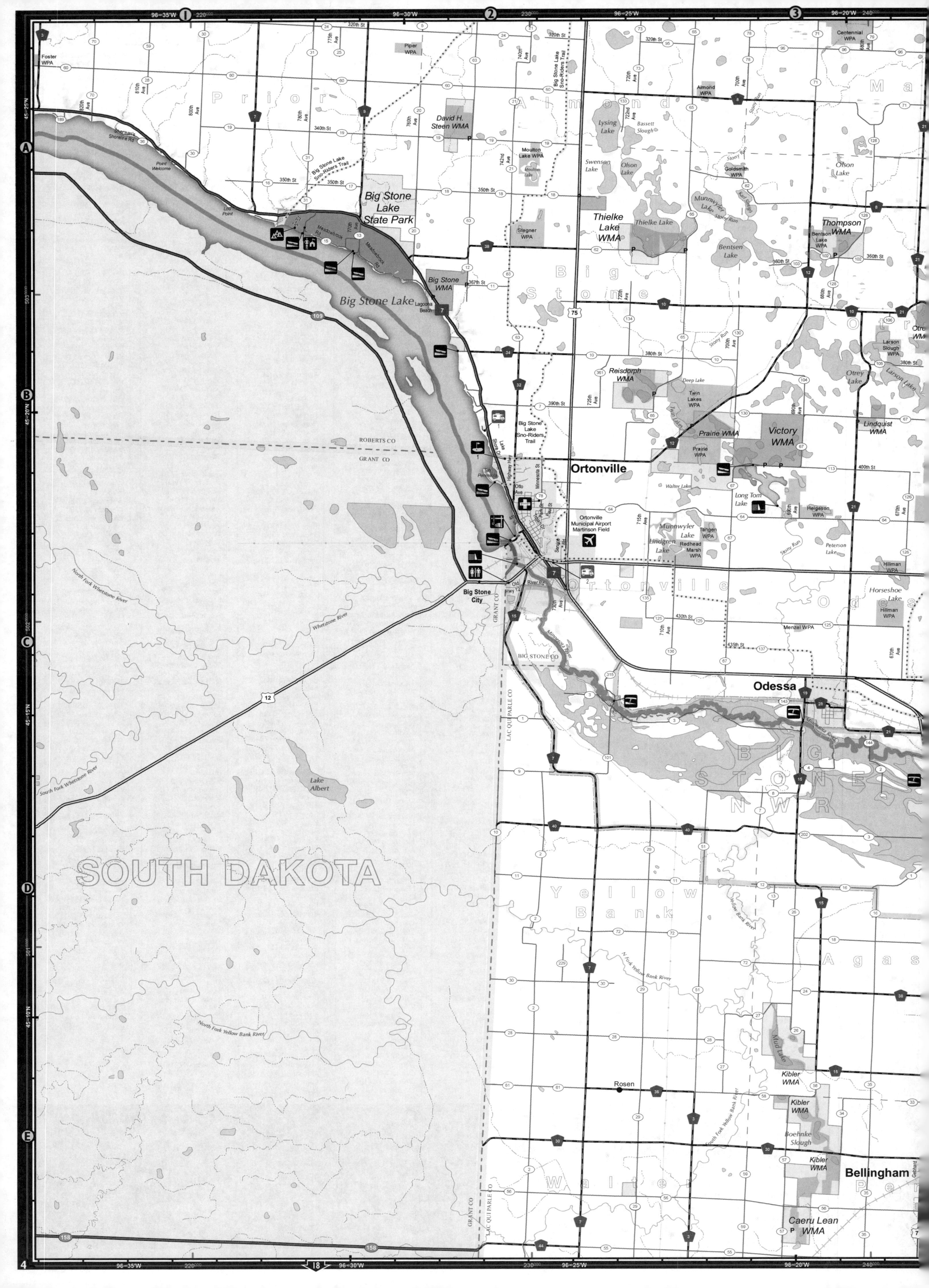

Foster WPA
Piper WPA
Centennial WPA
Almond WPA
David H. Steen WMA
Moulton Lake WPA
Lysing Lake
Bassett Slough
Swenson Lake
Olson Lake
Goldsmith WPA
Big Stone Lake Sno-Riders Trail
Point Welcome
Lac Point
Big Stone Lake State Park
Stegner WPA
Thielke Lake WMA
Thielke Lake
Munnwyler Lake
Bentsen Lake
Thompson WMA
Bentson Lake WPA
Big Stone WMA
Big Stone Lake
Lagoona Beach
Reisdorph WMA
Deep Lake
Twin Lakes WPA
Prairie WMA
Prairie WPA
Victory WMA
Larson Slough WPA
Otrey Lake
Larson Lake
Lindquist WMA
ROBERTS CO
GRANT CO
Ortonville
Walter Lakes
Long Tom Lake
Helgeson WPA
Ortonville Municipal Airport Martinson Field
Munnwyler Lake
Tangen WPA
Lindgren Lake
Redhead Marsh WPA
Peterson Lake
Hillman WPA
Horseshoe Lake
Big Stone City
North Fork Whetstone River
Whetstone River
Menzel WPA
BIG STONE CO
LAC QUI PARLE CO
Odessa
Minnesota River
BIG STONE NWR
South Fork Whetstone River
Lake Albert
SOUTH DAKOTA
Yellow Bank
Yellow Bank River
N Fork Yellow Bank River
North Fork Yellow Bank River
Mud Lake
Kibler WMA
Rosen
South Fork Yellow Bank River
Boehnke Slough
Bellingham
Caeru Lean WMA
Prior
Almond
Big Stone
Ortonville
Odessa
Yellow Bank
Agassiz
Walter
Perry

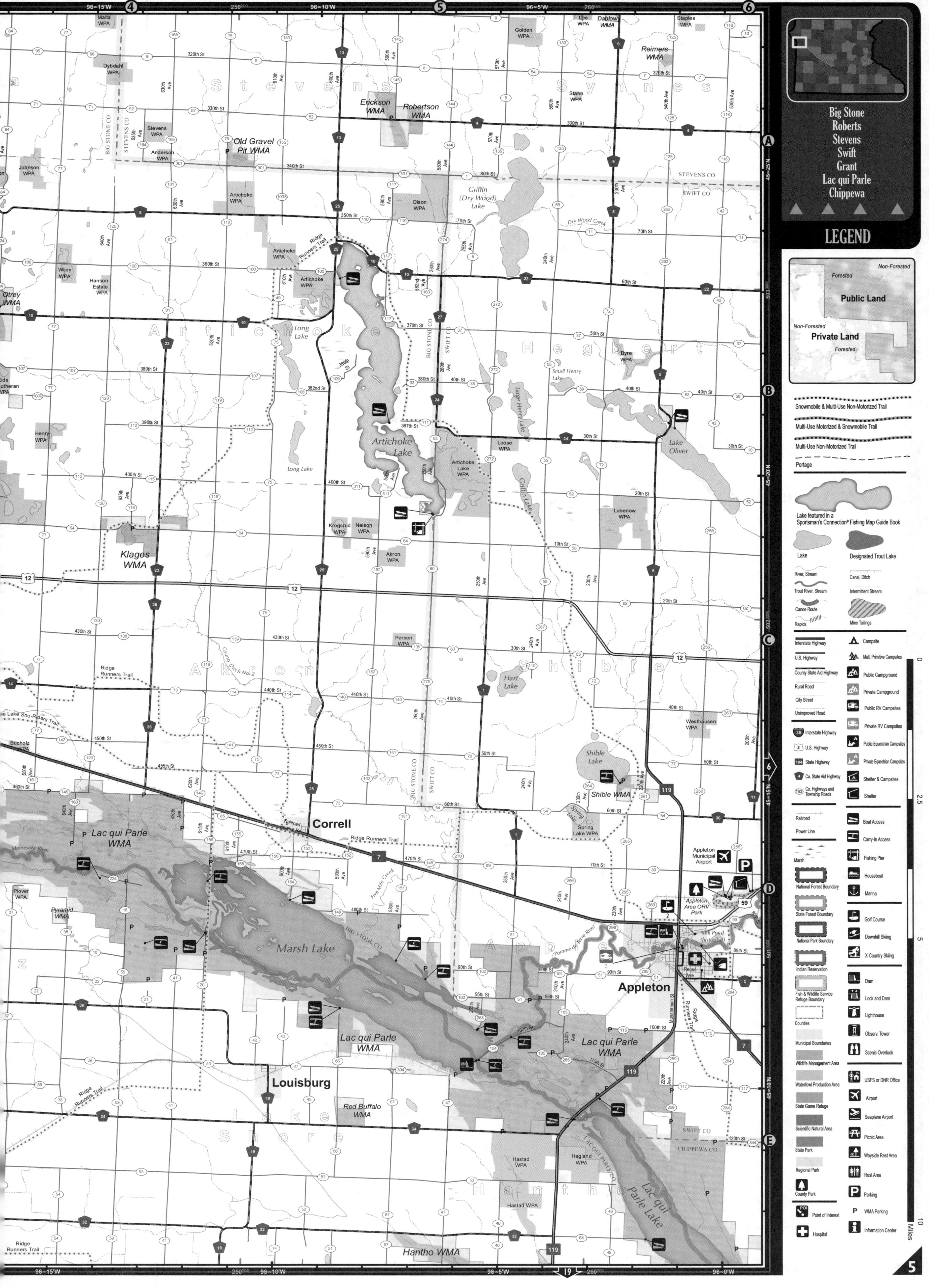

Big Stone
Roberts
Stevens
Swift
Grant
Lac qui Parle
Chippewa
LEGEND
Public Land
Private Land
Forested
Non-Forested
Snowmobile & Multi-Use Non-Motorized Trail
Multi-Use Motorized & Snowmobile Trail
Multi-Use Non-Motorized Trail
Portage
Lake featured in a Sportsman's Connection® Fishing Map Guide Book
Lake
Designated Trout Lake
River, Stream
Canal, Ditch
Trout River, Stream
Intermittent Stream
Canoe Route
Rapids
Mine Tailings
Interstate Highway
U.S. Highway
County State Aid Highway
Rural Road
City Street
Unimproved Road
Interstate Highway
U.S. Highway
State Highway
Co. State Aid Highway
Co. Highways and Township Roads
Railroad
Power Line
Marsh
National Forest Boundary
State Forest Boundary
National Park Boundary
Indian Reservation
Fish & Wildlife Service Refuge Boundary
Counties
Municipal Boundaries
Wildlife Management Area
Waterfowl Production Area
State Game Refuge
Scientific Natural Area
State Park
Regional Park
County Park
Point of Interest
Hospital
Campsite
Mult. Primitive Campsites
Public Campground
Private Campground
Public RV Campsites
Private RV Campsites
Public Equestrian Campsites
Private Equestrian Campsites
Shelter & Campsites
Shelter
Boat Access
Carry-In Access
Fishing Pier
Houseboat
Marina
Golf Course
Downhill Skiing
X-Country Skiing
Dam
Lock and Dam
Lighthouse
Observ. Tower
Scenic Overlook
USFS or DNR Office
Airport
Seaplane Airport
Picnic Area
Wayside Rest Area
Rest Area
Parking
WMA Parking
Information Center
Miles
Stevens
Synnes
Artichoke
Hegbert
Akron
Shible
Appleton
Lake Shore
Hantho
Artichoke Lake
Long Lake
Griffin (Dry Wood) Lake
Lake Oliver
Shible Lake
Hart Lake
Marsh Lake
Lac qui Parle Lake
Klages WMA
Shible WMA
Lac qui Parle WMA
Red Buffalo WMA
Hantho WMA
Old Gravel Pit WMA
Erickson WMA
Robertson WMA
Reimers WMA
Correll
Louisburg
Appleton
Appleton Municipal Airport
Appleton Area ORV Park
Ridge Runners Trail
STEVENS CO
SWIFT CO
BIG STONE CO
CHIPPEWA CO
96°15'W
96°10'W
96°5'W
96°0'W
45°25'N
45°20'N
45°15'N
45°10'N

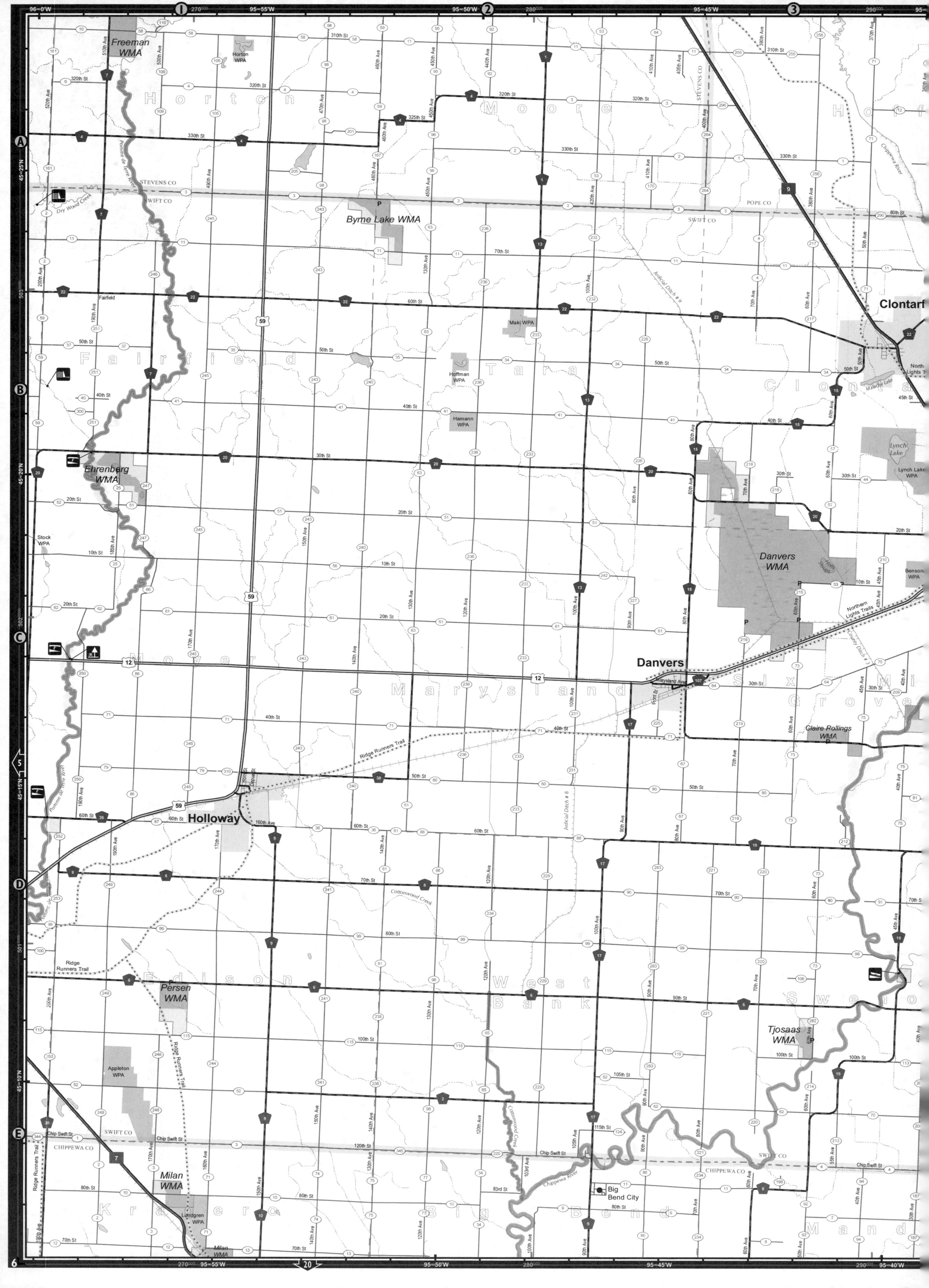
Freeman WMA
Horton WPA
Horton
Moore
Hoff
Byrne Lake WMA
STEVENS CO
SWIFT CO
POPE CO
Dry Wood Creek
Fairfield
Maki WPA
Hoffman WPA
Hamann WPA
Tara
Clontarf
North Lights Trail
Lynch Lake WPA
Ehrenberg WMA
Stock WPA
Danvers WMA
Benson WPA
Northern Lights Trails
Danvers
Maryland
Six Mile Grove
Claire Rollings WMA
Ridge Runners Trail
Holloway
Cottonwood Creek
Judicial Ditch # 8
Judicial Ditch # 9
Edison
Persen WMA
West Bank
Swenoda
Tjosaas WMA
Appleton WPA
CHIPPEWA CO
Milan WMA
Lundgren WPA
Kragero
Big Bend
Big Bend City
Chippewa River
Mandt
Pomme de Terre River
30th St
60th St
70th St
80th St
90th St
100th St
Chip Swift St

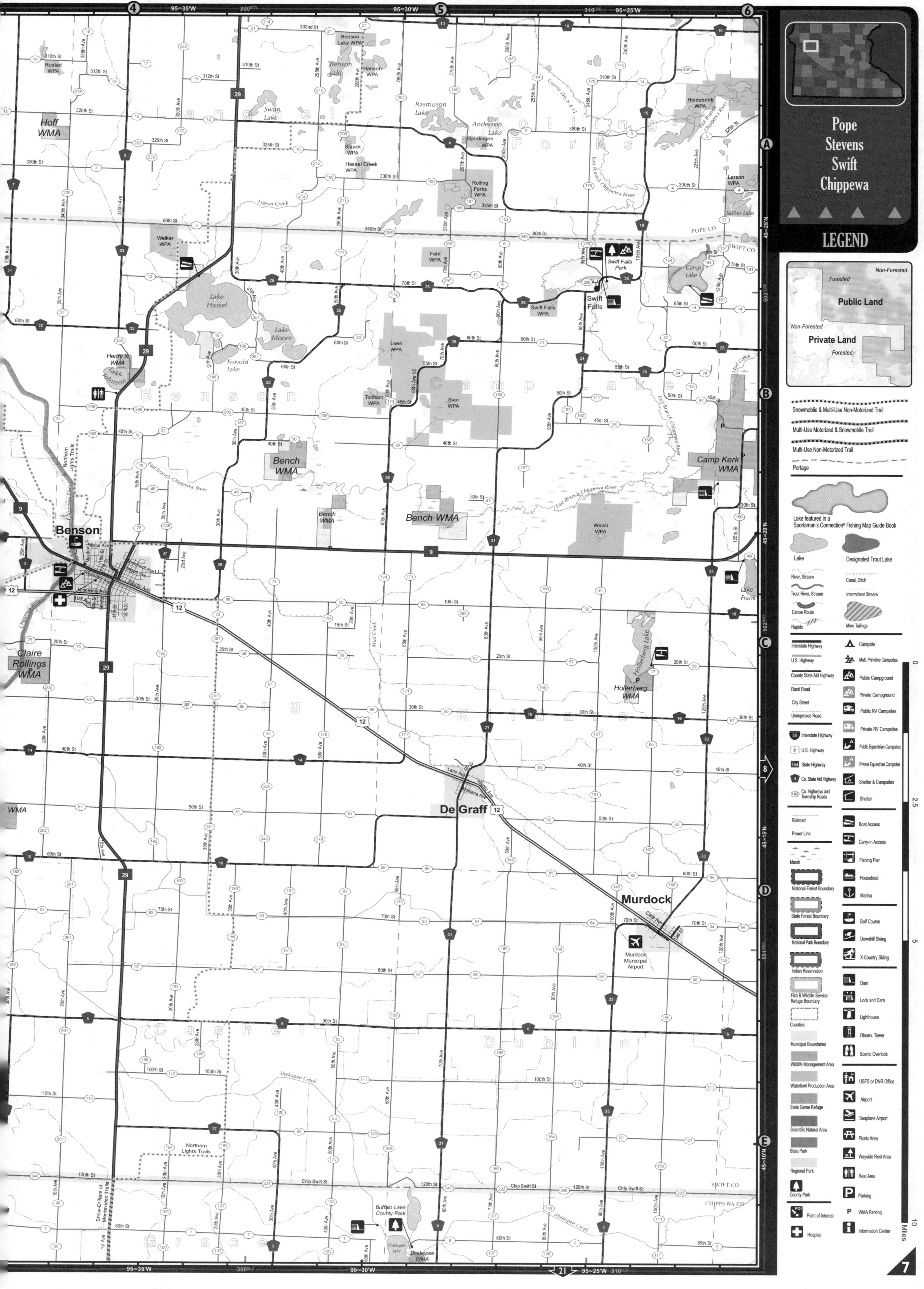

Pope
Stevens
Swift
Chippewa
LEGEND
Public Land
Private Land
Forested
Non-Forested
Snowmobile & Multi-Use Non-Motorized Trail
Multi-Use Motorized & Snowmobile Trail
Multi-Use Non-Motorized Trail
Portage
Lake featured in a Sportsman's Connection® Fishing Map Guide Book
Lake
Designated Trout Lake
River, Stream
Canal, Ditch
Trout River, Stream
Intermittent Stream
Canoe Route
Rapids
Mine Tailings
Interstate Highway
U.S. Highway
County State Aid Highway
Rural Road
City Street
Unimproved Road
Interstate Highway
U.S. Highway
State Highway
Co. State Aid Highway
Co. Highways and Township Roads
Railroad
Power Line
Marsh
National Forest Boundary
State Forest Boundary
National Park Boundary
Indian Reservation
Fish & Wildlife Service Refuge Boundary
Counties
Municipal Boundaries
Wildlife Management Area
Waterfowl Production Area
State Game Refuge
Scientific Natural Area
State Park
Regional Park
County Park
Point of Interest
Hospital
Campsite
Mult. Primitive Campsites
Public Campground
Private Campground
Public RV Campsites
Private RV Campsites
Public Equestrian Campsites
Private Equestrian Campsites
Shelter & Campsites
Shelter
Boat Access
Carry-In Access
Fishing Pier
Houseboat
Marina
Golf Course
Downhill Skiing
X-Country Skiing
Dam
Lock and Dam
Lighthouse
Observ. Tower
Scenic Overlook
USFS or DNR Office
Airport
Seaplane Airport
Picnic Area
Wayside Rest Area
Rest Area
Parking
WMA Parking
Information Center
0
2.5
5
10
Miles
95°35'W
95°30'W
95°25'W
45°25'N
45°20'N
45°15'N
45°10'N
Benson
De Graff
Murdock
Swift Falls
Hoff WMA
Rustad WPA
Benson Lake WPA
Benson Lake
Hanson WPA
Swan Lake
Rasmuson Lake
Anderson Lake
Gjerdingen WPA
Staack WPA
Hassel Creek WPA
Rolling Forks WPA
Heidebrink WPA
Larson WPA
Sather Lake
Welker WPA
Fahl WPA
Swift Falls Park
Swift Falls WPA
Camp Lake
Lake Hassel
Lake Moore
Frovold Lake
Henry X WMA
Lake Johnson
Loen WPA
Tolifson WPA
Svor WPA
Bench WMA
Camp Kerk WMA
Welsh WPA
Lake Frank
Claire Rollings WMA
Hollerberg Lake
Hollerberg WMA
Murdock Municipal Airport
Buffalo Lake County Park
Shakopee Lake
Shakopee WMA
Northern Lights Trails
Snow-Drifters of Montevideo Trails
Hassel Creek
East Branch Chippewa River
Mud Creek
Shakopee Creek
County Ditch # 15
Chippewa River
POPE CO
SWIFT CO
CHIPPEWA CO
Lake Hassel
Benson
Camp Lake
Kildare
Cashel
Dublin
Grace
Torning
Lake
Rolling Forks
8
21

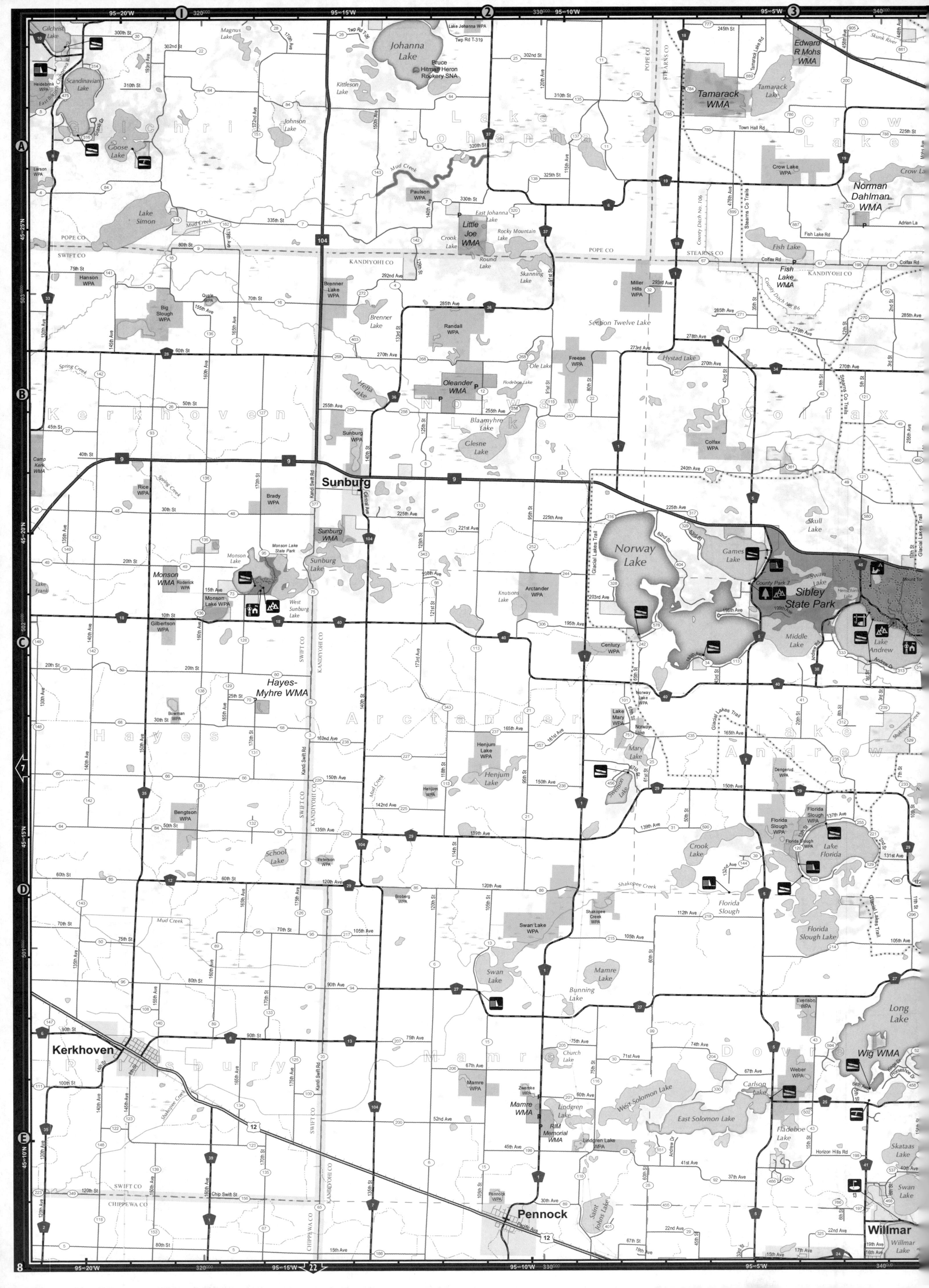

Gilchrist Lake
Magnus Lake
Johanna Lake
Bruce Hitman Heron Rookery SNA
Lake Johanna WPA
Kittleson Lake
Johnson Lake
Scandinavian Lake
Heidebrink WPA
Goose Lake
Larson WPA
Edward R Mohs WMA
Tamarack WMA
Tamarack Lake
Skunk River
Crow Lake WPA
Crow Lake
Norman Dahlman WMA
Mud Creek
Paulson WPA
Lake Simon
East Johanna Lake
Little Joe WMA
Crook Lake
Rocky Mountain Lake
Round Lake
Skanning Lake
Fish Lake
Fish Lake WMA
Miller Hills WPA
Section Twelve Lake
Hanson WPA
Big Slough WPA
Quale WPA
Brenner Lake WPA
Brenner Lake
Randall WPA
Freese WPA
Hystad Lake
Ole Lake
Oleander WMA
Hefta Lake
Blaamyhre Lake
Glesne Lake
Sunburg WPA
Colfax WPA
Camp Kerk WMA
Rice WPA
Brady WPA
Sunburg
Skull Lake
Sunburg WMA
Sunburg Lake
Monson Lake State Park
Monson Lake
Monson WMA
Roderick WPA
Monson Lake WPA
West Sunburg Lake
Lake Frank
Norway Lake
Games Lake
Swan Lake
Sibley State Park
County Park 7
Knutsons Lake
Arctander WPA
Middle Lake
Lake Andrew
Gilbertson WPA
Century WPA
Hayes-Myhre WMA
Bowman WPA
Norway Lake WPA
Lake Mary WPA
Norway Lake
Mary Lake
Henjum Lake WPA
Henjum Lake
Henjum WPA
Swenson Lake
Dengerud WPA
Bengtson WPA
School Lake
Peterson WPA
Crook Lake
Florida Slough WPA
Lake Florida
Florida Slough
Florida Slough Lake
Broberg WPA
Shakopee Creek WPA
Swan Lake WPA
Swan Lake
Mamre Lake
Bunning Lake
Evenson WPA
Long Lake
Wig WMA
Kerkhoven
Church Lake
Mamre WPA
Weber WPA
Carlson Lake
West Solomon Lake
East Solomon Lake
Zwemke WPA
Mamre WMA
Lindgren Lake
RIM Memorial WMA
Lindgren Lake WPA
Fladeboe Lake
Skataas Lake
Swan Lake
Pennock WPA
Pennock
Saint Johns Lake
Willmar
Willmar Lake
Kerkhoven
Norway Lake
Arctander
Hayes
Lake Andrew
Colfax
Crow Lake
Johanna
Gilchrist
Mamre
Dovre
Pillsbury
POPE CO
SWIFT CO
KANDIYOHI CO
STEARNS CO
CHIPPEWA CO
Glacial Lakes Trail
Stearns Co Trails
Shakopee Creek
Spring Creek
Mud Creek
95°20'W
95°15'W
95°10'W
95°5'W
45°25'N
45°20'N
45°15'N
45°10'N

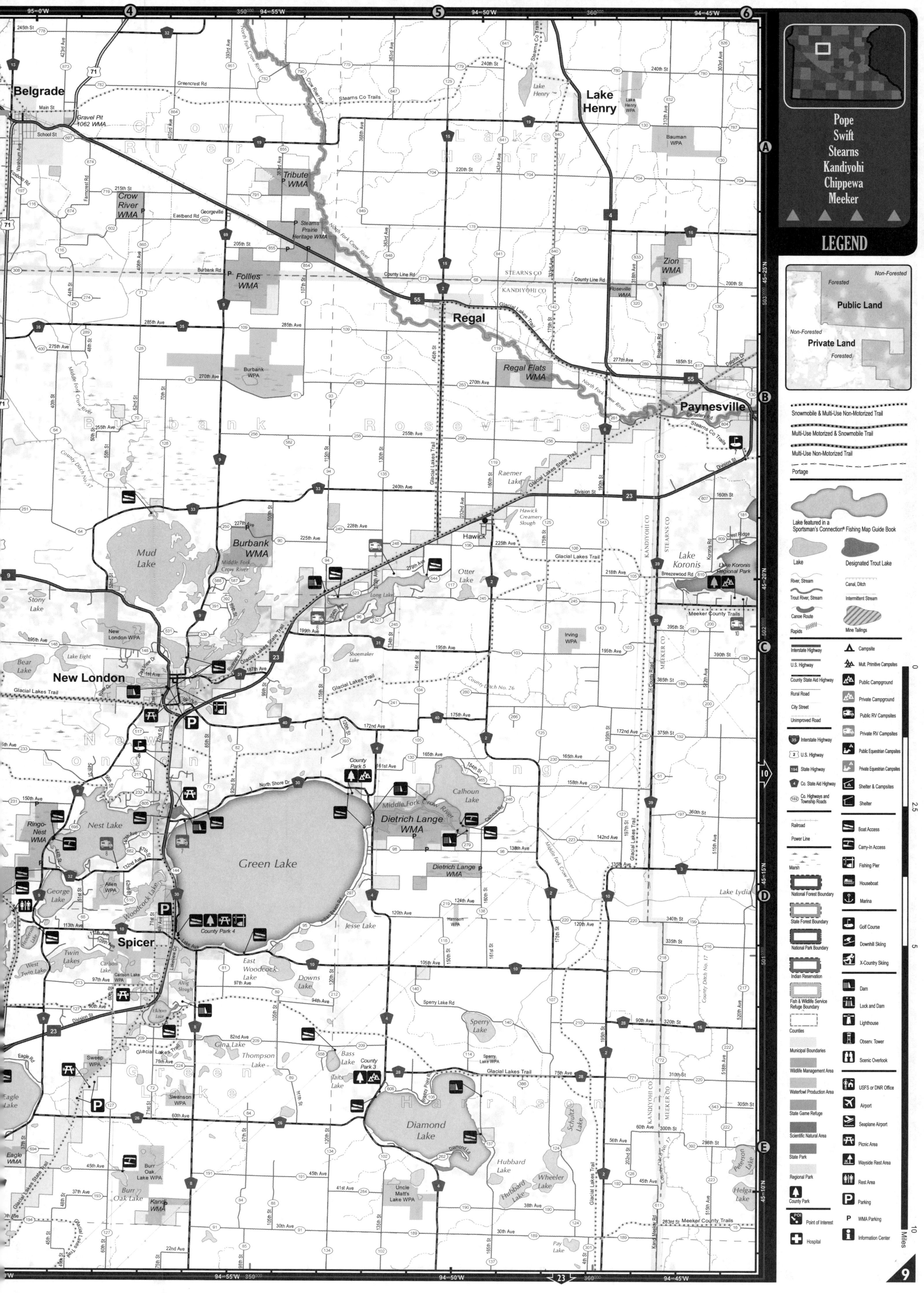

Pope
Swift
Stearns
Kandiyohi
Chippewa
Meeker
LEGEND
Forested
Non-Forested
Public Land
Private Land
Snowmobile & Multi-Use Non-Motorized Trail
Multi-Use Motorized & Snowmobile Trail
Multi-Use Non-Motorized Trail
Portage
Lake featured in a Sportsman's Connection® Fishing Map Guide Book
Lake
Designated Trout Lake
River, Stream
Canal, Ditch
Trout River, Stream
Intermittent Stream
Canoe Route
Rapids
Mine Tailings
Interstate Highway
U.S. Highway
County State Aid Highway
Rural Road
City Street
Unimproved Road
Interstate Highway
U.S. Highway
State Highway
Co. State Aid Highway
Co. Highways and Township Roads
Railroad
Power Line
Marsh
National Forest Boundary
State Forest Boundary
National Park Boundary
Indian Reservation
Fish & Wildlife Service Refuge Boundary
Counties
Municipal Boundaries
Wildlife Management Area
Waterfowl Production Area
State Game Refuge
Scientific Natural Area
State Park
Regional Park
County Park
Point of Interest
Hospital
Campsite
Mult. Primitive Campsites
Public Campground
Private Campground
Public RV Campsites
Private RV Campsites
Public Equestrian Campsites
Private Equestrian Campsites
Shelter & Campsites
Shelter
Boat Access
Carry-In Access
Fishing Pier
Houseboat
Marina
Golf Course
Downhill Skiing
X-Country Skiing
Dam
Lock and Dam
Lighthouse
Observ. Tower
Scenic Overlook
USFS or DNR Office
Airport
Seaplane Airport
Picnic Area
Wayside Rest Area
Rest Area
Parking
WMA Parking
Information Center
Miles
Belgrade
Lake Henry
Regal
Paynesville
New London
Spicer
Hawick
Green Lake
Nest Lake
Mud Lake
Diamond Lake
Lake Koronis
Calhoun Lake
Dietrich Lange WMA
Crow River WMA
Tribute WMA
Steams Prairie Heritage WMA
Follies WMA
Burbank WMA
Burbank WPA
Regal Flats WMA
Zion WMA
Bauman WPA
Lake Henry WPA
Ringo-Nest WMA
Allen WPA
George Lake
Irving WPA
Harrison WPA
Sweep WPA
Swenson WPA
Eagle WMA
Burr Oak Lake WPA
Kandi WMA
Uncle Matt's Lake WPA
Sperry Lake WPA
Lake Koronis Regional Park
County Park 3
County Park 4
County Park 5
Glacial Lakes State Trail
Glacial Lakes Trail
Stearns Co Trails
Meeker County Trails
North Fork Crow River
Middle Fork Crow River
STEARNS CO
KANDIYOHI CO
MEEKER CO
Crow River
Lake Henry
Burbank
Roseville
New London
Irving
Green Lake
Harrison
95°0'W
94°55'W
94°50'W
94°45'W
45°25'N
45°20'N
45°15'N
45°10'N

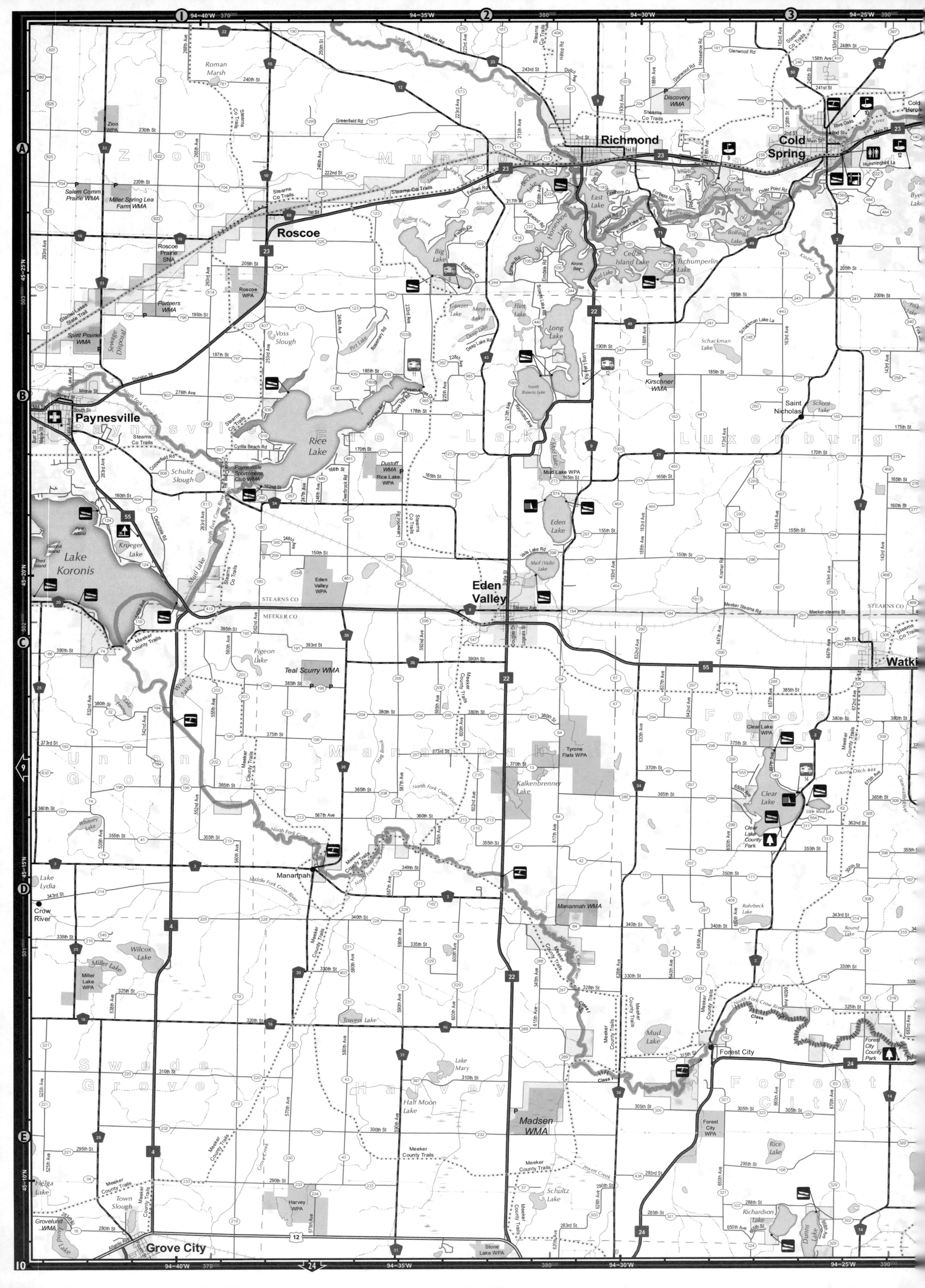

Richmond
Cold Spring
Roscoe
Paynesville
Eden Valley
Watkins
Manannah
Forest City
Grove City
Crow River
Saint Nicholas
Zion
Munson
Wakefield
Paynesville
Eden Lake
Luxemburg
Union Grove
Manannah
Forest Prairie
Swede Grove
Harvey
Forest City
Rice Lake
Lake Koronis
Big Lake
Horseshoe Lake
Cedar Island Lake
Tschumperlin Lake
Long Lake
North Browns Lake
Eden Lake
Mud Lake
Krueger Lake
Clear Lake
Schultz Slough
Voss Slough
Roman Marsh
Schultz Lake
Half Moon Lake
Towers Lake
Wilcox Lake
Miller Lake
Pigeon Lake
Whitney Lake
Lake Lydia
Helga Lake
Town Slough
Kalkenbrenner Lake
Rohrbeck Lake
Round Lake
Rice Lake
Richardson Lake
Dunns Lake
Lake Mary
Zion WPA
Roscoe WPA
Partners WMA
Spirit Prairie WMA
Salem Comm Prairie WMA
Miller Spring Lea Farm WMA
Roscoe Prairie SNA
Discovery WMA
Kirschner WMA
Dustoff WMA
Rice Lake WPA
Mud Lake WPA
Eden Valley WPA
Teal Scurry WMA
Tyrone Flats WPA
Manannah WMA
Madsen WMA
Miller Lake WPA
Harvey WPA
Groveland WMA
Forest City WPA
Clear Lake WPA
Stone Lake WPA
Paynesville Sportsmens Club WMA
Clear Lake County Park
Forest City County Park
Glacial Lakes State Trail
Stearns Co Trails
Meeker County Trails
Sewage Disposal
North Fork Crow River
Middle Fork Crow River
Sauk River
STEARNS CO
MEEKER CO
94°40'W
94°35'W
94°30'W
94°25'W
45°25'N
45°20'N
45°15'N
45°10'N

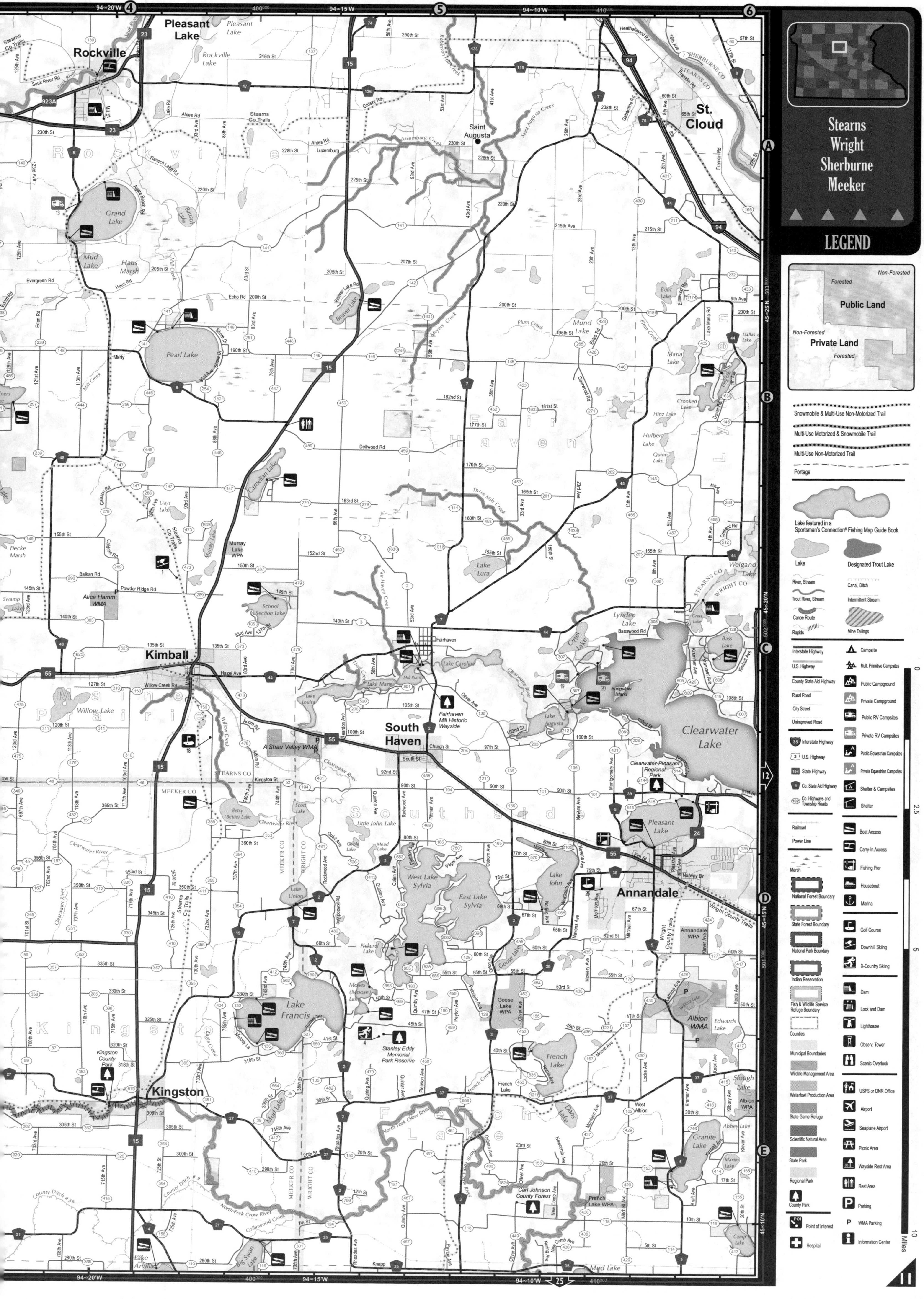

Stearns
Wright
Sherburne
Meeker
LEGEND
Public Land
Private Land
Forested
Non-Forested
Snowmobile & Multi-Use Non-Motorized Trail
Multi-Use Motorized & Snowmobile Trail
Multi-Use Non-Motorized Trail
Portage
Lake featured in a Sportsman's Connection® Fishing Map Guide Book
Lake
Designated Trout Lake
River, Stream
Canal, Ditch
Trout River, Stream
Intermittent Stream
Canoe Route
Rapids
Mine Tailings
Interstate Highway
U.S. Highway
County State Aid Highway
Rural Road
City Street
Unimproved Road
Interstate Highway
U.S. Highway
State Highway
Co. State Aid Highway
Co. Highways and Township Roads
Campsite
Mult. Primitive Campsites
Public Campground
Private Campground
Public RV Campsites
Private RV Campsites
Public Equestrian Campsites
Private Equestrian Campsites
Shelter & Campsites
Shelter
Railroad
Power Line
Marsh
National Forest Boundary
State Forest Boundary
National Park Boundary
Indian Reservation
Fish & Wildlife Service Refuge Boundary
Counties
Municipal Boundaries
Wildlife Management Area
Waterfowl Production Area
State Game Refuge
Scientific Natural Area
State Park
Regional Park
County Park
Point of Interest
Hospital
Boat Access
Carry-In Access
Fishing Pier
Houseboat
Marina
Golf Course
Downhill Skiing
X-Country Skiing
Dam
Lock and Dam
Lighthouse
Observ. Tower
Scenic Overlook
USFS or DNR Office
Airport
Seaplane Airport
Picnic Area
Wayside Rest Area
Rest Area
Parking
WMA Parking
Information Center
0
2.5
5
10
Miles
Pleasant Lake
Rockville
Rockville Lake
St. Cloud
Saint Augusta
Grand Lake
Mud Lake
Haus Marsh
Pearl Lake
Beaver Lake
Mund Lake
Maria Lake
Crooked Lake
Hinz Lake
Hulbert Lake
Quinn Lake
Bunt Lake
Carnelian Lake
Days Lake
Murray Lake WPA
Fiecke Marsh
Alice Hamm WMA
School Section Lake
Lake Lura
Weigand Lake
Lynden Lake
Bass Lake
Kimball
Fairhaven
Fairhaven Mill Historic Wayside
Lake Caroline
Lake Marie
Lake Louisa
Willow Lake
South Haven
A Shau Valley WMA
Lake Augusta
Clearwater Lake
Bungalow Island
Clearwater-Pleasant Regional Park
Pleasant Lake
Annandale
Betsy (Bettie) Lake
Scott Lake
Little John Lake
West Lake Sylvia
East Lake Sylvia
Lake John
Lake Union
Pickerel Lake
Moses (Moose) Lake
Lake Francis
Stanley Eddy Memorial Park Reserve
Goose Lake WPA
French Lake
Annandale WPA
Albion WMA
Edwards Lake
Kingston County Park
Kingston
Mud Lake
Dans Lake
West Albion
Slough Lake
Albion WPA
Abbey Lake
Granite Lake
Maxim Lake
Carl Johnson County Forest
French Lake WPA
Camp Lake
Big Swan Lake
Lake Arvilla
Mud Lake
North Fork Crow River
Clearwater River
Sauk River
Three Mile Creek
Luxemburg Creek
Saint Augusta Creek
Fair Haven Creek
Stearns Co Trails
Wright County Trails
STEARNS CO
MEEKER CO
WRIGHT CO
SHERBURNE CO
Rockville
Fair Haven
Maine Prairie
South Side
Kingston
French Lake
94°20'W
94°15'W
94°10'W
45°25'N
45°20'N
45°15'N
45°10'N
A
B
C
D
E
4
5
6
12
25

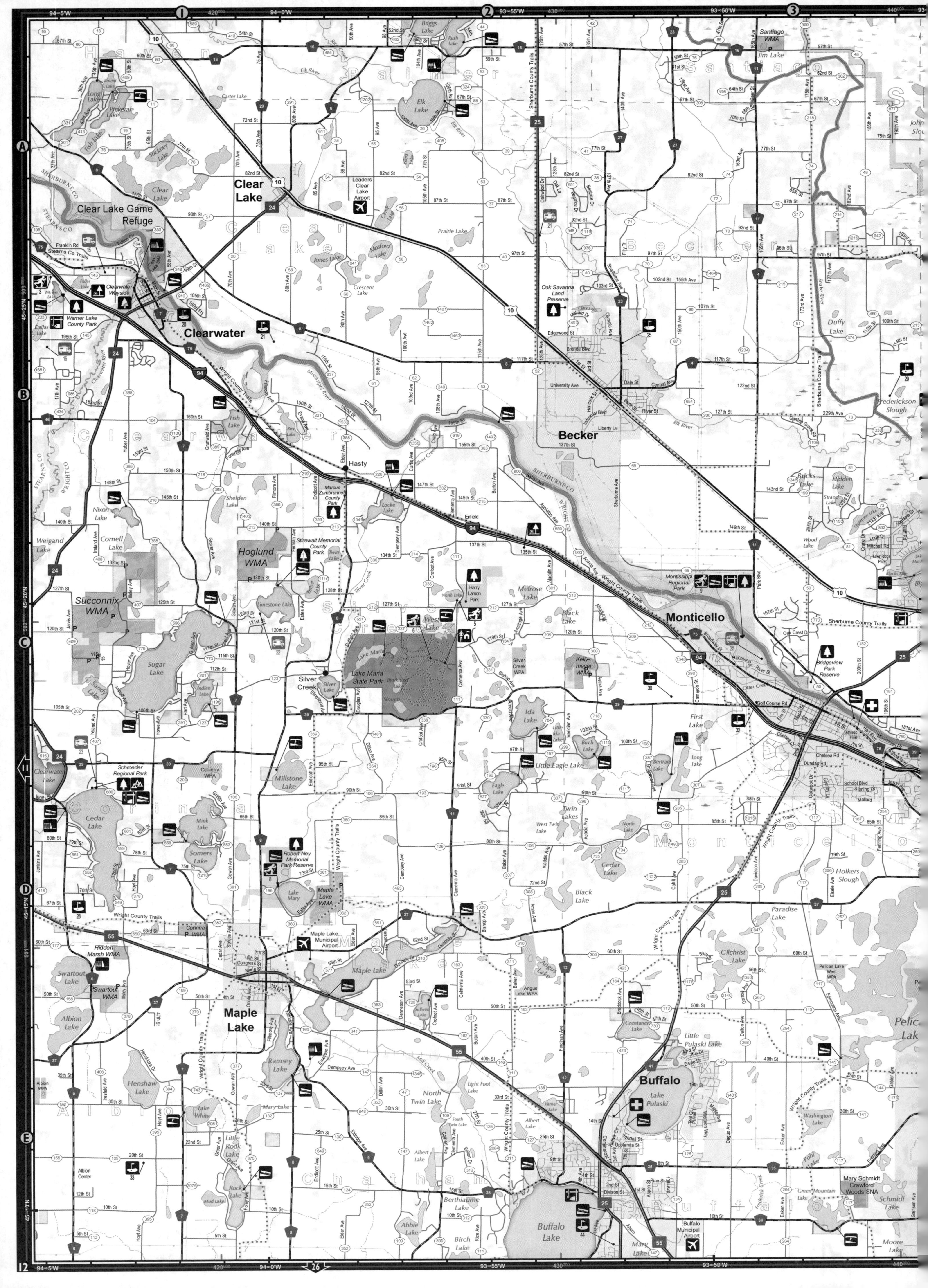

Clear Lake
Clear Lake Game Refuge
Clearwater
Clearwater Wayside
Warner Lake County Park
Leaders Clear Lake Airport
Becker
Oak Savanna Land Preserve
Santiago WMA
Jim Lake
Monticello
Montissippi Regional Park
Bridgeview Park Reserve
Hasty
Enfield
Marcus Zumbrunnen County Park
Stirewalt Memorial County Park
Hoglund WMA
Succonnix WMA
Harry Larson Park
Lake Maria State Park
Silver Creek
Silver Creek WPA
Kelly-meyer WMA
Schroeder Regional Park
Corinna WPA
Robert Ney Memorial Park Reserve
Maple Lake WMA
Maple Lake Municipal Airport
Hidden Marsh WMA
Swartout WMA
Maple Lake
Angus Lake WPA
Buffalo
Buffalo Municipal Airport
Mary Schmidt Crawford Woods SNA
Albion Center
Mississippi River
Elk River
Clearwater River
Sugar Lake
Cedar Lake
Clearwater Lake
Ida Lake
Lake Pulaski
Buffalo Lake
Pelican Lake
Fredrickson Slough
Holkers Slough
Sherburne County Trails
Wright County Trails
Stearns Co Trails
12
26

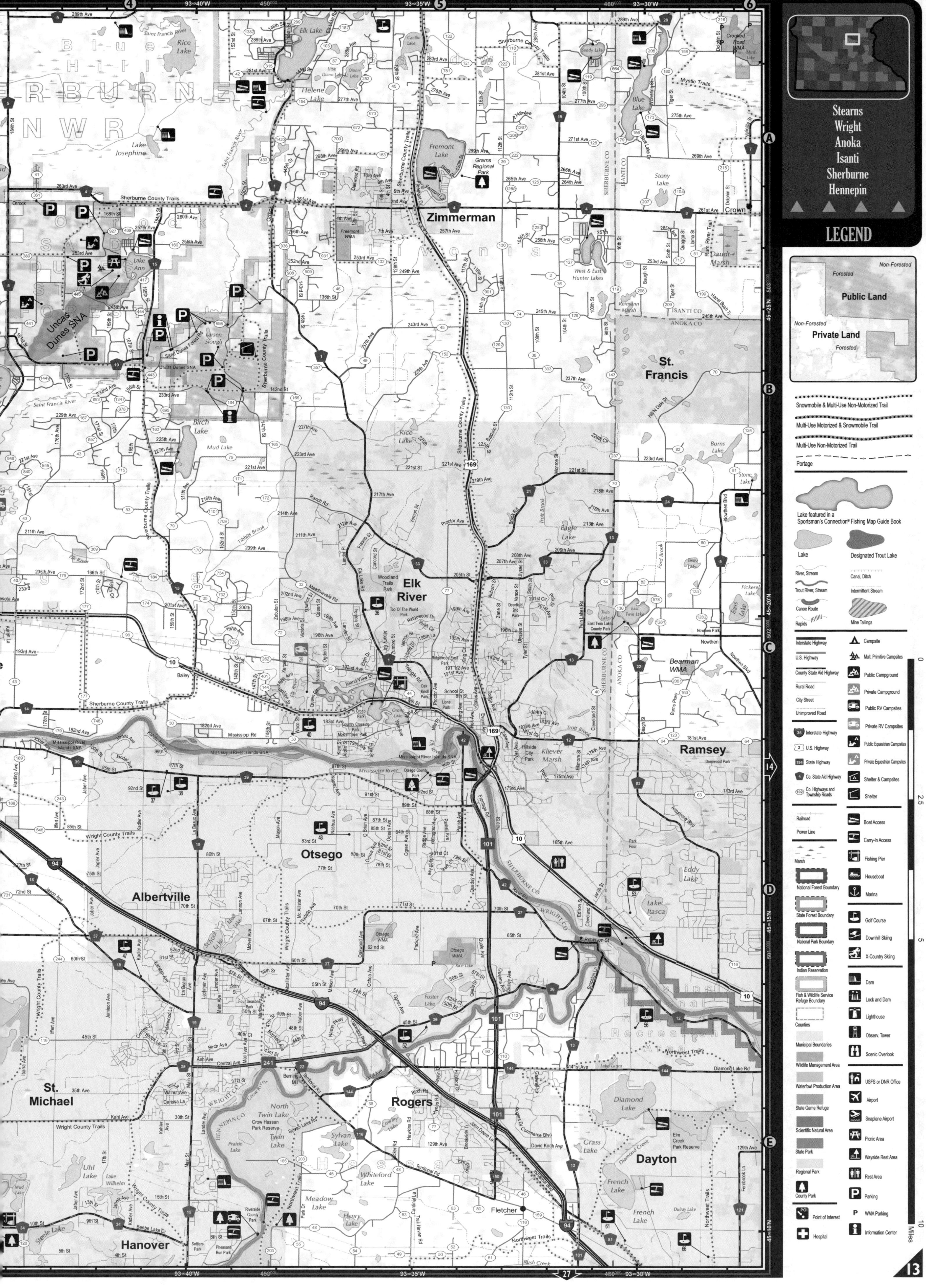

Stearns
Wright
Anoka
Isanti
Sherburne
Hennepin
LEGEND
Public Land
Private Land
Forested
Non-Forested
Snowmobile & Multi-Use Non-Motorized Trail
Multi-Use Motorized & Snowmobile Trail
Multi-Use Non-Motorized Trail
Portage
Lake featured in a Sportsman's Connection® Fishing Map Guide Book
Lake
Designated Trout Lake
Zimmerman
St. Francis
Elk River
Ramsey
Otsego
Albertville
St. Michael
Rogers
Dayton
Hanover
Fletcher
Uncas Dunes SNA
Sherburne NWR
Mississippi River
Lake Itasca
Diamond Lake
Fremont Lake
Elk Lake
Blue Lake
Eagle Lake
Eddy Lake
93°40'W
93°35'W
93°30'W
45°25'N
45°20'N
45°15'N
45°10'N
Miles

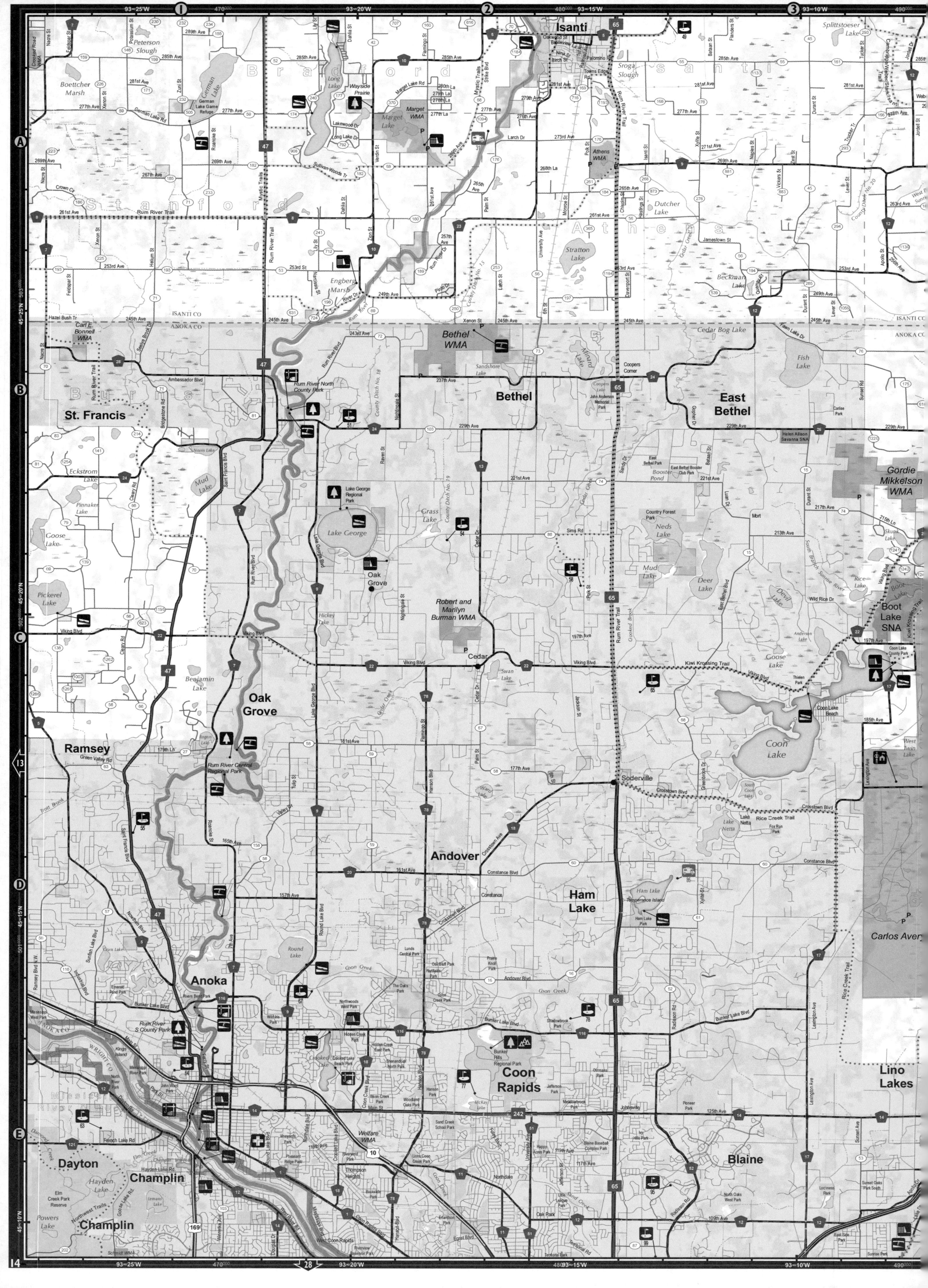

93°25'W
470
93°20'W
480
93°15'W
93°10'W
490
1
2
3
A
B
C
D
E
45°25'N
45°20'N
45°15'N
45°10'N
Isanti
Bradford
Isanti
Stanford
Athens
Burns
St. Francis
Bethel
East Bethel
Oak Grove
Ramsey
Andover
Ham Lake
Anoka
Coon Rapids
Lino Lakes
Dayton
Champlin
Blaine
Cedar
Soderville
Coopers Corner
Peterson Slough
Boettcher Marsh
German Lake
German Lake Game Refuge
Long Lake
Wayside Prairie
Marget Lake
Marget WMA
Sroga Slough
Splittstoeser Lake
Athens WMA
Dutcher Lake
Stratton Lake
Beckman Lake
Engberg Marsh
Carl E. Bonnell WMA
Bethel WMA
Sandshore Lake
Minard Lake
Cedar Bog Lake
Fish Lake
Rum River North County Park
Lake George Regional Park
Lake George
Grass Lake
Oak Grove
Eckstrom Lake
Mud Lake
Pinnaker Lake
Goose Lake
Pickerel Lake
Norris Lake
Robert and Marilyn Burman WMA
Hickey Lake
Benjamin Lake
Swan Lake
Gordie Mikkelson WMA
Helen Allison Savanna SNA
Country Forest Park
Neds Lake
Mud Lake
Deer Lake
Devil Lake
Boot Lake SNA
Goose Lake
Coon Lake County Park
Coon Lake
Coon Lake Beach
Rum River Central Regional Park
Rogers Lake
Ward Lake
Lake Netta
Ham Lake
Temperance Island
Ham Lake Park
Carlos Avery
Round Lake
Bunker Hills Regional Park
Rum River S County Park
Crooked Lake
Welfare WMA
Hayden Lake
Powers Lake
Elm Creek Park Reserve
Mississippi River
Rum River
Coon Creek
Kiwi Krossing Trail
Crosstown Blvd
Rice Creek Trail
Viking Blvd
Bunker Lake Blvd
Constance Blvd
Andover Blvd
Main St
Northdale
Rum River Trail
Mystic Trails
Rum River Blvd
Lake George Blvd
Round Lake Blvd
Hanson Blvd
University Ave
Radisson Rd
Lexington Ave
Sunset Rd
Northwest Trails
West Coon Rapids
ISANTI CO
ANOKA CO
13
28
14

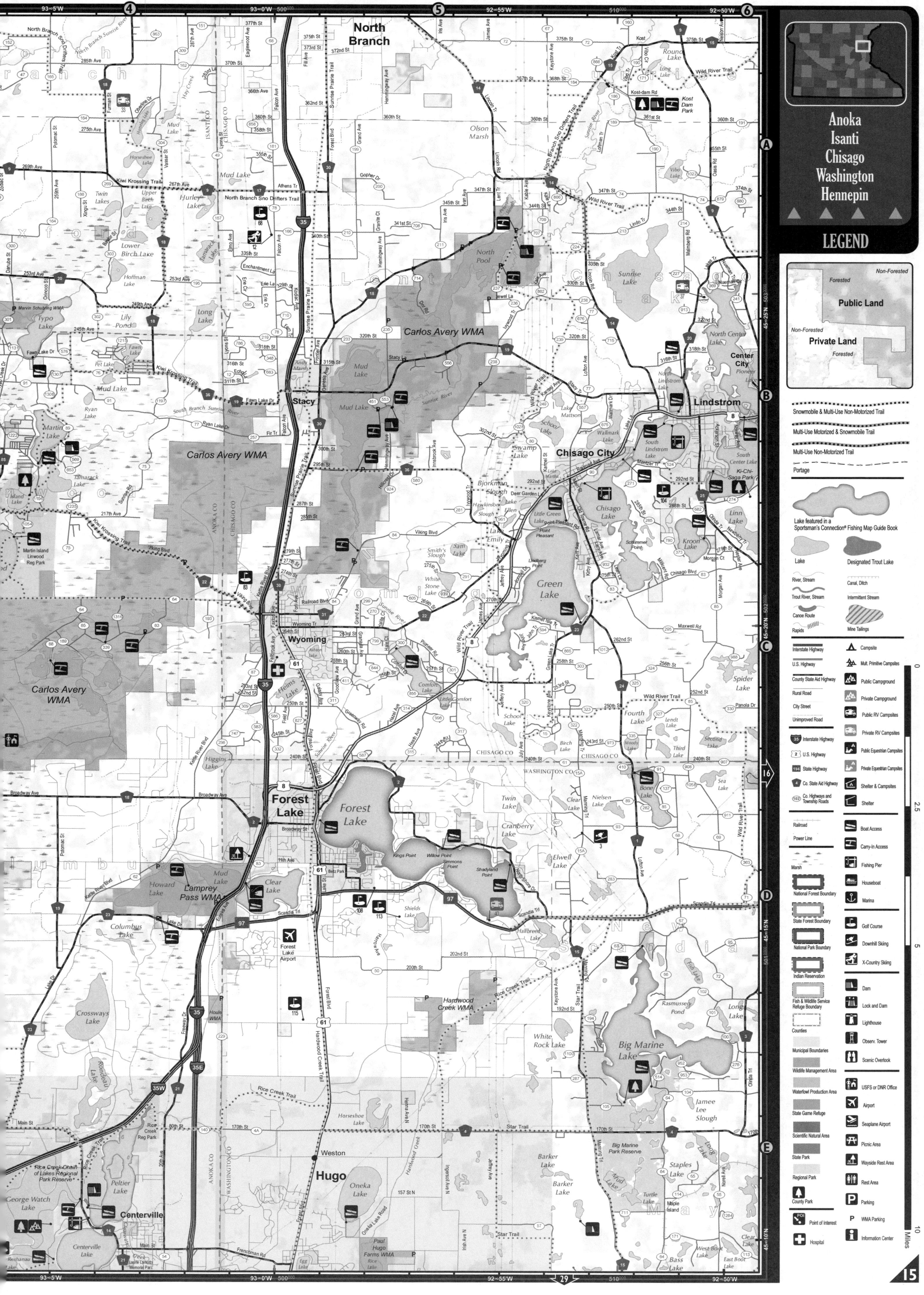

Anoka
Isanti
Chisago
Washington
Hennepin
LEGEND
Forested
Non-Forested
Public Land
Non-Forested
Private Land
Forested
Snowmobile & Multi-Use Non-Motorized Trail
Multi-Use Motorized & Snowmobile Trail
Multi-Use Non-Motorized Trail
Portage
Lake featured in a Sportsman's Connection® Fishing Map Guide Book
Lake
Designated Trout Lake
River, Stream
Canal, Ditch
Trout River, Stream
Intermittent Stream
Canoe Route
Mine Tailings
Rapids
Interstate Highway
U.S. Highway
County State Aid Highway
Rural Road
City Street
Unimproved Road
Interstate Highway
U.S. Highway
State Highway
Co. State Aid Highway
Co. Highways and Township Roads
Railroad
Power Line
Marsh
National Forest Boundary
State Forest Boundary
National Park Boundary
Indian Reservation
Fish & Wildlife Service Refuge Boundary
Counties
Municipal Boundaries
Wildlife Management Area
Waterfowl Production Area
State Game Refuge
Scientific Natural Area
State Park
Regional Park
County Park
Point of Interest
Hospital
Campsite
Mult. Primitive Campsites
Public Campground
Private Campground
Public RV Campsites
Private RV Campsites
Public Equestrian Campsites
Private Equestrian Campsites
Shelter & Campsites
Shelter
Boat Access
Carry-In Access
Fishing Pier
Houseboat
Marina
Golf Course
Downhill Skiing
X-Country Skiing
Dam
Lock and Dam
Lighthouse
Observ. Tower
Scenic Overlook
USFS or DNR Office
Airport
Seaplane Airport
Picnic Area
Wayside Rest Area
Rest Area
Parking
WMA Parking
Information Center
0
2.5
5
10
Miles
93°5'W
93°0'W
92°55'W
92°50'W
45°25'N
45°20'N
45°15'N
45°10'N
North Branch
Stacy
Wyoming
Forest Lake
Lindstrom
Chisago City
Center City
Hugo
Centerville
Weston
Carlos Avery WMA
Lamprey Pass WMA
Hardwood Creek WMA
Paul Hugo Farms WMA
Marvin Schubring WMA
Houle WMA
Kost Dam Park
Martin Island Linwood Reg Park
Rice Creek Reg Park
Rice Creek Chain of Lakes Regional Park Reserve
Big Marine Park Reserve
Ki-Chi-Saga Park
Forest Lake Airport
Forest Lake
Green Lake
Chisago Lake
Big Marine Lake
Clear Lake
Mud Lake
Howard Lake
Columbus Lake
Crossways Lake
Rondeau Lake
Peltier Lake
Centerville Lake
George Watch Lake
Oneka Lake
Horseshoe Lake
Typo Lake
Long Lake
Lily Pond
Martin Lake
Linwood Lake
Island Lake
Tamarack Lake
Fawn Lake
Pet Lake
Ryan Lake
Lower Birch Lake
Hoffman Lake
Twin Lakes
Upper Birch Lake
Hurley Lake
Horseshoe Lake
North Pool
Olson Marsh
Sunrise Lake
North Center Lake
South Center Lake
South Lindstrom Lake
North Lindstrom Lake
Linn Lake
Kroon Lake
Little Green Lake
School Lake
Swamp Lake
Lake Mattson
Wallmark Lake
Bjorkman Slough
Hawkinson Slough
Lake Emily
Sam Lake
Smith's Slough
White Stone Lake
Heims Lake
Comfort Lake
Little Comfort Lake
School Lake
Fourth Lake
Second Lake
Third Lake
Birch Lake
Moody Lake
Spider Lake
Bone Lake
Sea Lake
Twin Lake
Clear Lake
Nielsen Lake
Cranberry Lake
Elwell Lake
Shields Lake
Hallbreed Lake
Rasmussen Pond
Long Lake
White Rock Lake
Jamee Lee Slough
Barker Lake
Staples Lake
Turtle Lake
Maple Island
West Boot Lake
East Boot Lake
Bass Lake
Clear Lake
Higgins Lake
Round Lake
Long Lake
Vibo Lake
Mud Lake
Kings Point
Willow Point
Simmons Point
Shadyland Point
Point Pleasant
Schrammer Point
Lindberg Point
Wild River Trail
Rice Creek Trail
Kiwi Krossing Trail
North Branch Sno Drifters Trail
Star Trail
Broadway Ave
Scandia Trl
ANOKA CO
CHISAGO CO
ISANTI CO
WASHINGTON CO
16
29

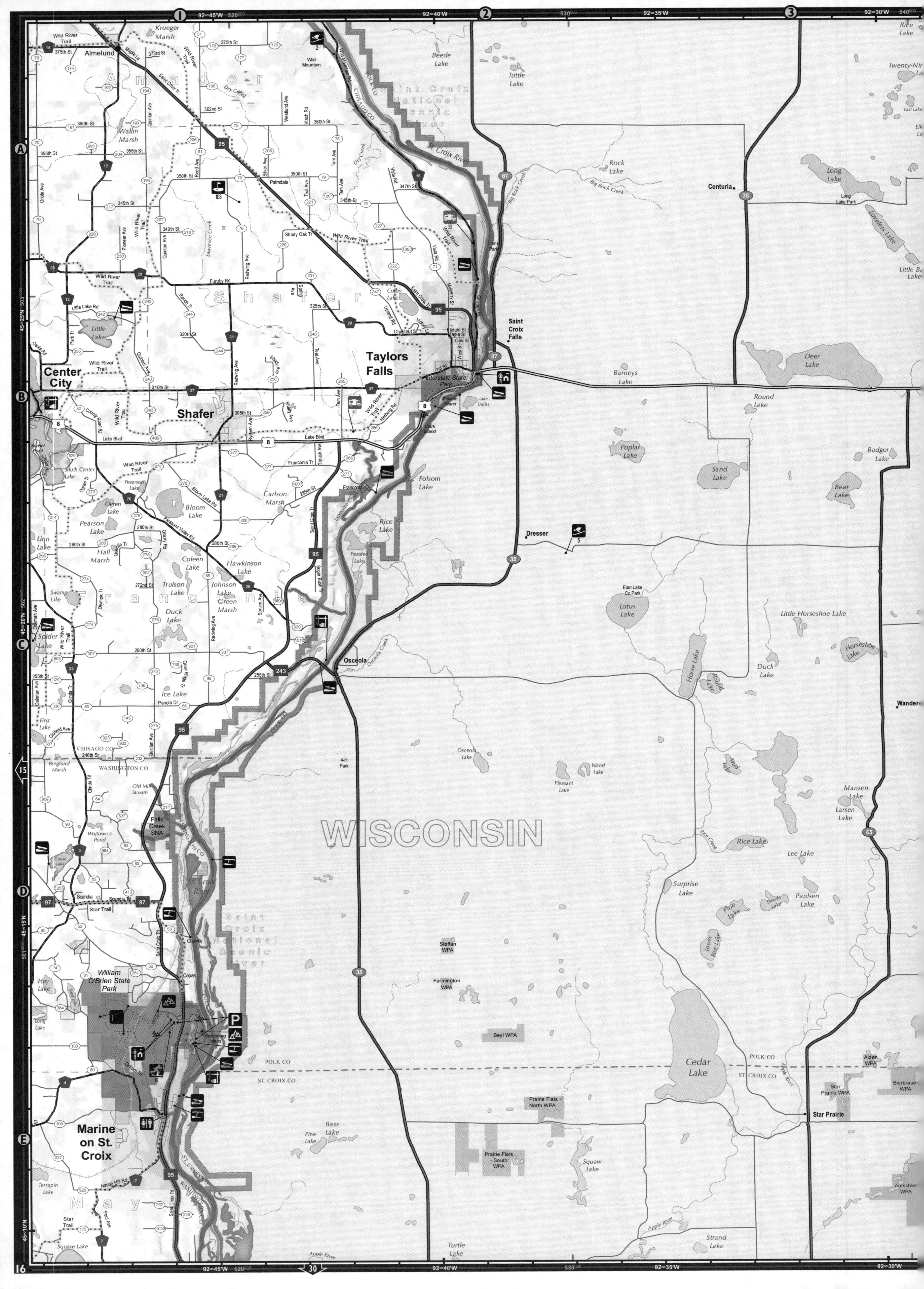

92°45'W
92°40'W
92°35'W
92°30'W
Almelund
Wild River Trail
Krueger Marsh
Wild Mountain
Beede Lake
Tuttle Lake
Saint Croix National Scenic River
Chisago Co
Polk Co
Wallin Marsh
St. Croix River
Rock Lake
Big Rock Creek
Centuria
Long Lake
Long Lake Park
Loveless Lake
Little Lake
Center City
Shafer
Taylors Falls
Interstate State Park
Saint Croix Falls
Deer Lake
Barneys Lake
Round Lake
Lake Dalles
Folsom Island
Clark Island
Poplar Lake
Badger Lake
Sand Lake
Bear Lake
South Center Lake
Peterson Lake
Ogren Lake
Bloom Lake
Carlson Marsh
Franconia
Folsom Lake
Pearson Lake
Linn Lake
Hall Marsh
Coleen Lake
Hawkinson Lake
Rice Lake
Peaslee Lake
Dresser
Trulson Lake
Johnson Lake
Green Marsh
Duck Lake
Swamp Lake
East Lake Co Park
Lotus Lake
Little Horseshoe Lake
Spider Lake
Osceola
Osceola Creek
Horse Lake
Horseshoe Lake
Duck Lake
Ice Lake
First Lake
Wanderoos
Chisago Co
Washington Co
Bergland Marsh
Osceola Lake
4-H Park
Island Lake
Pleasant Lake
Old Mill Stream
Falls Creek SNA
Wojtowicz Pond
Mansen Lake
Larsen Lake
WISCONSIN
Rice Creek
Rice Lake
Lee Lake
Goose Lake
Scandia
Star Trail
Surprise Lake
Pine Lake
Paulsen Lake
Swede Lake
Lower Pine Lake
Steffan WPA
Farmington WPA
Hay Lake
William O'Brien State Park
Copas
Long Lake
Beyl WPA
Polk Co
St. Croix Co
Cedar Lake
Alden WPA
Star Prairie WPA
Star Prairie
Bierbrauer WPA
Prairie Flats - North WPA
Marine on St. Croix
Bass Lake
Pine Lake
Prairie Flats - South WPA
Squaw Lake
Terrapin Lake
Amschler WPA
Star Trail
Apple River
Strand Lake
Turtle Lake
Square Lake
45°25'N
45°20'N
45°15'N
45°10'N
15
30

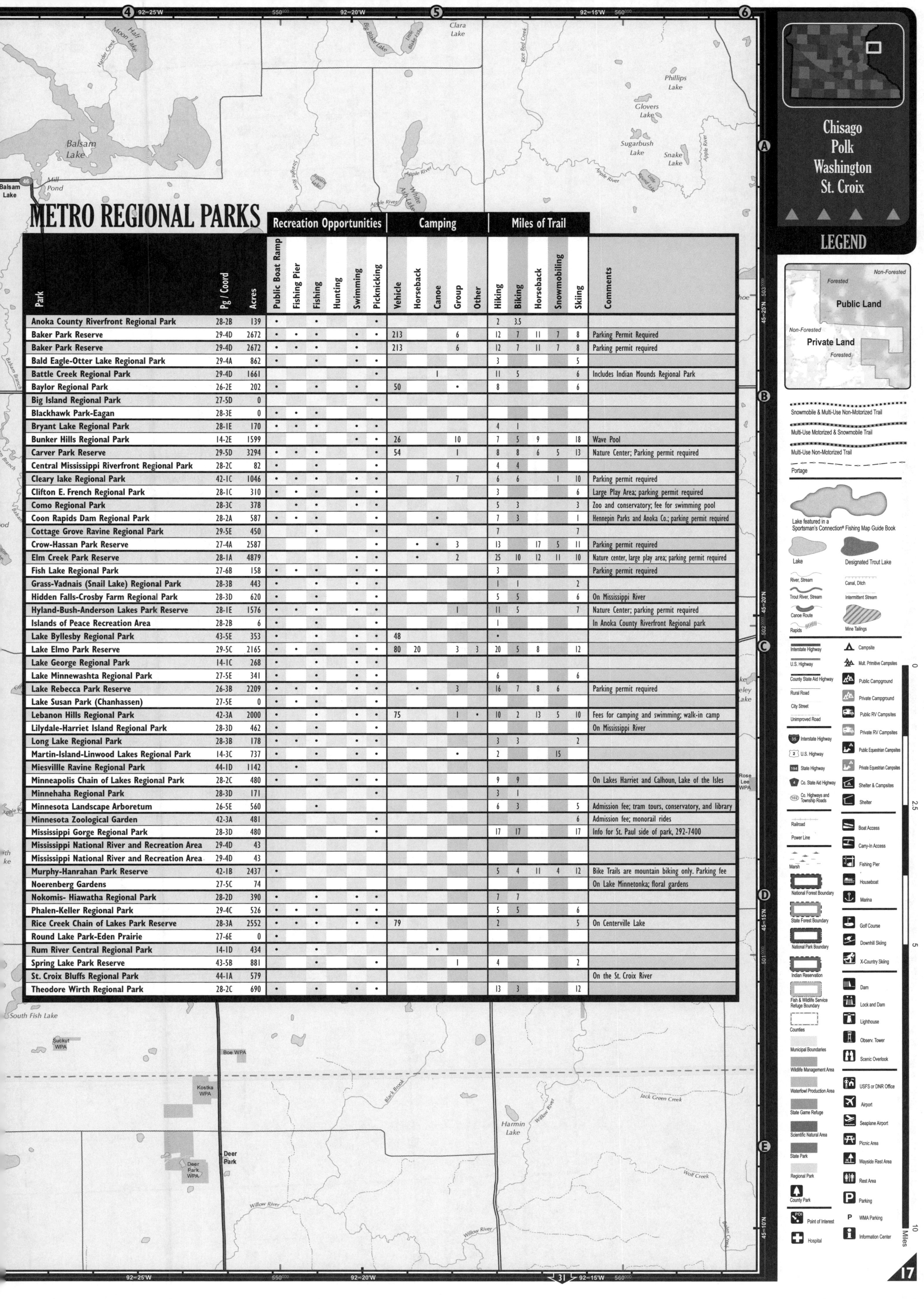

METRO REGIONAL PARKS

Park	Pg / Coord	Acres	Recreation Opportunities: Public Boat Ramp	Fishing Pier	Fishing	Hunting	Swimming	Picnicking	Camping: Vehicle	Horseback	Canoe	Group	Other	Miles of Trail: Hiking	Biking	Horseback	Snowmobiling	Skiing	Comments
Anoka County Riverfront Regional Park	28-2B	139	•		•			•						2	3.5				
Baker Park Reserve	29-4D	2672	•	•	•		•	•	213			6		12	7	11	7	8	Parking Permit Required
Baker Park Reserve	29-4D	2672	•	•	•		•		213			6		12	7	11	7	8	Parking permit required
Bald Eagle-Otter Lake Regional Park	29-4A	862	•		•		•	•						3				5	
Battle Creek Regional Park	29-4D	1661						•			1			11	5			6	Includes Indian Mounds Regional Park
Baylor Regional Park	26-2E	202	•		•		•		50			•		8				6	
Big Island Regional Park	27-5D	0						•											
Blackhawk Park-Eagan	28-3E	0	•	•	•														
Bryant Lake Regional Park	28-1E	170	•	•	•		•	•						4	1				
Bunker Hills Regional Park	14-2E	1599					•	•	26			10		7	5	9		18	Wave Pool
Carver Park Reserve	29-5D	3294	•	•	•			•	54			1		8	8	6	5	13	Nature Center; Parking permit required
Central Mississippi Riverfront Regional Park	28-2C	82	•		•			•						4	4				
Cleary lake Regional Park	42-1C	1046	•	•	•		•	•				7		6	6		1	10	Parking permit required
Clifton E. French Regional Park	28-1C	310	•	•	•		•	•						3				6	Large Play Area; parking permit required
Como Regional Park	28-3C	378		•	•		•	•						5	3			3	Zoo and conservatory; fee for swimming pool
Coon Rapids Dam Regional Park	28-2A	587	•	•	•			•			•			7	3			1	Hennepin Parks and Anoka Co.; parking permit required
Cottage Grove Ravine Regional Park	29-5E	450			•			•						7				7	
Crow-Hassan Park Reserve	27-4A	2587						•		•	•	3		13		17	5	11	Parking permit required
Elm Creek Park Reserve	28-1A	4879					•	•		•		2		25	10	12	11	10	Nature center, large play area; parking permit required
Fish Lake Regional Park	27-6B	158	•	•	•		•	•						3					Parking permit required
Grass-Vadnais (Snail Lake) Regional Park	28-3B	443	•		•		•	•						1	1			2	
Hidden Falls-Crosby Farm Regional Park	28-3D	620	•		•			•						5	5			6	On Mississippi River
Hyland-Bush-Anderson Lakes Park Reserve	28-1E	1576	•	•	•		•	•				1		11	5			7	Nature Center; parking permit required
Islands of Peace Recreation Area	28-2B	6	•		•			•						1					In Anoka County Riverfront Regional park
Lake Byllesby Regional Park	43-5E	353	•		•		•	•	48					•					
Lake Elmo Park Reserve	29-5C	2165	•	•	•		•	•	80	20		3	3	20	5	8		12	
Lake George Regional Park	14-1C	268	•		•		•	•											
Lake Minnewashta Regional Park	27-5E	341	•		•		•	•						6				6	
Lake Rebecca Park Reserve	26-3B	2209	•	•	•		•	•		•		3		16	7	8	6		Parking permit required
Lake Susan Park (Chanhassen)	27-5E	0	•	•	•			•											
Lebanon Hills Regional Park	42-3A	2000	•		•		•	•	75			1	•	10	2	13	5	10	Fees for camping and swimming; walk-in camp
Lilydale-Harriet Island Regional Park	28-3D	462	•		•			•											On Mississippi River
Long Lake Regional Park	28-3B	178	•	•	•		•	•						3	3			2	
Martin-Island-Linwood Lakes Regional Park	14-3C	737	•		•		•	•				•		2			15		
Miesvillle Ravine Regional Park	44-1D	1142		•															
Minneapolis Chain of Lakes Regional Park	28-2C	480	•		•		•	•						9	9				On Lakes Harriet and Calhoun, Lake of the Isles
Minnehaha Regional Park	28-3D	171						•						3	1				
Minnesota Landscape Arboretum	26-5E	560			•									6	3			5	Admission fee; tram tours, conservatory, and library
Minnesota Zoological Garden	42-3A	481						•										6	Admission fee; monorail rides
Mississippi Gorge Regional Park	28-3D	480						•						17	17			17	Info for St. Paul side of park, 292-7400
Mississippi National River and Recreation Area	29-4D	43																	
Mississippi National River and Recreation Area	29-4D	43																	
Murphy-Hanrahan Park Reserve	42-1B	2437	•											5	4	11	4	12	Bike Trails are mountain biking only. Parking fee
Noerenberg Gardens	27-5C	74																	On Lake Minnetonka; floral gardens
Nokomis- Hiawatha Regional Park	28-2D	390	•		•		•	•						7	7				
Phalen-Keller Regional Park	29-4C	526	•	•	•		•	•						5	5			6	
Rice Creek Chain of Lakes Park Reserve	28-3A	2552	•	•	•		•	•	79					2				5	On Centerville Lake
Round Lake Park-Eden Prairie	27-6E	0	•																
Rum River Central Regional Park	14-1D	434	•		•						•								
Spring Lake Park Reserve	43-5B	881			•			•				1		4				2	
St. Croix Bluffs Regional Park	44-1A	579																	On the St. Croix River
Theodore Wirth Regional Park	28-2C	690	•		•		•	•						13	3			12	

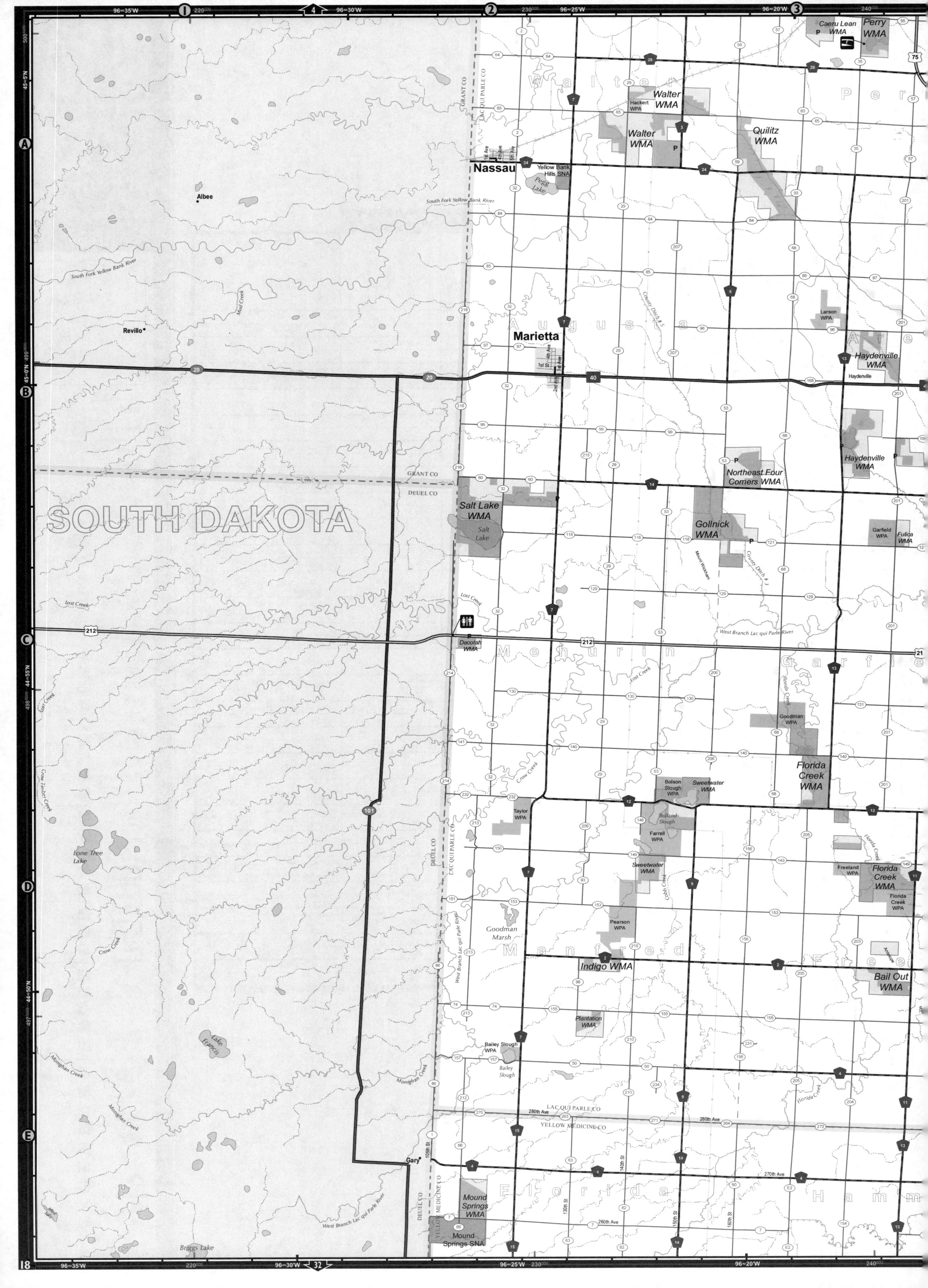
SOUTH DAKOTA
Nassau
Marietta
Albee
Revillo
Gary
Walter WMA
Hackert WPA
Quilitz WMA
Caeru Lean WMA
Perry WMA
Yellow Bank Hills SNA
Pegg Lake
South Fork Yellow Bank River
Mud Creek
Larson WPA
Haydenville WMA
Haydenville
Northeast Four Corners WMA
Salt Lake WMA
Salt Lake
Gollnick WMA
Garfield WPA
Fulica WMA
County Ditch # 5
County Ditch # 3
Lost Creek
West Branch Lac qui Parle River
Dacotah WMA
Goodman WPA
Florida Creek WMA
Bolson Slough WPA
Sweetwater WMA
Taylor WPA
Farrell WPA
Freeland WPA
Florida Creek WPA
Pearson WPA
Goodman Marsh
Indigo WMA
Bail Out WMA
Plantation WMA
Bailey Slough WPA
Bailey Slough
Lone Tree Lake
Lake Francis
Crow Creek
Crow Timber Creek
Monighan Creek
Briggs Lake
Mound Springs WMA
Mound Springs SNA
GRANT CO
DEUEL CO
LAC QUI PARLE CO
YELLOW MEDICINE CO
280th Ave
270th Ave
260th Ave
130th St
140th St
150th St
160th St
Walter
Augusta
Arena
Perry
Mehurin
Garfield
Manfred
Freeland
Florida
Hammer
96°35'W
96°30'W
96°25'W
96°20'W
45°5'N
45°0'N
44°55'N
44°50'N
A
B
C
D
E
1
2
3
4
32

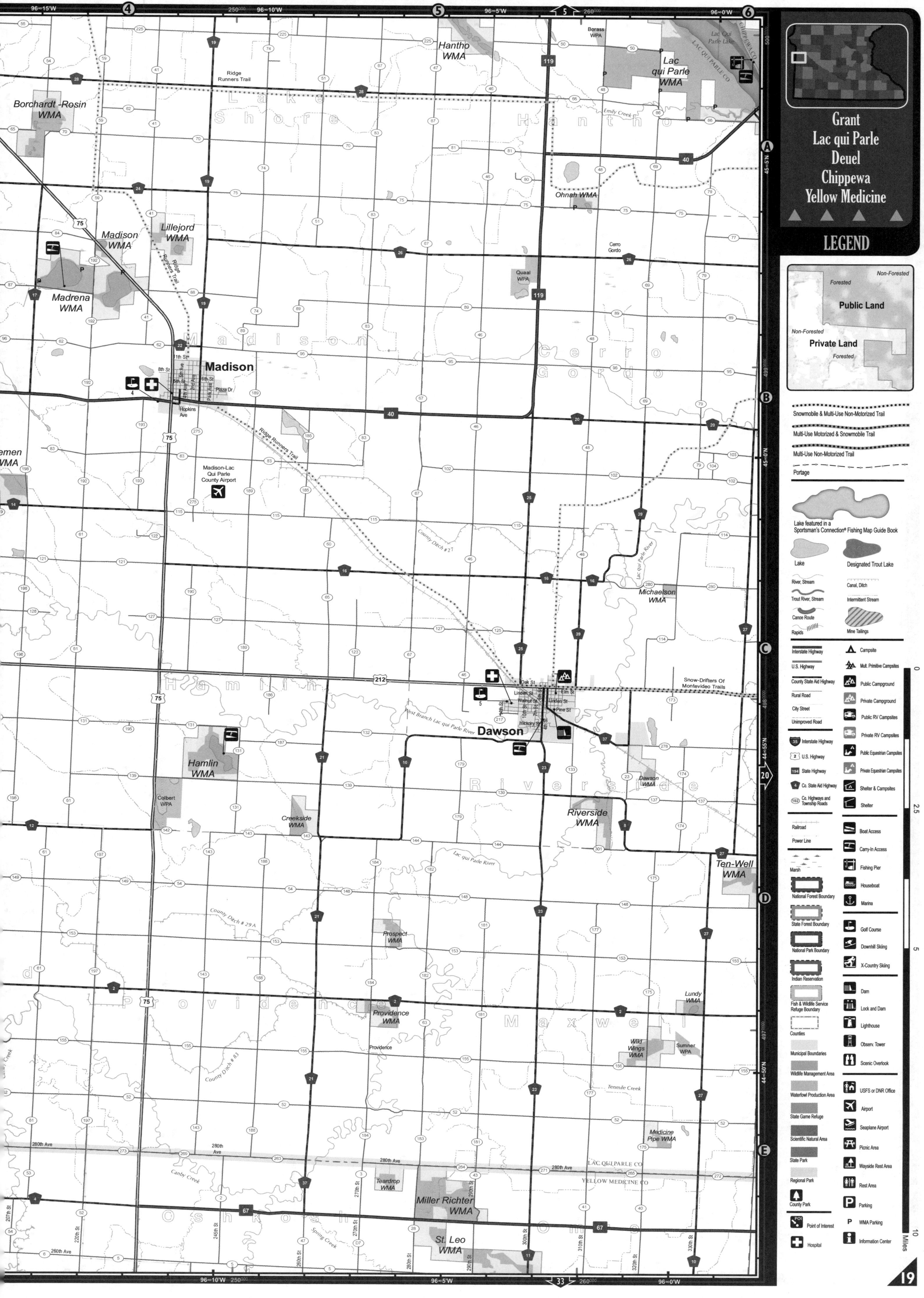

Grant
Lac qui Parle
Deuel
Chippewa
Yellow Medicine
LEGEND
Public Land
Private Land
Forested
Non-Forested
Snowmobile & Multi-Use Non-Motorized Trail
Multi-Use Motorized & Snowmobile Trail
Multi-Use Non-Motorized Trail
Portage
Lake featured in a Sportsman's Connection® Fishing Map Guide Book
Lake
Designated Trout Lake
Madison
Dawson
Borchardt -Rosin WMA
Hantho WMA
Lac qui Parle WMA
Madison WMA
Lillejord WMA
Madrena WMA
Ohnah WMA
Quaal WPA
Madison-Lac Qui Parle County Airport
Michaelson WMA
Hamlin WMA
Creekside WMA
Riverside WMA
Dawson WMA
Colbert WPA
Ten-Well WMA
Prospect WMA
Providence WMA
Lundy WMA
Wild Wings WMA
Sumner WPA
Medicine Pipe WMA
Teardrop WMA
Miller Richter WMA
St. Leo WMA
Ridge Runners Trail
Snow-Drifters Of Montevideo Trails
Lac qui Parle River
West Branch Lac qui Parle River
LAC QUI PARLE CO
YELLOW MEDICINE CO
19

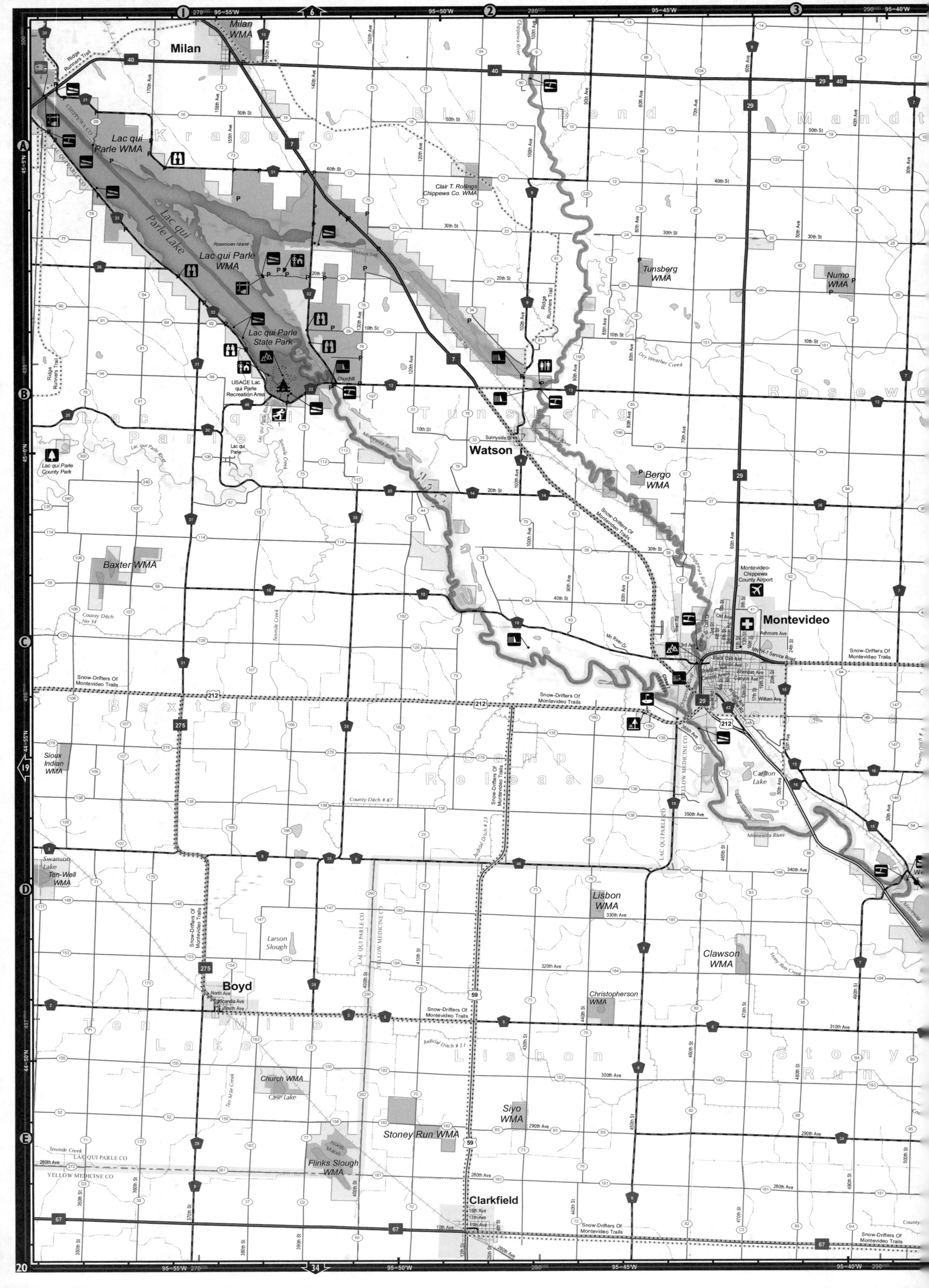

Milan
Milan WMA
Lac qui Parle WMA
Lac qui Parle Lake
Lac qui Parle State Park
USACE Lac qui Parle Recreation Area
Lac qui Parle County Park
Clair T. Rollings Chippewa Co. WMA
Tunsberg WMA
Numo WMA
Watson
Bergo WMA
Baxter WMA
Montevideo
Montevideo-Chippewa County Airport
Sioux Indian WMA
Swanson Lake
Ten-Well WMA
Lisbon WMA
Clawson WMA
Larson Slough
Boyd
Christopherson WMA
Church WMA
Case Lake
Siyo WMA
Stoney Run WMA
Flinks Slough WMA
North Marsh
Clarkfield
Carlton Lake
Snow-Drifters Of Montevideo Trails
Ridge Runners Trail
Minnesota River
Chippewa River
Lac qui Parle River
Dry Weather Creek
Tenmile Creek
Stony Run Creek
Watson Sag
Big Bend
Kragero
Mandt
Rosewood
Tunsberg
Lac qui Parle
Baxter
Camp Release
Ten Mile Lake
Lisbon
Stony Run
CHIPPEWA CO
LAC QUI PARLE CO
YELLOW MEDICINE CO
Lac qui Parle
Churchill
Sunnyside
Rosemoen Island
County Ditch No 34
County Ditch # 87
Judicial Ditch # 23
Judicial Ditch # 21
95°55'W
95°50'W
95°45'W
95°40'W
45°5'N
45°0'N
44°55'N
44°50'N
6
34
19
20

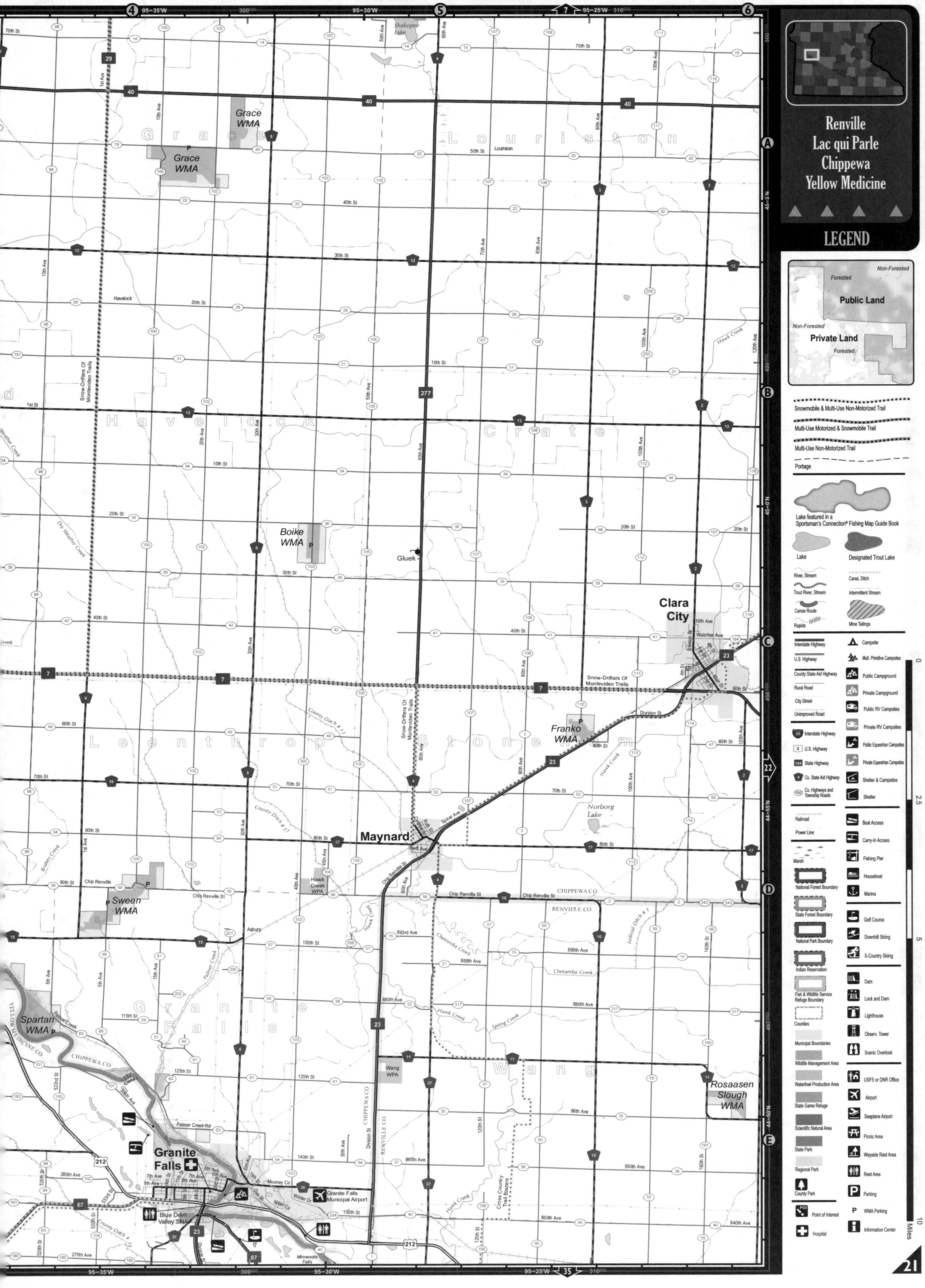

Renville
Lac qui Parle
Chippewa
Yellow Medicine
LEGEND
Public Land
Private Land
Forested
Non-Forested
Snowmobile & Multi-Use Non-Motorized Trail
Multi-Use Motorized & Snowmobile Trail
Multi-Use Non-Motorized Trail
Portage
Lake featured in a Sportsman's Connection® Fishing Map Guide Book
Lake
Designated Trout Lake
River, Stream
Canal, Ditch
Trout River, Stream
Intermittent Stream
Canoe Route
Rapids
Mine Tailings
Interstate Highway
U.S. Highway
County State Aid Highway
Rural Road
City Street
Unimproved Road
State Highway
Co. State Aid Highway
Co. Highways and Township Roads
Railroad
Power Line
Marsh
National Forest Boundary
State Forest Boundary
National Park Boundary
Indian Reservation
Fish & Wildlife Service Refuge Boundary
Counties
Municipal Boundaries
Wildlife Management Area
Waterfowl Production Area
State Game Refuge
Scientific Natural Area
State Park
Regional Park
County Park
Point of Interest
Hospital
Campsite
Mult. Primitive Campsites
Public Campground
Private Campground
Public RV Campsites
Private RV Campsites
Public Equestrian Campsites
Private Equestrian Campsites
Shelter & Campsites
Shelter
Boat Access
Carry-In Access
Fishing Pier
Houseboat
Marina
Golf Course
Downhill Skiing
X-Country Skiing
Dam
Lock and Dam
Lighthouse
Observ. Tower
Scenic Overlook
USFS or DNR Office
Airport
Seaplane Airport
Picnic Area
Wayside Rest Area
Rest Area
Parking
WMA Parking
Information Center
0
2.5
5
10
Miles
Grace
Louriston
Havelock
Crate
Leenthrop
Stoneham
Granite Falls
Wang
Grace WMA
Boike WMA
Franko WMA
Sween WMA
Spartan WMA
Rosaasen Slough WMA
Hawk Creek WPA
Wang WPA
Clara City
Maynard
Granite Falls
Gluek
Havelock
Louriston
Asbury
Norborg Lake
Shakopee Lake
Blue Devil Valley SNA
Granite Falls Municipal Airport
Minnesota Falls
Snow-Drifters Of Montevideo Trails
Cross Country Trail Blazers
Hawk Creek
Chetamba Creek
Palmer Creek
Spring Creek
Dry Weather Creek
County Ditch # 11
County Ditch # 37
Judicial Ditch # 1
CHIPPEWA CO
RENVILLE CO
YELLOW MEDICINE CO
95°35'W
95°30'W
95°25'W
45°5'N
45°0'N
44°55'N
44°50'N

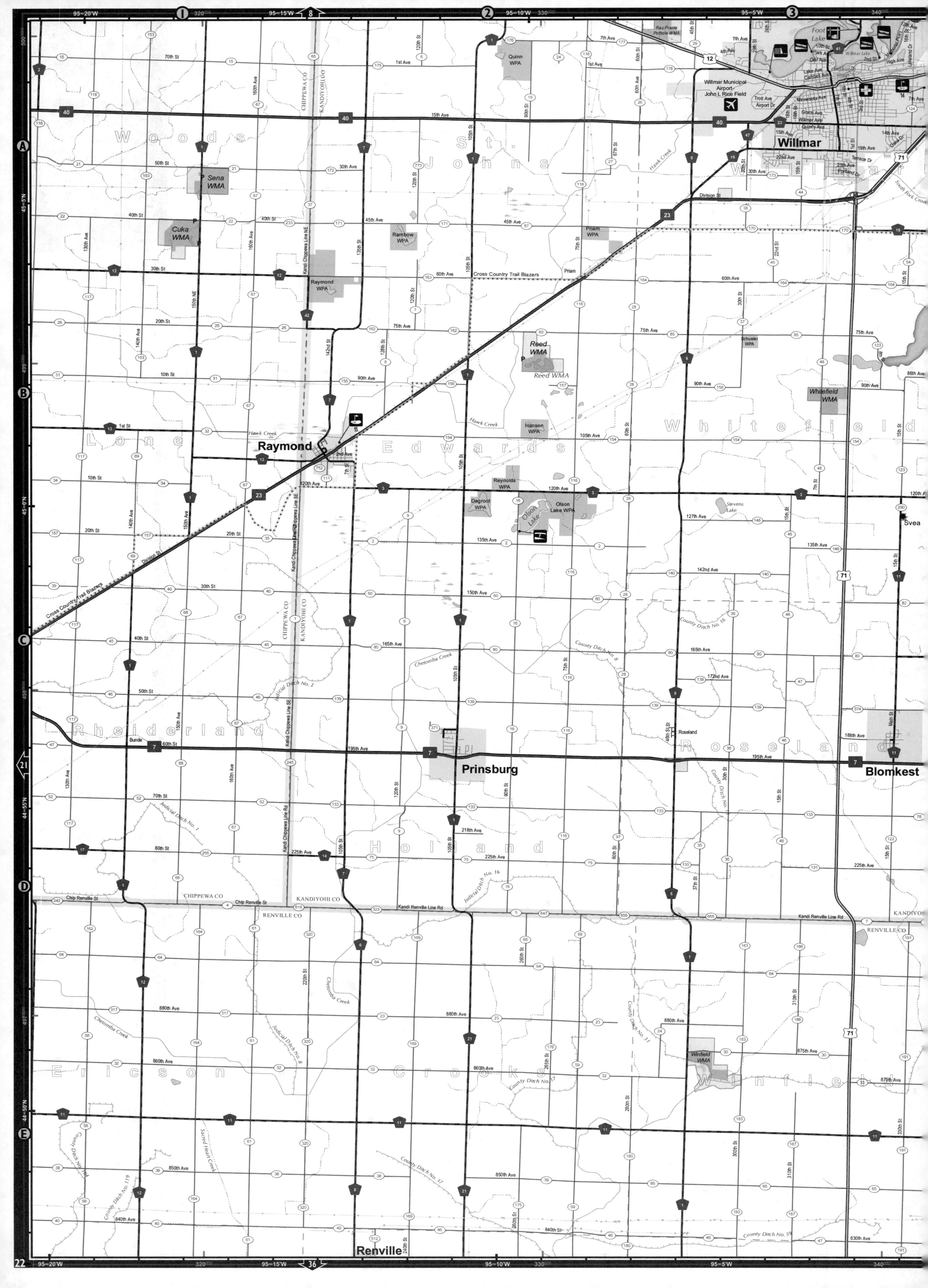

95°20'W
320
95°15'W
8
95°10'W
330
95°5'W
340
1
2
3
A
B
C
D
E
45°5'N
45°0'N
44°55'N
44°50'N
Woods
St. Johns
Willmar
Lone Tree
Edwards
Whitefield
Rheiderland
Roseland
Holland
Ericson
Crooks
Winfield
Willmar
Raymond
Prinsburg
Blomkest
Renville
Svea
Priam
Bunde
Roseland
Willmar Municipal Airport John L Rice Field
Foot Lake
Willmar Lake
Sena WMA
Cuka WMA
Quinn WPA
Rambow WPA
Raymond WPA
Reed WMA
Hanson WPA
Reynolds WPA
Degroot WPA
Olson Lake WPA
Olson Lake
Pniam WPA
Schueler WPA
Whitefield WMA
Winfield WMA
Rau Prairie Pothole WMA
Stevens Lake
Hawk Creek
Chetomba Creek
Sacred Heart Creek
South Fork Crow
Cross Country Trail Blazers
Judicial Ditch No. 1
Judicial Ditch No. 2
Judicial Ditch No. 8
Judicial Ditch No. 16
County Ditch No. 8
County Ditch No. 16
County Ditch No. 17
County Ditch No. 31
County Ditch No. 37
County Ditch No. 59
County Ditch No. 119
CHIPPEWA CO
KANDIYOHI CO
RENVILLE CO
Kandi Chippewa Line NE
Kandi Chippewa Line SE
Kandi Chippewa Line Rd
Chip Renville St
Kandi Renville Line Rd
15th Ave
30th Ave
45th Ave
60th Ave
75th Ave
90th Ave
105th Ave
120th Ave
135th Ave
150th Ave
165th Ave
195th Ave
225th Ave
880th Ave
860th Ave
850th Ave
840th Ave
70th St
50th St
40th St
30th St
20th St
10th St
1st St
60th St
80th St
21
22
36

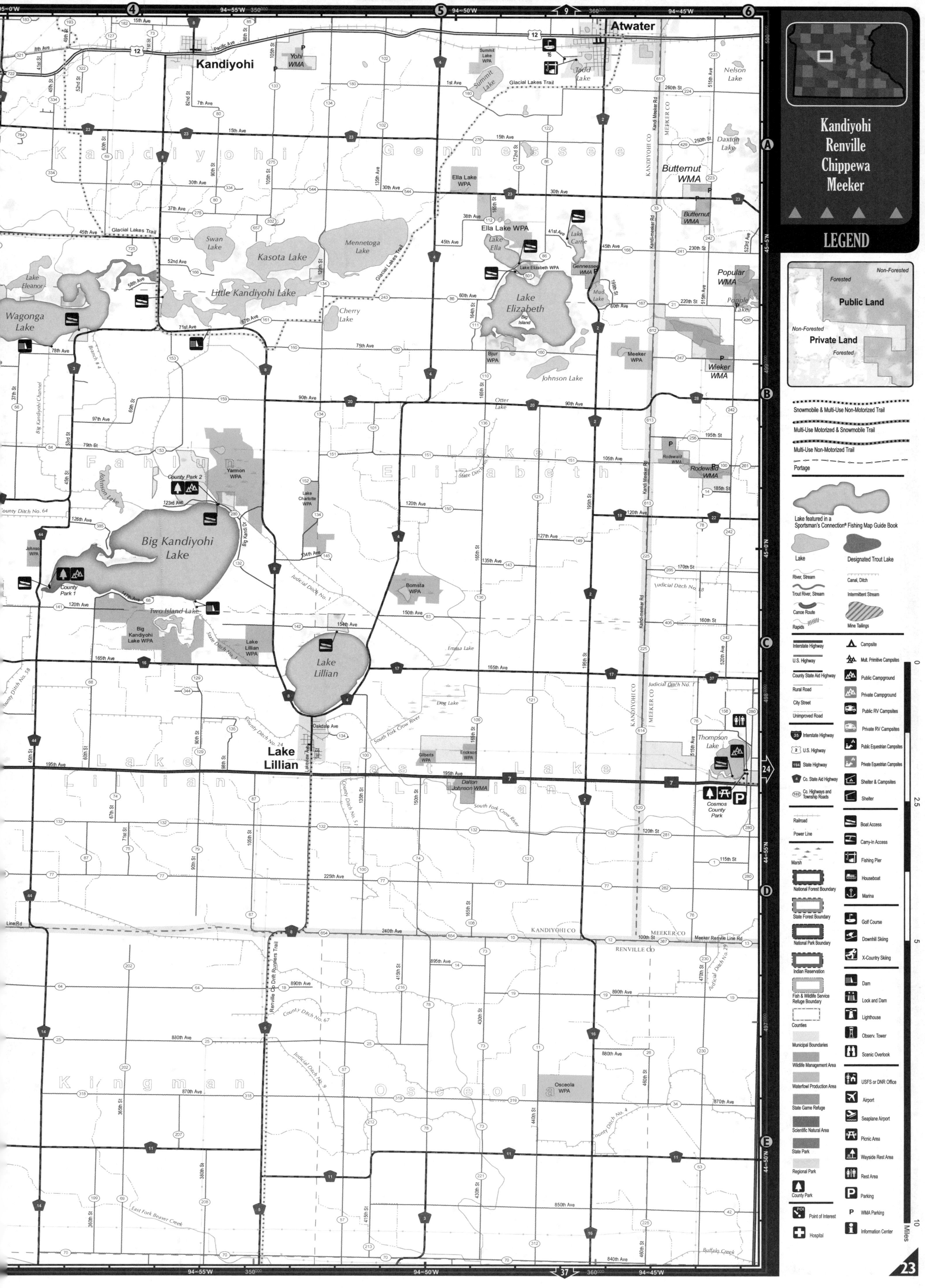
Kandiyohi
Renville
Chippewa
Meeker
LEGEND
Public Land
Private Land
Forested
Non-Forested
Snowmobile & Multi-Use Non-Motorized Trail
Multi-Use Motorized & Snowmobile Trail
Multi-Use Non-Motorized Trail
Portage
Lake featured in a Sportsman's Connection® Fishing Map Guide Book
Lake
Designated Trout Lake
River, Stream
Canal, Ditch
Trout River, Stream
Intermittent Stream
Canoe Route
Mine Tailings
Rapids
Interstate Highway
U.S. Highway
County State Aid Highway
Rural Road
City Street
Unimproved Road
Interstate Highway
U.S. Highway
State Highway
Co. State Aid Highway
Co. Highways and Township Roads
Railroad
Power Line
Marsh
National Forest Boundary
State Forest Boundary
National Park Boundary
Indian Reservation
Fish & Wildlife Service Refuge Boundary
Counties
Municipal Boundaries
Wildlife Management Area
Waterfowl Production Area
State Game Refuge
Scientific Natural Area
State Park
Regional Park
County Park
Point of Interest
Hospital
Campsite
Mult. Primitive Campsites
Public Campground
Private Campground
Public RV Campsites
Private RV Campsites
Public Equestrian Campsites
Private Equestrian Campsites
Shelter & Campsites
Shelter
Boat Access
Carry-In Access
Fishing Pier
Houseboat
Marina
Golf Course
Downhill Skiing
X-Country Skiing
Dam
Lock and Dam
Lighthouse
Observ. Tower
Scenic Overlook
USFS or DNR Office
Airport
Seaplane Airport
Picnic Area
Wayside Rest Area
Rest Area
Parking
WMA Parking
Information Center
Miles
Atwater
Kandiyohi
Lake Lillian
Big Kandiyohi Lake
Lake Lillian
Lake Elizabeth
Kasota Lake
Little Kandiyohi Lake
Wagonga Lake
Mennetoga Lake
Swan Lake
Summit Lake
Todd Lake
Nelson Lake
Daxton Lake
Cherry Lake
Johnson Lake
Two Island Lake
Thompson Lake
Cosmos County Park
County Park 1
County Park 2
Yohi WMA
Ella Lake WPA
Butternut WMA
Popular WMA
Meeker WPA
Wieker WMA
Yarmon WPA
Bomsta WPA
Osceola WPA
Dalton Johnson WMA
Kandiyohi
Gennessee
Fahlun
Lake Elizabeth
Lake Lillian
East Lake Lillian
Kingman
Osceola
Glacial Lakes Trail
South Fork Crow River
East Fork Beaver Creek
Buffalo Creek
Renville Co Drift Runners Trail
KANDIYOHI CO
MEEKER CO
RENVILLE CO
94°55'W
94°50'W
94°45'W
45°5'N
45°0'N
44°55'N
44°50'N
24
37
9

10

94°40'W
370000
94°35'W
380000
94°30'W
94°25'W
390000
Grove City
Litchfield
Darwin
Rosendale
Cosmos
Cedar Mills
Strout
Beckville
Greenleaf
Casey
Corvuso
Heatwole
Lakeside
Churchill
West Lynn
Hutchinson Municipal Airport
Litchfield Municipal Airport
Lake Ripley Game Refuge
Gopher Campfire Game Refuge
Acton
Litchfield
Darwin
Danielson
Greenleaf
Ellsworth
Cosmos
Cedar Mills
Acoma
Brookfield
Boon Lake
Lynn
Acton WPA
Hanson Lake WPA
Litchfield WPA
Grass Lake WPA
Peifer School WPA
Casey Lake WPA
Acton WMA
Popular WMA
Rosendale WPA
Hen Haven WMA
Greenleaf WPA
Mahlon James WMA
Greenleaf WMA
Provencher WMA
Lake Harden WPA
Cosmos WPA
Cedar Mills WPA
Brookfield WPA
Prieve WMA
Boon Lake WMA
Boon Lake Slough WMA
Boon Lake WPA
Phare Lake WPA
Dahl WMA
Barber Lake WPA
Eagle Lake WPA
Ras-Lynn WMA
Hutchinson WMA
West Ripley Park
Lake Manuella County Park
Piepenburg Park
Stahl's Lake County Park
Luce Line State Trail
Meeker County Trails
Long Lake
Sather Lake
Grove Creek
Grass Lake
Thoen Lake
Hanson Lake
Chicken Lake
Stone Lake
Lake Ripley
East Lake Ripley
Lake Harold
Hope Lake
Mud Lake
Youngstrom Lake
Minnesota Lake
Star Lake
Hoosier Lake
Evenson Lake
Round Lake
East Andrew Nelson Lake
Lake Andrew Nelson
Casey Lake
Lake Manuella
Washington Creek
Stella Lake
Lake Washington
Lake Darwin
Stevens Lake
South Buckley Lake
Lake Minnie Belle
Benton Lake
Hurley Lake
Sioux Lake
Greenleaf Lake
Lake Willie
King Lake
Belle Lake
Lake Erie
Eighty Acre Lake
Birch Lake
Porter Lake
School House Lake
Long Lake
Goose Lake
Atkinson Lake
Lake Harding
Hoff Lake
Cedar Lake
Belle Lake
Dettman Lake
Stahls Lake
Popp Slough
Mud Lake
Clear Lake
French Lake
Pierce Lake
Campbell Lake
Otter Lake
Campbell Lake
Pipe Lake
King Creek
Belle Creek
South Fork Crow River
Judicial Ditch #18
Judicial Ditch #1
Judicial Ditch No. 29
County Ditch # 18
Boon Lake
Hodgson Lake
Lake Allen
Phare Lake
Allie Lake
Barber Lake
Mud Lake
County Ditch # 4
County Ditch # 7 A
Buffalo Creek
MEEKER CO
RENVILLE CO
MCLEOD CO
Meeker Renville Line Rd
Vista Rd
York Rd
Grade Rd
Lake Rd
Belle St
Common St
Curran St
Meeker County Trails

23

38

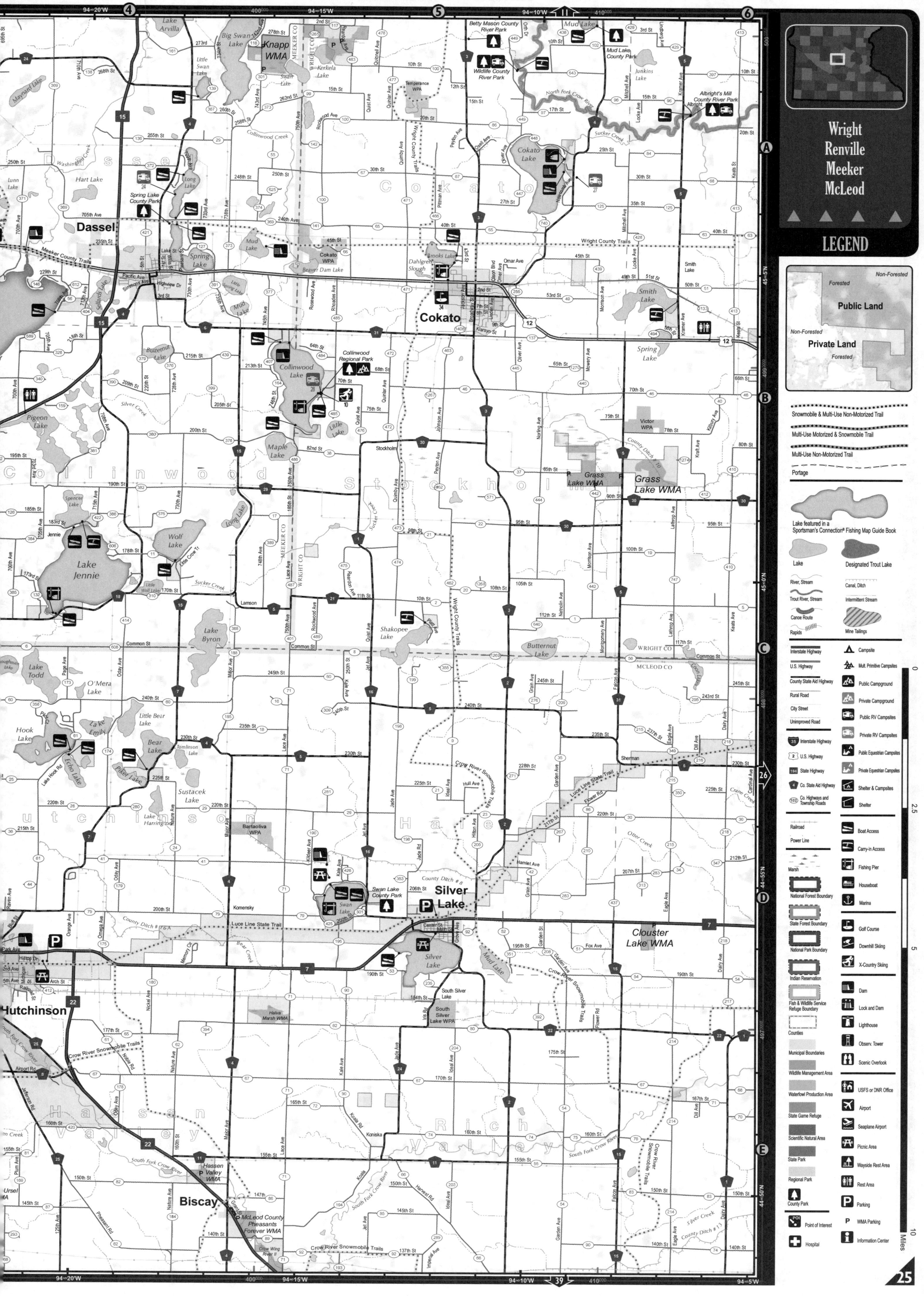

Wright
Renville
Meeker
McLeod
LEGEND
Public Land
Private Land
Forested
Non-Forested
Snowmobile & Multi-Use Non-Motorized Trail
Multi-Use Motorized & Snowmobile Trail
Multi-Use Non-Motorized Trail
Portage
Lake featured in a Sportsman's Connection® Fishing Map Guide Book
Lake
Designated Trout Lake
River, Stream
Canal, Ditch
Trout River, Stream
Intermittent Stream
Canoe Route
Rapids
Mine Tailings
Interstate Highway
U.S. Highway
County State Aid Highway
Rural Road
City Street
Unimproved Road
Interstate Highway
U.S. Highway
State Highway
Co. State Aid Highway
Co. Highways and Township Roads
Railroad
Power Line
Marsh
National Forest Boundary
State Forest Boundary
National Park Boundary
Indian Reservation
Fish & Wildlife Service Refuge Boundary
Counties
Municipal Boundaries
Wildlife Management Area
Waterfowl Production Area
State Game Refuge
Scientific Natural Area
State Park
Regional Park
County Park
Point of Interest
Hospital
Campsite
Mult. Primitive Campsites
Public Campground
Private Campground
Public RV Campsites
Private RV Campsites
Public Equestrian Campsites
Private Equestrian Campsites
Shelter & Campsites
Shelter
Boat Access
Carry-in Access
Fishing Pier
Houseboat
Marina
Golf Course
Downhill Skiing
X-Country Skiing
Dam
Lock and Dam
Lighthouse
Observ. Tower
Scenic Overlook
USFS or DNR Office
Airport
Seaplane Airport
Picnic Area
Wayside Rest Area
Rest Area
Parking
WMA Parking
Information Center
Miles
Dassel
Cokato
Silver Lake
Hutchinson
Biscay
Knapp WMA
Lake Jennie
Collinwood Lake
Collinwood Regional Park
Cokato Lake
Spring Lake County Park
Swan Lake County Park
Betty Mason County River Park
Wildlife County River Park
Mud Lake County Park
Albright's Mill County River Park
Grass Lake WMA
Victor WPA
Clouster Lake WMA
Bartaoliva WPA
South Silver Lake WPA
Halva Marsh WMA
Hassen Valley WMA
McLeod County Pheasants Forever WMA
Luce Line State Trail
Crow River Snowmobile Trails
Wright County Trails
Meeker County Trails
North Fork Crow River
South Fork Crow River
WRIGHT CO
MEEKER CO
MCLEOD CO
Collinwood
Stockholm
Cokato
Hutchinson
Hale
Hassan Valley
Rich Valley
94°20'W
94°15'W
94°10'W
94°5'W
45°5'N
45°0'N
44°55'N
44°50'N

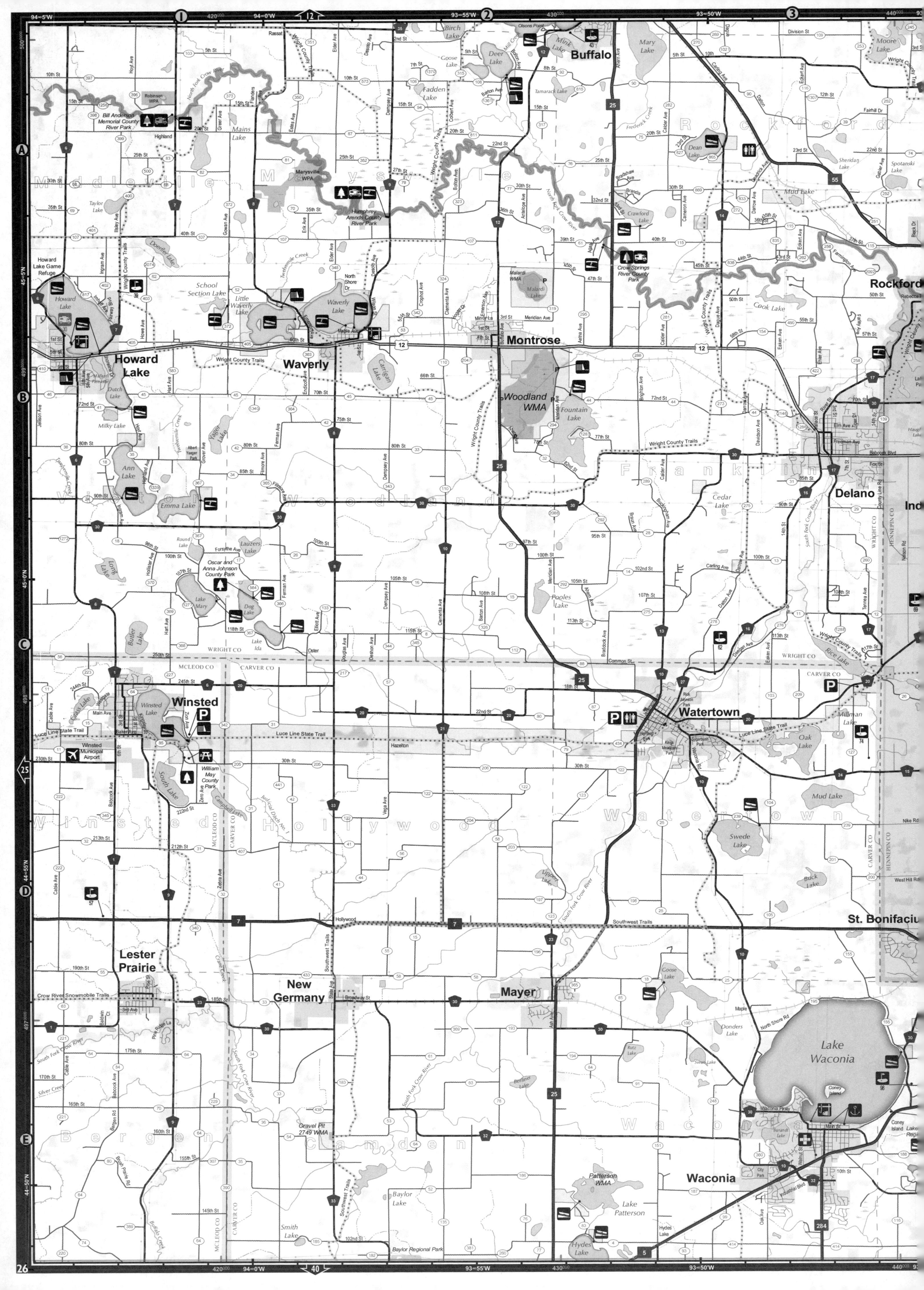

Buffalo
Howard Lake
Waverly
Montrose
Rockford
Delano
Winsted
Watertown
Lester Prairie
New Germany
Mayer
Waconia
St. Bonifacius
Woodland WMA
Marysville WPA
Robinson WPA
Malardi WMA
Howard Lake Game Refuge
Bill Anderson Memorial County River Park
Humphrey Arends County River Park
Crow Springs River County Park
Oscar and Anna Johnson County Park
William May County Park
Winsted Municipal Airport
Gravel Pit 2749 WMA
Patterson WMA
Baylor Regional Park
Lake Waconia
Coney Island
Mary Lake
Deer Lake
Birch Lake
Goose Lake
Fadden Lake
Mink Lake
Dean Lake
Crawford Lake
Mud Lake
Moore Lake
Sheridan Lake
Spotanski Lake
Taylor Lake
Doerfler Lake
School Section Lake
Little Waverly Lake
Waverly Lake
Carrigan Lake
Fountain Lake
Dutch Lake
Milky Lake
Ann Lake
Emma Lake
Round Lake
Lauzers Lake
Long Lake
Lake Mary
Dog Lake
Lake Ida
Butler Lake
Pooles Lake
Cedar Lake
Rice Lake
Cook Lake
Winsted Lake
Grass Lake
South Lake
Campbell Lake
Millman Lake
Oak Lake
Swede Lake
Buck Lake
Mud Lake
Upper Lake
Goose Lake
Donders Lake
Rutz Lake
Swan Lake
Berliner Lake
Baylor Lake
Smith Lake
Lake Patterson
Hydes Lake
Wright County Trails
Luce Line State Trail
Southwest Trails
Crow River Snowmobile Trails
North Fork Crow River
South Fork Crow River
Middleville
Marysville
Rockford
Woodland
Franklin
Victor
Winsted
Hollywood
Watertown
Bergen
Camden
Waconia
WRIGHT CO
MCLEOD CO
CARVER CO
HENNEPIN CO
Hollywood
Hazelton
Oster
Rassat
12
25
40

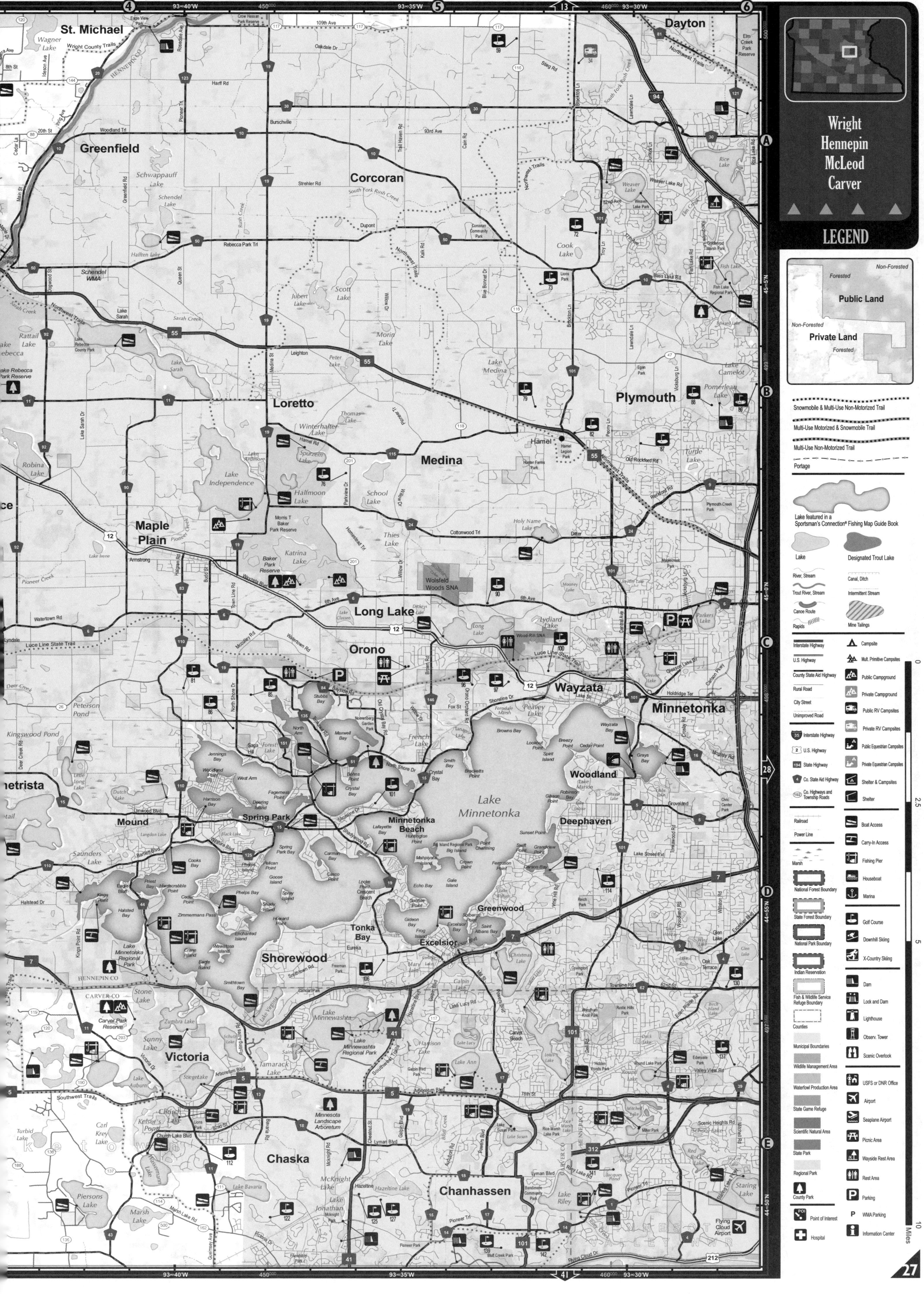

Wright
Hennepin
McLeod
Carver
LEGEND
Public Land
Private Land
Forested
Non-Forested
Snowmobile & Multi-Use Non-Motorized Trail
Multi-Use Motorized & Snowmobile Trail
Multi-Use Non-Motorized Trail
Portage
Lake featured in a Sportsman's Connection® Fishing Map Guide Book
Lake
Designated Trout Lake
Campsite
Mult. Primitive Campsites
Public Campground
Private Campground
Public RV Campsites
Private RV Campsites
Shelter & Campsites
Shelter
Boat Access
Carry-In Access
Fishing Pier
Houseboat
Marina
Golf Course
Downhill Skiing
X-Country Skiing
Dam
Lock and Dam
Lighthouse
Observ. Tower
Scenic Overlook
USFS or DNR Office
Airport
Seaplane Airport
Picnic Area
Wayside Rest Area
Rest Area
Parking
WMA Parking
Information Center
Point of Interest
Hospital
Miles
St. Michael
Dayton
Greenfield
Corcoran
Loretto
Plymouth
Medina
Maple Plain
Long Lake
Orono
Wayzata
Minnetonka
Woodland
Deephaven
Mound
Spring Park
Minnetonka Beach
Lake Minnetonka
Greenwood
Excelsior
Tonka Bay
Shorewood
Victoria
Chaska
Chanhassen

Dayton
Champlin
Elm Creek Park Reserve
Anoka County Airport
Blaine
Lexington
Coon Rapids
Coon Rapids Dam Reg Park
Circle Pines
Osseo
Mounds View
Shoreview
Brooklyn Park
Spring Lake Park
Maple Grove
Arden Hills
Brooklyn Center
Fridley
Crystal Airport
Crystal
Hilltop
New Brighton
Columbia Heights
Plymouth
Robbinsdale
St. Anthony
New Hope
Medicine Lake
Lauderdale
Falcon Heights
Golden Valley
Minnetonka
St. Louis Park
Minneapolis
St. Paul
Hopkins
Lake Calhoun
Lake Harriet
Edina
Lilydale
Mendota Heights
Mendota
Minneapolis-Saint Paul International Airport
Richfield
Eden Prairie
Fort Snelling State Park
Bloomington
Eagan
Burnsville
Highland Park
Minnehaha Falls
Fort Snelling
Hennepin Trail Corridor Bike Trail
Long Lake Regional Park
Rice Creek North Regional Park
Anoka County Riverfront Regional Park
Clifton French Regional Park
Bryant Lake Regional Park
Hyland-Bush Lakes Park
Lake Harvey
Turtle Lake
Medicine Lake
Bass Lake
Eagle Lake
93°25'W
93°20'W
93°15'W
93°10'W
45°5'N
45°0'N
44°55'N
44°50'N

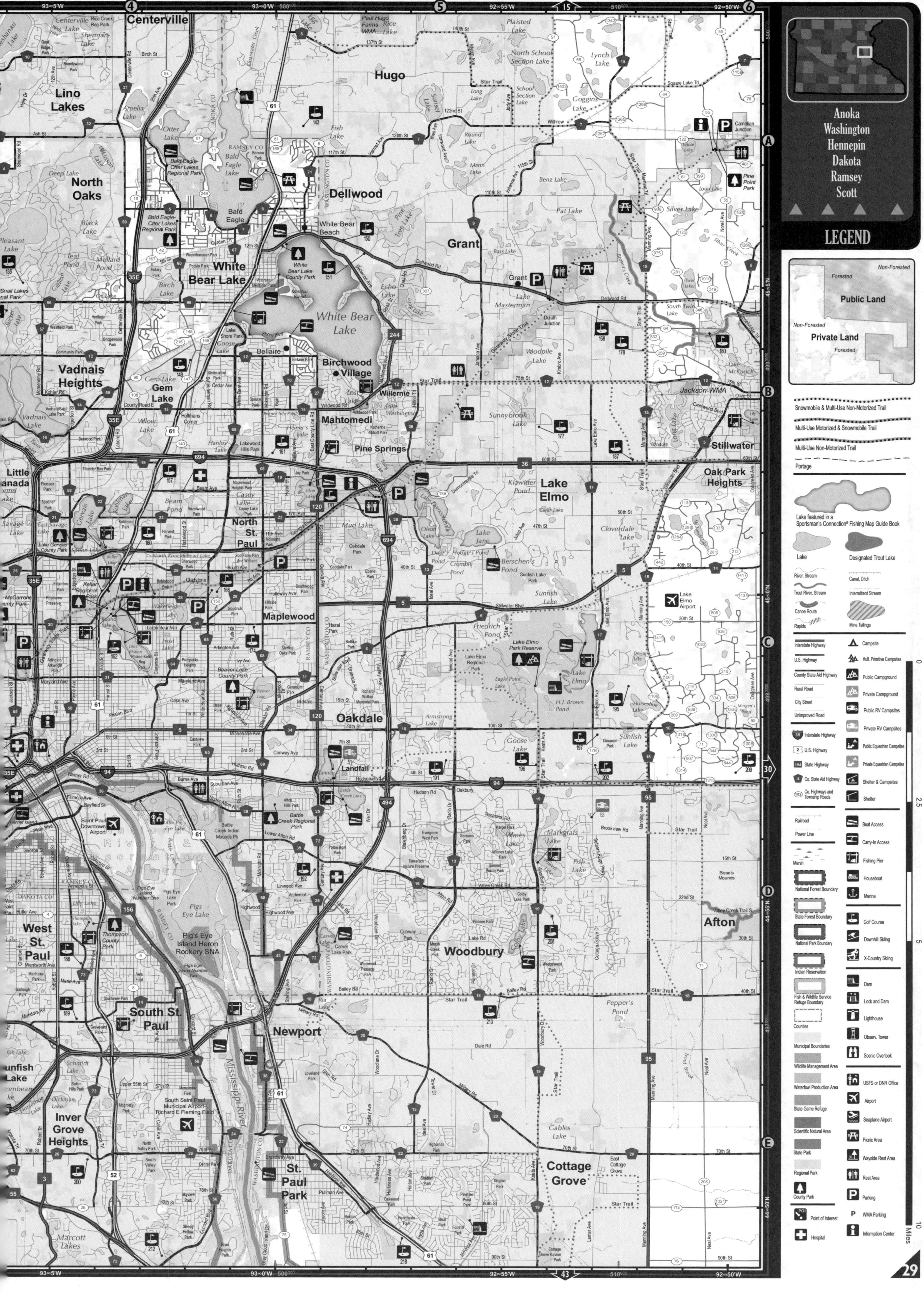

Centerville
Lino Lakes
North Oaks
Hugo
Dellwood
Grant
White Bear Lake
White Bear Lake
Birchwood Village
Vadnais Heights
Gem Lake
Willernie
Mahtomedi
Pine Springs
Little Canada
North St. Paul
Lake Elmo
Oak Park Heights
Stillwater
Maplewood
Oakdale
Landfall
Woodbury
Afton
West St. Paul
South St. Paul
Newport
Inver Grove Heights
St. Paul Park
Cottage Grove
Mississippi River
Lake Elmo Park Reserve
Battle Creek Regional Park
Pig's Eye Lake
Pig's Eye Island Heron Rookery SNA
Saint Paul Downtown Airport
Lake Elmo Airport
South Saint Paul Municipal Airport Richard E Fleming Field
Jackson WMA
Anoka
Washington
Hennepin
Dakota
Ramsey
Scott
LEGEND
Forested
Non-Forested
Public Land
Private Land
Snowmobile & Multi-Use Non-Motorized Trail
Multi-Use Motorized & Snowmobile Trail
Multi-Use Non-Motorized Trail
Portage
Lake featured in a Sportsman's Connection® Fishing Map Guide Book
Lake
Designated Trout Lake
River, Stream
Canal, Ditch
Trout River, Stream
Intermittent Stream
Canoe Route
Rapids
Mine Tailings
Interstate Highway
U.S. Highway
County State Aid Highway
Rural Road
City Street
Unimproved Road
Interstate Highway
U.S. Highway
State Highway
Co. State Aid Highway
Co. Highways and Township Roads
Railroad
Power Line
Marsh
National Forest Boundary
State Forest Boundary
National Park Boundary
Indian Reservation
Fish & Wildlife Service Refuge Boundary
Counties
Municipal Boundaries
Wildlife Management Area
Waterfowl Production Area
State Game Refuge
Scientific Natural Area
State Park
Regional Park
County Park
Point of Interest
Hospital
Campsite
Mult. Primitive Campsites
Public Campground
Private Campground
Public RV Campsites
Private RV Campsites
Public Equestrian Campsites
Private Equestrian Campsites
Shelter & Campsites
Shelter
Boat Access
Carry-In Access
Fishing Pier
Houseboat
Marina
Golf Course
Downhill Skiing
X-Country Skiing
Dam
Lock and Dam
Lighthouse
Observ. Tower
Scenic Overlook
USFS or DNR Office
Airport
Seaplane Airport
Picnic Area
Wayside Rest Area
Rest Area
Parking
WMA Parking
Information Center
Miles

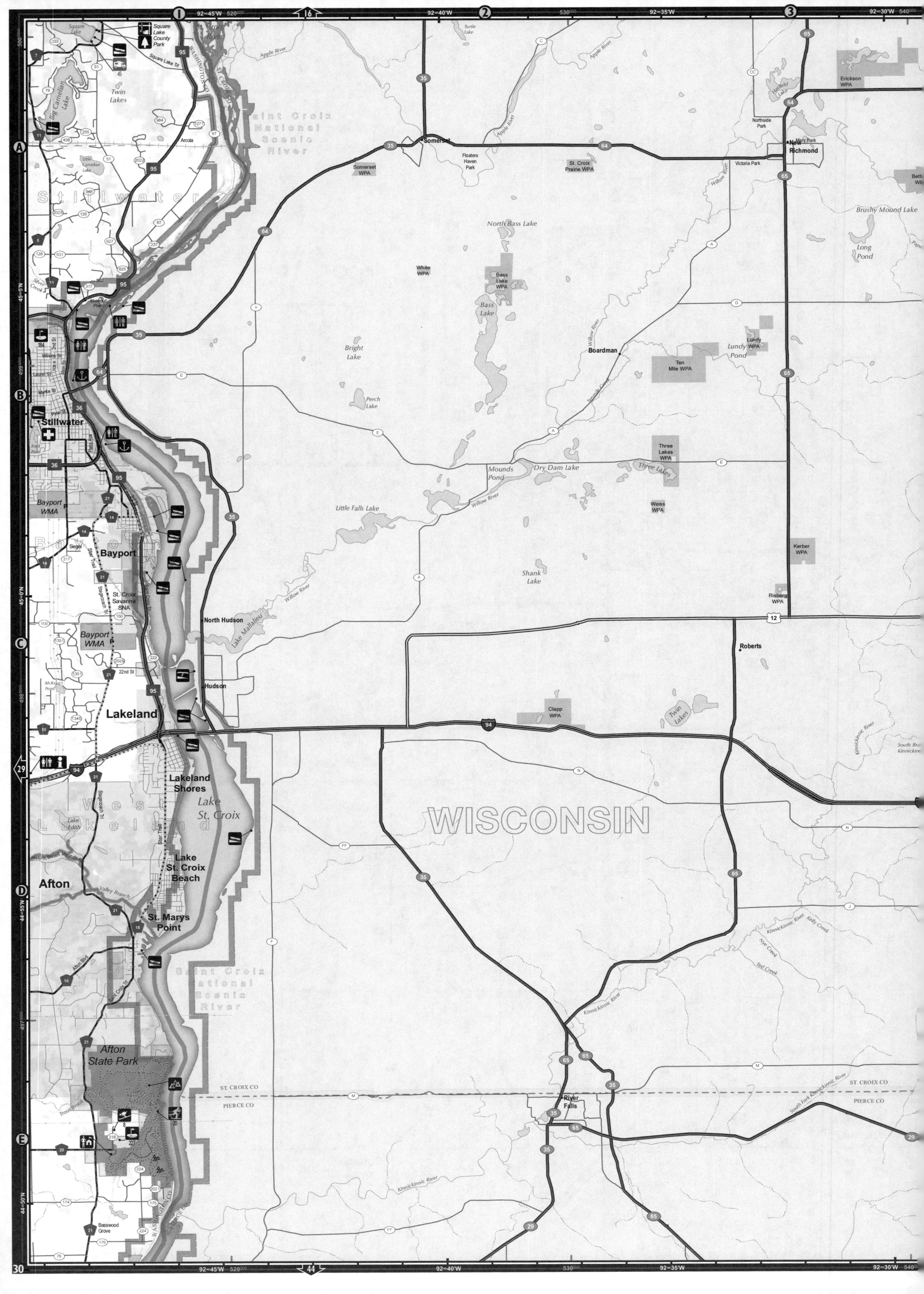

WISCONSIN
Stillwater
Bayport
Lakeland
Lakeland Shores
Lake St. Croix Beach
St. Marys Point
Afton
Afton State Park
Somerset
New Richmond
North Hudson
Hudson
Roberts
River Falls
Boardman
Lake St. Croix
Saint Croix National Scenic River
Twin Lakes
Square Lake County Park
Somerset WPA
St. Croix Prairie WPA
White WPA
Bass Lake WPA
Ten Mile WPA
Lundy WPA
Three Lakes WPA
Weiss WPA
Kerber WPA
Risberg WPA
Clapp WPA
Erickson WPA
Bayport WMA
St. Croix Savanna SNA
North Bass Lake
Bass Lake
Bright Lake
Perch Lake
Mounds Pond
Dry Dam Lake
Little Falls Lake
Shank Lake
Lake Mallalieu
Lundy Pond
Brushy Mound Lake
Long Pond
Willow River
Apple River
Kinnickinnic River
ST. CROIX CO
PIERCE CO
WASHINGTON CO
92°45'W
92°40'W
92°35'W
92°30'W
45°5'N
45°0'N
44°55'N
44°50'N

Washington
St. Croix
Pierce
LEGEND
Public Land
Private Land
Forested
Non-Forested
Snowmobile & Multi-Use Non-Motorized Trail
Multi-Use Motorized & Snowmobile Trail
Multi-Use Non-Motorized Trail
Portage
Lake featured in a Sportsman's Connection® Fishing Map Guide Book
Lake
Designated Trout Lake
River, Stream
Canal, Ditch
Trout River, Stream
Intermittent Stream
Canoe Route
Rapids
Mine Tailings
Interstate Highway
U.S. Highway
County State Aid Highway
Rural Road
City Street
Unimproved Road
Interstate Highway
U.S. Highway
State Highway
Co. State Aid Highway
Co. Highways and Township Roads
Railroad
Power Line
Marsh
National Forest Boundary
State Forest Boundary
National Park Boundary
Indian Reservation
Fish & Wildlife Service Refuge Boundary
Counties
Municipal Boundaries
Wildlife Management Area
Waterfowl Production Area
State Game Refuge
Scientific Natural Area
State Park
Regional Park
County Park
Point of Interest
Hospital
Campsite
Mult. Primitive Campsites
Public Campground
Private Campground
Public RV Campsites
Private RV Campsites
Public Equestrian Campsites
Private Equestrian Campsites
Shelter & Campsites
Shelter
Boat Access
Carry-In Access
Fishing Pier
Houseboat
Marina
Golf Course
Downhill Skiing
X-Country Skiing
Dam
Lock and Dam
Lighthouse
Observ. Tower
Scenic Overlook
USFS or DNR Office
Airport
Seaplane Airport
Picnic Area
Wayside Rest Area
Rest Area
Parking
WMA Parking
Information Center
0
2.5
5
10
Miles
Forest
Willow River
Dry Run
South Fork Willow River
Bushy Lake
Glen Hills Co Park
Parker Creek
Spring Valley
Martell
Mines Creek
Cave Creek
Eau Galle River
Goose Creek
92°25'W
92°20'W
92°15'W
45°5'N
45°0'N
44°55'N
44°50'N
17
45
Karla Caspari

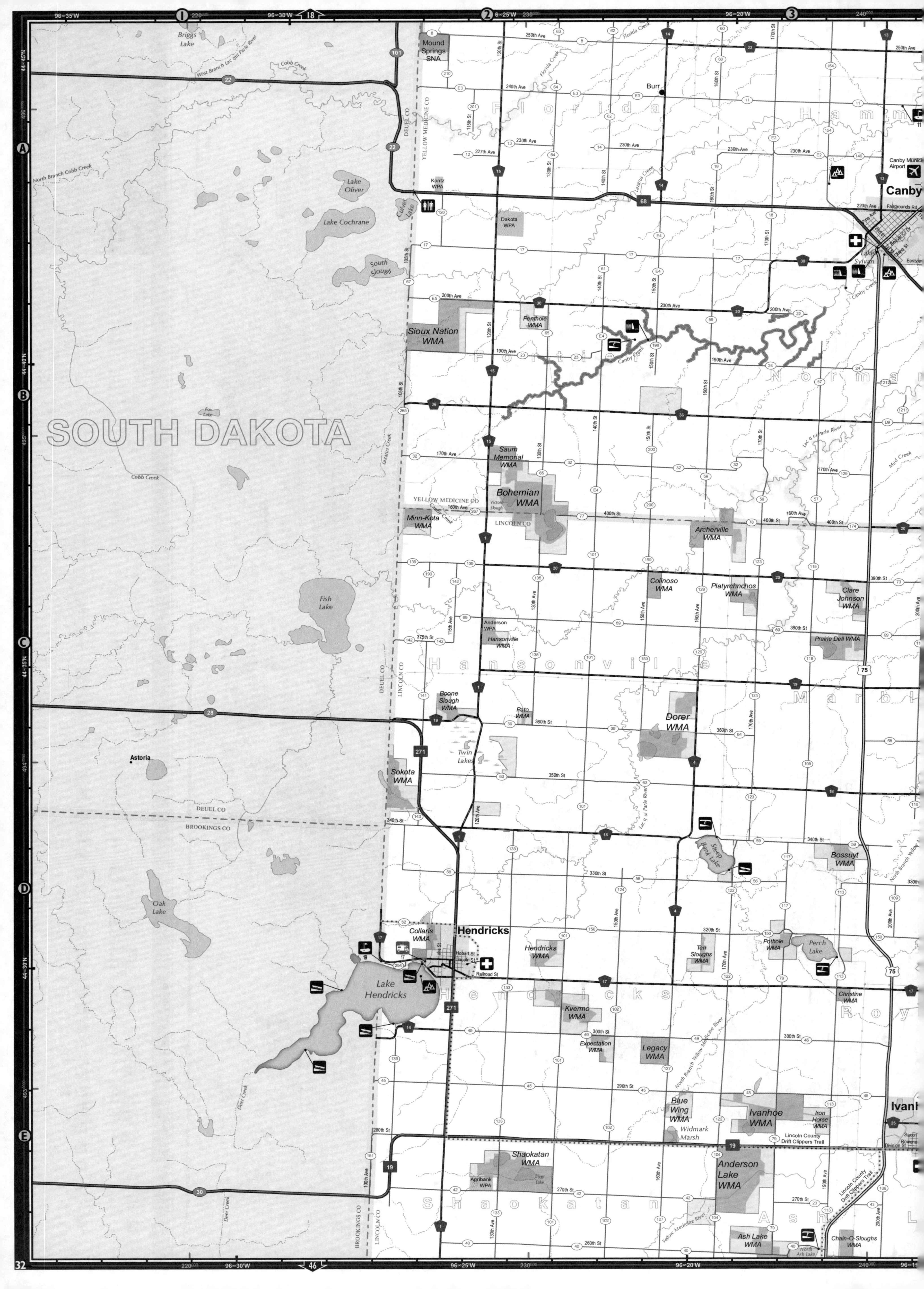
SOUTH DAKOTA
Briggs Lake
Lake Oliver
Lake Cochrane
South Slough
Fish Lake
Oak Lake
Astoria
DEUEL CO
BROOKINGS CO
YELLOW MEDICINE CO
LINCOLN CO
Mound Springs SNA
Kontz WPA
Dakota WPA
Sioux Nation WMA
Penthole WMA
Saum Memorial WMA
Bohemian WMA
Minn-Kota WMA
Archerville WMA
Colinoso WMA
Platyrchnchos WMA
Clare Johnson WMA
Prairie Dell WMA
Anderson WPA
Hansonville WMA
Boone Slough WMA
Pato WMA
Twin Lakes
Dorer WMA
Sokota WMA
Bossuyt WMA
Steep Bank Lake
Collaris WMA
Hendricks
Lake Hendricks
Hendricks WMA
Ten Sloughs WMA
Pothole WMA
Perch Lake
Christine WMA
Kvermo WMA
Expectation WMA
Legacy WMA
Blue Wing WMA
Widmark Marsh
Ivanhoe WMA
Iron Horse WMA
Lincoln County Drift Clippers Trail
Shaokatan WMA
Agribank WPA
Anderson Lake WMA
Ash Lake WMA
Chain-O-Sloughs WMA
Burr
Canby
Canby Municipal Airport
Florida
Hammer
Fortier
Norman
Hansonville
Marble
Hendricks
Royal
Shaokatan
Ash Lake
Ivanhoe

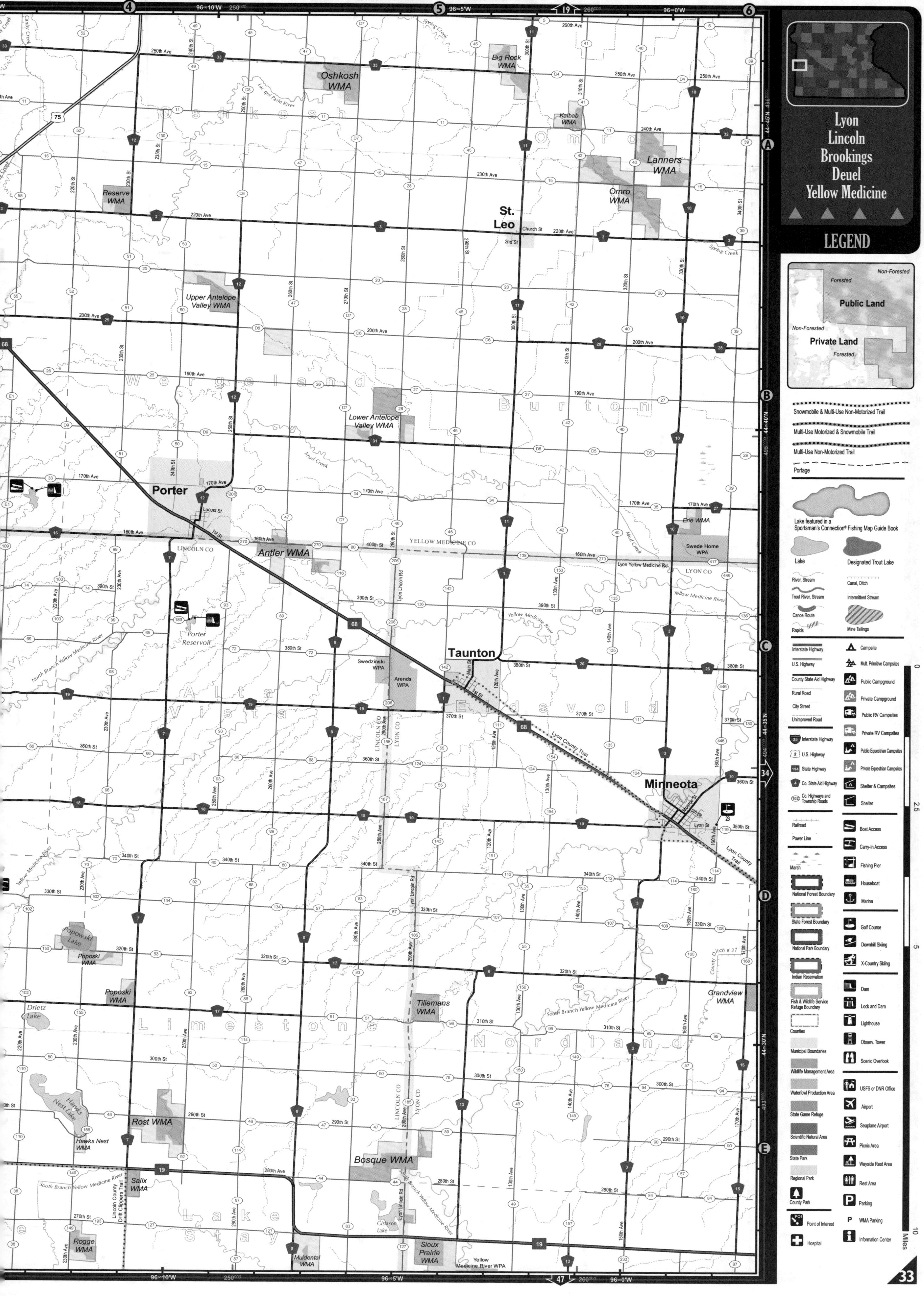

Lyon
Lincoln
Brookings
Deuel
Yellow Medicine
LEGEND
Public Land
Private Land
Forested
Non-Forested
Snowmobile & Multi-Use Non-Motorized Trail
Multi-Use Motorized & Snowmobile Trail
Multi-Use Non-Motorized Trail
Portage
Lake featured in a Sportsman's Connection® Fishing Map Guide Book
Lake
Designated Trout Lake
River, Stream
Canal, Ditch
Trout River, Stream
Intermittent Stream
Canoe Route
Rapids
Mine Tailings
Interstate Highway
U.S. Highway
County State Aid Highway
Rural Road
City Street
Unimproved Road
Interstate Highway
U.S. Highway
State Highway
Co. State Aid Highway
Co. Highways and Township Roads
Railroad
Power Line
Marsh
National Forest Boundary
State Forest Boundary
National Park Boundary
Indian Reservation
Fish & Wildlife Service Refuge Boundary
Counties
Municipal Boundaries
Wildlife Management Area
Waterfowl Production Area
State Game Refuge
Scientific Natural Area
State Park
Regional Park
County Park
Point of Interest
Hospital
Campsite
Mult. Primitive Campsites
Public Campground
Private Campground
Public RV Campsites
Private RV Campsites
Public Equestrian Campsites
Private Equestrian Campsites
Shelter & Campsites
Shelter
Boat Access
Carry-In Access
Fishing Pier
Houseboat
Marina
Golf Course
Downhill Skiing
X-Country Skiing
Dam
Lock and Dam
Lighthouse
Observ. Tower
Scenic Overlook
USFS or DNR Office
Airport
Seaplane Airport
Picnic Area
Wayside Rest Area
Rest Area
Parking
WMA Parking
Information Center
Miles
Porter
Taunton
Minneota
St. Leo
Oshkosh WMA
Big Rock WMA
Kaibab WMA
Lanners WMA
Omro WMA
Reserve WMA
Upper Antelope Valley WMA
Lower Antelope Valley WMA
Erie WMA
Swede Home WPA
Antler WMA
Porter Reservoir
Swedzinski WPA
Arends WPA
Popowski Lake
Poposki WMA
Grandview WMA
Tillemans WMA
Drietz Lake
Hawks Nest Lake
Hawks Nest WMA
Rost WMA
Bosque WMA
Salix WMA
Rogge WMA
Muldental WMA
Sioux Prairie WMA
Yellow Medicine River WPA
Gislason Lake
Lincoln County Drift Clippers Trail
Lyon County Trail
Oshkosh
Omro
Wergeland
Burton
Alta Vista
Eidsvold
Limestone
Nordland
Lake Stay
LINCOLN CO
YELLOW MEDICINE CO
LYON CO
Lac qui Parle River
Yellow Medicine River
North Branch Yellow Medicine River
South Branch Yellow Medicine River
Spring Creek
Mud Creek
County Ditch # 37
Canby Creek
96°10'W
96°5'W
96°0'W
44°45'N
44°40'N
44°35'N
44°30'N

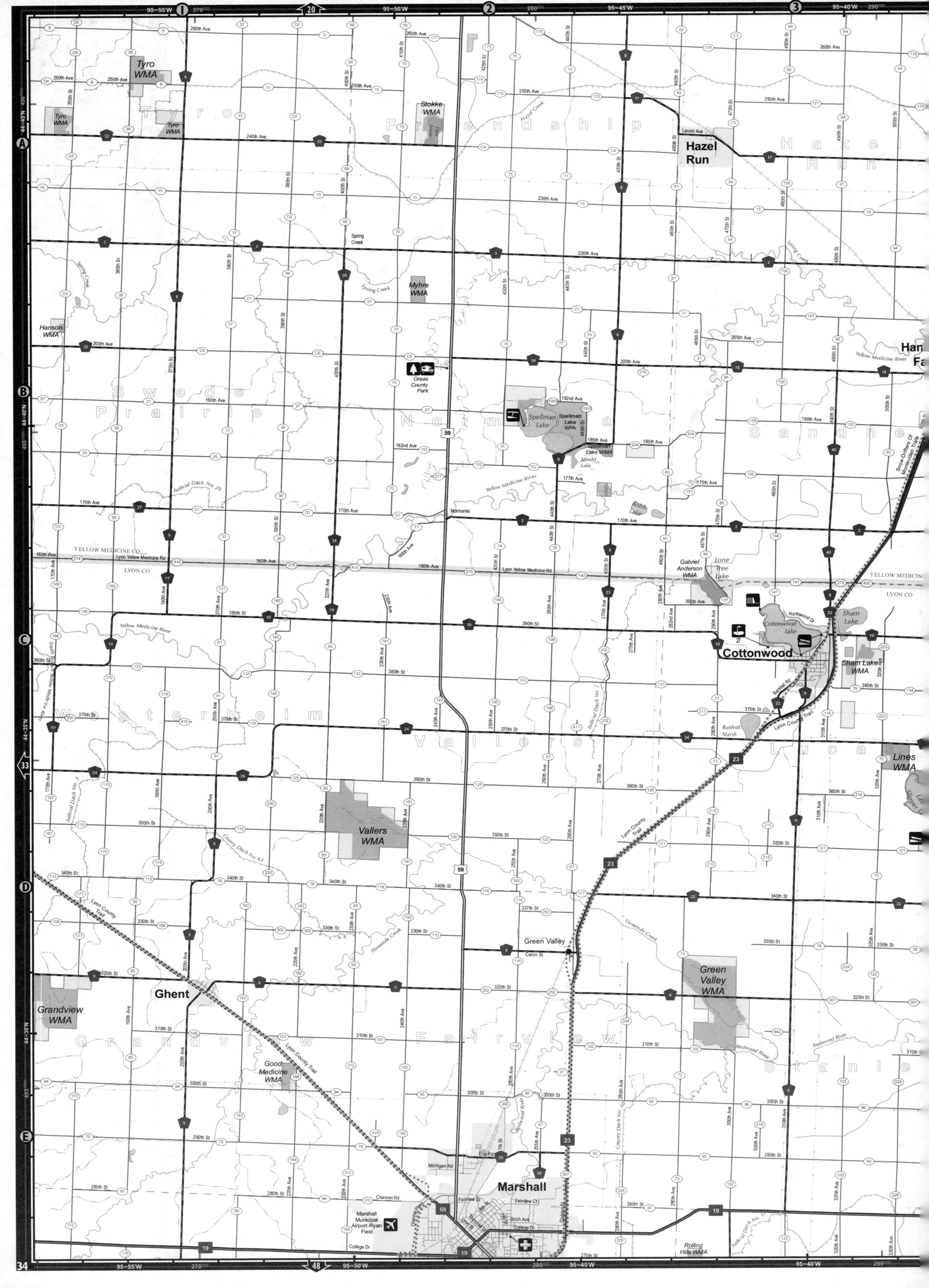
Tyro WMA
Stokke WMA
Hazel Run
Myhre WMA
Hanson WMA
Oraas County Park
Spellman Lake WPA
Normania
Gabriel Anderson WMA
Lone Tree Lake
Cottonwood
Sham Lake WMA
Lines WMA
Vallers WMA
Green Valley
Green Valley WMA
Ghent
Grandview WMA
Good Medicine WMA
Marshall
Marshall Municipal Airport-Ryan Field
Rolling Hills WMA
YELLOW MEDICINE CO
LYON CO
Lyon County Trail

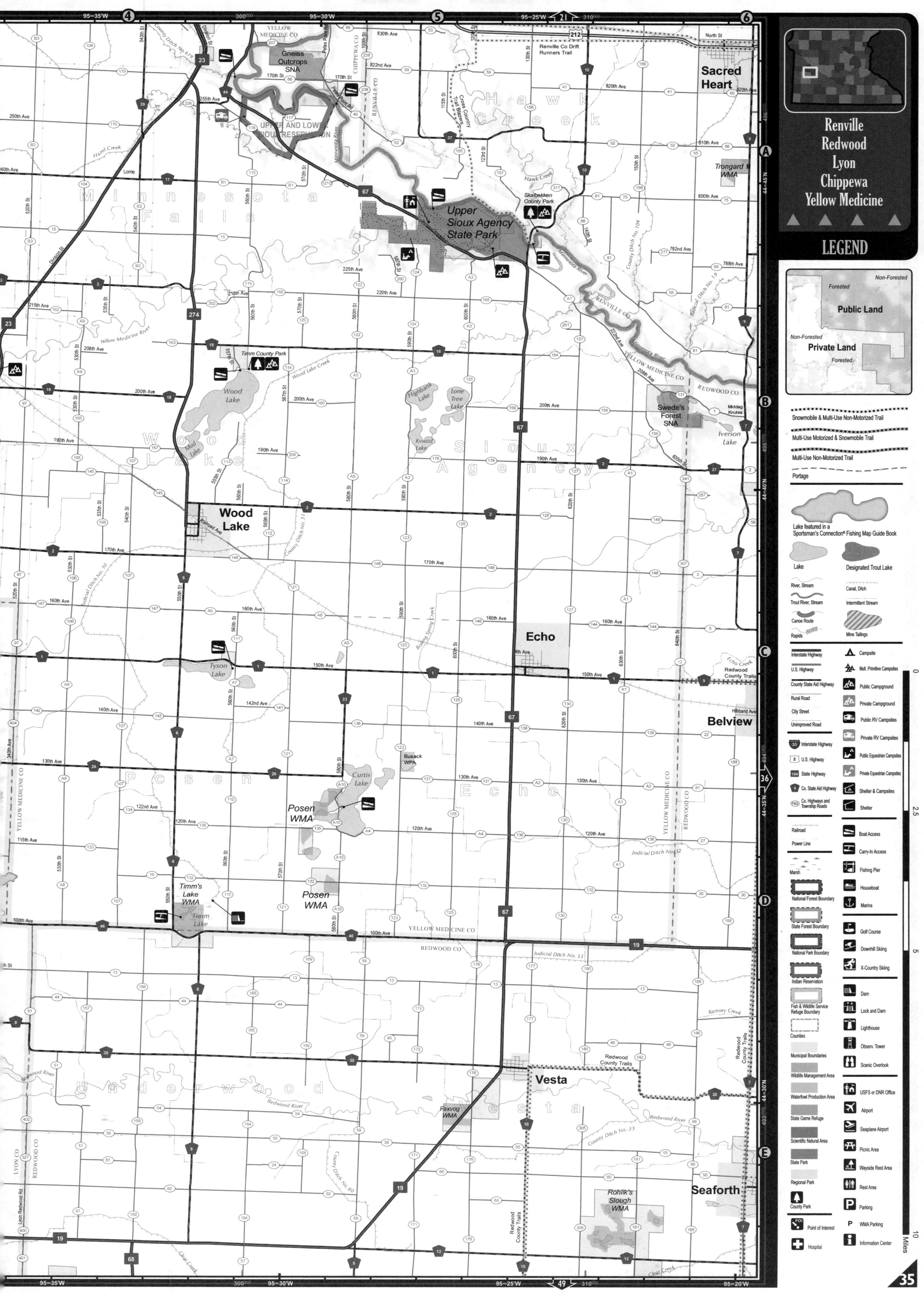
Renville
Redwood
Lyon
Chippewa
Yellow Medicine
LEGEND
Public Land
Private Land
Forested
Non-Forested
Sacred Heart
Upper Sioux Agency State Park
Gneiss Outcrops SNA
Upper and Lower Sioux Reservation
Skalbekken County Park
Timm County Park
Wood Lake
Echo
Belview
Vesta
Seaforth
Swede's Forest SNA
Trongard WMA
Posen WMA
Timm's Lake WMA
Faxvog WMA
Rohlik's Slough WMA
Busack WPA
Lone Tree Lake
Highbank Lake
Kvistid Lake
Mud Lake
Tyson Lake
Curtis Lake
Timm Lake
Iverson Lake
Minnesota River
Redwood River
Yellow Medicine River
Redwood County Trails
Renville Co Drift Runners Trail
Cross Country Trail Blazers
Minnesota Falls
Hawk Creek
Wood Lake
Sioux Agency
Posen
Echo
Underwood
Vesta
YELLOW MEDICINE CO
REDWOOD CO
RENVILLE CO
CHIPPEWA CO
LYON CO
Snowmobile & Multi-Use Non-Motorized Trail
Multi-Use Motorized & Snowmobile Trail
Multi-Use Non-Motorized Trail
Portage
Lake featured in a Sportsman's Connection® Fishing Map Guide Book
Lake
Designated Trout Lake
River, Stream
Canal, Ditch
Trout River, Stream
Intermittent Stream
Canoe Route
Rapids
Mine Tailings
Interstate Highway
U.S. Highway
County State Aid Highway
Rural Road
City Street
Unimproved Road
State Highway
Co. State Aid Highway
Co. Highways and Township Roads
Railroad
Power Line
Marsh
National Forest Boundary
State Forest Boundary
National Park Boundary
Indian Reservation
Fish & Wildlife Service Refuge Boundary
Counties
Municipal Boundaries
Wildlife Management Area
Waterfowl Production Area
State Game Refuge
Scientific Natural Area
State Park
Regional Park
County Park
Point of Interest
Hospital
Campsite
Mult. Primitive Campsites
Public Campground
Private Campground
Public RV Campsites
Private RV Campsites
Public Equestrian Campsites
Private Equestrian Campsites
Shelter & Campsites
Shelter
Boat Access
Carry-In Access
Fishing Pier
Houseboat
Marina
Golf Course
Downhill Skiing
X-Country Skiing
Dam
Lock and Dam
Lighthouse
Observ. Tower
Scenic Overlook
USFS or DNR Office
Airport
Seaplane Airport
Picnic Area
Wayside Rest Area
Rest Area
Parking
WMA Parking
Information Center
Miles
95°35'W
95°30'W
95°25'W
95°20'W
44°45'N
44°40'N
44°35'N
44°30'N

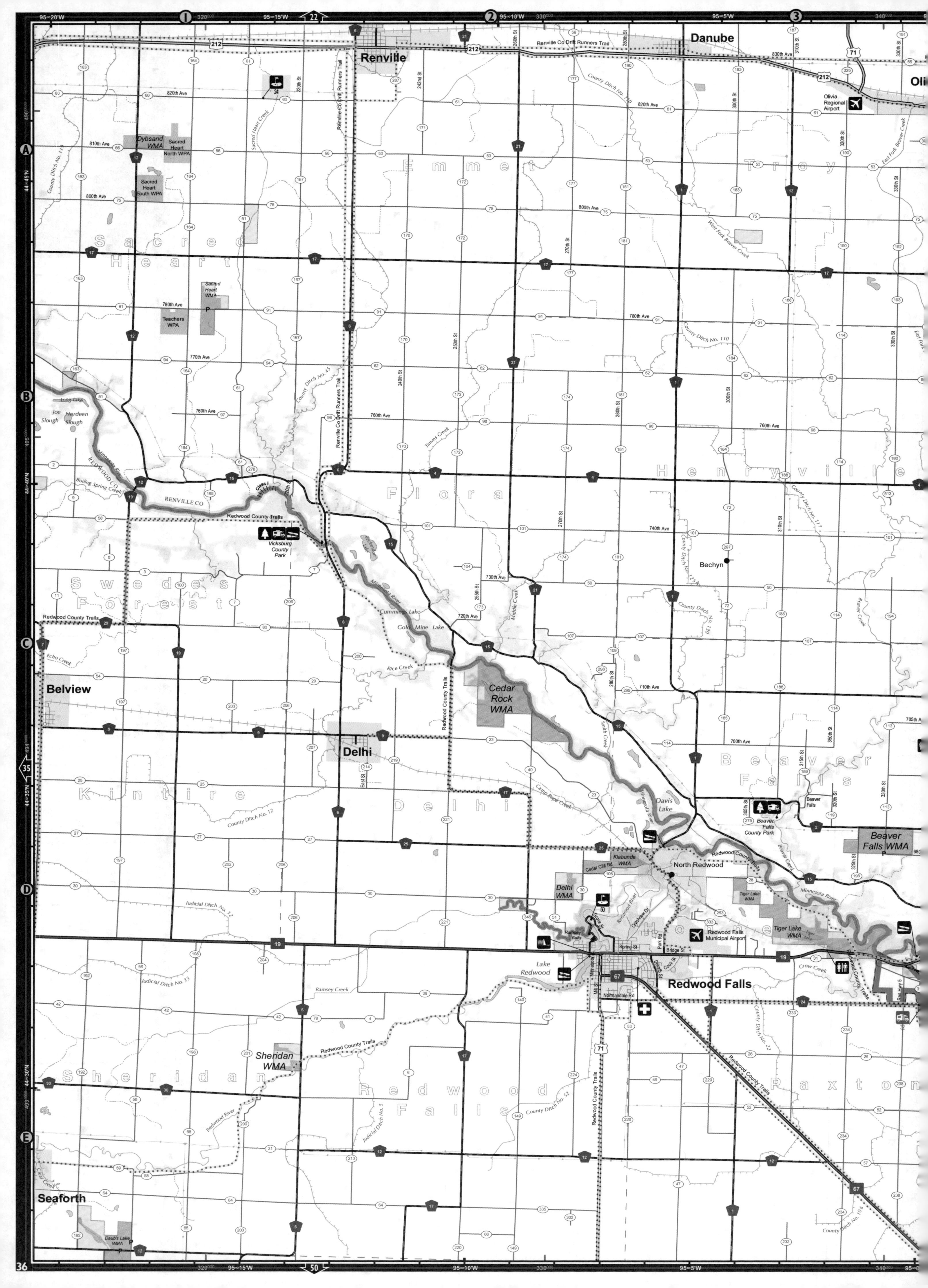

22
Renville
Danube
Oli
Olivia Regional Airport
Renville Co Drift Runners Trail
Dybsand WMA
Sacred Heart North WPA
Sacred Heart South WPA
Emmet
Troy
Sacred Heart
Sacred Heart WMA
Teachers WPA
Flora
Henryville
Long Lake
Joe Slough
Nordeen Slough
REDWOOD CO
RENVILLE CO
Redwood County Trails
Vicksburg County Park
Bechyn
Swedes Forest
Cummings Lake
Gold Mine Lake
Minnesota River
Cedar Rock WMA
Belview
Delhi
Kintire
Beaver Falls
Beaver Falls County Park
Beaver Falls WMA
Davis Lake
Klabunde WMA
North Redwood
Delhi WMA
Tiger Lake WMA
Redwood Falls Municipal Airport
Lake Redwood
Redwood Falls
Sheridan WMA
Sheridan
Paxton
Seaforth
Daub's Lake WMA
50
35
36

Renville
Redwood
Brown
LEGEND
Public Land
Private Land
Forested
Non-Forested
Snowmobile & Multi-Use Non-Motorized Trail
Multi-Use Motorized & Snowmobile Trail
Multi-Use Non-Motorized Trail
Portage
Lake featured in a Sportsman's Connection® Fishing Map Guide Book
Lake
Designated Trout Lake
River, Stream
Canal, Ditch
Trout River, Stream
Intermittent Stream
Canoe Route
Rapids
Mine Tailings
Interstate Highway
U.S. Highway
County State Aid Highway
Rural Road
City Street
Unimproved Road
Interstate Highway
U.S. Highway
State Highway
Co. State Aid Highway
Co. Highways and Township Roads
Railroad
Power Line
Marsh
National Forest Boundary
State Forest Boundary
National Park Boundary
Indian Reservation
Fish & Wildlife Service Refuge Boundary
Counties
Municipal Boundaries
Wildlife Management Area
Waterfowl Production Area
State Game Refuge
Scientific Natural Area
State Park
Regional Park
County Park
Point of Interest
Hospital
Campsite
Mult. Primitive Campsites
Public Campground
Private Campground
Public RV Campsites
Private RV Campsites
Public Equestrian Campsites
Private Equestrian Campsites
Shelter & Campsites
Shelter
Boat Access
Carry-In Access
Fishing Pier
Houseboat
Marina
Golf Course
Downhill Skiing
X-Country Skiing
Dam
Lock and Dam
Lighthouse
Observ. Tower
Scenic Overlook
USFS or DNR Office
Airport
Seaplane Airport
Picnic Area
Wayside Rest Area
Rest Area
Parking
WMA Parking
Information Center
Miles
Bird Island
Hector
Hector Municipal Airport
Franklin
Fairfax
Birch Coulee County Park
Cedar Mountain SNA
Anderson Lake County Park
Anderson Lake
Minnesota River
Renville Co Drift Runners Trail
Redwood County Trails
Bird Island
Melville
Norfolk
Palmyra
Birch Cooley
Bandon
Camp
Sherman
Eden
East Fork Beaver Creek
Buffalo Creek
Birch Coulee Creek
Three Mile Creek
Fort Ridgely Creek
Judicial Ditch No. 15
Judicial Ditch No. 12
County Ditch No. 66
County Ditch No. 124
County Ditch No. 85A
County Ditch No. 115
County Ditch No. 106A
County Ditch No. 109A
County Ditch No. 34
County Ditch No. 31
County Ditch No. 109
Woelfel Slough
REDWOOD CO
RENVILLE CO
BROWN CO
94°55'W
94°50'W
94°45'W
44°45'N
44°40'N
44°35'N
44°30'N
23
38
51

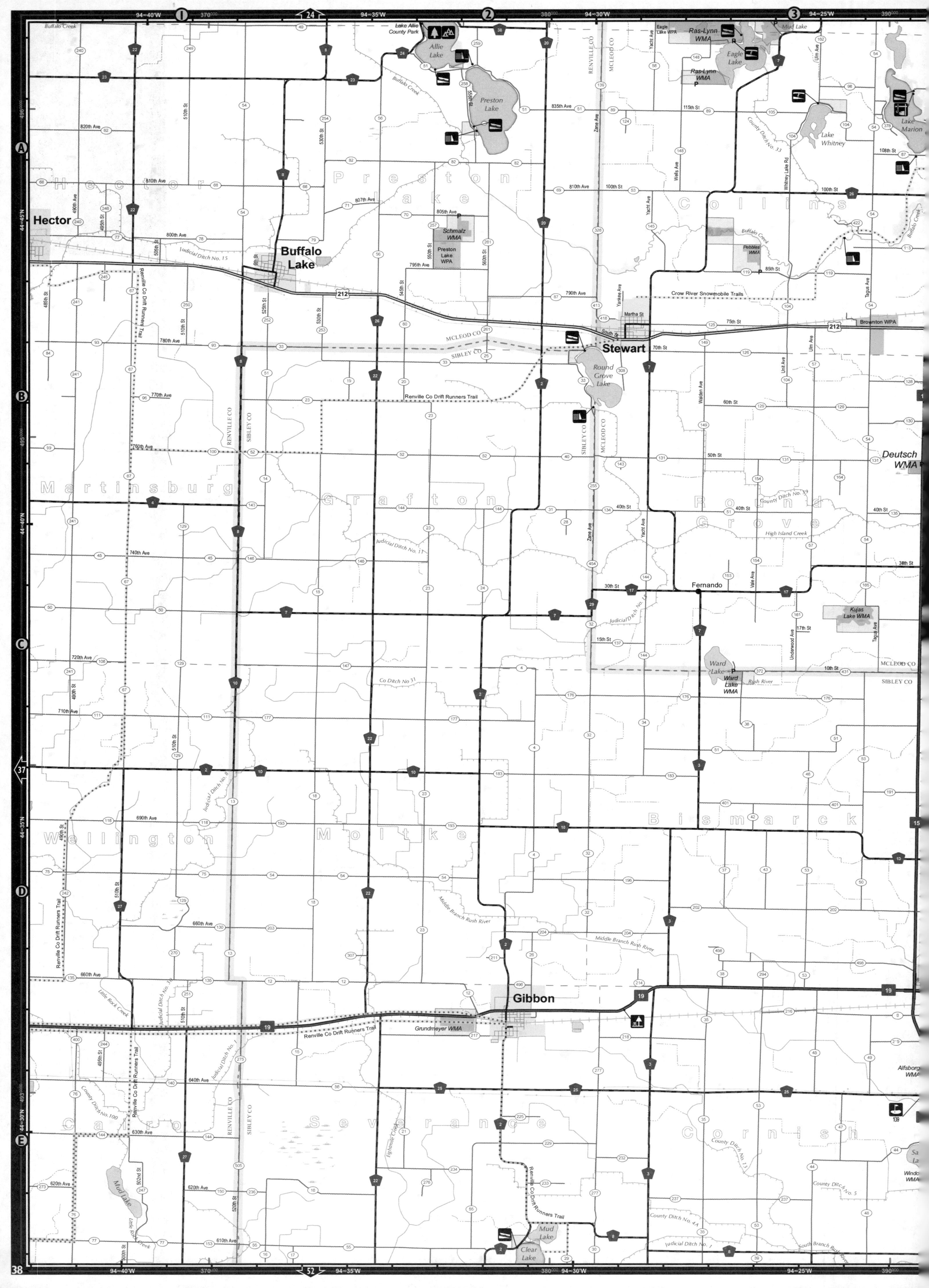
Hector
Buffalo Lake
Stewart
Gibbon
Fernando
Preston Lake
Grafton
Martinsburg
Wellington
Moltke
Bismarck
Round Grove
Collins
Severance
Cornish
Allie Lake
Lake Allie County Park
Preston Lake
Schmalz WMA
Preston Lake WPA
Ras-Lynn WMA
Eagle Lake
Mud Lake
Lake Whitney
Lake Marion
Pebbles WMA
Round Grove Lake
Deutsch WMA
Kujas Lake WMA
Ward Lake
Ward Lake WMA
Grundmeyer WMA
Alfsborg WMA
Brownton WPA
Clear Lake
Mud Lake
Renville Co Drift Runners Trail
Crow River Snowmobile Trails
RENVILLE CO
MCLEOD CO
SIBLEY CO
Judicial Ditch No. 15
Judicial Ditch No. 11
Middle Branch Rush River
Rush River
High Island Creek
Buffalo Creek
Little Rock Creek
Co Ditch No 31
County Ditch No. 100
94°40'W
94°35'W
94°30'W
94°25'W
44°45'N
44°40'N
44°35'N
44°30'N

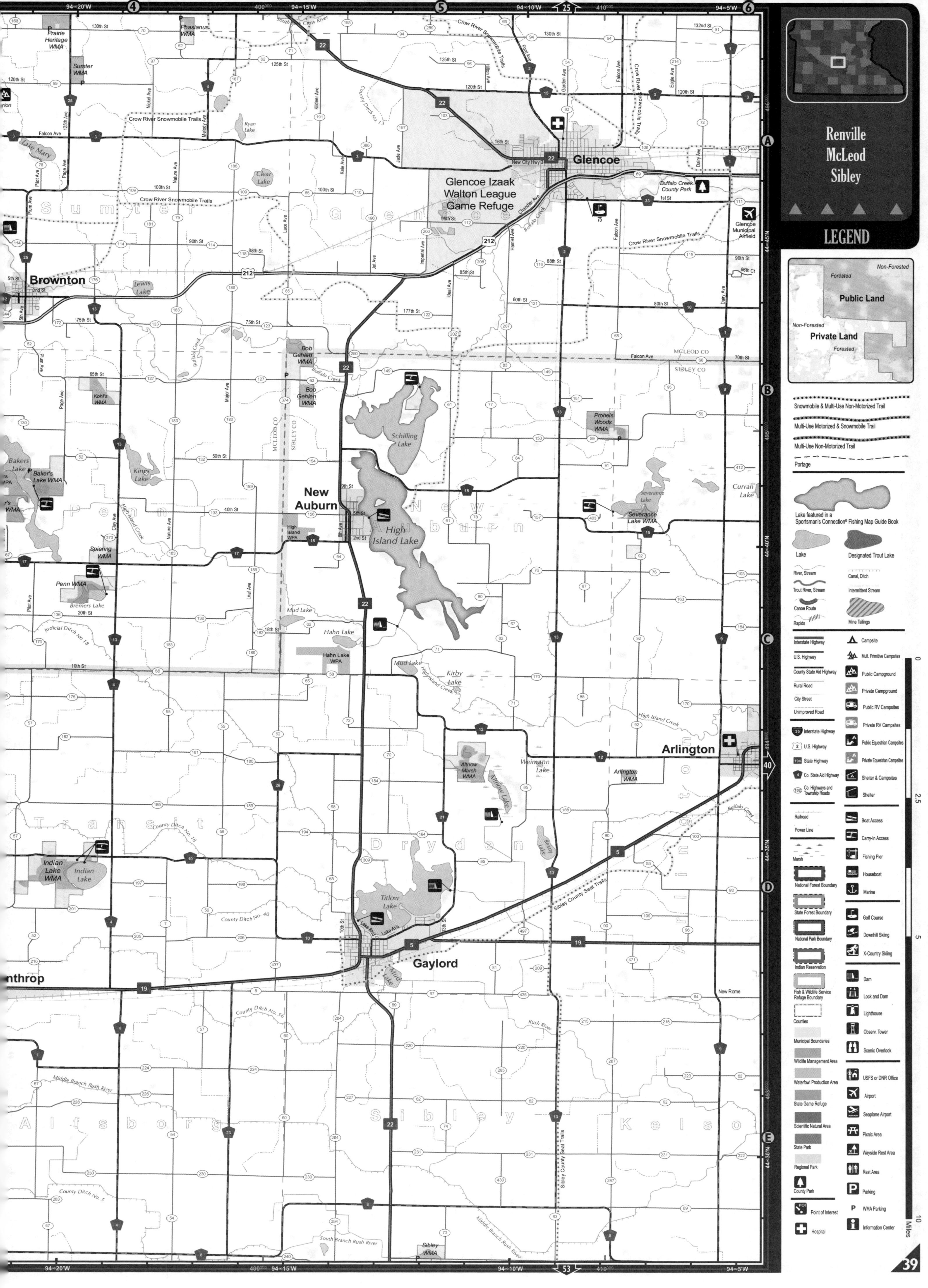

Renville
McLeod
Sibley
LEGEND
Glencoe
Glencoe Izaak Walton League Game Refuge
Brownton
New Auburn
High Island Lake
Schilling Lake
Arlington
Gaylord
Titlow Lake
Prairie Heritage WMA
Sumter WMA
Phasianus WMA
Bob Gehlen WMA
Kohl's WMA
Bakers Lake
Baker's Lake WMA
Kings Lake
Spiering WMA
Penn WMA
Bremers Lake
Mud Lake
Hahn Lake
Hahn Lake WPA
Kirby Lake
Althow Marsh WMA
Althow Lake
Weimann Lake
Arlington WMA
Prohels Woods WMA
Severance Lake
Severance Lake WMA
Curran Lake
Indian Lake WMA
Indian Lake
Sibley WMA
Buffalo Creek County Park
Glencoe Municipal Airfield
Lake Mary
Clear Lake
Ryan Lake
Lewis Lake
Crow River Snowmobile Trails
Sibley County Seat Trails
High Island Creek
Buffalo Creek
Rush River
Middle Branch Rush River
South Branch Rush River
County Ditch No. 18
County Ditch No. 40
County Ditch No. 56
County Ditch No. 5
Judicial Ditch No 18
MCLEOD CO
SIBLEY CO
Sumter
Glencoe
Penn
New Auburn
Transit
Dryden
Arlington
Alfsborg
Sibley
Kelso
New Rome
Winthrop
94°20'W
94°15'W
94°10'W
94°5'W
44°45'N
44°40'N
44°35'N
44°30'N
Public Land
Private Land
Forested
Non-Forested
Snowmobile & Multi-Use Non-Motorized Trail
Multi-Use Motorized & Snowmobile Trail
Multi-Use Non-Motorized Trail
Portage
Lake featured in a Sportsman's Connection® Fishing Map Guide Book
Lake
Designated Trout Lake
River, Stream
Canal, Ditch
Trout River, Stream
Intermittent Stream
Canoe Route
Rapids
Mine Tailings
Interstate Highway
U.S. Highway
County State Aid Highway
Rural Road
City Street
Unimproved Road
Interstate Highway
U.S. Highway
State Highway
Co. State Aid Highway
Co. Highways and Township Roads
Railroad
Power Line
Marsh
National Forest Boundary
State Forest Boundary
National Park Boundary
Indian Reservation
Fish & Wildlife Service Refuge Boundary
Counties
Municipal Boundaries
Wildlife Management Area
Waterfowl Production Area
State Game Refuge
Scientific Natural Area
State Park
Regional Park
County Park
Point of Interest
Hospital
Campsite
Mult. Primitive Campsites
Public Campground
Private Campground
Public RV Campsites
Private RV Campsites
Public Equestrian Campsites
Private Equestrian Campsites
Shelter & Campsites
Shelter
Boat Access
Carry-In Access
Fishing Pier
Houseboat
Marina
Golf Course
Downhill Skiing
X-Country Skiing
Dam
Lock and Dam
Lighthouse
Observ. Tower
Scenic Overlook
USFS or DNR Office
Airport
Seaplane Airport
Picnic Area
Wayside Rest Area
Rest Area
Parking
WMA Parking
Information Center
0
2.5
5
10
Miles

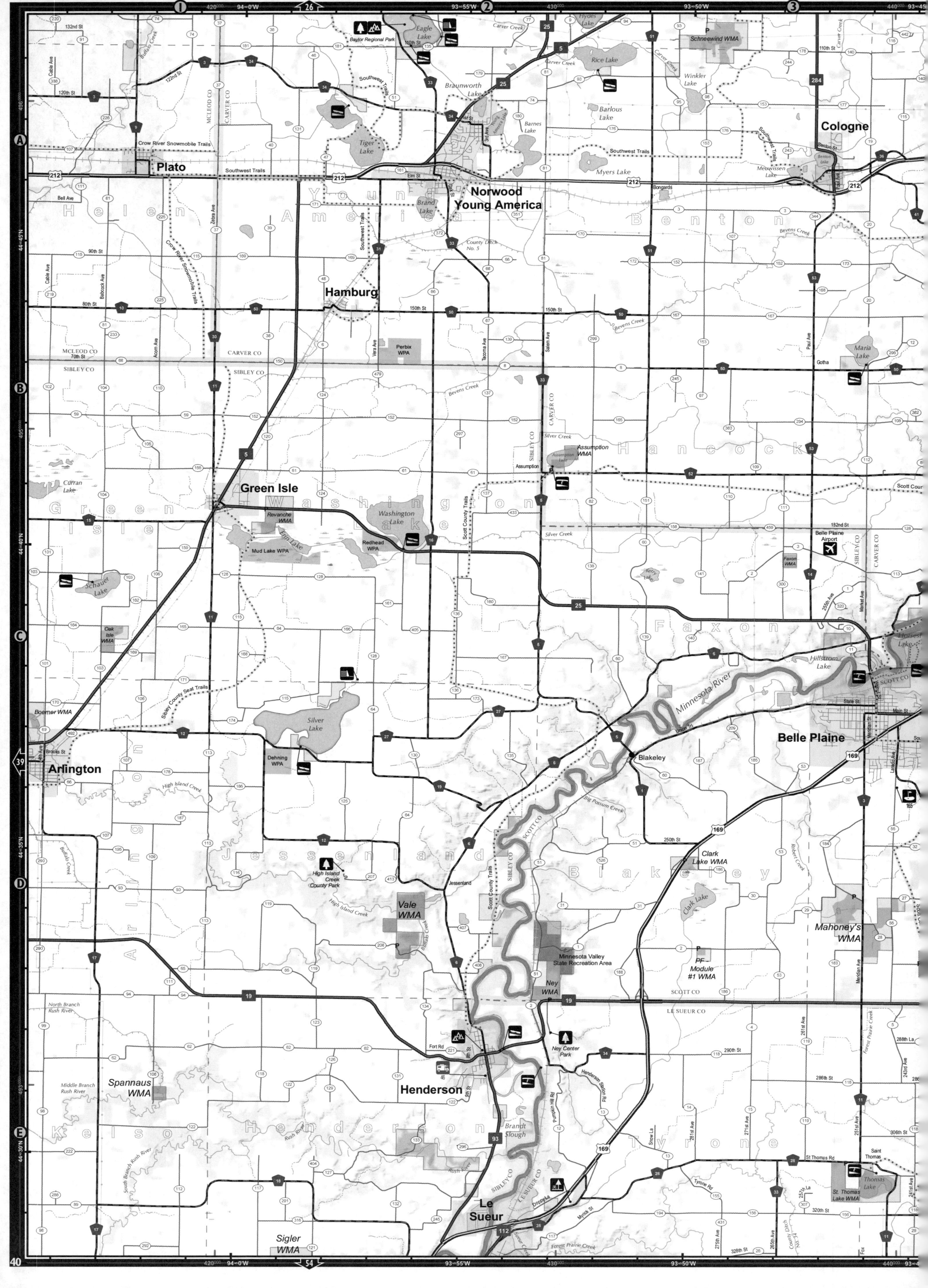

Plato
Norwood Young America
Cologne
Hamburg
Green Isle
Arlington
Belle Plaine
Blakeley
Henderson
Le Sueur
Eagle Lake
Baylor Regional Park
Rice Lake
Schneewind WMA
Braunworth Lake
Winkler Lake
Barlous Lake
Barnes Lake
Tiger Lake
Myers Lake
Brand Lake
Crow River Snowmobile Trails
Southwest Trails
Helen
Young America
Benton
Hancock
Green Isle
Washington Lake
Faxon
Arlington
Jessenland
Blakeley
Kelso
Henderson
Tyrone
Perbix WPA
Maria Lake
Assumption WMA
Curran Lake
Revanche WMA
Mud Lake WPA
Redhead WPA
Schauer Lake
Belle Plaine Airport
Faxon WMA
Oak Isle WMA
Silver Lake
Boerner WMA
Dehning WPA
Minnesota River
Hillstrom Lake
High Island Creek County Park
Vale WMA
Clark Lake WMA
Clark Lake
Mahoney's WMA
Minnesota Valley State Recreation Area
Ney WMA
PF-Module #1 WMA
Ney Center Park
Spannaus WMA
Brandt Slough
St. Thomas Lake WMA
Thomas Lake
Sigler WMA
MCLEOD CO
CARVER CO
SIBLEY CO
SCOTT CO
LE SUEUR CO

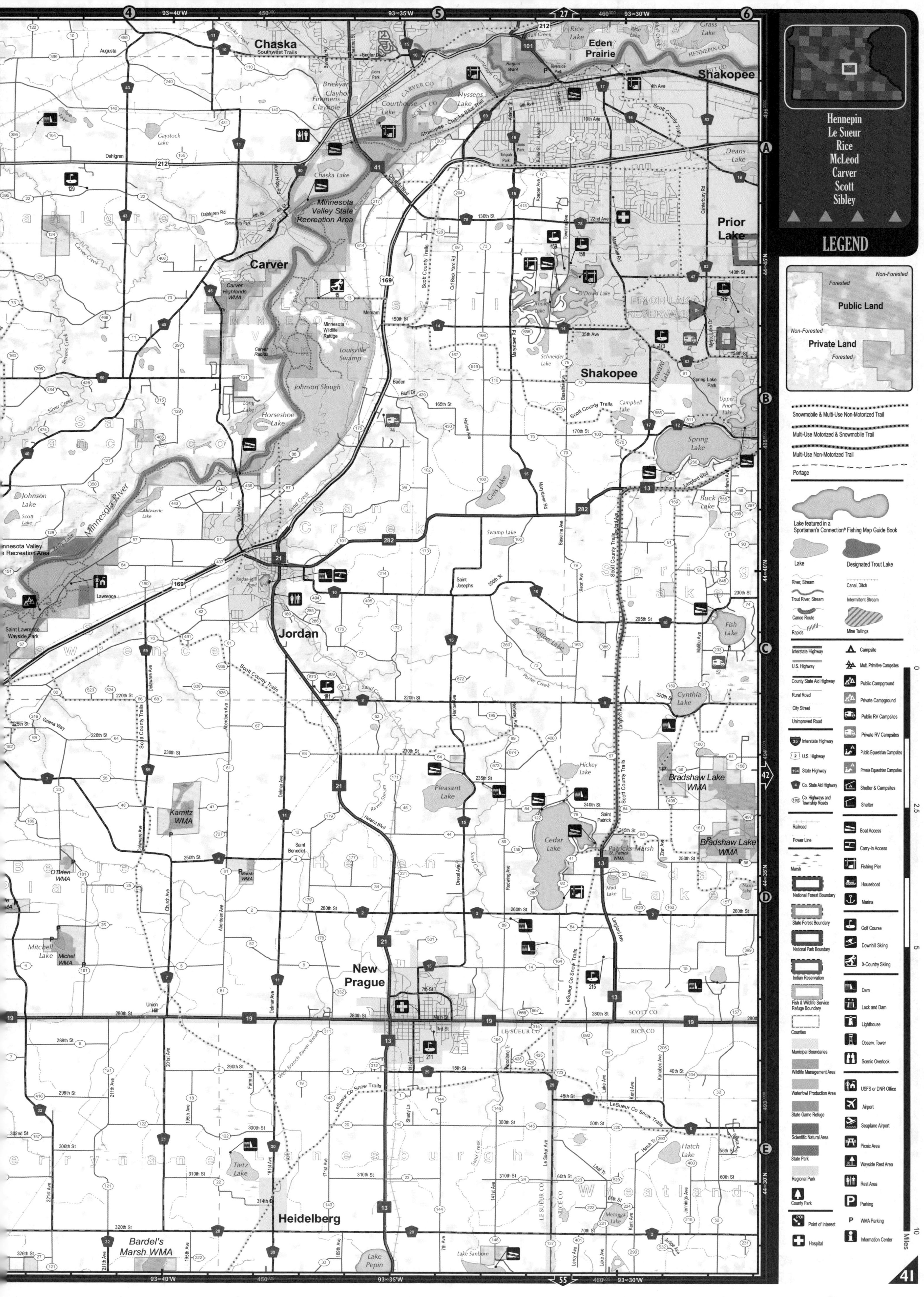

93°40'W
93°35'W
93°30'W
450000
460000
27
42
55
44°45'N
44°40'N
44°35'N
44°30'N
Chaska
Southwest Trails
Eden Prairie
Shakopee
Prior Lake
Carver
Jordan
New Prague
Heidelberg
Augusta
Dahlgren
Dahlgren Rd
Caystock Lake
Brickyard Clayhole
Firemens Clayhole
Courthouse Lake
Chaska Lake
Nyssens Lake
Minnesota Valley State Recreation Area
Minnesota Valley N.W.R.
Rice Lake
Grass Lake
Riley Creek
Bluff Creek
Assumption Creek
Raguet WMA
Deans Lake
Shakopee - Chaska Bike Trail
Carver Creek
Carver Highlands WMA
Minnesota Wildlife Refuge
Louisville Swamp
Carver Rapids
Johnson Slough
Horseshoe Lake
Long Lake
Johnson Lake
Scott Lake
Minnesota River
Minnesota Valley State Recreation Area
Sand Creek
Silver Creek
Bevens Creek
Thole Lake
O'Dowd Lake
Prior Lake Reservation
Schneider Lake
Howard Lake
Spring Lake Park
Upper Prior Lake
Campbell Lake
Spring Lake
Buck Lake
Geis Lake
Swamp Lake
Fish Lake
Sutton Lake
Porter Creek
Cynthia Lake
Hickey Lake
Pleasant Lake
Cedar Lake
Saint Patrick
Patricks Marsh
St. Patrick WMA
Mud Lake
Bradshaw Lake WMA
Kamitz WMA
O'Brien WMA
Marsh WMA
Mitchell Lake
Michel WMA
Raven Stream
West Branch Raven Stream
Saint Benedict
Saint Josephs
Union Hill
Lawrence
Saint Lawrence Wayside Park
Merriam
Baden
Bluff Dr
Scott County Trails
LeSueur Co Snow Trails
Helena Blvd
Tietz Lake
Hatch Lake
Metogga Lake
Lake Pepin
Lake Sanborn
Bardel's Marsh WMA
SCOTT CO
LE SUEUR CO
RICE CO
CARVER CO
HENNEPIN CO
Dahlgren
Louisville
Sand Creek
Spring Lake
Cedar Lake
Helena
Belle Plaine
Lanesburgh
Wheatland
Jackson
Hennepin
Le Sueur
Rice
McLeod
Carver
Scott
Sibley
LEGEND
Forested
Non-Forested
Public Land
Private Land
Snowmobile & Multi-Use Non-Motorized Trail
Multi-Use Motorized & Snowmobile Trail
Multi-Use Non-Motorized Trail
Portage
Lake featured in a Sportsman's Connection® Fishing Map Guide Book
Lake
Designated Trout Lake
River, Stream
Canal, Ditch
Trout River, Stream
Intermittent Stream
Canoe Route
Rapids
Mine Tailings
Interstate Highway
U.S. Highway
County State Aid Highway
Rural Road
City Street
Unimproved Road
Interstate Highway
U.S. Highway
State Highway
Co. State Aid Highway
Co. Highways and Township Roads
Railroad
Power Line
Marsh
National Forest Boundary
State Forest Boundary
National Park Boundary
Indian Reservation
Fish & Wildlife Service Refuge Boundary
Counties
Municipal Boundaries
Wildlife Management Area
Waterfowl Production Area
State Game Refuge
Scientific Natural Area
State Park
Regional Park
County Park
Point of Interest
Hospital
Campsite
Mult. Primitive Campsites
Public Campground
Private Campground
Public RV Campsites
Private RV Campsites
Public Equestrian Campsites
Private Equestrian Campsites
Shelter & Campsites
Shelter
Boat Access
Carry-In Access
Fishing Pier
Houseboat
Marina
Golf Course
Downhill Skiing
X-Country Skiing
Dam
Lock and Dam
Lighthouse
Observ. Tower
Scenic Overlook
USFS or DNR Office
Airport
Seaplane Airport
Picnic Area
Wayside Rest Area
Rest Area
Parking
WMA Parking
Information Center
0
2.5
5
10
Miles

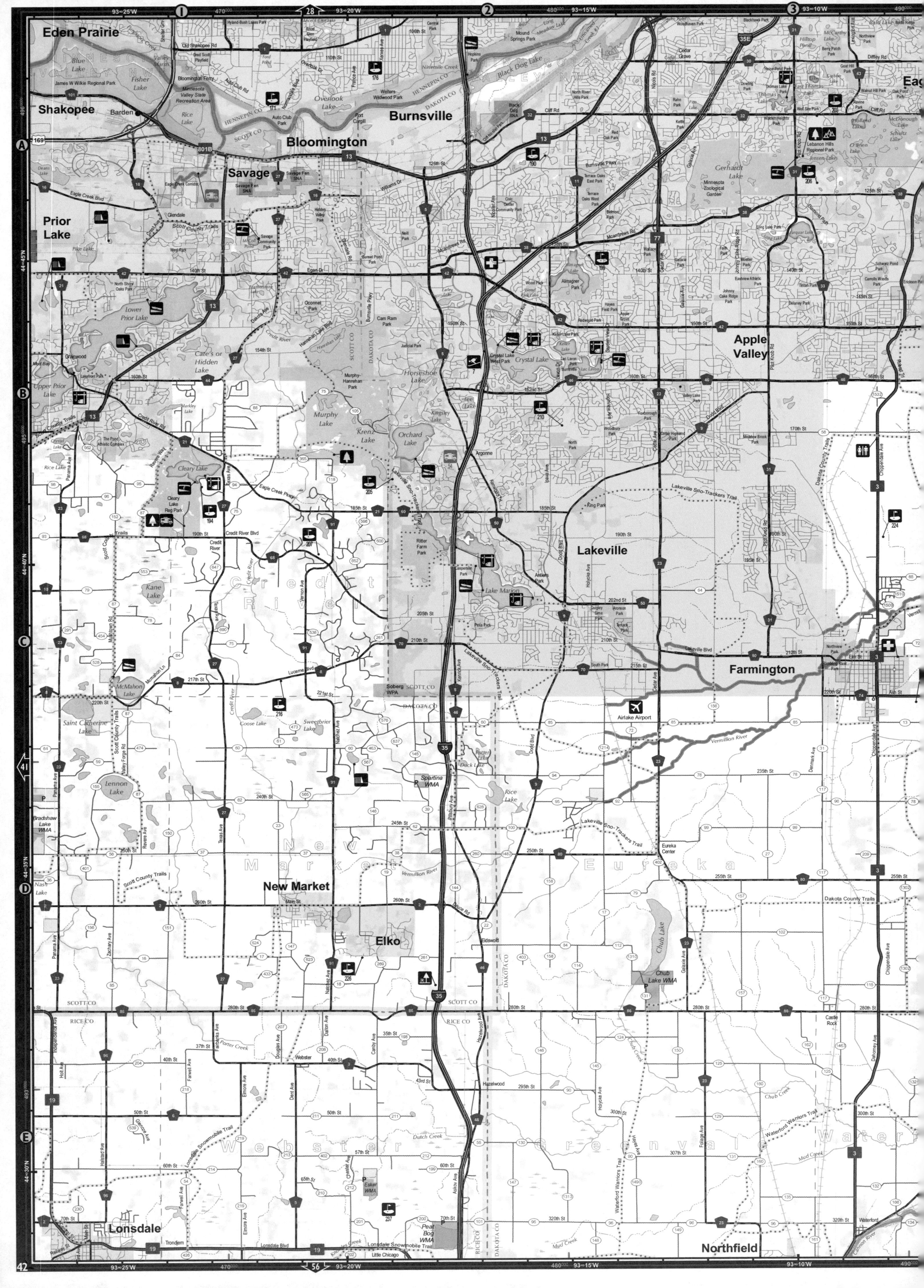

93°25'W
93°20'W
93°15'W
93°10'W
28
Eden Prairie
Shakopee
Barden
Bloomington
Burnsville
Savage
Prior Lake
Eagle Creek Blvd
Egan Dr
Lower Prior Lake
Cate's or Hidden Lake
Upper Prior Lake
Murphy-Hanrehan Park
Murphy Lake
Krenz Lake
Orchard Lake
Horseshoe Lake
Crystal Lake
Apple Valley
Minnesota Zoological Garden
Gerhardt Lake
Lebanon Hills Regional Park
Cleary Lake
Credit River
Kane Lake
McMahon Lake
Lake Marion
Lakeville
Lakeville Sno-Trackers Trail
Farmington
Airlake Airport
Vermillion River
Saint Catherine Lake
Lennon Lake
Rice Lake
New Market
Elko
Chub Lake
Chub Lake WMA
Eureka Center
Eureka
Credit River
New Market
Scott County Trails
Dakota County Trails
SCOTT CO
DAKOTA CO
RICE CO
Castle Rock
Hazelwood
Webster
Lonsdale
Lonsdale Snowmobile Trail
Waterford Warriors Trail
Waterford
Northfield
Little Chicago
Peat Bog WMA
Esker WMA
Greenvale
Webster
160th St
185th St
210th St
250th St
260th St
280th St
320th St
41
56
35
35E
A
B
C
D
E
44°45'N
44°40'N
44°35'N
44°30'N

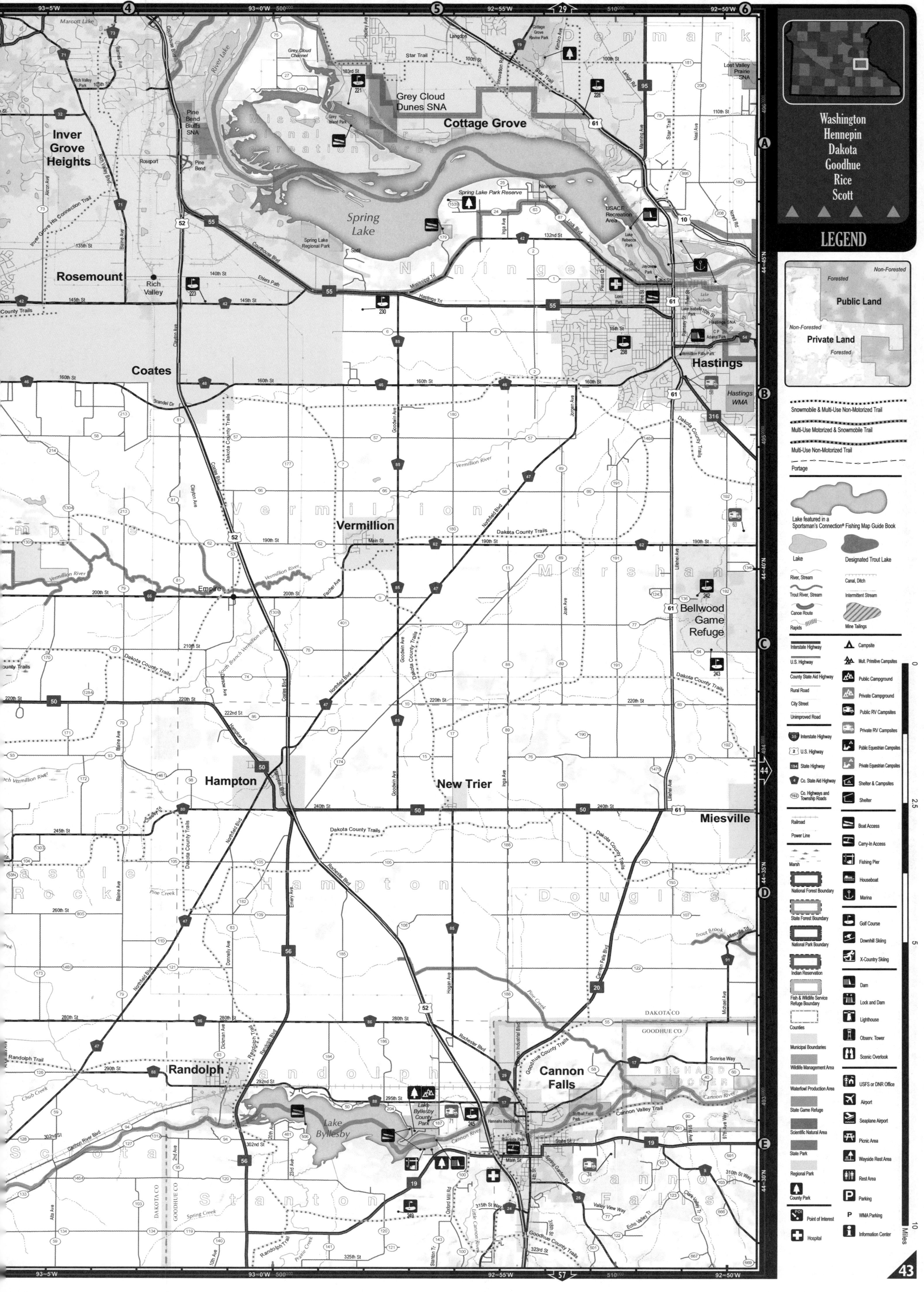

Inver Grove Heights
Rosemount
Rich Valley
Coates
Cottage Grove
Grey Cloud Dunes SNA
Pine Bend Bluffs SNA
Spring Lake
Spring Lake Regional Park
Spring Lake Park Reserve
USACE Recreation Area
Lake Rebecca Park
Hastings
Hastings WMA
Vermillion
Empire
Bellwood Game Refuge
Hampton
New Trier
Miesville
Randolph
Cannon Falls
Lake Byllesby
Lake Byllesby County Park
Denmark
Nininger
Marshan
Castle Rock
Douglas
Sciota
Stanton
Vermillion River
Dakota County Trails
DAKOTA CO
GOODHUE CO
Washington
Hennepin
Dakota
Goodhue
Rice
Scott
LEGEND
Public Land
Private Land
Forested
Non-Forested
Snowmobile & Multi-Use Non-Motorized Trail
Multi-Use Motorized & Snowmobile Trail
Multi-Use Non-Motorized Trail
Portage
Lake featured in a Sportsman's Connection® Fishing Map Guide Book
Lake
Designated Trout Lake
River, Stream
Canal, Ditch
Trout River, Stream
Intermittent Stream
Canoe Route
Rapids
Mine Tailings
Interstate Highway
U.S. Highway
County State Aid Highway
Rural Road
City Street
Unimproved Road
Interstate Highway
U.S. Highway
State Highway
Co. State Aid Highway
Co. Highways and Township Roads
Railroad
Power Line
Marsh
National Forest Boundary
State Forest Boundary
National Park Boundary
Indian Reservation
Fish & Wildlife Service Refuge Boundary
Counties
Municipal Boundaries
Wildlife Management Area
Waterfowl Production Area
State Game Refuge
Scientific Natural Area
State Park
Regional Park
County Park
Point of Interest
Hospital
Campsite
Mult. Primitive Campsites
Public Campground
Private Campground
Public RV Campsites
Private RV Campsites
Public Equestrian Campsites
Private Equestrian Campsites
Shelter & Campsites
Shelter
Boat Access
Carry-In Access
Fishing Pier
Houseboat
Marina
Golf Course
Downhill Skiing
X-Country Skiing
Dam
Lock and Dam
Lighthouse
Observ. Tower
Scenic Overlook
USFS or DNR Office
Airport
Seaplane Airport
Picnic Area
Wayside Rest Area
Rest Area
Parking
WMA Parking
Information Center
Miles
93°5'W
93°0'W
92°55'W
92°50'W
44°45'N
44°40'N
44°35'N
44°30'N

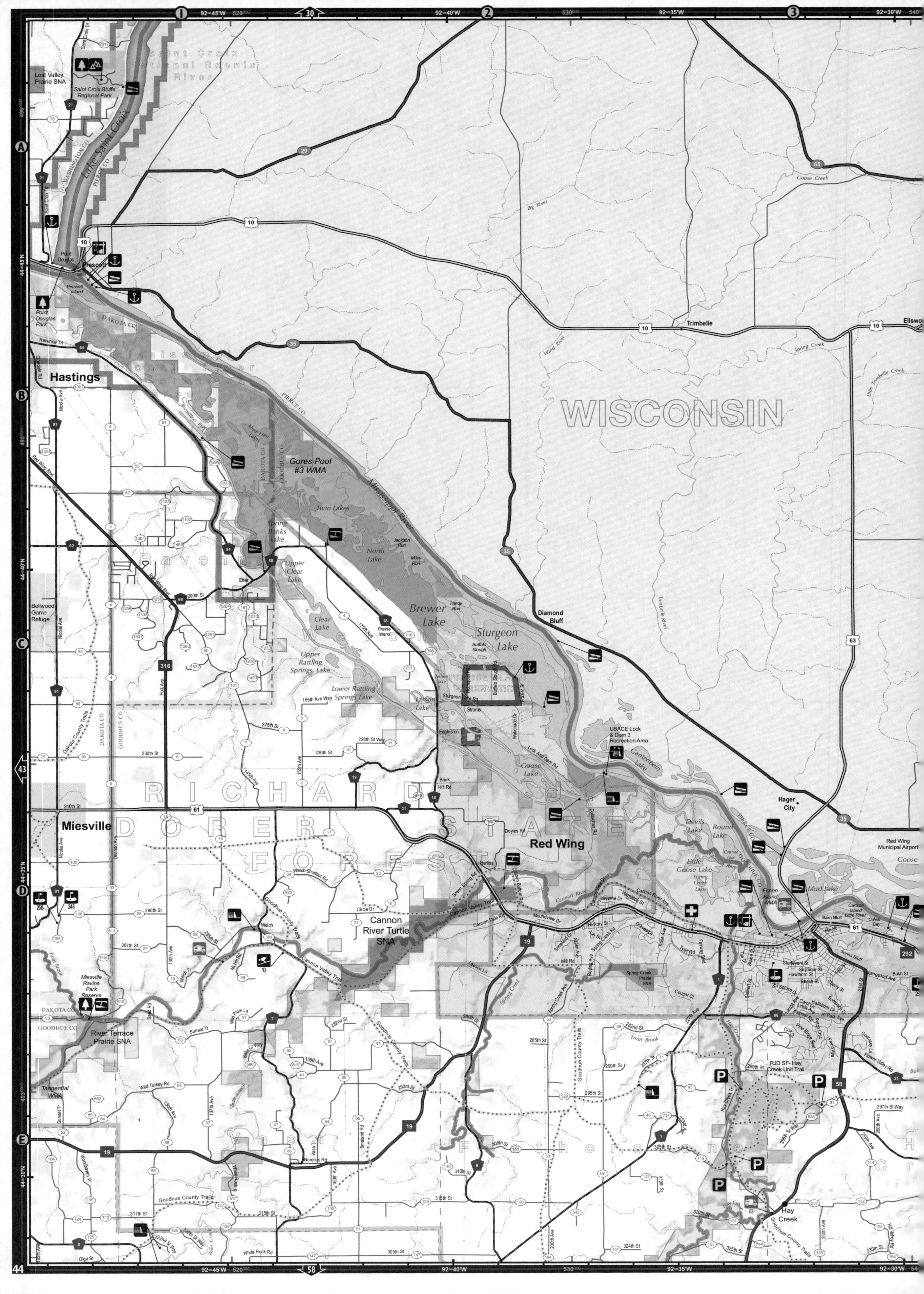

WISCONSIN
Hastings
Prescott
Red Wing
Miesville
Diamond Bluff
Trimbelle
Hager City
Hay Creek
Welch
RICHARD DORER STATE FOREST
Saint Croix National Scenic River
Lake Saint Croix
Mississippi River
Gores Pool #3 WMA
Cannon River Turtle SNA
River Terrace Prairie SNA
Tangential WMA
Lost Valley Prairie SNA
Saint Croix Bluffs Regional Park
Point Douglas Park
Bellwood Game Refuge
Miesville Ravine Park Reserve
USACE Lock & Dam 3 Recreation Area
Spring Creek Prairie SNA
RJD SF- Hay Creek Unit Trail
Red Wing Municipal Airport
Sturgeon Lake
Brewer Lake
North Lake
Twin Lakes
Spring Banks Lake
Upper Clear Lake
Clear Lake
Upper Rattling Springs Lake
Lower Rattling Springs Lake
Goose Lake
Devils Lake
Round Lake
Little Goose Lake
Mud Lake
Cannon River
Goodhue County Trails
Cannon Valley Trail
Ravenna
DAKOTA CO
GOODHUE CO
PIERCE CO
WASHINGTON CO

Washington
Dakota
Goodhue
Pierce
Pepin
LEGEND
Public Land
Private Land
Lake Pepin
Maiden Rock
Bay City
Wacouta
Frontenac State Park
Frontenac
Old Frontenac
Stockholm
Nugget Lake
PIERCE CO
PEPIN CO

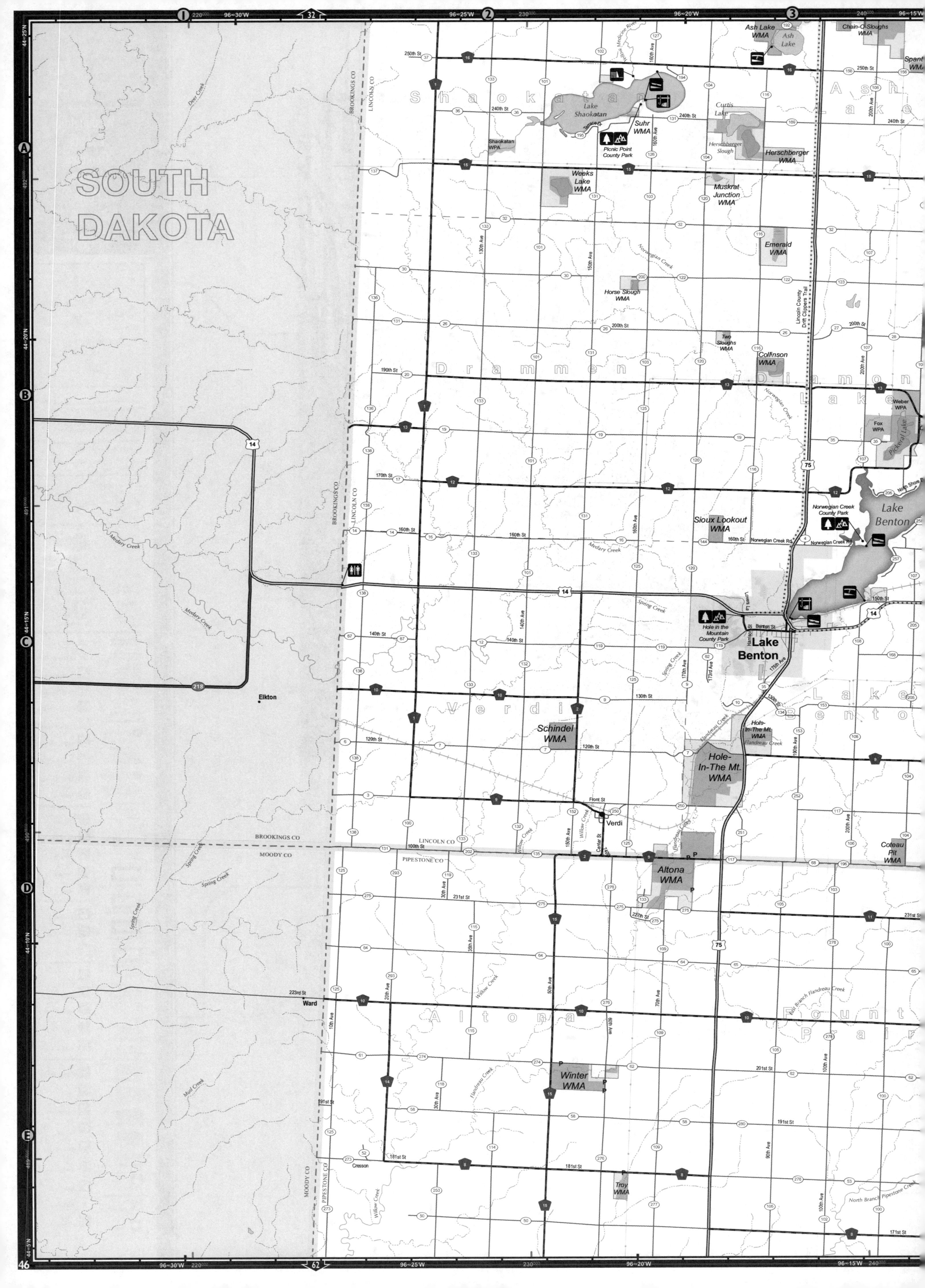

SOUTH DAKOTA
BROOKINGS CO
LINCOLN CO
MOODY CO
PIPESTONE CO
Lake Shaokatan
Lake Benton
Verdi
Elkton
Ward
Cresson
Ash Lake WMA
Suhr WMA
Picnic Point County Park
Shaokatan WPA
Weeks Lake WMA
Curtis Lake
Herschberger Slough
Herschberger WMA
Muskrat Junction WMA
Emerald WMA
Horse Slough WMA
Two Sloughs WMA
Collinson WMA
Sioux Lookout WMA
Norwegian Creek County Park
Weber WPA
Fox WPA
Hole in the Mountain County Park
Hole-In-The Mt. WMA
Schindel WMA
Altona WMA
Coteau Pit WMA
Winter WMA
Troy WMA
Chain-O-Sloughs WMA
Lincoln County Drift Clippers Trail
Medary Creek
Norwegian Creek
Spring Creek
Flandreau Creek
Willow Creek
Mud Creek
Deer Creek
Shaokatan
Drammen
Verdi
Altona
Diamond Lake
Lake Benton
Ash Lake
Fountain Prairie

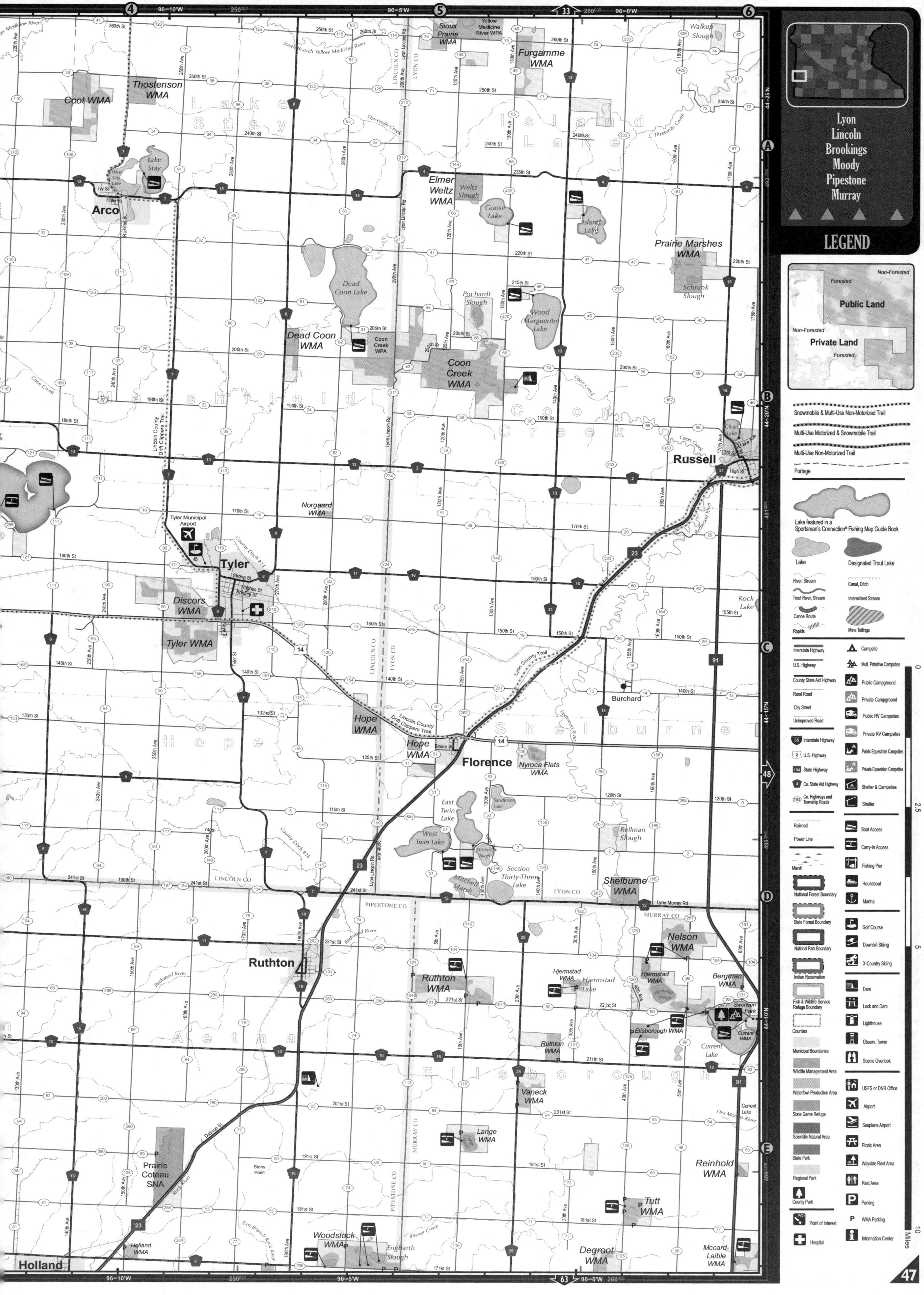

Lyon
Lincoln
Brookings
Moody
Pipestone
Murray
LEGEND
Public Land
Private Land
Forested
Non-Forested
Snowmobile & Multi-Use Non-Motorized Trail
Multi-Use Motorized & Snowmobile Trail
Multi-Use Non-Motorized Trail
Portage
Lake featured in a Sportsman's Connection® Fishing Map Guide Book
Lake
Designated Trout Lake
River, Stream
Canal, Ditch
Trout River, Stream
Intermittent Stream
Canoe Route
Rapids
Mine Tailings
Interstate Highway
U.S. Highway
County State Aid Highway
Rural Road
City Street
Unimproved Road
Railroad
Power Line
Marsh
National Forest Boundary
State Forest Boundary
National Park Boundary
Indian Reservation
Fish & Wildlife Service Refuge Boundary
Counties
Municipal Boundaries
Wildlife Management Area
Waterfowl Production Area
State Game Refuge
Scientific Natural Area
State Park
Regional Park
County Park
Point of Interest
Hospital
Campsite
Mult. Primitive Campsites
Public Campground
Private Campground
Public RV Campsites
Private RV Campsites
Public Equestrian Campsites
Private Equestrian Campsites
Shelter & Campsites
Shelter
Boat Access
Carry-In Access
Fishing Pier
Houseboat
Marina
Golf Course
Downhill Skiing
X-Country Skiing
Dam
Lock and Dam
Lighthouse
Observ. Tower
Scenic Overlook
USFS or DNR Office
Airport
Seaplane Airport
Picnic Area
Wayside Rest Area
Rest Area
Parking
WMA Parking
Information Center
Miles
Arco
Tyler
Russell
Florence
Ruthton
Holland
Burchard
Coot WMA
Thostenson WMA
Sioux Prairie WMA
Yellow Medicine River WPA
Furgamme WMA
Elmer Weltz WMA
Prairie Marshes WMA
Dead Coon WMA
Coon Creek WPA
Coon Creek WMA
Norgaard WMA
Discors WMA
Tyler WMA
Hope WMA
Nyroca Flats WMA
Shelburne WMA
Nelson WMA
Hjermstad WMA
Bergman WMA
Ruthton WMA
Ellsborough WMA
Current WMA
Swenson Park
Vaneck WMA
Lange WMA
Prairie Coteau SNA
Reinhold WMA
Tutt WMA
Woodstock WMA
Holland WMA
Degroot WMA
Mccard-Laible WMA
Lake Stay
Goose Lake
Island Lake
Dead Coon Lake
Wood (Marguerite) Lake
Clear Lake
Rock Lake
East Twin Lake
West Twin Lake
Sanderson Lake
Rellman Slough
Section Thirty-Three Lake
Mitchell Marsh
Hjermstad Lake
Current Lake
Walkup Slough
Schrunk Slough
Pochardt Slough
Engbarth Slough
Lake Stay
Island Lake
Coon Creek
Marshfield
Hope
Shelburne
Aetna
Ellsborough
LINCOLN CO
LYON CO
PIPESTONE CO
MURRAY CO
Lincoln County Drift Clippers Trail
Lyon County Trail
Tyler Municipal Airport
Stony Point
Lyon Murray Rd
Lyon Lincoln Rd
Division St
Redwood River
Des Moines River
96°10'W
96°5'W
96°0'W
44°25'N
44°20'N
44°15'N
44°10'N

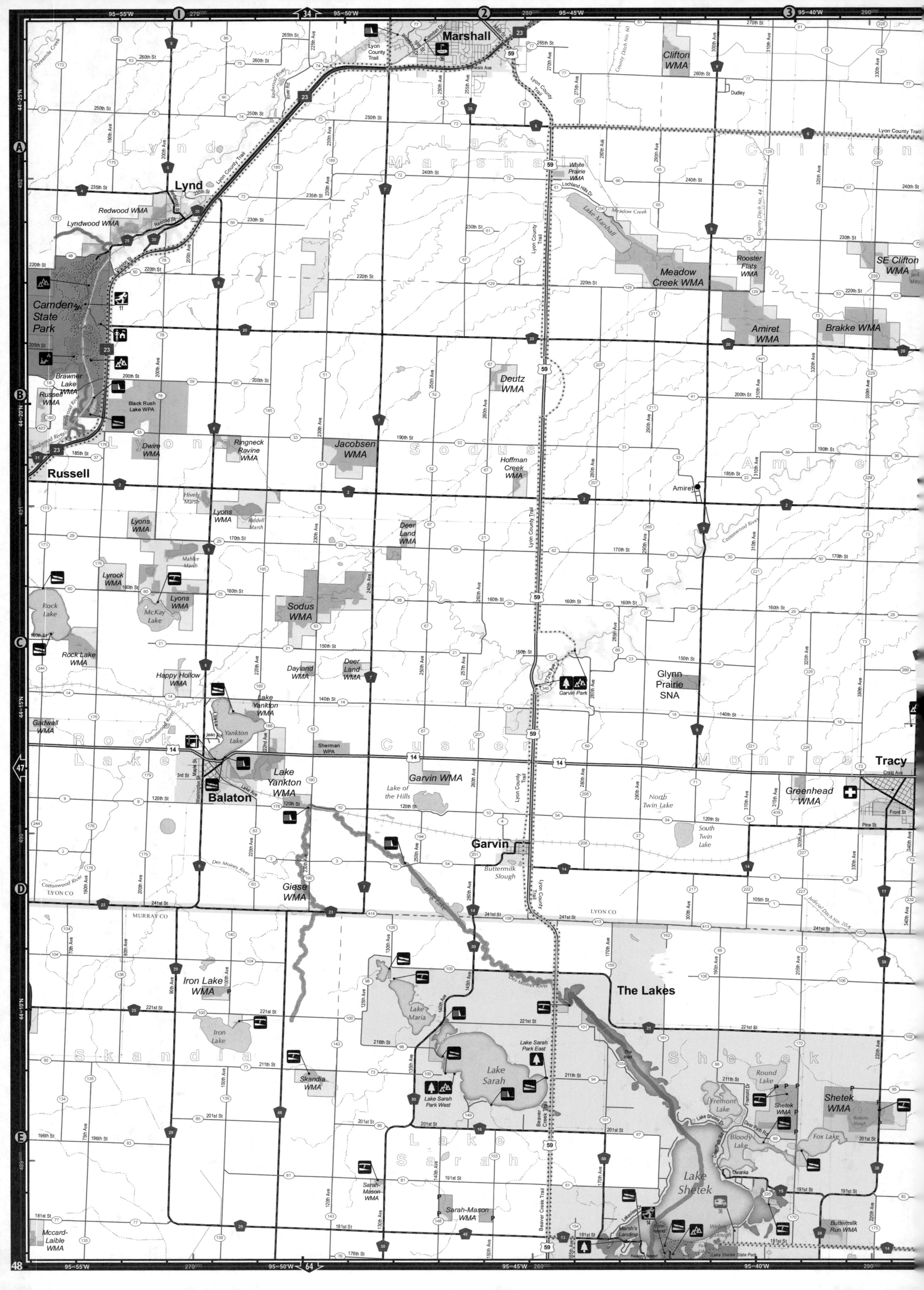

Marshall
Lyon County Trail
Clifton WMA
Dudley
Lynd
Redwood WMA
Lyndwood WMA
Camden State Park
Brawner Lake WMA
Russell WMA
Black Rush Lake WPA
Russell
Dwire WMA
Ringneck Ravine WMA
Jacobsen WMA
Deutz WMA
Hoffman Creek WMA
White Prairie WMA
Lake Marshall
Meadow Creek WMA
Rooster Flats WMA
SE Clifton WMA
Amiret WMA
Brakke WMA
Amiret
Lyons WMA
Hively Marsh
Riddell Marsh
Mahlke Marsh
Deer Land WMA
Lyrock WMA
McKay Lake
Rock Lake
Rock Lake WMA
Sodus WMA
Happy Hollow WMA
Dayland WMA
Gadwall WMA
Lake Yankton WMA
Yankton Lake
Sherman WPA
Garvin Park
Glynn Prairie SNA
Garvin WMA
Lake of the Hills
North Twin Lake
South Twin Lake
Tracy
Greenhead WMA
Balaton
Garvin
Buttermilk Slough
Giese WMA
Des Moines River
Cottonwood River
Redwood River
LYON CO
MURRAY CO
Iron Lake WMA
Iron Lake
The Lakes
Lake Maria
Lake Sarah
Lake Sarah Park East
Lake Sarah Park West
Skandia WMA
Sarah-Mason WMA
Round Lake
Fremont Lake
Shetek WMA
Bloody Lake
Fox Lake
Lake Shetek
Owanka
Marsh's Landing
Lake Shetek State Park
Buttermilk Run WMA
Mccard-Laible WMA
Beaver Creek Trail
Lynd
Marshall
Clifton
Lyons
Sodus
Amiret
Rock Lake
Custer
Monroe
Skandia
Shetek
Lake Sarah

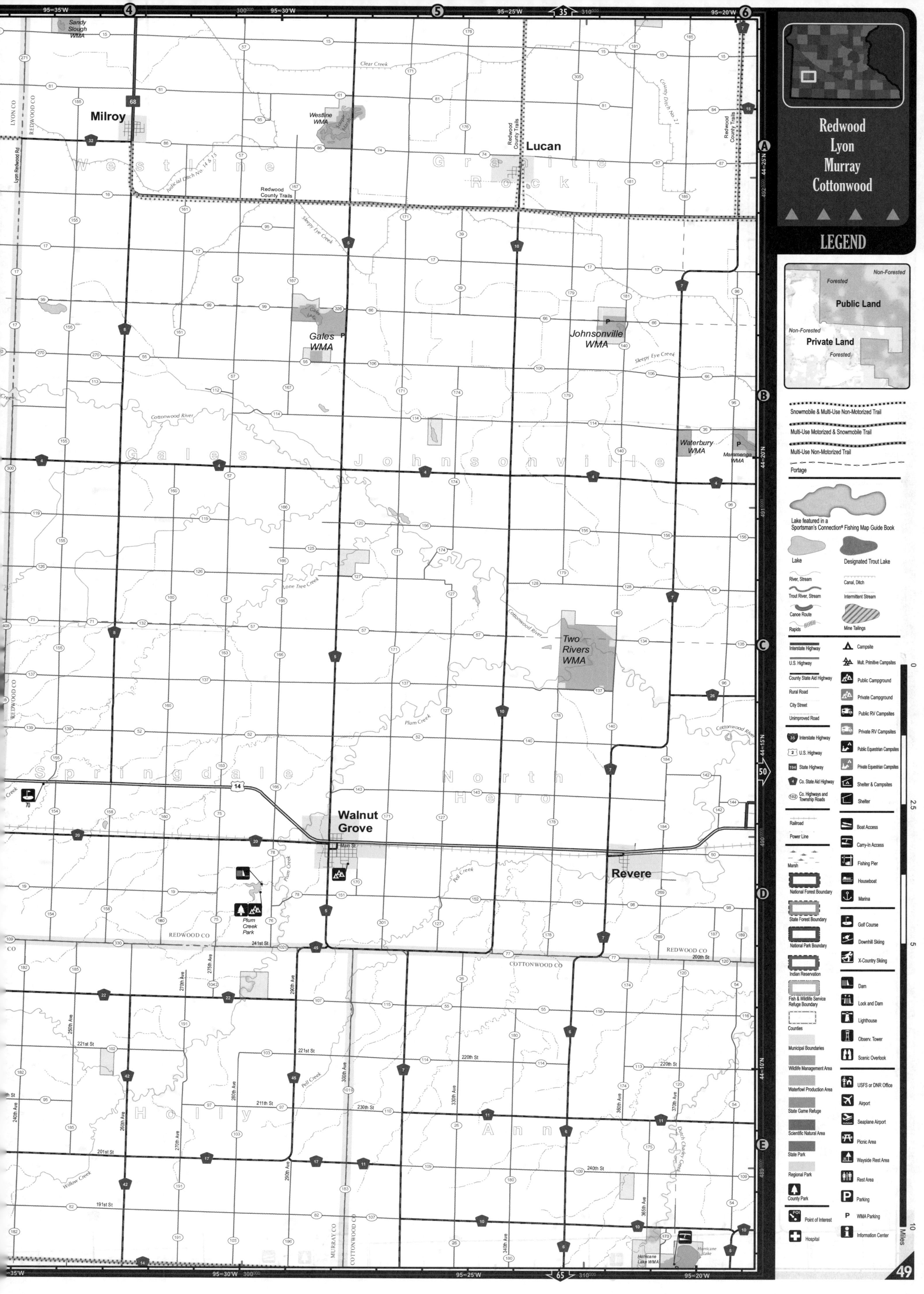
Redwood
Lyon
Murray
Cottonwood
LEGEND
Public Land
Private Land
Forested
Non-Forested
Snowmobile & Multi-Use Non-Motorized Trail
Multi-Use Motorized & Snowmobile Trail
Multi-Use Non-Motorized Trail
Portage
Lake featured in a Sportsman's Connection® Fishing Map Guide Book
Lake
Designated Trout Lake
Milroy
Lucan
Walnut Grove
Revere
Westline
Granite Rock
Gales
Johnsonville
Springdale
North Hero
Holly
Ann
Sandy Slough WMA
Westline WMA
Gales WMA
Johnsonville WMA
Waterbury WMA
Mammenga WMA
Two Rivers WMA
Plum Creek Park
Hurricane Lake WMA
Cottonwood River
Sleepy Eye Creek
Plum Creek
Lone Tree Creek
Pell Creek
Clear Creek
Willow Creek
Dutch Charley Creek
Redwood County Trails
REDWOOD CO
COTTONWOOD CO
MURRAY CO
LYON CO
Lyon Redwood Rd
95°35'W
95°30'W
95°25'W
95°20'W
44°25'N
44°20'N
44°15'N
44°10'N
Miles

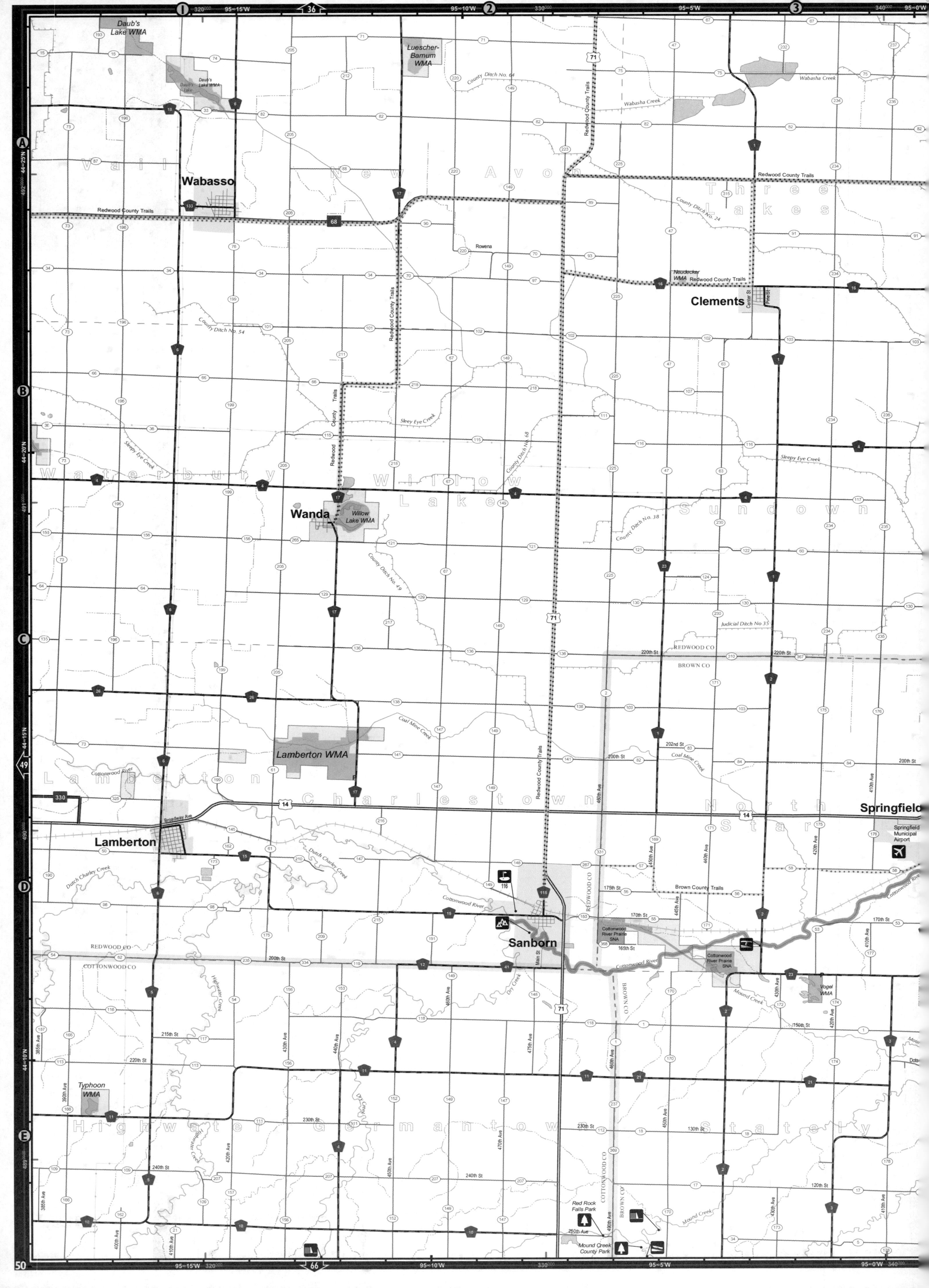

Daub's Lake WMA
Luescher-Barnum WMA
Wabasso
Redwood County Trails
County Ditch No. 64
Wabasha Creek
County Ditch No. 24
Rowena
Neudecker WMA
Clements
Center St
Pine St
County Ditch No. 54
Sleepy Eye Creek
County Ditch No. 68
Wanda
Willow Lake WMA
County Ditch No. 38
County Ditch No. 49
Judicial Ditch No 35
220th St
REDWOOD CO
BROWN CO
Coal Mine Creek
202nd St
200th St
Lamberton WMA
Cottonwood River
Springfield
Springfield Municipal Airport
Broadway Ave
Lamberton
Dutch Charley Creek
175th St
170th St
165th St
Brown County Trails
Sanborn
Main St
Cottonwood River Prairie SNA
COTTONWOOD CO
Highwater Creek
Dry Creek
Mound Creek
Vogel WMA
150th St
215th St
220th St
230th St
240th St
Typhoon WMA
130th St
120th St
Red Rock Falls Park
Mound Creek County Park
250th Ave
Vail
New Avon
Three Lakes
Waterbury
Willow Lake
Sundown
Lamberton
Charlestown
North Star
Highwater
Germantown
Stately

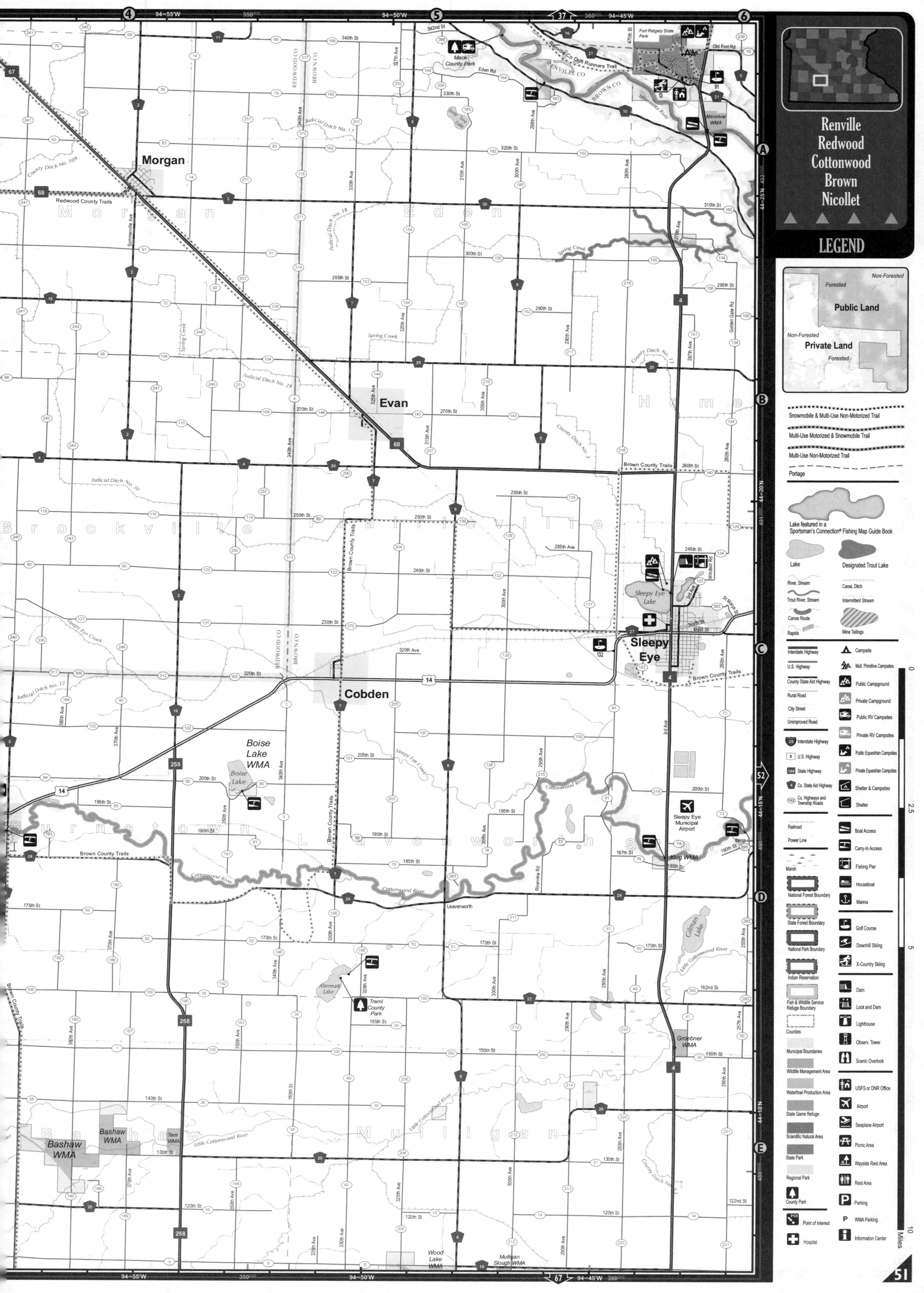
Renville
Redwood
Cottonwood
Brown
Nicollet
LEGEND
Public Land
Private Land
Forested
Non-Forested
Snowmobile & Multi-Use Non-Motorized Trail
Multi-Use Motorized & Snowmobile Trail
Multi-Use Non-Motorized Trail
Portage
Lake featured in a Sportsman's Connection® Fishing Map Guide Book
Lake
Designated Trout Lake
River, Stream
Canal, Ditch
Trout River, Stream
Intermittent Stream
Canoe Route
Mine Tailings
Rapids
Interstate Highway
U.S. Highway
County State Aid Highway
Rural Road
City Street
Unimproved Road
State Highway
Co. State Aid Highway
Co. Highways and Township Roads
Railroad
Power Line
Marsh
National Forest Boundary
State Forest Boundary
National Park Boundary
Indian Reservation
Fish & Wildlife Service Refuge Boundary
Counties
Municipal Boundaries
Wildlife Management Area
Waterfowl Production Area
State Game Refuge
Scientific Natural Area
State Park
Regional Park
County Park
Point of Interest
Hospital
Campsite
Mult. Primitive Campsites
Public Campground
Private Campground
Public RV Campsites
Private RV Campsites
Public Equestrian Campsites
Private Equestrian Campsites
Shelter & Campsites
Shelter
Boat Access
Carry-In Access
Fishing Pier
Houseboat
Marina
Golf Course
Downhill Skiing
X-Country Skiing
Dam
Lock and Dam
Lighthouse
Observ. Tower
Scenic Overlook
USFS or DNR Office
Airport
Seaplane Airport
Picnic Area
Wayside Rest Area
Rest Area
Parking
WMA Parking
Information Center
Miles
Morgan
Evan
Sleepy Eye
Cobden
Leavenworth
Iberia
Fort Ridgely State Park
Mack County Park
Minnriver WMA
Renville Co Drift Runners Trail
Redwood County Trails
Brown County Trails
Minnesota River
Cottonwood River
Little Cottonwood River
Spring Creek
Sleepy Eye Creek
Sleepy Eye Lake
Boise Lake WMA
Boise Lake
Aftermath Lake
Treml County Park
Gilman Lake
Groebner WMA
Krug WMA
Bashaw WMA
Terri WMA
Wood Lake WMA
Mulligan Slough WMA
Sleepy Eye Municipal Airport
Judicial Ditch No. 17
Judicial Ditch No. 18
Judicial Ditch No. 29
Judicial Ditch No. 30
Judicial Ditch No. 12
County Ditch No. 109
County Ditch No. 13
County Ditch No. 5
Redwood Co
Brown Co
Renville Co
Morgan
Eden
Home
Brookville
Prairieville
Burnstown
Leavenworth
Bashaw
Mulligan
94°55'W
94°50'W
94°45'W
44°25'N
44°20'N
44°15'N
44°10'N

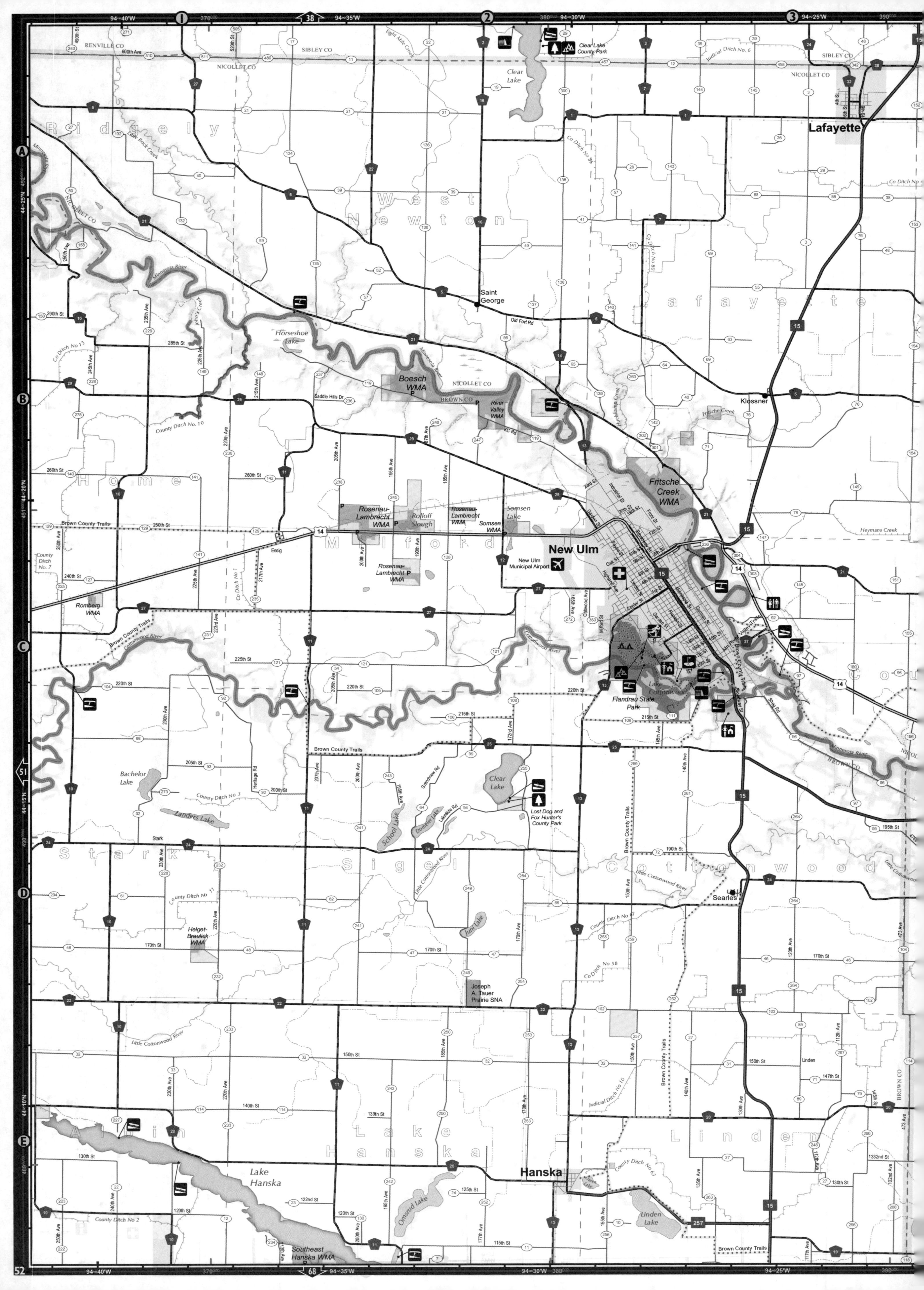

Lafayette
Klossner
Saint George
New Ulm
New Ulm Municipal Airport
Searles
Hanska
Linden
Essig
Stark
Clear Lake County Park
Clear Lake
Boesch WMA
River Valley WMA
Fritsche Creek WMA
Rosenau-Lambrecht WMA
Rolloff Slough
Somsen Lake
Somsen WMA
Romberg WMA
Flandrau State Park
Lake Cottonwood
Horseshoe Lake
Bachelor Lake
Zanders Lake
School Lake
Juni Lake
Lost Dog and Fox Hunter's County Park
Helget-Braulick WMA
Joseph A. Tauer Prairie SNA
Lake Hanska
Southeast Hanska WMA
Omsrud Lake
Linden Lake
Minnesota River
Cottonwood River
Little Cottonwood River
Brown County Trails
Ridgely
West Newton
Lafayette
Home
Milford
Stark
Sigel
Cottonwood
Lake Hanska
Linden
Albin
SIBLEY CO
NICOLLET CO
RENVILLE CO
BROWN CO

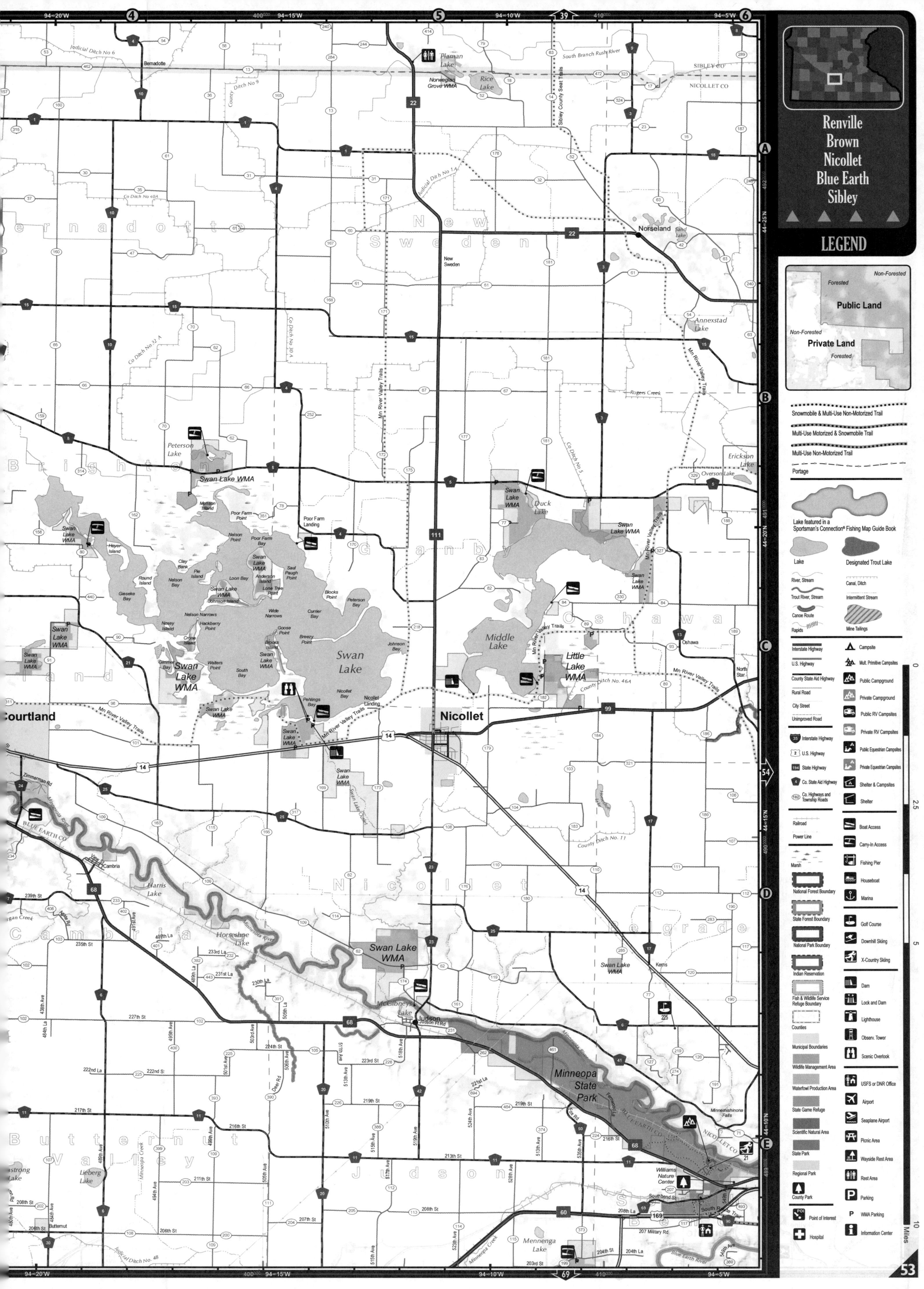

Renville
Brown
Nicollet
Blue Earth
Sibley
LEGEND
Public Land
Private Land
Forested
Non-Forested
Snowmobile & Multi-Use Non-Motorized Trail
Multi-Use Motorized & Snowmobile Trail
Multi-Use Non-Motorized Trail
Portage
Lake featured in a Sportsman's Connection® Fishing Map Guide Book
Lake
Designated Trout Lake
River, Stream
Canal, Ditch
Trout River, Stream
Intermittent Stream
Canoe Route
Rapids
Mine Tailings
Interstate Highway
U.S. Highway
County State Aid Highway
Rural Road
City Street
Unimproved Road
Interstate Highway
U.S. Highway
State Highway
Co. State Aid Highway
Co. Highways and Township Roads
Railroad
Power Line
Marsh
National Forest Boundary
State Forest Boundary
National Park Boundary
Indian Reservation
Fish & Wildlife Service Refuge Boundary
Counties
Municipal Boundaries
Wildlife Management Area
Waterfowl Production Area
State Game Refuge
Scientific Natural Area
State Park
Regional Park
County Park
Point of Interest
Hospital
Campsite
Mult. Primitive Campsites
Public Campground
Private Campground
Public RV Campsites
Private RV Campsites
Public Equestrian Campsites
Private Equestrian Campsites
Shelter & Campsites
Shelter
Boat Access
Carry-In Access
Fishing Pier
Houseboat
Marina
Golf Course
Downhill Skiing
X-Country Skiing
Dam
Lock and Dam
Lighthouse
Observ. Tower
Scenic Overlook
USFS or DNR Office
Airport
Seaplane Airport
Picnic Area
Wayside Rest Area
Rest Area
Parking
WMA Parking
Information Center
0
2.5
5
10
Miles
94°20'W
94°15'W
94°10'W
94°5'W
44°25'N
44°20'N
44°15'N
44°10'N
39
54
69
A
B
C
D
E
4
5
6
Bernadotte
Judicial Ditch No 6
Plaman Lake
Rice Lake
Norwegian Grove WMA
South Branch Rush River
Sibley County Seat Trails
SIBLEY CO
NICOLLET CO
Norseland
Sand Lake
New Sweden
Annexstad Lake
Mn River Valley Trails
Rogers Creek
Erickson Lake
Overson Lake
Peterson Lake
Swan Lake WMA
Poor Farm Landing
Duck Lake
Swan Lake
Middle Lake
Little Lake WMA
Oshawa
North Star
Nicollet
Courtland
Nicollet Landing
Zimmerman Rd
BLUE EARTH CO
Minnesota River
Cambria
Harris Lake
Horseshoe Lake
Swan Lake WMA
Kerns
McCabneys Lake
Judson
Minneopa State Park
Minneopa Falls
Williams Nature Center
South Bend
Mennenga Lake
Lieberg Lake
Butternut
Blue Earth River
Minneopa Creek
Judicial Ditch No. 48
County Ditch No. 11
County Ditch No. 46A
Co Ditch No 5
Judicial Ditch No 14

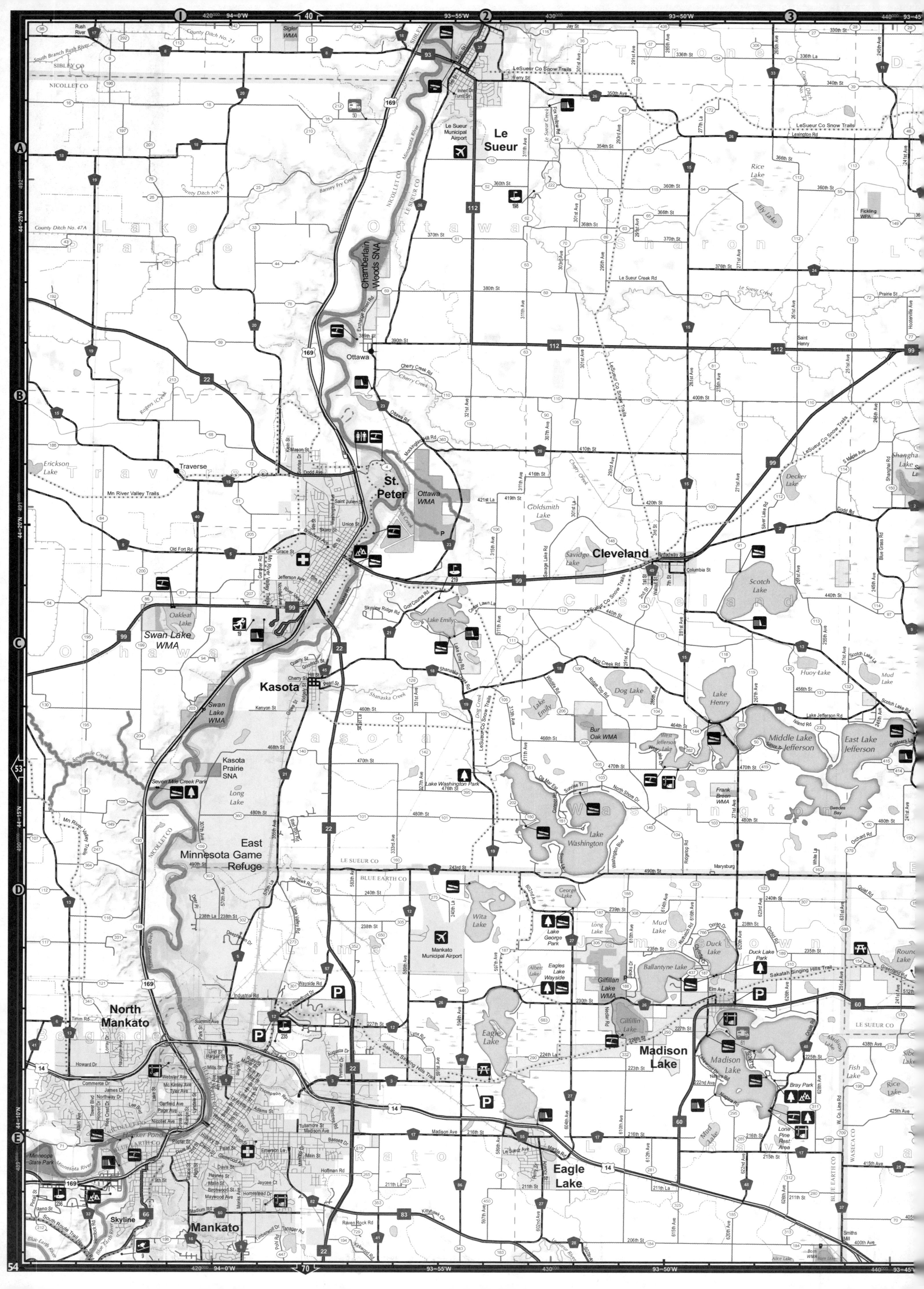

Le Sueur
St. Peter
Ottawa
Traverse
Cleveland
Kasota
North Mankato
Mankato
Skyline
Madison Lake
Eagle Lake
Saint Henry
Marysburg
Smiths Mill
Le Sueur Municipal Airport
Mankato Municipal Airport
Chamberlain Woods SNA
Ottawa WMA
Swan Lake WMA
Kasota Prairie SNA
Seven Mile Creek Park
East Minnesota Game Refuge
Sigler WMA
Fickling WPA
Bur Oak WMA
Frank Breen WMA
Gilfillan Lake WMA
Lake George Park
Eagles Lake Wayside
Duck Lake Park
Bray Park
Lone Pine Rest Area
Minneopa State Park
Sakatah Singing Hills Trail
LeSueur Co Snow Trails
Mn River Valley Trails
Minnesota River
Rice Lake
Fly Lake
Erickson Lake
Oakleaf Lake
Savidge Lake
Goldsmith Lake
Scotch Lake
Lake Emily
Dog Lake
Lake Henry
Middle Lake Jefferson
East Lake Jefferson
West Jefferson Lake
Huoy Lake
Mud Lake
Decker Lake
Shanghai Lake
Long Lake
Lake Washington
Wita Lake
George Lake
Albert Lake
Ballantyne Lake
Duck Lake
Eagle Lake
Gilfillan Lake
Madison Lake
Fish Lake
Sibert Lake
Round Lake
Swedes Bay
Tyrone
Lake Prairie
Ottawa
Sharon
Traverse
Cleveland
Oshawa
Kasota
Washington
Lime
Jamestown
Belgrade
Mankato
Le Ray
Janesville
SIBLEY CO
NICOLLET CO
LE SUEUR CO
BLUE EARTH CO
WASECA CO

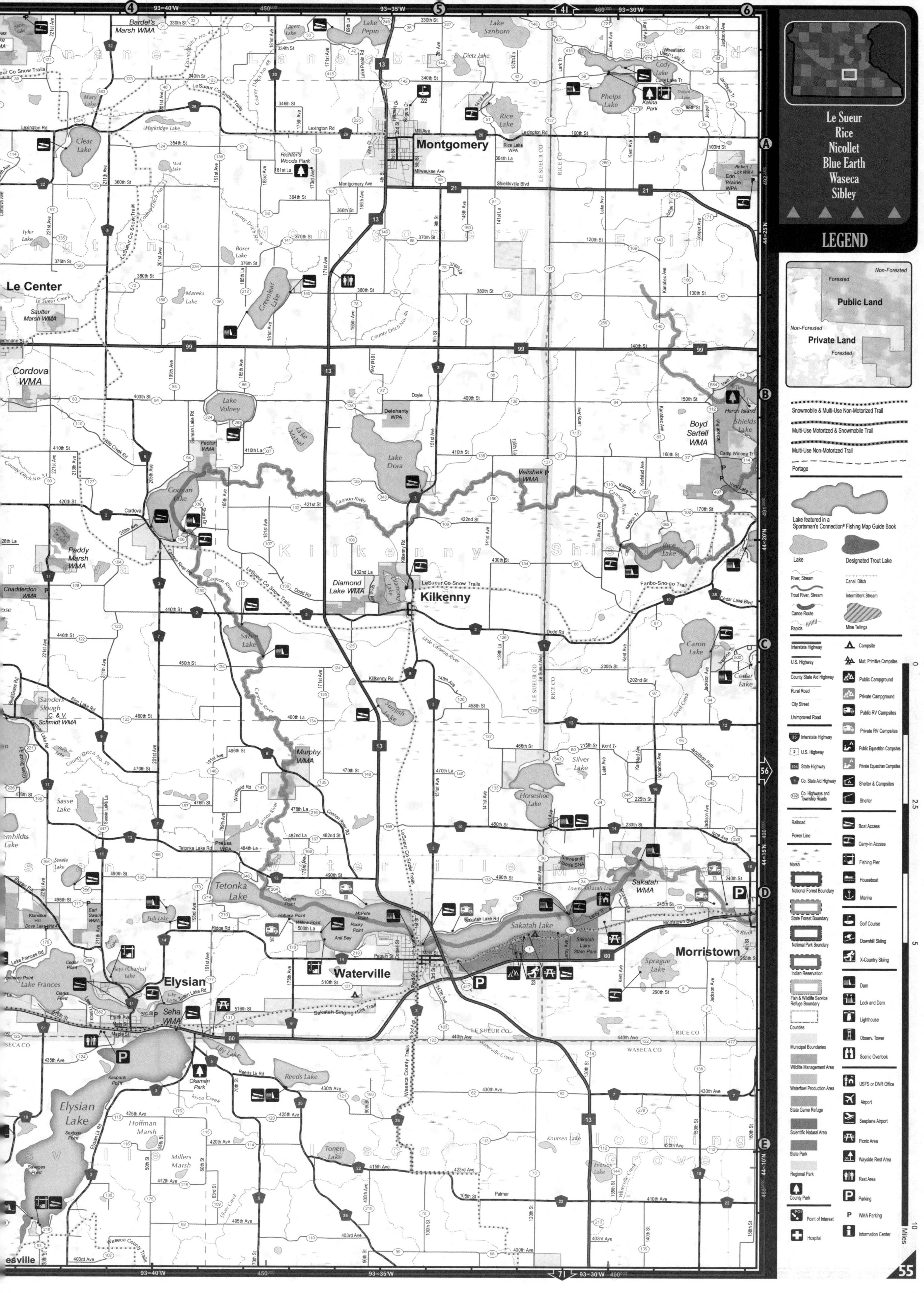

Le Sueur
Rice
Nicollet
Blue Earth
Waseca
Sibley
LEGEND
Public Land
Private Land
Forested
Non-Forested
Snowmobile & Multi-Use Non-Motorized Trail
Multi-Use Motorized & Snowmobile Trail
Multi-Use Non-Motorized Trail
Portage
Lake featured in a Sportsman's Connection® Fishing Map Guide Book
Lake
Designated Trout Lake
River, Stream
Canal, Ditch
Trout River, Stream
Intermittent Stream
Canoe Route
Rapids
Mine Tailings
Interstate Highway
U.S. Highway
County State Aid Highway
Rural Road
City Street
Unimproved Road
Interstate Highway
U.S. Highway
State Highway
Co. State Aid Highway
Co. Highways and Township Roads
Railroad
Power Line
Marsh
National Forest Boundary
State Forest Boundary
National Park Boundary
Indian Reservation
Fish & Wildlife Service Refuge Boundary
Counties
Municipal Boundaries
Wildlife Management Area
Waterfowl Production Area
State Game Refuge
Scientific Natural Area
State Park
Regional Park
County Park
Point of Interest
Hospital
Campsite
Mult. Primitive Campsites
Public Campground
Private Campground
Public RV Campsites
Private RV Campsites
Public Equestrian Campsites
Private Equestrian Campsites
Shelter & Campsites
Shelter
Boat Access
Carry-In Access
Fishing Pier
Houseboat
Marina
Golf Course
Downhill Skiing
X-Country Skiing
Dam
Lock and Dam
Lighthouse
Observ. Tower
Scenic Overlook
USFS or DNR Office
Airport
Seaplane Airport
Picnic Area
Wayside Rest Area
Rest Area
Parking
WMA Parking
Information Center
Miles
Montgomery
Le Center
Kilkenny
Waterville
Elysian
Morristown
Cordova WMA
Paddy Marsh WMA
Sanders Slough C. & V. Schmidt WMA
Boyd Sartell WMA
Diamond Lake WMA
Murphy WMA
Sakatah WMA
Sakatah Lake State Park
Seha WMA
Delehanty WPA
Clear Lake
Greenleaf Lake
Lake Volney
Lake Dora
Gorman Lake
Sabre Lake
Tetonka Lake
Sakatah Lake
Silver Lake
Horseshoe Lake
Rice Lake
Caron Lake
Cedar Lake
Sprague Lake
Elysian Lake
Lake Frances
Reeds Lake
Lily Lake
Phelps Lake
Cody Lake
Lake Sanborn
Lake Pepin
Cannon River
LeSueur Co Snow Trails
Sakatah Singing Hills Trail
Waseca County Trails
LE SUEUR CO
RICE CO
WASECA CO
93°40'W
93°35'W
93°30'W
44°25'N
44°20'N
44°15'N
44°10'N
41
56
71
55

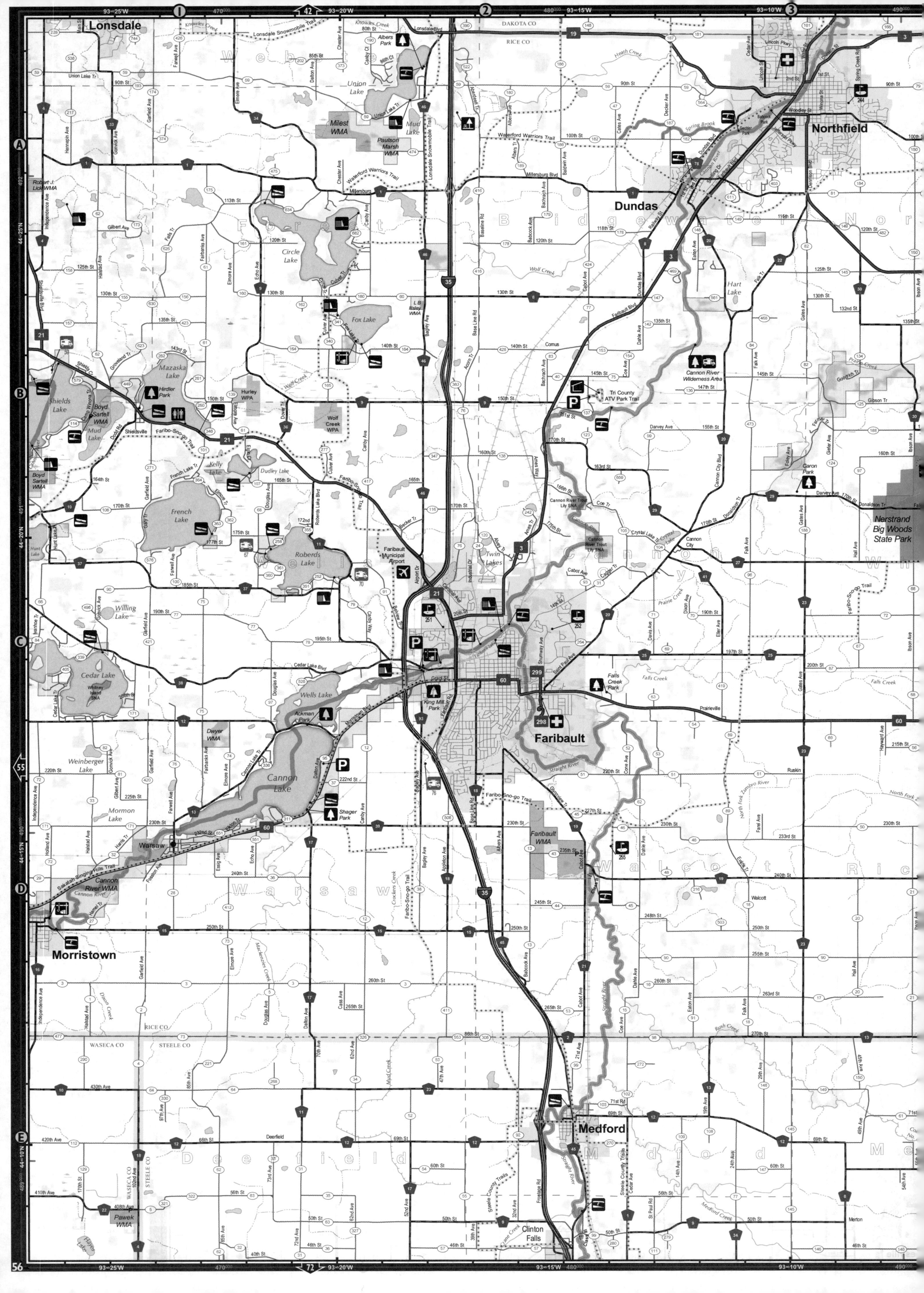

93°25'W
470000
42
93°20'W
480000
93°15'W
93°10'W
490000
1
2
3
A
B
C
D
E
55
72
Lonsdale
DAKOTA CO
RICE CO
Lonsdale Snowmobile Trail
Albers Park
Union Lake
Milest WMA
Paulson Marsh WMA
Mud Lake
Waterford Warriors Trail
Millersburg
Millersburg Blvd
Northfield
Dundas
Robert J. Lick WMA
Circle Lake
Fox Lake
L B Ilsley WMA
Mazaska Lake
Hirdler Park
Hurley WPA
Shields Lake
Boyd Sartell WMA
Mud Lake
Shieldsville
Fariba-Sno-go Trail
Wolf Creek WPA
Wolf Creek
Kelly Lake
Dudley Lake
French Lake
Roberds Lake
Hunt Lake
Faribault Municipal Airport
Twin Lakes
Tri County ATV Park Trail
Cannon River Wilderness Area
Hart Lake
Comus
Caron Park
Nerstrand Big Woods State Park
Cannon River Trout Lily SNA
Cannon City
Willing Lake
Cedar Lake
Whitney Island SNA
Wells Lake
Ackman Park
King Mill Park
Falls Creek Park
Falls Creek
Prairieville
Faribault
Straight River
Dwyer WMA
Weinberger Lake
Cannon Lake
Mormon Lake
Shager Park
Warsaw
Sakatah Singing Hills Trail
Cannon River WMA
Faribault WMA
Ruskin
North Fork Zumbro River
Walcott
Morristown
Crockers Creek
Mackenzie Creek
Dixon Creek
Rush Creek
WASECA CO
STEELE CO
Medford
Deerfield
Steele County Trails
Clinton Falls
Merton
Pawek WMA
Medford Creek
Mud Creek
Webster
Forest
Bridgewater
Wheeling
Cannon City
Wells
Warsaw
Walcott
Richland
Deerfield
Medford
44°25'N
44°20'N
44°15'N
44°10'N

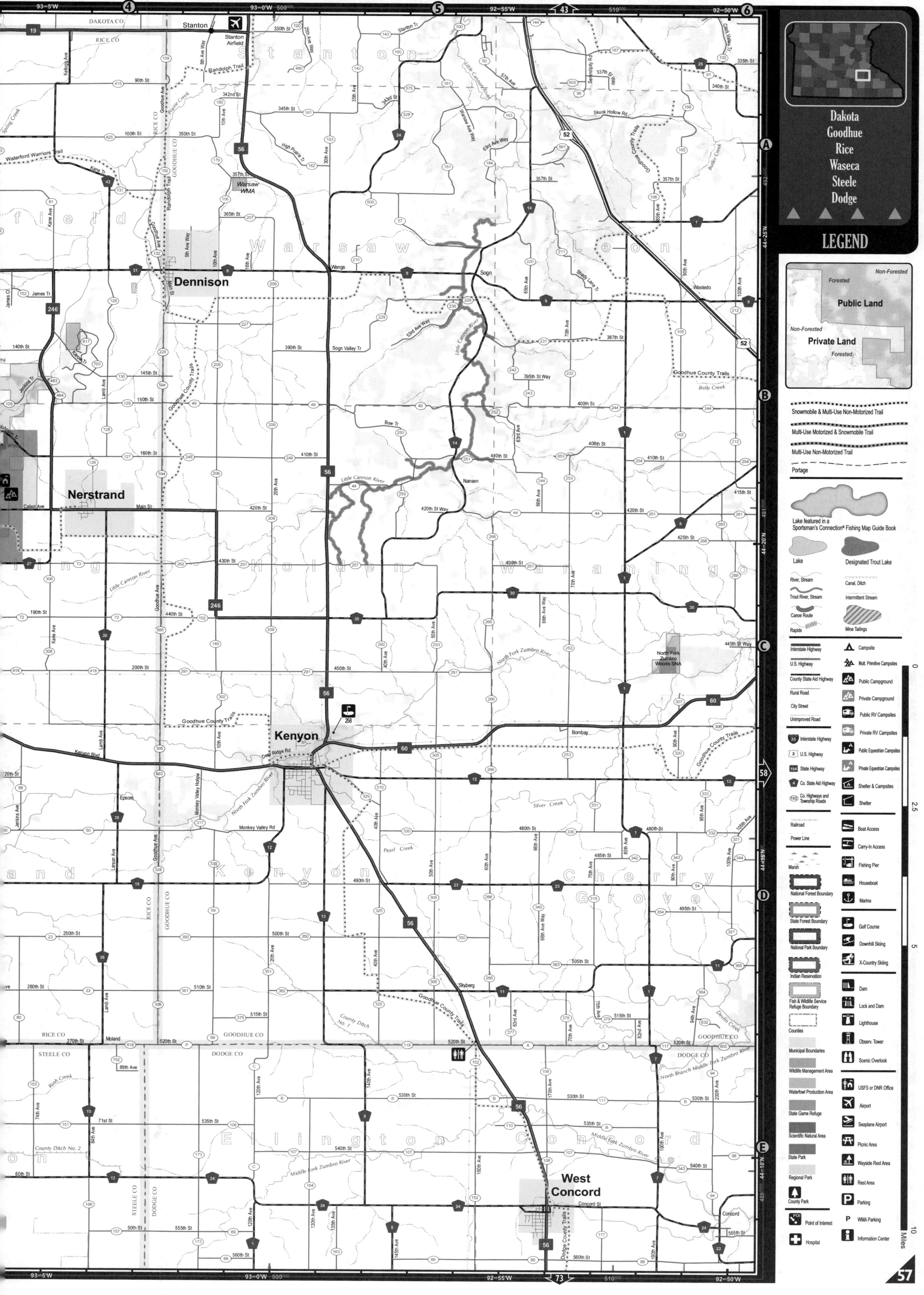

Dakota
Goodhue
Rice
Waseca
Steele
Dodge
LEGEND
Public Land
Private Land
Forested
Non-Forested
Snowmobile & Multi-Use Non-Motorized Trail
Multi-Use Motorized & Snowmobile Trail
Multi-Use Non-Motorized Trail
Portage
Lake featured in a Sportsman's Connection® Fishing Map Guide Book
Lake
Designated Trout Lake
Interstate Highway
U.S. Highway
County State Aid Highway
Rural Road
City Street
Unimproved Road
Campsite
Public Campground
Private Campground
Golf Course
Airport
Stanton
Dennison
Nerstrand
Kenyon
West Concord
Wangs
Sogn
Nansen
Wastedo
Skyberg
Moland
Epsom
Bombay
Concord
Stanton Airfield
Warsaw WMA
North Fork Zumbro Woods SNA
Little Cannon River
North Fork Zumbro River
Middle Fork Zumbro River
North Branch Middle Fork Zumbro River
Goodhue County Trails
Waterford Warriors Trail
RICE CO
GOODHUE CO
DAKOTA CO
STEELE CO
DODGE CO
Miles

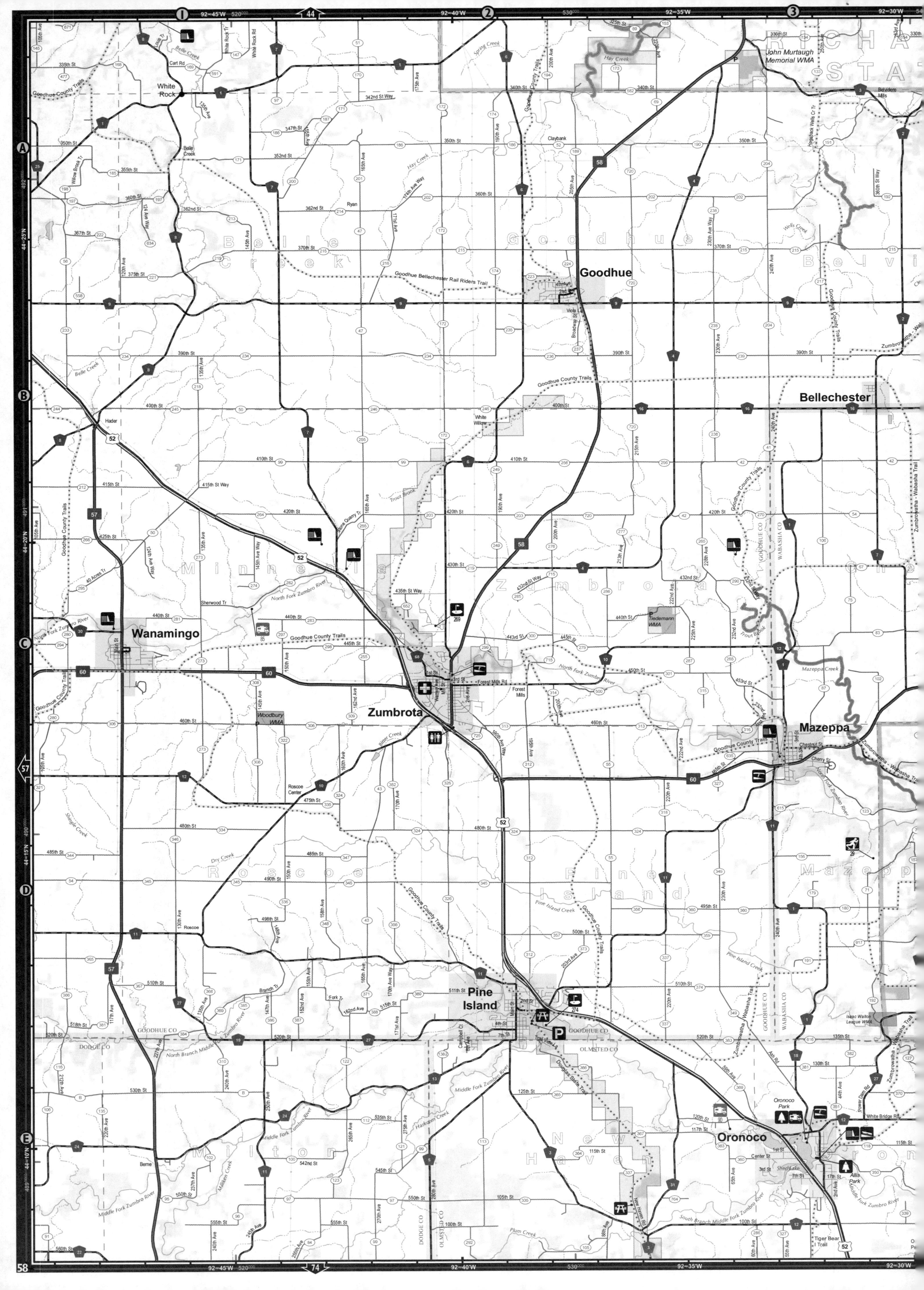

Goodhue
Bellechester
Wanamingo
Zumbrota
Mazeppa
Pine Island
Oronoco
White Rock
Hader
White Willow
Roscoe
Roscoe Center
Belvidere Mills
John Murtaugh Memorial WMA
Woodbury WMA
Tiedemann WMA
Isaac Walton League WMA
Oronoco Park
Allis Park
Goodhue County Trails
Goodhue Bellechester Rail Riders Trail
Douglas State Trail
Zumbrowatha - Wabasha Trail
North Fork Zumbro River
Middle Fork Zumbro River
South Branch Middle Fork Zumbro River
Pine Island Creek
Mazeppa Creek
Trout Brook
Belle Creek
Hay Creek
Spring Creek
GOODHUE CO
DODGE CO
OLMSTED CO
WABASHA CO
92°45'W
92°40'W
92°35'W
92°30'W
44°25'N
44°20'N
44°15'N
44°10'N

44
57
74

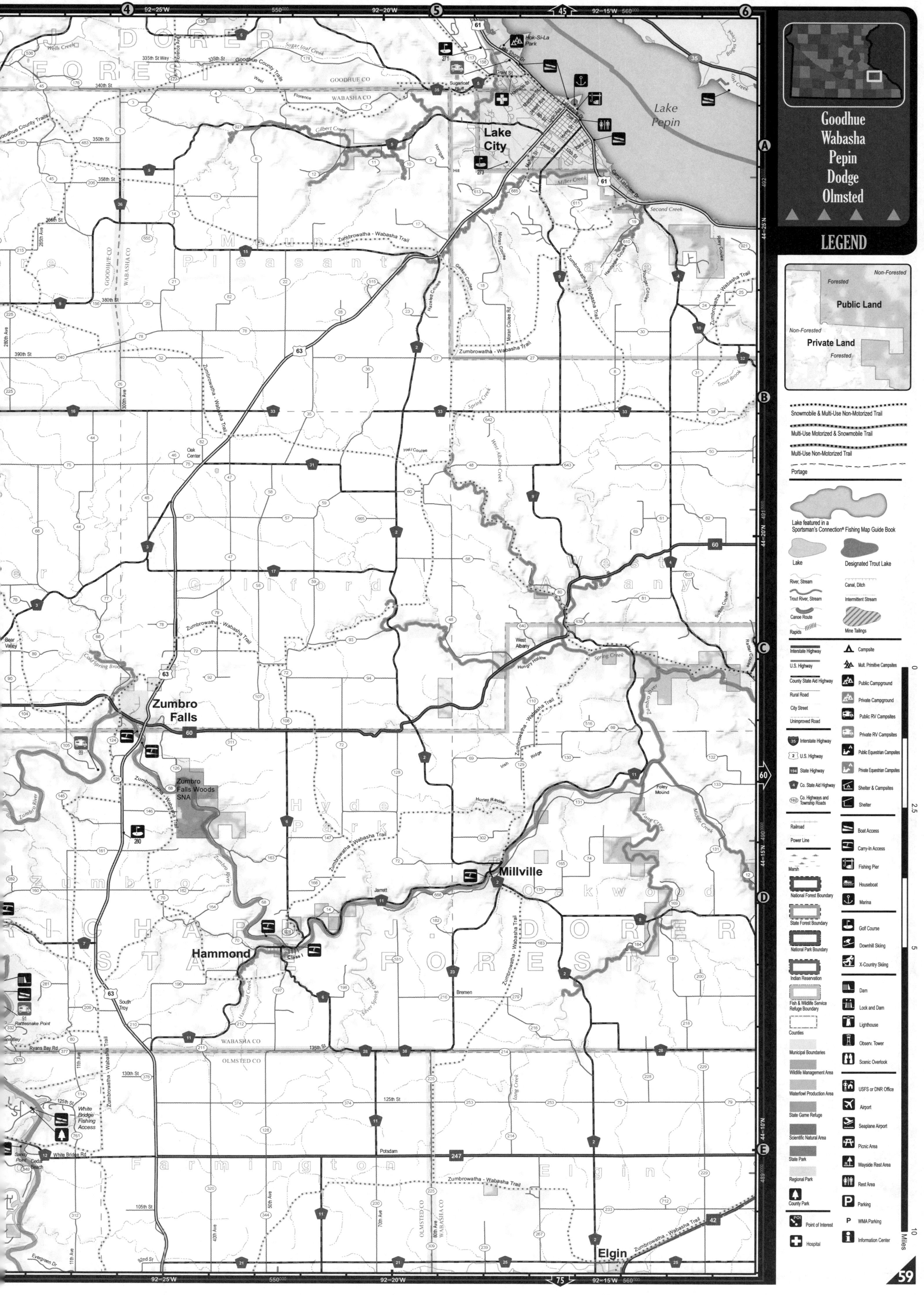

Goodhue
Wabasha
Pepin
Dodge
Olmsted
LEGEND
Public Land
Private Land
Forested
Non-Forested
Snowmobile & Multi-Use Non-Motorized Trail
Multi-Use Motorized & Snowmobile Trail
Multi-Use Non-Motorized Trail
Portage
Lake featured in a Sportsman's Connection® Fishing Map Guide Book
Lake
Designated Trout Lake
River, Stream
Canal, Ditch
Trout River, Stream
Intermittent Stream
Canoe Route
Rapids
Mine Tailings
Interstate Highway
U.S. Highway
County State Aid Highway
Rural Road
City Street
Unimproved Road
Interstate Highway
U.S. Highway
State Highway
Co. State Aid Highway
Co. Highways and Township Roads
Railroad
Power Line
Marsh
National Forest Boundary
State Forest Boundary
National Park Boundary
Indian Reservation
Fish & Wildlife Service Refuge Boundary
Counties
Municipal Boundaries
Wildlife Management Area
Waterfowl Production Area
State Game Refuge
Scientific Natural Area
State Park
Regional Park
County Park
Point of Interest
Hospital
Campsite
Mult. Primitive Campsites
Public Campground
Private Campground
Public RV Campsites
Private RV Campsites
Public Equestrian Campsites
Private Equestrian Campsites
Shelter & Campsites
Shelter
Boat Access
Carry-In Access
Fishing Pier
Houseboat
Marina
Golf Course
Downhill Skiing
X-Country Skiing
Dam
Lock and Dam
Lighthouse
Observ. Tower
Scenic Overlook
USFS or DNR Office
Airport
Seaplane Airport
Picnic Area
Wayside Rest Area
Rest Area
Parking
WMA Parking
Information Center
Miles
Lake Pepin
Lake City
Hok-Si-La Park
Sugarloaf Bluff
Zumbro Falls
Zumbro Falls Woods SNA
Millville
Hammond
Elgin
West Albany
Oak Center
Foley Mound
Bremen
Potsdam
South Troy
Bear Valley
White Bridge Fishing Access
Rattlesnake Point
Zumbrowatha - Wabasha Trail
Goodhue County Trails
Richard J. Dorer State Forest
Mount Pleasant
Lake
Gilford
West Albany
Hyde Park
Zumbro
Oakwood
Farmington
Elgin
Zumbro River
Gilbert Creek
Miller Creek
Second Creek
Spring Creek
Long Creek
Trout Brook
Cold Spring Brook
Hammond Creek
Silver Spring Creek
Hungry Hollow
Hurley Ravine
Wells Creek
Sugar Loaf Creek
Goodhue Co
Wabasha Co
Olmsted Co
92°25'W
92°20'W
92°15'W
44°25'N
44°20'N
44°15'N
44°10'N

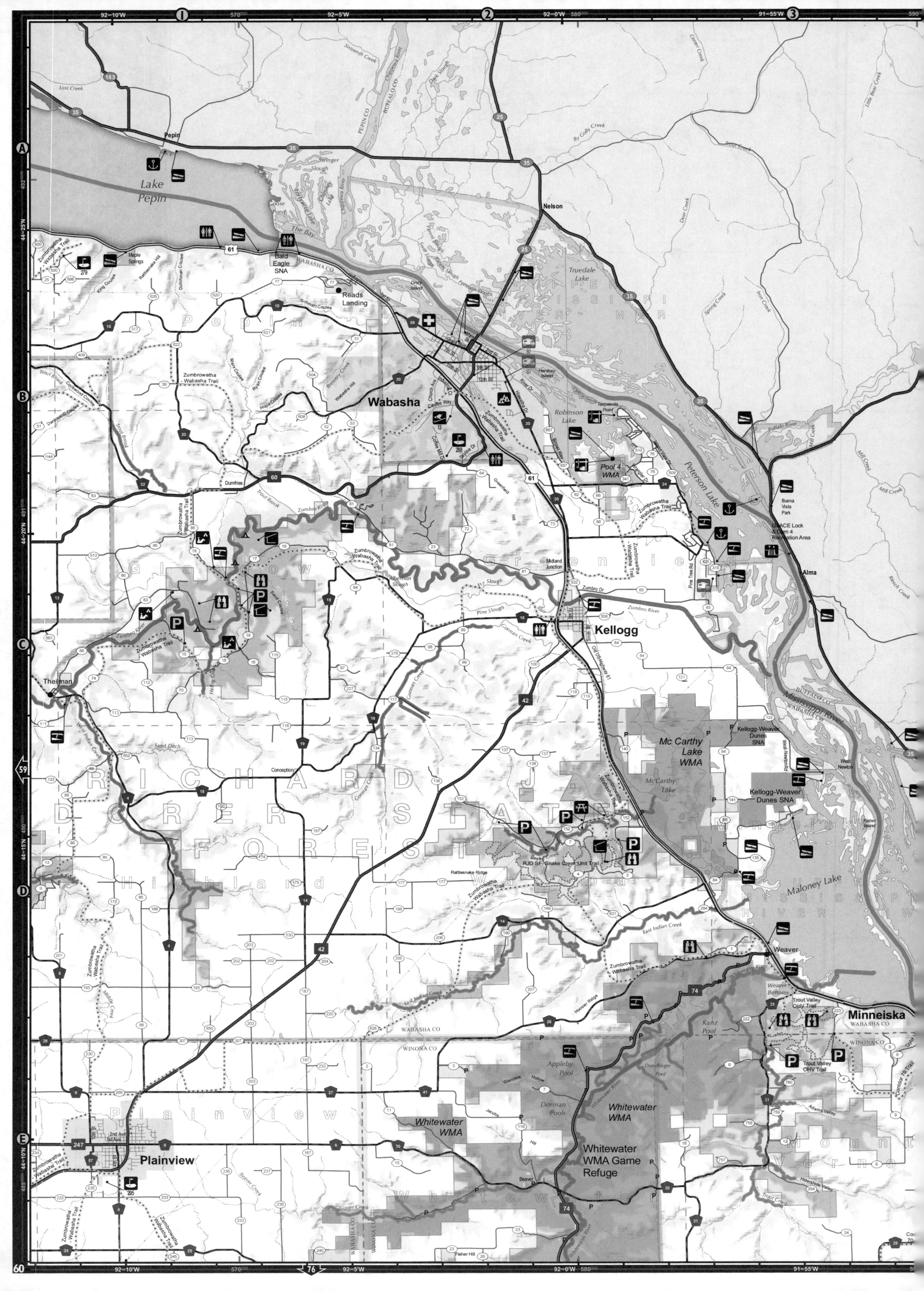

92°10'W
570000
92°5'W
92°0'W 580000
91°55'W
590
Lost Creek
Pepin
Lake Pepin
Swinger Slough
Nelson
Cedar Creek
Little Bear Creek
By Golly Creek
Trout Creek
Deer Creek
Truedale Lake
Spring Creek
Iron Creek
Maple Springs
King Coulee
Rattlesnake Hill
Bald Eagle SNA
WABASHA CO
Reads Landing
The Bay
Drury Island
Zumbrowatha - Wabasha Trail
Pepin
Wabasha
Hershey Island
Robinson Lake
Teepeeota Point
Pool 4 WMA
Peterson Lake
Buffalo River
Mill Creek
Buena Vista Park
USACE Lock & Dam 4 Recreation Area
Alma
Dumfries
Trout Brook
Zumbro River
Midland Junction
Zumbro Dr
Fly Slough
Pine Slough
Kellogg
Smith St
Old US Highway 61
Gorman Creek
Rinch Creek
BUFFALO CO
WABASHA CO
Mississippi River
Theilman
West Indian Creek
Sand Ditch
Conception
Mc Carthy Lake WMA
McCarthy Lake
Kellogg-Weaver Dunes SNA
West Newton
Fisher Island
RICHARD J. DORER STATE FOREST
Rattlesnake Ridge
RJD SF - Snake Creek Unit Trail
Maloney Lake
East Indian Creek
Weaver
Weaver Bottoms
Trout Valley OHV Trail
Minneiska
Hoosier Ridge
Kanz Pool
Appleby Pool
Dondlinger Pool
Glendale
Hollow
Jacobs
Dorman Pools
Whitewater WMA
Whitewater WMA Game Refuge
Whitewater River
Adams Valley
Corridor 70 Trail
WABASHA CO
WINONA CO
Plainview
Beaver Creek
Beaver
Hill
Trout Creek
Fisher Hill
Middle Creek
Hidershide Valley
Plainview
Whitewater
Mount Vernon
Highland
Glasgow
Greenfield
44°25'N
44°20'N
44°15'N
44°10'N
492
491
490
489
59
76

Buffalo
Trempealeau
Wabasha
Pepin
Winona
LEGEND
Public Land
Private Land
Forested
Non-Forested
Snowmobile & Multi-Use Non-Motorized Trail
Multi-Use Motorized & Snowmobile Trail
Multi-Use Non-Motorized Trail
Portage
Lake featured in a Sportsman's Connection® Fishing Map Guide Book
Lake
Designated Trout Lake
River, Stream
Canal, Ditch
Trout River, Stream
Intermittent Stream
Canoe Route
Rapids
Mine Tailings
Interstate Highway
U.S. Highway
County State Aid Highway
Rural Road
City Street
Unimproved Road
Interstate Highway
U.S. Highway
State Highway
Co. State Aid Highway
Co. Highways and Township Roads
Railroad
Power Line
Marsh
National Forest Boundary
State Forest Boundary
National Park Boundary
Indian Reservation
Fish & Wildlife Service Refuge Boundary
Counties
Municipal Boundaries
Wildlife Management Area
Waterfowl Production Area
State Game Refuge
Scientific Natural Area
State Park
Regional Park
County Park
Point of Interest
Hospital
Campsite
Mult. Primitive Campsites
Public Campground
Private Campground
Public RV Campsites
Private RV Campsites
Public Equestrian Campsites
Private Equestrian Campsites
Shelter & Campsites
Shelter
Boat Access
Carry-In Access
Fishing Pier
Houseboat
Marina
Golf Course
Downhill Skiing
X-Country Skiing
Dam
Lock and Dam
Lighthouse
Observ. Tower
Scenic Overlook
USFS or DNR Office
Airport
Seaplane Airport
Picnic Area
Wayside Rest Area
Rest Area
Parking
WMA Parking
Information Center
0
2.5
5
10
Miles
WISCONSIN
Modena
Waumandee
Cochrane
Fountain City
Whitman
John A. Latsch State Park
Thorpe WMA
USACE Lock & Dam 5 Recreation Area
Chimney Rock
5.1 Reservoir
Buffalo River
Elk Creek
South Fork Elk Creek
Little Tamarack Creek
Tamarack Creek
Pratt Creek
Thompson Creek
Waumandee Creek
Screech Owl Creek
Eagle Creek
Keller Creek
Trempealeau River
Deering Valley Creek
BUFFALO CO
WINONA CO
TREMPEALEAU CO
Island No 55
Island No 57
Island No 58
Andre Klopper
91°50'W
91°45'W
91°40'W
91°35'W
44°25'N
44°20'N
44°15'N
44°10'N

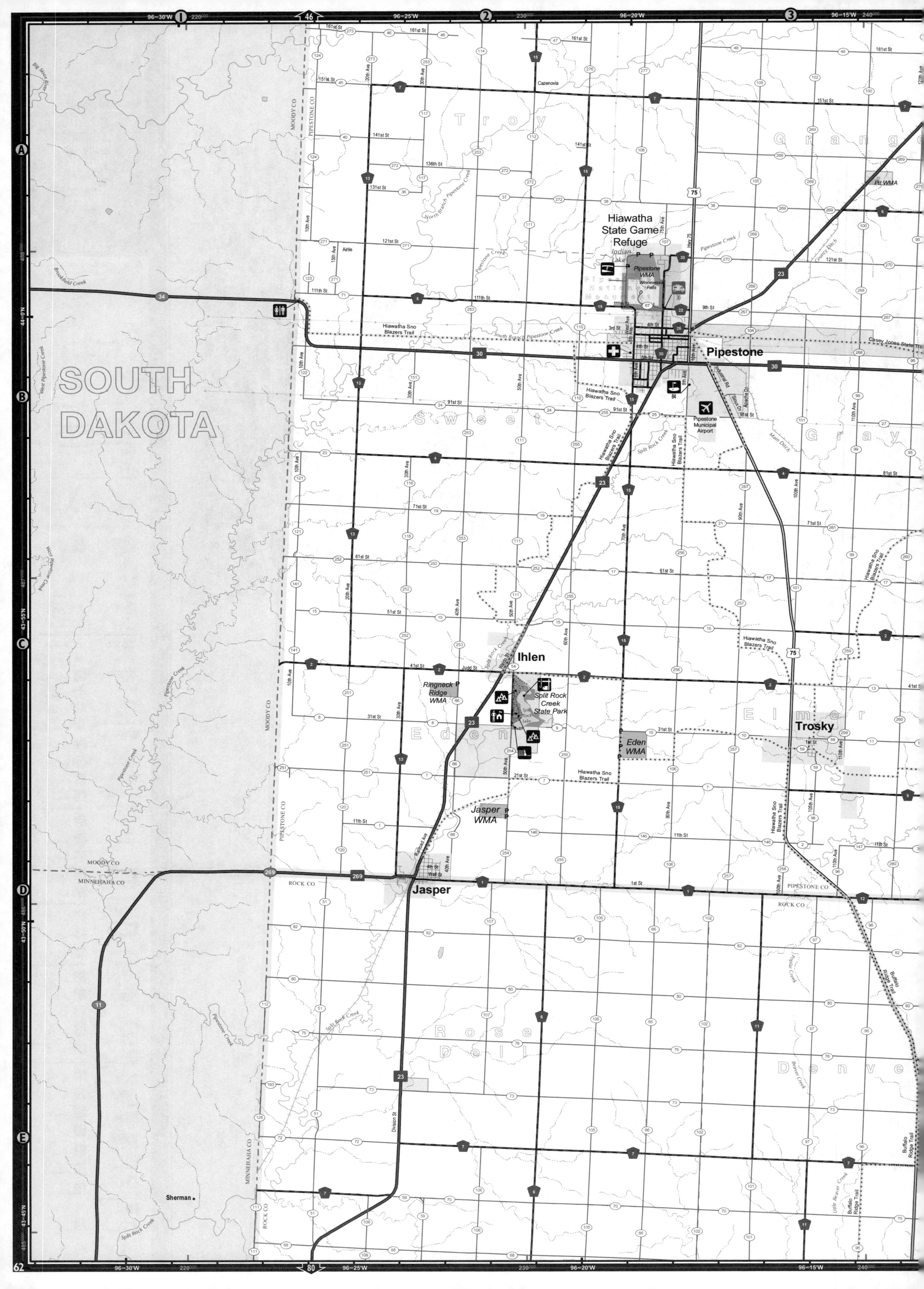

SOUTH DAKOTA
Pipestone
Hiawatha State Game Refuge
Pipestone WMA
Pipestone Municipal Airport
Ihlen
Split Rock Creek State Park
Ringneck Ridge WMA
Eden WMA
Jasper WMA
Trosky
Jasper
Airlie
Cazenovia
Sherman
Pit WMA
Troy
Grange
Sweet
Gray
Eden
Elmer
Rose Dell
Denver
Hiawatha Sno Blazers Trail
Casey Jones State Trail
Buffalo Ridge Trail
MOODY CO
PIPESTONE CO
MINNEHAHA CO
ROCK CO
96°30'W
96°25'W
96°20'W
96°15'W
44°0'N
43°55'N
43°50'N
43°45'N

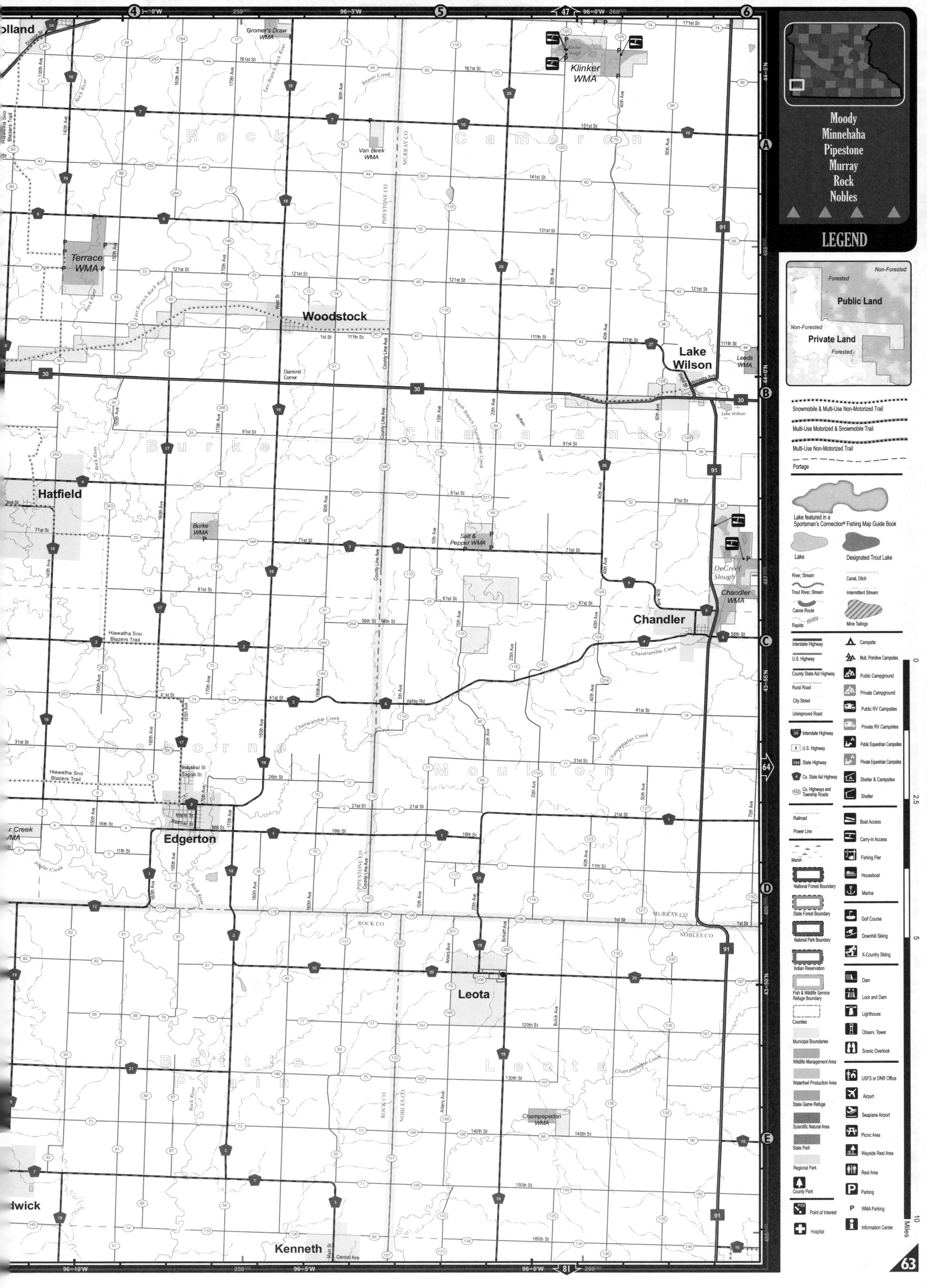
Moody
Minnehaha
Pipestone
Murray
Rock
Nobles
LEGEND
Forested
Non-Forested
Public Land
Private Land
Snowmobile & Multi-Use Non-Motorized Trail
Multi-Use Motorized & Snowmobile Trail
Multi-Use Non-Motorized Trail
Portage
Lake featured in a Sportsman's Connection® Fishing Map Guide Book
Lake
Designated Trout Lake
River, Stream
Canal, Ditch
Trout River, Stream
Intermittent Stream
Canoe Route
Mine Tailings
Rapids
Interstate Highway
U.S. Highway
County State Aid Highway
Rural Road
City Street
Unimproved Road
Interstate Highway
U.S. Highway
State Highway
Co. State Aid Highway
Co. Highways and Township Roads
Railroad
Power Line
Marsh
National Forest Boundary
State Forest Boundary
National Park Boundary
Indian Reservation
Fish & Wildlife Service Refuge Boundary
Counties
Municipal Boundaries
Wildlife Management Area
Waterfowl Production Area
State Game Refuge
Scientific Natural Area
State Park
Regional Park
County Park
Point of Interest
Hospital
Campsite
Mult. Primitive Campsites
Public Campground
Private Campground
Public RV Campsites
Private RV Campsites
Public Equestrian Campsites
Private Equestrian Campsites
Shelter & Campsites
Shelter
Boat Access
Carry-In Access
Fishing Pier
Houseboat
Marina
Golf Course
Downhill Skiing
X-Country Skiing
Dam
Lock and Dam
Lighthouse
Observ. Tower
Scenic Overlook
USFS or DNR Office
Airport
Seaplane Airport
Picnic Area
Wayside Rest Area
Rest Area
Parking
WMA Parking
Information Center
Miles
Holland
Gromer's Draw WMA
Klinker WMA
Klinker Slough
Van Beek WMA
Terrace WMA
Woodstock
Diamond Corner
Lake Wilson
Leeds WMA
Hatfield
Burke WMA
Salt & Pepper WMA
DeGreef Slough
Chandler WMA
Chandler
Hiawatha Sno Blazers Trail
Edgerton
Leota
Champepedan WMA
Kenneth
Rock
Cameron
Burke
Chanarambie
Osborne
Moulton
Battle Plain
Leota
Rock River
East Branch Rock River
Beaver Creek
North Branch Chanarambie Creek
Chanarambie Creek
Champepadan Creek
Poplar Creek
Buffalo Ridge
MURRAY CO
PIPESTONE CO
ROCK CO
NOBLES CO
96°10'W
96°5'W
96°0'W
44°5'N
44°0'N
43°55'N
43°50'N

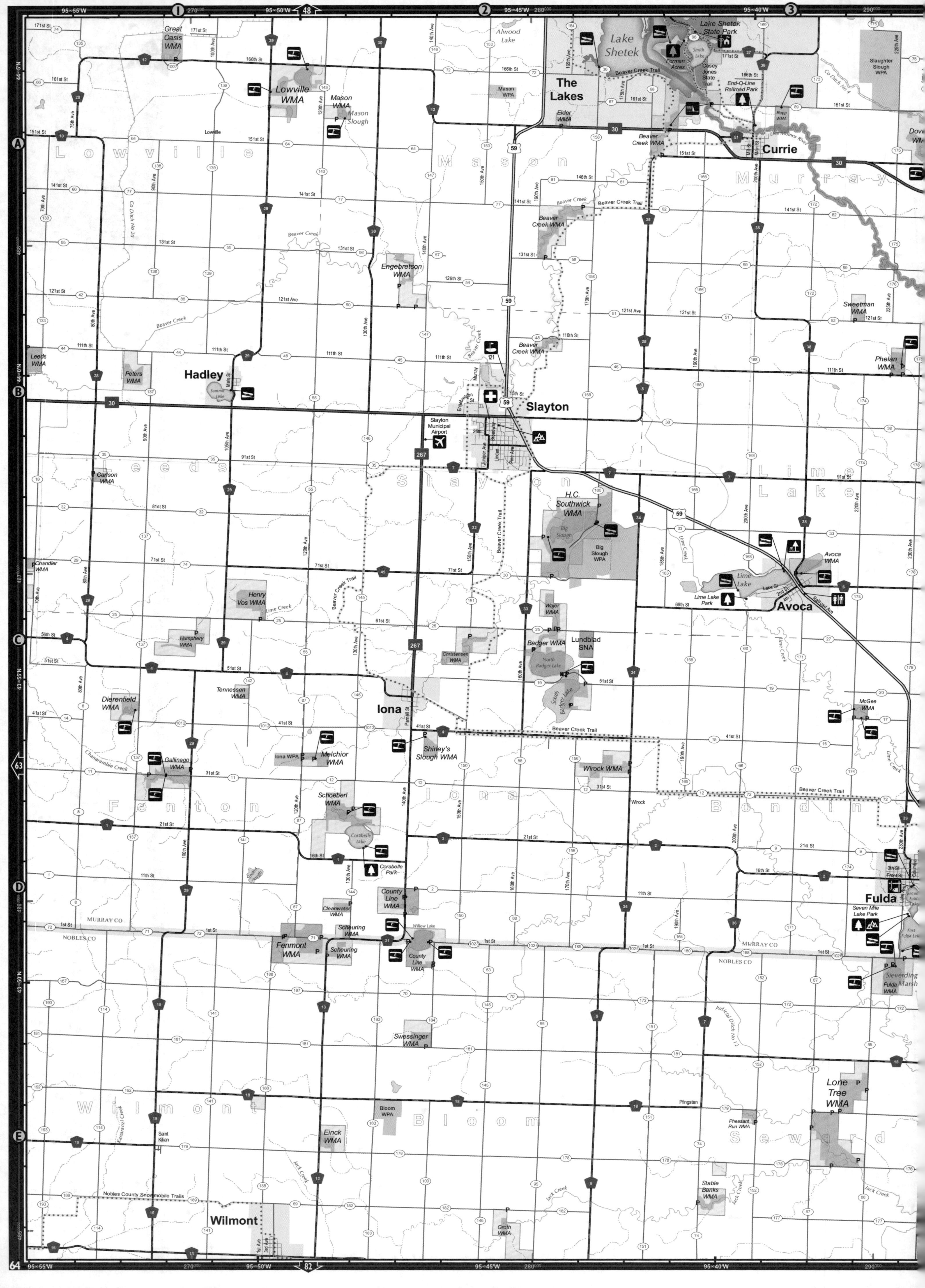

95°55'W
95°50'W
95°45'W
95°40'W
48
The Lakes
Lake Shetek
Lake Shetek State Park
Great Oasis WMA
Alwood Lake
Lowville WMA
Mason WMA
Mason Slough
Mason WPA
Elder WMA
Forman Acres
Smith Lake
Casey Jones State Trail
End-O-Line Railroad Park
Rupp WMA
Slaughter Slough WPA
Beaver Creek WMA
Currie
Des Moines River
Lowville
Mason
Murray
Beaver Creek Trail
Beaver Creek
Co Ditch No 20
Engebretson WMA
Sweetman WMA
Leeds WMA
Peters WMA
Hadley
Summit Lake
Phelan WMA
Slayton
Slayton Municipal Airport
Leeds
Slayton
Lime Lake
Carlson WMA
H.C. Southwick WMA
Big Slough
Big Slough WPA
Chandler WMA
Henry Vos WMA
Lime Creek
Avoca WMA
Lime Lake Park
Avoca
Humphrey WMA
Wajer WMA
Badger WMA
Lundblad SNA
North Badger Lake
South Badger Lake
Christensen WMA
Tennessen WMA
Dierenfield WMA
Iona
McGee WMA
Shirley's Slough WMA
Iona WPA
Melchior WMA
Gallinago WMA
Chanarambie Creek
Wirock WMA
Wirock
Fenton
Iona
Bondin
Schoeberl WMA
Corabelle Lake
Corabelle Park
County Line WMA
Cleanwater WMA
Scheuring WMA
Willow Lake
Fenmont WMA
Fulda
Seven Mile Lake Park
First Fulda Lake
Sieverding Marsh
Fulda WMA
MURRAY CO
NOBLES CO
Judicial Ditch No 12
Swessinger WMA
Lone Tree WMA
Wilmont
Bloom
Seward
Bloom WPA
Pfingsten
Pheasant Run WMA
Saint Kilian
Kanaranzi Creek
Einck WMA
Jack Creek
Stable Banks WMA
Nobles County Snowmobile Trails
Groth WMA
63
82

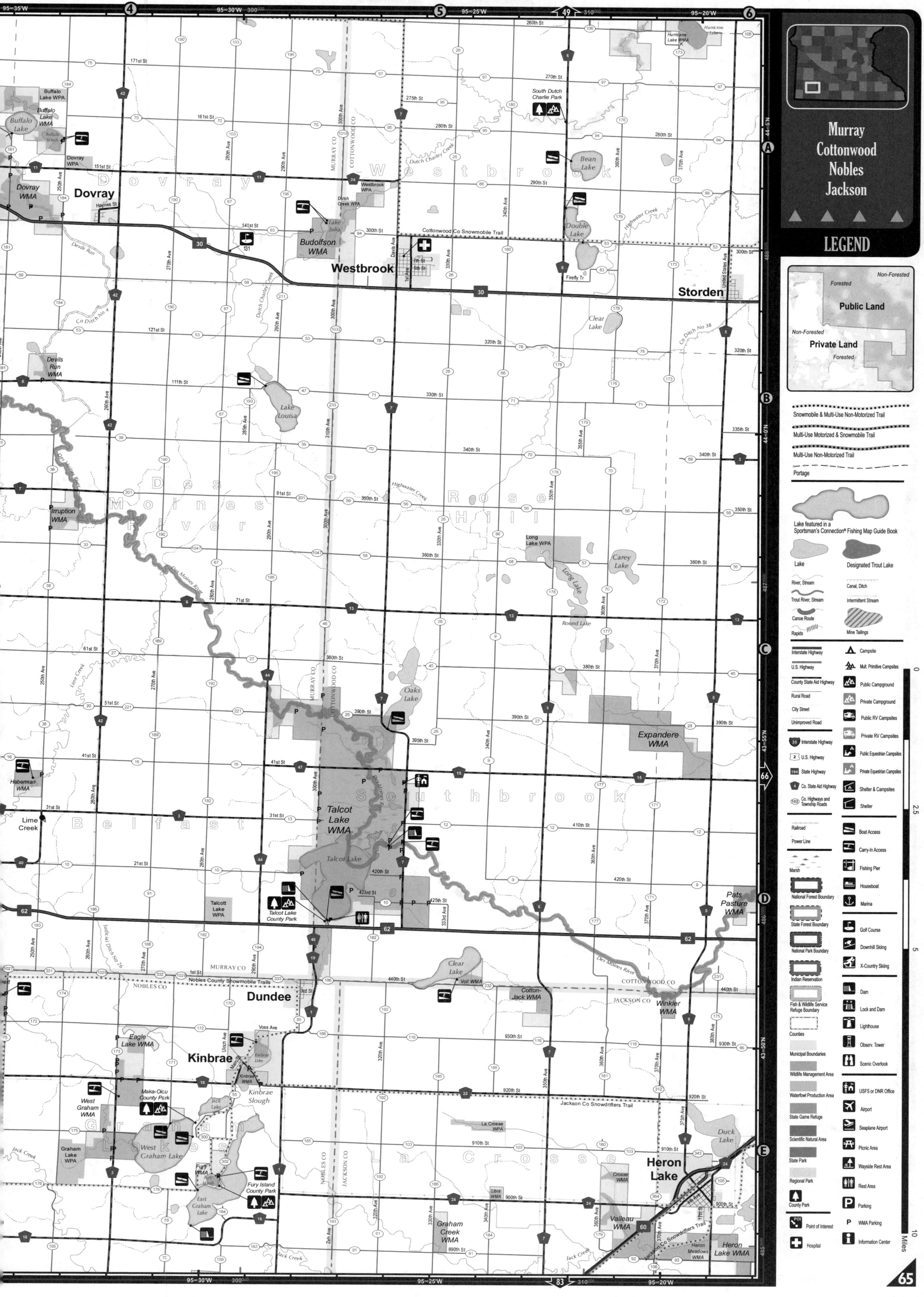

Murray
Cottonwood
Nobles
Jackson
LEGEND
Forested
Non-Forested
Public Land
Private Land
Snowmobile & Multi-Use Non-Motorized Trail
Multi-Use Motorized & Snowmobile Trail
Multi-Use Non-Motorized Trail
Portage
Lake featured in a Sportsman's Connection® Fishing Map Guide Book
Lake
Designated Trout Lake
River, Stream
Canal, Ditch
Trout River, Stream
Intermittent Stream
Canoe Route
Mine Tailings
Rapids
Interstate Highway
U.S. Highway
County State Aid Highway
Rural Road
City Street
Unimproved Road
Interstate Highway
U.S. Highway
State Highway
Co. State Aid Highway
Co. Highways and Township Roads
Railroad
Power Line
Marsh
National Forest Boundary
State Forest Boundary
National Park Boundary
Indian Reservation
Fish & Wildlife Service Refuge Boundary
Counties
Municipal Boundaries
Wildlife Management Area
Waterfowl Production Area
State Game Refuge
Scientific Natural Area
State Park
Regional Park
County Park
Point of Interest
Hospital
Campsite
Mult. Primitive Campsites
Public Campground
Private Campground
Public RV Campsites
Private RV Campsites
Public Equestrian Campsites
Private Equestrian Campsites
Shelter & Campsites
Shelter
Boat Access
Carry-In Access
Fishing Pier
Houseboat
Marina
Golf Course
Downhill Skiing
X-Country Skiing
Dam
Lock and Dam
Lighthouse
Observ. Tower
Scenic Overlook
USFS or DNR Office
Airport
Seaplane Airport
Picnic Area
Wayside Rest Area
Rest Area
Parking
WMA Parking
Information Center
Miles
Dovray
Westbrook
Storden
Dundee
Kinbrae
Heron Lake
Lime Creek
Buffalo Lake
Buffalo Lake WPA
Buffalo Lake WMA
Dovray WPA
Dovray WMA
Budolfson WMA
Lake Julia
Westbrook WPA
Dutch Creek WPA
Bean Lake
Double Lake
Hurricane Lake
Hurricane Lake WMA
South Dutch Charlie Park
Cottonwood Co Snowmobile Trail
Clear Lake
Devils Run WMA
Lake Louisa
Irruption WMA
Long Lake WPA
Long Lake
Carey Lake
Round Lake
Oaks Lake
Expandere WMA
Haberman WMA
Talcot Lake WMA
Talcot Lake
Talcot Lake WPA
Talcot Lake County Park
Pats Pasture WMA
Volt WMA
Cotton-Jack WMA
Winkler WMA
Nobles County Snowmobile Trails
Eagle Lake WMA
Maka-Oicu County Park
Kinbrae Lake
Kinbrae WMA
Kinbrae Slough
Jack Lake
West Graham WMA
West Graham Lake
Graham Lake WPA
Fury Lake
Fury WMA
Fury Island County Park
East Graham Lake
La Crosse WPA
Jackson Co Snowdrifters Trail
Duck Lake
Cross WMA
Libra WMA
Valleau WMA
Graham Creek WMA
Heron Meadows WMA
Heron Lake WMA
Des Moines River
Highwater Creek
Dutch Charley Creek
Devils Run
Lime Creek
Jack Creek
Co Ditch No 4
Co Ditch No 38
Judicial Ditch No 26
MURRAY CO
COTTONWOOD CO
NOBLES CO
JACKSON CO
Westbrook
Dovray
Des Moines River
Rose Hill
Southbrook
Belfast
Graham Lakes
La Crosse
95°35'W
95°30'W
95°25'W
95°20'W
44°5'N
44°0'N
43°55'N
43°50'N
49
66
83
A
B
C
D
E
4
5
6

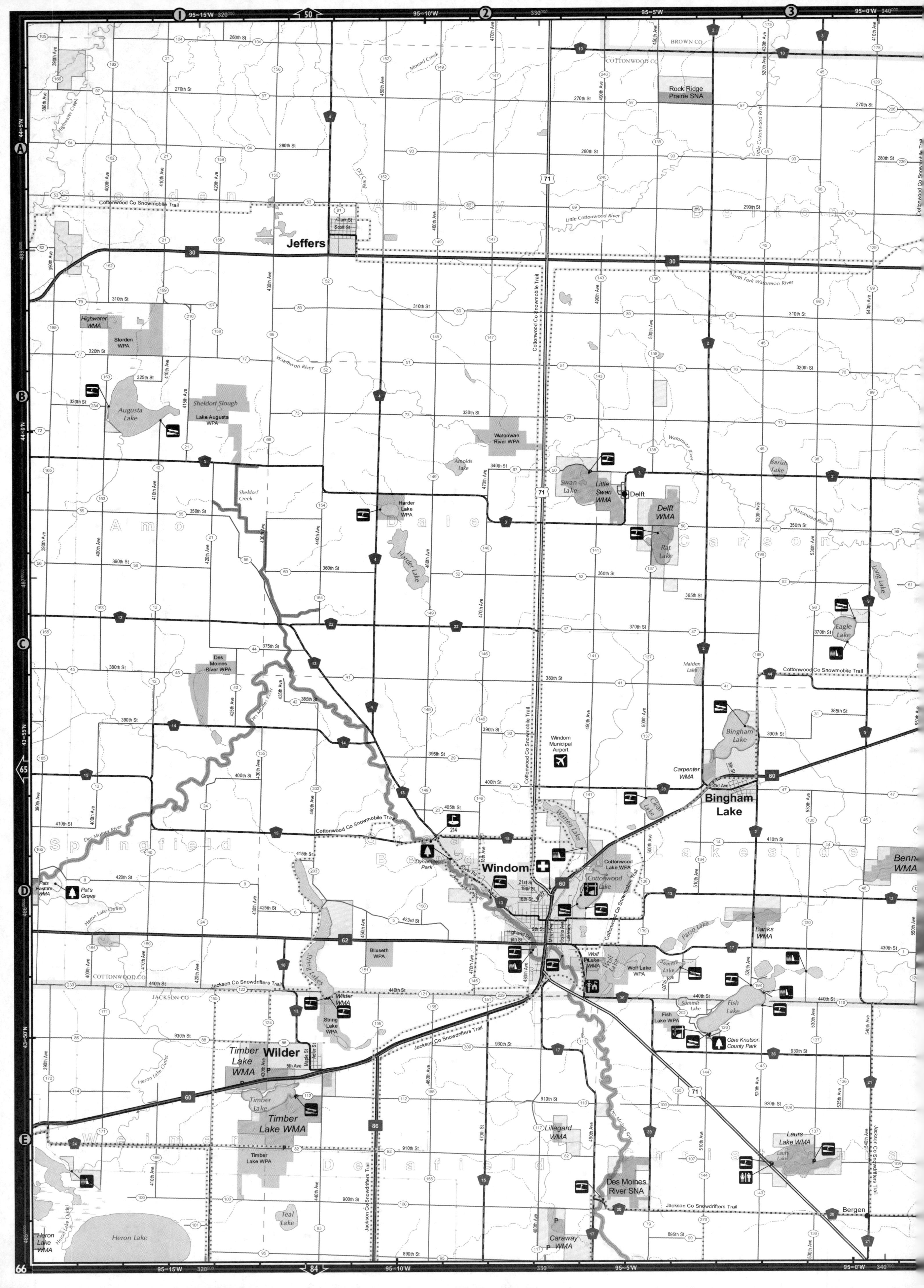

Jeffers
Windom
Bingham Lake
Wilder
Delft
Bergen
Augusta Lake
Sheldorf Slough
Lake Augusta WPA
Highwater WMA
Storden WPA
Rock Ridge Prairie SNA
Watonwan River WPA
Harder Lake WPA
Harder Lake
Swan Lake
Little Swan WMA
Delft WMA
Rat Lake
Eagle Lake
Long Lake
Bingham Lake
Carpenter WMA
Windom Municipal Airport
Des Moines River WPA
Dynamite Park
Cottonwood Lake WPA
Cottonwood Lake
Warren Lake
Clear Lake
Banks WMA
Parso Lake
Wolf Lake WPA
Wolf Lake WMA
Fish Lake
Fish Lake WPA
Sommit Lake
Obie Knutson County Park
Blixseth WPA
String Lakes
Wilder WMA
String Lake WPA
Timber Lake WMA
Timber Lake
Timber Lake WPA
Heron Lake
Heron Lake WMA
Heron Lake Outlet
Teal Lake
Lillegard WMA
Des Moines River SNA
Caraway WMA
Laurs Lake WMA
Pat's Pasture WMA
Pat's Grove
Maiden Lake
Barish Lake
Arnolds Lake
Des Moines River
Watonwan River
Little Cottonwood River
North Fork Watonwan River
Sheldorf Creek
Mound Creek
Highwater Creek
Dry Creek
Cottonwood Co Snowmobile Trail
Jackson Co Snowdrifters Trail
BROWN CO
COTTONWOOD CO
JACKSON CO
Springfield
Amboy
Delton
Amo
Dale
Carson
Great Bend
Lakeside
Germantown
Weimer
Delafield
Christiania

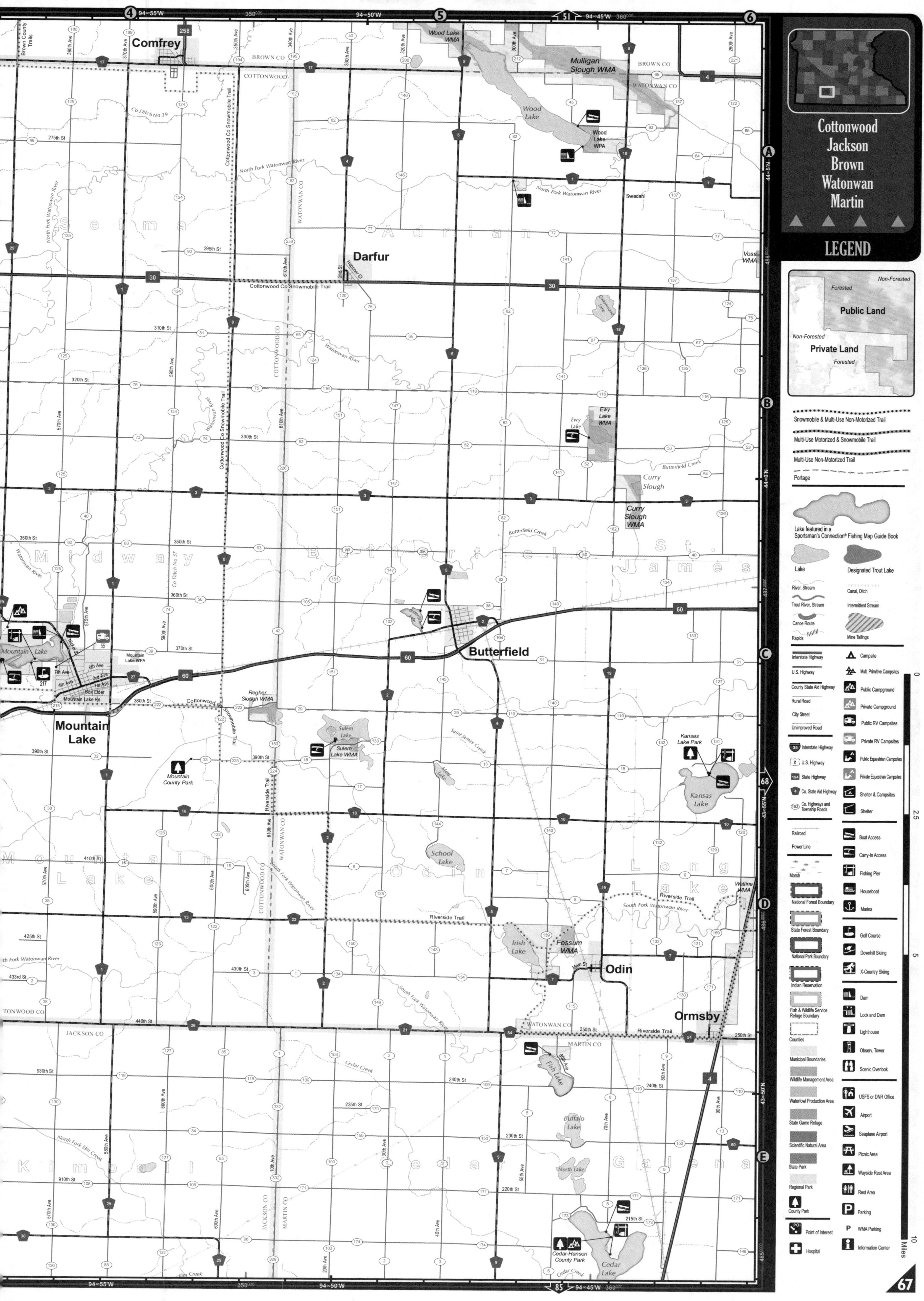
Cottonwood
Jackson
Brown
Watonwan
Martin
LEGEND
Public Land
Private Land
Forested
Non-Forested
Snowmobile & Multi-Use Non-Motorized Trail
Multi-Use Motorized & Snowmobile Trail
Multi-Use Non-Motorized Trail
Portage
Lake featured in a Sportsman's Connection® Fishing Map Guide Book
Lake
Designated Trout Lake
River, Stream
Trout River, Stream
Canoe Route
Rapids
Canal, Ditch
Intermittent Stream
Mine Tailings
Interstate Highway
U.S. Highway
County State Aid Highway
Rural Road
City Street
Unimproved Road
Interstate Highway
U.S. Highway
State Highway
Co. State Aid Highway
Co. Highways and Township Roads
Railroad
Power Line
Marsh
National Forest Boundary
State Forest Boundary
National Park Boundary
Indian Reservation
Fish & Wildlife Service Refuge Boundary
Counties
Municipal Boundaries
Wildlife Management Area
Waterfowl Production Area
State Game Refuge
Scientific Natural Area
State Park
Regional Park
County Park
Point of Interest
Hospital
Campsite
Mult. Primitive Campsites
Public Campground
Private Campground
Public RV Campsites
Private RV Campsites
Public Equestrian Campsites
Private Equestrian Campsites
Shelter & Campsites
Shelter
Boat Access
Carry-In Access
Fishing Pier
Houseboat
Marina
Golf Course
Downhill Skiing
X-Country Skiing
Dam
Lock and Dam
Lighthouse
Observ. Tower
Scenic Overlook
USFS or DNR Office
Airport
Seaplane Airport
Picnic Area
Wayside Rest Area
Rest Area
Parking
WMA Parking
Information Center
0
2.5
5
10
Miles
Comfrey
Darfur
Butterfield
Mountain Lake
Odin
Ormsby
Wood Lake WMA
Mulligan Slough WMA
Wood Lake
Wood Lake WPA
Sveadahl
Voss WMA
Ewy Lake
Ewy Lake WMA
Curry Slough
Curry Slough WMA
Mountain Lake WPA
Regher Slough WMA
Sulem Lake
Sulem Lake WPA
Mountain County Park
Kansas Lake Park
Kansas Lake
School Lake
Irish Lake
Fossum WMA
Watline WMA
Fish Lake
Buffalo Lake
North Lake
Cedar-Hanson County Park
Cedar Lake
Cottonwood Co Snowmobile Trail
Riverside Trail
North Fork Watonwan River
South Fork Watonwan River
Watonwan River
Butterfield Creek
Saint James Creek
Cedar Creek
North Fork Elm Creek
Selma
Adrian
Midway
Butterfield
St. James
Mountain Lake
Odin
Long Lake
Kimball
Cedar
Galena
BROWN CO
COTTONWOOD
WATONWAN CO
COTTONWOOD CO
JACKSON CO
MARTIN CO
94°55'W
94°50'W
94°45'W
44°5'N
44°0'N
43°55'N
43°50'N
51
68
85

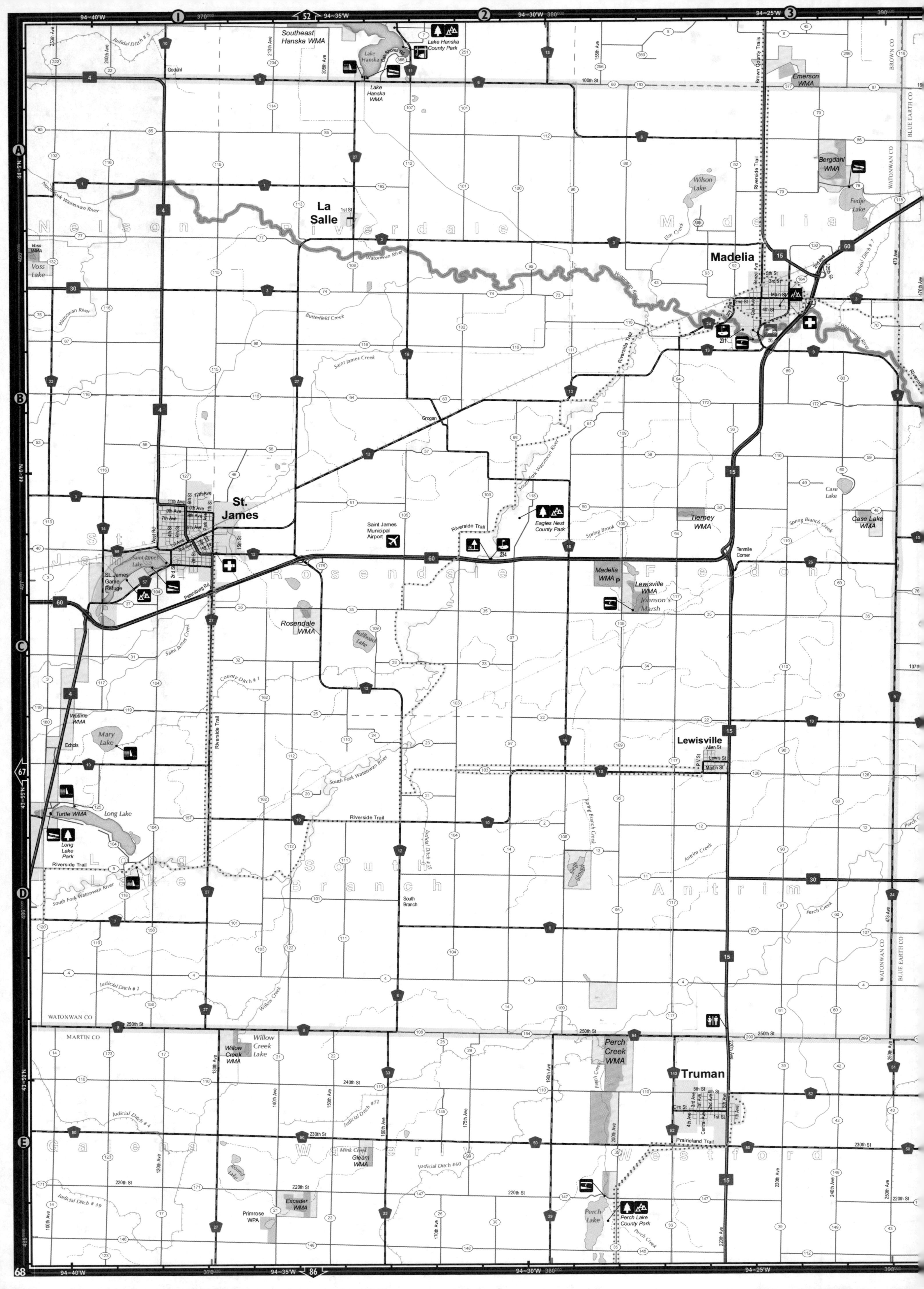

Southeast Hanska WMA
Lake Hanska
Lake Hanska County Park
Lake Hanska WMA
Godahl
La Salle
Nelson
Riverdale
Madelia
North Fork Watonwan River
Watonwan River
Voss WMA
Voss Lake
Butterfield Creek
Saint James Creek
Wilson Lake
Elm Creek
Madelia
Emerson WMA
Bergdahl WMA
Fedje Lake
Brown County Trails
Riverside Trail
BROWN CO
BLUE EARTH CO
WATONWAN CO
Grogan
St. James
Saint James Lake
St. James Game Refuge
Petersburg Rd
Saint James Municipal Airport
Eagles Nest County Park
South Fork Watonwan River
Spring Brook
Tierney WMA
Tenmile Corner
Case Lake
Case Lake WMA
Spring Branch Creek
St. James
Rosendale
Fieldon
Madelia WMA
Lewisville WMA
Johnson's Marsh
Rosendale WMA
Bullhead Lake
County Ditch #1
Walline WMA
Mary Lake
Echols
Lewisville
Turtle WMA
Long Lake
Long Lake Park
Riverside Trail
Judicial Ditch #15
Antrim Creek
Perch Creek
Long Lake
South Branch
Antrim
Judicial Ditch #2
Willow Creek
WATONWAN CO
MARTIN CO
250th St
Willow Creek Lake
Willow Creek WMA
Perch Creek WMA
Truman
Judicial Ditch #4
Judicial Ditch #72
Galena
Waverly
Westford
Mink Creek
Gleam WMA
Round Lake
Judicial Ditch #60
Prairieland Trail
Judicial Ditch #39
Exceder WMA
Primrose WPA
Perch Lake
Perch Lake County Park
94°40'W
94°35'W
94°30'W
94°25'W
44°5'N
44°0'N
43°55'N
43°50'N

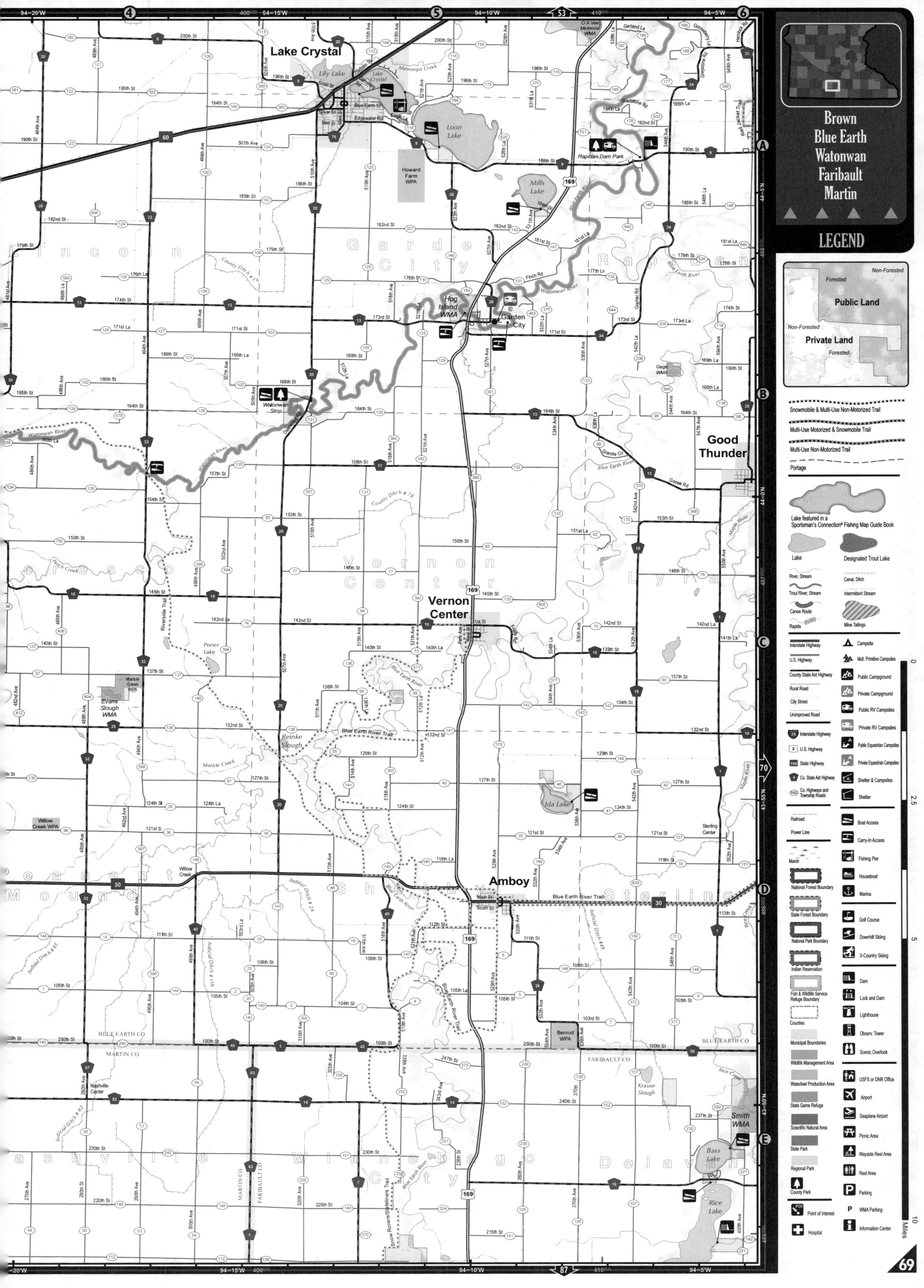

Brown
Blue Earth
Watonwan
Faribault
Martin
LEGEND
Public Land
Private Land
Forested
Non-Forested
Snowmobile & Multi-Use Non-Motorized Trail
Multi-Use Motorized & Snowmobile Trail
Multi-Use Non-Motorized Trail
Portage
Lake featured in a Sportsman's Connection® Fishing Map Guide Book
Lake
Designated Trout Lake
River, Stream
Canal, Ditch
Trout River, Stream
Intermittent Stream
Canoe Route
Rapids
Mine Tailings
Interstate Highway
U.S. Highway
County State Aid Highway
Rural Road
City Street
Unimproved Road
Interstate Highway
U.S. Highway
State Highway
Co. State Aid Highway
Co. Highways and Township Roads
Railroad
Power Line
Marsh
National Forest Boundary
State Forest Boundary
National Park Boundary
Indian Reservation
Fish & Wildlife Service Refuge Boundary
Counties
Municipal Boundaries
Wildlife Management Area
Waterfowl Production Area
State Game Refuge
Scientific Natural Area
State Park
Regional Park
County Park
Point of Interest
Hospital
Campsite
Mult. Primitive Campsites
Public Campground
Private Campground
Public RV Campsites
Private RV Campsites
Public Equestrian Campsites
Private Equestrian Campsites
Shelter & Campsites
Shelter
Boat Access
Carry-In Access
Fishing Pier
Houseboat
Marina
Golf Course
Downhill Skiing
X-Country Skiing
Dam
Lock and Dam
Lighthouse
Observ. Tower
Scenic Overlook
USFS or DNR Office
Airport
Seaplane Airport
Picnic Area
Wayside Rest Area
Rest Area
Parking
WMA Parking
Information Center
Miles
Lake Crystal
Lily Lake
Lake Crystal
Minneopa Creek
Loon Lake
Howard Farm WPA
O A Vee Memorial WMA
Rapidan Dam Park
Mills Lake
Garden City
Hog Island WMA
Watonwan Stop
Watonwan River
Blue Earth River
Good Thunder
Vernon Center
Porter Lake
Marble Creek WPA
Evans Slough WMA
Reinke Slough
Blue Earth River Trail
Riverside Trail
Ida Lake
Sterling Center
Willow Creek WPA
Willow Creek
Amboy
Benrud WPA
BLUE EARTH CO
MARTIN CO
FARIBAULT CO
Nashville Center
Krause Slough
Smith WMA
Bass Lake
Rice Lake
Rice Creek
Maple River
Perch Creek
Judicial Ditch # 24
Judicial Ditch # 49
Judicial Ditch # 82
Judicial Ditch # 85
Judicial Ditch # 116
County Ditch # 36
County Ditch # 78
Snow Rovers/Stateliners Trail
Lincoln
Garden City
Rapidan
Decoria
Vernon Center
Lyra
Pleasant Mound
Shelby
Sterling
Nashville
Winnebago City
Delavan
94°20'W
94°15'W
94°10'W
94°5'W
44°5'N
44°0'N
43°55'N
43°50'N
53
70
87
69

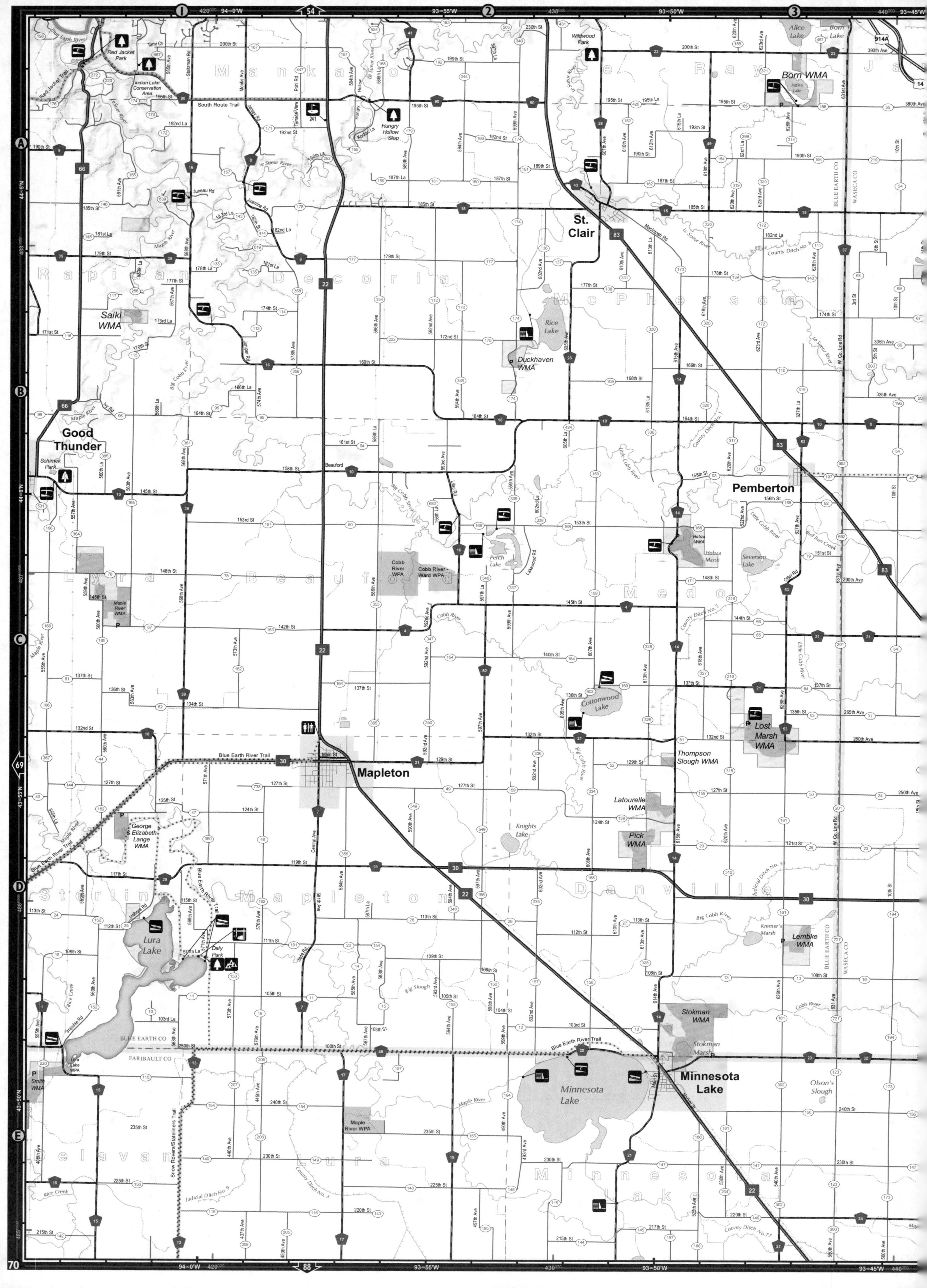

Red Jacket Park
Indian Lake Conservation Area
Wildwood Park
Born WMA
Alice Lake
Born Lake
Hungry Hollow Stop
Saiki WMA
St. Clair
Rice Lake
Duckhaven WMA
Good Thunder
Schimek Park
Pemberton
Hobza WMA
Hobza Marsh
Severson Lake
Cobb River WPA
Cobb River - Ward WPA
Perch Lake
Maple River WMA
Cottonwood Lake
Lost Marsh WMA
Thompson Slough WMA
Mapleton
Latourelle WMA
Pick WMA
Knights Lake
George & Elizabeth Lange WMA
Lura Lake
Daly Park
Lembke WMA
Kremer's Marsh
Stokman WMA
Stokman Marsh
Minnesota Lake
Olson's Slough
Lura Lake WPA
Smith WMA
Maple River WPA
Blue Earth River Trail
Red Jacket Trail
South Route Trail
Snow Rovers/Statelines Trail
BLUE EARTH CO
FARIBAULT CO
WASECA CO
Mankato
Le Ray
Rapidan
Decoria
McPherson
Lyra
Beauford
Medo
Sterling
Mapleton
Danville
Delavan
Lura
Minnesota Lake

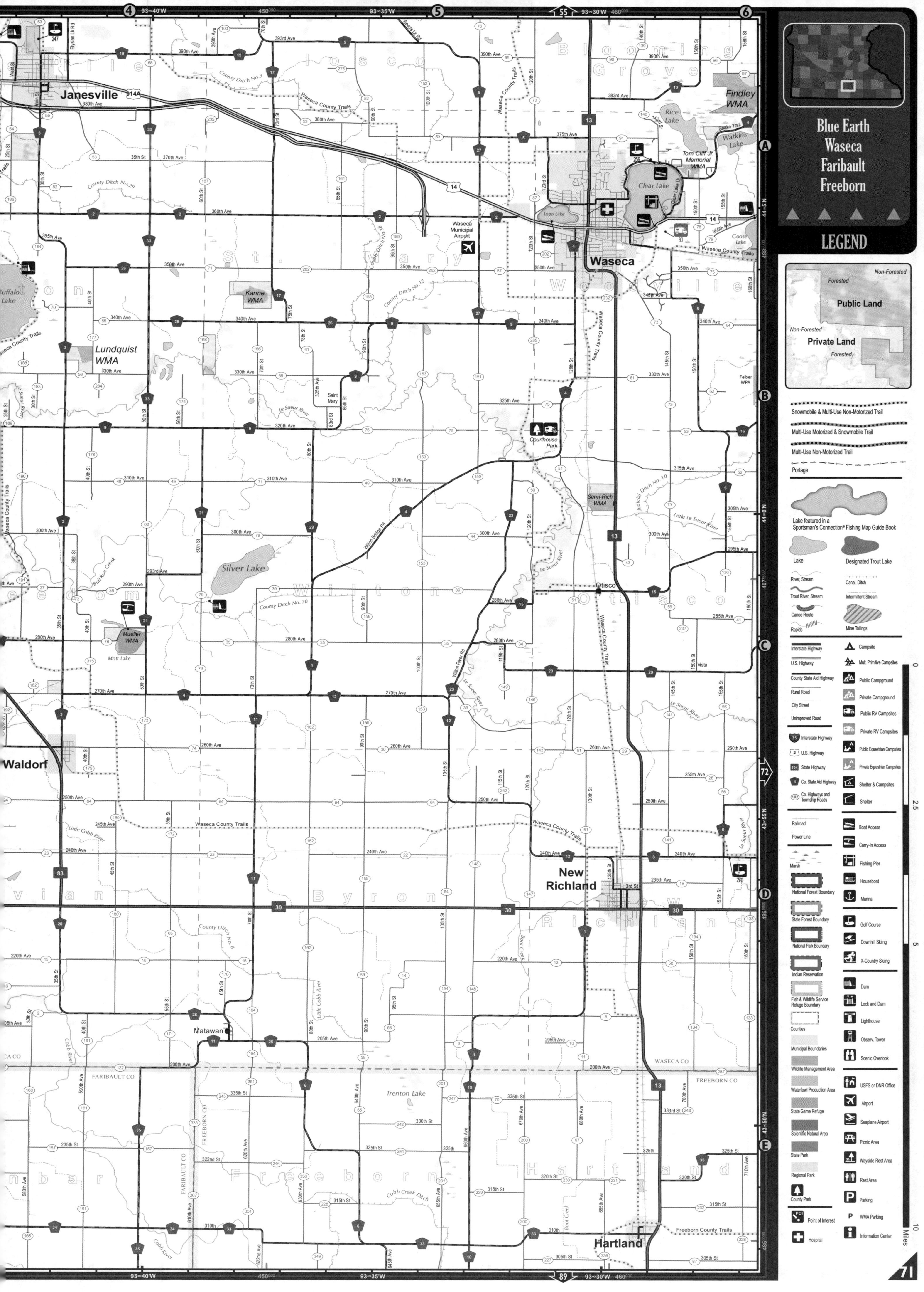

Blue Earth
Waseca
Faribault
Freeborn
LEGEND
Public Land
Private Land
Forested
Non-Forested
Snowmobile & Multi-Use Non-Motorized Trail
Multi-Use Motorized & Snowmobile Trail
Multi-Use Non-Motorized Trail
Portage
Lake featured in a Sportsman's Connection® Fishing Map Guide Book
Lake
Designated Trout Lake
Janesville
Waseca
New Richland
Hartland
Waldorf
Matawan
Otisco
Clear Lake
Silver Lake
Lundquist WMA
Findley WMA
Kanne WMA
Mueller WMA
Senn-Rich WMA
Tom Cliff Jr. Memorial WMA
Rice Lake
Watkins Lake
Loon Lake
Goose Lake
Trenton Lake
Waseca Municipal Airport
Courthouse Park
Le Sueur River
Little Le Sueur River
Waseca County Trails
Freeborn County Trails
WASECA CO
FREEBORN CO
FARIBAULT CO
93°40'W
93°35'W
93°30'W
44°5'N
44°0'N
43°55'N
43°50'N

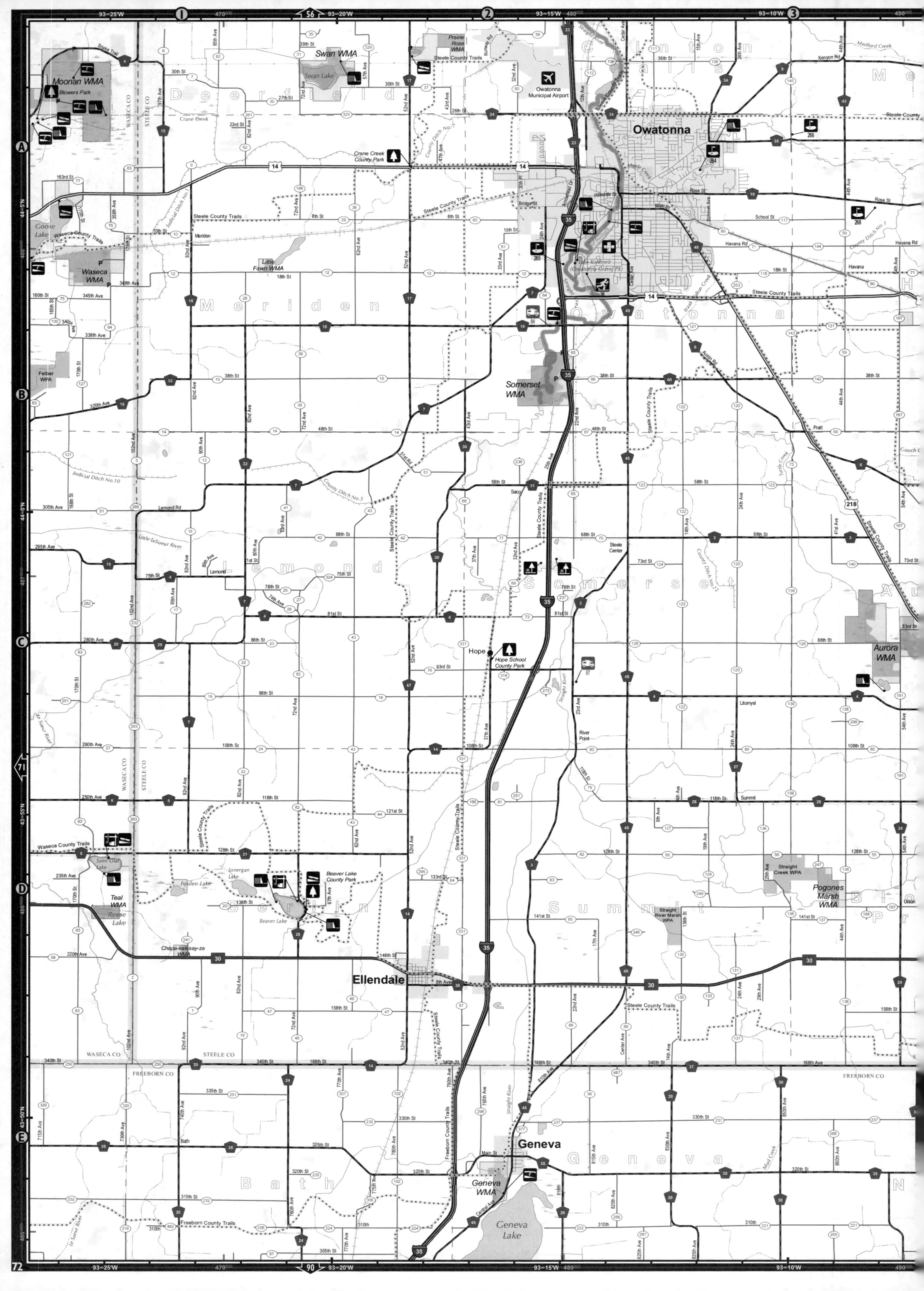

Owatonna
Owatonna Municipal Airport
Ellendale
Geneva
Moonan WMA
Blowers Park
Swan WMA
Swan Lake
Prairie Rose WMA
Crane Creek County Park
Goose Lake
Waseca WMA
Little Fawn WMA
Felber WPA
Meriden
Somerset WMA
Saco
Steele Center
Lemond
Hope
Hope School County Park
River Point
Litomysl
Summit
Aurora WMA
Saint Olaf Lake
Teal WMA
Reese Lake
Fosilen Lake
Lonergan Lake
Beaver Lake
Beaver Lake County Park
Chapa-kak-say-za WMA
Straight Creek WPA
Pogones Marsh WMA
Straight River Marsh WPA
Geneva WMA
Geneva Lake
Bath
Union
Pratt
Steele County Trails
Waseca County Trails
Freeborn County Trails
Judicial Ditch No.10
County Ditch No.5
Little LeSueur River
Straight River
Le Sueur River
Crane Creek
Turtle Creek
Mud Creek
Medford Creek
WASECA CO
STEELE CO
FREEBORN CO
Deerfield
Meriden
Owatonna
Lemond
Somerset
Berlin
Summit
Geneva
Bath
Clinton Falls
93°25'W
93°20'W
93°15'W
93°10'W
44°5'N
44°0'N
43°55'N
43°50'N

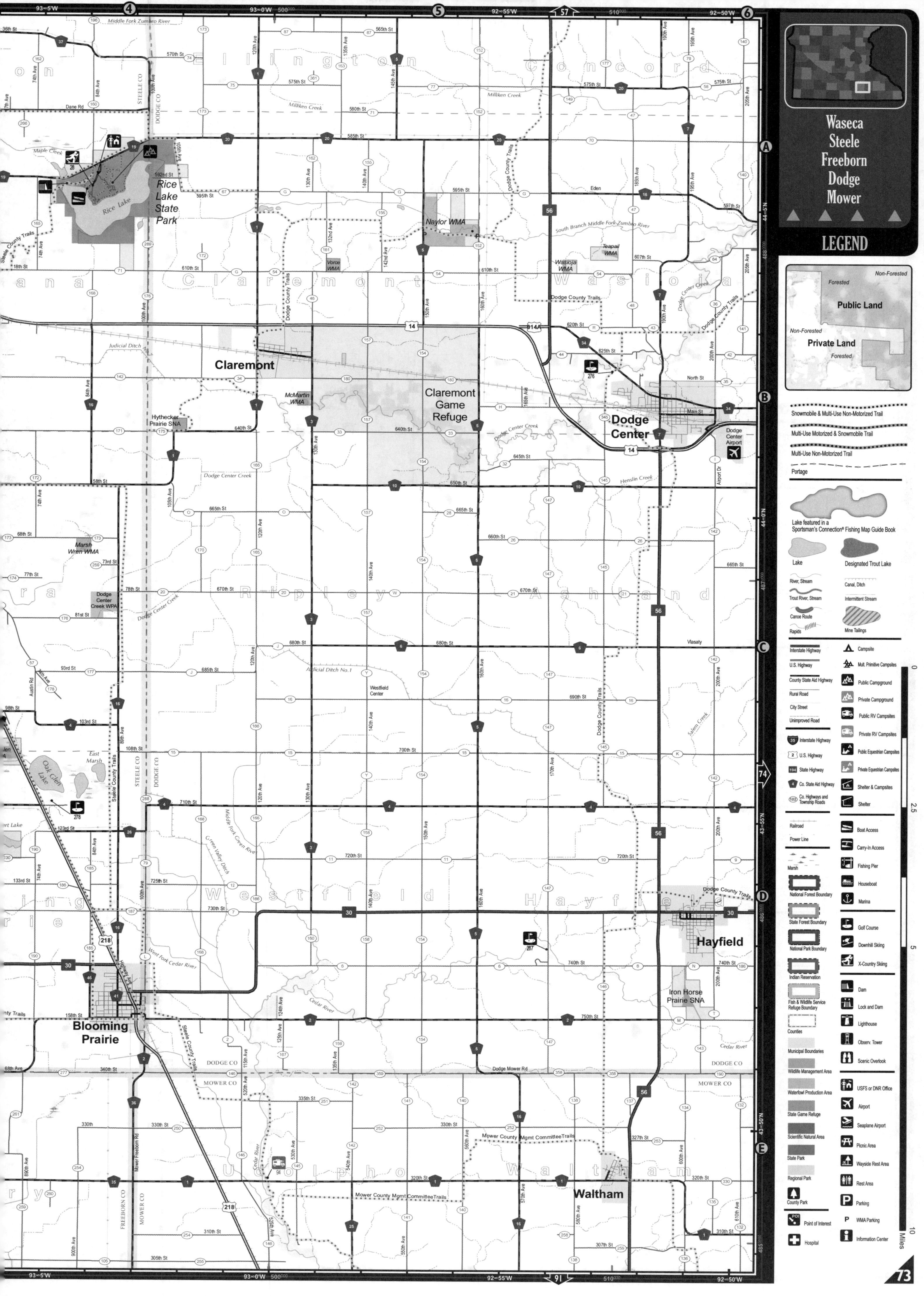

Waseca
Steele
Freeborn
Dodge
Mower
LEGEND
Public Land
Private Land
Forested
Non-Forested
Snowmobile & Multi-Use Non-Motorized Trail
Multi-Use Motorized & Snowmobile Trail
Multi-Use Non-Motorized Trail
Portage
Lake featured in a Sportsman's Connection® Fishing Map Guide Book
Lake
Designated Trout Lake
River, Stream
Canal, Ditch
Trout River, Stream
Intermittent Stream
Canoe Route
Rapids
Mine Tailings
Interstate Highway
U.S. Highway
County State Aid Highway
Rural Road
City Street
Unimproved Road
Interstate Highway
U.S. Highway
State Highway
Co. State Aid Highway
Co. Highways and Township Roads
Railroad
Power Line
Marsh
National Forest Boundary
State Forest Boundary
National Park Boundary
Indian Reservation
Fish & Wildlife Service Refuge Boundary
Counties
Municipal Boundaries
Wildlife Management Area
Waterfowl Production Area
State Game Refuge
Scientific Natural Area
State Park
Regional Park
County Park
Point of Interest
Hospital
Campsite
Mult. Primitive Campsites
Public Campground
Private Campground
Public RV Campsites
Private RV Campsites
Public Equestrian Campsites
Private Equestrian Campsites
Shelter & Campsites
Shelter
Boat Access
Carry-In Access
Fishing Pier
Houseboat
Marina
Golf Course
Downhill Skiing
X-Country Skiing
Dam
Lock and Dam
Lighthouse
Observ. Tower
Scenic Overlook
USFS or DNR Office
Airport
Seaplane Airport
Picnic Area
Wayside Rest Area
Rest Area
Parking
WMA Parking
Information Center
0
2.5
5
10
Miles
Rice Lake State Park
Rice Lake
Claremont
Claremont Game Refuge
McMartin WMA
Hythecker Prairie SNA
Dodge Center
Dodge Center Airport
Naylor WMA
Vorce WMA
Wasioja WMA
Teapail WMA
Marsh Wren WMA
Dodge Center Creek WPA
Westfield Center
Hayfield
Iron Horse Prairie SNA
Blooming Prairie
Oak Glen Lake
East Marsh
Waltham
Eden
Vlasaty
Ellington
Concord
Claremont
Wasioja
Ripley
Ashland
Westfield
Hayfield
Udolpho
Waltham
STEELE CO
DODGE CO
MOWER CO
FREEBORN CO
Dodge County Trails
Steele County Trails
Mower County Mgmt Committee Trails
Middle Fork Zumbro River
South Branch Middle Fork Zumbro River
Milliken Creek
Maple Creek
Judicial Ditch No. 1
Dodge Center Creek
Henslin Creek
Salem Creek
Middle Fork Green River
Green Valley Ditch
West Fork Cedar River
Cedar River
93°5'W
93°0'W
92°55'W
92°50'W
44°5'N
44°0'N
43°55'N
43°50'N
A
B
C
D
E
4
5
6
57
74
91

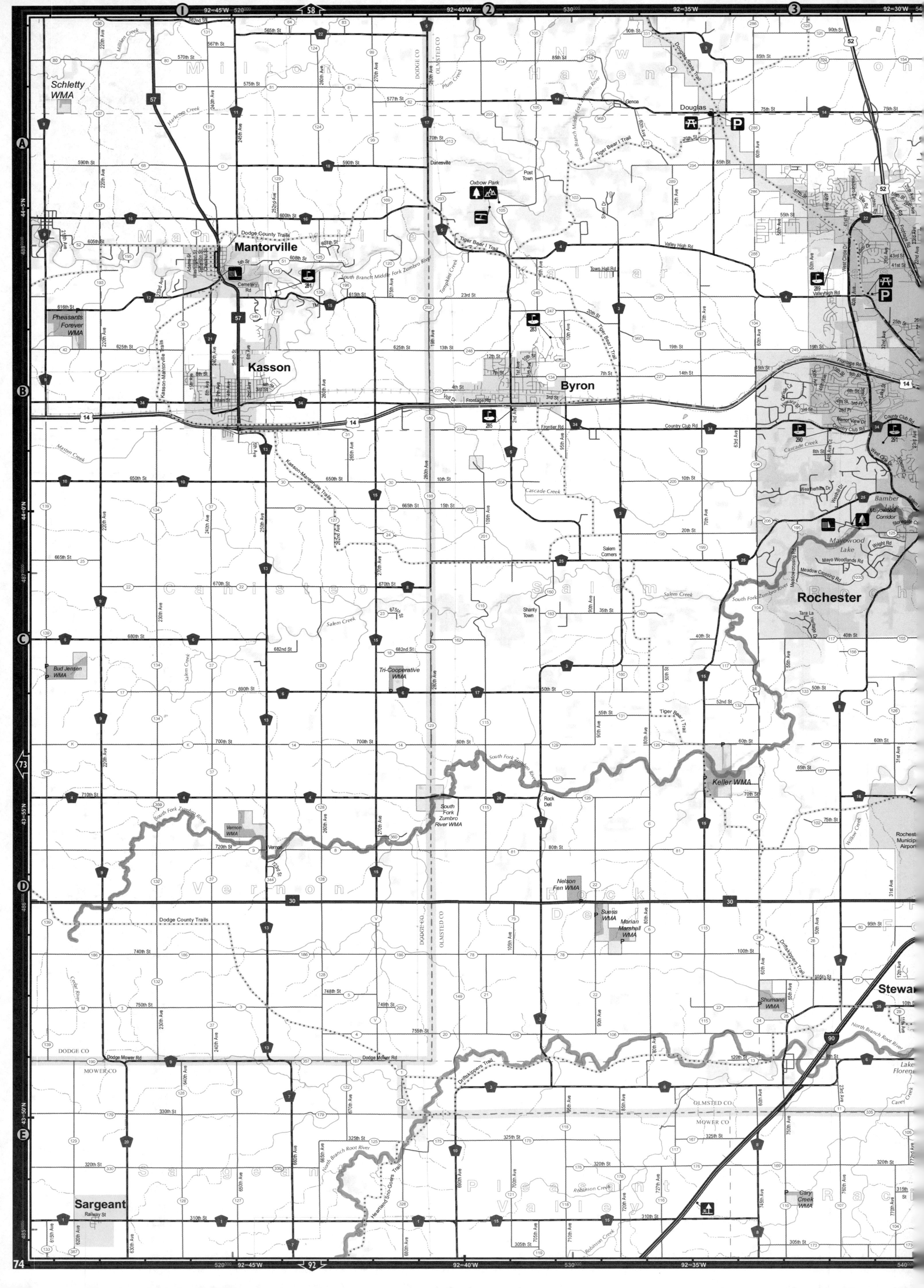

Mantorville
Kasson
Byron
Rochester
Douglas
Genoa
Post Town
Danesville
Salem Corners
Shanty Town
Rock Dell
Vernon
Sargeant
Milton
Mantorville
Kalmar
New Haven
Canisteo
Salem
Vernon
Rock Dell
Sargeant
Pleasant Valley
Schletty WMA
Pheasants Forever WMA
Bud Jensen WMA
Tri-Cooperative WMA
Vernon WMA
South Fork Zumbro River WMA
Keller WMA
Nelson Fen WMA
Suess WMA
Marian Marshall WMA
Shumann WMA
Cary Creek WMA
Oxbow Park
Mayowood Corridor
Mayowood Lake
Bamber Lake
South Fork Zumbro River
North Branch Root River
Salem Creek
Cascade Creek
Dodge County Trails
Kasson-Mantorville Trails
Tiger Bear I Trail
Douglas State Trail
Driftskippers Trail
Heartland Sno-Goers Trail
DODGE CO
OLMSTED CO
MOWER CO
92°45'W
92°40'W
92°35'W
92°30'W
44°5'N
44°0'N
43°55'N
43°50'N

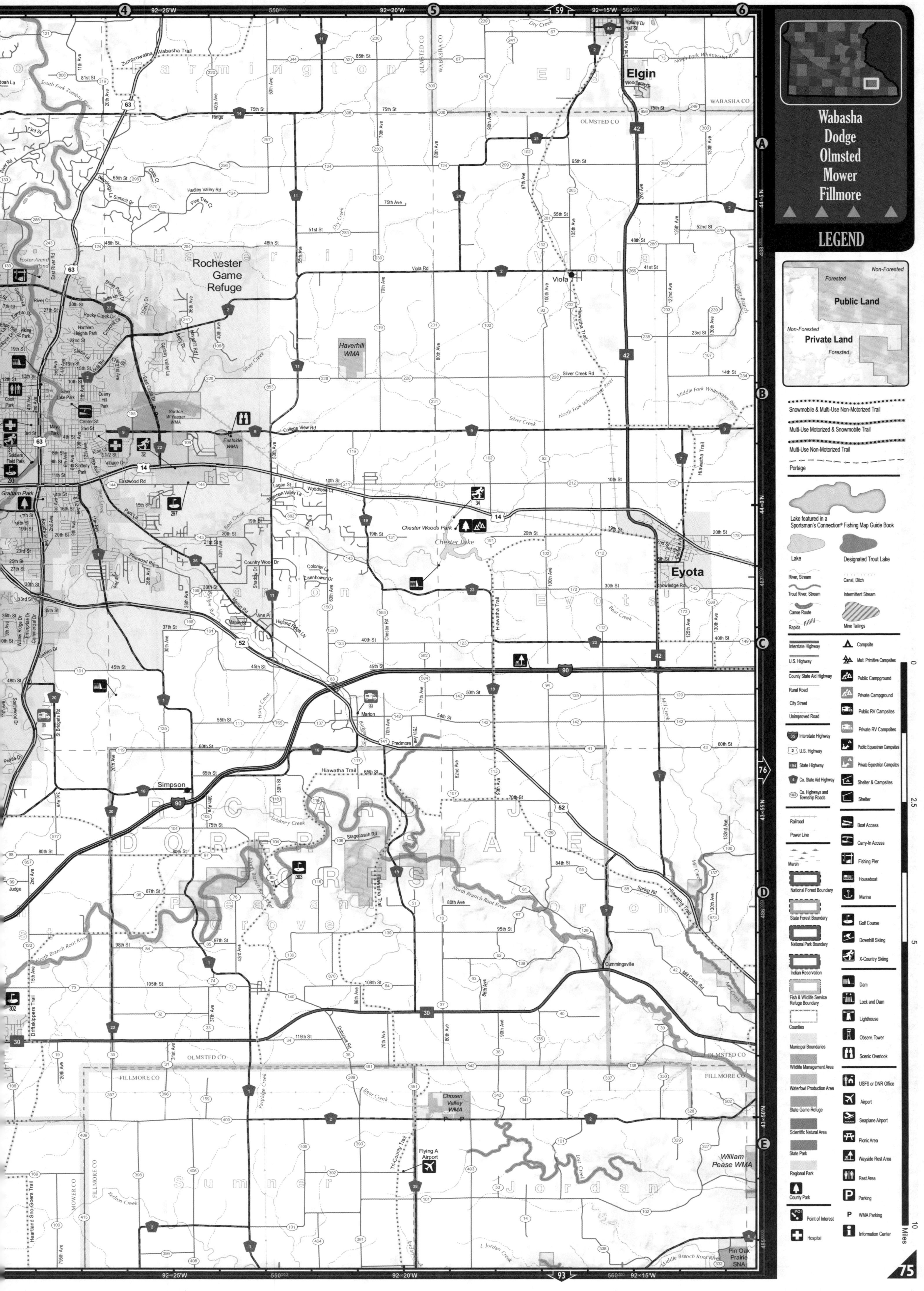

Wabasha
Dodge
Olmsted
Mower
Fillmore
LEGEND
Non-Forested
Forested
Public Land
Non-Forested
Private Land
Forested
Snowmobile & Multi-Use Non-Motorized Trail
Multi-Use Motorized & Snowmobile Trail
Multi-Use Non-Motorized Trail
Portage
Lake featured in a Sportsman's Connection® Fishing Map Guide Book
Lake
Designated Trout Lake
River, Stream
Canal, Ditch
Trout River, Stream
Intermittent Stream
Canoe Route
Rapids
Mine Tailings
Interstate Highway
U.S. Highway
County State Aid Highway
Rural Road
City Street
Unimproved Road
Interstate Highway
U.S. Highway
State Highway
Co. State Aid Highway
Co. Highways and Township Roads
Railroad
Power Line
Marsh
National Forest Boundary
State Forest Boundary
National Park Boundary
Indian Reservation
Fish & Wildlife Service Refuge Boundary
Counties
Municipal Boundaries
Wildlife Management Area
Waterfowl Production Area
State Game Refuge
Scientific Natural Area
State Park
Regional Park
County Park
Point of Interest
Hospital
Campsite
Mult. Primitive Campsites
Public Campground
Private Campground
Public RV Campsites
Private RV Campsites
Public Equestrian Campsites
Private Equestrian Campsites
Shelter & Campsites
Shelter
Boat Access
Carry-In Access
Fishing Pier
Houseboat
Marina
Golf Course
Downhill Skiing
X-Country Skiing
Dam
Lock and Dam
Lighthouse
Observ. Tower
Scenic Overlook
USFS or DNR Office
Airport
Seaplane Airport
Picnic Area
Wayside Rest Area
Rest Area
Parking
WMA Parking
Information Center
0
2.5
5
10
Miles
4
5
6
59
76
93
A
B
C
D
E
92°25'W
92°20'W
92°15'W
44°5'N
44°0'N
43°55'N
43°50'N
Elgin
Rochester Game Refuge
Haverhill WMA
Gordon W Yeager WMA
Eastside WMA
Viola
Eyota
Chester Woods Park
Chester Lake
Marion
Predmore
Simpson
Judge
Cummingsville
RICHARD J. DORER STATE FOREST
Chosen Valley WMA
Flying A Airport
William Pease WMA
Pin Oak Prairie SNA
Farmington
Elgin
Haverhill
Viola
Marion
Eyota
Pleasant Grove
Oronoco
Sumner
Jordan
OLMSTED CO
WABASHA CO
FILLMORE CO
MOWER CO
South Fork Zumbro River
North Fork Whitewater River
Middle Fork Whitewater River
North Branch Root River
Middle Branch Root River
Silver Creek
Bear Creek
Dry Creek
Mill Creek
Lost Creek
Whitney Creek
Kedron Creek
L Jordan Creek
Hiawatha Trail
Heartland Sno-Goers Trail
Driftskippers Trail
Tri-County Trail
Zumbrowalkers Wabasha Trail
Foster-Arend Park
Quarry Hill Park
Silver Lake Park
Soldiers Field Park
Graham Park
Slatterly Park
Northern Heights Park
Cook Park
Mayo Park

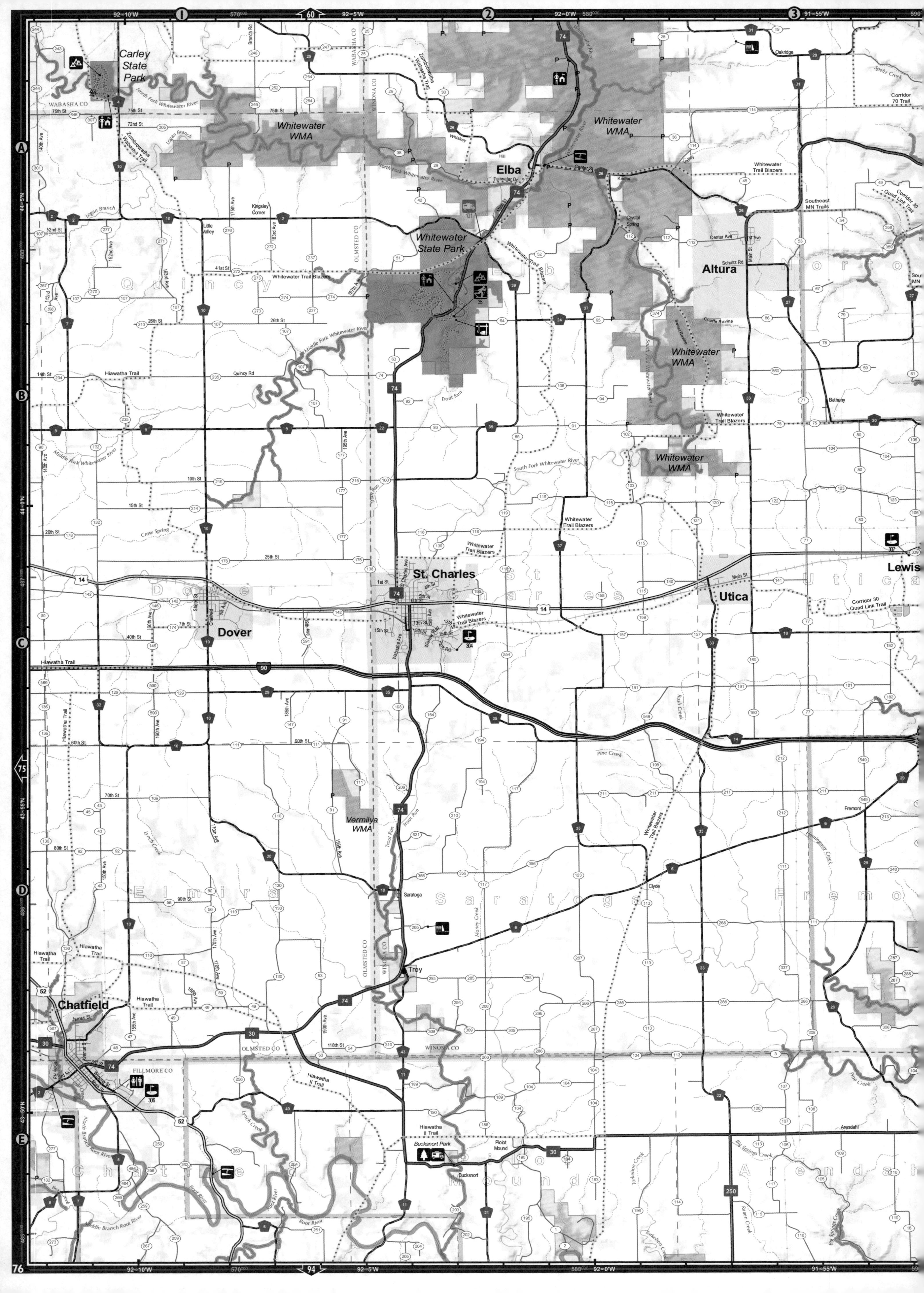

Carley State Park
Whitewater WMA
Elba
Whitewater State Park
Altura
Quincy
St. Charles
Dover
Utica
Lewis
Vermilya WMA
Saratoga
Troy
Chatfield
Bucksnort Park
Pilot Mound
Bucksnort
Elmira
Saratoga
Fremont
Chatfield
Arendahl
Oakridge
Crystal Spring
Clyde
Bethany
Hiawatha Trail
Whitewater Trail Blazers
Zumbrowatha Wabasha Trail
Corridor 70 Trail
Corridor 30 Quad Link Trail
Southeast MN Trails
North Fork Whitewater River
Middle Fork Whitewater River
South Fork Whitewater River
Root River
North Branch Root River
Middle Branch Root River
WABASHA CO
WINONA CO
OLMSTED CO
FILLMORE CO

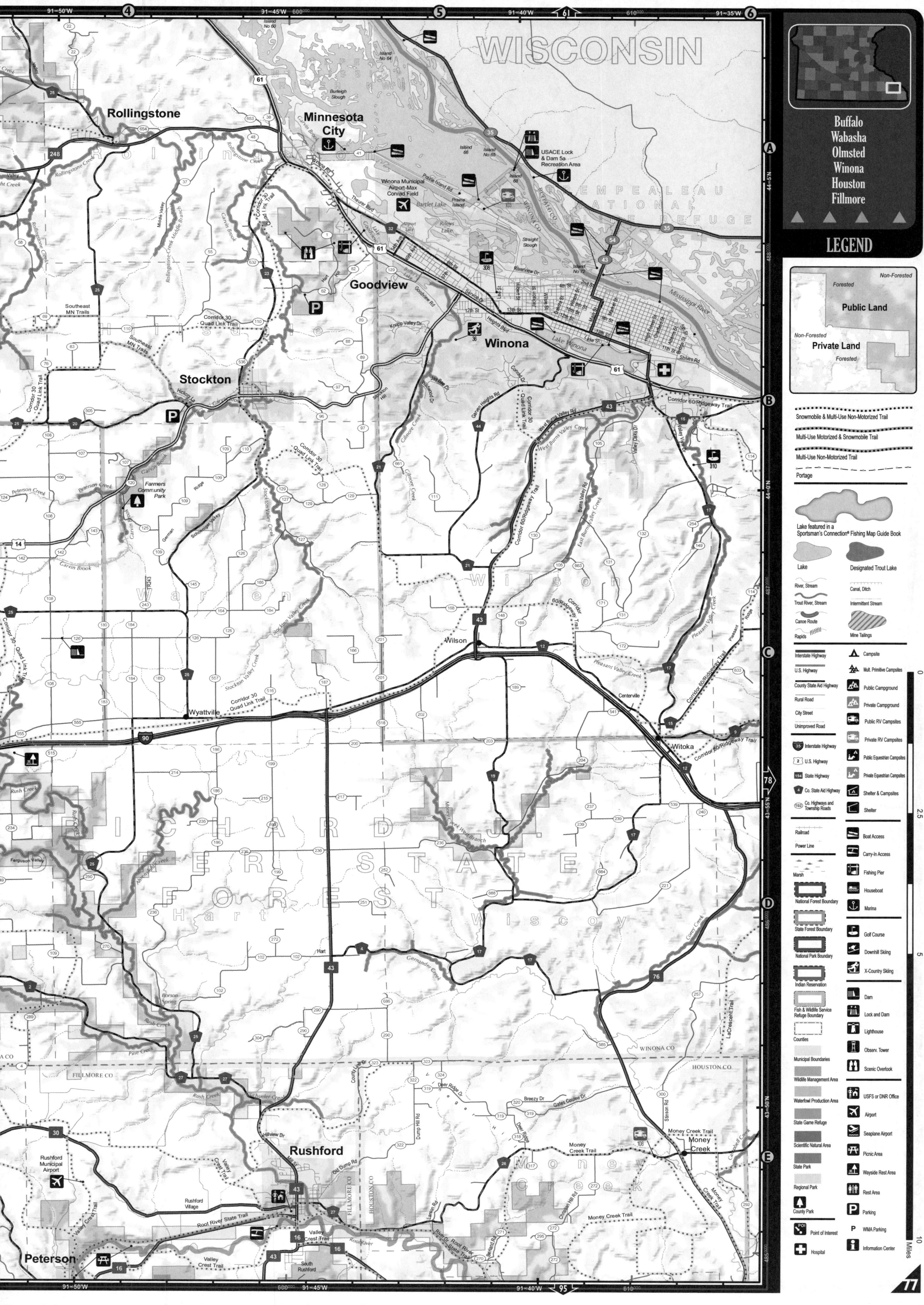

WISCONSIN
Rollingstone
Minnesota City
Goodview
Winona
Stockton
Wilson
Wyattville
Witoka
Centerville
Hart
Rushford
Rushford Village
Peterson
Money Creek
Buffalo
Wabasha
Olmsted
Winona
Houston
Fillmore
LEGEND
Public Land
Private Land
Forested
Non-Forested
USACE Lock & Dam 5a Recreation Area
Winona Municipal Airport-Max Conrad Field
Farmers Community Park
Rushford Municipal Airport
Richard J. Dorer State Forest
Trempealeau National Wildlife Refuge
Mississippi River
Lake Winona
Corridor 30 Quad Link Trail
Corridor 60/Ridgeway Trail
Southeast MN Trails
Money Creek Trail
Root River State Trail
Valley Crest Trail
WINONA CO
HOUSTON CO
FILLMORE CO
Snowmobile & Multi-Use Non-Motorized Trail
Multi-Use Motorized & Snowmobile Trail
Multi-Use Non-Motorized Trail
Portage
Lake featured in a Sportsman's Connection® Fishing Map Guide Book
Lake
Designated Trout Lake
River, Stream
Canal, Ditch
Trout River, Stream
Intermittent Stream
Canoe Route
Rapids
Mine Tailings
Interstate Highway
U.S. Highway
County State Aid Highway
Rural Road
City Street
Unimproved Road
Interstate Highway
U.S. Highway
State Highway
Co. State Aid Highway
Co. Highways and Township Roads
Railroad
Power Line
Marsh
National Forest Boundary
State Forest Boundary
National Park Boundary
Indian Reservation
Fish & Wildlife Service Refuge Boundary
Counties
Municipal Boundaries
Wildlife Management Area
Waterfowl Production Area
State Game Refuge
Scientific Natural Area
State Park
Regional Park
County Park
Point of Interest
Hospital
Campsite
Mult. Primitive Campsites
Public Campground
Private Campground
Public RV Campsites
Private RV Campsites
Public Equestrian Campsites
Private Equestrian Campsites
Shelter & Campsites
Shelter
Boat Access
Carry-In Access
Fishing Pier
Houseboat
Marina
Golf Course
Downhill Skiing
X-Country Skiing
Dam
Lock and Dam
Lighthouse
Observ. Tower
Scenic Overlook
USFS or DNR Office
Airport
Seaplane Airport
Picnic Area
Wayside Rest Area
Rest Area
Parking
WMA Parking
Information Center
Miles
0
2.5
5
10
91°50'W
91°45'W
91°40'W
91°35'W
44°5'N
44°0'N
43°55'N
43°50'N

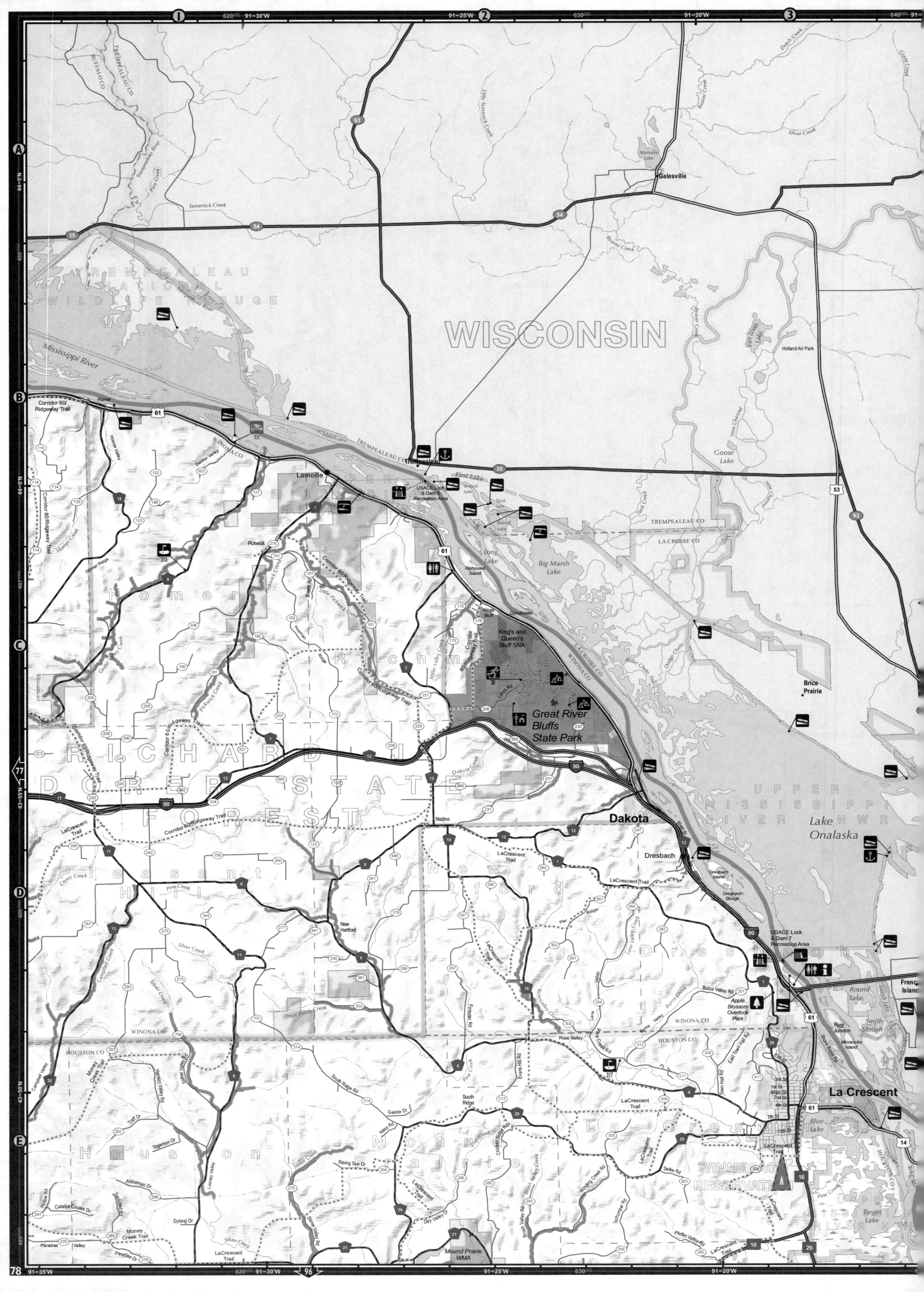

WISCONSIN
TREMPEALEAU NATIONAL WILDLIFE REFUGE
Mississippi River
Galesville
Trempealeau
Lamoille
Pickwick
Homer
Richmond
Great River Bluffs State Park
King's and Queen's Bluff SNA
USACE Lock & Dam 6 Recreation Area
Big Marsh Lake
Long Lake
Goose Lake
Brice Prairie
Holland Air Park
Van Loon Lake
Marinuka Lake
RICHARD J DORER STATE FOREST
Dakota
Dresbach
Nodine
New Hartford
Pleasant Hill
UPPER MISSISSIPPI RIVER NWR
Lake Onalaska
USACE Lock & Dam 7 Recreation Area
Apple Blossom Overlook Park
La Crescent
WINNEBAGO RESERVATION
Mound Prairie WMA
Houston
Mound Prairie
La Crescent
Dresbach
TREMPEALEAU CO
LA CROSSE CO
WINONA CO
HOUSTON CO
BUFFALO CO
Corridor 60/Ridgeway Trail
LaCrescent Trail
Money Creek Trail

Buffalo
Trempealeau
Winona
Houston
Jackson
Monroe
La Crosse
LEGEND
Public Land
Private Land
Forested
Non-Forested
Snowmobile & Multi-Use Non-Motorized Trail
Multi-Use Motorized & Snowmobile Trail
Multi-Use Non-Motorized Trail
Portage
Lake featured in a Sportsman's Connection® Fishing Map Guide Book
Lake
Designated Trout Lake
River, Stream
Canal, Ditch
Trout River, Stream
Intermittent Stream
Canoe Route
Rapids
Mine Tailings
Interstate Highway
U.S. Highway
County State Aid Highway
Rural Road
City Street
Unimproved Road
Interstate Highway
U.S. Highway
State Highway
Co. State Aid Highway
Co. Highways and Township Roads
Railroad
Power Line
Marsh
National Forest Boundary
State Forest Boundary
National Park Boundary
Indian Reservation
Fish & Wildlife Service Refuge Boundary
Counties
Municipal Boundaries
Wildlife Management Area
Waterfowl Production Area
State Game Refuge
Scientific Natural Area
State Park
Regional Park
County Park
Point of Interest
Hospital
Campsite
Mult. Primitive Campsites
Public Campground
Private Campground
Public RV Campsites
Private RV Campsites
Public Equestrian Campsites
Private Equestrian Campsites
Shelter & Campsites
Shelter
Boat Access
Carry-In Access
Fishing Pier
Houseboat
Marina
Golf Course
Downhill Skiing
X-Country Skiing
Dam
Lock and Dam
Lighthouse
Observ. Tower
Scenic Overlook
USFS or DNR Office
Airport
Seaplane Airport
Picnic Area
Wayside Rest Area
Rest Area
Parking
WMA Parking
Information Center
0
2.5
5
10
Miles
West Salem
Veterans Memorial Park
Bangor
La Crosse
LaCrosse River
Dutch Creek
Bostwick Creek
Sour Creek
Davis Creek
Burns Creek
Pammel Creek
Mormon Creek
91°10'W
91°5'W
91°0'W
44°5'N
44°0'N
43°55'N
43°50'N
I. McCormick

97

SOUTH DAKOTA
IOWA
Springwater
Mound
Beaver Creek
Luverne
Martin
Clinton
Garretson
Valley Springs
Beaver Creek
Luverne
Hills
Steen
Bruce
Larchwood
Lester
Springwater WMA
Little Beaver Creek WMA
Luverne Municipal Airport
Buffalo Ridge Trail
Division St
Dodge St
Warren St
Hatting St
Koehn Ave
Barck Ave
1st St
MINNEHAHA CO
ROCK CO
LYON CO
West Pipestone Creek
Split Rock Creek
Beaver Creek
Springwater Creek
Mud Creek
Four Mile Creek
Blood Run
Ash Creek
Moon Creek
Little Beaver Creek
96°30'W
96°25'W
96°20'W
96°15'W
43°40'N
43°35'N
43°30'N
43°25'N

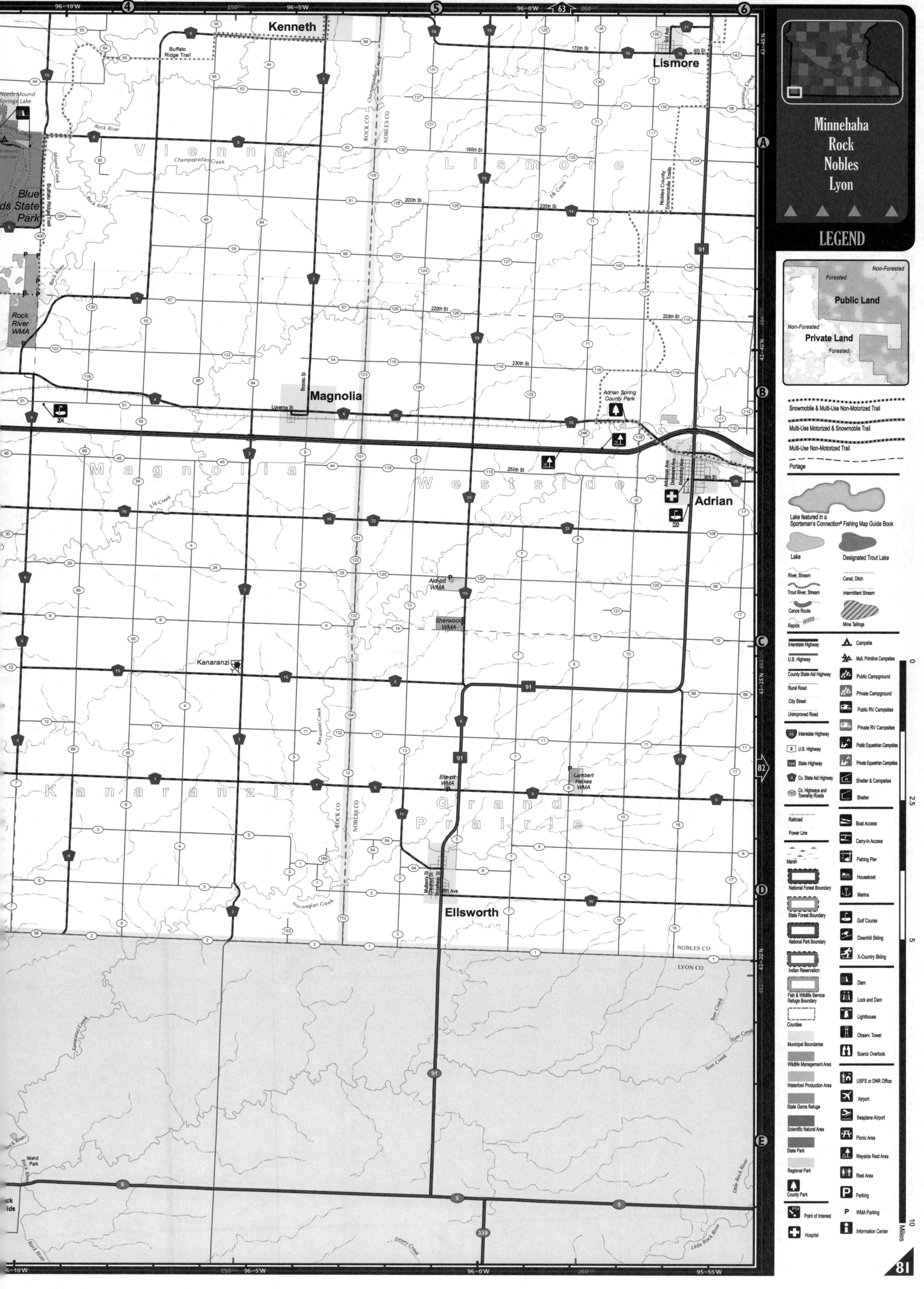

Minnehaha
Rock
Nobles
Lyon
LEGEND
Public Land
Private Land
Forested
Non-Forested
Snowmobile & Multi-Use Non-Motorized Trail
Multi-Use Motorized & Snowmobile Trail
Multi-Use Non-Motorized Trail
Portage
Lake featured in a Sportsman's Connection® Fishing Map Guide Book
Lake
Designated Trout Lake
Kenneth
Lismore
Magnolia
Adrian
Ellsworth
Kanaranzi
Vienna
Lismore
Magnolia
Westside
Kanaranzi
Grand Prairie
Blue Mounds State Park
Rock River WMA
Adrian Spring County Park
Aid-pit WMA
Sherwood WMA
Ellis-pit WMA
Lambert Heikes WMA
Buffalo Ridge Trail
Nobles County Snowmobile Trail
ROCK CO
NOBLES CO
LYON CO
96°10'W
96°5'W
96°0'W
95°55'W
43°45'N
43°40'N
43°35'N
43°30'N
Miles

Wilmont
Groth WMA
Nobles County Snowmobile Trails
Larkin
Summit Lake
Elk
Midway County Park
Reading
County Ditch No. Five
Bluebird Prairie WMA
East Branch Kanaranzi Creek
Herlein-Boote WMA
Worthington
Little Rock Creek
Rushmore
Olney
Dewald
Worthington
Lambert Prairie WMA
Lake Okabena
Stony Point
Dewald WMA
Judicial Ditch No. 1
Compass Prairie SNA
Pickeral County Park
Ocheda Lake
Little Rock
Ransom
Bigelow
John Erickson WMA
Peterson WMA
Wachter WMA
Sunrise Prairie County Park
West Branch Little Rock River
Lake Bella WPA
Lake Bella
Bigelow WMA
Bigelow
Lake Bella WMA
NOBLES CO
LYON CO
OSCEOLA CO
Otter Creek
Little Ocheyedan River
Ocheyedan River
Little Rock
Little Rock River
Tom Creek

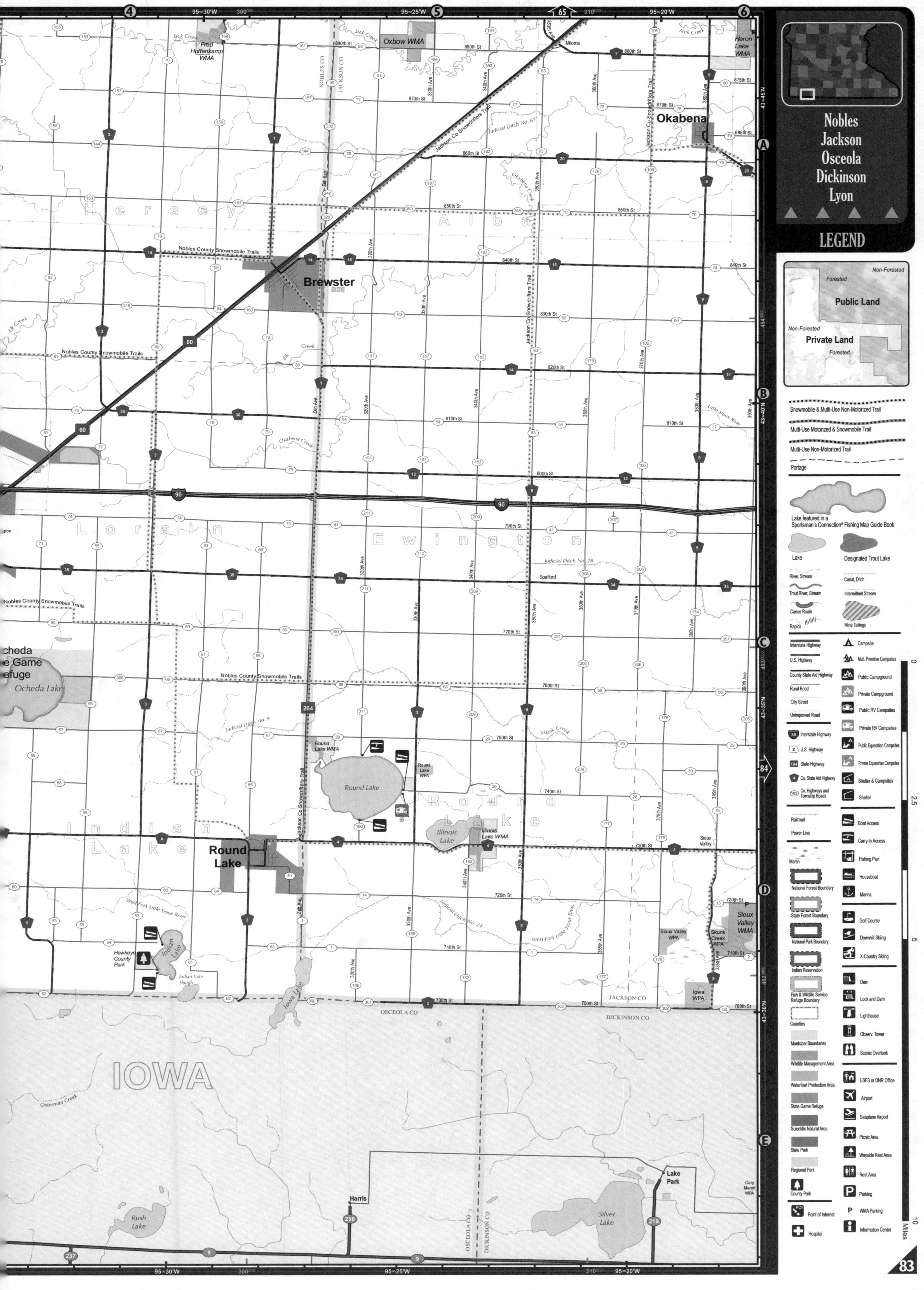

Nobles
Jackson
Osceola
Dickinson
Lyon
LEGEND
Public Land
Private Land
Forested
Non-Forested
Snowmobile & Multi-Use Non-Motorized Trail
Multi-Use Motorized & Snowmobile Trail
Multi-Use Non-Motorized Trail
Portage
Lake featured in a Sportsman's Connection® Fishing Map Guide Book
Lake
Designated Trout Lake
River, Stream
Canal, Ditch
Trout River, Stream
Intermittent Stream
Canoe Route
Rapids
Mine Tailings
Interstate Highway
U.S. Highway
County State Aid Highway
Rural Road
City Street
Unimproved Road
Railroad
Power Line
Marsh
National Forest Boundary
State Forest Boundary
National Park Boundary
Indian Reservation
Fish & Wildlife Service Refuge Boundary
Counties
Municipal Boundaries
Wildlife Management Area
Waterfowl Production Area
State Game Refuge
Scientific Natural Area
State Park
Regional Park
County Park
Point of Interest
Hospital
Campsite
Mult. Primitive Campsites
Public Campground
Private Campground
Public RV Campsites
Private RV Campsites
Public Equestrian Campsites
Private Equestrian Campsites
Shelter & Campsites
Shelter
Boat Access
Carry-In Access
Fishing Pier
Houseboat
Marina
Golf Course
Downhill Skiing
X-Country Skiing
Dam
Lock and Dam
Lighthouse
Observ. Tower
Scenic Overlook
USFS or DNR Office
Airport
Seaplane Airport
Picnic Area
Wayside Rest Area
Rest Area
Parking
WMA Parking
Information Center
Miles
Okabena
Brewster
Round Lake
Spafford
Miloma
Sioux Valley
Harris
Lake Park
IOWA
Oxbow WMA
Fred Hoffenkamp WMA
Heron Lake WMA
Round Lake WMA
Illinois Lake WMA
Sioux Valley WMA
Sioux Valley WPA
Skunk Creek WPA
Iowa WPA
Round Lake WPA
Hawkeye County Park
Ocheda Lake
Round Lake
Illinois Lake
Indian Lake
Indian Lake Slough
Iowa Lake
Rush Lake
Silver Lake
Cory Marsh WPA
Hersey
Alba
Lorain
Ewington
Indian Lake
Round Lake
Nobles County Snowmobile Trails
Jackson Co Snowdrifters Trail
Judicial Ditch No. 67
Judicial Ditch No. 28
Judicial Ditch No. 9
Judicial Ditch No. 24
Jack Creek
Elk Creek
Okabena Creek
Little Sioux River
Skunk Creek
West Fork Little Sioux River
Osterman Creek
NOBLES CO
JACKSON CO
OSCEOLA CO
DICKINSON CO
95°30'W
95°25'W
95°20'W
43°45'N
43°40'N
43°35'N
43°30'N
65
84

Heron Lake
South Heron Lake
Lake Flaherty
Lake Independence
Kilen Woods State Park
Prairie Bush Clover SNA
Belmont County Park
Sandy Point County Park
Community Point County Park
Sparks Environmental County Park
Lakefield
Toe WMA
Boot Lake
Clear Lake
Jackson
Jackson Municipal Airport
Summers WMA
Husen WMA
Hunter WPA
Holy Trinity WPA
Pletz Marsh
Bisaillon WPA
Little Sioux WMA
Sioux Forks WPA
Skunk Lake
Skunk Lake WMA
Sangl WMA
Rush Lake
Andersons Marsh
Loon Lake
Chandler Lake
Brown County Park
Anderson County Park
Little Spirit Lake
Robertson County Park
Minneota WMA
Spirit Lake WPA
JACKSON CO
DICKINSON CO
Grovers Lake
Diamond Lake WPA
Spirit Lake
Sunken Lake
Marble Lake
Kettleson Hogsback WPA
Welsh Lake WPA
Orleans
Cory Marsh WPA
Santee Prairie WPA
Jemmerson Slough WPA
Jackson Co Snowdrifters Trail
Des Moines River
West Heron Lake
Heron Lake
Belmont
West
Hunter
Des Moines
Sioux Valley
Minneota
Middletown

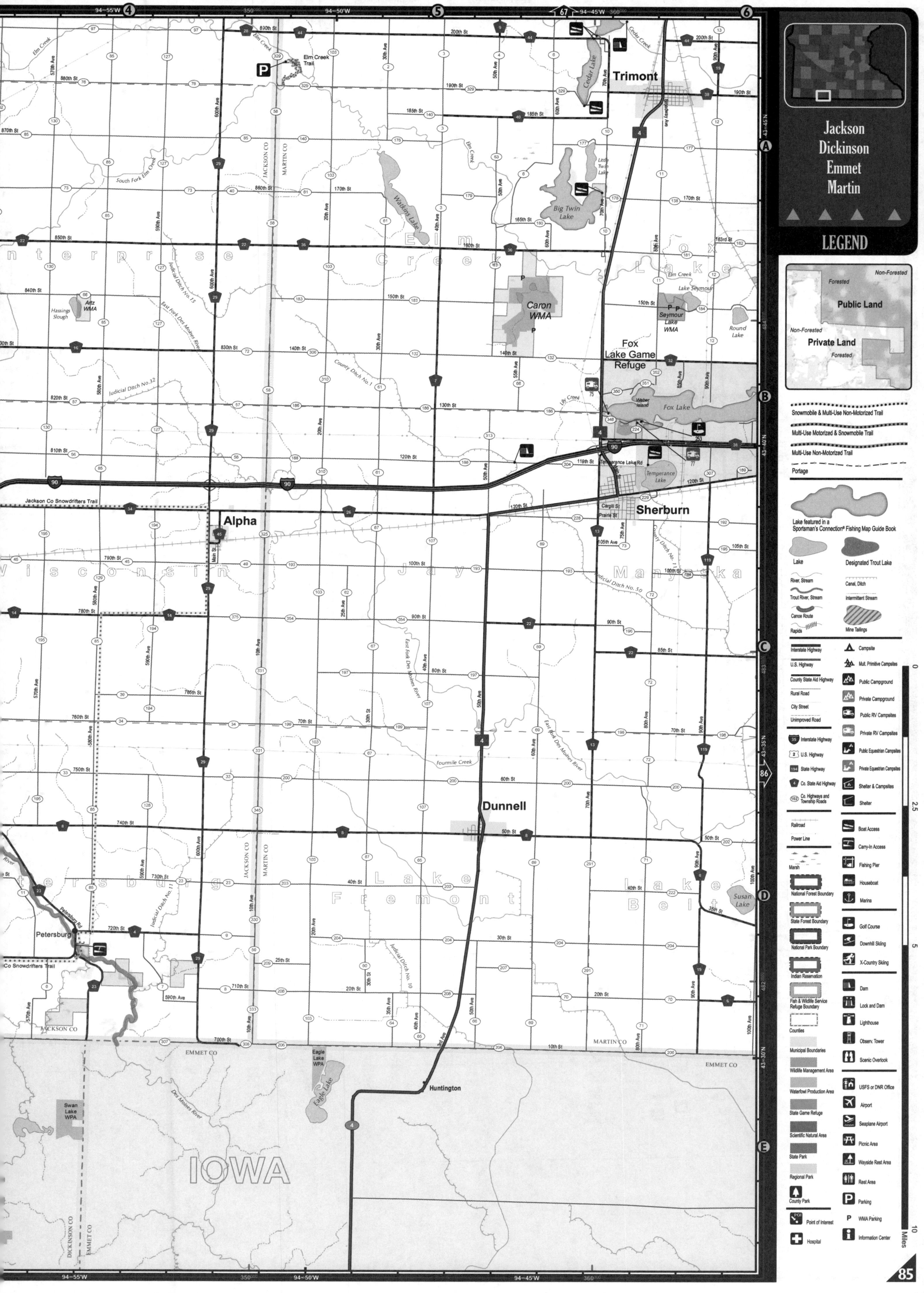
Jackson
Dickinson
Emmet
Martin
LEGEND
Public Land
Private Land
Trimont
Fox Lake Game Refuge
Sherburn
Alpha
Dunnell
Petersburg
Huntington
IOWA
Caron WMA
Seymour Lake WMA
Big Twin Lake
Fox Lake
Temperance Lake
Cedar Lake
Watkins Lake
Round Lake
Susan Lake
Eagle Lake WPA
Swan Lake WPA
Artz WMA
Hassings Slough
JACKSON CO
MARTIN CO
EMMET CO
DICKINSON CO
Jackson Co Snowdrifters Trail
Elm Creek Trail
Des Moines River
East Fork Des Moines River
Fourmile Creek
Elm Creek
Cedar Creek
Miles

Northrop
Granada
Welcome
Fairmont
Fairmont Municipal Airport
Manyaska
Ceylon
Mud Bardwell Game Refuge
East Chain
Dolliver
Fox Lake
Rolling Green
Rutland
Lake Belt
Tenhassen
Silver Lake
Fraser
Big Tuttle (Okamanpeedan) Lake
Bright Lake
Pierce Lake
Clayton Lake
Hall Lake
Budd Lake
Sisseton Lake
George Lake
Amber Lake
Martin Lake
Buffalo Lake
Eagle Lake
Creek Lake
Clear Lake
Fish Lake
Wilmert Lake
Iowa Lake
Rose Lake
Lake Imogene
Prairieland Trail
MARTIN CO
EMMET CO
KOSSUTH CO

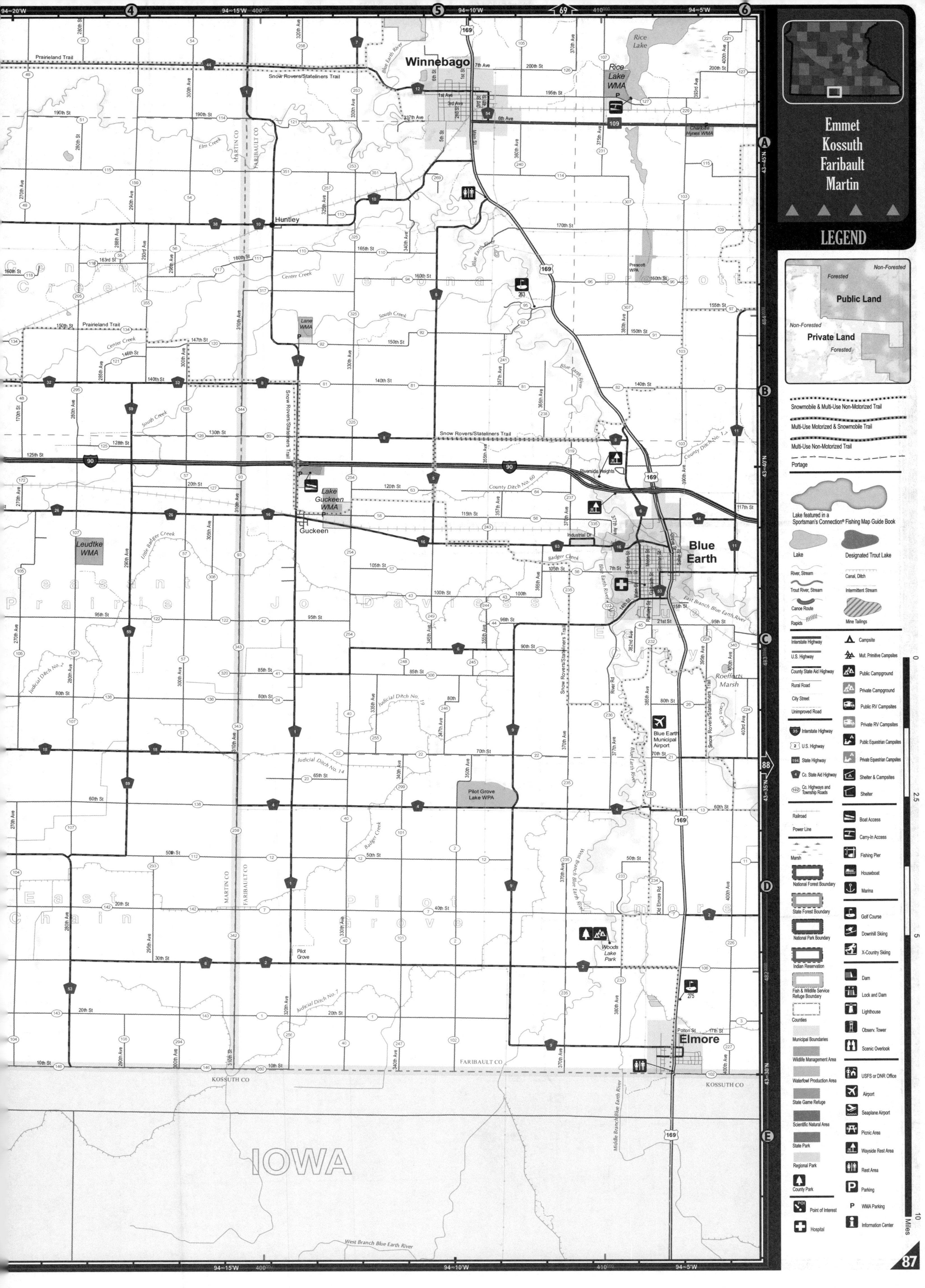

Emmet
Kossuth
Faribault
Martin
LEGEND
Public Land
Private Land
Forested
Non-Forested
Snowmobile & Multi-Use Non-Motorized Trail
Multi-Use Motorized & Snowmobile Trail
Multi-Use Non-Motorized Trail
Portage
Lake featured in a Sportsman's Connection® Fishing Map Guide Book
Lake
Designated Trout Lake
River, Stream
Canal, Ditch
Trout River, Stream
Intermittent Stream
Canoe Route
Rapids
Mine Tailings
Interstate Highway
U.S. Highway
County State Aid Highway
Rural Road
City Street
Unimproved Road
Interstate Highway
U.S. Highway
State Highway
Co. State Aid Highway
Co. Highways and Township Roads
Railroad
Power Line
Marsh
National Forest Boundary
State Forest Boundary
National Park Boundary
Indian Reservation
Fish & Wildlife Service Refuge Boundary
Counties
Municipal Boundaries
Wildlife Management Area
Waterfowl Production Area
State Game Refuge
Scientific Natural Area
State Park
Regional Park
County Park
Point of Interest
Hospital
Campsite
Mult. Primitive Campsites
Public Campground
Private Campground
Public RV Campsites
Private RV Campsites
Public Equestrian Campsites
Private Equestrian Campsites
Shelter & Campsites
Shelter
Boat Access
Carry-In Access
Fishing Pier
Houseboat
Marina
Golf Course
Downhill Skiing
X-Country Skiing
Dam
Lock and Dam
Lighthouse
Observ. Tower
Scenic Overlook
USFS or DNR Office
Airport
Seaplane Airport
Picnic Area
Wayside Rest Area
Rest Area
Parking
WMA Parking
Information Center
Miles
Winnebago
Huntley
Blue Earth
Guckeen
Elmore
Pilot Grove
Riverside Heights
Rice Lake
Rice Lake WMA
Charlotte Hynes WMA
Lane WMA
Lake Guckeen WMA
Leudtke WMA
Pilot Grove Lake WPA
Prescott WPA
Woods Lake Park
Roeffers Marsh
Blue Earth Municipal Airport
Prairieland Trail
Snow Rovers/Stateliners Trail
Blue Earth River
East Branch Blue Earth River
West Branch Blue Earth River
Middle Branch Blue Earth River
Center Creek
South Creek
Elm Creek
Little Badger Creek
Badger Creek
County Ditch No. 60
Judicial Ditch No. 19
Judicial Ditch No. 14
Judicial Ditch No. 7
MARTIN CO
FARIBAULT CO
KOSSUTH CO
IOWA
Center Creek
Verona
Prescott
Pleasant Prairie
Jo Daviess
Blue Earth City
East Chain
Pilot Grove
Elmore
94°20'W
94°15'W
94°10'W
94°5'W
43°45'N
43°40'N
43°35'N
43°30'N
87

Delavan
Easton
Frost
Bricelyn
Rake
IOWA
Prescott
Barber
Walnut Lake
Blue Earth City
Emerald
Brush Creek
Elmore
Rome
Seely
Walnut Lake WMA
South Walnut Lake
Rice Lake
Pihls Park
Wells Municipal Airport
Snow Rovers/Stateliners Trail
East Branch Blue Earth River
Middle Branch Blue Earth River
FARIBAULT CO
KOSSUTH CO
WINNEBAGO CO
93°55'W
93°50'W
93°45'W
94°0'W
43°45'N
43°40'N
43°35'N
43°30'N

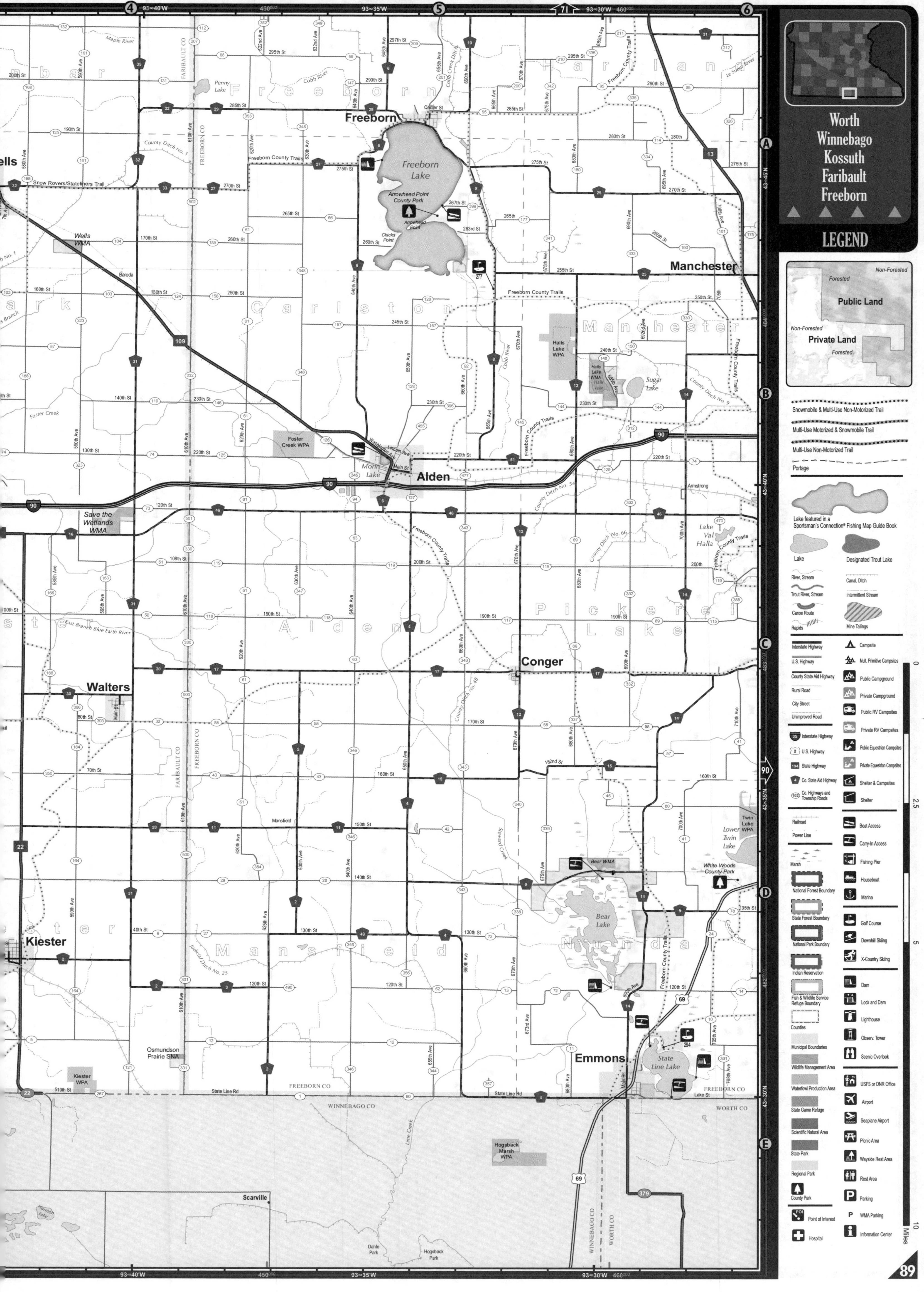

Worth
Winnebago
Kossuth
Faribault
Freeborn
LEGEND
Public Land
Private Land
Freeborn
Freeborn Lake
Manchester
Alden
Conger
Walters
Kiester
Emmons
Bear Lake
State Line Lake
Scarville

72

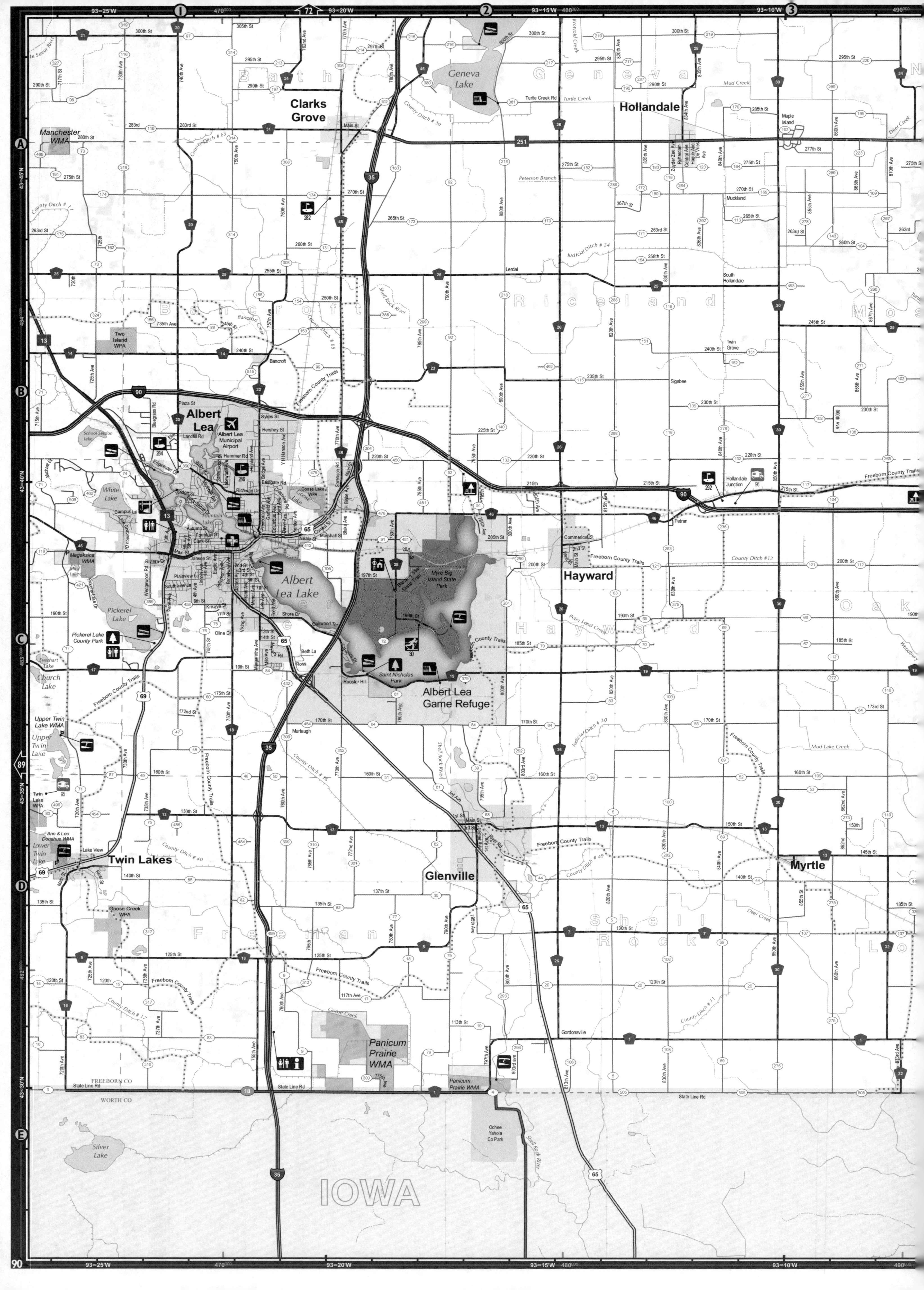

93°25'W
470000
93°20'W
93°15'W
480000
93°10'W
490000
43°45'N
43°40'N
43°35'N
43°30'N
Bath
Geneva
Geneva Lake
Clarks Grove
Hollandale
Manchester WMA
Maple Island
Muckland
South Hollandale
Lerdal
Bancroft
Riceland
Two Island WPA
Twin Grove
Sigsbee
Albert Lea
Albert Lea Municipal Airport
School Section Lake
White Lake
Campus Lake
Goose Lake WPA
Magaksica WMA
Albert Lea Lake
Myre Big Island State Park
Blazing Star State Trail
Hollandale Junction
Petran
Hayward
Pickerel Lake
Pickerel Lake County Park
Fountain Lake
Saint Nicholas Park
Rooster Hill
Albert Lea Game Refuge
Freeborn County Trails
Church Lake
Upper Twin Lake WMA
Upper Twin Lake
Murtaugh
Twin Lake WPA
Ann & Leo Donahue WMA
Lower Twin Lake
Twin Lakes
Glenville
Myrtle
Goose Creek WPA
Freeman
Shell Rock
Shell Rock River
Panicum Prairie WMA
Gordonsville
FREEBORN CO
WORTH CO
State Line Rd
Ochee Yahola Co Park
Silver Lake
IOWA

89

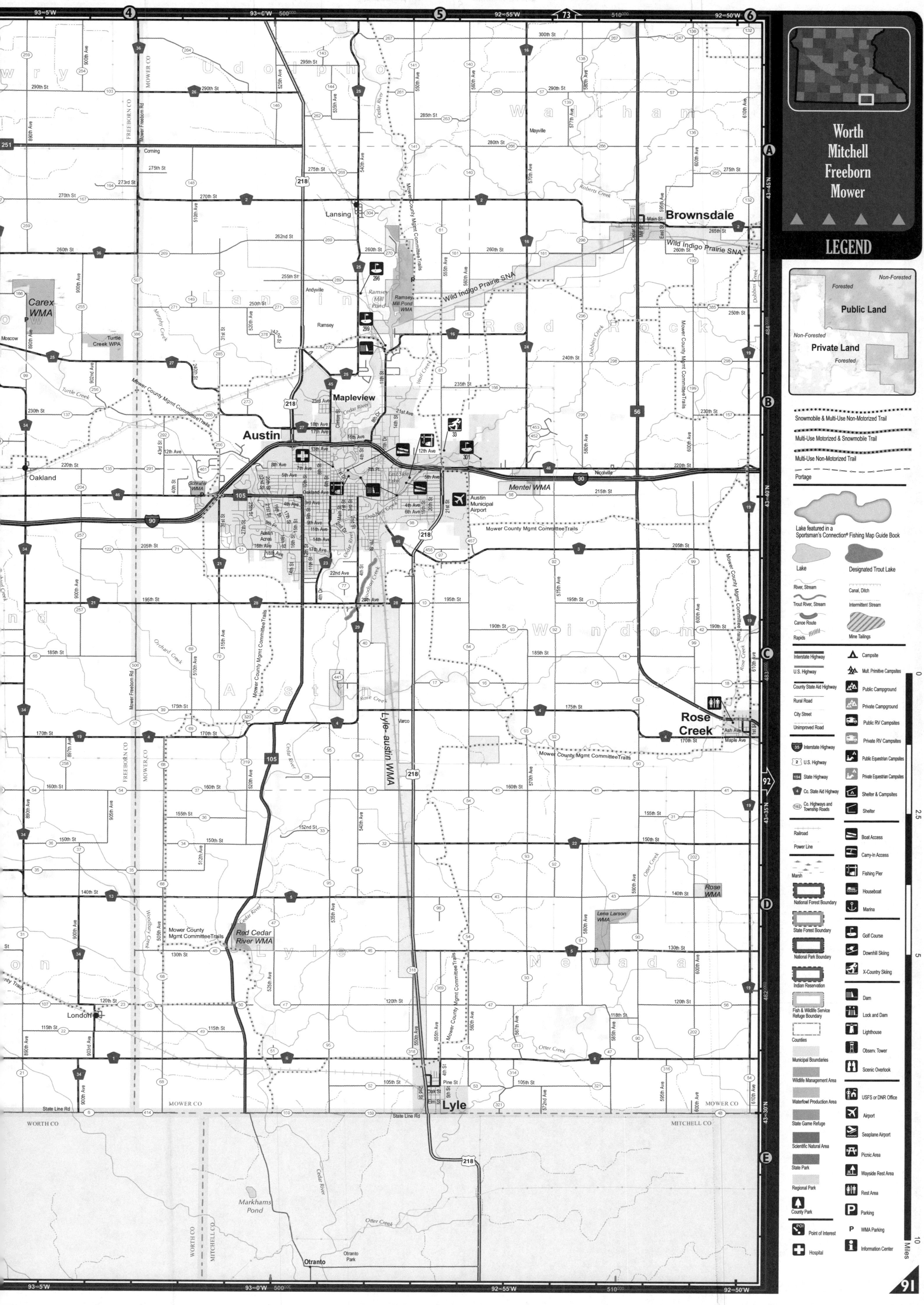

Worth
Mitchell
Freeborn
Mower
LEGEND
Public Land
Private Land
Forested
Non-Forested
Snowmobile & Multi-Use Non-Motorized Trail
Multi-Use Motorized & Snowmobile Trail
Multi-Use Non-Motorized Trail
Portage
Lake featured in a Sportsman's Connection® Fishing Map Guide Book
Lake
Designated Trout Lake
River, Stream
Canal, Ditch
Trout River, Stream
Intermittent Stream
Canoe Route
Rapids
Mine Tailings
Interstate Highway
U.S. Highway
County State Aid Highway
Rural Road
City Street
Unimproved Road
State Highway
Co. State Aid Highway
Co. Highways and Township Roads
Railroad
Power Line
Marsh
National Forest Boundary
State Forest Boundary
National Park Boundary
Indian Reservation
Fish & Wildlife Service Refuge Boundary
Counties
Municipal Boundaries
Wildlife Management Area
Waterfowl Production Area
State Game Refuge
Scientific Natural Area
State Park
Regional Park
County Park
Point of Interest
Hospital
Campsite
Mult. Primitive Campsites
Public Campground
Private Campground
Public RV Campsites
Private RV Campsites
Public Equestrian Campsites
Private Equestrian Campsites
Shelter & Campsites
Shelter
Boat Access
Carry-In Access
Fishing Pier
Houseboat
Marina
Golf Course
Downhill Skiing
X-Country Skiing
Dam
Lock and Dam
Lighthouse
Observ. Tower
Scenic Overlook
USFS or DNR Office
Airport
Seaplane Airport
Picnic Area
Wayside Rest Area
Rest Area
Parking
WMA Parking
Information Center
Miles
Austin
Mapleview
Brownsdale
Rose Creek
Lyle
Lansing
Oakland
Moscow
London
Otranto
Corning
Mayville
Andyville
Ramsey
Varco
Nicolville
Carex WMA
Turtle Creek WPA
Ramsey Mill Pond WMA
Wild Indigo Prairie SNA
Mentel WMA
Austin Municipal Airport
Austin Acres
Lyle-austin WMA
Red Cedar River WMA
Lena Larson WMA
Rose WMA
Markhams Pond
Otranto Park
Mower County Mgmt Committee Trails
Cedar River
Turtle Creek
Murphy Creek
Orchard Creek
Roberts Creek
Dobbins Creek
Wolf Creek
Rose Creek
Otter Creek
Woodbury Creek
MOWER CO
FREEBORN CO
WORTH CO
MITCHELL CO
State Line Rd
93°5'W
93°0'W
92°55'W
92°50'W
43°45'N
43°40'N
43°35'N
43°30'N

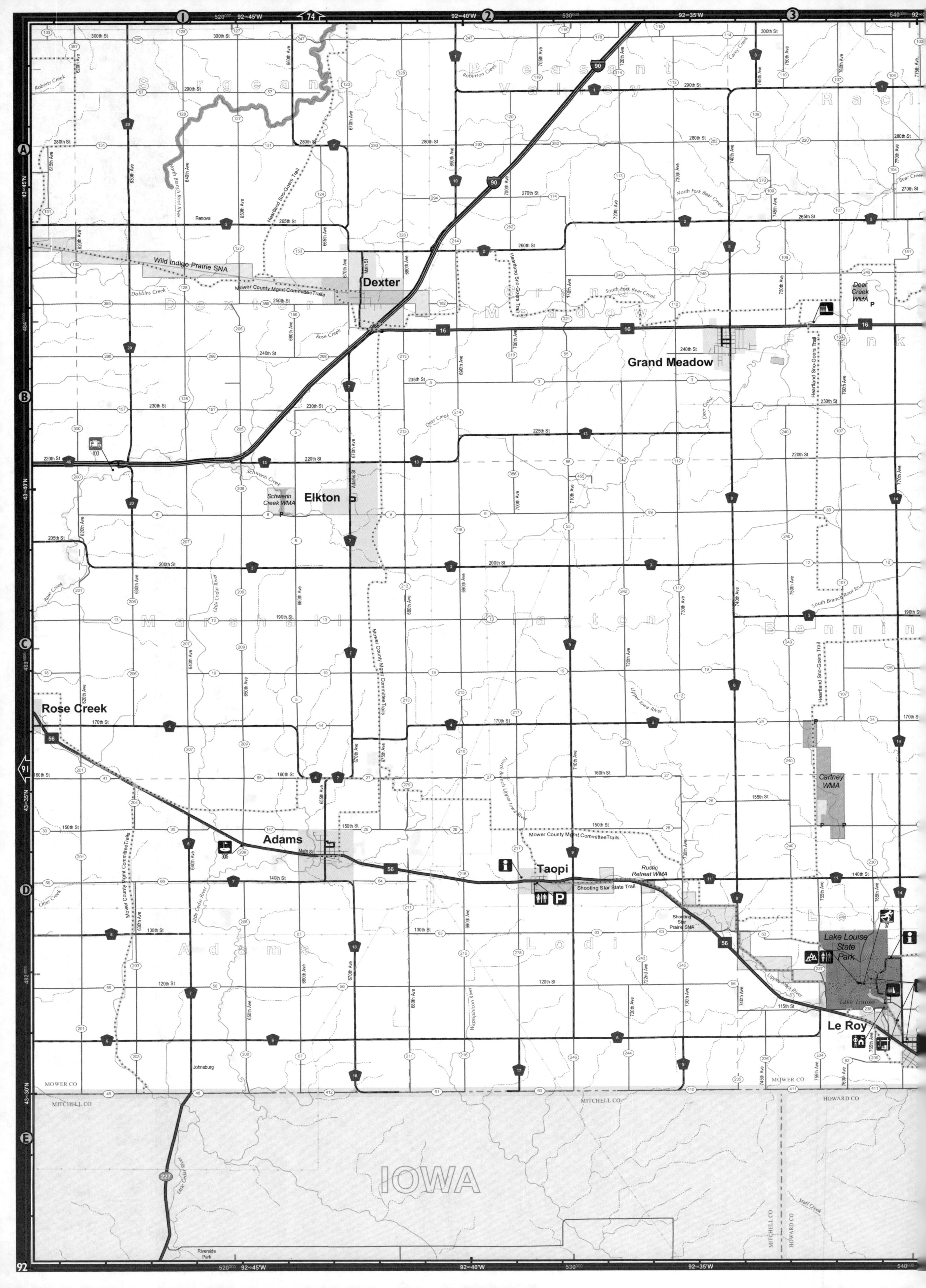

Dexter
Grand Meadow
Elkton
Rose Creek
Adams
Taopi
Le Roy
Lake Louise State Park
Lake Louise
Cartney WMA
Deer Creek WMA
Schwerin Creek WMA
Rustic Retreat WMA
Shooting Star Prairie SNA
Wild Indigo Prairie SNA
Shooting Star State Trail
Heartland Sno-Goers Trail
Mower County Mgmt Committee Trails
Johnsburg
Renova
Riverside Park
IOWA
MOWER CO
MITCHELL CO
HOWARD CO
Sargeant
Pleasant Valley
Dexter
Grand Meadow
Marshall
Clayton
Bennington
Adams
Lodi
Racine
Frankford
North Branch Root River
South Branch Root River
North Fork Bear Creek
South Fork Bear Creek
Upper Iowa River
North Branch Upper Iowa River
Little Cedar River
Wapsipinicon River
Rose Creek
Deer Creek
Dobbins Creek
Schwerin Creek
Robinson Creek
Roberts Creek
Otter Creek
Carey Creek
Bear Creek
Staff Creek
92°45'W
92°40'W
92°35'W
43°45'N
43°40'N
43°35'N
43°30'N

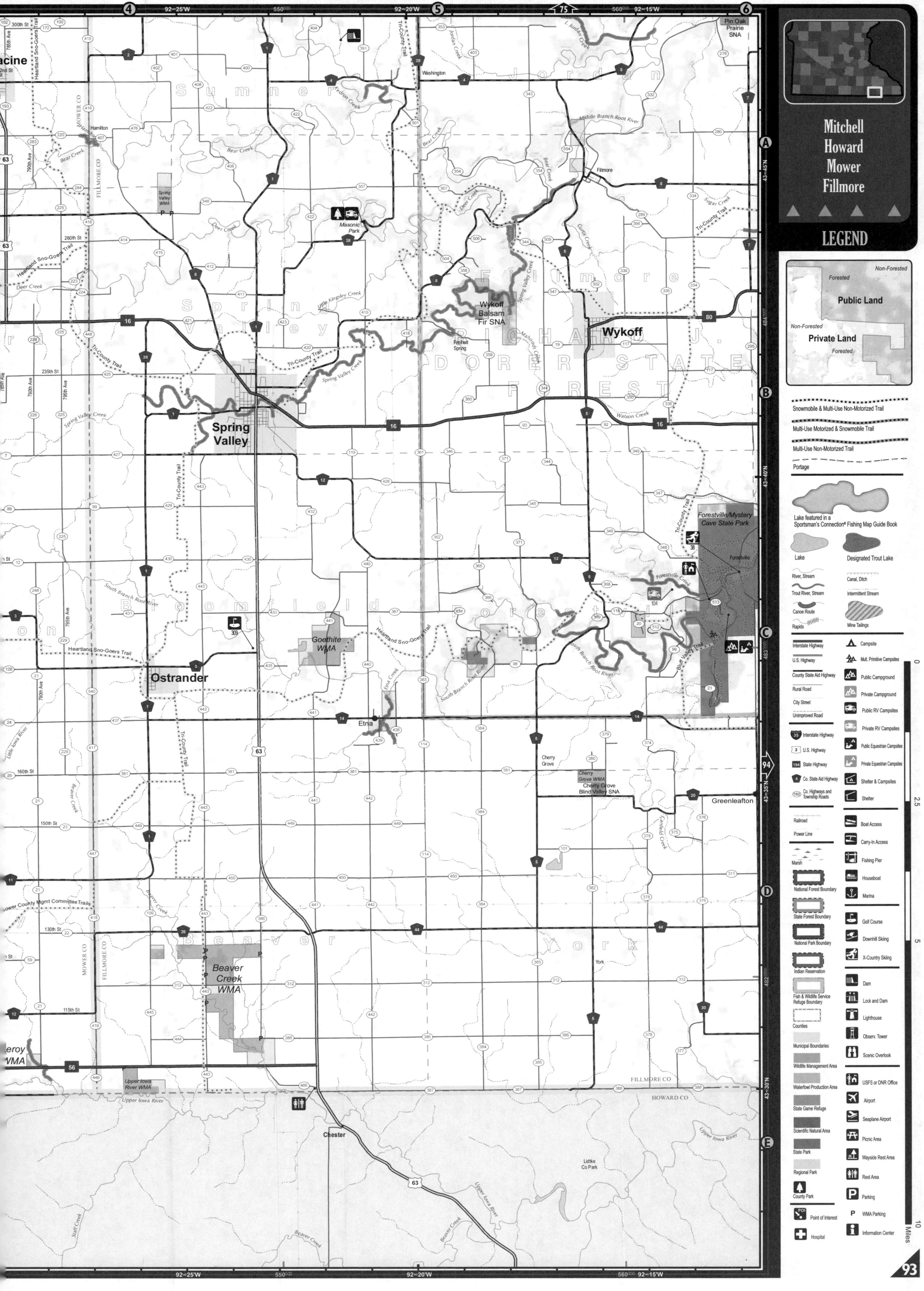
Mitchell
Howard
Mower
Fillmore
LEGEND
Public Land
Private Land
Forested
Non-Forested
Spring Valley
Wykoff
Ostrander
Wykoff Balsam Fir SNA
Forestville/Mystery Cave State Park
Goethite WMA
Beaver Creek WMA
Cherry Grove WMA
Cherry Grove Blind Valley SNA
Upper Iowa River WMA
Masonic Park
Greenleafton
Etna
Chester
Fillmore
Washington
Hamilton
Cherry Grove
York
Pin Oak Prairie SNA
Forestville
Tri-County Trail
Heartland Sno-Goers Trail
FILLMORE CO
HOWARD CO
MOWER CO

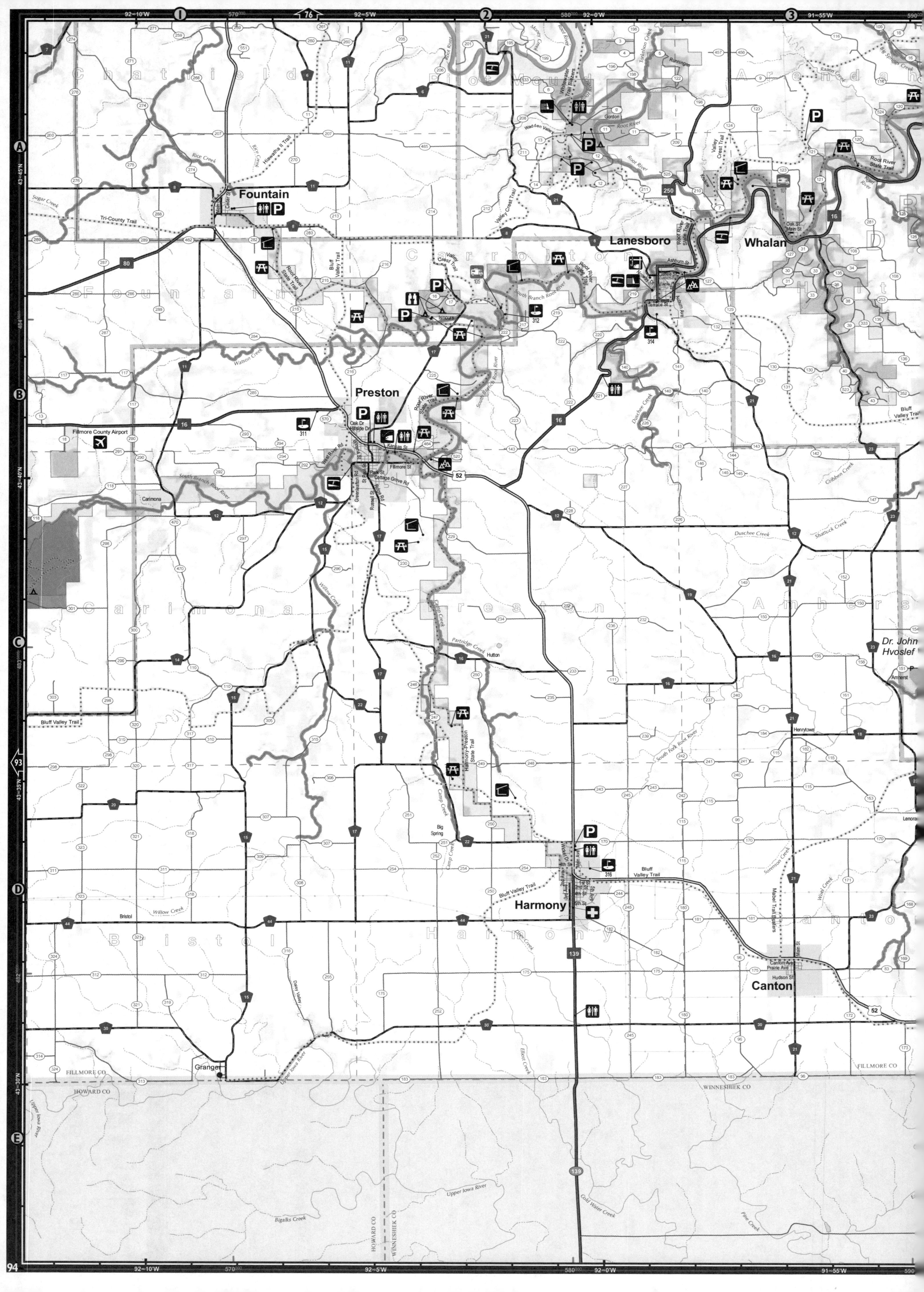

Fountain
Preston
Lanesboro
Whalan
Harmony
Canton
Chatfield
Pilot Mound
Arendahl
Carrolton
Fountain
Carimona
Preston
Amherst
Bristol
Harmony
Canton
Fillmore County Airport
Root River State Trail
Harmony-Preston State Trail
Bluff Valley Trail
Tri-County Trail
Hiawatha II Trail
Valley Crest Trail
Whitewater Trail Blazers
Mabel Trail Blazers
Dr. John Hvoslef Trail
Root River
South Branch Root River
South Fork Root River
Upper Iowa River
Camp Creek
Willow Creek
Partridge Creek
Duschee Creek
Watson Creek
Rice Creek
Sugar Creek
Shattuck Creek
Cold Water Creek
Pine Creek
Bigalks Creek
Elliott Creek
Deer Creek
Crooked Creek
Big Spring
Hutton
Henrytown
Granger
Carimona
Gordon
Lenora
Amherst
FILLMORE CO
HOWARD CO
WINNESHIEK CO
92°10'W
92°5'W
92°0'W
91°55'W
43°45'N
43°40'N
43°35'N
43°30'N
76
93

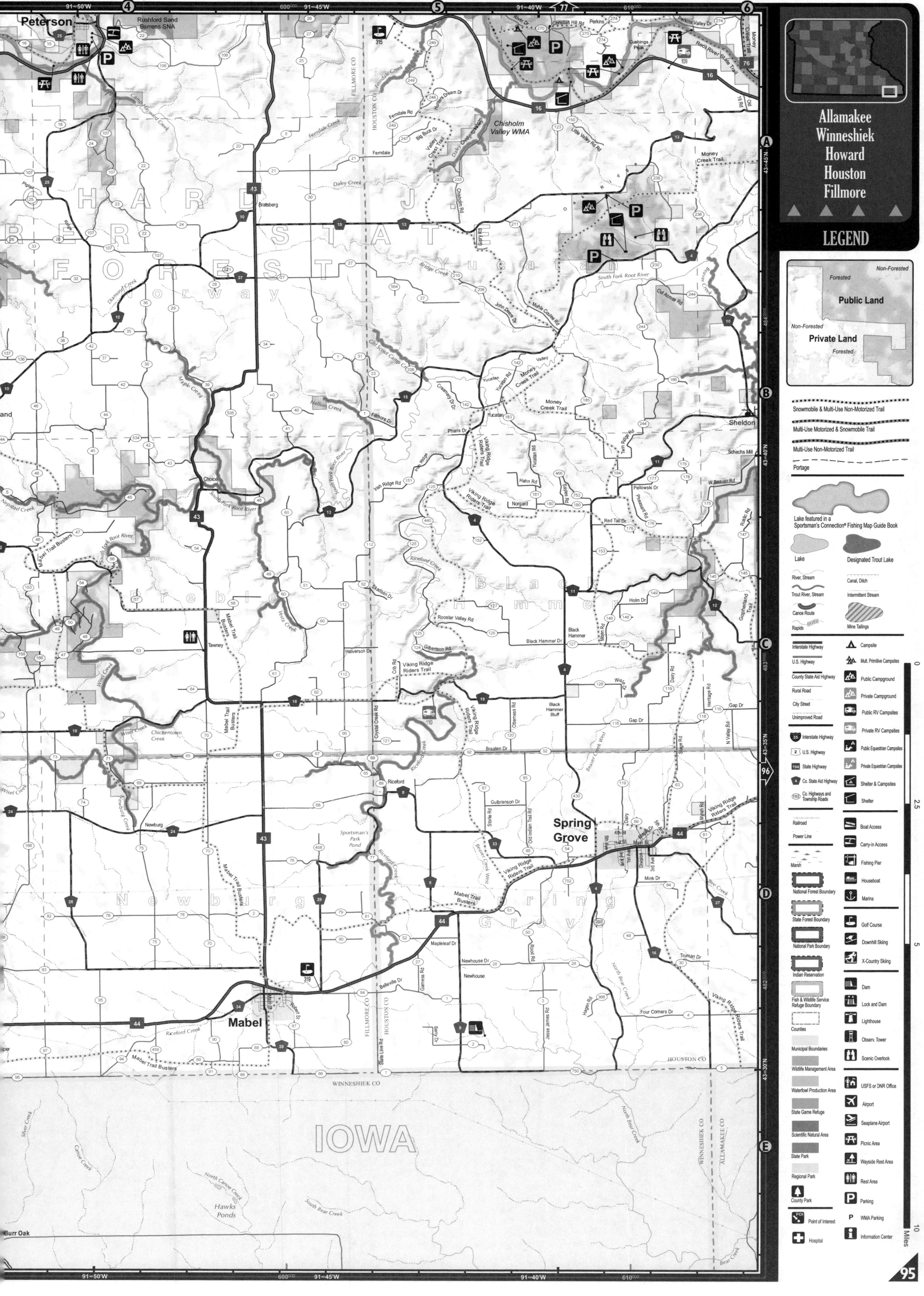
Peterson
Rushford Sand Barrens SNA
Chisholm Valley WMA
Allamakee
Winneshiek
Howard
Houston
Fillmore
LEGEND
Public Land
Private Land
Forested
Non-Forested
Snowmobile & Multi-Use Non-Motorized Trail
Multi-Use Motorized & Snowmobile Trail
Multi-Use Non-Motorized Trail
Portage
Lake featured in a Sportsman's Connection® Fishing Map Guide Book
Lake
Designated Trout Lake
Sheldon
Spring Grove
Mabel
Riceford
Newburg
Newhouse
Black Hammer
Yucatan
Choice
Tawney
Bratsberg
Ferndale
Sportsman's Park Pond
IOWA
Hawks Ponds
Burr Oak
WINNESHIEK CO
ALLAMAKEE CO
HOUSTON CO
FILLMORE CO
91°50'W
91°45'W
91°40'W
43°45'N
43°40'N
43°35'N
43°30'N
Miles

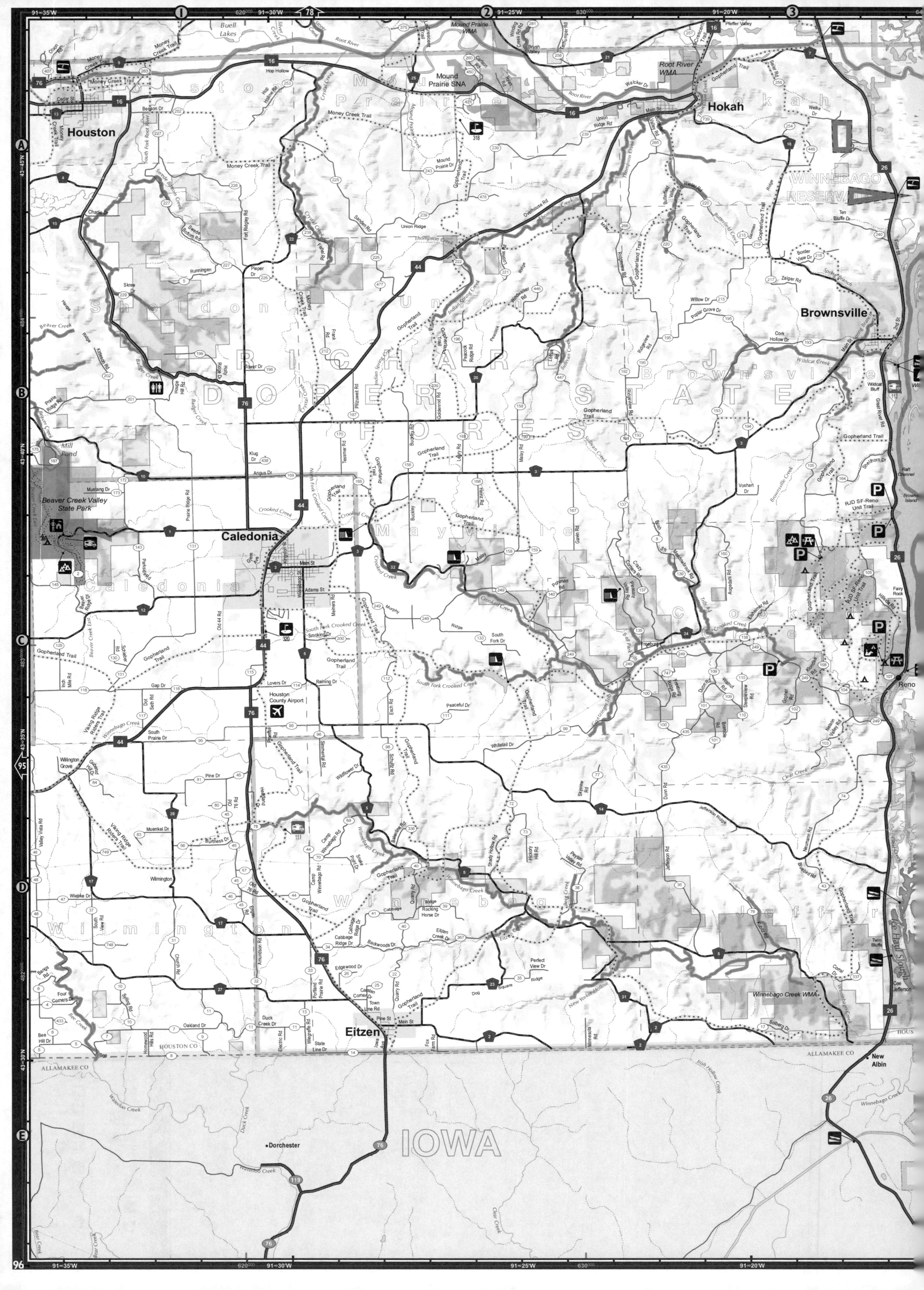
Houston
Hokah
Brownsville
Caledonia
Eitzen
Reno
New Albin
Dorchester
IOWA
RICHARD J DORER STATE FOREST
Winnebago Reservation
Beaver Creek Valley State Park
Mound Prairie SNA
Mound Prairie WMA
Root River WMA
Winnebago Creek WMA
Houston County Airport
Root River
Gopherland Trail
Money Creek Trail
Viking Ridge Riders Trail
RJD SF-Reno Unit Trail
ALLAMAKEE CO
HOUSTON CO
Mill Pond
Buell Lakes
91°35'W
91°30'W
91°25'W
91°20'W
43°45'N
43°40'N
43°35'N
43°30'N

Allamakee
Houston
Vernon
La Crosse
LEGEND
Public Land
Private Land
Forested
Non-Forested
Snowmobile & Multi-Use Non-Motorized Trail
Multi-Use Motorized & Snowmobile Trail
Multi-Use Non-Motorized Trail
Portage
Lake featured in a Sportsman's Connection® Fishing Map Guide Book
Lake
Designated Trout Lake
WISCONSIN
Stoddard
Genoa
USACE Lock & Dam 8 Recreation Area
Victory
Zabolio Lake
Waller Lakes
Elgar Lake
Big Lake
Minnesota Slough
LA CROSSE CO
VERNON CO
Mormon Creek
Bad Axe River
North Fork Bad Axe River
Sidie Hollow County Park
Esofea Park
Max Blain

FISHING

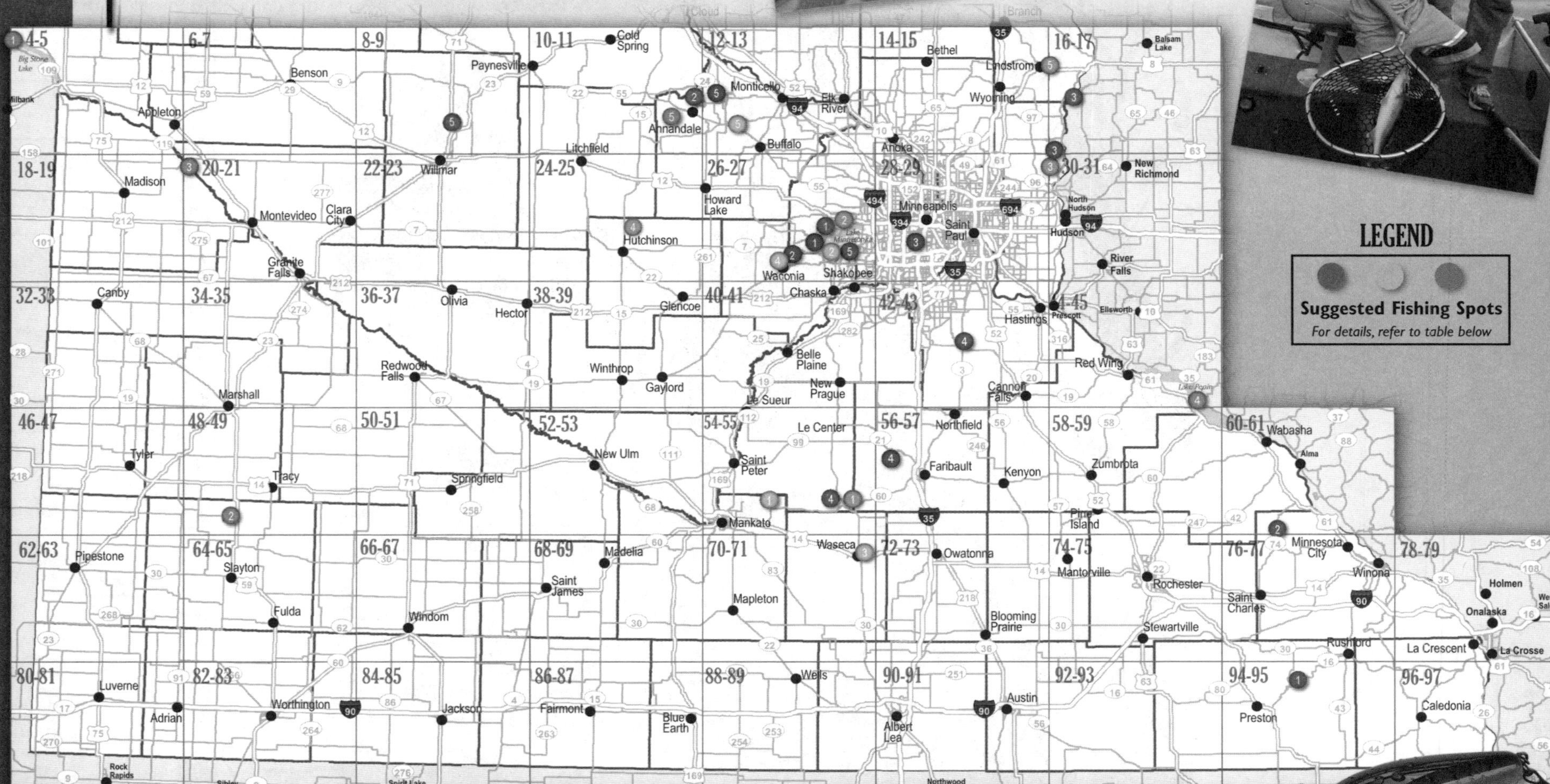

Minnesota seems custom-made for anglers. With more than 5,000 fishable lakes, 15,000 miles of fishable warmwater streams, and 1,900 miles of trout streams, anglers could spend many happy lifetimes plying the waters here. Gamefish are abundant, ranging from local favorites such as walleye, northern pike, and panfish, to brook trout, smallmouth bass, and muskellunge. In all, 158 fish species call Minnesota home, and there are as many ways to catch them as there are names of fish.

Not only are there lots of fish and lots of places to fish, but there are plenty of locations that make it easy for anglers to get out on the water. In all, there are more than 3,000 public lake accesses across the state. It's no surprise that Minnesota is one of the most popular destinations for anglers across the United States. Fishing is so popular in Minnesota that the state's governor participates in the season opener every year, and has since 1948. Fishing is also a great activity for families and a perfect way to introduce youngsters to the great outdoors.

MAY WE SUGGEST...

With thousands of lakes to choose from, it can be difficult decide on a short list. This map and these tables indicate a few of the more obvious (even legendary) destinations, and a couple lesser known (not lesser quality) waters. We encourage you to use these as a starting point, and refer to the information in the larger tables to discover your own favorite spots.

WALLEYE			BASS			NORTHERN PIKE		
# / NAME	COUNTY	PG.#/COORD.	# / NAME	COUNTY	PG.#/COORD.	# / NAME	COUNTY	PG.#/COORD.
1) Big Stone Lake	Big Stone	4/1A	1) Lake Minnetonka	Hennepin	27/5D	1) Lower Lake Sakatah	Rice/ Le Sueur	55/5D
2) Lake Sarah	Marray	48/2E	2) Clearwater Lake	Wright	11/6C	2) Lake Minnetonka	Hennepin	27/5D
3) Lac qui Parle	Lac qui Parle	20/1A	3) St. Croix River	various	16 & 30	3) Big Carnelian Lake	Washington	30/1A
4) Lake Pepin	Goodhue	45/5E	4) Lake Hanska	Brown	52/1E	4) Lake Washington	Meeker	25/4B
5) Sylvia Lake	Wright	11/5D	5) Green Lake	Kandiyohi	9/4D	5) North Center Lake	Chisago	15/6B

MUSKIE			TROUT			PANFISH		
# / NAME	COUNTY	PG.#/COORD.	# / NAME	COUNTY	PG.#/COORD.	# / NAME	COUNTY	PG.#/COORD.
1) Lake Minnetonka	Hennepin	27/5D	1) Root River	various	74-78,92-96	1) Lake Washington	Le Sueur	54/2D
2) Lake Waconia	Carver	26/3E	2) Whitewater River	various	60, 75 & 76	2) Lake Minnetonka	Hennepin	27/5D
3) Lake Harriet	Hennepin	28/2D	3) Square Lake	Washington	30/1A	3) Clear Lake	Waseca	71/6A
4) French Lake	Rice	56/1C	4) Vermillion River	various	42-44	4) Lake Waconia	Carver	26/3E
5) Sugar Lake	Wright	12/1C	5) Christmas Lake	Hennepin	27/5D	5) Maple Lake	Wright	12/2D

Lake Fishing -Warm Water Species

Southern Minnesota is dotted with lakes, rivers, and miles of trout streams. Within this region are some of the state's biggest and best fisheries such as Lake Waconia, Lake Minnetonka, Lake Pepin, and the Mississippi River. From prairie potholes and bullhead ponds to scenic trout waters and broad rivers, southern Minnesota has something for all anglers.

Although spring and fall are generally the two best fishing seasons, there can be fantastic action on calm summer evenings as well as in the middle of winter, when area lakes typically support a thick mantle of ice.

(For complete fishing regulations, contact the Minnesota DNR Information Center, 500 Lafayette Rd., St. Paul, MN 55155-4040; phone: (651) 296-6157, (800) 657-3929; Web: www.dnr.state.mn.us.)

Walleye *(Sander vitreus)*

Preferred Water Temperatures: 55 to 70 degrees

The walleye is Minnesota's state fish and is avidly pursued by anglers from spring through winter. Thanks to a combination of abundant natural spawning habitat and an aggressive stocking program, the species is found across the state, in rivers and big and small lakes. An average North Star State walleye weighs about 1 to 3 pounds, but fish bigger than 10 pounds are caught every year.

Walleyes (sometimes called marble-eyes) are very sensitive to light, and typically feed in shallow water during early morning and early evening hours only to avoid the bright daytime sunlight. During the day, walleyes will often move into deeper water or near available cover such as boulders or logs. On cloudy or windy days they may remain in shallower water if the sun's glare is sufficiently reduced. Fishing is usually best on windy and cloudy days, when there is a good "walleye chop" on the water. Because walleyes are light sensitive, many anglers wait until after dark to pursue them.

The best walleye fishing is typically during spring and fall when the fish are most active. Walleyes often key in on rocks and submerged weeds during the day. Jigging with leeches, minnows, or nightcrawlers over such areas can be effective for finding fish, as can be trolling with crankbaits past rock reefs or along weed lines. Walleye are schooling fish and often congregate with like-sized fish; thus, once one fish is caught in an area there will usually be others of similar size nearby.

SPRING - In spring, walleyes will locate in shallow water on rock piles and shoals, sandbars, near river mouths, and other areas with hard, rocky bottoms providing favorable spawning substrate. Small (1/16- to 1/2-ounce) jigs tipped with minnows, leeches, or nightcrawlers are tops for spring walleyes.

Early-season Walleye Fishing Tips

Fish shallow: unless fishing a clear lake on a bright day, walleyes will typically be in less than 10 feet of water. Knowing this can make fish easy to find, but not necessarily easy to catch. In shallow water, walleyes can spook very easily, so presentation and boat control are vital to success. The best way to approach fish is by drifting, keeping in position with a trolling motor.

Warm water in spring is walleye water: finding water that's just a degree or two warmer than the rest of the lake or river you're fishing can make all the difference between hooking up with fish or going home empty. These areas with warmer water will hold fish that are active and feeding. As a rule, the north shores of lakes, particularly bays, as well as river mouths generally warm first in spring. Lakes with dark, stained water will also warm quicker than clear-water lakes. Clear lakes will also have earlier and shallower weed growth.

SUMMER - By early summer, walleyes leave shoreline zones for sand/gravel points, weed beds, shoreline flats, and rock reefs. Drifting or slow-trolling near weed edges with 'crawler harnesses or leech-tipped Lindy rigs is a proven walleye tactic. Many anglers also do well using minnow-imitating baits such as Rapalas or deep-diving crankbaits.

FALL - Fair-weather anglers probably won't like fall walleye fishing. It's often during the coldest, rainiest, or windy days that the fish are most actively feeding. Those willing to brave the elements, however, have a shot at catching the biggest fish of the year. Most walleyes caught in fall are females – the ones that grow to trophy size. Look for them near weedbed edges and rock humps, where baitfish will be concentrated. A jig tipped with a minnow, leech, or nightcrawler is dynamite for autumn 'eyes. Jig on or near bottom, keeping contact with the lake floor while jigging. Fish deep water during the day and shallower water in the evening.

WINTER - Ice fishing for walleyes is popular, and the fish are again most active during low-light conditions. Minnow-tipped jigs, jigging spoons, and tip-ups with minnows are common wintertime walleye rigs. Look for fish in shallow bays and along shorelines during winter.

Fish Fact: The Minnesota state record walleye was caught in Cook County's Seagull River on May 13, 1979. The fish weighed 17 pounds, 8 ounces and measured 35.8 inches long!

General Walleye Fishing Tips

Go orange and yellow for 'eyes: Orange, yellow and yellow-green are the colors most visible to walleyes, so be sure to keep a supply of lures in these colors in the tackle box.

Fish dark water: Lakes with dark or stained water warm faster in spring. They will also stay warm longer than clear-water lakes.

Fish the wind: Although windy conditions can make for challenging boat positioning, sometimes a steady wind that blows for a couple of days can affect water temps along the windy shore, creating pockets of warmer water that attract baitfish and in turn attract walleyes.

Sauger *(Sander Canadensis)*

Preferred Water Temperatures: 55 to 70 degrees

Minnesotans love walleyes…so much so that they've dubbed this species the state fish. But the closely related sauger doesn't receive much of this love or attention.

Saugers are similar in appearance and habits to walleyes, although their distribution is more limited. Saugers are smaller than walleyes, and rarely grow larger than 3 pounds – a 5-pounder is a huge sauger. They are also skinnier and more cylindrical in shape. Saugers are darker and have brown blotches on their bodies. The easiest way to distinguish between the two species is to note the presence of dark spots on the dorsal fin and the absence of a white tip on the lower part of the tail in saugers.

A sauger's eyes are ideally suited to low-light visibility – even better than a walleye's. It's no coincidence, then, that saugers are frequently found in turbid rivers. They are also usually found in deeper water than walleyes. When angling for them, fish just as you would for walleyes, using jigs tipped with minnows or other popular walleye baits, but focus your efforts in deeper water. Because they stay deep, sauger are more likely to bite during the day than walleyes.

In rivers, saugers may bite best early or late in the day – even more so than walleyes. River fish may also bite best on cloudy, rainy, windy days. Nasty weather is more likely to positively affect the bite than it does with walleyes.

Saugers are not widespread in Minnesota. They're most commonly fished for in Lake of the Woods, but they are also found in Rainy Lake and other lakes of the far north, as well as lakes along the Wisconsin/Minnesota border and in some of the state's large rivers.

Muskie *(Esox masquinongy)*

Preferred Water Temperatures: 60 to 70 degrees

Muskellunge, or muskies, are one of the most prized fish swimming in Minnesota waters. They have very definite habitat requirements and are relatively scarce in any lake or river they inhabit. Muskies are notoriously difficult to catch and have often been called the fish of 10,000 casts. Few muskie anglers are deterred, however, by the species' notorious reputation. For many anglers, fishing for muskies can border on obsession.

Muskies are loners, living a solitary existence among weed lines, rock shelves and shoals, and other areas of natural cover. The best fishing for muskies often occurs late in the morning or during the afternoon, particularly on cloudy days.

Keying in on good muskie habitat means finding structure: Points, weedy bays, islands, gravel bars, breaklines, and drop-offs are all likely Esox haunts. These fish-attracting areas are even better if located near deeper water, as muskies seek such naturally occurring transitions. These spots should be fished from shallow water into deeper water.

SPRING - Like other gamefish, muskies are drawn to the shallows in early spring. This is where water will warm quicker and where weed growth will be heaviest. Focus on shallow bays with emergent vegetation and reed beds. Spring muskies are typically spooky and need to be targeted carefully. Try making long casts to the shallows with small bucktail spinners, crankbaits, or jerkbaits, and use a slow retrieve.

SUMMER - Areas of submergent vegetation or structure such as rocky reefs will hold fish in midsummer. Topwater lures are great for working shallow reefs, while bucktails and spinnerbaits are effective for buzzing weed edges. Use bright colors.

FALL - For many anglers, fall affords the best opportunity at a trophy muskie. The big predators have had a full season to put on pounds and they're particularly ravenous before winter sets in. A long-espoused theory is that the bigger the bait the bigger the fish that will bite it. There's some truth to this, but not all muskies (or even northern pike) that chase huge baits will be monsters. Often smaller fish will attack an out-sized bait out of sheer aggressiveness. Drifting large suckers (12 inches or bigger) near weed edges, casting big bucktails, or slow-trolling crankbaits can all be extremely effective on autumn Esox.

WINTER - Muskies remain inactive when water temperatures are near freezing and feed sporadically during winter; thus, they are rarely caught by ice fishermen.

Fish Fact: The biggest muskies – those reaching the magic 50-inch mark – are almost always females. It can take 15 years or more for a muskie to grow 50 inches.

Tips For Boating More Muskies

Fish where muskies abound: Fishing on lakes with abundant populations of muskies is the best strategy to put the odds in an angler's favor.

Cast, cast, and cast again: As obvious as it sounds, you can't catch fish unless your lure or bait is in the water. Successful muskie anglers don't let an hour or even a day of no-catch fishing discourage them. Persistence is a big part of the game – the odds are if you keep at it, a muskie will eventually strike your offering.

Revisit hotspots: If you raise a muskie or it follows your lure but doesn't strike, make a note of the location and return later. It's often possible to get a second look from the same fish the same day or the following day.

Change it up: Muskies are notorious for following lures all the way to the boat but not striking. Anglers have devised techniques to entice trigger-shy fish into fully committing. The most popular method is to work lures such as bucktails in a "figure-eight" pattern at the end of a retrieve. This involves putting the rod tip into the water and moving it below the surface as if you were writing the number 8 on an imaginary chalkboard. Often, this simple change of direction can make a hesitant fish charge a lure. Another frequently used tactic involves changing speed during the retrieve – cranking faster or slowing down, letting the lure flutter – to simulate what real baitfish do when pursued.

Lake Fishing -Warm Water Species

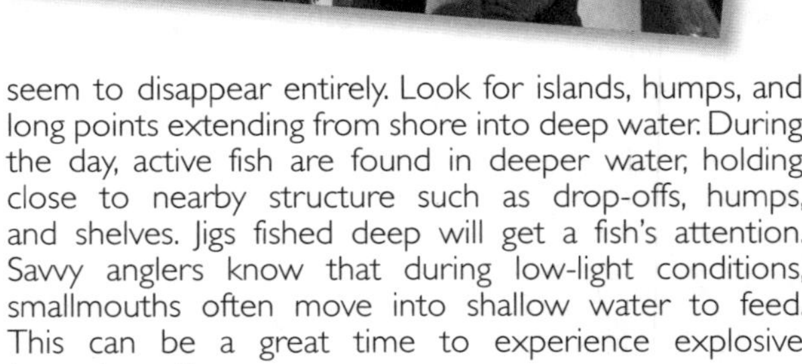

Northern Pike *(Esox lucius)*

Preferred Water Temperatures: 50 to 70 degrees

Northern pike are the most widespread gamefish in Minnesota. They are aggressive feeders and will strike nearly any lure or bait offered. Pike typically lurk in quiet areas thick with vegetation such as weedy bays and estuaries in the spring and summer; in late summer and autumn they will move into deeper water.

SPRING - Pike begin to spawn as the ice goes out in early spring. They will seek out shallow, weedy bays and points. Look for them in 8 feet of water or less. The northern shorelines of lakes and bays receive the sun's southern exposure and usually warm quickest in spring. Effective spring tactics include casting spoons and spinnerbaits to bays and feeder creeks.

As water temps warm, pike shift to deeper water with submerged weed beds or other forms of cover or structure.

SUMMER - In summer, pike can be found along weed edges, points, and drop-offs in water as deep as 40 feet. Spoons, crankbaits, and large spinnerbaits are all effective summertime lures. Deep-water trolling can also be very effective.

FALL - In autumn, pike return to shallower water where mature vegetation is present. The fish feed actively and can be caught casting or trolling along weed beds and lines. When water temperature drops and the fall turnover occurs, northern pike become very active again. They return to the weedy shallows, rocky bars, or below rapids in rivers or streams. Throw big bucktails, crankbaits, and jerkbaits.

WINTER - Look for pike in shallow bays (from 3 to 12 feet of water), and near points and drop-offs. Tip-ups rigged with live minnows will do the trick on under-the-ice pike.

Fish Fact: The Minnesota state record northern pike has stood since May 16, 1929, when a lucky angler pulled a 45-pound, 12-ounce pike from Basswood Lake in Lake County.

Largemouth Bass *(Micropterus salmoides)*

Preferred Water Temperatures: 70 to 75 degrees

One of the best-kept secrets is Minnesota's largemouth bass fishery. In this state where walleyes rule, surprisingly few anglers bother to chase bucketmouths, which is great news for bass fishermen. Anglers won't find the scale-busting bigmouths that are present in the south, but for pure numbers of fish in the 2- to 6-pound range, Minnesota is, perhaps, the best state for largemouth bass.

Largemouth bass prefer warm, weedy, and slow-moving waters. They spend a lot of time in the shallows, among reeds, lily pads and other vegetation, boat docks, and other cover, where they can ambush prey.

SPRING - At about the time Minnesota bass season opens, largemouths will typically be concentrated in shallow bays with weeds – places where they will spawn and remain afterward until the water warms. Not all bays are created equal – the best ones will have a variety of vegetation and some type of additional structure. Spinnerbaits or Texas-rigged plastics worked through the shallow, weedy bays are proven springtime bass techniques. As the weeds become thicker, fan-cast weedless spoons and frogs, or pitch Texas-rigged tubes or jig-and-pig combos directly into holes and on the edges of the heavy cover.

SUMMER - Look for bass near natural and manmade stucture. Flip Texas-rigged plastics or jig-and-pig combos tight to lily pads, weed edges, boat docks, and stumps. During calm, low-light conditions, topwater lures can provide some thrilling action. On clear lakes with heavy recreational traffic, night fishing for largemouths can be an excellent summer option. Try big lures using slow, steady retrieves.

FALL - As the days get shorter and colder, largemouth bass will seek deeper water. As shallow weeds start to die, deeper green weeds will concentrate active bass looking to fatten up for the winter. Deep-diving crankbaits, Texas-rigged plastics, and jig-and-pig combos all work well for autumn bucketmouths.

WINTER - Because largemouth bass prefer warm water and warm weather, they are largely inactive in winter and rarely bite on baits offered through the ice.

Smallmouth Bass *(Micropterus dolomieu)*

Preferred Water Temperatures: 65 to 70 degrees

Pound for pound, the smallmouth bass is one of the feistiest freshwater fish anglers will encounter. Noted for putting up a battle regardless of size, smallmouth routinely make bulldog-like runs toward bottom, and may go airborne several times when hooked. Once the hook is set, hold on. Whether they dive deep or shoot the surface, battling a big bronzeback is always a first-class experience.

At home in clear, rocky lakes and rivers, smallmouth bass favor structure such as rocky shorelines, points, and shoals, and may often be found in relatively deep water. Areas with a good mix of small, medium, and large rocks tend to hold the most fish.

SPRING - Find shallow, rocky flats and there will likely be smallies nearby. Areas with a mix of gravel and sand, with cover such as fallen logs or boulders, are prime spawning areas. Look for fish around islands, points, and shoals. After spawning, the fish will hang tight to rocky shallows until water temperatures rise. Work from shallow to deeper water with small crankbaits, jigs, and suspending jerkbaits.

SUMMER - The challenge of summer smallmouth bass fishing is finding fish, as smallies retreat to open water and can seem to disappear entirely. Look for islands, humps, and long points extending from shore into deep water. During the day, active fish are found in deeper water, holding close to nearby structure such as drop-offs, humps, and shelves. Jigs fished deep will get a fish's attention. Savvy anglers know that during low-light conditions, smallmouths often move into shallow water to feed. This can be a great time to experience explosive topwater action.

FALL - Autumn is normally the best time for a shot at a trophy-sized smallie. October and November can be the best months for connecting with the largest fish. Cooling temperatures trigger a serious, shallow-water feed before fish move to deeper water for the lean winter months. As water temps drop into the 50s, the best areas are typically rocky flats in 5 to 10 feet of water. The fish tend to be aggressive, and a wide range of presentations will work. As the water continues to cool, follow the fish out to deeper holding areas like rock humps or steep edges of points. The fish typically hang in water from 10 to 25 feet, maybe deeper depending on prevailing structure. Slow, deliberate presentations like a small, twin-tailed grub on a football-head jig, will be your best bet.

Panfish

Ask any angler about the first fish he or she ever caught and the answer is likely to be "panfish." In many ways panfish – a group that includes bluegills, crappies, perch, and other sunfish – are perfect fish for beginning anglers. They are found in most lake and river systems, they are generally abundant, and they are usually aggressive feeders and can often be found in shallow water close to shore.

Panfish can be caught using any number of methods, from a hook and bobber dangling from a cane pole to an expertly placed popping bug dropped into the lily pads with fly-fishing gear.

Although many anglers lump bluegills, perch, and crappies together into the collective panfish category, the species occupy different niches within any particular water system and generally require different techniques to catch.

Bluegill *(Lepomis macrochirus)*

Preferred Water Temperatures: 65 to 75 degrees

Bluegills are the most abundant sunfish in Minnesota and one of the most popular gamefish with anglers of all ages. Bluegills favor warm, still waters with abundant vegetation and are found in approximately 65 percent of the state's lakes and many slower-moving streams. Their abundance and willingness to strike a variety of lures and baits makes them a favorite with beginning and experienced anglers alike. Bluegills also feed throughout the day - a bonus for anglers who like to sleep in.

SPRING - As water temps warm to about 70 degrees and weed beds begin developing, bluegills will become active. They will concentrate in the shallows, where males build spawning beds which are vigorously defended. These saucer-shaped nests are generally quite visible and are often found among many other bluegill beds. Males will charge lures to protect the beds.

SUMMER - The fish move into deeper water (10 feet or greater) as water temperatures rise. Look for bigger bluegills among deep weed beds and structure such as weed-covered humps and bars. Bluegills often suspend just above the thermocline. Drifting with small worms under a bobber works well. Fly anglers can have a ball casting popping bugs in the lily pads.

FALL - Bluegills will move up from their deeper summer haunts as water temps begin to cool. They'll hold close to weed edges and other cover. Drop small baits near cover to fall 'gills.

WINTER - Bluegills feed actively all winter long and are popular with ice anglers. Target areas with submergent vegetation and fish near bottom in 10 to 20 feet of water. Small jigs tipped with a waxworm are an excellent combination. Keep drilling holes until you locate fish.

Black Crappie *(Pomoxis nigromaculatus)*

Preferred Water Temperatures: 65 to 75 degrees

Black crappies are the more widely distributed crappie in Minnesota. They favor clear, cool lakes with abundant vegetation. Crappies often travel in schools during summer and winter, at which time anglers can have a field day with these tasty fish.

SPRING - The best crappie fishing is often just after ice-out when the fish will move into shallow, weedy bays and similar areas to feed and spawn. Fish will often be in water less than 5 feet deep. Slip-bobber rigs baited with small fathead minnows should be worked over the developing weeds or tight to reeds, docks and shoreline cover. By late spring, the fish leave the shallows and move to deep water. During this period they can be difficult to locate, and many anglers choose to pursue other species.

SUMMER - Finding crappies in summer can be challenging. The fish usually retreat to deep water (20 to 40 feet) or suspend along weed lines. Fish for crappies with small minnows under a float, or free-line small jigs.

FALL - After lakes turn over, loose schools of crappies will move to deeper water and suspend. Drop a jig and minnow close to deep weedbeds.

WINTER - Try fishing in shallow bays in 4 to 8 feet of water. Teardrop jigs tipped with waxworms should be fished in a gentle up-and-down motion.

Yellow Perch *(Perca flavescens)*

Preferred Water Temperatures: 55 to 70 degrees

Yellow perch are one of Minnesota's favorite panfish. These relatives of the walleye are best known for making fine table fare. Most perch run in the 6- to 9-inch range, with any fish 12 inches or longer qualifying for "jumbo" status.

Perch are typically found in deeper water, with schools of fish actively on the move in search of minnows. Structure such as rocks, reefs, drop-offs, and mats of submergent vegetation will attract baitfish and in turn will attract perch.

Locating perch generally requires a boat, and unlike most gamefish, perch don't seem to be bothered by the sound of a running motor. Once a school of fish is located, slow down and slow-troll or drift minnow-tipped jigs.

SPRING - Look for perch in 10 to 20 feet of water, near bottom, in late spring. Target weedy areas, sand flats, and rocky shoals with jigs.

SUMMER - During warm summer days, perch will key on weed edges, bars, and humps, and may be found in water deeper than 40 feet, depending on the lake. Minnows and nightcrawler pieces fished near bottom are excellent summer baits. Slow-trolling with live-bait rigs or spinners can also be effective.

FALL - As water temps begin to cool, perch will move into shallower water to feed. Windy days can be awesome, as baitfish get pushed into the shallows. Again, rocky areas can be very productive. On calm days, fish the deeper breaks.

WINTER - First ice is often the best ice for winter perch fishing. Jig for perch at 10 to 25 feet, using small, live minnows; weighted ice flies and insect larvae; or small jigging spoons.

Ice Fishing

Just because lakes freeze over in winter doesn't mean anglers stop fishing. In winter, the land of 10,000 lakes becomes the land of 10,000 icehouses (and then some) as anglers travel by truck, snowmobile, and sled across frozen water in search of walleyes, panfish, perch, pike, saugers, and more. Minnesota has so much water that it can be difficult to know where to start. In reality, there are few bad choices. If you have a favorite body of water, it only takes a change in technique and clothing to hit the ice in search of fish.

Walleyes and saugers become aggressive feeders as ice first forms on the lake. In early winter, the fish typically hold in shallower water, along sandy bottoms, getting fat on shiners before making a gradual descent into deeper waters. First ice also finds perch and northern pike feeding actively.

As winter progresses, fish move steadily toward deeper water where the temperatures are warmest, and anglers follow. It's not unusual to travel several miles onto the ice to follow the moving fish.

Walleye fishermen often go with a one-two punch of jigging complemented by a baited tip-up. Lures such as the silver Swedish Pimple or the fish-imitating Jigging Rapala are actively twitched up and down to entice a strike. For northern pike, live bait is tough to beat. Fishing a chub, shiner, or sucker a few feet below the surface can bring great results and some heart-stopping moments when a toothy pike slams into the bait.

For perch, the bite is often fast and furious as large schools gather along the sandy shorelines to feed. A popular method of fishing is a jigging spoon, perhaps tipped with a piece of minnow. These baits should be worked right near the bottom.

The traditional method is to drop the spoon through a hole and let it sink to the desired depth. Once there, lift the rod and bring the spoon up a foot or so and then let it drop again. As it drops, the natural motion will make it flutter and wobble and is often when the perch will strike. When the fishing is hot, the spoon won't even make it down before being taken by a hungry fish.

Lake trout can be found at all depths during the winter angling season, so it is not necessary to locate the deepest water in order to find fish. What trout anglers often look for is a point, reef, or some other type of prominent structure located relatively close to deeper areas of a lake. Steep ledge areas are also classic lake trout spots in the winter.

The most popular method to entice lakers through the ice is jigging. Ice anglers use various types of jigging spoons, Jigging Rapalas, tube jigs, and airplane jigs. These lures can be used without bait, however, sometimes it helps to tip them with a small live minnow or a piece of cisco, smelt, or other dead bait. Lakers can be caught at many different depths, so don't concentrate solely on the bottom. Start by dropping your lure to the bottom, then jig in motions that pull the lure up about a foot, dropping it back down and repeating the process several times. Then reel up a few feet and begin the process again until you've repeated this motion all the way to the surface. Lake trout will often follow bait several feet as it moves from deeper to shallower water, sometimes hitting within 10 feet of the ice. Just because you don't see a lake trout on your electronics doesn't mean there isn't one there, just on the periphery, ready to strike.

Ice Fishing Gear

Ice fishing and ice fishing gear have undergone a revival of sorts. The emphasis is being placed on personal comfort and convenience, coupled with technology. Today's icehouses have become portable mini-motels with creature comforts ranging from gas heat and padded seats to bunk beds and toilets. Portable shelters can be set up and taken down in less time than a camping tent. Augers for drilling holes are fast and efficient and anglers can simply fire up a gasoline-powered machine to break through the thickest ice.

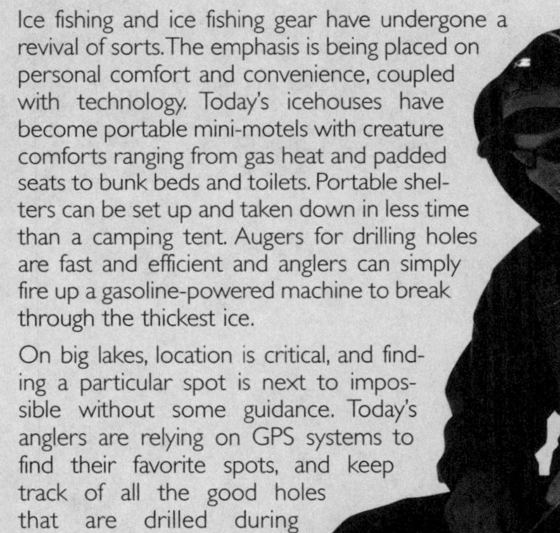

On big lakes, location is critical, and finding a particular spot is next to impossible without some guidance. Today's anglers are relying on GPS systems to find their favorite spots, and keep track of all the good holes that are drilled during a day.

GPS can also be a lifesaver. On the larger lakes, it is not uncommon to travel a couple miles or more to get to the fish. In the event of a winter storm, that GPS unit may be the difference between getting lost and making it back to shore safely.

Underwater cameras are also becoming more popular with anglers on the ice. These devices give anglers a view of the watery world below and bring sandbars, gravel beds, and vegetation to life. Cameras can even be hooked up to full-size televisions and allow everyone in a fishing party to watch what's happening underneath them.

With all the emphasis on high tech, it is still possible to catch plenty of fish with basic equipment. The tip-up is a ubiquitous piece of ice-fishing gear that has been around and continues to produce. It is extremely popular for live-bait fishing and requires little effort to use. A tip-up is placed over a drilled hole, with a spool of line and a flag attached to a piece of steel that signals a strike. You simply bait a hook, lower the line, and rig it to the steel and wait for the flag to indicate a bite. The tip-up is nice because it can be used to fish live bait in one hole, freeing anglers to fish another rod with a jigging spoon or other lure in a second hole.

Ice Safety

Although lakes in Minnesota typically freeze solid, some with more than 3 feet of ice, caution is necessary whenever venturing out onto the ice. The old saying "there is no safe ice" is good to keep in mind.

The DNR does a good job of keeping areas notorious for having thin or weak ice marked with flags to keep people away from potential danger. Most resorts and local radio stations give "ice reports," which update the status of lakes and the depth of ice. It is important to stay informed of current conditions and not to venture out before safe ice forms. Many anglers carry a length of rope and a personal flotation device in case of emergency.

Recommended safe ice:

4 inches - foot travel
5 inches - snowmobile or ATV
8 to 12 inches - car/small truck
12 to 15 inches - medium-sized truck

Lake Fishing -Warm Water Species

Channel Catfish *(Ictalurus punctatus)*

Preferred Water Temperatures: 70 to 75 degrees

Channel catfish are the most widespread catfish in Minnesota. They are found in lakes, reservoirs, ponds, big rivers, and streams. Most anglers fish on the bottom for channel cats, using prepared stinkbaits. Although channels will occasionally strike live bait and even lures, they prefer dead or inert matter such as chicken livers, gizzards, or nightcrawlers.

Channel cats are slow growing, but fish bigger than 20 pounds aren't uncommon. Catfish are most active at night (hot, muggy weather and heavy rainfall seems to really put them on the feed). In rivers and lakes, cats will move into the shallows in the evenings to eat. The key to catfishing is to find structure such as rocks or submerged timber, to fish near bottom, and to fish slow.

SPRING - Dead minnows or cut bait fished near bottom are good bets for spring catfish.

SUMMER - Fish on bottom with chicken livers, cheese, or other aromatic baits.

FALL - Prepared stinkbaits, nightcrawlers, crayfish, and shrimp all work well on fall channels. They'll also bite on a number of lures, including jigs, crankbaits, and spinners – the bigger the better.

WINTER - Few ice anglers specifically target catfish, but it's possible to attract a few fish using cut bait, nightcrawlers, or minnows. Drop the bait near bottom and let it remain motionless.

Flathead Catfish *(Pylodictis olivaris)*

Preferred Water Temperatures: 70 to 80 degrees

Flathead catfish are the largest catfish in Minnesota. The state record weighed 70 pounds.

Like channel catfish and bullheads, flatheads have scaleless bodies. They have four pairs of barbels on their faces that help them detect food, and sharp spines on their pectoral and dorsal fins. As their name suggests, they have a wide, flat head. A flathead's lower jaw sticks out farther than its upper jaw, which is one way to distinguish it from a channel cat. Flatheads have brown and yellow coloration that changes to gray or olive as the fish matures.

Many people are afraid of being "stung" by catfish. However, when people talk about being "stung" by catfish, they really are being poked by the sharp spines on the fins, and fish slime aggravates the wound, causing the "stinging" feeling. Small catfish can be handled in a manner that prevents "stinging." Put your hand over the fish's belly and slide your fingers underneath the pectoral fins protruding out either side of the body. This keeps the spiny pectoral and dorsal fins away from your hands. When handling larger fish, it's a good idea to wear gloves.

Flatheads are found in large rivers. They stay out of the main current flow, and instead, lie right on the bottom near rocks, sunken logs and in deep holes. Although small catfish will eat insects and other aquatic life, large cats feed almost exclusively on fish, and a big flathead can take down a pretty good-sized fish.

Flatheads mate at an unusual time of year – right in the middle of summer. The female lays her eggs in a sheltered spot. The male guards the eggs, even stirring them with his tail to oxygenate them, and guards the young after they hatch.

Although anglers often associate catfish with smelly baits like rotten chicken livers, that reputation belongs to channel cats. Flatheads are fish eaters, and the best baits are large, live minnows. Locate a deep hole out of the main current flow and pitch a live minnow weighted with a sinker heavy enough to keep your bait on the bottom. A stout rod equipped with a bait-casting reel and 20-pound line (or heavier) is the way to go for catfish. The best fishing is at night.

Bullheads

Preferred Water Temperatures: 70 to 75 degrees

Bullheads are one of the most common fish in Minnesota. They look very much like small catfish. They have no scales, relatively large heads and sensitive barbels on their face that help them detect food. Bullheads have sharp spines in their dorsal and pectoral fins. When people talk about being "stung" by bullheads, they really are being poked by these sharp spines, and fish slime aggravates the wound, causing the "stinging" feeling.

There are three bullhead species native to the state: brown, black and yellow. All look similar. Brown bullheads are the largest. The state record weighed 7 pounds, 1 ounce. Brown bullheads are dark green or brown in color, which distinguishes them from the lighter-colored yellow bullheads. They are similar in color to black bullheads, but lack the lighter crescent-shaped marking found near the tail of black bullheads. The state record yellow bullhead weighed 3 pounds, 10 ounces, while the state record black bullhead weighed 3 pounds, 13 ounces.

The fish spawn between April and June. They lay far fewer eggs than some species – only about 2,000 to 6,000 eggs – but both the male and female play a role in protecting the young, which helps their offspring survive. Females scoop out a hole in the soft bottom in which to lay her eggs. The male then guards the nest. After the young bullheads hatch, both parents protect them.

Bullheads live in a variety of different waters, including clear lakes and muddy ponds. They can tolerate a variety

of water temperatures, but are best known for their ability to survive in turbid waters with very low oxygen levels. In fact, in lakes that winterkill, bullheads may be the only fish species to survive.

Bullheads are opportunistic bottom feeders. They eat snails, leeches, worms, small fish, clams or almost anything else they can find. Bass, walleyes and northern pike eat small bullheads.

Many anglers despise bullheads, which they catch incidentally while fishing for bluegills or perch. This aversion to bullheads comes from the fish's rather ugly appearance and the concern over being "stung." However, the fish can be handled in a manner that prevents "stinging." Put your hand over the fish's belly and slide your fingers underneath the pectoral fins protruding out either side of the body. This keeps the spiny pectoral and dorsal fins away from your hands.

Although some people reject bullheads, there are many who embrace them. They are easy to catch, common across the state, and quite abundant. There is little concern of overharvesting this species, and the daily bag limit is 100 fish. A simple technique to catch these "whiskered" fish is to throw out a worm or nightcrawler on a spring or summer day and let it sit on the bottom of a good bullhead lake and wait for a bite.

White Bass *(Marone chrysops)*

Preferred Water Temperatures: 65 to 75 degrees

White bass are not widespread in Minnesota, but occur in large rivers and reservoirs in the southern part of the state. Where they do occur, they are found in large numbers and provide a real treat for anglers. The panfish are aggressive and will readily attack jigs, minnows, small crankbaits and spinners. They grow to a nice average length – often 12 inches or better – and fight with a spirit that belies their size. Plus, liberal limits allow anglers to catch 30 fish per day, and there is no closed season.

As their name suggests, white bass are white and have faint black horizontal bars along their body. They are members of the temperate bass family and are closely related to striped bass, although they are much smaller; the Minnesota state record weighs 4 pounds. Despite their name, they are unrelated to largemouth and smallmouth bass.

White bass make massive spawning runs in rivers sometime between late April and early June. A female white bass may lay a half-million eggs, although very few will survive. White bass do not build nests or guard their eggs. Rather, they simply drop them over gravel. Fishing during the spawning run can be fantastic, as fish congregate below dams, and limit catches are common. Three-way rigs, consisting of an egg sinker on a short line and a plain hook with a minnow or a streamer on another will get your bait to the bottom in heavy river current and produce fish. In shallower water where the fish are spawning, spinners and jigs with plastic grubs are productive.

White bass are good to eat, although later in the summer when the water warms, some people find their flesh to be a bit mushy. However, fish taken during the spawn have firm flesh and are excellent when fried or smoked. Fish caught in winter will also be firm, but few anglers target white bass in winter. At times, white bass can taste a bit fishy. Removing the "mud line" – the dark red area of the fillet, can avert this problem. To do this, fillet a white bass as normal, however, as you separate the fillet from the scales with your knife, allow a thin section of the meat to remain on the skin by raising the knife slightly off the scales.

White bass commonly form large schools in open water, as any walleye crankbait troller will begrudgingly attest. When you find these large schools, action can be intense. In summer, watch for flocks of seagulls circling overhead, as they will be hunting for baitfish (particularly gizzard shad) driven to the surface or injured by schools of marauding white bass. If you witness such a sight, approach quickly but quietly to avoid spooking the school. Stop the boat just at the edge of casting range and throw spinners, spoons or just about any small, flashy lure, particularly if it's white or silver. The action will be fast, but won't last long before the fish move. Stay alert and follow the school if you can.

LENGTH TO WEIGHT CONVERSION TABLE

Average Weight (pounds)

	Inland Lakes & Rivers Species								Inland Trout (Lakes)			
Inches	Largemouth Bass	Smallmouth Bass	Walleye	Northern Pike	Muskellunge	Channel Catfish	Flathead Catfish	Black Crappie	Rainbow Trout	Lake Trout	Brown Trout	Brook Trout
3.5	.0186	.0212	.0132	.0072	.0041	.0082	.0132	.0198	0.015	0.011	0.018	0.014
4.5	.0409	.0454	.0282	.0158	.0098	.0188	.0292	.0441	0.032	0.023	0.039	0.030
5.5	.0765	.0834	.0519	.0297	.0197	.0362	.0551	.0835	0.059	0.044	0.071	0.056
6.5	0.129	0.138	0.086	0.050	0.035	0.063	0.094	0.142	0.097	0.075	0.118	0.095
7.5	0.202	0.213	0.133	0.079	0.057	0.100	0.147	0.224	0.148	0.118	0.181	0.148
8.5	0.299	0.311	0.195	0.117	0.088	0.151	0.219	0.333	0.220	0.175	0.264	0.220
9.5	0.423	0.436	0.273	0.165	0.129	0.217	0.311	0.475	0.306	0.250	0.369	0.312
10.5	0.578	0.590	0.369	0.226	0.182	0.302	0.427	0.653	0.411	0.343	0.498	0.427
11.5	0.77	0.78	0.49	0.30	0.25	0.41	0.57	0.87	0.54	0.46	0.66	0.57
12.5	1.00	1.00	0.63	0.39	0.33	0.53	0.74	1.14	0.70	0.60	0.84	0.74
13.5	1.27	1.27	0.79	0.50	0.43	0.69	0.95	1.45	0.87	0.76	1.06	0.94
14.5	1.59	1.57	0.98	0.62	0.55	0.87	1.19	1.82	1.08	0.96	1.32	1.18
15.5	1.95	1.92	1.21	0.77	0.70	1.08	1.46	2.25	1.33	1.18	1.61	1.45
16.5	2.38	2.32	1.46	0.94	0.86	1.33	1.78		1.60	1.44	1.94	1.77
17.5	2.86	2.77	1.74	1.13	1.06	1.61	2.15		1.90	1.74	2.32	2.12
18.5	3.40	3.28	2.06	1.34	1.28	1.93	2.56		2.26	2.08	2.74	2.53
19.5	4.01	3.84	2.42	1.58	1.54	2.29	3.03		2.64	2.46	3.21	2.98
20.5	4.68	4.47	2.82	1.85	1.82	2.70	3.55		3.08	2.88	3.73	3.49
21.5	5.44	5.17	3.26	2.15	2.15	3.16	4.13		3.54	3.35	4.30	4.05
22.5	6.27	5.93	3.74	2.48	2.51	3.66	4.76		4.05	3.87	4.93	4.68
23.5	7.18	6.76	4.26	2.85	2.92	4.22	5.47		4.63	4.45	5.62	5.36
24.5	8.18	7.67	4.84	3.24	3.37	4.84	6.2 4		5.25	5.08	6.37	6.11
25.5	9.27	8.66	5.46	3.68	3.87	5.52	7.08		5.92	5.76	7.19	6.93
26.5			6.14	4.15	4.42	6.26	8.00		6.65	6.51	8.07	
27.5			6.87	4.66	5.02	7.07	8.99		7.44	7.33	9.02	
28.5			7.66	5.22	5.67	7.95	10.07		8.28	8.21	10.05	
29.5			8.50	5.81	6.39	8.90	11.23		9.18	9.16	11.14	
30.5			9.41	6.46	7.16	9.92	12.48		10.15	10.19	12.32	
31.5			10.40	7.10	8.00	11.00	13.80			11.30	13.60	
32.5			11.40	7.90	8.90	12.20	15.30			12.50	14.90	
33.5			12.50	8.70	9.90	13.50	16.80			13.70	16.30	
34.5			13.70	9.50	11.00	14.90	18.40			15.10	17.80	
35.5			14.90	10.40	12.10	16.30	20.20			16.50	19.50	
36.5				11.40	13.30	17.90	22.00			18.00		
37.5				12.40	14.60	19.50	24.00			19.60		
38.5				13.40	16.00	21.30	26.10			21.40		
39.5				14.50	17.50	23.20	28.30			23.20		
40.5					19.00							
41.5					20.42							
42.5					21.93							
43.5					23.52							
44.5					25.20							

Lake Fishing -Cold Water Species

Many rivers and streams in Minnesota's south are managed for trout, and are typically stocked with brook trout, rainbow trout, and brown trout. Many of these fisheries are located in the southeast, home to Minnesota's beautiful bluff country.

In addition, some lakes in the region are stocked with trout. These put-and-take fisheries are great places to introduce youngsters to angling.

Brook Trout *(Salvelinus fontinalis)*

Preferred Water Temperatures: 55 to 65 degrees

These beautifully colored fish are actually members of the char family. Because of their many red spots, brook trout are sometimes called "speckled trout." Brook trout are found in cool, clean, and well-oxygenated streams. They are intolerant of warm water and streams with marginal water quality.

Because they are very aggressive and often found near the edges of streams and rivers, most brook trout are caught before reaching sizes much bigger than 10 inches.

A 12-inch brookie is usually cause for celebration, and anything larger is reaching trophy size.

Brook trout are most active in spring and fall when the water is cool. Fish near overhanging trees, submerged wood, and rocks. As waters warm, brook trout move deeper, becoming harder to find. Look for pockets of deeper water or pools beneath waterfalls.

SPRING - Fish with small spinners or live bait; fly anglers do well with nymphs.

SUMMER - Flies and spinners work well on brookies in rivers and streams throughout summer. Live bait (where permitted) is also effective.

FALL - Brook trout are fall spawners. In river and stream systems, work near feeder creeks.

WINTER - Some streams in southern Minnesota have a special catch-and-release winter trout season from Jan. 1 to March 31. Check trout regulations for more information

Brown Trout *(Salmo trutta)*

Preferred Water Temperatures: 65 to 75 degrees

Although they are not native to Minnesota, brown trout have occupied a spot in North Star State streams, rivers, and Lake Superior for more than 100 years. Brown trout, or brownies as they are often referred to, are native to Europe.

Of the three stream trout species present in Minnesota, browns are most tolerant of warm water and can survive in waters uninhabitable by brook and rainbow trout. However, they can be the most difficult to catch. Feeding primarily at night and with a natural suspicion of artificial lures, brown trout can be very frustrating prey for anglers. Many a brown trout fisherman has experienced evenings when fish were feeding everywhere, on apparently everything, but would not bite on a lure. This is especially true when a mayfly hatch is on.

SPRING - Throw spinners, spoons, crankbaits, or nightcrawlers.

SUMMER - Fish at night with large dry flies or crankbaits. Mouse patterns are favorites with fly anglers.

FALL - Brown trout are fall spawners and will be found close to shore in autumn. Throw spinners and crankbaits along shorelines, lake inlets, and feeder creeks and streams.

WINTER - Use jig-and-minnow combos.

Rainbow Trout *(Oncorhynchus mykiss)*

Preferred Water Temperatures: 60 to 70 degrees

A flash of silver leaping from the water is an apt description of the scrappy rainbow trout. Like brown trout, rainbow trout are not native to Minnesota waters, but they have been stocked here for many decades and are now present in many lakes, rivers, and streams. Unlike brook and brown trout, rainbow trout reproduce in the spring.

Rainbows are able to thrive in waters too warm for brook trout but too cold for browns. Thus, they are often found in the same streams, at the margins of where the other two species range. In this and other respects, rainbows are the "trout in the middle," and often occupy waters holding brook or brown trout. They are less difficult to fool than a brown but not quite so easily caught as a brookie. Rainbow trout are strong and acrobatic battlers, often taking to the air when hooked. They favor stretches of fast-moving water such as ripples and stream bends.

SPRING - Use nightcrawlers, spoons, spinners, and crankbaits.

SUMMER - Dry flies, nymphs, spinners, spoons, and crankbaits are top lures. Nightcrawlers, marshmallows, and salmon eggs are excellent baits.

FALL - Fish on bottom with nightcrawlers or throw small lures.

WINTER - Target bays, drop-offs, and shallow, shoreline flats in 4 to 10 feet of water. Jigs or ice flies tipped with minnows or waxworms work well.

Following is a list of lakes accessible to the public with viable sport fisheries that are featured in Sportsman's Connection Fishing Map Guides. Each fishing map guide includes contour fishing maps, lake stocking and survey data and other fishing information.

www.scmaps.com or fine retailers everywhere

SPORTSMAN'S connection

SO Southern Minnesota Area Fishing Map Guide
EM East Metro Area Fishing Map Guide
WM West Metro Area Fishing Map Guide
AST Alexandria Area & Stearns / Todd Counties Fishing Map Guide

Southern Minnesota Fishing Lakes

ACCESS TYPE LEGEND
CD - Carry Down **CR** - Concrete Ramp **ER** - Earthen Ramp **GR** - Gravel Ramp **MR** - Metal Ramp **NC** - Navigable Channel **ND** - No Designated Access **PV** - Private **U** - Unknown **UR** - Unknown Ramp

Name	County	Pg / Coord	Acres	Max Depth	Clarity (ft)	Access Type	Camping	Pier	SC Guide	Walleye	Northern	Muskie	LM Bass	SM Bass	Bluegill	Crappie	Lake Trout	Rnbw Trout	Brown Trout	Brook Trout
Albert Lea	Freeborn	90-1C	2,654	5	3.6	CR			SO	•	•		•		•	•				
Alice	Washington	16-1E	25	9	5.0	CD		•	EM	•	•			•	•	•				
Alimagnet	Dakota	42-2B	89	11	3.0	CD			WM	•	•		•		•	•				
Allie	Renville	38-2A	451	12	4.0	CR			WM	•	•		•		•	•				
Amber	Martin	86-2C	180	19	1.3	CR		•	SO	•	•				•	•				
Andrew	Kandiyohi	8-3C	814	26	7.8	CR		•	WM	•	•		•		•	•				
Ann	Carver	27-5E	116	45	7.0	CR		•	WM		•		•		•	•				
Ann	Wright	26-1B	386	18	7.0	CR			WM	•	•		•		•	•				
Ann	Sherburne	13-4B	184	26	11.5	CR	•		EM		•		•		•	•				
Artichoke	Big Stone	5-5B	1,964	15	1.8	CR		•	AST	•	•		•		•	•				
Auburn	Carver	27-4E	261	84	7.9	CR			WM		•		•		•	•				
Augusta	Wright	11-5C	177	82	10.5	CR			WM	•	•		•		•	•				
Bald Eagle	Ramsey	29-4A	1,268	36	2.6	CR			EM	•	•	•	•		•	•				
Ballantyne	Blue Earth	54-3D	350	58	3.0	CR			SO	•	•				•	•				
Bass	Kandiyohi	9-5E	52	31	4.0	GR			WM	•	•				•	•				
Bass	Wright	11-6C	218	34	13.7	CR			WM	•	•		•	•	•	•				
Bass	Faribault	69-6E	203	20	4.5	CR			SO	•	•		•		•	•				
Battle Creek (Mud)	Washington	29-5D	103	14	8.0	CR		•	EM		•				•	•				
Bavaria	Carver	27-4E	162	66	5.0	GR			WM		•		•		•	•				
Beaver	Steele	72-1D	94	27	4.0	CR		•	SO	•	•		•		•	•				
Beaver	Stearns	11-5B	152	27	7.0	CR			AST		•		•		•	•				
Becker	Stearns	10-2A	176	20	8.5	CR			AST	•	•		•		•	•				
Beebe	Wright	13-4E	300	27	7.2	CR		•	WM	•	•		•		•	•				
Bella	Nobles	82-3D	182	14	1.1	CR			SO	•	•				•	•				
Belle	Meeker	24-3C	826	25	2.8	CR			WM	•	•		•		•	•				
Bennett	Ramsey	28-3C	23	9	5.0	CD	•	•	EM	•	•		•		•	•				
Benton	Lincoln	46-3C	2,857	9	1.5	CR		•	SO	•	•		•		•	•				
Bertram	Wright	12-3D	100	44	4.0	CR			WM		•		•		•	•				
Big	Stearns	10-2A	403	42	4.8	CR	•		AST	•	•		•		•	•				
Big	Sherburne	12-3C	251	48	9.5	CR		•	EM	•	•		•		•	•				
Big Stone	Big Stone	4-1A	12,610	16	11.9	CR	•	•	AST	•	•		•		•	•				
Birch	Sherburne	13-4B	151	18	2.5	CR			EM	•	•		•		•	•				
Birch	Wright	12-2C	76	52	7.7	CR			WM	•	•		•		•	•				
Blackhawk	Dakota	28-3E	54	12	4.3	ER		•	WM		•		•		•	•				
Bloody	Murray	48-3E	248	9	1.0	CR			SO	•	•				•	•				
Blue	Isanti	13-6A	309	31	5.0	CR			EM	•	•		•		•	•				
Bolting	Stearns	10-3A	104	36	3.5	NC			AST	•	•			•	•	•				
Bone (Bonny)	Washington	15-6D	210	30	9.5	CR			EM	•	•				•	•				
Brawner	Lyon	48-1B	28	18	10.5	CR			SO				•		•					
Bright	Martin	86-1D	645	7	0.9	CR			SO	•	•					•				
Brooks	Wright	25-5A	96	21	15.0	CR		•	WM		•		•		•					
Brownie	Hennepin	28-2C	12	47	4.0	CR			WM						•	•				
Browns, North	Stearns	10-2B	324	41	4.5	CR			AST	•	•		•		•	•				
Bryant	Hennepin	28-1E	161	45	5.4	CR		•	WM	•	•		•		•	•				
Budd	Martin	86-2C	222	23	1.8	CR			SO	•	•		•		•	•				
Buffalo	Wright	12-2E	1,552	33	2.7	CR		•	WM	•	•		•		•	•				
Buffalo	Murray	65-4A	124	8	1.3	CR			SO	•	•					•				
Bush	Hennepin	28-1E	172	28	16.8	CR		•	WM	•	•		•		•	•				
Butterfield	Watonwan	67-5C	N/A	10	1.0	CR			SO		•		•		•	•				
Byllesby	Dakota	43-5E	1,435	50	2.6	CR		•	WM	•	•				•	•				
Calhoun	Kandiyohi	9-5D	618	13	5.7	CR			WM	•	•		•		•	•				
Calhoun	Hennepin	28-2D	401	82	12.5	CR		•	WM	•	•		•		•	•				
Camp	Swift	7-6B	203	26	3.8	CR			AST	•	•		•		•	•				
Camp	Wright	11-6E	108	52	3.0	CR			WM	•	•		•		•	•				
Cannon	Rice	56-1D	1,591	15	2.0	CR			SO	•	•		•		•	•				
Carnelian	Stearns	11-4B	164	36	11.0	GR			AST	•	•		•		•	•				
Carnelian, Big	Washington	30-1A	463	66	9.0	CR			EM	•	•		•		•	•				
Caroline	Wright	11-5C	126	45	n/a	NC			WM	•	•		•		•	•				
Carrie	Kandiyohi	23-5A	81	26	9.2	GR			WM	•	•		•		•	•				
Carver	Washington	29-5D	51	36	n/a	ER			EM		•		•		•	•				
Cedar	Rice	56-1C	804	42	2.0	CR			SO	•	•		•		•	•				
Cedar	Martin	85-6A	710	7	2.1	CR			SO	•	•					•				
Cedar	Wright	12-1D	837	108	7.2	CR	•	•	WM	•	•		•		•	•				
Cedar	Hennepin	28-2C	169	51	5.5	CD		•	WM	•	•		•		•	•				
Cedar	Scott	41-5D	779	13	3.1	CR		•	WM	•	•		•		•	•				
Cedar Island	Stearns	10-2A	998	75	2.3	CR			AST	•	•		•	•	•	•				
Cenaiko	Anoka	28-2A	29	36	11.5	CD			EM							•	•	•	•	•
Centerville	Anoka	15-4E	455	19	3.2	CR	•		EM	•	•		•		•	•				
Chain, East	Martin	86-3D	485	6	0.8	CR			SO	•	•					•				
Champlin Mill Pond	Hennepin	14-1E	34	11	5.8	CD		•	WM		•				•	•				
Charlotte	Wright	26-3A	235	46	16.0	CR			WM	•	•		•		•	•				
Chisago (Kaner's)	Chisago	15-6C	873	34	6.5	NC			EM	•	•		•		•	•				
Christmas	Hennepin	27-5D	257	87	18.8	CR			WM	•	•		•		•			•		
Church	Carver	27-4E	12	54	2.0	CD			WM				•		•	•				
Circle	Rice	56-1A	624	14	n/a	CR			SO	•	•		•		•	•				
Clear	Jackson	84-2C	415	9	1.5	CR		•	SO	•	•				•	•				
Clear	Martin	86-1D	273	7	1.4	CR			SO	•						•				
Clear	Washington	15-4D	424	28	4.5	CR		•	EM	•	•				•	•				
Clear	Waseca	71-6A	652	34	2.8	CR	•		SO	•	•		•		•	•				
Clear	Le Sueur	55-4A	268	18	2.3	CR			SO	•	•		•		•	•				
Clear	Meeker	10-3D	497	18	1.5	CR	•		WM	•	•			•	•	•				
Clear	Lyon	47-6B	68	11	1.3	CR			SO	•	•		•		•	•				
Clear	Brown	52-2D	335	8	n/a	CR			SO	•			•		•	•				
Clear	Sibley	52-2A	469	8	n/a	CR			SO	•	•				•	•				
Clearwater	Wright	11-6C	3,158	73	7.4	CR	•		WM	•	•		•		•	•				
Cleary	Scott	42-1B	143	9	2.1	CD		•	WM	•			•		•					
Cody	Rice	55-6A	257	14	0.7	CR		•	SO	•	•		•		•	•				
Cokato	Wright	25-5A	539	52	10.0	CR	•	•	WM	•	•		•	•	•	•				
Colby	Washington	29-5D	70	11	2.0	CD			EM	•	•				•	•				
Collinwood	Wright	25-5B	584	28	2.5	CR	•	•	WM	•	•		•		•	•				
Comfort, Big	Chisago	15-5C	219	47	5.5	CR			EM	•	•				•	•				
Comfort, Little	Chisago	15-5C	36	56	3.8	CR			EM	•	•		•		•	•				
Como	Ramsey	28-3C	66	15	1.5	U		•	EM	•	•				•	•				
Constance	Wright	12-2E	161	23	2.0	CR			WM	•	•		•		•	•				
Coon	Anoka	14-3C	1,259	27	7.8	CR			EM	•	•		•	•	•	•				
Corabelle	Murray	64-2D	107	6	n/a	CR			SO		•					•				
Cottonwood	Cottonwood	66-2D	140	10	2.0	CR		•	SO	•	•		•		•	•				
Cottonwood	Lyon	34-3C	323	7	2.3	CR			SO	•	•				•					
Courthouse	Carver	41-5A	10	57	7.0	CD		•	WM	•	•					•	•	•	•	•
Crooked	Stearns	11-6B	65	35	10.5	CR			AST		•				•	•				
Crooked	Anoka	14-1E	117	26	6.0	CR		•	EM	•	•		•	•	•	•				
Crosby	Ramsey	28-3D	48	19	10.5	CD			EM		•				•	•				
Crystal	Blue Earth	69-5A	393	8	1.2	CR		•	SO	•	•				•	•				
Crystal	Dakota	42-2B	280	37	2.9	CR		•	WM		•		•		•	•				
Crystal	Hennepin	28-2B	78	39	3.3	GR		•	WM	•	•		•		•	•				
Current	Murray	47-6E	377	9	1.2	CR			SO	•	•					•				
Dead Coon	Lincoln	47-5B	569	9	2.4	CR			SO	•	•					•				
Dean	Wright	26-3A	173	20	3.5	CR			WM	•	•		•		•	•				
Deer	Wright	26-2A	163	27	4.5	CR			WM	•	•				•	•				
Demontreville	Washington	29-5B	143	24	16.5	CR			EM	•	•		•		•	•				
Diamond	Kandiyohi	9-5E	1,565	27	3.0	CR			WM	•	•				•	•				
Dog	Wright	26-1C	94	25	2.5	CR			WM		•		•		•	•				
Duck	Blue Earth	54-3D	282	25	n/a	CR			SO	•	•				•	•				
Dudley	Rice	56-1B	124	60	14.0	CR			SO		•		•		•	•				
Dunns	Meeker	10-3E	142	20	1.2	CR			WM	•	•				•	•				
Dutch	Hennepin	27-4D	159	45	2.3	GR			WM	•	•		•		•	•				
Dutch	Wright	26-1B	153	21	2.3	CR			WM		•		•		•	•				
Eagle	Blue Earth	54-2E	914	9	1.0	CR			SO	•	•				•	•				
Eagle	Kandiyohi	9-4E	824	67	8.5	CR			WM	•	•		•	•	•	•				
Eagle	Sherburne	13-4B	381	18	2.0	CR			EM	•	•		•		•	•				
Eagle	Carver	40-2A	233	14	n/a	CR	•		WM	•	•		•		•	•				
Eagle	Hennepin	28-1B	291	34	4.3	CR			WM	•	•	•	•		•	•				
Eagle (Little)	Wright	12-2D	244	38	4.2	GR			WM	•	•		•		•	•				
East Twin	Anoka	13-6C	158	68	9.6	ER			EM	•	•		•		•	•				
Eden	Stearns	10-2C	263	77	5.5	CR			AST	•	•		•		•	•				
Elizabeth	Kandiyohi	23-5B	1,054	9	4.0	CR			WM	•	•		•		•	•				
Elk, Big	Sherburne	12-2A	360	9	1.9	CR			EM	•	•		•		•	•				
Elk, Little	Sherburne	13-5A	353	15	2.5	CR			EM	•	•		•		•	•				
Elkhorn	Kandiyohi	9-4D	87	41	20.8	CR			WM	•	•		•		•	•				
Ella	Kandiyohi	23-5A	136	12	10.5	CR			WM	•	•		•		•	•				
Elmo	Washington	29-5C	206	140	14.0	CR		•	EM	•	•		•		•	•		•	•	
Elysian	Waseca	55-4E	1,902	13	n/a	CR		•	SO	•	•				•	•				
Emily	Le Sueur	54-2C	235	37	2.0	CR			SO	•	•		•		•	•				
Erie	Meeker	24-3C	182	34	4.5	CR			WM	•	•		•		•	•				
Farquar	Dakota	42-3A	67	10	0.8	CD			WM							•				
Fish	Wright	12-1B	98	38	3.0	CR			WM	•	•		•	•	•	•				
Fish	Martin	67-5E	175	5	0.9	CR			SO	•	•					•				
Fish	Hennepin	27-6A	223	48	2.7	CR		•	WM		•		•		•	•				
Fish	Le Sueur	55-4D	78	55	17.5	CR			SO		•				•	•				
Fish	Jackson	66-3D	300	26	5.0	CR			SO	•				•	•	•				
Fish	Scott	41-6C	171	28	6.5	CR	•		WM	•	•		•		•	•				
Fish	Dakota	28-3E	28	33	6.0	CR		•	WM		•		•		•	•				
Florida	Kandiyohi	8-3D	674	40	10.5	CR			WM	•	•		•		•	•				
Foot	Kandiyohi	22-3A	694	24	3.0	GR		•	WM	•	•		•		•	•				
Forest	Washington	15-5D	2,251	37	6.3	CR	•		EM	•	•	•	•		•	•				
Fountain	Freeborn	90-1B	534	14	2.0	CR		•	SO	•	•				•	•				
Fox	Rice	56-2B	308	47	2.0	CR		•	SO	•	•				•	•				
Fox	Murray	48-3E	174	8	1.2	CR			SO	•	•				•	•				
Fox	Martin	85-6B	1,041	20	2.5	CR	•	•	SO	•	•	•			•	•				
Francis	Meeker	11-5D	921	17	7.0	CR			WM	•	•		•		•	•				
Francis	Le Sueur	55-4D	797	60	8.5	CR			SO	•	•		•		•	•				
Freeborn	Freeborn	89-5A	2,222	6	0.4	CR			SO							•				
Fremont	Sherburne	13-5A	484	8	3.3	CR			EM		•		•		•	•				
French	Wright	11-5E	332	50	5.0	CR			WM	•	•		•		•	•				
French	Rice	56-1C	816	56	14.0	CR			WM	•		•			•	•				
French	McLeod	24-3C	94	23	3.2	NC			WM	•	•				•	•				
Fulda, First	Murray	64-3D	179	7	1.0	CR		•	SO	•	•		•		•	•				
Fulda, Second	Murray	64-3D	60	5	1.6	CR		•	SO	•	•				•	•				
Games	Kandiyohi	8-3C	515	42	8.5	CR			WM	•	•		•		•	•				
George	Martin	86-2B	84	11	1.5	CR			SO	•	•				•	•				
George	Kandiyohi	9-4D	231	34	15.5	CR			WM	•	•		•		•	•				
George	Anoka	14-2C	495	32	13.8	CR			EM	•	•		•		•	•				

Name	County	Pg / Coord	Acres	Max Depth	Clarity (ft)	Access Type	Camping	Pier	SC Guide	Walleye	Northern	Muskie	LM Bass	SM Bass	Bluegill	Crappie	Lake Trout	Rnbw Trout	Brown Trout	Brook Trout
George	Blue Earth	54-2D	80	28	1.3	CR			SO		•		•		•	•				
German	Le Sueur	55-4C	899	51	5.0	CR			SO	•	•		•		•	•				
Gervais	Ramsey	29-4C	234	41	3.0	NC			EM	•	•		•		•	•				
Gleason	Hennepin	27-6C	142	16	8.0	CD			WM	•	•		•		•	•				
Golden	Anoka	28-3A	57	25	5.0	CR		•	EM	•	•		•		•	•				
Goodners	Stearns	11-4B	150	24	3.0	CR			AST		•		•		•	•				
Goose	Washington	16-1D	74	25	14.1	CR			EM		•		•		•	•				
Goose	Wright	26-2A	42	14	1.1	NC			WM		•		•		•	•				
Goose, East	Lyon	47-5A	139	9	1.7	CR			SO	•			•			•				
Gorman	Le Sueur	55-4B	499	14	6.0	CR			SO	•	•		•		•	•				
Graham, East	Nobles	65-4E	604	8	1.3	GR			SO	•	•					•				
Graham, West	Nobles	65-4E	515	8	1.1	CR			SO	•	•					•				
Grand	Stearns	11-4A	655	34	4.0	CR	•		AST	•	•		•		•	•				
Granite	Wright	11-6E	339	34	6.0	CR			WM	•	•		•		•	•				
Great Northern	Stearns	10-3A	356	19	n/a	NC			AST	•	•				•	•				
Green	Chisago	15-5C	1,714	32	7.0	CR			EM	•	•		•		•	•				
Green	Kandiyohi	9-4D	5,406	110	9.5	CR	•	•	WM	•	•		•	•	•	•				
Greenleaf	Meeker	24-3C	224	18	2.4	CR			WM	•	•				•	•				
Haften	Hennepin	27-4A	43	44	3.0	ER			WM		•		•		•	•				
Half Moon	Hennepin	27-5B	28	25	4.0	CD			WM	•	•		•		•	•				
Hall	Martin	86-2C	513	27	2.4	CR			SO	•					•	•				
Ham	Anoka	14-3D	174	22	6.8	CR	•		EM		•				•	•				
Hanlos	Ramsey	29-4B	7	7	n/a	ND			EM		•				•	•				
Hanska	Brown	52-1E	1,773	16	n/a	CR		•	SO	•	•		•		•	•				
Harriet	Hennepin	28-2D	335	87	9.5	CR		•	WM	•	•	•	•		•	•				
Henderson	Kandiyohi	9-4D	73	57	13.7	CR			WM	•	•		•		•	•				
Hendricks	Lincoln	32-2E	1,557	12	2.0	CR	•		SO	•	•					•				
Hiawatha	Hennepin	28-2D	53	33	5.0	CD		•	WM	•	•				•	•				
Holland	Dakota	42-3A	32	55	13.6	CD			WM		•		•		•	•		•	•	
Hook	McLeod	25-4C	327	18	0.9	CR			WM	•	•		•		•	•				
Horseshoe	Le Sueur	55-5D	393	26	2.2	CR			SO	•	•				•	•				
Horseshoe	Stearns	10-2A	550	57	3.0	CR			AST	•	•		•	•	•	•				
Howard	Wright	26-1B	717	39	3.5	CR	•	•	WM	•	•		•		•	•				
Hunt	Rice	56-1C	159	27	1.7	CR			SO	•	•		•		•	•				
Hunter	Sherburne	13-5A	58	6	1.0	CR			EM				•		•	•				
Hunter, E	Sherburne	13-6A	54	7	1.5	NC			EM						•	•				
Hydes	Carver	26-2E	214	18	3.8	CR			WM	•	•		•		•	•				
Hyland	Hennepin	28-1E	84	12	10.0	CR		•	WM	•			•		•	•				
Ida	Blue Earth	69-6C	120	8	0.8	CR			SO	•	•		•		•	•				
Ida	Wright	12-2C	231	60	15.0	CR			WM		•		•		•	•				
Ida	Wright	26-1C	79	26	2.3	ER			WM		•		•		•	•				
Independence	Hennepin	27-4B	844	58	3.0	CR		•	WM	•	•	•	•		•	•				
Indian	Nobles	83-4D	204	6	1.6	CR			SO	•	•				•	•				
Indian	Wright	12-1C	146	31	3.0	CR			WM	•	•		•		•	•				
Island	Lyon	47-5A	163	8	0.5	CR			SO		•									
Island	Ramsey	28-3B	59	11	2.1	CR		•	EM	•	•		•		•	•				
Jane	Washington	29-5C	145	39	17.0	CR			EM		•		•		•	•				
Jefferson, East	Le Sueur	54-3C	700	37	4.0	CR	•		SO	•	•		•		•	•				
Jefferson, West	Le Sueur	54-3C	441	24	1.5	CR			SO	•	•		•		•	•				
Jennie	Meeker	25-4C	1,056	15	3.5	CR		•	WM	•	•		•		•	•				
Johanna	Ramsey	28-3B	213	43	9.5	CR			EM	•	•		•		•	•				
Johanna	Pope	8-2A	1,584	10	8.0	CR			AST	•	•		•		•	•				
John	Wright	11-5D	411	28	7.3	CR			WM	•	•		•		•	•				
Jordan Mill Pond	Scott	41-4C	17	7	1.5	CD			WM	•	•				•	•				
Josephine	Ramsey	28-3B	118	44	6.8	CR			EM	•	•		•		•	•				
Kandiyohi, Big	Kandiyohi	23-4C	2,692	15	2.8	CR			WM	•	•			•	•	•				
Kansas	Watonwan	67-6D	398	7	1.8	CR		•	SO	•	•		•		•	•				
Keller	Ramsey	29-4C	72	8	2.0	NC			EM	•			•		•	•				
Keller	Dakota	42-2B	51	7	n/a	CD			WM		•		•		•	•				
Kelly	Rice	56-1B	62	0	n/a	CR			SO		•		•		•	•				
Knaus	Stearns	10-3A	205	20	n/a	CR			AST	•	•		•		•	•				
Kohlman	Ramsey	29-4B	74	9	2.0	NC			EM	•			•		•	•				
Kohlmeier (Kohlmier)	Steele	72-2A	32	14	13.0	CR		•	SO	•	•				•	•				
Koronis	Stearns	10-1C	3,014	132	5.2	CR	•		AST	•	•		•	•	•	•				
Krays	Stearns	10-3A	85	40	n/a	NC			AST	•	•				•	•				
Kroon	Chisago	15-6C	192	30	6.2	CR			EM	•	•		•		•	•				
Laclavon	Dakota	42-2B	55	32	10.0	CD			WM		•		•	•	•	•		•		
Lady Slipper	Lyon	34-3D	247	11	1.2	CR			SO	•					•					
Lake Of The Isles	Hennepin	28-2C	109	31	2.0	CR			WM	•	•		•		•	•				
Langton	Ramsey	28-3B	30	5	4.5	CD		•	EM						•	•				
Lillian	Kandiyohi	23-5C	1,149	7	2.3	CR			WM	•	•		•	•	•	•				
Lily	Washington	29-6B	35	51	6.5	CR		•	EM	•	•		•		•	•				
Lily	Waseca	55-4E	59	23	12.0	CR			SO	•	•		•		•	•				
Lime	Murray	64-3C	338	7	0.8	CR			SO		•					•				
Limestone	Wright	12-1C	188	34	8.3	ER	•		WM	•	•		•		•	•				
Lindstrom, North	Chisago	15-6B	137	29	6.0	GR			EM	•	•		•		•	•				
Lindstrom, South	Chisago	15-6B	499	34	7.8	CR		•	EM	•	•		•		•	•				
Linwood	Anoka	15-4C	559	42	4.0	CR		•	EM	•	•		•		•	•				
Little	Chisago	16-1B	159	23	3.4	CR			EM	•	•				•	•				
Locke	Wright	12-2B	156	49	4.3	CR			WM	•	•		•	•	•	•				
Loeb (Marydale)	Ramsey	28-3C	9	28	6.0	ND		•	EM	•	•		•	•	•	•				
Lone	Hennepin	28-1D	22	27	n/a	CD		•	WM						•	•				
Long	Ramsey	28-3B	183	30	4.5	CR		•	EM	•	•				•	•				
Long	Watonwan	68-1D	264	13	2.9	CR			SO	•	•		•		•	•				
Long	Stearns	10-2B	460	35	3.5	CR	•		AST	•	•		•	•	•	•				
Long	Isanti	14-1A	390	15	1.5	CR			EM	•	•		•		•	•				
Long	Kandiyohi	9-5C	286	46	16.2	CR	•		WM	•	•		•		•	•				
Long	Hennepin	27-5C	261	33	n/a	CR			WM	•	•				•	•		•		
Long	Meeker	25-4A	163	28	9.7	CR	•		WM	•	•		•		•	•				
Long	Kandiyohi	8-3E	1,575	16	10.6	CR			WM	•	•		•		•	•				
Long	Stearns	11-6B	49	38	10.5	CR			AST	•	•		•		•	•				
Long	Sherburne	12-1A	182	26	16.0	CD			EM	•	•		•		•	•				
Long Tom	Big Stone	4-3B	133	15	3.8	CR			AST	•	•		•		•	•				
Long, Little	Hennepin	27-4D	108	76	15.8	CR			WM		•				•			•		

Name	County	Pg / Coord	Acres	Max Depth	Clarity (ft)	Access Type	Camping	Pier	SC Guide	Walleye	Northern	Muskie	LM Bass	SM Bass	Bluegill	Crappie	Lake Trout	Rnbw Trout	Brown Trout	Brook Trout
Loon	Jackson	84-2D	679	7	2.7	CR	•	•	SO	•	•					•				
Loon	Blue Earth	69-5A	755	7	1.1	CR			SO	•	•				•	•				
Loon	Waseca	71-5A	122	9	1.1	CR			SO		•		•		•	•				
Lost	Washington	29-5B	9	26	7.0	ND		•	EM		•		•		•	•				
Lotus	Carver	27-5E	246	29	n/a	CR		•	WM	•	•		•		•	•				
Louisa	Wright	11-5C	194	44	3.7	NC			WM	•	•		•		•	•				
Louisa	Murray	65-4B	298	8	0.8	ER			SO	•	•					•				
Lower Penn	Hennepin	28-2E	31	7	1.0	CR			WM						•	•				
Lucy	Carver	27-5E	92	20	5.0	ER			WM		•		•		•	•				
Lura	Blue Earth	70-1D	1,224	9	n/a	CR	•	•	SO	•	•		•		•	•				
Madison	Blue Earth	54-3E	1,113	59	4.0	CR	•	•	SO	•	•		•		•	•				
Manuella	Meeker	24-3B	286	51	8.8	CR			WM	•	•			•	•	•				
Maple	Wright	12-2D	777	76	8.8	CR			WM	•	•		•		•	•				
Marie	Stearns	11-5C	147	36	3.5	CD			WM	•	•		•		•	•				
Marine, Big	Washington	15-6E	1,756	60	9.0	CR			EM	•	•		•		•	•				
Marion	Dakota	42-2C	560	21	8.8	CR		•	WM	•	•		•		•	•				
Marion	McLeod	38-3A	594	12	n/a	CR		•	WM	•	•		•		•	•				
Martha	Wright	27-4A	97	22	11.0	CR			WM		•		•		•	•				
Martin	Anoka	15-4B	234	20	1.5	CR			EM	•	•		•		•	•				
Mary	Wright	12-1D	209	102	5.5	GR			WM	•	•		•		•	•				
Mary	Wright	26-1C	196	47	6.5	CR			WM	•	•		•		•	•				
Mazaska	Rice	56-1B	685	50	2.3	CR			SO	•	•		•		•	•				
McCarrons	Ramsey	28-3C	68	57	8.4	CR		•	EM	•	•				•	•				
McColl Pond	Scott	42-1A	21	11	5.8	CD		•	WM				•		•	•				
McMahon (Carl's)	Scott	42-1C	110	14	2.5	CR			WM	•	•		•		•	•				
Medicine	Hennepin	28-1C	886	49	5.5	CR		•	WM	•	•		•		•	•				
Mink	Wright	12-1D	301	39	n/a	CR			WM	•	•		•		•	•				
Minnetonka	Hennepin	27-5D	14,004	113	10.9	CR		•	WM	•		•								
Minnewashta	Carver	27-5E	738	70	13.5	CR		•	WM	•	•		•		•	•				
Minnie Belle	Meeker	24-2B	545	49	16.0	CR		•	WM	•	•		•		•	•				
Mitchell	Sherburne	12-3C	170	33	10.5	CR			EM	•	•		•		•	•				
Mitchell	Hennepin	27-6E	112	19	2.5	CR		•	WM	•	•		•		•	•				
Monson	Swift	8-1C	152	21	7.8	CR			AST	•	•		•		•	•				
Mooney	Hennepin	27-5C	118	10	n/a	GR			WM		•				•	•				
Moore	Anoka	28-2B	108	22	n/a	CD			EM	•	•		•		•	•				
Moose (Moses)	Wright	11-5D	88	43	15.5	CR			WM		•		•		•	•				
Morin	Freeborn	89-5B	21	7	2.5	CR			SO	•					•	•				
Mountain	Cottonwood	67-4C	241	8	2.0	CR	•	•	SO	•	•		•		•	•				
Mud (Vails)	Stearns	10-2C	151	20	5.0	CR			AST	•	•		•		•	•				
Mud, Little	Meeker	10-3D	37	42	2.9	CR			WM				•	•	•	•		•		
Nest	Kandiyohi	9-4D	945	40	9.8	CR			WM	•	•		•	•	•	•				
Nixon	Wright	12-1C	56	67	9.0	CR			WM		•		•		•	•				
Nokomis	Hennepin	28-2D	204	33	2.0	CR		•	WM	•			•		•	•				
North Center	Chisago	15-6B	725	46	3.4	CR	•		EM	•	•		•		•	•				
Norway	Kandiyohi	8-2C	2,344	33	3.5	CR			WM	•	•		•		•	•				
O'Dowd	Scott	41-5B	258	22	1.8	CR		•	WM	•	•		•		•	•				
Ocheda	Nobles	82-3D	1,917	5	1.0	CR			SO	•	•					•				
Okabena	Nobles	82-3C	751	16	3.0	CR	•	•	SO	•	•		•		•	•				
Olson	Washington	29-5C	79	15	5.1	CR			EM	•	•		•		•	•				
Orchard	Dakota	42-2B	234	33	8.8	CR			WM	•	•		•		•	•				
Orono	Sherburne	13-5C	281	18	0.8	CR	•		EM	•	•			•	•	•				
Otter	McLeod	24-3D	583	6	1.0	CR			WM	•	•		•		•	•				
Otter	Anoka	29-4A	332	21	9.0	CR			EM		•				•	•				
Owasso	Ramsey	28-3B	384	37	7.0	CR			EM	•	•	•	•		•	•				
Parkers	Hennepin	27-6C	97	37	13.5	CR			WM		•				•	•				
Parley	Carver	27-4E	242	18	6.0	CR			WM	•	•				•	•				
Pearl	Stearns	11-4B	733	17	3.7	CR			AST	•	•		•		•	•				
Peltier	Anoka	15-4E	465	18	2.8	CR		•	EM	•	•		•		•	•				
Pepin	Goodhue	45-5E	25,060	60	n/a	CR			SO	•	•					•				
Perch	Lincoln	32-3D	224	16	2.0	CD			SO	•	•		•		•					
Phalen	Ramsey	29-4C	198	91	5.5	CR		•	EM	•	•		•		•	•				
Pickerel	Sherburne	12-1A	121	21	9.0	CD			EM		•				•	•				
Pike (Eagle)	Hennepin	28-1B	57	22	4.4	NC			WM		•		•		•	•				
Pleasant	Wright	11-6D	509	74	11.5	CR		•	WM	•	•		•		•	•				
Point	Kandiyohi	8-3E	164	32	5.8	CR			WM	•	•		•		•	•				
Pool 2, Mississippi River	Dakota	43-5A	11,810	0	n/a	CR		•	EM	•	•		•		•	•				
Powderhorn	Hennepin	28-2D	12	22	3.0	ND		•	WM		•				•	•				
Preston	Renville	38-2A	670	11	1.5	CR			WM	•	•		•		•	•				
Prior, Lower	Scott	42-1B	810	60	9.5	CR		•	WM	•	•				•	•				
Prior, Upper	Scott	42-1B	354	50	3.5	CR			WM	•	•		•		•	•				
Pulaski	Wright	12-3E	702	87	8.0	CR			WM	•	•		•		•	•				
Quigley (Carlson)	Dakota	42-3A	11	19	n/a	CD			WM	•			•		•	•				
Ramsey	Wright	12-1E	275	80	4.0	CR			WM	•	•		•		•	•				
Rays (Charles)	Le Sueur	55-4D	156	32	1.5	GR		•	SO	•	•				•	•				
Rebecca	Dakota	43-6A	77	15	2.5	CR			WM	•	•	•	•	•	•	•				
Rebecca	Hennepin	26-3B	254	30	2.5	CR			WM			•			•	•				
Red Rock	Hennepin	27-6E	92	16	10.0	CR			WM	•	•		•		•	•				
Reeds	Waseca	55-5E	187	58	12.5	GR			SO	•	•		•		•	•				
Reitz	Carver	26-3E	79	36	3.5	CR			WM		•		•		•	•				
Rice	Hennepin	27-6A	314	11	2.5	CD			WM		•		•		•	•				
Rice	Stearns	10-1B	1,639	41	4.6	CR	•		AST	•	•			•	•	•				
Richardson	Meeker	10-3E	111	47	2.9	CR			WM	•	•		•		•	•				
Riley	Carver	27-5E	297	49	3.5	CR		•	WM	•	•		•		•	•				
Ringo	Kandiyohi	9-4D	716	10	1.2	CR			WM	•	•		•		•	•				
Ripley	Meeker	24-2A	558	18	5.1	CR			WM	•	•		•		•	•				
Roberds	Rice	56-1C	625	43	2.5	CR	•		SO	•	•				•	•				
Rock	Wright	12-1E	175	37	5.8	CR			WM	•	•		•		•	•				
Rock	Lyon	48-1C	439	7	1.0	CR			SO	•	•					•				
Roemhildts	Le Sueur	55-4D	72	60	6.5	CR			SO		•		•		•	•				
Rogers	Dakota	28-3E	99	8	6.0	CD		•	WM	•	•		•		•	•				
Round	Jackson	83-5D	1,024	9	1.0	CR	•		SO	•	•					•				
Round	Hennepin	27-6E	33	37	14.3	CR		•	WM	•			•		•	•				
Rush	Sherburne	12-2A	142	11	1.9	CR			EM	•	•		•		•	•				
Sabre	Le Sueur	55-4C	263	13	7.0	ER			SO	•	•		•		•	•				

Southern Minnesota Fishing Lakes

Name	County	Pg / Coord	Acres	Max Depth	Clarity (ft)	Access Type	Camping	Pier	SC Guide	Walleye	Northern	Muskie	LM Bass	SM Bass	Bluegill	Crappie	Lake Trout	Rnbw Trout	Brown Trout	Brook Trout
Sakatah, Lower	Le Sueur	55-5D	310	7	2.0	U	•		SO	•	•		•		•	•				
Sandy	Sherburne	13-5A	62	41	11.5	CD			EM		•		•		•	•				
Sarah	Murray	48-2E	1,093	11	2.5	CR			SO	•	•					•				
Sarah	Hennepin	27-4B	574	59	1.8	GR			WM		•		•		•	•				
Scandinavian	Pope	8-1A	424	49	10.0	CR			AST	•	•		•		•	•				
Schneider	Stearns	10-3A	54	52	n/a	NC			AST	•	•				•	•				
School Grove	Lyon	35-4D	318	11	1.6	CR			SO	•	•					•				
School Section	Stearns	11-4C	188	12	9.0	CR			AST		•		•		•	•				
Schutz	Carver	27-4E	105	49	n/a	CD			WM		•		•		•	•				
Shady Oak	Hennepin	28-1D	85	35	n/a	CD		•	WM		•		•		•	•				
Shaokotan	Lincoln	46-2A	995	10	2.2	CR		•	SO	•	•				•					
Shetek	Murray	48-3E	3,596	10	n/a	CR			SO	•	•					•				
Shields	Rice	56-1B	872	42	8.0	CR	•		SO	•	•		•		•	•				
Silver	Wright	12-1C	78	42	7.0	ER			WM	•	•				•	•				
Silver	McLeod	25-5D	472	10	n/a	CR			WM	•	•		•		•	•				
Silver	Ramsey	28-3B	69	47	4.0	GR			EM	•	•				•	•				
Silver	Ramsey	29-5B	72	18	6.8	CR		•	EM	•	•		•	•	•	•				
Silver	Sibley	40-1C	621	8	1.0	CR			SO	•					•	•				
Silver, South	Martin	86-2D	245	22	2.5	CR	•		SO	•	•		•		•	•				
Sisseton	Martin	86-2B	140	19	2.0	CR		•	SO	•			•		•	•				
Skifstrom	Wright	25-5A	55	65	5.5	GR			WM		•				•	•				
Sleepy Eye	Brown	51-6C	227	21	2.5	CR		•	SO		•		•		•	•				
Smith	Murray	64-3A	93	9	n/a	ND			SO		•									
Snail	Ramsey	28-3B	150	30	9.0	CR			EM	•	•		•		•	•				
Solomon, East	Kandiyohi	8-3E	706	14	12.0	CR			WM	•	•		•		•	•				
Somers	Wright	12-1D	158	21	n/a	CR			WM	•	•		•		•	•				
South Center	Chisago	15-6B	835	109	3.0	CR			EM	•	•		•		•	•				
Spoon	Ramsey	29-4C	6	6	2.0	CR			EM		•				•	•				
Spring	Meeker	25-4A	218	30	4.0	CR			WM		•		•		•	•				
Spring	Scott	41-6B	580	37	2.5	CR			WM	•	•		•		•	•				
Spurzem	Hennepin	27-5B	70	38	2.7	CR			WM		•		•		•	•				
Square	Washington	30-1A	195	68	21.6	CR	•	•	EM		•		•		•	•		•		
St. Croix	Washington	30-1D	8,209	78	3.3	CR		•	EM	•	•	•		•	•	•				
St. James	Watonwan	68-1C	252	16	n/a	CR			SO	•	•		•		•	•				
St. Joe (Little Joe)	Carver	27-5E	14	52	10.0	ER			WM		•		•		•					
St. Olaf	Waseca	72-1D	99	33	7.0	CR		•	SO		•		•		•	•				
Stahls (Stahlis)	McLeod	24-3C	142	37	4.8	CR			WM	•	•		•		•	•				
Star	Meeker	24-2B	557	15	2.8	CR			WM	•	•				•	•				
Starring	Hennepin	27-6E	155	16	3.1	CR		•	WM		•				•	•				
Stay, East	Lincoln	47-4A	224	6	0.8	CR			SO	•	•									
Steele	Le Sueur	55-4D	69	27	2.1	GR			SO		•		•		•	•				
Steep Bank (Dane)	Lincoln	32-3D	208	6	1.5	CR			SO	•										
Steiger (Victoria)	Carver	27-4E	158	37	3.2	GR		•	WM	•	•		•		•	•				
Stella	Meeker	24-3B	553	75	5.5	CR			WM	•	•		•	•	•	•				
Sugar	Wright	12-1C	1,015	69	8.0	CR			WM	•	•	•	•		•	•				
Sullivan	Wright	12-2D	73	58	6.0	CR			WM	•	•		•		•	•				
Summit	Murray	64-1B	77	7	1.5	ER			SO	•	•		•		•	•				
Sunfish	Le Sueur	55-5C	119	30	n/a	CR			SO		•		•		•	•				
Susan (Suzan)	Carver	27-5E	93	17	7.5	CR		•	WM	•	•		•		•	•				
Swan	McLeod	25-5D	343	10	n/a	CR		•	WM	•	•				•	•				
Swan, Big	Meeker	25-4A	628	32	4.1	CR			WM	•	•			•	•	•				
Swan, Little	Meeker	25-4A	45	31	6.5	CR			WM	•	•		•		•	•				
Swenson	Kandiyohi	8-2D	109	14	6.0	CR			WM	•	•				•	•				
Sylvia	Wright	11-5D	652	78	17.0	CR			WM	•	•		•		•	•				
Taft	Hennepin	28-2D	12	45	4.5	CD			WM	•	•		•		•	•				
Tanners	Washington	29-5C	70	46	10.5	CR	•	•	EM	•	•				•	•				
Tetonka	Le Sueur	55-5D	1,336	35	9.0	CR	•	•	SO	•	•		•	•	•	•				
Thole/Schneider	Scott	41-5B	105	12	2.0	CR			WM	•	•		•		•	•				
Turtle	Ramsey	28-3A	408	28	4.5	CR			EM	•	•		•		•	•				
Twin, Big	Martin	85-5A	457	18	0.7	ER			SO	•	•		•		•	•				
Twin, East	Lyon	47-5D	352	22	3.2	CR			SO	•				•	•					
Twin, West	Lyon	47-5D	232	10	9.5	CD			SO						•					
Typo	Isanti	15-4B	295	6	1.5	CR			EM	•	•		•		•	•				
Union	Rice	56-2A	403	10	1.2	CD			SO	•	•				•					
Union	Wright	11-5D	88	35	4.0	CR			WM	•	•		•		•	•				
Vadnais, East	Ramsey	29-4B	394	58	8.0	ND			EM	•	•		•	•	•	•				
Virginia	Carver	27-4D	110	34	10.5	CR			WM	•	•	•	•		•	•				
Volney	Le Sueur	55-4B	283	67	15.0	CR			SO	•	•				•	•				
Wabasso	Ramsey	28-3B	46	66	13.0	CR			EM		•		•		•	•				
Waconia	Carver	26-3E	2,996	37	4.0	CR		•	WM	•	•	•	•		•	•				
Wagonga	Kandiyohi	23-4B	1,664	15	1.9	CR			WM	•	•					•				
Warner	Stearns	12-1B	27	38	8.0	CR		•	AST		•		•		•	•				
Washington	Le Sueur	54-2D	1,487	51	2.2	CR			SO	•	•		•		•	•				
Washington	Meeker	25-4B	2,639	17	3.9	CR			WM	•	•		•	•	•	•				
Wasserman (Plancher)	Carver	27-4E	153	41	2.0	CR			WM		•		•		•	•				
Waverly, Big	Wright	26-2B	485	70	3.0	CR		•	WM	•	•		•		•	•				
Waverly, Little	Wright	26-1B	330	12	3.5	CR			WM	•	•		•		•	•				
Weaver	Hennepin	27-6A	149	57	3.4	CR		•	WM	•	•		•		•	•				
Wells (Bully Wells)	Rice	56-2C	634	4	1.5	CR		•	SO	•	•		•		•	•				
West Sylvia (Twin)	Wright	11-5D	872	97	n/a	CR			WM	•	•		•		•	•				
Whaletail	Hennepin	27-4D	558	25	1.5	CR			WM		•		•		•	•				
White Bear	Washington	29-5B	2,416	83	15.5	CR		•	EM	•	•	•	•	•	•	•				
Willie	Meeker	24-2C	182	17	2.8	CR			WM	•	•		•		•	•				
Willmar	Kandiyohi	22-3A	435	14	2.0	CR			WM	•	•		•		•	•				
Wilmert	Martin	86-2D	362	8	2.1	CR			SO	•					•	•				
Winona	Winona	77-6B	319	38	4.1	CR		•	SO	•	•		•		•	•				
Winsted	McLeod	26-1C	376	12	2.1	CR			WM		•				•	•				
Wirth	Hennepin	28-2C	38	25	3.5	CR		•	WM	•	•		•		•	•				
Wolf (Big Wolf)	Meeker	25-4C	259	11	5.0	CR			WM	•	•		•		•	•				
Wood (Marguerite)	Lyon	47-5B	367	14	7.0	CR			SO	•	•		•		•					
Yankton	Lyon	48-1C	387	8	n/a	CR		•	SO	•	•				•	•				
Zumbra (Sunny)	Carver	27-4D	162	58	7.3	GR			WM		•		•		•	•				
Zumwalde	Stearns	10-3A	106	23	n/a	U			AST	•	•				•	•				

A FEW KNOTS YOU SHOULD KNOW

PALOMAR KNOT

A popular and easy to tie knot for small terminal tackle connections. It is one of the few recommended knots for use with braided lines.

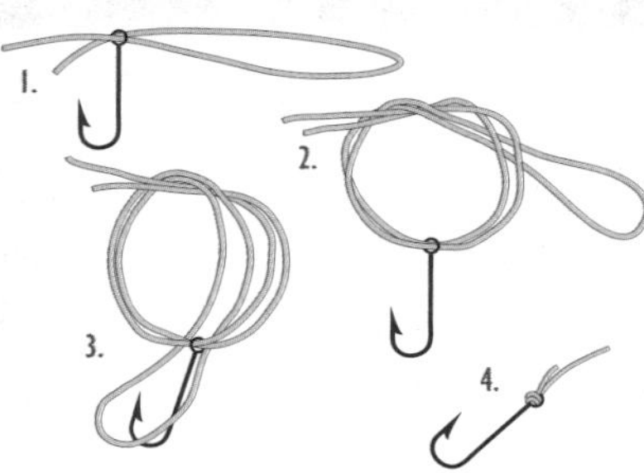

1. Double 4 to 6 inches of line and pass loop through eye of hook or lure. **2.** Tie a loose overhand knot in doubled line with hook hanging from bottom. **3.** Holding overhand knot between thumb and forefinger, pass loop of line over hook or lure. **4.** Pull both standing line and tag end to tighten knot down onto eye. Clip tag end.

IMPROVED CLINCH KNOT

This knot has become one of the most popular knots for tying terminal tackle connections. It is quick and easy to tie and is strong and reliable. However, it is not recommended for use with braided lines.

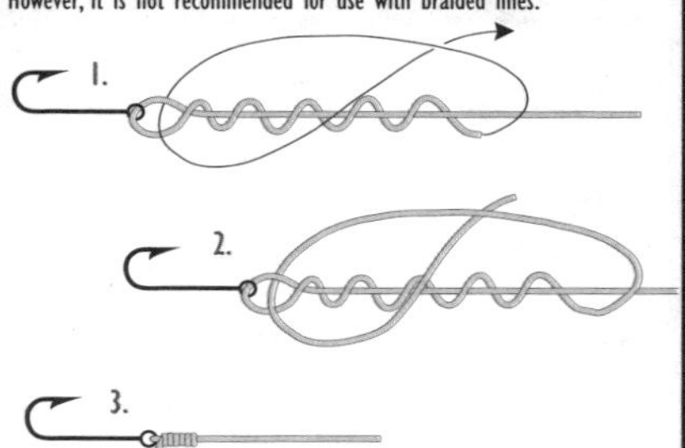

1. Thread end of line through eye of hook or lure. Double back and make 5 or more turns around the standing line. Bring the end of the line through the first loop formed behind the eye, then through the big loop. **2.** Wet knot and pull slightly on the tag end to draw up coils. **3.** Pull on the standing line to form knot with coils pressed neatly together. Slide tight against eye and clip tag end.

BLOOD KNOT

Use this knot to join sections of leader or line together. It works best with lines of approximately equal diameter.

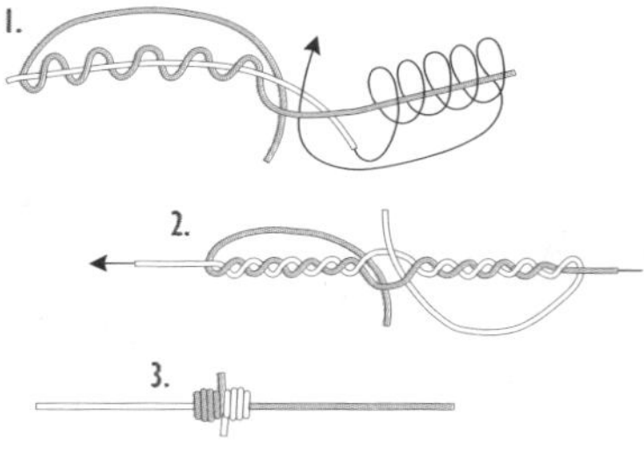

1. Overlap ends of lines to be joined. Twist one around the other making 5 turns. Bring tag end back between the two lines. Repeat with other end, wrapping in opposite direction the same number of turns. **2.** Slowly pull lines or leaders in opposite directions. Turns will wrap and gather. **3.** Pull tight and clip ends closely.

SAN DIEGO JAM KNOT

This knot can be tied with confidence in braided and monofilament line, but works exceptionally well with flourocarbon line.

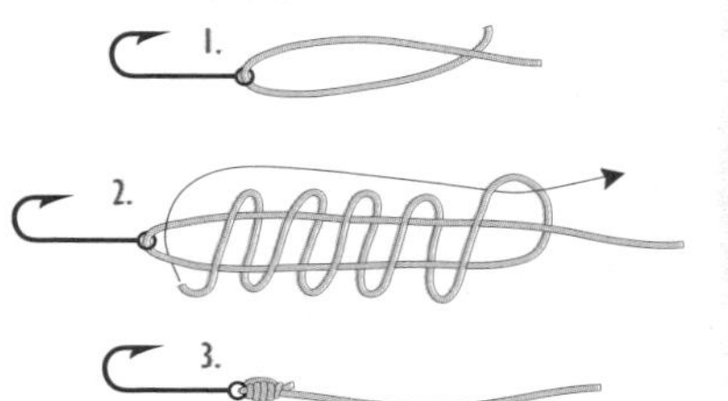

1. Pass line through hook or lure. Let a heavy lure hang down or pinch hook between little finger and palm of opposite hand. **2.** Loop tag end over index finger and make 7 wraps (5 with heavy line) around the double line, then feed tag end between double lines below last wrap and bring back through loop made by index finger. **3.** Moisten lines and pull tag end tight. Slide knot down to eye and tighten.

-Also note, most monofilament line will deteriorate when exposed to sunlight. In order to maintain maximum strength, change line often. Good line and a strong knot are your link to the fish of a lifetime.

Rivers and Streams

Fly Fishing

For many anglers, river and stream fishing means fly fishing. The term "fly fishing" is aptly descriptive. Using small hooks adorned with feathers, yarn, and other materials, anglers seek to imitate the natural prey of stream trout, such as mayflies, stoneflies, grasshoppers, caddis flies, ants, mosquitoes, gnats and much more. These are the "flies" of fly fishing.

Unlike other freshwater fishing methods, such as spincasting, spinning, or baitcasting – where anglers cast lures or baits, letting the weight of them pull line from a reel – in fly fishing it's the line that is "cast." The weight of the fly line propels the essentially weightless flies used for fishing. Fly lines are thicker and heavier than monofilament fishing line and are coated to float on the water. A leader of tapered monofilament line connects to the tippet, which is a supple, nearly invisible line to which the fly is tied. Fly lines come in different models and configurations (floating, single taper, double taper, weight forward), with each graded according to its weight. A 7-weight line is heavier and thicker than a 5-weight line. The line is matched to the rod. For example, a 5-weight line is used with a 5-weight rod. Rods range in weight from 1 up to 14: The higher the number, the stouter the rod. In most stream trout situations, rods ranging from 3 weight to 6 weight should be adequate. Larger 8-weight rods would be better suited to salmon fishing, with the really large rods being reserved for saltwater applications. Compared to traditional casting rods, fly rods are longer and more flexible to make casting the line easier.

Unlike spinning or casting reels, fly reels are designed for storing line, rather than for casting. Once a fish is hooked, anglers "reel" in the fish by stripping in the line with one hand, while holding onto the rod with the other. The retrieved line is allowed to fall at the angler's feet (where it usually drifts downstream).

The two most common casts used in fly fishing are the forward cast and roll cast. To make a forward cast, strip a few yards of line off the reel with the rod held at the 11:00 position. In a smooth motion, sweep the rod tip behind you to the 1:00 position. The slack line will follow the rod and form a tight loop in the air. Just as the line straightens out, bring the rod forward again. Repeat the process making "false casts" and gradually paying out more line. When the desired amount of line is swishing overhead, making a final cast forward and allow the line to lay out and fall gently to the water.

The roll cast is useful when fishing in close quarters, particularly when there are trees or other obstructions behind you. With the line laid out on the water in front of you, raise your rod to the 1:00 position. Your line will come toward you across the surface of the water. Then, with a flick of the wrist, cast your arm forward and down to the water. The idea is to make the line "roll" off the water and forward, without ever coming behind you.

Fly fishing does require practice to achieve proficiency, but such effort is well rewarded. There is a grace to fly casting that can't be replicated with other equipment, and savvy anglers can often finesse their offerings into spots using fly gear that would be impossible with a conventional rod and reel.

Mayflies

One of the most common phrases used by fly fishermen is "matching the hatch." This simply means selecting a presentation to reflect what fish are currently feeding on. Of all the "hatches," the one most closely tied to fly fishing is the mayfly hatch. These insects have a fascinating life cycle and are regarded with awe by many anglers.

A mayfly lives most of its pre-adult life underwater as a "nymph," clinging to rocks, logs, and other natural structure, or burrowed into stream beds. When the nymph matures, it swims to the water's surface or crawls onto a rock or plant and molts into a winged subadult, called a "subimago" or dun. Fully-winged, duns are not yet sexually mature. They'll fly to a nearby tree or bush to undergo a final molt into a fully developed adult called a "spinner." Adult mayflies have no mouthparts and are unable to eat; therefore, their only function is to reproduce.

Male and female spinners take to the skies, coupling in midair and then dropping back to the water in an event known as "spinner fall." Once completed, females will deposit eggs on the water or even underwater, where the eggs will settle on bottom. Spinners die after mating or soon after (the span of an adult mayfly's life is one day or less). During spinner fall trout will feed voraciously, gobbling up spent mayflies as they fall to the surface. Such an event – when thousands of mayflies are circling over water, rising and falling – is one of nature's most extraordinary displays.

When a hatch is underway, getting trout to bite on anything but the temporary mayfly bonanza can be almost impossible. Thus, anglers have tailored fly patterns to imitate the mayfly hatch. Such flies are fished on the water's surface and are called "dry flies." Some of the most popular fly patterns mimic march browns, light cahills, tricos, and hexagenia species.

Minnesota is called the land of 10,000 lakes, but how quickly we sometimes forget about its 69,200 miles of rivers and streams. These provide quality fishing in their own right – maybe even better fishing than that found in many lakes because they often receive less fishing pressure and recreational boat traffic. Southern Minnesota's rivers offer a diverse variety of fishing opportunities, from walleyes and catfish on the Mississippi to brookies and browns on the Root.

The most famous of southern Minnesota's rivers is the Mississippi. A cultural icon, important to commercial fishermen, fish and wildlife, transportation and countless other applications, it is also home to some great fishing for walleyes, white bass, catfish and other species. The Minnesota River, which feeds the Mississippi, provides angling for the same general variety of species, just on a smaller scale.

The trout streams of southeastern Minnesota provide a unique angling experience. Southern Minnesota waters are often better suited to bullheads than trout, but these streams burble up from cold springs in the hilly region of the state that the glaciers missed. These limestone streams are very productive and support abundant insect life, which allows the streams to produce a staggering number of trout. The cold springs keep the streams cool, even in summer.

Between the extremes of tiny limestone trout streams and big muddy rivers of national importance, you'll find the rest of southern Minnesota's rivers and streams. Some hold desirable gamefish populations, others feature carp and bullheads. Even if a river itself doesn't offer good fishing, no doubt it feeds another river that does.

River fishing has a few basics that are pretty universal. Dams are excellent places to fish in spring, when fish, particularly walleyes, move upriver on their spawning runs. Dams prevent fish from moving farther upstream and concentrate fish. In summer, water levels drop and fish seek deep holes where the water is cooler. Smallmouths are structure-oriented and are frequently found in and around rock riffles where they prey on crayfish. Panfish, northern pike and largemouth bass often seek out the slack water provided by backwater areas, where they lurk in vegetation. Big northern pike look for cool water. Look for them where a feeder stream – especially a trout stream – flows into the main river. In trout streams, brook trout will be found in the cool headwaters. As the rivers continue, they often warm slightly, and this is where you'll find brown trout. The biggest browns are found in marginal trout habit, where the water is seemingly too warm to support trout. Browns tolerate warmer water than brookies, and the increased temperature produces more forage.

When fishing in rivers, keep in mind that the fish don't want to work any harder than necessary to maintain their position. In other words, they generally don't like to fight the current. Therefore, look for them in places that break the current flow. Rocks, root balls, fallen trees and even garbage carelessly thrown in the river break the current flow. This creates a calm "eddy" both downstream and upstream of the structure, and this is where fish lie. You'll also find fish hiding below undercut stream banks and in deep holes.

No matter what quarry you desire, you're likely to find a river in southern Minnesota that can produce!

Mississippi River

The Mississippi River is an American icon, and a good portion of it runs through or alongside Minnesota. The Minnesota section of the river alone comprises more than 400 miles of its 2,300 miles of overall length. At its source at Lake Itasca, the river is only about 30 feet wide, but by the time it reaches the Twin Cities, it is quite wide, and at Lake Pepin, it is several miles wide.

Thoughts of the "Big Muddy" conjure up visions of carefree youths aboard rafts and of freedom and adventure. But the river is also all business, as a site of shipping and commerce. Tourism, recreation and fish and wildlife habitat are also important functions of the river.

Indeed, the "Old Man" is home to hundreds of fish, wildlife and bird species. It serves as an important wintering area for eagles and as a migration corridor for waterfowl. It also supports a diverse fishery for both recreational and commercial anglers. Catfish, walleyes and smallmouth bass are of major importance to these anglers.

The river's changing character dictates how anglers target their quarry. In spring, walleyes, white bass and other species make major spawning runs, congregating below dams, which block their upstream migration. Angling pressure below dams at this time can be intense, but the fishing is equally good. The pools that form above dams resemble lakes more than rivers. Measuring several miles long and sometimes several miles wide, they have weaker current. Wing dams are always good bets, particularly for smallmouth bass and walleyes. These structures form eddies on

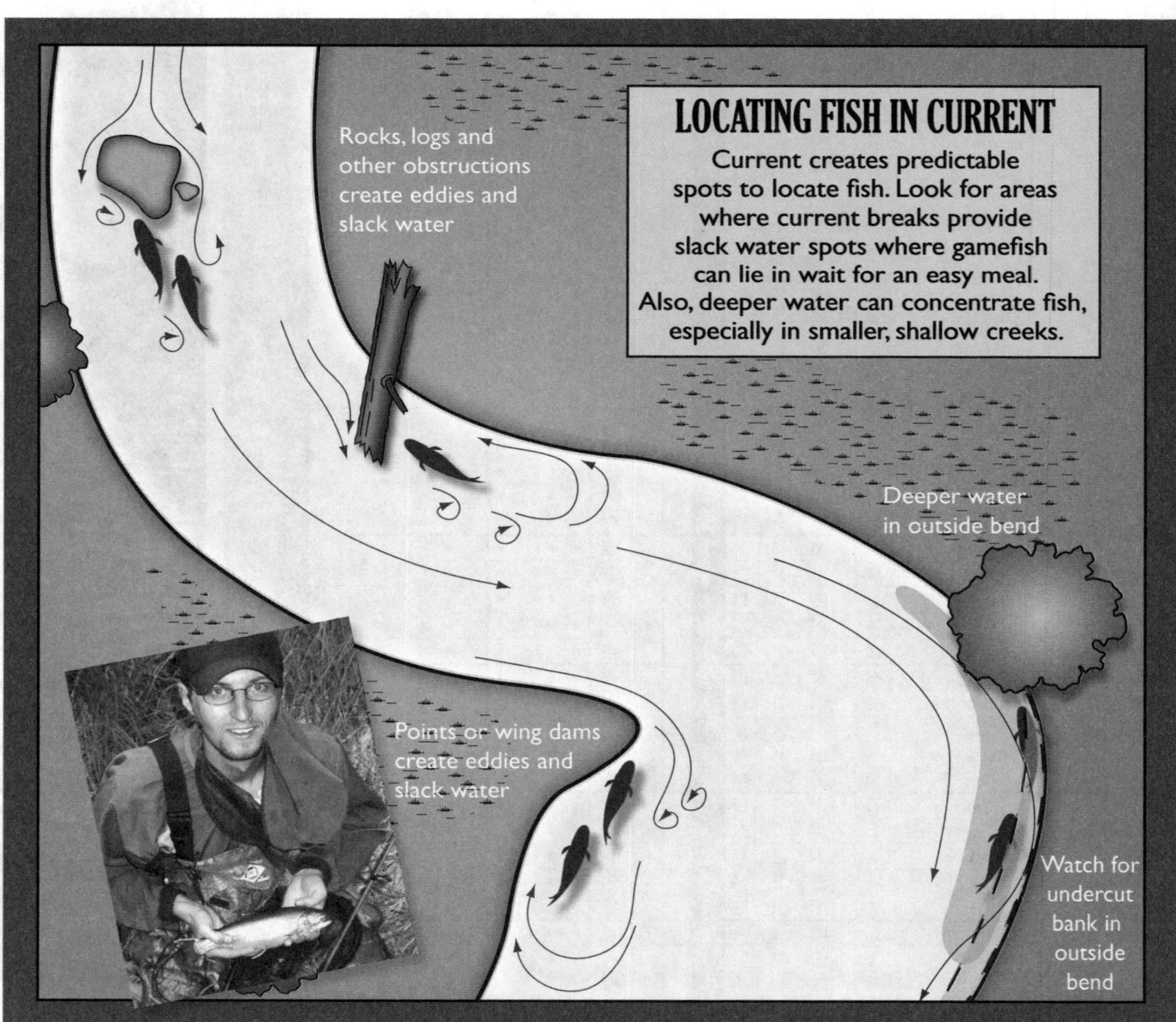

Rivers and Streams

Southeast Minnesota Trout Streams

KEY: - - - Marginal Trout Fishery

Name	County	Pg / Coord	Brown	Brook	Rainbow
Ahrensfeld Creek	Winona	77-4D	•	•	
Albany Creek, West	Wabasha	59-5C	•		
Badger Creek	Houston	96-1B	•	•	
Ball Park Tributary	Houston	96-2C	•		
Bear Creek	Winona	76-3A	•	•	
Beaver Creek	Winona	60-2E	•		
Beaver Creek, East	Houston	96-1B	•		
Beaver Creek, West	Houston	95-6C	•	•	
Bee Creek	Houston	96-1E	•	•	
Belle Creek	Goodhue	44-1E	•		
Berg Creek	Houston	96-2D	-	-	-
Borson Spring	Winona	77-4D	•		
Brush Valley Creek	Houston	78-2E	•		
Bullard Creek	Goodhue	45-4E	•	•	
Burns Valley Creek, East	Winona	77-6B	•	•	
Burns Valley Creek, West	Winona	77-5B	•	•	
Butterfield Creek	Houston	96-3A	•	•	
Camp Creek	Fillmore	94-2C	•		•
Camp Hayward Creek	Fillmore	95-4A	•	•	
Campbell Creek	Winona	78-1E		•	
Canfield Creek	Fillmore	93-6C	•		
Cannon River, Little	Goodhue	57-5B	•		•
Cedar Valley Creek	Winona	78-1C	•	•	
Chickentown Creek	Fillmore	95-4C		•	
Clear Creek	Goodhue	58-3A		•	
Cold Spring Brook	Wabasha	59-4C	•	•	
Coolridge Creek	Winona	76-3D	•	•	
Corey Creek	Winona	77-6D		•	
Crooked Creek	Houston	96-2C	•	•	•
Crooked Creek, South Fork	Houston	96-2C	•	•	
Crystal Creek	Houston	96-1A	•		
Dakota Creek	Winona	78-2C	•	•	
Daley Creek	Houston	95-5A	•	•	
Deering Valley Creek	Winona	61-4E	•		
Diamond Creek	Fillmore	94-3A	•	•	
Duschee Creek	Fillmore	94-3B	•	•	•
Eitzen Creek	Houston	96-2D	•		
Etna Creek	Fillmore	93-5C	•		
Ferndale Creek	Houston	95-5A	•	•	
Forestville Creek	Fillmore	93-6C	•		
Foster Arend Pond	Olmsted	75-4A			•
Frego Creek	Fillmore	94-3D	•		
Garvin Brook	Winona	77-4B	•	•	
Gernander Creek	Winona	77-5D		•	
Gilbert Creek	Wabasha	59-5A	•	•	
Gilmore Creek	Winona	77-5B	•		
Girl Scout Camp Creek	Houston	95-5B		•	
Goetzinger Tributary	Houston	96-2C	-	-	-
Gorman Creek	Wabasha	60-2C	•	•	
Gribben Creek	Fillmore	94-3B	•		
Hallum Creek	Fillmore	95-5B		•	
Hamilton Creek	Mower	93-4A		•	
Hammond Creek	Wabasha	59-4D	•	•	
Hay Creek	Goodhue	44-3E	•		
Helbig Creek	Wabasha	60-1C		•	
Hemmingway Creek	Winona	76-3D	•	•	
Indian Creek, East	Wabasha	60-2D	•	•	
Indian Creek, West	Wabasha	60-1D	•		
Jordon Creek, Little	Fillmore	93-6A	•		
Kedron Creek	Fillmore	93-5A	•		
Kinney Creek	Olmsted	75-5D	•		
Lanesboro Park Pond	Fillmore	94-3B			•
Larson Creek	Houston	95-6C		•	
Logan Creek	Olmsted	76-1A	•		
Long Creek	Wabasha	59-6D	•		
Lost Creek	Fillmore	75-6E	•		
Lynch Creek	Fillmore	76-1E	•	•	
Mahoods Creek	Fillmore	93-5B	•		
Maple Creek	Fillmore	95-4B		•	
Mazeppa Creek	Wabasha	58-3C	•		
Middle Creek	Wabasha	59-6D	•	•	
Mill Creek	Olmsted	75-6D	•		•
Miller Creek	Wabasha	59-5A	•		
Miller Valley Creek	Winona	78-2C		•	
Money Creek	Winona	77-5D	•		
Money Creek, West Branch	Winona	77-5D	•		
Nepstad Creek	Fillmore	95-4B	•	•	
New Yorker Hollow	Houston	96-2D		•	
Newburg Creek	Fillmore	95-4D	•	•	
Partridge Creek	Fillmore	94-2C	•		
Pickwick Creek	Winona	78-1C	•		
Pickwick Creek, Little	Winona	78-2C	•	•	
Pine Creek	Winona	77-4E	•	•	
Pine Creek	Winona	78-2D	•	•	
Pine Creek, South Fork	Winona	78-1D	•	•	
Pleasant Valley Creek	Winona	77-6C	•	•	
Rice Creek	Fillmore	94-1A	•		
Riceford Creek	Houston	95-5D	•	•	
Rollingstone Creek	Winona	77-4A	•		
Rollingstone Creek, Middle Branch	Winona	77-4A	•		
Root River, Middle Branch	Fillmore	93-5A	•		
Root River, South Branch	Fillmore	94-1B	•		•
Root River, South Fork	Fillmore	95-4C	•	•	•
Rose Valley Creek	Winona	78-2D	•	•	
Rupprecht Creek	Winona	77-4B	•		
Rush Creek	Winona	77-4D	•		•
Schueler Creek	Fillmore	77-4E	•		
Second Creek	Wabasha	59-6A		•	
Shady Creek	Fillmore	94-1A		•	
Silver Creek	Houston	78-1E		•	
Snake Creek	Wabasha	60-2D		•	
Speltz Creek	Winona	77-4A	•	•	
Sportsman's Park Pond Creek	Fillmore	95-5D			•
Spring Brook	Rice	56-3A		•	
Spring Creek	Goodhue	44-2E	•	•	
Spring Creek	Wabasha	59-5C	•		
Spring Valley Creek	Fillmore	93-5B	•		•
Springs Creek, Big	Fillmore	94-3A	•		
Stockton Valley Creek	Winona	77-4C	•	•	
Storer Creek	Houston	78-1E	•	•	
Straight Creek	Winona	77-4A	•		
Sullivan Creek	Houston	96-2B	•	•	
Swede Bottom Creek	Houston	96-1A		•	
Thompson (Dexter) Creek	Houston	96-2A	•	•	
Torkelson Creek	Fillmore	94-3A	•		
Trib 5 to Crooked Creek	Houston	96-3C	•		
Trout Brook	Dakota	44-1D	•	•	
Trout Brook	Wabasha	60-1B		•	
Trout Ponds Creek	Winona	78-2D		•	
Trout Run Creek	Winona	76-2B	•	•	
Trout Valley Creek	Winona	60-3E	•	•	
Vesta Creek	Fillmore	95-4C		•	
Watson Creek	Fillmore	94-1B	•		
Whitewater River	Winona	60-2E	•		•
Whitewater River, Middle Branch	Winona	76-2B	•	•	•
Whitewater River, North Branch	Olmsted	76-1A	•		•
Whitewater River, South Branch	Winona	76-3B	•		•
Wildcat Creek	Houston	96-3B	•		
Willow Creek	Fillmore	94-2C	•		•
Winnebago Creek	Houston	96-2D	•	•	•
Wisel Creek	Fillmore	95-4C	•	•	
Zumbro River, North Fork	Wabasha	58-3D	•		

Other Trout Streams

Name	County	Pg / Coord	Brown	Brook	Rainbow
Assumption Creek	Carver	41-5A		•	
Black Dog Creek	Dakota	28-2E	-	-	-
Brown's Creek	Washington	29-6B	•		
Canby Creek	Yellow Medicine	32-3B	•		
Cannon River, Little	Goodhue	57-5B	•		
Cold Springs Creek	Stearns	10-3A		•	
Cottonwood Creek	Swift	6-2E	•		
County Ditch 055	Yellow Medicine	32-2B	•		
County Ditch 12	Brown	51-5A	•		
Eagle Creek	Scott	42-1A	•		
Eagle Creek, East Branch	Scott	42-1A	•		
Fairhaven Creek	Stearns	11-5C		•	
John's Creek	Brown	52-1B	•		
Kennaley's Creek	Dakota	28-3E	-	-	-
Kinzer Creek	Stearns	10-3A		•	
Lawrence Creek	Chisago	16-2B		•	
Luxemburg Creek	Stearns	11-5A	•		
Meyers Creek	Stearns	11-5B	•		
Mud Creek	Pope	8-2A	-	-	-
Old Mill Stream	Washington	16-1E		•	
Paul's Creek	Le Sueur	54-2B			•
Pine Creek	Dakota	43-5D	•		
Ramsey Creek	Redwood	36-2D	•		
Redwood River	Lyon	48-1B	•		•
Robinson Hill Creek	Stearns	11-5A	•		
Scheldorf Creek	Cottonwood	66-1C	•		•
Seven Mile Creek	Nicollet	54-1C	-	-	-
Snake River	Sherburne	12-3A	-	-	-
Spring Brook	Stearns	11-5C		•	
Spring Brook	Rice	56-3A		•	
Spring Creek	Brown	51-6A	•		
Thiel Creek	Stearns	11-5C		•	
Threemile Creek	Stearns	11-5C		•	
Trout Brook	Dakota	44-1D	•		
Valley Branch	Washington	30-1D	•	•	•
Valley Creek	Washington	30-1D	•	•	•
Vermillion River	Dakota	42-3C	•		•
Vermillion River, S. Branch	Dakota	43-4C	•		•
Washington Creek	Meeker	24-3B		•	
Willow Creek	Stearns	11-4C	•		
Woodson Creek	Mower	91-5C	•		

both the upstream and downstream side, and fish wait here for prey species to be swept across the wing dams. Backwater areas of the river are also important. Here, you're likely to find species such as largemouth bass, northern pike and panfish hiding in the weeds. These are important spawning areas as well.

Beginning at St. Cloud (for the purposes of this book), the river runs through quiet countryside consisting of forested bluffs. Riffles and numerous rapids mark the river. The Beaver Islands are found here - a group of more than 30 islands downstream of St. Cloud. As the river nears Anoka, power plants begin appearing along the river, and the landscape becomes more developed.

The fishing in this stretch of the Big Muddy is pretty good. Anglers will find walleyes, northerns, crappies and even some big muskies. Most notable, however, are the area's smallmouth bass. Not only do anglers catch good numbers of fish, but some of them grow quite large. A fish weighing five pounds or more is a possibility.

Unfortunately, most of the Mississippi carries a fish-consumption advisory. Women of child-bearing age and children should not eat fish from the part of the river below St. Anthony Falls. Others should eat no more than one meal of Mississippi River fish per month.

Downstream of Anoka the river measures up to a half-mile wide. The river cuts through limestone, sandstone and shale bluffs as it transitions from farmland to the suburbs. Despite the urban location, a natural buffer area has been maintained along much of the river, providing a natural-looking river with a cityscape backdrop.

Because of its proximity to the Twin Cities here, the river is a hub of transportation, and you'll find locks at St. Anthony Falls – the only waterfall on the entire river – and at the Ford Dam above Fort Snelling. The Minnesota River joins the Mississippi here.

Anglers in this stretch of the Mississippi may encounter walleyes, sauger, northern pike, muskies, panfish and largemouth and smallmouth bass – all in close proximity to a major metropolitan area.

After leaving the Twin Cities, Lock and Dam No. 2 forms Spring Lake – a wide spot in the river contained within the state's borders. Thus begins a series of dams and pools. From here on down to the Iowa border, Minnesota shares the Mississippi with Wisconsin. The river forms the border between these two states. Along this stretch, bluffs rise 150 feet above the river, creating breathtaking views. Bottomland trees including cottonwood, ash, elm and maple line the banks in low-lying areas. This area of the river contains 113 fish species.

Lock and Dam No. 3 at Red Wing forms Pool 3. The area below this dam is extremely popular with spring walleye anglers. Fishing is usually crowded, as folks from the Twin Cities and Eau Claire, WI seek the river's spawning walleyes.

Lock and Dam No. 4 forms the wide-sprawling Lake Pepin. This water spans 24 miles and contains 25,000 acres. The area is deep compared to the surrounding areas of the river – up to 60 feet – and is fairly clear.

The pool upstream of Lock and Dam Nos. 5 & 5A forms a complex series of side channels, backwaters and islands. This area, as well as several areas downstream make up part of the massive Upper Mississippi National Wildlife and Fish Refuge, which includes nearly 240,000 acres of water, islands and marshes.

Lock and Dam No. 6 at Trempealeau, WI forms Pool 6, which lies alongside Winona, MN. It also forms part of the above-mentioned refuge and includes numerous channels, sloughs, backwaters, islands and bars.

Lock and Dam No. 7 between La Crescent, MN and La Crosse, WI forms Pool 7, which consists largely of 7,700-acre Lake Onalaska. This lake is generally only about 4 or 5 feet deep, and maxes out in the 20s.

Lock and Dam No. 8 at Genoa, WI forms Pool 8, which contains numerous islands in its upper reaches. The river here is very wide throughout the length of the pool.

Lock and Dam No. 9 at Harpers Ferry, IA forms Pool 9. The Minnesota section of this water consists mostly of backwater sloughs and provides great fishing for bass, northerns and panfish.

Wherever you venture along the great river, you're sure to find interesting scenery, abundant fish and wildlife and great adventures.

HUNTING

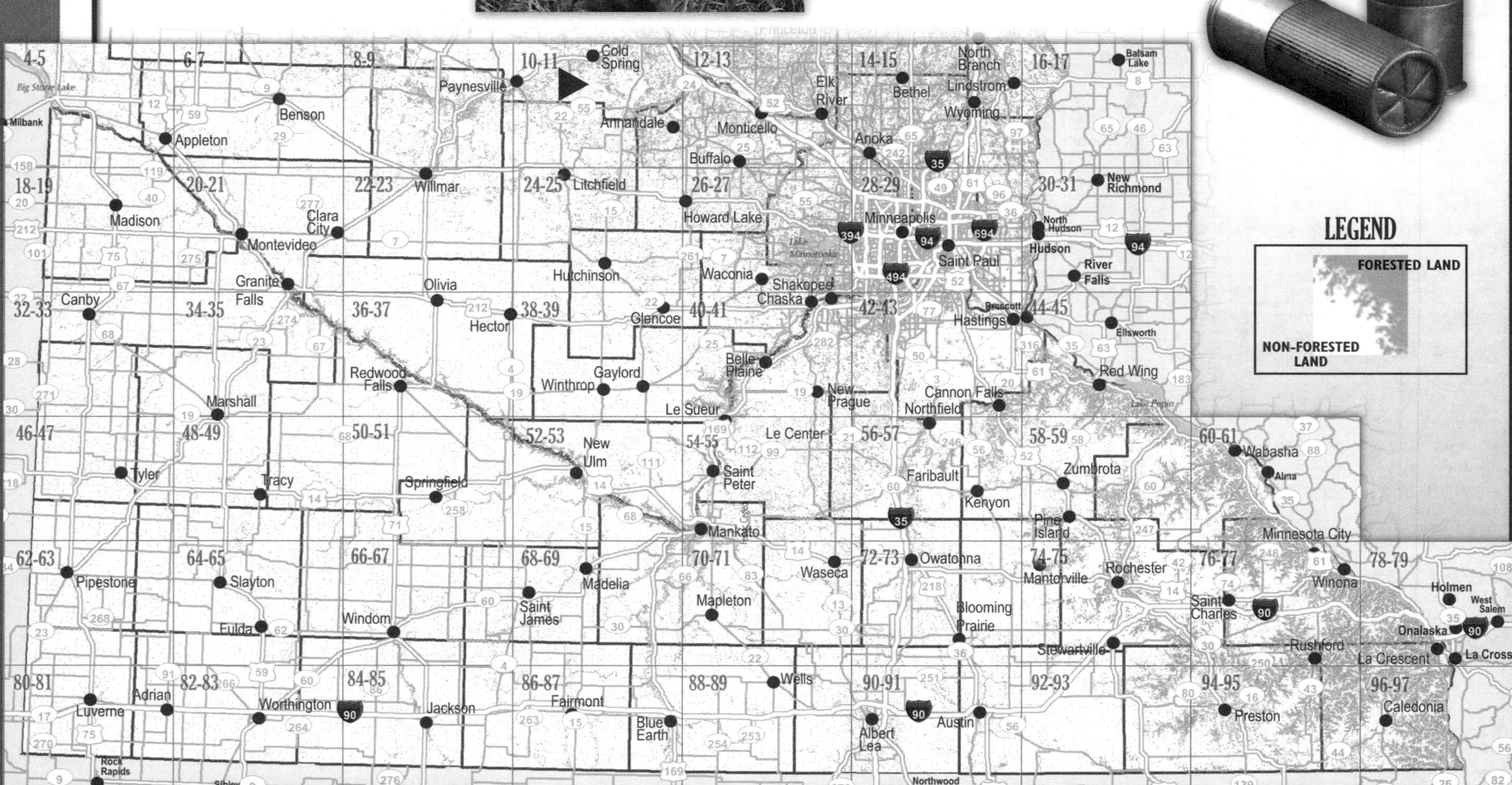

Minnesota is home to millions of acres of public hunting land. Although the majority of that public land consists of large state and national forests in the northern part of the state, there are still numerous public hunting opportunities in the southern half of the Gopher State.

The state has 1,380 wildlife management areas that encompass more than 1.2 million acres, many of which are found in the southern part of the state. These areas often have good hunting for deer, pheasants, doves, waterfowl and other small-game species. Wherever you live or hunt in Minnesota, there is sure to be a WMA somewhere nearby.

Another option for hunters, particularly those pursuing waterfowl and upland game, are waterfowl production areas. These federally managed areas usually consist of wetlands as well as upland nesting cover. Most are open to public hunting.

Although southern Minnesota doesn't have the sprawling forests of the north, it does have some state forest land. Most notably, the Richard J. Dorer Hardwood State Forest encompasses a large area in southeastern Minnesota and provides great habitat for deer, turkeys and other game animals.

In addition, some state parks, state game refuges and state scientific and natural areas may be open to some types of hunting. Check current hunting regulations, or contact the specific state park or local wildlife management office for more information.

With all this public land available, hunters shouldn't have too much trouble finding a place to chase their quarry. To help you along, we've provided detailed maps indicating public and private land. They should only be used as a general guide, however, because the maps may not be able to show small private parcels, and land ownership can change hands. Consult a current plat book for more detailed information. Also, beware that just because land isn't posted, that doesn't mean it's not private.

Despite the abundance of public hunting lands, sometimes hunting on private land can be as good or better. Hunters who are polite and courteous can sometimes get permission to hunt on private property. If that is your goal, call or stop by the landowner's house at a decent time of day and introduce yourself. Politely ask permission to hunt on the landowner's property. Offer to help the landowner with chores, or to share part of your harvest. Some landowners will be receptive, while others won't. Either way, thank the landowner for his or her time. If you are granted access, treat the property with respect and leave it better than you found it.

Whether you hunt public or private land, the beautiful terrain and good game populations found in Minnesota can provide quality hunting. Adequate public land ensures there are places for everyone to hunt.

Hunting -Big Game White-tailed Deer

White-tailed deer are Minnesota's most popular big game animal – some 500,000 hunters take to the woods and fields each fall in search of deer, usually harvesting 200,000 or more deer annually. White-tailed deer are incredibly adaptable and live in every county in the state. They are at home in farm fields, forests, swamps and even urban areas. More than 1 million deer live in Minnesota, and the challenge of hunting them (deer have keen senses of smell, are largely nocturnal, and can run up to 40 miles per hour) makes white-tailed deer the king of game animals for many hunters.

White-tailed deer in Minnesota and other northern states grow much bigger than their counterparts in the south and areas with less-severe winter climates. Because of the often-extreme winter conditions in northern locales, deer have adapted to the cold by growing larger, which reduces an animal's surface-area-to-volume ratio. Larger animals radiate less body heat and stay warmer in cold temperatures. It's illustrative of an adaptive mechanism known as Bergmann's rule, which proposes that the body mass of a warm-blooded species increases as mean temperature decreases. Thus, warm-blooded animals living in cold climates tend to be larger than members of their species living in warmer climates. A typical adult male white-tailed deer weighs between 100-300 pounds, with 170 pounds about average. However, bucks weighing more than 400 pounds have been harvested in Minnesota.

Although deer hunting is typically considered a late-fall/early winter activity, many hunters begin scouting for areas to hunt long before the season opens. In fact, those serious about finding that big buck of a lifetime often start "hunting" in spring, just after the snow melts, looking for sheds (antlers dropped by male deer in winter). Males grow a new set of antlers each year, and the location they drop them in the season before is a good starting point when looking for them again in fall.

In agricultural areas, deer can often be seen feeding in fields on late-summer evenings. Locating such areas is another part of the preseason hunting effort. Because deer are herbivores (plant eaters), they will usually be found near ready food sources such as clovers, grasses, corn, and soybeans in the summer. Come autumn, high-energy foods such as acorns and wild fruits become a more important part of a deer's diet. Agricultural areas, containing year-round sources of high-protein foods, will attract deer. Big bucks favor habitat near water, and will often key in on river drainages, and locations with dense cover, in edge areas where woods meet fields, and where there are multiple avenues of escape.

Deer are creatures of habit, and they generally use the same paths when traveling from feeding areas to bedding areas – places of shelter where they often remain during daytime. Beds – circular depressions formed in grass or snow – reveal where deer are resting. Other visible clues to a deer's presence include hoof prints and droppings. Deer are creatures of the edge, preferring areas of woods near fields with available food.

Male deer leave other clues of their presence, such as scrapes and rubs. Scrapes are usually made as the fall breeding season, known as "the rut," approaches. During this time, bucks will begin to clear areas in the ground with their hoofs. These can range in size from Frisbees to the size of a small vehicle. After pawing an area clean, a buck will stand in the scrape and urinate over his hind hocks to emit secretions into the scrape. Deer will also chew on and rub overhanging limbs, depositing scent through glands located in the head. More than one deer may use the same scrape, as individual animals often investigate scrapes made by other deer and then will leave their own scent on the existing scrape. The biggest and most dominant bucks usually begin making scrapes earlier in the season, before other deer. Often, a series of scrapes will be made between feeding and bedding areas.

Rubs on the trunks of trees and shrubs are a sure give-away to the presence of bucks. Rubs look like "scars," and are made by bucks in one of two ways: In early autumn, they will use the woody vegetation to remove velvet from their antlers. Later, in preparation for the rut, bucks will "spar" or "fight" with a small tree, sort of like a boxer does prior to an actual fight. Such rubs help deer alleviate aggression and prepare for battle with other deer in their quest for dominance and breeding rights.

Besides these visual clues, hunters also rely heavily on data from the Department of Natural Resources, which often undertakes intensive studies of deer populations, calculating density, mortality, hunter success, and providing yearly hunting reports.

Deer Harvest Density charts, as shown on this page, provide hunters with quick overviews of county-by-county harvest rates. Numbers such as 459, in Faribault County at the far southern end of the state, indicate a specific deer management unit. A quick glance at the 2002 chart reveals that the harvest density for Faribault County was on the low end compared to other nearby counties. In Faribault County, hunters harvested 0 to 1.5 deer per square mile of deer range. Looking at the same county data for 2003 shows a slightly higher figure (0 to 1.8 deer harvested per square mile of deer range). The totals for 2004 are down, with just 0 to 1.4 deer harvested per square mile of deer range. For 2005, the numbers dropped again, with a high of 1.3 deer harvested per square mile of range.

Studying those sections with the darkest shading, the areas of highest harvest density by zone can quickly be decoded. And comparing the four charts, from 2002 to 2005, certain areas such as 346 in Winona County, stand out as locations that have recorded some of the highest harvest densities in southern Minnesota for the four years represented. In 2003, hunters in unit 346 harvested 5.2 to 10.1 deer per square mile. In 2004, the harvest in unit 346 was 8.0 to 12.2 deer per square mile, while in 2005, the harvest dropped slightly to 7.1 to 11.6 deer par square mile.

When studying these charts, one should remember that deer harvest density alone doesn't fully reveal the quality of the hunting opportunities within a particular area. In lightly populated counties such as Faribault, fewer hunters will be present than in counties closer to large population centers or in those areas with larger overall deer populations.

It's necessary to compare this information with other data, such as buck harvest per square mile, antlerless harvest per square mile, and total harvest per square mile, to get a more complete picture of the deer population in any location. Those hunters who do their homework in August-October are often rewarded with venison in the freezer come November.

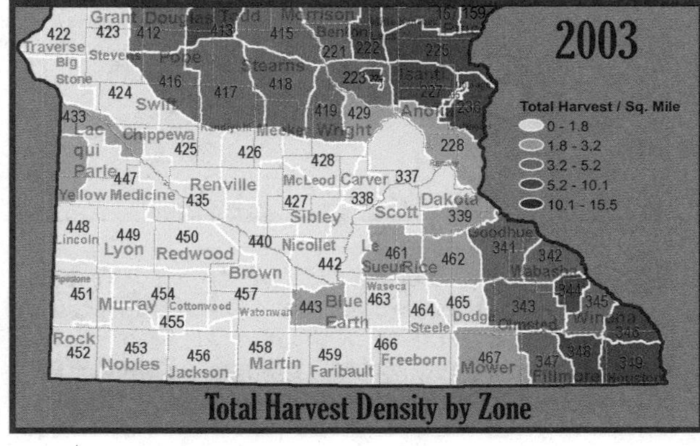

Total Harvest Density by Zone

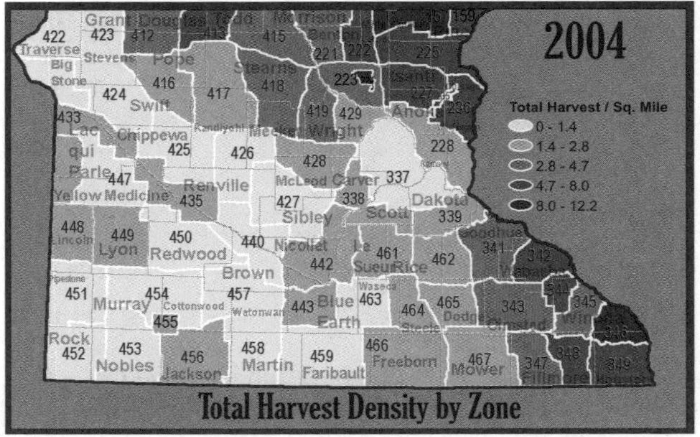

Total Harvest Density by Zone

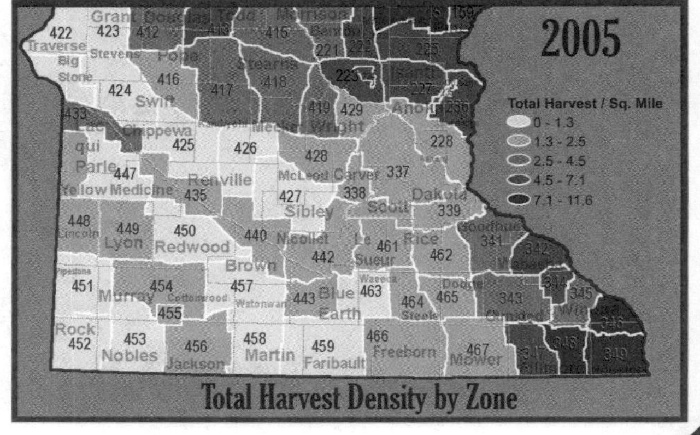

Total Harvest Density by Zone

Total Harvest Density by Zone

Hunting -Wildlife Management Areas

LEGEND

Wildlife Management Area

Because of the great number of WMAs in southern Minnesota, this overview map is intended to show general density and approximate placement only. For details, refer to the table on the following pages and larger maps earlier in this book.

Bruce MacQueen

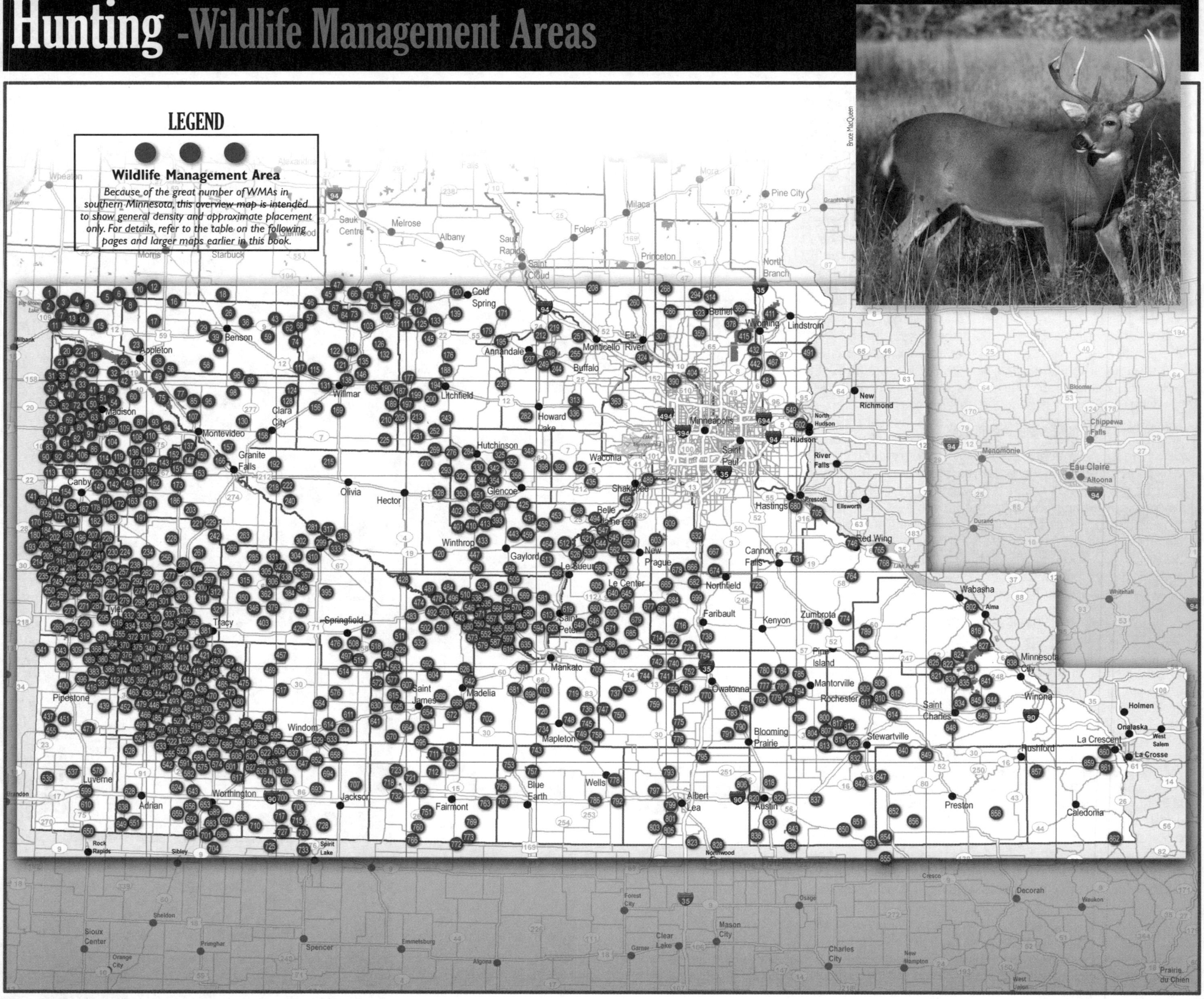

The wealth and breadth of Minnesota's natural resources are perhaps best represented in the state's Wildlife Management Area system. Wildlife Management Areas, commonly called WMAs, encompass 1.2 million acres of the North Star State, across a multitude of habitat types, such as forests, swamps, prairies, wetlands, and peatlands.

Protecting lands and waters that have productive habitat for fish and wildlife as well as fish- and wildlife-oriented recreation is the stated goal of WMAs. As such, these lands are administered differently than state parks or forests. Here, wildlife managers actively plant food plots, restore native plants and wetlands, perform prescribed burns, manipulate water levels, and improve habitat for nesting birds. Many WMAs have observation decks or areas for wildlife viewing.

The current system of WMAs had its beginnings in 1951, when the state of Minnesota created a Save The Wetlands program to purchase and preserve the rapidly diminishing areas of wildlife habitat at the time due to development and farming.

Today WMAs serve three broad purposes:

1) To protect wildlife habitat for future generations
2) To provide citizens with opportunities for hunting, fishing and wildlife watching
3) To promote important wildlife-based tourism in the state.

WMAs are open to a variety of activities including:

- Hunting, in accordance with state regulations
- Fishing, in accordance with all regulations
- Camping, at designated areas
- Hiking, both on and off designated trails
- Bicycling, on designated trails
- Picking fruit and mushrooms
- Wildlife viewing

Activities requiring a permit and/or fee include:

- Trapping
- Camping, outside of the hunting season

(For additional information, contact the Minnesota DNR Information Center, 500 Lafayette Road., St. Paul, MN 55155-4040; phone: (651) 296-6157, (800) 657-3929; Web: www.dnr.state.mn.us.)

WMAs benefit much more than just local fish and wildlife – these public lands contribute to an outdoor lifestyle enjoyed by many and the state's economy as well. It is estimated that 15 percent of Minnesotans hunt and 52 percent of Minnesota residents watch wildlife. WMAs are home to a variety of small and big game animals including white-tailed deer, black bear, moose, squirrels, ruffed grouse, woodcock, waterfowl, pheasants, turkeys, and mourning doves. Thus, WMAs are very popular destinations for wildlife watchers and hunters. In fact, hunters and wildlife watchers spend more than $1 billion annually on their collective activities. Of that $1 billion, the U.S. Fish and Wildlife Service estimates that $250 million is spent by deer hunters alone.

Antler Growth

Typical white-tailed deer antler development from age 1.5 to 5.5

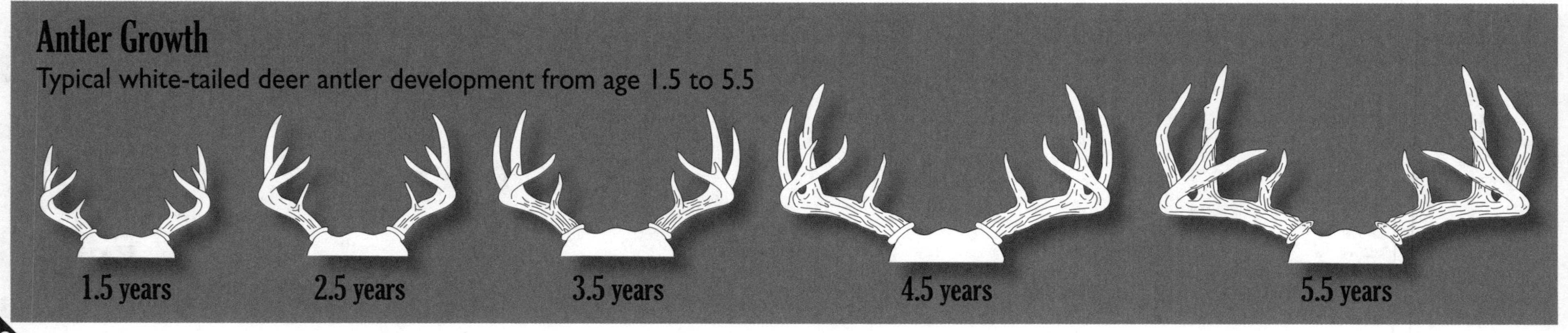

Name	Number	County	Nearest Town	Pg / Coord	Acres	Deer	Bear	Small Game	Forest Birds	Sharptail	Pheasant	Waterfowl	Turkey	Cropland	Grassland	Emergent Wetland	Open Water	Lowland	Upland
						Game Species								**% Cover Type**					
A Shau Valley WMA	195	Stearns, Wright	Kimball	11-5C	210	•		•	•		•	•	•	0.7	0.9	2.7	-	-	95.8
Area is within a traditional deer and turkey wintering area. Hunting, trapping, and wildlife viewing are popular activities. Situated in steeply rolling hardwood forest habitat. Wonderful vistas of western border "Big Woods" hardwood forest.																			
Acton WMA	200	Meeker	Grove City	24-1A	40	•		•			•	•		-	15.9	78.4	-	-	2.2
Minimally managed due to its small size and predominance of wetlands. Terrain is flat. In a highly agricultural area.																			
Aid-pit WMA	628	Nobles	Ellsworth	81-5C	5	•		•			•			-	-	-	-	-	44.0
Abandoned DOT gravel pit that is 70% covered by trees. A seasonal pond is located in the pit area. Rest of unit is grass.																			
Albion WMA	237	Wright	Annandale	11-6D	545	•		•			•	•	•	-	6.7	62.2	-	12.0	19.2
Good hunting, trapping, hiking, and wildlife and bird viewing.																			
Alfsborg WMA	447	Sibley	Winthrop	38-3E	73	•					•			-	11.5	64.7	-	-	19.4
WMA is mainly lowland meadow dominated by reed canary grass. Managed for pheasant habitat.																			
Alice Hamm WMA	179	Stearns	Kimball	11-4C	121	•		•			•	•	•	1.0	51.9	18.0	-	28.0	1.1
Hunting, trapping, wildlife viewing, and hiking. WMA is situated in an area of marginally drained cropland. Mgmt. for grassland and wetland ecosystems. A corn food plot is usually available for winter wildlife. Turkeys sometimes seen.																			
Altnow Marsh WMA	443	Sibley	Gaylord	39-5C	147	•					•	•		-	17.3	82.4	-	-	-
WMA is a wetland/open-grassland complex. Limited parking area. Wheelchair access limited to access lane.																			
Altona WMA	309	Lincoln, Pipestone	Lake Benton	46-3D	552	•		•			•			8.2	48.8	37.2	-	-	2.2
Good viewing of grassland areas available from the hills on the unit's east side.																			
Amiret WMA	311	Lyon	Marshall	48-3B	669	•		•			•	•		4.5	37.8	57.2	-	-	0.5
Duck boat access. Four other WMAs are within two miles of unit, offering more wildlife-related opportunities.																			
Anderson Lake WMA	223	Lincoln	Ivanhoe	32-3E	592	•		•			•	•		10.6	29.0	53.2	-	-	7.3
Duck boat access. WMA is a wetland/prairie complex with some woody plantings. Yellow Medicine River runs through unit.																			
Ann and Leo Donahue WMA For more information call 507-280-5066.	805	Freeborn	Twin Lakes	90-1D	87			•			•	•		-	9.3	65.8	1.3	4.2	18.8
Antler WMA For more information call 507-537-6250.	183	Yellow Medicine, Lincoln	Porter	33-5C	174	•		•			•			7.1	58.3	-	-	-	34.6
Archerville WMA For more information call 507-537-6250.	167	Yellow Medicine, Lincoln	Porter	32-3C	237	•		•			•		•	14.3	44.4	2.4	-	-	38.9
Arlington WMA	459	Sibley	Arlington	39-6D	21						•			-	-	77.6	-	-	22.4
Permission from an adjacent landowner is required to enter WMA. Shrub planting established to provide winter cover for pheasants.																			
Armbrust WMA For more information call 507-831-2900.	726	Martin	Truman	86-2A	66	•		•			•	•	•	-	50.7	49.3	-	-	0.2
Artz WMA For more information call 507-831-2900.	707	Jackson	Jackson	85-4B	16			•			•	•		-	12.3	87.0	-	-	-
Ash Lake WMA For more information call 507-537-6250.	232	Lincoln	Ivanhoe	46-3A	300	•		•			•	•		13.3	61.9	21.8	-	-	3.0
Assumption WMA	468	Carver	Belle Plaine	40-2B	67			•			•	•		1.0	5.1	92.0	1.6	-	0.1
Majority of visitors hunt waterfowl. Trapping, mainly for mink and muskrat. Three waterfowl production areas and two other WMAs are within 5 miles of unit.																			
Athens WMA	314	Isanti	Isanti	14-2A	192	•	•	•	•		•	•	•	-	13.0	56.9	-	-	30.0
Species include terns and Blanding's turtles. Primarily large, Type 4 wetland with cattails interspersed with scattered prairie fields and upland hardwood forests. Mgmt. is primarily maintenance of current cover types. Limited wildlife viewing due to nature and location of cover types.																			
Aurora WMA For more information call 507-280-5066.	783	Steele	Bixby	72-3C	639	•		•			•	•		-	32.3	37.5	1.0	22.5	5.4
Avoca WMA	500	Murray	Avoca	64-3C	60	•		•			•	•		-	25.3	-	69.5	-	5.3
WMA is a deep marsh containing high populations of undesirable fish resulting in poor water quality and little wildlife.																			
Badger WMA	506	Murray	Slayton	64-2C	403	•		•			•	•		-	8.2	83.5	-	-	8.3
Includes portions of North and South Badger lakes (designated wildlife lakes totaling 550 acres) and a fringe of surrounding upland. Water levels managed for waterfowl production and hunting.																			
Bail Out WMA For more information call 320-289-2493.	106	Lac Qui Parle	Providence	18-3D	155	•		•			•			8.9	41.5	43.1	-	-	4.0
Baker's Lake WMA	393	McLeod	Brownton	39-4B	294	•		•	•		•	•		10.0	3.2	53.5	1.4	-	31.9
WMA consists of two tracts split by Baker's Lake, a designated Migratory Waterfowl Feeding and Resting Area that prohibits boat motors during waterfowl hunting season. Consult MN hunting regulations for more information.																			
Banks WMA	633	Cottonwood	Bingham Lake	66-3D	155	•		•	•		•	•		13.4	23.3	13.3	35.4	-	14.7
WMA is a wetland/prairie complex surrounding an unnamed lake. Boat access to the 60+ acre lake on this unit.																			
Bardel's Marsh WMA	612	Le Sueur	Heidelberg	41-4E	78	•					•	•		-	-	88.9	-	8.8	2.3
Bardel's Marsh WMA is mostly marsh with cattails, bulrushes, and phragmites. Limited parking. Access requires a 1/4-mile walk.																			
Bashaw WMA - Dahl Tract All units: For more information call 320-231-5163.	515	Brown	Comfrey	51-4E	240	•		•			•			9.7	38.4	50.3	0.2	1.4	-
Bashaw WMA - DM and E Tract	508	Brown	Comfrey	51-4E	12	•		•			•			-	16.8	41.2	-	-	42.9
Bashaw WMA - Tracts 2-7 and 9	514	Brown	Comfrey	51-4E	280	•		•			•			12.0	20.4	35.2	-	31.5	1.0
Baxter WMA - Baxter East Unit Both units: For more information call 320-289-2493.	93	Lac Qui Parle	Dawson	20-1C	80	•		•			•	•		28.8	13.7	50.9	-	-	6.5
Baxter WMA - Baxter Main Unit	94	Lac Qui Parle	Dawson	20-1C	187	•		•			•	•		4.1	40.1	49.0	-	-	6.8
Bayport WMA	602	Washington	Bayport	30-1C	452	•		•	•		•	•	•	18.9	46.5	4.5	0.9	-	28.6
Archery deer hunting opportunities during firearms deer hunting season. Hike and observe purple coneflowers and black-eyed susans in the planted prairie. WMA restricted to fine shot only. No single-projectile rifles or shotgun slugs are allowed, including .22-caliber rifles.																			
Bear WMA For more information call 507-280-5066.	803	Freeborn	Twin Lakes	89-6D	64			•			•			-	1.6	69.4	3.1	5.0	19.1
Bearman WMA	307	Anoka	Nowthen	13-6C	38	•		•			•		•	9.3	-	58.5	-	11.3	20.9
This WMA is 38 acres and consists of grassland, woodland, and wetland habitats.																			
Beaver Creek WMA	854	Fillmore	Ostrander	93-4D	711	•		•	•		•	•	•	5.2	56.6	17.0	-	-	21.2
Hunting, trapping, and wildlife viewing. Special-use permit required for beaver trapping when allowed.																			
Beaver Creek WMA - Central Unit	441	Murray	Slayton	64-2A	166	•		•			•			2.6	-	-	-	-	97.4
This sub-unit is oak forest along Beaver Creek. Grass parking lot in NE corner.																			
Beaver Creek WMA - Northeast Unit	436	Murray	Currie	64-3A	192	•		•			•	•		6.6	2.2	16.7	-	73.1	1.3
Managed for a large deer herd that winters here every year. Three parking lots throughout unit.																			
Beaver Creek WMA - Southwest Unit	462	Murray	Slayton	64-2B	37	•		•			•	•	•	-	-	-	-	-	100.0
Good raccoon and squirrel hunting. Water levels managed for waterfowl production and hunting.																			
Beaver Falls WMA For more information call 320-231-5163.	318	Renville	Morton	36-3D	351	•		•			•	•		2.1	73.9	14.8	4.8	-	4.4
Bench WMA For more information call 320-289-2493.	36	Swift	Benson	7-5B	477	•		•			•	•		-	21.7	72.7	2.9	2.1	0.6
Bennett WMA For more information call 507-831-2900.	634	Cottonwood	Bingham Lake	66-3D	344	•		•			•	•		-	53.3	44.0	0.5	-	1.8
Bergdahl WMA For more information call 507-831-2900.	642	Watonwan	Madelia	68-3A	181	•		•	•		•	•	•	8.4	2.3	64.6	-	1.1	23.8
Bergman WMA	370	Murray	Ruthton	47-6D	34	•		•			•	•	•	-	28.9	38.7	-	-	32.2
Two emergent marshes, some uplands, and a grove of mature trees. View the marsh from the township road on the east boundary. Parking lot in unit's SE corner.																			
Bergo WMA	107	Chippewa	Montevideo	20-2B	40	•		•			•	•		-	62.3	29.2	-	-	8.5
Lowland brush, native grass, and wetland in an isolated location in the Chippewa River bottoms, adjacent to private wildlife habitat.																			
Bethel WMA	323	Isanti, Anoka	Bethel	14-2B	677	•	•	•	•		•	•	•	0.8	16.0	25.3	4.8	31.9	21.2
Fall hunting, cross-country skiing and/or snowshoeing in winter. Managed for a variety of waterfowl, woodland, and grassland wildlife. Bring hip boots.																			
Big John's WMA	650	Rock	Ash Creek	81-4D	67	•		•			•			-	19.2	-	-	52.2	-
WMA is a riparian forest along the Rock River with some adjacent grasslands.																			
Big Rock WMA For more information call 507-537-6250.	148	Yellow Medicine	St. Leo	33-5A	132	•		•			•	•		-	52.8	43.5	1.3	-	2.4
Big Stone WMA For more information call 320-289-2493.	2	Big Stone	Ortonville	4-2B	232	•		•	•		•		•	51.8	30.7	5.5	-	-	12.1
Bigelow WMA	691	Nobles	Bigelow	82-2D	82	•		•			•			-	6.4	93.4	-	-	-
Access to most of WMA is possible through private land or when the ice in the ditch is frozen only.																			
Blue Wing WMA For more information call 507-537-6250.	216	Lincoln	Ivanhoe	32-3E	58	•		•			•			-	45.5	54.2	-	-	-
Bluebird Prairie WMA	624	Nobles	Reading	82-2B	78	•		•			•			19.0	39.4	27.0	-	-	14.7
Grass parking lot in unit's NW corner. Unit managed primarily for upland gamebird habitat and wintering cover.																			
Bob Gehlen WMA	397	McLeod, Sibley	New Auburn	39-5B	167	•		•			•	•		-	35.5	51.4	5.6	7.5	-
WMA consists of two separate parcels. The north unit is a wetland/prairie complex with Buffalo Creek running through it. The south sub-unit is also a wetland/prairie complex. Access to the north unit requires a 1/2-mile walk. Access south unit from the township road. A food plot exists on the north unit. Wheelchair access limited to primitive parking lot.																			
Boerner WMA	464	Sibley	Arlington	40-1C	27				•					-	-	22.2	-	77.8	-
Woodland adjacent to High Island Creek. WMA is closed to hunting and trapping of all species.																			
Boesch WMA - Tract 1, 1c-d and 10 For more information call 320-231-5163.	478	Brown	New Ulm	52-2B	70	•		•					•	6.6	-	38.9	-	34.9	19.0
Boesch WMA - Tracts 1a, 1b, 3-5 For more information call 320-231-5163.	474	Brown	New Ulm	52-2B	156	•		•	•			•	•	12.3	6.7	20.1	-	42.3	18.7
Bohemian WMA For more information call 507-537-6250.	160	Yellow Medicine, Lincoln	Hendricks	32-2B	665	•		•			•	•		4.3	49.3	6.7	37.5	-	2.2
Boike WMA	130	Chippewa	Clara City	21-5C	104	•		•			•			-	43.7	47.0	2.7	-	1.3
Grassland, brush, scattered cottonwood, and a few dugout wetland areas. WMA is split down the middle by a township road. Road access on the north end and a road bisecting the unit provide handicapped access.																			
Boise Lake WMA For more information call 320-231-5163.	472	Brown	Springfield	51-4D	6							•		-	84.1	-	-	-	15.9
Boon Lake Slough WMA For more information call 320-231-5163.	270	Renville	Hutchinson	24-1E	89	•		•			•	•		12.4	27.9	47.3	-	3.8	8.6
Boon Lake WMA For more information call 320-231-5163.	269	Renville	Hutchinson	24-2D	24	•		•			•	•		-	-	92.9	-	-	7.1
Boone Slough WMA For more information call 507-537-6250.	175	Lincoln	Hendricks	32-2C	71	•		•			•	•		-	2.3	97.7	-	-	-
Bootleg WMA	694	Jackson	Lakefield	84-2B	87	•		•			•	•		-	15.4	7.8	68.4	-	7.9
WMA has a boat access to Boot Lake. For more information call 507-831-2900.																			
Borchardt-Rosin WMA For more information call 320-289-2493.	41	Lac Qui Parle	Madison	19-4A	258	•		•			•	•		-	15.6	82.1	-	-	1.0
Born WMA	709	Blue Earth	Smiths Mill	54-3E	185	•		•			•	•		-	32.7	60.7	-	3.1	3.5
WMA includes two small (less than 100 acres), shallow lakes and several fields of native warm-season grasses and forbs.																			
Bosque WMA For more information call 507-537-6250.	238	Lincoln, Lyon	Marshall	33-5E	293	•		•			•		•	21.9	27.2	-	-	-	51.0
Bossuyt WMA For more information call 507-537-6250.	196	Lincoln	Ivanhoe	32-3D	82	•		•			•	•		-	35.4	64.6	-	-	-
Boyd Sartell WMA - Main Unit	687	Rice	Shieldsville	55-6B	836	•		•			•	•	•	1.8	27.6	41.8	0.8	4.4	22.2
Both units: Excellent year-round wildlife watching. Look for gray fox, blue-winged teal, sandhill cranes, trumpeter swans, egrets, bitterns, pied-billed grebes, Cooper's hawks, and chorus frogs.																			
Boyd Sartell WMA - Rainbow Island Unit	684	Rice	Shieldsville	56-1B	155	•		•			•	•	•	10.5	2.7	41.3	0.6	12.4	31.3
Bradshaw Lake WMA	609	Scott	New Market	41-6D	729	•		•	•		•	•	•	2.4	46.1	32.8	5.7	1.8	11.1
Sandhill cranes can often be seen in spring in the WMA's wetland areas.																			
Brakke WMA For more information call 507-537-6250.	321	Lyon	Marshall	48-3B	267	•		•			•			1.9	21.3	39.3	-	-	37.6
Brawner Lake WMA For more information call 507-537-6250.	292	Lyon	Russell	48-1B	136	•		•			•		•	-	26.8	-	-	-	73.2
Bud Jensen WMA For more information call 507-280-5066.	798	Dodge	Dodge Center	74-1C	102	•					•			0.3	47.5	34.0	2.9	10.1	5.3
Budolfson WMA - West Unit	475	Murray, Cottonwood	Westbrook	65-5A	437	•		•			•	•		9.2	18.1	37.4	13.3	4.0	10.1
Carry-in water access for Lake Julia, a shallow wildlife lake. WMA consists of abandoned gravel pits, grasslands, marginal farmland, and farm groves that provide winter cover and food for wintering wildlife.																			
Buffalo Lake WMA - Northwest Unit	448	Murray	Currie	65-4A	125	•		•			•			-	67.7	30.3	-	-	2.1
WMA consists of two tracts. NW sub-unit contains five wetland basins and associated grassland uplands managed for waterfowl and upland gamebird production. This sub-unit is a wildlife sanctuary - no trespassing from Sept. 1 until end of duck season.																			
Buffalo Lake WMA - Southeast Unit	454	Murray	Dovray	65-4A	110	•		•			•	•	•	-	19.3	68.8	-	12.0	-
SE sub-unit is primarily a large marsh with associated grass uplands and part of the east shore of Buffalo Lake.																			
Buffalo Ridge WMA	368	Pipestone	Holland	47-4E	41	•		•			•			53.0	30.4	-	-	-	16.5
Cropland farmed as food plots for wintering deer herd. WMA is adjacent to 300+ acre Prairie Coteau SNA - a till hill prairie. A tremendous view of the surrounding landscape can be had from here. Hunting prohibited on the SNA.																			
Bur Oak WMA	648	Le Sueur	Cleveland	54-2C	212				•					7.9	22.4	41.6	-	3.5	24.1
Managed to provide a refuge and wintering area for deer, turkeys, pheasants, and other wildlife.																			
Burbank WMA	103	Kandiyohi	New London	9-4C	447	•		•			•	•	•	-	28.2	27.7	23.5	4.5	15.1
Variety of wildlife habitats. Wild turkeys occasionally seen.																			
Burke WMA	439	Pipestone	Woodstock	63-4C	106	•		•			•			8.4	6.8	77.7	-	-	7.1
Mostly creek valley with a poor-quality wet prairie, fens, and some remnant hillside prairies.																			

Name	Number	County	Nearest Town	Pg / Coord	Acres	Deer	Bear	Small Game	Forest Birds	Sharptail	Pheasant	Waterfowl	Turkey	Cropland	Grassland	Emergent Wetland	Open Water	Lowland	Upland
Buttermilk Run WMA	430	Murray	Currie	48-3E	56	•		•			•			-	14.2	75.3	-	-	10.6
Mgmt. objective is to maintain a pheasant wintering area.																			
Butternut WMA	187	Meeker	Grove City	23-6A	33	•		•	•		•	•	•	-	38.2	28.6	12.0	-	20.6
Both units: WMA is a mix of wooded, wetland, and grassland habitats. Food plots are also present.																			
Butternut WMA	190	Meeker	Grove City	23-6A	121	•		•	•		•	•	•	9.2	17.2	21.1	21.4	-	30.0
Byrne Lake WMA For more information call 320-289-2493.	16	Stevens, Swift	Holloway	6-2A	217	•		•			•	•		9.6	35.5	49.6	-	-	5.3
C. and V. Schmidt WMA	671	Le Sueur	Cordova	55-4C	48									-	-	100.0	-	-	-
Almost entirely cattail marsh with very little open water. Closed to hunting, but open to trapping.																			
Caeru Lean WMA - Main Unit For more information call 320-289-2493.	30	Lac Qui Parle	Bellingham	18-3A	113	•		•			•	•		-	37.6	52.5	-	-	10.0
Caeru Lean WMA - North Unit For more information call 320-289-2493.	28	Lac Qui Parle	Bellingham	4-3E	74	•		•			•	•		-	52.1	47.9	-	-	-
Camp Kerk WMA For more information call 320-289-2493.	43	Swift	Murdock	7-6B	1,023	•		•	•		•	•		-	40.0	51.7	0.9	-	7.4
Cannon River WMA	722	Rice	Morristown	56-1D	152	•					•	•		-	14.4	43.6	9.8	20.8	11.6
Both units: Good spring bird watching. Look for bald eagles, hooded mergansers, wood ducks, woodcock, trumpeter swans, black and Forster's terns, ring-billed gulls, painted turtles, and green herons.																			
Cannon River WMA - Thomas West Unit	724	Rice	Morristown	56-1D	119						•	•		-	20.8	47.2	11.2	7.3	13.5
Caraway WMA For more information call 507-831-2900.	652	Jackson	Lakefield	66-2E	132	•		•			•	•		10.3	35.7	48.7	-	-	5.0
Carex WMA For more information call 507-280-5066.	806	Freeborn	Moscow	91-4B	332	•					•	•	•	-	45.9	27.6	0.6	12.2	13.6
Carl E. Bonnell WMA	286	Anoka	St. Francis	14-1B	39	•	•	•	•		•		•	-	-	-	-	49.2	50.5
During spring, many warbler species, including yellow-rumped and yellow warblers, can be seen.																			
Carlos Avery WMA - Carlos Avery Unit	415	Chisago, Anoka	Forest Lake	15-4C	16,501	•	•	•	•		•	•	•	2.2	3.1	58.5	5.0	6.2	24.6
Both units: Very popular for bird watching. Managed primarily for deer, waterfowl, and turkeys. 20 pools managed for waterfowl habitat. 4,500 acres posted as Wildlife Sanctuary and closed to trespassing. Trapping permits required for all species. Area closed from 10 p.m.-4 a.m. each night. 18 wheelchair-accessible blinds available during turkey season or as part of a special deer hunt conducted by Capable Partners.																			
Carlos Avery WMA - Sunrise Unit	411	Chisago	Forest Lake	15-5B	7,246	•	•	•	•		•	•	•	1.4	13.4	26.8	22.4	14.0	21.8
Carlson WMA	461	Murray	Lake Wilson	64-1B	26	•		•			•			-	85.8	-	-	-	14.6
Pheasant hunting is possible. WMA has a small, high-quality remnant prairie and seeded prairie with two woody-cover plantings.																			
Caron WMA For more information call 507-831-2900.	718	Martin	Sherburn	85-5B	412	•		•			•	•		5.5	58.3	33.4	-	-	2.1
Carpenter WMA For more information call 507-831-2900.	614	Cottonwood	Bingham Lake	66-3D	61	•		•			•	•		5.4	64.1	10.7	4.3	-	15.5
Cartney WMA	851	Mower	Le Roy	92-3D	479	•		•			•	•		5.1	25.4	66.7	-	-	2.7
Excellent pheasant hunting and opportunity to observe native prairie plants.																			
Carver Highlands WMA	495	Carver	Carver	41-4B	302			•			•		•	19.2	77.5	-	-	-	0.4
This WMA's three parcels are located adjacent to State Recreation Area Land and very close to USFWS land, along the MN River. WMA managed mainly for grassland wildlife. It is predominantly upland grasses at three disjunct parcels, two of which are along Cty. Rd. 45 and the third is next to Cty. Rd. 50, 0.3 miles east of Cty. Rd. 45.																			
Cary Creek WMA	832	Mower	Racine	74-3E	56	•		•			•			7.9	65.3	27.0	-	-	-
Pheasant hunting is the primary activity on this unit.																			
Case Lake WMA For more information call 507-831-2900.	675	Watonwan	Madelia	68-3B	34	•		•			•	•		-	15.8	35.2	44.8	-	4.5
Cedar Rock WMA	281	Renville, Redwood	Redwood Falls	36-2C	641	•		•	•		•	•	•	9.9	35.2	7.2	3.8	5.9	37.9
Look for migrating raptors. For more information call 320-231-5163.																			
Ceylon WMA For more information call 507-831-2900.	766	Martin	Ceylon	86-1D	150	•		•			•	•		-	24.4	50.3	17.2	-	7.9
Chadderdon WMA	660	Le Sueur	Le Center	55-4C	133	•		•			•	•		3.1	0.9	68.3	-	25.2	2.6
Complex of grassland/wetland with some forested wetland. A food plot has been established.																			
Chain-O-Sloughs WMA For more information call 507-537-6250.	233	Lincoln	Ivanhoe	46-3A	281	•		•			•	•		7.8	53.2	36.4	-	-	2.6
Champepedan WMA	528	Nobles	Leota	63-5E	81	•		•			•			-	100.0	-	-	-	-
WMA is managed for upland game birds. Champepadan Creek must be forded to access most of unit.																			
Chandler WMA - North Unit	463	Murray	Chandler	63-6C	39	•		•			•	•		-	11.9	85.3	-	-	2.8
A remote esker in the central portion of the unit contains native prairie.																			
Chandler WMA - South Unit	466	Murray	Chandler	63-6C	370	•		•			•	•		12.1	18.2	66.4	-	0.9	2.5
WMA is mainly a large permanent marsh with some associated uplands containing food plots, nesting cover, and woody plantings.																			
Chapa-kak-say-za WMA	776	Steele	New Richland	72-1D	21									19.9	26.7	3.9	-	-	47.1
Closed to hunting and trapping. For more information call 507-280-5066.																			
Charlotte Hynes WMA	757	Faribault	Winnebago	87-6A	72	•		•			•	•	•	-	46.6	37.8	-	-	15.5
Wheelchair access limited to adjacent cty/township roads and gravel parking lot off Hwy. 109. For more information call 507-225-3572.																			
Chen Bay WMA For more information call 507-537-6250.	271	Lincoln	Lake Benton	46-3B	249	•		•			•	•		2.7	31.1	65.0	-	-	1.2
Cherry Grove WMA For more information call 507-932-4133.	856	Fillmore	Cherry Grove	93-5D	78	•		•			•			99.2	-	-	-	-	0.8
Chisholm Valley WMA For more information call 507-932-4133.	857	Houston	Rushford	95-5A	80	•		•	•				•	6.2	-	-	-	-	93.0
Chosen Valley WMA	840	Fillmore	Chatfield	75-5E	197	•		•			•	•		3.2	68.6	8.7	0.2	-	19.3
Recreation dominated by hunting and trapping. Primarily upland gamebird habitat composed of native warm-season and cool-season grasses.																			
Christensen WMA	493	Murray	Iona	64-2C	124	•		•			•			8.5	78.3	-	-	0.8	12.4
WMA managed for upland gamebirds.																			
Christine WMA For more information call 507-537-6250.	207	Lincoln	Ivanhoe	32-3D	41	•		•			•	•		28.6	36.6	33.2	-	-	1.7
Christopherson WMA For more information call 507-537-6250.	147	Yellow Medicine	Clarkfield	20-2E	143	•		•			•	•		-	41.5	50.0	-	-	8.3
Chub Lake WMA	667	Dakota	Castle Rock	42-3D	203	•		•	•		•	•	•	-	32.5	23.6	0.5	-	43.4
Chub Lake has a small, non-paved access for hunting or canoeing. Many forest songbirds can be viewed or heard here.																			
Church WMA For more information call 320-289-2493.	143	Lac Qui Parle	Boyd	20-1E	95	•		•			•	•		-	49.3	50.8	-	-	-
Clair T. Rollings Chippewa Co. WMA	77	Chippewa	Milan	20-2A	120	•		•			•	•		15.0	29.2	32.4	1.4	0.1	18.1
Field hunting for Canada geese. Area consists of three 40s in three sections containing a wetland flowage, woody plantings, grasslands, an old woodlot, and a food plot. The flowage into the unit is identified as C.D. #13. An old farmstead occupied part of the NW 40, but old buildings were torn down and the area was planted with grass and trees. Wheelchair access limited to gravel roads adjacent to each 40-acre parcel.																			
Claire Rollings WMA For more information call 320-289-2493.	39	Swift	Benson	7-4C	401	•		•	•		•	•	•	8.4	43.3	16.1	1.7	8.2	22.4
Clare Johnson WMA For more information call 507-537-6250.	178	Lincoln	Canby	32-3C	83	•		•			•	•		-	46.3	53.7	-	-	-
Clark Lake WMA	521	Scott	Belle Plaine	40-3D	34	•		•			•			25.1	44.2	25.7	-	-	5.4
Numerous grassland bird species. Red-tailed hawks and American kestrels patrol open spaces. WMA is mostly established prairie with a portion of a wetland connected to Clark Lake and a small corn food plot. Managed for grassland species. Wheelchair access limited to parking lot along Hwy. 169.																			
Clawson WMA For more information call 507-537-6250.	150	Yellow Medicine	Clarkfield	20-3D	79	•		•			•			-	72.8	-	-	-	27.2
Cleanwater WMA	522	Murray	Iona	64-2D	35	•		•			•			-	83.3	16.7	-	-	-
Partially drained wetland with associated native-grass uplands. Managed to provide nesting cover for ground-nesting wildlife.																			
Clifton WMA For more information call 507-537-6250.	280	Lyon	Marshall	48-3A	173	•		•			•	•		-	45.1	53.6	-	-	1.3
Clouster Lake WMA	348	McLeod	Silver Lake	25-6D	80	•		•			•			1.6	13.4	78.8	-	-	6.3
WMA consists mostly of drained lake bed, dominated by reed canary grass. Several small upland areas are present.																			
Colinoso WMA For more information call 507-537-6250.	168	Lincoln	Canby	32-3C	81	•		•			•	•		26.8	64.8	6.3	-	-	2.0
Collaris WMA For more information call 507-537-6250.	193	Lincoln	Hendricks	32-2D	73	•		•			•	•		-	51.6	48.4	-	-	-
Collinson WMA For more information call 507-537-6250.	265	Lincoln	Lake Benton	46-3B	87	•		•			•	•		-	46.1	44.9	-	-	8.9
Coon Creek WMA For more information call 507-537-6250.	279	Lincoln, Lyon	Russell	47-5B	1,049	•		•			•	•		1.1	34.6	58.9	3.6	-	1.8
Coot WMA For more information call 507-537-6250.	254	Lincoln	Arco	47-4A	348	•		•			•	•		16.8	42.2	41.0	-	-	-
Cordova WMA	645	Le Sueur	Le Center	55-4B	55	•		•			•			-	11.1	88.0	-	-	0.7
WMA consists of two separate units. Both are wetland/grassland complexes.																			
Corinna WMA	246	Wright	Maple Lake	12-1D	79	•		•			•	•	•	1.9	25.3	16.5	-	45.7	10.7
Hunting, trapping, wildlife viewing, and hiking.																			
Coteau Pit WMA For more information call 507-537-6250.	319	Lincoln	Lake Benton	46-3D	81	•		•			•	•		31.1	32.3	-	-	-	-
Cotton-Jack WMA For more information call 507-831-2900.	598	Jackson	Heron Lake	65-5D	156	•		•			•	•		14.7	34.6	46.1	0.1	-	2.7
County Line WMA - North Unit	523	Murray	Iona	64-2D	165	•		•			•	•		6.7	56.7	26.9	-	1.0	5.8
This North sub-unit has uncommon wet prairie in the NE corner. Plants include rattlesnake master and bottled gentian. Sub-unit contains several wetlands and associated uplands with native grasses, woody cover plantings, and food plots.																			
County Line WMA - South Unit	533	Murray, Nobles	Iona	64-2D	164	•		•			•	•		6.2	36.5	53.5	-	-	3.8
South sub-unit contains 90-acre Willow Lake, which is managed for waterfowl. Associated uplands contain food plots, woody cover plantings, and native grasslands. This unit is managed primarily for upland game.																			
Creekside WMA For more information call 320-289-2493.	104	Lac Qui Parle	Dawson	19-5D	100	•		•			•			-	7.4	88.7	-	0.6	3.3
Crooked Road WMA	268	Isanti	Spencer Brook	13-6A	381	•		•	•		•	•	•	-	17.1	31.8	34.1	-	17.1
Many wading birds and raptors present. Species of note include trumpeter swans, terns, and Blanding's turtles.																			
Crosse WMA For more information call 507-831-2900.	622	Jackson	Heron Lake	65-6E	67	•		•			•	•		-	46.1	53.4	-	-	0.6
Crow River WMA	73	Stearns	Belgrade	9-4A	155	•		•			•	•		-	55.4	44.6	-	-	-
Hunting, trapping, wildlife viewing, and hiking. Excellent for pheasant, waterfowl, and other grassland-nesting wildlife.																			
Crow Wing River II For more information call 507-225-3572.	358	McLeod	Biscay	25-4E	60									-	33.3	16.2	13.5	37.0	-
Cuka WMA	128	Chippewa	Raymond	22-1A	197	•		•			•	•		-	41.7	52.3	0.5	-	4.6
Heaviest public use during pheasant and deer seasons.																			
Current WMA - Central Unit	377	Murray	Lake Wilson	47-6E	9			•			•	•		-	38.8	48.2	-	5.9	-
WMA consists of two separate sub-units. This sub-unit is a small grass area on the east shore of Current Lake.																			
Current WMA - Island Unit	375	Murray	Lake Wilson	47-6E	4						•	•		-	26.2	73.8	-	-	-
A sand beach is popular for swimming and fishing. This sub-unit is a small island of sand and rock with some grass, cattails, and a few trees. This land was purchased to build a dam on Current Lake. In low-water years, the area provides access to an island for duck hunting.																			
Curry Slough WMA For more information call 507-831-2900.	625	Watonwan	Saint James	67-6B	111	•		•			•	•		22.6	15.3	53.1	0.3	5.0	3.4
Daak WMA For more information call 320-231-5163.	293	Renville	Buffalo Lake	24-2E	40	•		•			•	•		-	11.1	89.2	-	-	-
Dacotah WMA For more information call 320-289-2493.	70	Lac Qui Parle	Marietta	18-2C	49	•		•			•	•		-	34.5	62.7	-	-	3.0
Dalton Johnson WMA	225	Kandiyohi	Cosmos	23-5D	150	•		•			•	•		-	92.9	5.8	-	1.5	-
WMA contains 37 acres of restored wetlands, 100 acres of former cropland seeded to a combination of native plants, old farm grove, 3-acre food plot, and a small natural wetland. It will take a few years to mature. Access from highway, driveway, and parking area.																			
Danvers WMA For more information call 320-289-2493.	29	Swift	Benson	6-3C	2,949	•		•			•	•		2.3	44.3	50.9	0.2	-	2.4
Daub's Lake WMA - Baune Tract All tracts: For more information call 320-289-2493.	331	Redwood	Wabasso	36-1E	120	•		•			•			19.6	45.8	19.7	-	-	14.8
Daub's Lake WMA - Tract 20	327	Redwood	Wabasso	36-1E	37	•		•			•	•	•	-	15.5	52.5	-	32.0	-
Daub's Lake WMA - Tracts 1-2, 4-5 and 16	349	Redwood	Wabasso	50-1A	184	•		•			•			0.4	5.4	81.6	8.5	2.1	2.1
Daub's Lake WMA - Tracts 12, 12a, 12b	335	Redwood	Wabasso	50-1A	137	•		•			•			8.0	56.5	23.8	-	-	11.7
Daub's Lake WMA - Tracts 8-10a	338	Redwood	Wabasso	50-1A	117	•		•			•			18.2	46.8	26.3	-	2.9	5.5
David H. Steen WMA For more information call 320-289-2493.	1	Big Stone	Clinton	4-2A	184	•					•	•		-	75.1	-	23.2	-	1.7
Dawson WMA For more information call 320-289-2493.	108	Lac Qui Parle	Dawson	19-6D	27	•		•			•			-	28.9	71.1	-	-	-
Dayland WMA For more information call 507-537-6250.	345	Lyon	Balaton	48-1C	21	•		•			•	•		-	-	-	-	-	100.0
Dead Coon WMA For more information call 507-537-6250.	272	Lincoln	Tyler	47-5B	101	•		•			•	•		14.1	20.3	16.8	-	-	48.8
Deer Creek WMA	842	Mower	Grand Meadow	92-3B	40	•		•			•			-	93.5	1.2	-	-	5.2
Pheasant and some deer hunting opportunities. WMA is a mixture of dry-mesic to wet-mesic grassland. 25 acres planted to native grasses and forbs; 5 acres to a bur oak savanna project. Managed for pheasants, deer, and grassland wildlife. Access via 3/4-mile walk from Hwy 16.																			
Deer Lane WMA For more information call 507-537-6250.	347	Lyon	Balaton	48-2C	117	•		•			•	•		-	51.7	19.4	-	-	28.8
Degroot WMA - East Unit	406	Murray	Lake Wilson	63-6A	6	•		•			•	•		-	-	62.1	-	36.2	-
WMA contains two sub-units with small prairie wetlands and some medium-quality prairie. This East sub-unit is a small wetland and willow patch.																			
Degroot WMA - West Unit	405	Murray	Lake Wilson	47-6E	72	•		•			•			-	43.9	48.2	-	2.2	5.7

Name	Number	County	Nearest Town	Pg / Coord	Acres	Deer	Bear	Small Game	Forest Birds	Sharptail	Pheasant	Waterfowl	Turkey	Cropland	Grassland	Emergent Wetland	Open Water	Lowland	Upland
						Game Species								**% Cover Type**					
WMA contains two sub-units with small prairie wetlands and some medium-quality prairie. This West sub-unit is composed of wetlands, upland grassland, and woody cover plantings. Flowing water creates a more diverse wetland community.																			
Delft WMA For more information call 507-831-2900.	576	Cottonwood	Delft	66-3C	352	•		•			•	•		3.5	23.7	49.0	19.2	-	4.1
Delhi WMA For more information call 320-231-5163.	302	Redwood	Redwood Falls	36-2D	81	•		•			•			24.4	36.7	33.0	-	1.5	4.5
Des Belt WMA For more information call 507-831-2900.	760	Martin	Ceylon	86-1D	82	•		•	•		•	•		11.0	30.2	17.1	6.8	12.9	22.2
Deutsch WMA	385	McLeod	Brownton	38-3B	81						•			-	44.8	48.0	-	-	6.9
WMA consists of two separate tracts of land that are wetland/prairie complexes. Woody planting has been established for winter pheasant cover.																			
Deutz WMA For more information call 507-537-6250.	303	Lyon	Marshall	48-2B	43	•		•			•			-	87.5	-	-	-	12.7
Devils Run WMA	480	Murray	Dovray	65-4B	90	•		•			•			-	52.2	43.8	-	-	3.9
High hills; scenic hiking. WMA is a stream valley with steep grassland slopes, some emergent wetlands, and woody cover plantings. Quality prairie in unit's NW corner. WMA managed for upland gamebirds.																			
Dewald WMA	659	Nobles	Rushmore	82-2C	16			•			•			-	100.0	-	-	-	-
WMA is a small creek valley grassland with the Rock River running through it.																			
Diamond Lake WMA	679	Le Sueur	Kilkenny	55-5C	274	•		•			•	•		-	22.1	56.1	-	4.8	17.0
Carry-in access to Diamond Lake on the lake's east side. WMA consists of forest and grassland adjacent to Diamond Lake and another smaller lake to the west. Several fields planted to prairie grasses and wildflowers and are maintained by periodic prescribed burning. Hardwood seedlings planted to restore a fragment of Big Woods forest.																			
Dierenfield WMA	485	Murray	Chandler	64-1C	56	•		•			•	•		-	6.8	86.4	-	3.8	3.4
Medium-sized permanent marsh with no associated uplands. A woody planting protects marsh vegetation for wintering pheasants.																			
Dietrich Lange WMA (1)	132	Kandiyohi	Spicer	9-5D	201	•		•	•		•	•		0.8	41.0	51.3	-	1.9	4.5
Unit composed of two areas with 1/4 mile of private land between parcels. Main part of unit contains the flowage area between lakes Calhoun and Green with large tracts of emergent vegetation and open channel. A food plot is on the unit's north part. Public access to Lake Calhoun also exists along the south shore. The west end of the North unit is a State Wildlife Sanctuary, closed Sept. 1 through close of waterfowl season. Check for signs. Access limited to strips and/or roads adjacent to the unit.																			
Dietrich Lange WMA (2)	126	Kandiyohi	Spicer	9-5D	701	•		•	•		•	•		2.5	13.5	55.9	11.2	5.1	11.0
Unit composed of two areas with 1/4 mile of private land between the two parcels. The main part of the unit contains the flowage area between lakes Calhoun and Green with large tracts of emergent vegetation and open channel. A food plot is maintained on the north part of the unit. A public access to Lake Calhoun also exists on this WMA, along the south shore of the lake. The West end of the North unit is posted as a State Wildlife Sanctuary, closed Sept. 1 through close of waterfowl season. Check for the signs. Access limited to access strips and/or roads adjacent to the unit.																			
Discors WMA For more information call 507-537-6250.	290	Lincoln	Tyler	47-4C	43	•		•			•	•		-	17.1	82.7	-	-	-
Discovery WMA	120	Stearns	Richmond	10-3A	129	•		•			•	•	•	-	65.1	35.0	-	-	-
Hunting, trapping, wildlife viewing, and hiking. Grassland benefits dozens of upland bird nesters. Restored prairie grasslands have a diverse mix of wildflowers. June/July are good times to view the flowering grasslands.																			
Dorer WMA For more information call 507-537-6250.	185	Lincoln	Hendricks	32-3C	338	•		•			•	•		3.4	24.9	53.4	15.7	-	2.5
Dove Lake WMA	688	Le Sueur	Elysian	55-4D	258	•		•	•		•	•	•	10.8	25.8	37.8	-	-	24.9
WMA consists of two tracts. Eastern tract contains a drained lakebed, grassy hills, and a forested knob that is a remnant of the Big Woods. Western tract has a cattail marsh, forest, and hayland. A parking lot is on the eastern tract. Walk-in access to the western tract via CSAH 130. A prairie grass field and a food plot exist on this WMA. A no-shooting buffer zone is posted around residence at NE end of WMA. Wheelchair access limited to the gravel parking lot and adjacent cty/township roads. A primitive trail runs from the parking lot along the edge of a prairie grass field to a seasonal wetland.																			
Dovray WMA - Central Unit	456	Murray	Dovray	64-3A	281	•		•			•	•		2.8	18.2	75.7	-	1.7	1.5
All units: Popular with waterfowl hunters. Part of a complex of five large wetlands connected by the same drainage outlet with associated uplands containing native grasslands, woody plantings, and food plots.																			
Dovray WMA - North Unit	450	Murray	Dovray	64-3A	86	•		•			•	•		-	24.8	75.2	-	-	-
Access to the large marsh off the highway is restricted to vehicles carrying watercraft. No other motorized vehicles are allowed.																			
Dovray WMA - Northwest Unit	445	Murray	Dovray	64-3A	13	•		•			•	•		-	43.2	28.8	-	-	28.0
Dovray WMA - South Unit	465	Murray	Dovray	65-4A	379	•		•			•	•		7.5	18.9	68.5	-	-	5.1
Dr. Johnan C. Hvoslef WMA	858	Fillmore	Amherst	94-3C	233	•		•	•		•		•	-	35.6	0.4	2.1	-	62.1
Hunting, trapping, fishing, and wildlife viewing. Good spring and fall migrant viewing. Area open to archery hunting only from Sept. 1-Oct. 31 and during spring turkey season. Firearms hunting (no centerfire rifles) allowed from Nov. 1-Dec. 15.																			
Duckhaven WMA	719	Blue Earth	St. Clair	70-2B	40			•			•	•		-	-	80.7	-	19.3	-
For more information call 507-225-3572. Wheelchair access limited to adjacent cty/township roads.																			
Dustoff WMA	133	Stearns	Eden Valley	10-2B	37	•		•			•	•		-	69.0	15.5	-	3.7	11.2
Good hunting, trapping, wildlife viewing, and hiking. WMA includes restored prairie, open-water wetlands, and a tree/shrub thicket on the west end. Wheelchair access limited to public roads and mowed parking lots.																			
Dwire WMA For more information call 507-537-6250.	298	Lyon	Russell	48-1B	40	•		•			•	•		-	-	4.0	-	-	-
Dwyer WMA	716	Rice	Warsaw	56-1C	56	•					•	•		-	0.5	72.6	0.2	14.1	11.2
Good spring wildlife watching. Look for blue-winged teal, marsh wrens, sora rails, bitterns, and green herons.																			
Dybsand WMA For more information call 320-231-5163.	222	Renville	Sacred Heart	36-1A	78	•		•			•	•		11.5	17.3	66.7	-	-	4.5
Eagle Lake WMA	584	Nobles	Kinbrae	65-4E	52	•		•			•			4.8	89.0	-	-	-	6.2
WMA contains a portion of a drained lakebed and associated upland planted to native grasses and a food plot.																			
Eagle WMA	135	Kandiyohi	Willmar	9-4E	50	•		•			•	•		-	32.0	51.1	-	8.5	7.6
Small unit consists of shallow, emergent wetland, upland grass, and small areas of lowland deciduous trees.																			
Earl Swain WMA	690	Le Sueur	Elysian	55-4D	107	•		•	•		•	•	•	17.8	28.2	30.0	-	-	24.0
WMA contains a restored cattail marsh, grass-covered hills, and a remnant of the Big Woods. Water levels in the marsh are managed to benefit waterfowl and wetland wildlife.																			
East Chain WMA For more information call 507-831-2900.	769	Martin	East Chain	86-3D	239	•		•	•		•	•	•	1.9	28.1	60.0	-	1.9	8.0
Eastside WMA	814	Olmsted	Rochester	75-4B	119	•		•			•			-	29.5	39.4	12.8	9.9	8.5
Excellent waterfowl and wetland wildlife viewing. About 7 acres of an old crop field have been planted to native grasses and forbs. Pheasants, deer, and small game hunting. No waterfowl hunting allowed.																			
Eden WMA	451	Pipestone	Ihlen	62-2C	159	•		•			•	•		17.9	72.0	-	-	-	10.1
WMA consists of poor-quality native prairie remnants, native grass, woody plantings, and food plots.																			
Edward R Mohs WMA	47	Stearns	Brooten	8-3A	209	•		•			•	•	•	0.2	-	82.3	-	10.2	7.3
Hunting, trapping, wildlife viewing, and hiking. Large reed canary grasslands and willow thickets dominate. Area is part of a large deer, pheasant, and turkey wintering area. Access to Tamarack Lake by foot travel only. Unit's southern portion offers more-diverse cover. Wheelchair access limited to public roads and mowed parking lots.																			
Ehrenberg WMA For more information call 320-289-2493.	17	Swift	Holloway	6-1B	168	•		•	•		•	•	•	7.8	37.0	46.6	-	-	7.3
Einck WMA	555	Nobles	Wilmont	64-1E	50	•		•			•	•		-	20.2	76.6	-	-	3.4
WMA is a small, semi-permanent marsh with associated grasslands and a woody planting.																			
Elder WMA	434	Murray	Currie	64-2A	21	•		•			•			-	95.1	-	-	-	4.9
WMA is predominantly an upland bird production area.																			
Ells-pit WMA	649	Nobles	Ellsworth	81-5D	5			•			•			-	-	-	-	-	-
WMA is a small abandoned gravel pit with trees and shrubs.																			
Ellsborough WMA	374	Murray	Ruthton	47-6E	80	•		•			•	•		-	63.1	23.9	-	-	13.1
Good example of prairie pothole habitat. WMA is predominantly an upland bird production area.																			
Elmer Weltz WMA For more information call 507-537-6250.	267	Lyon	Lynd	47-5A	161	•		•			•	•		15.1	58.7	23.0	-	-	3.3
Emerald WMA For more information call 507-537-6250.	258	Lincoln	Lake Benton	46-3A	77	•		•			•	•		-	25.2	72.7	-	-	2.1
Emerson WMA For more information call 320-231-5163.	626	Brown	Madelia	68-3A	119	•		•			•	•		10.6	4.8	81.2	-	-	3.5
Engebretson WMA - East Unit	449	Murray	Slayton	64-2B	3	•		•			•			-	67.9	-	-	-	32.1
WMA consists of two sub-units. East sub-unit is a small area of trees and grass.																			
Engebretson WMA - West Unit	444	Murray	Slayton	64-2B	48	•		•			•	•	•	-	70.5	-	-	23.8	6.0
West sub-unit is a wooded river valley with some grassland. Beaver Creek runs through unit. Wild turkeys found here. Irregular boundaries: Pay attention to signs.																			
Erickson WMA For more information call 320-634-0342.	6	Stevens	Alberta	5-5A	160	•		•			•	•		-	23.5	72.1	-	-	4.1
Erie WMA For more information call 507-537-6250.	191	Yellow Medicine	St. Leo	33-6C	69	•		•			•	•		-	56.3	43.6	-	-	-
Esker WMA	666	Rice	Little Chicago	42-2E	48	•		•			•	•		-	27.7	17.0	0.4	8.2	45.1
Look for beavers, deer, coyotes, raccoons, ring-necked ducks, pied-billed grebes, green herons, and gray tree frogs. Watch warblers in spring. Vehicle access to parking area using cartway trail not recommended when wet and muddy; please walk in. A unique glacial esker is located on WMA's east side.																			
Espen Island WMA	746	Goodhue	Red Wing	44-3D	13			•	•			•		-	-	-	-	100.0	-
WMA consists entirely of bottomland hardwood forest and is frequently flooded. Hunting for small game, forest birds, and waterfowl. Wetland and forest wildlife viewing. Bald eagles often seen along Mississippi River.																			
Evans Slough WMAF or more information call 507-225-3572.	702	Blue Earth	Vernon Center	69-4C	85	•		•			•	•		-	-	97.3	-	-	2.8
Ewy Lake WMA For more information call 507-831-2900.	615	Watonwan	Sveadahl	67-6B	227	•		•			•	•		11.9	32.9	44.4	-	-	10.6
Exceder WMA For more information call 507-831-2900.	712	Martin	Welcome	68-1E	100	•		•			•	•		13.7	36.4	42.5	-	-	7.2
Expandere WMA For more information call 507-831-2900.	561	Cottonwood	Storden	65-6C	896	•		•			•	•		4.4	19.7	72.0	-	0.9	2.0
Expectation WMA For more information call 507-537-6250.	206	Lincoln	Hendricks	32-2E	47	•		•			•	•		-	38.6	49.2	-	-	12.4
Factor WMA	657	Le Sueur	Cordova	55-4B	135	•		•			•	•		-	9.0	57.2	1.8	-	32.0
WMA is on the NE side of Gorman Lake and is a wetland/shrubland complex with some open grassy areas. Access by boat only.																			
Faribault WMA	738	Rice	Faribault	56-2D	522			•			•			22.6	39.8	11.7	0.5	4.2	20.7
Good bird watching. Look for pheasants, deer, red fox, mink, savannah and Henslow's sparrows, crossbills, bobolinks, garter snakes, long-eared owls, and mourning doves.																			
Faxon WMA	494	Sibley	Belle Plaine	40-3C	41	•		•			•			18.9	-	81.1	-	-	-
WMA is a wetland/grassland complex. A food plot has been established on the WMA. Wheelchair access limited to adjacent township road.																			
Faxvog WMA For more information call 320-231-5163.	285	Redwood	Vesta	35-5E	105	•		•			•		•	25.9	51.0	18.3	0.3	2.5	1.9
Fenmont WMA	524	Murray, Nobles	Wilmont	64-1D	276	•		•			•	•		6.1	48.0	40.2	-	-	3.1
Ample road access makes good wildlife viewing. WMA contains permanent and semi-permanent wetlands with associated uplands, woody plantings, and food plots.																			
Findley WMA For more information call 507-225-3572.	741	Waseca	Waseca	71-6A	287	•		•	•		•	•	•	-	12.1	75.5	-	-	12.3
Fish Lake WMA	67	Stearns	Brooten	8-3A	1							•		-	100.0	-	-	-	-
Unit serves as primitive access to Fish Lake. Spring and fall bird migrations can be observed on or around Fish Lake. Nearly all of Fish Lake's shoreline is private. Wheelchair access limited to public roads and mowed parking lots.																			
Flinks Slough WMA For more information call 320-289-2493.	152	Lac Qui Parle, Yellow Medicine	Boyd	20-1E	358	•		•			•	•		2.1	29.7	67.8	-	-	0.4
Florida Creek WMA - Lost Unit All units: For more information call 320-289-2493.	86	Lac Qui Parle	Madison	18-3D	40	•		•			•	•		-	-	100.0	-	-	-
Florida Creek WMA - Middle Unit	84	Lac Qui Parle	Madison	18-3D	43	•		•			•	•		-	-	100.0	-	-	-
Florida Creek WMA - North West Unit	82	Lac Qui Parle	Madison	18-3D	455	•		•			•	•		12.0	6.6	75.5	-	-	6.0
Florida Creek WMA - South East Unit	91	Lac Qui Parle	Madison	18-3D	311	•		•			•	•		6.2	5.0	86.2	-	-	2.6
Follies WMA	79	Stearns, Kandiyohi	New London	9-4B	502	•		•			•	•		-	27.4	41.5	0.3	29.2	1.5
WMA lies on flat land and contains former crop fields seeded to native and non-native grasses, native prairie that was once pastured, and large areas of cattail marsh.																			
Fossum WMA - Thorn Unit For more information call 507-831-2900.	670	Watonwan	Odin	67-5D	69	•		•		•	•	•		-	-	-	-	-	-
Fox Lake WMA	732	Martin	Sherburn	85-6B	37			•			•			-	26.3	57.2	-	11.4	5.4
WMA is a wetland complex with some grassland and lowland brush located within the Fox Lake Game Refuge. Check boundary signs to stay within WMA.																			
Frank Breen WMA This small WMA is primarily wetland.	663	Le Sueur	Cleveland	54-3D	22						•			-	-	95.5	-	-	4.5
Franko WMA	158	Chippewa	Clara City	21-5C	67	•		•			•	•		-	31.3	66.8	-	0.5	0.3
Unit is primarily a shallow marsh with a narrow perimeter of grass, a small tree planting, and scattered volunteer deciduous trees. Parking limited to end of access strip.																			
Fred Hoffenkamp WMA	617	Nobles	Brewster	83-4A	87	•		•			•			-	88.0	5.5	-	-	6.4
WMA is creek valley grassland with some woody-cover areas. Unit managed for upland gamebirds.																			
Freeman WMA	12	Stevens	Hancock	6-1A	322	•					•			27.8	65.4	1.4	-	-	4.9
Excellent area to view mesic grassland bird species including upland sandpipers, bobolinks, western meadowlarks, and clay-colored sparrows. Significant amount of native prairie and restored prairie. Managed for upland gamebirds and prairie and wetland. Uncommon native wildflowers, such as pasque flowers, prairie smoke, Canada anemone, coneflowers, purple prairie clover, and wild sunflowers.																			
Freemont WMA	260	Sherburne	Zimmerman	13-5A	165	•		•	•			•	•	-	24.5	53.1	-	-	22.4
Hunting, trapping, wildlife viewing, and hiking. North Unit is mostly bur/pin oak forest with scattered openings. A larger sedge/cattail wetland flanks the border. South Unit is approximately 1/3 remnant prairie and within Zimmerman city limits, where a shooting-restriction ordinance is in place.																			
Fritsche Creek WMA	510	Nicollet	Klossner	52-3B	385	•		•			•	•	•	2.3	-	23.3	-	71.9	2.5
Hiking, wildlife viewing, hunting, fishing, and cross-country skiing. Managed for deer, turkeys, and waterfowl. Several rare mollusks found here. Active water bird nesting colony. Breeding bald eagles seen here. Good bird watching.																			
Fulda WMA	559	Nobles	Fulda	64-3D	157	•		•			•	•		6.1	17.4	72.4	-	-	4.1
WMA is an 80-acre permanent marsh with associated grassland, woody cover plantings, and food plot. Carry-in water access to the marsh.																			

Name	Number	County	Nearest Town	Pg / Coord	Acres	Game Species: Deer	Bear	Small Game	Forest Birds	Sharptail	Pheasant	Waterfowl	Turkey	% Cover Type: Cropland	Grassland	Emergent Wetland	Open Water	Lowland	Upland
Fulica WMA For more information call 320-289-2493.	72	Lac Qui Parle	Madison	18-3C	21	•		•			•	•		-	41.5	58.5	-	-	-
Furgamme WMA For more information call 507-537-6250.	262	Lyon	Marshall	47-5A	152	•		•			•	•		9.3	21.6	59.5	-	-	9.5
Fury WMA WMA is a small, permanent marsh adjacent to East Graham Lake.	608	Nobles	Kinbrae	65-4E	26							•		-	-	-	76.2	23.8	-
Gabriel Anderson WMA For more information call 507-537-6250.	221	Yellow Medicine, Lyon	Cottonwood	34-3C	110	•		•			•	•		-	14.2	85.8	-	-	-
Gadwall WMA For more information call 507-537-6250.	339	Lyon	Balaton	48-1C	32	•		•			•	•		-	34.8	60.9	-	-	4.3
Gage WMA For more information call 507-225-3572. No wheelchair access to this unit.	698	Blue Earth	Garden City	69-6B	34	•		•	•		•	•	•	0.9	-	-	33.9	65.5	-
Gales WMA - Main Unit Both units: For more information call 320-231-5163.	346	Redwood	Walnut Grove	49-5B	239	•		•			•	•		6.5	39.8	39.0	12.0	-	2.8
Gales WMA - Tract 9	350	Redwood	Walnut Grove	49-5B	29	•		•			•	•		-	28.3	51.0	-	18.2	2.4
Gallinago WMA	499	Murray	Chandler	64-1D	139	•		•			•	•		1.3	34.9	58.9	-	1.9	2.9
A township road passing through the area provides wildlife viewing opportunities. Limited waterfowl hunting. WMA is a shallow wetland-grassland area with woody cover and a food plot.																			
Garvin WMA For more information call 507-537-6250.	365	Lyon	Balaton	48-2D	82	•		•			•			-	79.2	15.0	-	-	5.8
Geneva WMA For more information call 507-280-5066.	795	Freeborn	Geneva	72-2E	86			•			•	•	•	-	17.0	41.0	3.6	33.9	2.6
Gennessee WMA	189	Kandiyohi	Atwater	23-5B	112	•		•			•		•	-	24.2	57.5	0.7	5.4	8.4
Contains old fields now in non-native grasses, a small piece of woods, old pasture, a small tree planting, large areas of cattail marsh, and shoreline on two small lakes. Feeder crib. Quite limited to approaches off CR 2.																			
George and Elizabeth Lange WMA For more information call 507-225-3572.	734	Blue Earth	Mapleton	70-1D	74	•		•	•		•	•	•	-	27.2	30.8	7.0	22.6	12.1
Giese WMA For more information call 507-537-6250.	373	Lyon	Balaton	48-1D	37	•		•			•	•		-	40.6	59.4	-	-	-
Gilfillan Lake WMA	676	Blue Earth	Madison Lake	54-2D	564	•		•	•		•	•	•	1.7	20.7	72.0	-	4.6	1.0
For more information call 507-225-3572. Wheelchair access limited to adjacent cty/township roads. Gravel parking lot on unit's east side.																			
Gleam WMA For more information call 507-831-2900.	711	Martin	Truman	68-2E	27	•		•			•	•		19.2	23.8	50.2	-	-	6.8
Goethite WMA	852	Fillmore	Spring Valley	93-5C	304	•		•	•		•	•	•	-	69.6	-	9.2	4.7	16.5
Hunting, trapping, fishing and wildlife viewing. Special-use permit required for beaver trapping when allowed.																			
Gollnick WMA For more information call 320-289-2493.	69	Lac Qui Parle	Marietta	18-3C	520	•		•			•			-	27.3	48.0	-	-	24.7
Good Medicine WMA For more information call 507-537-6250.	256	Lyon	Marshall	34-1E	57	•		•			•	•		2.1	11.8	83.8	-	-	-
Gordie Mikkelson WMA	378	Anoka	Martin Lake	14-3B	817	•	•	•	•		•		•	1.5	7.4	32.1	-	22.8	36.0
Windswept Prairie Environmental Education Area is a planted prairie established in 1999. Primarily managed for woodland and wooded wetland wildlife such as deer and turkeys.																			
Gordon W Yeager WMA - Northeast Unit	809	Olmsted	Rochester	75-4B	10	•		•	•		•		•	-	19.2	-	-	-	80.8
All units: Birding, berry picking, hiking, nature observation, and hunting. In winter, 10,000-15,000 geese feed on corn food plots. WMA is within Rochester Game Refuge. Managed to provide a winter feeding location for the migratory Interlake Giant Canada geese that winter at Rochester. No waterfowl hunting allowed. Some deer and small game hunting permitted, but unit is within Rochester city limits, so hunting is restricted to shotguns with fine shot for small game and archery hunting for big game.																			
Gordon W Yeager WMA - Northwest Unit	808	Olmsted	Rochester	75-4B	34	•		•	•		•		•	48.1	11.3	-	-	-	40.6
Gordon W Yeager WMA - Southeast Unit	811	Olmsted	Rochester	75-4B	159	•		•	•		•		•	-	6.4	-	0.7	21.9	65.3
Gordon W Yeager WMA - Southwest Tract	810	Olmsted	Rochester	75-4B	111	•		•	•		•		•	58.5	28.4	-	-	-	8.5
Gores Pool #3 WMA	705	Dakota, Goodhue	Hastings	44-1B	6,449	•		•	•			•		-	0.4	10.3	39.6	47.2	2.6
WMA is located along the Mississippi River, offering many recreational opportunites such as fishing and boating. Two boat launches within the unit and another where C.R. 68 crosses the Vermillion River. WMA consists entirely of Mississippi and Vermillion River floodplain forest and backwater marshes. Designated Migratory Waterfowl Refuge near the unit's south end is off-limits to all activities.																			
Grace WMA	96	Chippewa	Clara City	21-4A	159	•		•			•	•		8.0	64.6	20.9	-	1.0	5.4
Both units: Wide variety of native plants on the native prairie parcel. Two separate parcels. Some native prairie exists on the NE tract of this unit, which is rare in this area. Hundreds of acres of adjacent private cropland have been enrolled in CRP, with permanent cover established. Access restricted to adjacent roadways.																			
Grace WMA	98	Chippewa	Clara City	21-4A	443	•		•			•	•		6.8	50.3	27.2	9.5	0.5	4.2
Graham Creek WMA For more information call 507-831-2900.	620	Jackson	Heron Lake	65-5E	90	•		•			•	•		28.4	70.9	0.7	-	-	-
Grandview WMA For more information call 507-537-6250.	234	Lyon	Ghent	34-1D	438	•		•			•			10.9	31.2	51.3	-	-	6.5
Grass Lake WMA	282	Wright	Cokato	25-6B	379	•		•			•	•		0.1	15.7	75.6	-	3.2	5.4
Hunting, trapping, wildlife viewing, and hiking. Excellent prairie grassland and cattail-dominated wetland habitat, usually with good numbers of pheasants. Beautiful vistas of expansive grassland and wetland habitats blend with border areas of old farmsteads.																			
Gravel Pit 1062 WMA	66	Stearns	Belgrade	9-4A	15	•		•			•			-	68.0	-	-	8.7	24.0
WMA composed of restored prairie, lowland sedge, and willow. Limited hunting/trapping opportunities. Watch for wildflowers June-August.																			
Gravel Pit 1672 WMA For more information call 320-255-4279.	171	Stearns	Luxemburg	11-5B	4									-	100.0	-	-	-	-
Gravel Pit 1748 WMA	399	Carver	New Germany	26-1E	4	•		•			•			-	100.0	-	-	-	-
Old gravel pit covered by medium-high grass and a few trees and shrubs. WMA provides habitat for upland species.																			
Gravel Pit 2749 WMA	398	Carver	New Germany	26-1E	3	•		•			•			-	52.0	-	-	48.0	-
Old gravel pit covered by medium-high grass and a few trees and shrubs. WMA provides habitat for upland species.																			
Great Oasis WMA	417	Murray	Hadley	64-1A	124	•		•			•	•		25.0	12.7	20.7	-	-	41.7
Unique plant community is a remnant of the Big Woods. Site of earliest European settlement in Murray County. Contains designated old-growth basswood forest. Major deer wintering area.																			
Green Valley WMA For more information call 507-537-6250.	261	Lyon	Green Valley	34-3D	744	•		•			•	•		8.3	42.1	46.1	0.3	-	3.2
Greenhead WMA For more information call 507-537-6250.	381	Lyon	Tracy	48-3D	50	•		•			•	•		-	51.1	38.7	-	-	10.2
Greenleaf WMA	252	Meeker	Corvuso	24-2C	440	•		•	•		•	•	•	3.5	23.5	59.1	1.3	0.5	10.6
Unit lies in rolling topography and contains woodlands, large cattail marshlands with some open water, a food plot, fields of seeded natives, woody plantings, an old grove, and scattered deciduous trees.																			
Groebner WMA For more information call 320-231-5163.	529	Brown	Sleepy Eye	51-6E	78	•		•			•		•	17.6	69.8	3.1	1.7	3.8	4.3
Gromer's Draw WMA	389	Pipestone	Woodstock	63-4A	87	•		•			•			-	46.3	40.7	-	4.9	8.1
WMA is a wet prairie with food plots and woody cover planting managed for upland gamebirds.																			
Groth WMA - North Unit	582	Nobles	Wilmont	64-2E	24	•		•			•			-	-	97.9	-	1.7	-
WMA has two sub-units. North sub-unit is creek valley grassland with Jack Creek running through it.																			
Groth WMA - South Unit	591	Nobles	Reading	82-2A	73	•		•			•	•		2.5	26.0	69.5	-	-	1.9
WMA has two sub-units. South sub-unit contains a 35-acre permanent marsh managed for waterfowl with associated grasslands and woody cover plantings.																			
Grovelund WMA	177	Meeker	Grove City	10-1E	27						•	•		-	-	43.8	56.2	-	-
Unit is primarily the north tip of the open lake with a narrow band of lowland grass and cattail. Provides public access to Lund Lake. Limited to the adjacent roadside.																			
Grundmeyer WMA	420	Sibley	Gibbon	38-2E	94						•	•		-	35.4	61.9	-	-	2.6
WMA is a prairie/wetland complex. Remnant native prairie plants occur on the upland between the railroad right-of-way and the marsh. A woody planting has been established to provide winter cover for pheasants. No parking.																			
H.C. Southwick WMA - North Unit	482	Murray	Slayton	64-2C	545	•		•			•	•		-	16.9	74.6	-	5.4	3.2
Largest public hunting area in Murray County. An abandoned dike offers good wetland wildlife viewing. Major wintering area for deer and pheasants.																			
H.C. Southwick WMA - South Unit	486	Murray	Slayton	64-2C	25	•		•			•	•		-	63.3	-	-	29.8	7.3
Area is a creek valley grassland with Big Slough WPA bordering on the north.																			
Haberman WMA	531	Murray	Lime Creek	65-4D	96	•		•			•	•		6.9	68.9	12.9	-	1.5	9.9
Site of earliest European settlement in Murray County. Predominantly managed for upland birds.																			
Halls Lake WMA For more information call 507-280-5066.	797	Freeborn	Alden	89-6B	152									-	7.4	73.5	-	0.9	18.1
Halva Marsh WMA	325	McLeod	Silver Lake	25-4D	88	•		•			•	•		-	6.8	88.8	-	-	4.4
Wetland with some open grassland areas. Trees and shrubs were planted on the south side of the marsh to provide winter cover for pheasants. Wheelchair access limited to primitive parking area and adjacent cty/township roads.																			
Hamlin WMA For more information call 320-289-2493.	88	Lac Qui Parle	Madison	19-4C	279	•		•			•	•		26.4	9.2	63.5	-	-	1.0
Hanson WMA For more information call 507-537-6250.	181	Yellow Medicine	St. Leo	34-1B	12	•		•			•			-	56.3	0.8	-	-	42.9
Hansonville WMA For more information call 507-537-6250.	170	Lincoln	Hendricks	32-2C	35	•		•			•	•		20.4	30.5	48.9	-	-	-
Hantho WMA For more information call 320-289-2493.	42	Lac Qui Parle	Madison	5-5E	338	•		•			•	•		-	31.7	67.0	-	-	1.4
Happy Hollow WMA For more information call 507-537-6250.	340	Lyon	Balaton	48-1C	18	•		•			•	•		-	32.8	34.4	-	-	32.8
Hardwood Creek WMA	467	Washington	Forest Lake	15-5E	583	•	•	•	•		•		•	-	11.4	15.3	0.1	56.4	16.8
Large wooded swamp offers plenty of room for hunting and cross-country skiing or snowshoeing. Totals 583 acres in two parcels. Mgmt. emphasizes small planted prairies. Remainder of WMA is primarily wooded wetlands with wooded upland islands. WMA is part of the largest complex of native habitat remaining in Washington County. A 60-acre tamarack bog and high-quality maple-basswood forest are highlights. Wheelchair access limited to gravel parking lots on the north side of each parcel.																			
Hassen Valley WMA	342	McLeod	Biscay	25-4E	53	•		•			•	•		-	-	-	2.8	26.6	3.6
Fishing. WMA is an old gravel pit. Includes wooded land along the Crow River. Parking area located along SH 22.																			
Hastings WMA	680	Dakota	Hastings	43-6B	158	•		•	•		•			47.1	50.2	-	-	-	2.6
A rare, dry prairie can be found within the WMA. WMA provides habitat for upland species. A "shooting-prohibited" area exists on the west side. A flat field road borders about half the WMA.																			
Haverhill WMA	815	Olmsted	Dover	75-5B	189	•		•			•	•		72.2	27.8	-	-	-	-
Unit is farmed to provide winter food plots for the Interlake goose flock that winters at Rochester. Three fields have been planted to native prairie for nesting wildlife; there is one woody cover planting. Open to goose, waterfowl, small game, and deer hunting.																			
Hawks Nest WMA For more information call 507-537-6250.	226	Lincoln	Ivanhoe	33-4E	3	•		•			•	•		-	100.0	-	-	-	-
Haydenville WMA - East Unit All units: For more information call 320-289-2493.	65	Lac Qui Parle	Madison	18-3B	49	•		•			•			-	46.4	53.6	-	-	-
Haydenville WMA - Main Unit	63	Lac Qui Parle	Madison	18-3B	261	•		•			•	•		3.6	42.4	51.6	-	-	2.4
Haydenville WMA - Supplement Unit	52	Lac Qui Parle	Madison	18-3B	154	•		•			•	•		4.6	37.7	49.0	-	-	8.8
Hayes-Myhre WMA For more information call 320-289-2493.	74	Swift	Kerkhoven	8-1C	41	•		•			•	•		-	17.6	24.6	43.5	-	14.3
Helget-Braulick WMA For more information call 320-231-5163.	532	Brown	Hanska	52-1D	28	•		•			•	•		-	22.0	35.4	-	4.7	37.6
Hen Haven WMA	213	Meeker	Cosmos	24-1B	40	•		•	•		•	•		10.0	37.3	42.9	-	0.5	8.8
Unit is slightly rolling and composed of shallow wetlands, grassland cover, tree plantings, lowland deciduous cover, and small woodland patches.																			
Hendricks WMA For more information call 507-537-6250.	198	Lincoln	Hendricks	32-2D	131	•		•			•	•		5.7	37.3	55.4	-	-	1.5
Henry Vos WMA	477	Murray	Iona	64-1C	140	•		•			•	•		10.1	54.0	28.5	-	1.9	5.4
WMA is grassland interspersed with small wetlands. Unit has food plots, woody cover, and a native prairie. Primarily managed for upland game.																			
Henry X WMA For more information call 320-289-2493.	26	Swift	Benson	7-4B	83	•					•	•		-	54.6	5.6	21.6	2.9	11.6
Herlein-Boote WMA	643	Nobles	Reading	82-3B	561	•		•			•	•		13.5	31.7	52.1	-	0.2	2.5
WMA contains a 250-acre marsh managed for waterfowl with associated grasslands, woody cover, and food plots. Carry-in water access to the marsh on this unit.																			
Heron Lake WMA - North Heron Unit All units: For more information call 507-831-2900.	644	Jackson	Heron Lake	83-6A	238	•		•			•	•		18.6	35.6	37.7	2.2	2.4	3.4
Heron Lake WMA - North Marsh Unit	639	Jackson	Heron Lake	65-6E	176	•		•			•	•		10.9	58.8	30.3	-	0.1	-
Heron Lake WMA - West Heron Unit	662	Jackson	Okabena	84-1A	142	•		•			•	•		5.8	40.4	44.9	-	-	9.0
Heron Meadows WMA For more information call 507-831-2900.	636	Jackson	Heron Lake	65-6E	200	•		•			•	•		16.9	81.5	1.3	0.2	0.3	-
Herschberger WMA	247	Lincoln	Ivanhoe	46-3A	243	•		•			•	•		5.1	49.1	12.2	30.4	-	3.3
WMA is a wetland/grassland complex along the shores of Curtis Lake. Some native prairie on the unit.																			
Hidden Marsh WMA	244	Wright	Maple Lake	12-1D	39	•		•			•	•	•	-	-	90.5	-	-	7.2
Good hunting, trapping, wildlife viewing, and hiking. Marsh is very attractive for waterfowlers. Good bird watching.																			
Highwater WMA	517	Cottonwood	Storden	66-1B	80	•		•			•	•		8.5	2.9	77.8	-	-	10.8
WMA is a wetland/prairie complex accessible only through the Storden WPA that lies east of the unit.																			
Hjermstad WMA - Dather Slough Unit	367	Murray	Ruthton	47-5D	36	•		•			•	•		-	31.1	63.4	-	-	5.5
WMA consists of two sub-units. This sub-unit is a small wetland with associated grass uplands. Waterfowl hunters are advised to use a boat. Carry-in water access to the wetland.																			
Hjermstad WMA - East Unit	371	Murray	Ruthton	47-6D	237	•		•			•	•		-	28.1	1.1	67.0	-	1.2
WMA consists of two sub-units. East sub-unit contains 3 large, permanent marshes and associated upland grassland and woody cover plantings. Property boundaries are extremely close to the water's edge. Waterfowl hunters are advised to use a boat. Carry-in water access to Hjermstad Slough on the north end and a concrete access ramp to Current Lake on the southeast end of this sub-unit.																			
Hobza WMA	736	Blue Earth	Pemberton	70-3C	158	•		•			•	•		-	-	92.8	-	-	7.2
For more information call 507-225-3572. Wheelchair access limited to adjacent cty/township roads. A gravel parking lot is located on the unit's east side.																			
Hoff WMA	18	Pope	Hancock	7-4A	81	•					•	•		-	59.2	35.5	-	-	5.3
Predator hunting is possible. Excellent habitat for upland birds. Look for marshland birds such as rails, swamp sparrows, blackbirds, song sparrows, and bitterns in the wetlands. Native wildflowers and planted native grasses grow in the uplands. Limited waterfowl hunting.																			
Hoffman Creek WMA	326	Lyon	Garvin	48-2B	37	•		•			•			-	58.2	36.7	-	-	5.1
For more information call 507-537-6250.																			
Hog Island WMA	681	Blue Earth	Garden City	69-5B	15	•		•	•		•	•	•	-	62.1	-	-	37.9	-
For more information call 507-225-3572. Hunting prohibited, as WMA lies within Garden City city limits.																			
Hoglund WMA	219	Wright	Hasty	12-1C	362	•		•	•		•	•	•	-	14.4	45.1	-	-	40.4

Name	Number	County	Nearest Town	Pg / Coord	Acres	Game Species: Deer	Bear	Small Game	Forest Birds	Sharptail	Pheasant	Waterfowl	Turkey	% Cover Type: Cropland	Grassland	Emergent Wetland	Open Water	Lowland	Upland
Hunting, trapping, wildlife viewing, and hiking. Great area to take a youngster squirrel hunting. Nice area for turkeys and deer. Good place to observe spring bird migrations. Mushroom hunters might find this area productive.																			
Hole-In-The Mt. WMA	296	Lincoln	Lake Benton	46-3D	639	•		•			•			13.1	79.7	6.4	-	-	0.8
WMA consists of two tracts that are grass/open lands mixed with some wetlands and some native prairie.																			
Holland WMA	383	Pipestone	Holland	47-4E	39	•		•			•			-	17.0	74.0	-	-	8.7
WMA is mainly grassland with some remnant prairie and woody cover.																			
Hollerberg WMA For more information call 320-289-2493.	59	Swift	Murdock	7-6C	123	•		•			•	•		-	36.0	50.9	-	-	13.1
Hope WMA For more information call 507-537-6250.	316	Lincoln, Lyon	Florence	47-5C	214	•		•			•			5.2	3.5	88.8	-	-	2.5
Horse Slough WMA For more information call 507-537-6250.	259	Lincoln	Lake Benton	46-2B	23	•		•			•	•		-	34.6	65.4	-	-	-
Houle WMA	442	Anoka, Washington	Forest Lake	15-4D	79	•		•			•	•		-	2.8	94.2	3.1	-	-
Some late-season hunting/hiking opportunities after wetlands have frozen.																			
Humphery WMA	479	Murray	Hadley	64-1C	83	•		•			•	•		-	58.8	27.9	-	2.3	10.9
Contains uplands interspersed with small wetlands. A segment of abandoned railroad right-of-way contains native prairie. The undeveloped access trail leading into the unit may not be accessible at certain times of the year.																			
Hurricane Lake WMA For more information call 507-831-2900.	469	Cottonwood	Storden	49-6E	264	•		•			•	•		-	8.8	21.8	65.4	-	4.1
Husen WMA For more information call 507-831-2900.	708	Jackson	Lakefield	84-1C	79	•		•			•	•		-	35.6	52.5	-	5.8	6.0
Hutchinson WMA	284	McLeod	Hutchinson	24-3D	49									-	61.8	32.0	-	-	6.0
The Campbell Marsh Nature Trail is a one-mile loop providing a view of prairie and wetland habitats on the area. A woody cover planting provides winter cover for pheasants. Closed to hunting and trapping.																			
Illinois Lake WMA For more information call 507-831-2900.	710	Jackson	Sioux Valley	83-5D	93	•		•			•	•		-	25.6	65.9	-	-	8.1
Indian Lake WMA	433	Sibley	Winthrop	39-4D	222						•	•		4.0	10.4	84.5	-	-	1.2
A parking lot and carry-in boat access to the lake is located at the unit's NE corner. WMA is a wetland/prairie complex along the west shore of Indian Lake. Access to south end requires a 1/4-mile walk from the township road. An addition along CSAH 10 was seeded to prairie grasses and wildflowers in 2002. A food plot is located at the south end. Wheelchair access limited to primitive access lane, parking lot, and adjacent cty/township roads.																			
Indigo WMA - East Unit	92	Lac Qui Parle	Marietta	18-2D	21	•		•			•			-	32.4	67.6	-	-	-
Both units: For more information call 320-289-2493.																			
Indigo WMA - Main Unit	90	Lac Qui Parle	Marietta	18-2D	39	•		•			•			15.3	46.9	29.8	-	-	8.3
Iron Horse WMA For more information call 507-537-6250.	220	Lincoln	Ivanhoe	32-3E	33	•		•			•	•		-	59.7	40.3	-	-	-
Iron Lake WMA	382	Murray	Balaton	48-1D	53	•		•			•	•		-	54.5	35.7	-	-	10.0
WMA contains three wetlands, associated marginal grasslands, and woody cover. Waterfowl hunting is limited.																			
Irruption WMA	504	Murray	Avoca	65-4B	125	•		•			•	•		-	26.9	54.3	-	18.8	-
WMA contains two wetlands, grasslands and woody cover. A stream corridor with a portion of the Des Moines River and dense willow thickets are also found on this unit.																			
Isaac Walton League WMA For more information call 507-280-5066.	796	Wabasha	Oronoco	58-3E	78	•		•	•		•		•	-	5.7	-	-	12.5	74.6
Island WMA For more information call 507-831-2900.	751	Martin	Welcome	86-1C	45	•		•	•		•			-	4.5	50.8	1.8	-	43.0
Ivanhoe WMA For more information call 507-537-6250.	217	Lincoln	Ivanhoe	32-3E	382	•		•			•	•		8.2	51.0	14.1	19.1	-	7.6
Jackson WMA	549	Washington	Stillwater	29-6B	32									-	-	-	47.0	-	53.0
Within Stillwater city limits - no hunting allowed. Use of canoes or other non-motorized boats is available.																			
Jacobsen WMA For more information call 507-537-6250.	308	Lyon	Marshall	48-2B	290	•		•			•	•		18.6	41.8	35.7	-	-	3.9
James Willey WMA	683	Nobles	Worthington	82-3D	138	•		•			•	•		25.1	34.4	34.0	-	-	6.4
WMA contains a wetland, grasslands, woody cover and food plots.																			
Jasper WMA	455	Pipestone	Jasper	62-2D	80	•		•			•			-	88.0	10.0	-	-	1.9
WMA is grassland with a small wetland on its west side. Unit managed for upland gamebirds.																			
John Erickson WMA	686	Nobles	Worthington	82-3D	122	•		•			•	•		27.3	38.6	21.9	-	-	12.4
WMA contains three wetlands, grasslands, woody cover, and food plots.																			
John Murtaugh Memorial WMA	764	Goodhue	Hay Creek	58-3A	96	•		•			•			6.0	66.5	0.2	0.9	-	26.1
Numerous grassland bird species and some prairie bird species can be seen. Eastern meadowlarks sing in the open areas.																			
Johnsonville WMA For more information call 320-231-5163.	362	Redwood	Lucan	49-6B	113	•		•			•	•		3.5	42.5	50.2	-	-	3.7
Jossart WMA For more information call 320-289-2493.	44	Swift	Benson	7-4D	160	•		•	•		•		•	-	31.7	51.9	-	-	16.4
Kaibab WMA For more information call 507-537-6250.	155	Yellow Medicine	St. Leo	33-5A	54	•		•			•	•		-	36.2	42.3	3.0	18.7	-
Kandi WMA	146	Kandiyohi	Kandiyohi	9-4E	127	•					•	•		-	32.7	27.6	34.8	0.1	4.8
Unit has several wetlands, a small woody cover planting at the west boundary, and native and non-native grassland. Controlled access trail from CR 8 to a parking area at west end. Unit's NW corner touches a large WPA.																			
Kanne WMA	739	Waseca	Waseca	71-4B	78						•	•		6.1	-	94.1	-	-	-
For more information call 507-225-3572. Wheelchair access limited to adjacent cty/township roads.																			
Karnitz WMA	551	Scott	Belle Plaine	41-4D	187	•		•	•			•	•	-	2.7	55.9	0.4	21.4	19.6
Diverse forests; some areas of old growth. WMA located in an area of gently rolling hills that is primarily agricultural, with scattered woodlots and some wetlands. Wheelchair access limited to a gravel parking lot on south side.																			
Keller WMA	812	Olmsted	Rochester	74-3D	196	•		•	•		•	•	•	9.3	14.0	-	-	41.0	35.9
Good area for deciduous forest bird watching. Zumbro River runs through unit. WMA is mostly wooded with bottomland hardwoods and oaks. A 3-acre prairie is established; several reforested fields are planted to oak and walnut. A turkey food plot is present. Good area for spring flower walks and to listen for turkeys. Two parking lots.																			
Kelly-Meyer WMA	251	Wright	Monticello	12-2C	137	•		•			•	•		-	37.2	55.1	-	3.1	4.6
Hunting, trapping, wildlife viewing, and hiking. Borders a shallow, 100-acre lake. Good waterfowl hunting. Pheasant hunting is fair to poor depending on habitat and weather prior to hunting season.																			
Kemen WMA For more information call 320-289-2493.	71	Lac Qui Parle	Madison	19-4B	210	•		•			•			-	80.6	19.4	-	-	-
Kibler WMA - Main Unit All units: For more information call 320-289-2493.	27	Lac Qui Parle	Bellingham	4-3E	342	•		•			•	•		-	37.4	45.9	-	-	16.7
Kibler WMA - North East Unit	20	Lac Qui Parle	Bellingham	4-3E	12	•		•			•	•		-	-	100.0	-	-	-
Kibler WMA - North West Unit	22	Lac Qui Parle	Bellingham	4-3E	170	•		•			•	•		-	10.0	72.6	-	-	17.4
Kibler WMA - South East Unit	21	Lac Qui Parle	Bellingham	4-3E	7	•		•			•	•		-	-	100.0	-	-	-
Kibler WMA - West Unit	24	Lac Qui Parle	Bellingham	4-3E	23	•		•			•	•		-	53.4	46.6	-	-	-
Kinbrae WMA - North Unit	590	Nobles	Kinbrae	65-4E	45	•					•	•		-	-	8.2	91.8	-	-
WMA consists of two sub-units. North sub-unit contains some shoreline and part of the Kinbrae Lake basin. Carry-in access to Kinbrae Lake on sub-unit's SW corner.																			
Kinbrae WMA - South Unit	596	Nobles	Kinbrae	65-4E	63	•					•	•		17.5	25.1	3.9	43.1	-	6.6
WMA consists of two sub-units. South sub-unit contains some shore land and part of the Kinbrae Slough basin. It also has a food plot, a tree planting, and some grassland.																			
Kirschner WMA	139	Stearns	Richmond	10-3B	39	•		•	•		•	•		1.8	38.3	19.0	-	36.2	4.6
Hunting, trapping, wildlife viewing, and hiking. The southern wooded grove provides winter shelter for numerous prairie and woodland wildlife species.																			
Klabunde WMA For more information call 320-231-5163.	299	Redwood	North Redwood	36-2D	202	•		•	•		•		•	29.9	19.8	3.8	-	1.8	44.3
Klages WMA For more information call 320-289-2493.	15	Big Stone	Ortonville	5-4C	242	•					•	•		5.4	38.2	32.8	19.6	-	4.1
Klinker WMA	408	Murray	Lake Wilson	63-6A	344	•		•			•	•		11.4	32.6	50.3	-	4.5	0.9
Good place to view wetland wildlife from a vehicle. WMA is an important deer wintering area. Carry-in water accesses to the marsh and wetland on this unit.																			
Klug WMA For more information call 320-231-5163.	511	Brown	Sleepy Eye	51-6D	10	•		•	•					-	-	-	44.0	7.0	49.0
Knapp WMA	239	Wright, Meeker	Cokato	25-4A	434	•		•			•	•		0.6	19.4	75.9	-	-	4.0
Hunting, trapping, wildlife viewing, and hiking. Popular with waterfowl and pheasant hunters. Good spring and fall birding. Trumpeter swans have nested here.																			
Kohl's WMA	386	McLeod	Brownton	39-4B	87						•			16.5	-	83.5	-	-	-
Prairie/wetland complex. The cattail-dominated marsh is partially drained by a ditch at the south end and has no open water. No parking lot. A 12-acre field was planted to native prairie grasses and wildflowers in 2003.																			
Krahmer WMA For more information call 507-831-2900.	735	Martin	Welcome	86-1B	382	•		•			•	•		5.6	44.9	45.9	-	-	3.6
Kujas Lake WMA	402	McLeod	Brownton	38-3C	119						•	•		-	-	100.1	-	-	-
Wetland complex in a predominantly agricultural landscape. No parking lot.																			
Kvermo WMA For more information call 507-537-6250.	204	Lincoln	Hendricks	32-2E	102	•		•			•	•		-	19.0	80.9	-	-	-
L B Illsley WMA	699	Rice	Faribault	56-2B	10	•		•						-	11.2	14.3	-	-	67.4
Look for squirrels, deer, hairy woodpeckers, white-breasted nuthatches, blue jays, cottontail rabbits, raccoons, and pileated woodpeckers. Mgmt. emphasizes oak forest protection and acorn production for resident wildlife.																			
Lac qui Parle WMA - Controlled Hunt Zone	75	Lac Qui Parle, Chippewa	Watson	20-1A	8,520	•		•			•	•	•	20.8	23.7	0.5	44.0	0.1	10.7
Canada goose hunting is main recreational activity. 112 public goose hunting blinds available. Up to 50 bald eagles use refuge during the fall; a few nest here. Lac Qui Parle State Park lies just south of WMA headquarters. Lac Qui Parle Refuge (controlled hunting zone) lies in the Upper MN River Valley, with the refuge boundary surrounding lower Lac Qui Parle Lake. Refuge is a mixture of cropland, seasonal and permanent wetlands, and scattered grasslands. Refuge managed as a waterfowl feeding and resting area. Up to 150,000 Canada geese and 20,000 mallards have been recorded. Cropland mgmt. is a priority to ensure sufficient food for migratory birds. CHZ exists on the refuge. No person may hunt waterfowl or small game in the CHZ without first registering at WMA headquarters. Waterfowl and small game hunting is restricted to designated hunting stations. There are 19 handicapped-accessible blinds within the CHZ.																			
Lac Qui Parle WMA - Main Unit	25	Big Stone, Swift, Lac Qui Parle, Chippewa	Watson	5-5D	23,977	•		•			•	•	•	6.5	48.8	0.2	35.4	1.2	7.6
Hunting opportunities include waterfowl, pheasants, deer, and small game. Marsh Lake contains the largest white pelican colony in North America and the WMA offers excellent viewing for numerous wetland and grassland species. Lac Qui Parle WMA lies in the Upper Minnesota River Valley with Lac Qui Parle Lake (5,600 acres) and Marsh Lake (5,000 acres) being the prominent features. Large tracts of native prairie interspersed with numerous wetland basins surround both lakes. Food plots are dispersed throughout the unit to provide a food source for resident and migratory wildlife. The eastern one-half of Marsh Lake is non-motorized during open waterfowl seasons. Entire WMA is closed from 10 p.m.-5 a.m. Trappers must obtain a permit from the area wildlife manager. Check hunting regulations for further details. WMA has more than 60 parking lots and/or water accesses located throughout the unit. Wheelchair access is considered difficult on the WMA and moderate along the gravel shoulders of adjacent county roads.																			
Lake Bella WMA - Northwest Unit	701	Nobles	Bigelow	82-3D	18	•	•	•		•	•	•		-	100.0	-	-	-	-
This sub-unit is adjacent to part of Lake Bella WPA. WMA consists of two sub-units adjacent to Lake Bella. NW sub-unit contains grasslands, food plots, and a pond.																			
Lake Bella WMA - Southeast Unit	704	Nobles	Bigelow	82-3D	89	•		•			•	•		17.8	66.4	11.9	4.1	-	-
WMA consists of two sub-units adjacent to Lake Bella. SE sub-unit contains grasslands, food plots, and a pond.																			
Lake Guckeen WMA	767	Faribault	Guckeen	87-5B	146	•		•			•	•		-	63.3	12.2	19.5	-	5.0
For more information call 507-225-3572. Wheelchair access limited to adjacent cty/township roads. North tract has a gravel parking area at the boat launch.																			
Lake Hanska WMA For more information call 320-231-5163.	604	Brown	Hanska	68-2A	5	•		•			•	•		-	34.8	60.9	-	-	2.2
Lake Yankton WMA For more information call 507-537-6250.	356	Lyon	Lake Benton	48-1D	281	•		•			•	•		6.0	40.3	9.6	37.6	-	6.5
Lambert Heikes WMA	651	Nobles	Ellsworth	81-5D	31	•		•			•			-	27.2	60.6	-	-	12.5
WMA is grassland and woody cover. Norwegian Creek runs through the unit.																			
Lambert Prairie WMA - North Unit	653	Nobles	Worthington	82-2C	82	•		•			•	•		16.0	57.6	12.5	-	6.2	5.5
Both units: WMA consists of two separate, recently acquired sub-units composed of grassland, woody cover, wetlands, and food plots.																			
Lambert Prairie WMA - South Unit	656	Nobles	Worthington	82-2C	4	•		•			•	•		-	63.9	36.1	-	-	-
Lamberton WMA For more information call 320-231-5163.	429	Redwood	Lamberton	50-1C	642	•		•			•	•		3.8	39.4	46.0	4.6	0.5	4.9
Lamprey Pass WMA	432	Anoka, Washington	Forest Lake	15-4D	1,332	•		•	•		•	•	•	1.6	6.6	19.0	46.3	9.4	16.2
Howard and Mud lakes within Lamprey Pass WMA are two of the largest bodies of water in the metro area to offer non-motorized boating opportunities where motorized boats are not allowed. Breeding eagles can be observed. WMA primarily managed for waterfowl.																			
Lane WMA For more information call 507-225-3572. No wheelchair access.	756	Faribault	Guckeen	87-5B	60	•		•			•	•	•	-	59.6	30.9	4.5	-	4.8
Lange WMA	380	Murray	Ruthton	47-5E	63	•		•			•	•		-	-	92.4	-	-	7.6
Most of unit is a deep-water marsh that can be viewed from the township road. Two small woody cover plantings grow on the only available upland.																			
Lanners WMA For more information call 507-537-6250.	163	Yellow Medicine	St. Leo	33-6A	206	•		•			•	•		-	20.1	78.4	-	-	1.5
Latourelle WMA For more information call 507-225-3572. No wheelchair access.	748	Blue Earth	Minnesota Lake	70-3D	82	•		•			•	•	•	-	7.7	73.0	-	-	19.4
Laurs Lake WMA For more information call 507-831-2900.	658	Jackson	Bergen	66-3E	266	•		•	•		•	•		4.1	12.9	59.0	-	-	23.6
Leeds WMA	438	Murray	Lake Wilson	64-1B	154	•		•			•	•		23.4	16.0	43.5	-	7.1	10.0
WMA is part of the floodplain along Beaver Creek, with dense willow cover and varying wetland habitat, depending on beaver activity. Four small agricultural fields and hedgerows are managed for upland game.																			
Legacy WMA For more information call 507-537-6250.	209	Lincoln	Ivanhoe	32-3E	165	•		•			•	•		13.5	52.5	27.1	-	-	6.9
Lembke WMA	758	Blue Earth	Minnesota Lake	70-3D	89	•		•	•		•	•	•	-	28.2	50.1	-	6.3	15.3
For more information call 507-225-3572. Wheelchair access limited to adjacent cty and township roads. Gravel parking lot located off Cty Rd 161.																			
Lena Larson WMA	839	Mower	Lyle	91-6D	170	•		•			•			-	21.4	-	-	70.3	8.3
Good pheasant hunting; some deer hunting. Otter Creek runs through unit and provides some trapping. Visit the prairie in late July.																			
Leroy WMA	853	Mower	Le Roy	93-4E	6			•			•			-	100.0	-	-	-	-
Limited hunting because of unit's small size. Soil not suitable for growing row crops.																			
Leudtke WMA For more information call 507-831-2900.	763	Martin	Imogene	87-4C	162	•		•	•		•	•		-	45.4	45.5	-	-	9.1
Lewisville WMA For more information call 507-831-2900.	672	Watonwan	Saint James	68-2C	94	•		•			•	•		13.6	33.8	46.6	-	-	6.0

Name	Number	County	Nearest Town	Pg / Coord	Acres	Game Species: Deer	Bear	Small Game	Forest Birds	Sharptail	Pheasant	Waterfowl	Turkey	% Cover Type: Cropland	Grassland	Emergent Wetland	Open Water	Lowland	Upland
Libra WMA For more information call 507-831-2900.	618	Jackson	Heron Lake	65-5E	29	•		•			•	•		28.5	19.8	30.6	-	-	21.2
Lillegard WMA For more information call 507-831-2900.	647	Jackson	Wilder	66-2E	38			•			•	•		-	30.9	62.7	-	-	6.7
Lillejord WMA For more information call 320-289-2493.	51	Lac Qui Parle	Madison	19-4A	94	•		•			•	•		-	30.8	69.1	-	-	-
Lindquist WMA For more information call 320-289-2493.	14	Big Stone	Ortonville	4-3B	72	•					•	•		-	32.5	23.2	40.3	-	4.0
Lines WMA For more information call 507-537-6250.	242	Lyon	Cottonwood	34-3C	325	•		•			•	•		21.5	35.6	38.9	-	-	3.9
Lisbon WMA For more information call 507-537-6250.	137	Yellow Medicine	Clarkfield	20-2D	80	•		•			•	•		-	22.8	73.2	-	2.5	1.5
Litchfield WMA	194	Meeker	Litchfield	24-2A	121	•		•			•	•		4.1	52.6	33.0	0.2	4.2	4.7
WMA consists of shallow wetlands, planted native-grass fields, a food plot, planted woody cover, and scattered deciduous shrubs and trees. Access limited to adjacent roadbeds.																			
Little Beaver Creek WMA	537	Rock	Luverne	80-3A	55	•		•			•			10.7	70.6	5.4	-	-	13.2
WMA contains grassland, woody cover, and a food plot.																			
Little Fawn WMA For more information call 507-280-5066.	761	Steele	Owatonna	72-1A	20			•			•			-	33.0	52.7	-	10.8	2.0
Little Joe WMA	46	Pope, Kandiyohi	Brooten	8-2A	230	•		•	•		•	•	•	-	15.8	17.1	20.2	-	47.0
Good cross-country skiing and snowshoeing. Look for woodland songbirds such as cardinals, orioles, vireos, and warblers. Old-growth oaks provide roost areas for wild turkeys and nest sites for wood ducks. Managed primarily for deer and turkeys.																			
Little Lake WMA	600	Nicollet	Nicollet	53-5C	210	•		•			•	•		-	6.5	76.0	-	-	17.6
Unit receives little summer use. Pheasant hunting is possible, but not easy. A Forster's tern nesting colony is present. Thick cover makes walking difficult and limits wildlife viewing.																			
Little Sioux WMA For more information call 507-831-2900.	717	Jackson	Lakefield	84-1D	307	•		•			•	•		7.1	35.0	55.6	1.1	-	1.0
Little Swan WMA For more information call 507-831-2900.	564	Cottonwood	Delft	66-2B	412	•		•			•	•		7.4	23.8	55.4	-	1.1	12.3
Lone Tree WMA - North Unit	575	Nobles	Fulda	64-3E	164	•		•			•	•		5.1	92.1	-	-	1.0	1.7
WMA made up of two sub-units. North sub-unit contains a 35-acre wetland managed for waterfowl with associated small wetlands, grasslands, woody cover, and food plots.																			
Lone Tree WMA - South Unit	585	Nobles	Fulda	64-3E	319	•		•			•	•		11.0	60.4	28.6	-	-	-
WMA made up of two sub-units. South sub-unit is a creek floodplain containing grassland, woody cover, and food plots.																			
Lost Marsh WMA	747	Blue Earth	Pemberton	70-3C	329	•		•			•	•		8.2	-	90.8	-	-	1.0
For more information call 507-225-3572. Wheelchair access limited to adjacent cty/township roads. An unimproved gravel lane off 620th Ave. on unit's west side provides access to marsh.																			
Lower Antelope Valley WMA For more information call 507-537-6250.	172	Yellow Medicine	Porter	33-5B	221	•		•			•			-	17.4	74.3	-	6.7	1.6
Lowville WMA - North Unit	424	Murray	Hadley	64-1A	148	•		•			•	•		-	5.6	92.6	-	-	1.9
WMA made up of two sub-units. North sub-unit consists of two large permanent marshes. Carry-in water access on the north side.																			
Lowville WMA - South Unit	426	Murray	Hadley	64-1A	46	•		•			•	•		-	57.3	31.6	-	-	11.1
WMA made up of two sub-units. South sub-unit contains a permanent marsh grassland and woody cover.																			
Luescher-Barnum WMA For more information call 320-231-5163.	357	Redwood	Redwood Falls	50-2A	130	•		•			•	•		2.2	22.2	61.0	5.5	7.2	1.9
Lundquist WMA	737	Waseca	Alma City	71-4B	42			•			•			-	-	100.0	-	-	-
For more information call 507-225-3572. Wheelchair access limited to adjacent cty and township roads.																			
Lundy WMA For more information call 320-289-2493.	123	Lac Qui Parle	Boyd	19-6D	61	•		•			•	•		-	53.6	46.3	-	-	-
Lyle-Austin WMA	833	Mower	Austin	91-5C	116	•		•			•			-	-	-	-	-	100.0
Good location for prairie observation and pheasant hunting. Vegetation is a mix of native prairie plants with aspen clones; some encroachment by box elder and honeysuckle managed by tree removal and burning. Unit was part of a two-rail system. Area managed for native prairie. The former rail bed is a nice walking path for nature observation and hunting.																			
Lyndwood WMA	278	Lyon	Lynd	48-1A	72	•		•			•		•	15.5	3.8	-	-	-	80.9
For more information call 507-537-6250. WMA partially closed to slug hunting. Contact the Area Wildlife office for restrictions.																			
Lyons WMA For more information call 507-537-6250.	329	Lyon	Balaton	48-1C	529	•		•			•	•		6.7	31.4	49.7	10.6	-	1.6
Lyrock WMA For more information call 507-537-6250.	320	Lyon	Russell	48-1C	55	•		•			•	•		-	54.8	45.2	-	-	-
Madelia WMA For more information call 507-831-2900.	669	Watonwan	Saint James	68-2C	158	•		•	•		•	•		13.4	66.9	5.1	-	1.5	11.1
Madison WMA - Main Unit Both units: For more information call 320-289-2493.	54	Lac Qui Parle	Madison	19-4B	193	•		•			•	•		-	12.1	67.7	-	-	20.2
Madison WMA - North Unit	48	Lac Qui Parle	Madison	19-4A	35	•		•			•	•		-	4.6	93.7	-	-	1.4
Madrena WMA For more information call 320-289-2493.	50	Lac Qui Parle	Madison	19-4B	306	•		•			•	•		4.1	23.8	66.1	-	-	6.0
Madsen WMA	188	Meeker	Litchfield	10-2E	364	•		•			•	•		1.6	18.7	73.5	3.6	0.4	1.7
A bald eagle nest is located in a cottonwood tree along the east side. Do not disturb during nesting season.																			
Magaksica WMA For more information call 507-280-5066.	799	Freeborn	Albert Lea	90-1C	113			•			•	•	•	-	29.6	42.4	12.4	0.1	15.5
Mahlon James WMA	231	Meeker	Corvuso	24-1C	45	•		•			•	•		-	41.8	37.8	17.7	-	2.9
Slightly rolling topography covers unit. North end provides public access to a large deep-water marsh. Many acres of adjacent private land provide wildlife habitat around this unit. Parking area at SE end.																			
Mahoney's WMA	544	Scott	Belle Plaine	40-3D	322	•		•			•	•	•	0.4	34.0	46.5	11.1	2.0	6.0
WMA is a great place to watch migrating waterfowl. One small area is posted as a "no shooting allowed" area.																			
Malardi WMA	313	Wright	Montrose	26-2B	127	•		•			•	•		-	45.5	-	54.5	-	-
Hunting, trapping, wildlife viewing, and hiking. Fair to good waterfowl and pheasant hunting. Spring and fall diving duck migrations can be exceptional. Trumpeter swans have nested on the marsh.																			
Mammenga WMA For more information call 320-231-5163.	384	Redwood	Wanda	49-6B	121	•		•			•	•		6.9	36.6	48.0	8.7	-	-
Mamre WMA	115	Kandiyohi	Pennock	8-2E	80	•		•			•	•		15.1	45.4	28.8	5.7	-	4.7
Unit contains non-native grasslands, brush areas, a woody cover planting, food plot, and several wetlands. A waterfowl production area adjoins the northern boundary and another exists to the east. Access restricted to parking area on east side of CR #1.																			
Manannah WMA	176	Meeker	Litchfield	10-2D	203	•		•	•		•		•	35.8	23.8	11.6	-	2.1	25.6
Some orchids have been observed in the past. A small corner of native prairie is being renovated through woody cover removal and fire. This WMA is covered by woods, introduced grass, and a large amount of food plot. It is managed primarily as a deer wintering area.																			
Manchester WMA For more information call 507-280-5066.	793	Freeborn	Hartland	90-1A	113			•			•	•	•	5.2	25.9	42.1	0.4	0.7	25.2
Maple Lake WMA	255	Wright	Maple Lake	12-1D	245	•		•	•		•	•	•	0.9	8.8	73.8	-	4.6	11.7
Hunting, trapping, wildlife viewing, and hiking. WMA is composed of brome grasslands/brushlands bordering a 160-acre sedge/cattail-dominated wetland.																			
Maple River WMA	720	Blue Earth	Mapleton	70-1C	317	•		•			•	•		-	24.3	35.3	-	-	2.7
For more information call 507-225-3572. Wheelchair access limited to adjacent cty/township roads.																			
Marget WMA	294	Isanti	Isanti	14-2A	489	•		•	•		•	•	•	-	11.7	35.9	21.4	10.8	16.7
Numerous wading birds and Blanding's turtles are present. Northern harriers use the open spaces.																			
Marian Marshall WMA	819	Olmsted	Stewartville	74-2D	59	•		•			•			-	32.3	-	-	31.1	35.9
Pheasant and deer hunting are primary recreational opportunities. Access is from the township road south of the unit by a 1/4-mile graveled easement.																			
Mark and Ursel Smith WMA For more information call 507-225-3572.	330	McLeod	Hutchinson	25-4E	81									-	61.7	38.3	-	-	-
Marsh WMA	567	Scott	New Prague	41-4D	52	•		•			•	•		9.3	45.0	22.8	0.4	22.4	-
The west branch of Raven Stream runs through the WMA. Mgmt. is primarily for wetland and grassland wildlife species.																			
Marsh Wren WMA For more information call 507-280-5066.	781	Steele	Pratt	73-4C	40			•			•			-	10.9	42.3	-	30.6	14.2
Marvin Schubring WMA	369	Isanti, Anoka	Stacy	15-4B	285	•	•	•	•		•	•	•	-	9.7	24.5	-	24.7	41.1
Wildlife observation is limited to hiking within the various cover types. Cooper's and sharp-shinned hawks use the forests.																			
Mason WMA	427	Murray	Hadley	64-2A	35	•		•			•	•		-	17.1	72.3	-	1.4	8.9
This unit has a 10-acre emergent marsh with some upland and a woody cover planting. Carry-in water access to the marsh on the unit's south end.																			
Mazeppa WMA	789	Wabasha	Mazeppa	58-3D	4	•		•			•			-	-	-	-	-	-
This small WMA is a former gravel pit that has become overgrown.																			
McCarthy Lake WMA	816	Wabasha	Kellogg	60-3D	2,886	•		•	•		•	•	•	-	9.2	29.0	6.7	54.4	0.5
Hunting, trapping, fishing, and wildlife viewing. Sandhill cranes, eagles, tundra swans, and numerous shorebirds may be observed. Special-use permit required for beaver trapping when allowed.																			
McCord-Laible WMA	407	Murray	Hadley	47-6E	76	•		•			•	•		-	19.3	68.0	-	3.0	9.7
WMA contains small marshes, associated upland grassland, woody planting and a food plot. There is a carry-in water access to the marsh on the unit's west side.																			
McGee WMA	520	Murray	Avoca	64-3C	43	•		•			•	•		2.3	67.7	-	6.2	-	24.1
Limited duck hunting opportunities. Pond provides fishing for northern pike. Managed for upland game.																			
McLeod County Pheasants Forever WMA	352	McLeod	Biscay	25-4E	92	•		•			•	•	•	1.5	27.6	44.3	5.0	12.8	8.9
Fishing, bird watching, canoeing. Two tracts of land along the Crow River. Both have woods and grassy fields. Fields on this unit have been planted to prairie grasses and wildflowers to provide nesting habitat for pheasants and other birds. A food plot has been established on the northern tract.																			
McMartin WMA For more information call 507-280-5066.	782	Dodge	Claremont	73-5B	38									36.5	13.3	-	6.1	14.4	27.5
Meadow Creek WMA For more information call 507-537-6250.	297	Lyon	Marshall	48-3B	592	•		•			•			11.4	41.5	39.9	-	-	7.2
Medicine Pipe WMA For more information call 320-289-2493.	136	Lac Qui Parle	Boyd	19-6E	36	•		•			•			-	21.2	78.8	-	-	-
Melchior WMA	505	Murray	Iona	64-1C	54	•		•			•	•		-	27.0	58.6	-	-	14.2
The portion of the basin north of the unit is privately owned. WMA is prairie marsh with associated uplands and a woody cover planting. An 80-acre WPA is adjacent to the west. Carry-in water access to the marsh on its west side. Unit has three parking areas.																			
Mentel WMA	829	Mower	Austin	91-5B	22									-	1.9	88.8	-	-	9.3
Birding and hiking. A warm-water stream runs through the WMA. Closed to hunting and trapping.																			
Michaelson WMA For more information call 320-289-2493.	87	Lac Qui Parle	Dawson	19-6C	31	•					•	•		-	61.4	33.8	-	-	4.8
Michel WMA	562	Scott	Belle Plaine	41-4D	138	•		•			•	•	•	1.4	3.8	51.2	23.8	14.5	5.3
WMA contains wetland large enough to canoe on. Many furbearers live on or in this wetland. WMA acquired mostly for waterfowl and wetland species.																			
Milan WMA	56	Chippewa	Milan	20-1A	263	•		•			•	•		1.5	20.4	69.3	4.3	-	3.9
Milan WMA	49	Chippewa	Milan	6-1E	129	•		•			•	•		2.5	48.3	45.9	-	-	2.3
Both units: A small flowage traverses the unit, providing many acres of lowland habitat, including cattail and sedge wetlands. Some old dugouts exist on the unit and there is a small woody cover planting and food plot in the NE corner. A smaller, separate part of the unit exists one mile to the NW and is connected to the main parcel by a Federal WPA. Some native prairie exists on the unit.																			
Milest WMA	678	Rice	Little Chicago	56-2A	218	•						•		-	3.9	51.8	0.5	32.7	11.2
Watch for least bitterns, deer, pheasants, mallards, red-winged blackbirds, mink, muskrats, marsh wrens, and cottontail rabbits. Canoeing and trapping.																			
Miller Richter WMA For more information call 507-537-6250.	134	Lac Qui Parle, Yellow Medicine	St. Leo	19-5E	447	•		•			•	•		4.4	46.5	45.6	-	-	3.5
Miller Spring Lea Farm WMA	105	Stearns	Paynesville	10-1A	73			•			•			-	99.5	-	-	-	0.5
Hunting, trapping, wildlife viewing, and hiking. WMA is mostly restored prairie with some original unbroken prairie land. Most resident wildlife relocates in winter to core cover areas.																			
Minn-kota WMA For more information call 507-537-6250.	159	Yellow Medicine, Lincoln	Hendricks	32-2C	105	•		•			•	•		27.8	45.3	27.0	-	-	-
Minneota WMA For more information call 507-831-2900.	733	Jackson	Lakefield	84-1D	173	•		•			•	•		8.9	43.8	42.3	-	-	4.9
Minnriver WMA	428	Nicollet	Fairfax	51-6A	91	•		•			•	•		-	0.8	81.3	-	17.9	-
Look for eagles and turkey vultures. Explore the river by canoe. Fish for walleyes, catfish, and other species in the MN River. Numerous wildlife species use river corridor. Look for indigo buntings and cerulean warblers. First recorded turkey vulture nest in SW MN was found nearby.																			
Minowa WMA For more information call 507-831-2900.	772	Martin	Fairmont	86-3E	100	•		•			•	•		9.9	66.9	19.7	-	-	2.7
Monson WMA For more information call 320-289-2493.	62	Swift	Kerkhoven	8-1C	177	•		•	•		•	•		-	27.3	21.0	42.6	-	9.0
Moonan WMA	742	Waseca	Waseca	72-1A	955	•		•	•		•	•	•	1.1	8.1	79.7	-	6.2	4.9
For more information call 507-225-3572. On unit's south end, a gravel lane extends eastward from CSAH 4 to edge of wetland and upland native-grass fields.																			
Mound Prairie WMA - Main Unit	860	Houston	Hokah	96-2A	329	•		•			•	•	•	-	5.7	42.9	3.8	39.1	6.2
Both units: Hunting, trapping, fishing and wildlife viewing. Root River bisects the south boundary. A large wetland complex exists on unit.																			
Mound Prairie WMA - West Unit	859	Houston	Hokah	78-2E	49	•		•			•	•	•	-	23.0	17.0	11.9	48.0	-
Mound Springs WMA For more information call 507-537-6250.	113	Yellow Medicine	Canby	18-2E	196	•		•			•			62.9	36.2	0.9	-	-	-
Mountain Lake WMA For more information call 507-831-2900.	611	Cottonwood	Mountain Lake	67-4C	70	•		•		•	•	•		-	43.5	31.5	-	-	24.8
Mueller WMA	750	Waseca	Waldorf	71-4C	121			•			•	•		-	-	98.4	-	1.6	-
For more information call 507-225-3572. Wheelchair access limited to adjacent cty/township roads.																			
Muldental WMA For more information call 507-537-6250.	248	Lincoln	Ivanhoe	33-5E	27	•		•			•	•		-	7.4	92.6	-	-	-
Mulligan Slough WMA For more information call 320-231-5163.	563	Brown, Watonwan	Comfrey	67-5A	634	•		•	•		•	•	•	6.9	23.6	56.6	-	9.4	3.4
Murphy WMA	685	Le Sueur	Waterville	55-5C	140							•		-	2.7	71.8	4.4	1.4	19.2
WMA composed of two tracts. Both sub-units are wetland/forest complexes with the Cannon River running through them. Southern tract accessible by water only. Wheelchair access limited to adjacent county road.																			
Muskrat Junction WMA For more information call 507-537-6250.	250	Lincoln	Arco	46-3A	14	•		•			•	•		-	26.6	73.4	-	-	-
Myhre WMA For more information call 507-537-6250.	186	Yellow Medicine	Clarkfield	34-2B	81	•		•			•	•		6.0	24.0	64.7	-	-	5.2
Naylor WMA - Main Unit For more information call 507-280-5066.	779	Dodge	Claremont	73-5A	270	•		•			•	•		-	47.7	16.0	2.1	17.1	17.0

Name	Number	County	Nearest Town	Pg / Coord	Acres	Deer	Bear	Small Game	Forest Birds	Sharptail	Pheasant	Waterfowl	Turkey	Cropland	Grassland	Emergent Wetland	Open Water	Lowland	Upland
Naylor WMA - Naylor Pond Unit For more information call 507-280-5066.	780	Dodge	Claremont	73-5A	37	•		•			•	•		-	5.7	18.4	33.5	27.0	14.8
Nelson Fen WMA	813	Olmsted	Stewartville	74-2D	79	•		•			•		•	2.9	36.9	0.1	0.1	44.4	15.4
Hunting and birding. Established native grasses and wet meadow with aspen clones. A 3-acre food plot and two woody cover plantings are present.																			
Nelson WMA	366	Murray	Ruthton	47-6D	182	•		•			•	•		-	9.4	90.5	-	-	-
Good pheasant wintering area. Attracts migrating waterfowl. Unit is a large emergent wetland with a water-control structure and limited upland cover. Access to the water is from the township road. Managed for waterfowl.																			
Neudecker WMA For more information call 320-231-5163.	395	Redwood	Clements	50-3B	11	•		•	•		•			-	42.0	-	-	-	58.0
Ney WMA	526	Scott	Henderson	40-2D	156	•		•	•		•		•	-	45.2	-	-	-	54.8
WMA is located next to the scenic MN River valley. WMA preserves a large area of oak forest along the steep banks of the MN River and is ideal turkey and deer habitat.																			
Norgaard WMA For more information call 507-537-6250.	287	Lincoln	Tyler	47-5B	21	•		•			•	•		-	39.3	60.7	-	-	-
Norman Dahlman WMA	64	Stearns	Belgrade	8-3A	41	•		•			•		•	-	4.1	95.1	-	-	0.7
Hunting, trapping, wildlife viewing, and hiking. WMA is mostly a shallow, cattail-dominated wetland basin surrounded by brome/reed canary grasslands and willow. Area is part of a large deer, pheasant, and turkey wintering complex.																			
Northeast Four Corners WMA For more information call 320-289-2493.	61	Lac Qui Parle	Marietta	18-3B	173	•		•			•	•		19.7	24.3	42.8	-	-	13.3
Norwegian Grove WMA	509	Sibley, Nicollet	New Sweden	53-5A	21	•		•	•		•	•		-	-	16.8	-	-	82.7
Excellent place to look for spring warblers. Limited hunting, although the WMA provides access to waterfowl hunting.																			
Numo WMA	95	Chippewa	Montevideo	20-3B	140	•		•			•	•		-	41.4	47.8	-	-	9.7
WMA contains seeded native-grass fields, a non-native-grass field, a woody planting, and a large wetland. Parking next to an old farm grove in SW corner. Disabled access limited to parking area and adjacent township roads.																			
Nyroca Flats WMA For more information call 507-537-6250.	334	Lyon	Florence	47-5C	52	•		•			•	•		-	14.9	85.1	-	-	-
O A Vee Memorial WMA	661	Blue Earth	Mankato	69-5A	164	•		•			•	•		-	-	85.9	-	1.9	12.2
For more information call 507-225-3572. Wheelchair access limited to adjacent cty/township roads.																			
O'Brien WMA	545	Scott	Belle Plaine	41-4D	25	•		•	•		•	•	•	-	66.0	-	10.3	-	23.7
WMA consists of old pasture, a small woodland, and a few wetlands. Yellow-headed blackbirds can be seen in the wetlands.																			
Oak Glen WMA For more information call 507-280-5066.	790	Steele	Bixby	73-4C	88			•			•			8.3	7.5	12.8	0.3	64.2	6.6
Oak Isle WMA	458	Sibley	Arlington	40-1C	91	•		•			•	•		-	21.7	62.1	-	-	16.3
WMA contains marsh, forest, and grassland habitat. Several fields have been planted to prairie grasses.																			
Ohnah WMA For more information call 320-289-2493.	60	Lac Qui Parle	Madison	19-5A	45	•		•			•	•		-	58.1	30.3	-	-	11.7
Old Gravel Pit WMA	5	Stevens	Chokio	5-4A	81	•		•			•	•		-	48.4	12.4	17.2	4.7	17.2
Variety of habitats attract many migrating songbirds. Bank swallows and western meadowlarks present. Some predator hunting. WMA located in the MN River Prairie Landscape and is used by deer, pheasants, and nongame species.																			
Oleander WMA	57	Kandiyohi	Sunburg	8-2B	376	•		•	•		•	•		-	44.2	48.1	1.4	-	6.3
Unit contains large cattail marsh with some open-water holes. Upland consists of some seeded native grasses, non-native grass fields, a few prairie remnants, and a large, old farm grove with adjacent woody planting. Access trail enters at unit's south end, leading to a parking area. Another access trail enters the east side and ends at the old farm grove.																			
Omro WMA For more information call 507-537-6250.	164	Yellow Medicine	St. Leo	33-6A	331	•		•			•	•		1.7	14.2	77.8	4.7	-	1.6
Oshkosh WMA For more information call 507-537-6250.	142	Yellow Medicine	St. Leo	33-5A	250	•		•			•			28.9	39.8	22.9	1.5	-	7.0
Otrey WMA For more information call 320-289-2493.	9	Big Stone	Clinton	14-3B	173	•					•	•		-	9.4	35.7	52.9	-	1.7
Otsego WMA	324	Wright	Albertville	13-5D	201	•		•	•		•	•	•	-	4.2	6.6	37.1	4.5	47.6
Hunting, trapping, wildlife viewing, and hiking. West unit is a 40-acre tract of grassland- and shallow cattail-dominated wetland within the City of Otsego. East Unit is a 160-acre tract of hardwood and lowland forest with some grassland areas bordering 60-acre Rice Lake. Although within Otsego city limits, the two WMAs remain open to hunting and trapping. Contact Otsego City Hall for clarification.																			
Ottawa WMA	619	Le Sueur	Saint Peter	54-2C	577	•		•	•		•	•	•	-	-	95.5	-	0.2	4.3
Three spring-fed ponds on the area are stocked annually with trout.																			
Oxbow WMA For more information call 507-831-2900.	627	Jackson	Heron Lake	83-5A	236	•		•			•	•		17.3	69.3	9.9	0.3	-	2.5
P.F. Mulder WMA WMA is a floodplain forest along the Rock River.	610	Rock	Luverne	80-3C	87	•		•			•	•	•	2.4	-	-	-	95.3	2.3
Paddy Marsh WMA	655	Le Sueur	Le Center	55-4C	189	•					•	•		-	-	92.8	-	-	7.3
For more information call 507-225-3572. Wheelchair access limited to adjacent county road.																			
Panicum Prairie WMA - Grass Lake Unit	823	Freeborn	Gordonsville	90-2E	855									-	66.1	24.8	2.0	0.5	6.5
Both units: For more information call 507-280-5066.																			
Panicum Prairie WMA - Shell Rock Unit	828	Freeborn	Gordonsville	90-2E	193									-	37.3	46.3	5.3	9.6	1.1
Partners WMA	112	Stearns	Paynesville	10-1B	79	•		•			•			-	34.4	65.6	-	-	-
Hunting, trapping, wildlife viewing and hiking. Mostly composed of lowland grass and aspen/willow brushland. Core wintering area for pheasants and deer.																			
Pato WMA For more information call 507-537-6250.	180	Lincoln	Hendricks	32-2C	19	•		•			•	•		-	15.4	85.1	-	-	-
Pats Pasture WMA For more information call 507-831-2900.	595	Cottonwood	Heron Lake	65-6D	138	•		•			•			30.6	57.6	1.4	9.4	-	-
Patterson WMA	422	Carver	Waconia	26-2E	22	•		•	•			•	•	-	46.5	-	5.1	-	48.4
WMA consists of islands on Lake Patterson, which are surrounded by emergent vegetation and some areas of open water. The islands are managed for forest species and aquatic birds, such as egrets and herons. Access by boat only.																			
Paul Hugo Farms WMA	481	Washington	Hugo	15-5E	357	•		•	•		•	•	•	-	6.5	31.0	39.3	14.2	9.1
Rice Lake on Paul Hugo Farms WMA is one of the largest bodies of water in the Twin Cities metro area to offer canoe or other non-motorized boating opportunities where motorized boat traffic is not allowed. Breeding trumpeter swans can be observed on Rice Lake. WMA emphasizes waterfowl mgmt.																			
Paulson Marsh WMA	682	Rice	Little Chicago	56-2A	62	•					•	•		-	1.0	83.2	-	4.6	11.5
Look for Canada geese, beavers, deer, great blue herons, yellowthroats, muskrats, ring-necked ducks, and hairy woodpeckers. Wildlife watching, trapping, deer and waterfowl hunting, canoeing, and quiet nature enjoyment. Mgmt. emphasis on wetland protection, public hunting, and old-growth forest protection. Parking limited to 1-2 vehicles. Vehicle access on cartway trail not recommended when road is wet and muddy.																			
Pavelko WMA For more information call 507-831-2900.	728	Jackson	Lakefield	84-2D	58	•		•			•	•		10.2	27.1	11.6	41.5	-	9.3
Pawek WMA	740	Steele, Waseca	Waseca	56-1E	79	•		•	•		•	•	•	17.0	13.2	31.3	-	0.6	38.0
For more information call 507-225-3572. Wheelchair access limited to adjacent cty/township roads.																			
Paynesville Sportsmens Club WMA	125	Stearns	Paynesville	10-1B	68	•		•	•		•	•		-	-	69.8	2.8	27.6	-
Best time to see WMA is in winter, when the area is frozen. Other seasons provide great wildlife viewing if prepared for some wet, tough conditions. Fishing could be decent on the river at certain times of the year.																			
Peat Bog WMA	674	Rice	Millersburg	42-2E	154	•					•	•		2.2	14.7	68.9	-	8.6	5.3
Good location to look for water birds. Watch for American white pelicans, egrets, mallards, blue-winged teal, Canada geese, mink, and beaver. Wildlife watching and canoeing.																			
Pebbles WMA WMA is riparian timber with little upland.	353	McLeod	Stewart	38-3A	110	•		•			•	•		1.8	40.9	-	5.5	40.7	11.1
Penn WMA	413	McLeod	Brownton	39-4C	90						•	•		-	19.8	80.2	-	-	-
For more information call 507-225-3572. Wheelchair access limited to a primitive access lane and parking area.																			
Penthole WMA For more information call 507-537-6250.	144	Yellow Medicine	Canby	32-2B	31	•		•			•	•		-	46.5	47.1	0.6	-	5.4
Perch Creek WMA For more information call 507-831-2900.	713	Watonwan, Martin	Truman	68-2E	490	•		•			•	•		-	12.5	86.0	0.4	-	0.8
Perched Valley WMA	768	Goodhue	Frontenac	45-4E	233	•		•			•	•	•	0.9	4.2	13.9	6.9	64.4	9.8
Both units: Viewing of wetland and forest wildlife. Permit from area wildlife manager required for beaver trapping. A small portion east of Hwy. 61, including Wacouta Pond, is closed to hunting and trapping.																			
Perched Valley WMA - Wacouta Pond Unit	765	Goodhue	Frontenac	45-4D	127	•		•			•	•	•	-	4.6	2.5	22.7	10.5	59.6
Perry WMA For more information call 320-289-2493.	33	Lac Qui Parle	Bellingham	18-3A	213									5.1	42.6	52.3	-	-	-
Persen WMA For more information call 320-289-2493.	38	Swift	Appleton	6-1D	160	•		•	•		•			-	28.0	11.8	-	-	60.3
Peters WMA	446	Murray	Hadley	64-1B	73	•		•			•			-	67.4	21.2	-	3.0	8.1
WMA contains small wetlands with associated grassy uplands and woody cover plantings.																			
Peterson WMA - Southeast Unit	692	Nobles	Worthington	82-3D	112	•		•			•	•		14.9	40.6	33.9	-	-	8.9
WMA consists of two sub-units (SE and West). SE sub-unit contains a small wetland with associated upland grassland, with woody cover and food plots.																			
Peterson WMA - West Unit	689	Nobles	Worthington	82-3D	109	•		•			•	•		-	27.3	71.3	-	-	1.5
WMA consists of two sub-units (SE and West). West sub-unit contains a medium-sized marsh with associated upland grassland and woody cover plantings.																			
PF - Module #1 WMA	530	Scott	Belle Plaine	40-3D	12	•		•	•		•		•	10.1	47.1	19.3	-	5.9	16.8
Spring ephemerals such as Dutchmans breeches can be found in the small forest here. WMA managed for upland species such as pheasant and forest species.																			
PF - Module #3 WMA	547	Scott	Belle Plaine	41-4D	27	•		•			•	•		21.7	65.4	6.6	-	-	5.9
WMA managed mostly for upland game species preferring grasslands.																			
Phasianus WMA	354	McLeod	Biscay	39-4A	38						•			-	25.7	67.5	-	-	6.6
WMA is a wetland/prairie complex managed for pheasants with a food plot and tree plantings. Wheelchair access limited to primitive parking area and adjacent cty/township roads.																			
Pheasant Run WMA	574	Nobles	Fulda	64-3E	32	•		•			•			1.6	80.1	-	-	-	18.4
WMA is a grassland creek valley with an abandoned farm grove and food plot.																			
Pheasants Forever WMA For more information call 507-280-5066.	794	Dodge	Wasioja	74-1B	217	•					•			-	57.1	11.5	0.8	28.8	0.6
Phelan WMA	473	Murray	Avoca	64-3B	69	•		•			•	•		9.2	16.6	53.5	-	-	20.7
Squirrel hunting is possible here. Carry-in water access to the wetland on this unit.																			
Pick WMA	749	Blue Earth	Minnesota Lake	70-2D	180	•		•			•	•	•	-	1.3	89.0	0.5	8.6	0.6
For more information call 507-225-3572. Wheelchair access limited to adjacent cty/township roads.																			
Pipestone WMA	400	Pipestone	Pipestone	62-3A	113	•		•			•			-	78.8	-	7.6	-	13.4
WMA contains remnant native prairie grassland, a small impoundment, and woody cover plantings. WMA is within the Hiawatha State Game Refuge. Open to hunting small game with shotguns with fine nontoxic shot, trapping, and archery deer hunting. Closed to waterfowl and firearms deer hunting.																			
Pit WMA Small WMA consisting of seeded native grasses and a willow patch.	396	Pipestone	Pipestone	62-3A	14			•			•			6.5	68.3	-	-	25.2	-
Plantation WMA For more information call 320-289-2493.	101	Lac Qui Parle	Marietta	18-2E	69	•		•			•	•		-	58.6	31.3	-	-	10.2
Platyrchnchos WMA For more information call 507-537-6250.	174	Lincoln	Canby	32-3C	85	•		•			•	•		10.9	33.2	53.2	-	-	2.6
Pletz Slough WMA For more information call 507-831-2900.	715	Jackson	Lakefield	84-1C	118	•		•			•	•		-	29.1	69.2	-	-	1.9
Pogones Marsh WMA For more information call 507-280-5066.	791	Steele	Blooming Prairie	72-3D	113			•			•	•	•	-	19.6	31.6	1.8	44.4	2.9
Pool 4 WMA	802	Wabasha	Wabasha	60-2B	142	•		•	•		•	•		-	53.4	0.9	15.7	30.0	-
Hunting, trapping, fishing, and wildlife viewing. Water access available to Mississippi River and backwaters. Primarily lowland hardwoods consisting of maple, ash, river birch, willow and cottonwood. Cool-season grasses make up lowland and upland fields. Managed to maintain diverse communities. Accessible fishing pier/observation deck.																			
Poplar Creek WMA	471	Pipestone	Edgerton	63-4D	87	•		•			•			14.7	76.3	2.2	-	-	6.7
Unit is a grassland creek valley with woody cover areas and a food plot. Poplar Creek runs through this WMA.																			
Poposki WMA For more information call 507-537-6250.	211	Lincoln	Ivanhoe	33-4D	288	•		•			•	•		3.8	31.1	10.4	54.1	-	0.6
Popular WMA	197	Meeker	Grove City	23-6B	206	•		•	•		•	•	•	8.1	14.3	27.6	17.9	2.7	29.3
This unit provides public access to Popple Lake on its eastern edge and other deep freshwater marshes.																			
Posen WMA For more information call 507-537-6250.	263	Yellow Medicine	Wood Lake	35-5D	155									-	20.2	79.9	-	-	-
Pothole WMA For more information call 507-537-6250.	201	Lincoln	Ivanhoe	32-3D	47	•		•			•	•		-	23.0	67.3	-	-	9.7
Prairie Dell WMA For more information call 507-537-6250.	182	Lincoln	Ivanhoe	32-3C	200	•		•			•	•		12.9	45.4	35.8	-	-	6.1
Prairie Heritage WMA	344	McLeod	Brownton	39-4A	76						•			0.7	67.2	25.6	-	-	6.8
For more information call 507-225-3572. Wheelchair access limited to gravel parking lot and adjacent cty/township roads.																			
Prairie Marshes WMA	274	Lyon	Russell	47-6A	278	•		•			•	•		-	64.7	35.3	-	-	-
WMA is a wetland/grassland complex with some native prairie. Camden State Park is 1.5 miles east of unit.																			
Prairie Rose WMA For more information call 507-280-5066.	754	Steele	Owatonna	72-2A	118			•			•	•	•	1.1	46.9	48.4	0.6	2.3	0.5
Prairie WMA For more information call 320-289-2493.	11	Big Stone	Ortonville	4-3B	186	•					•	•		-	67.5	13.0	19.4	-	-
Prieve WMA	276	McLeod	Hutchinson	24-2D	40						•	•		-	13.7	86.3	-	-	-
For more information call 507-225-3572. Wheelchair access limited to adjacent cty/township roads.																			
Prohels Woods WMA	425	Sibley	Arlington	39-6B	134	•		•	•		•	•		-	-	83.8	-	-	16.1
WMA is a wetland/forest complex in an agricultural landscape. Wheelchair access limited to primitive parking area and adjacent cty road.																			
Prospect WMA For more information call 320-289-2493.	114	Lac Qui Parle	Dawson	19-5D	71	•		•			•	•		-	54.4	40.4	-	-	5.4
Provencher WMA	243	Meeker	Cedar Mills	24-2C	86	•		•			•	•		-	42.8	42.6	6.1	1.7	5.8
Unit contains a large mature woody cover planting, several wetlands, upland grass areas, and non-native and native seeding. Disabled access limited to gravel road on north side.																			
Providence WMA For more information call 320-289-2493.	119	Lac Qui Parle	Boyd	19-5E	95	•		•			•	•		-	13.7	85.2	-	-	1.1
Pyramid WMA Observe prairie chickens. For more information call 320-289-2493.	19	Lac Qui Parle	Bellingham	5-4D	20	•		•			•			-	58.8	41.2	-	-	-
Quilitz WMA For more information call 320-289-2493.	40	Lac Qui Parle	Nassau	18-3A	384	•		•			•	•		0.5	3.7	94.9	-	0.9	-

Name	Number	County	Nearest Town	Pg / Coord	Acres	Deer	Bear	Small Game	Forest Birds	Sharptail	Pheasant	Waterfowl	Turkey	Cropland	Grassland	Emergent Wetland	Open Water	Lowland	Upland
						Game Species								**% Cover Type**					
Raguet WMA	489	Carver, Scott	Shakopee	41-5A	270	•		•	•		•	•		-	34.7	16.0	3.5	5.4	40.4
Many furbearers can be found here. Unit is entirely within the MN River floodplain. It contains floodplain forest, wetlands, and grassland. Firearms hunting restricted to shotgun with fine shot only. Archery deer hunting only and only in designated areas. Wheelchair access limited to parking lot on SE corner.																			
Ramsey Mill Pond WMA	818	Mower	Lansing	91-5B	335	•		•			•	•	•	1.7	36.3	4.5	-	39.5	18.0
Diverse habitats attract many wildlife species. Area is adjacent to the Red Cedar River, but there is no boat access from this parcel. Potential for walk-in fishing or waterfowl hunting.																			
Ras-Lynn WMA	322	McLeod	Stewart	38-3A	1,214	•		•			•	•		0.5	13.7	66.0	17.1	-	2.7
WMA consists of several tracts of land around Eagle Lake, Mud Lake, and Lake Carla. Managed for pheasants and waterfowl.																			
Rau Prairie Pothole WMA	131	Kandiyohi	Willmar	22-3A	105	•		•			•	•		-	77.2	6.9	11.1	-	5.0
Unit is being developed with woody cover, native grass/forb nesting cover fields, and several wetland restorations.																			
Raven WMA	553	Scott	Belle Plaine	40-3D	73	•		•			•	•		7.9	51.1	29.9	1.8	-	9.5
WMA consists mostly of established prairie, with a few wetlands, a wet meadow, a large wood-cover planting, and a food plot. Surrounding area is heavily farmed and relatively flat. Unit managed for grassland species and is excellent habitat for prairie wildlife. Prescribed burning invigorates the prairie.																			
Red Buffalo WMA For more information call 320-289-2493.	32	Lac Qui Parle	Louisburg	5-5E	109	•		•			•	•		24.7	32.4	40.8	-	-	2.2
Red Cedar River WMA	836	Mower	Lyle	91-4D	74	•		•	•		•	•	•	-	-	-	1.1	98.9	-
Recreational opportunities exist all year for hunting and nature observation.																			
Redwood WMA For more information call 507-537-6250.	277	Lyon	Lynd	48-1A	40	•		•			•		•	-	19.5	-	-	-	80.5
Reed WMA	156	Kandiyohi	Priam	22-2B	117	•		•			•	•		-	33.9	53.0	13.0	-	-
Contains native prairie and natural wetlands. Some open water, primarily at the east end.																			
Regal Flats WMA	102	Kandiyohi	Regal	9-5B	282	•		•			•	•	•	18.4	26.4	-	2.1	39.0	-
Unit is a newer acquisition and habitat development is ongoing. Should be an excellent area for wintering deer.																			
Regher Slough WMA For more information call 507-831-2900.	630	Cottonwood	Mountain Lake	67-4C	65	•		•			•	•		-	20.3	42.9	36.8	-	-
Reimers WMA	10	Stevens	Alberta	5-6A	26						•	•		-	8.0	71.6	20.3	-	-
Look for marsh wrens and yellow-headed blackbirds. Hunting opportunities, primarily for waterfowl, are limited. Predator hunting is possible.																			
Reinhold WMA	391	Murray	Lake Wilson	47-6E	21	•					•			-	21.5	-	-	-	78.5
Wildlife habitat value is limited. WMA is a mature cottonwood stand that floods temporarily due to agricultural drainage.																			
Reisdorph WMA For more information call 320-289-2493.	7	Big Stone	Ortonville	4-2B	215	•		•			•	•		-	46.4	2.6	38.9	-	12.1
Reserve WMA For more information call 507-537-6250.	149	Yellow Medicine	Canby	33-4A	133	•		•			•	•		3.8	76.5	16.0	-	-	3.8
Revanche WMA	453	Sibley	Green Isle	40-1C	114	•		•	•		•	•		5.4	20.4	54.2	-	-	20.1
For more information call 507-225-3572. Wheelchair access limited to gravel parking lot and primitive field lane running from parking lot to the woods.																			
Rice Lake WMA	753	Faribault	Winnebago	87-6A	136	•		•	•		•	•	•	2.1	68.8	8.9	-	-	20.3
For more information call 507-225-3572. Wheelchair access limited to adjacent cty/township roads.																			
Riecks Slough WMA For more information call 320-231-5163.	497	Brown	Springfield	51-4E	131	•		•			•	•		-	26.3	69.3	-	-	4.3
RIM Memorial WMA	117	Kandiyohi	Pennock	8-2E	77	•		•			•	•		11.5	65.0	14.5	2.5	-	6.8
Unit borders West Lindgren Lake and contains some small potholes, seeded native grass/forb field, a small flowage, a woody planting, and some non-native grass cover. Limited to access from CR #1.																			
Ringneck Ravine WMA For more information call 507-537-6250.	301	Lyon	Lynd	48-1B	69	•		•			•			33.4	12.4	54.2	-	-	-
Ringneck Ridge WMA WMA consists of grasslands, woody cover plantings, and food plots.	437	Pipestone	Ihlen	62-2C	82	•		•			•			31.1	48.5	-	-	-	20.2
Ringo-Nest WMA	116	Kandiyohi	Spicer	9-4D	543	•		•	•		•	•		3.8	33.5	46.8	0.2	10.1	4.3
Large cattail wetlands, woody cover plantings, lowland brush, old farm grove, native prairie remnants, and several small food plots.																			
River Valley WMA - Tract 21 All tracts: For more information call 320-231-5163.	487	Brown	New Ulm	52-2B	14	•		•	•				•	-	92.8	7.2	-	-	-
River Valley WMA - Tracts 1-2, 2a, 4-6, 8 and 10-11	484	Brown	New Ulm	52-2B	246	•		•	•		•	•	•	3.3	21.3	21.6	-	32.6	21.2
Riverside WMA For more information call 320-289-2493.	109	Lac Qui Parle	Dawson	19-5D	146	•		•			•	•		3.2	44.3	30.3	3.4	-	16.7
Robert and Marilyn Burman WMA	359	Anoka	Cedar	14-2C	204	•	•	•	•		•	•	•	-	29.4	19.2	0.6	13.2	37.6
Cedar Creek runs through this WMA and may offer some fishing opportunities. Hunting and viewing opportunities for many different species.																			
Robert J. Lick WMA	665	Rice	Lonsdale	55-6A	179	•		•			•	•	•	-	18.6	42.7	-	13.5	25.0
Watch for mallards, wood ducks, Canada geese, muskrats, Wilson's snipe, bitterns, and green herons.																			
Robertson WMA	8	Stevens	Chokio	5-5A	76	•		•			•	•		11.4	23.0	18.6	39.5	-	5.8
Look for great blue herons and great egrets. Waterfowl, pheasant, deer, and small game hunting. Look for wildlife near food plot and woody cover. WMA consists of two tracts, one on each side of Cty Rd 4. Some grassy nesting cover, a food plot, and two small woody plantings. Managed for prairie wildlife. Parking along Cty Rd 4.																			
Rock Lake WMA For more information call 507-537-6250.	332	Lyon	Balaton	48-1C	100	•		•			•	•		-	24.9	74.0	-	-	1.2
Rock River WMA WMA is floodplain forest with some grasslands and food plots.	578	Rock	Luverne	81-4B	421	•		•			•	•		19.3	40.9	8.5	-	27.8	2.5
Rodewald WMA - East Unit	210	Meeker	Cosmos	23-6B	112	•		•			•	•		-	36.6	46.8	11.5	-	4.7
Both units: Variety of habitats available or under development for wildlife.																			
Rodewald WMA - West Unit	205	Meeker	Cosmos	23-6B	114	•		•			•	•		8.2	43.8	28.4	4.6	-	14.7
Rogge WMA For more information call 507-537-6250.	236	Lincoln	Ivanhoe	33-4E	106	•		•			•	•		7.8	18.9	69.7	-	-	3.7
Rohlik's Slough WMA - Main Unit For more information call 320-231-5163.	305	Redwood	Seaforth	35-6E	263	•		•			•	•		-	8.4	81.0	7.0	2.2	1.5
Rohlik's Slough WMA - Paul's Slough Unit	306	Redwood	Seaforth	35-6E	38	•		•			•	•		-	5.1	71.0	13.3	4.3	6.1
Rolling Hills WMA For more information call 507-537-6250.	275	Lyon	Marshall	34-3E	33	•		•			•	•		-	64.6	35.4	-	-	-
Romberg WMA For more information call 320-231-5163.	483	Brown	Sleepy Eye	52-1C	19			•			•	•		-	54.1	45.9	-	-	-
Rooney Run WMA For more information call 507-831-2900.	721	Martin	Trimont	86-1A	111	•		•			•	•	•	-	8.4	74.4	0.3	-	17.0
Rooster Flats WMA For more information call 507-537-6250.	300	Lyon	Amiret	48-3A	126	•		•			•			20.8	43.7	8.4	-	6.9	20.0
Root River WMA	861	Houston	Hokah	96-3A	346	•		•	•		•	•	•	18.7	46.9	3.9	2.9	-	25.9
Hunting, trapping, fishing, and wildlife viewing. The Root River bisects the south boundary.																			
Rosaasen Slough WMA For more information call 320-231-5163.	192	Renville	Sacred Heart	21-6E	93	•		•			•	•		-	21.7	66.4	-	9.3	2.9
Rose WMA	843	Mower	Lyle	91-6D	51	•		•			•		•	-	34.6	4.9	-	-	60.5
Deer, turkey, and some pheasant hunting. WMA has been allowed to mature to a bottomland hardwood forest.																			
Rosenau-Lambrecht WMA - Sandmann Tract 1	502	Brown	New Ulm	52-2C	31	•		•			•	•		8.0	29.4	62.6	-	-	-
All tracts: For more information call 320-231-5163.																			
Rosenau-Lambrecht WMA - Sandmann Tract 2	501	Brown	New Ulm	52-2C	8	•		•			•	•		-	8.8	91.3	-	-	-
Rosenau-Lambrecht WMA - Tract 10	496	Brown	New Ulm	52-2B	16	•		•			•	•		-	74.2	12.3	-	-	14.2
Rosenau-Lambrecht WMA - Tracts 1 and 6-8	492	Brown	New Ulm	52-2C	275	•		•			•	•		4.7	45.0	31.5	6.9	3.5	8.5
Rosendale WMA For more information call 507-831-2900.	654	Watonwan	Saint James	68-1C	19	•		•			•	•		-	18.8	75.4	-	-	5.8
Roseville WMA	99	Kandiyohi	Regal	9-6B	64	•					•	•		-	7.9	26.3	59.6	-	4.1
Unit is primarily a deep-water cattail wetland with a small, woody cover planting on its west end.																			
Rost WMA For more information call 507-537-6250.	227	Lincoln	Ivanhoe	33-4E	251	•		•			•	•		5.7	39.8	53.4	-	-	1.0
Round Lake WMA For more information call 507-831-2900.	696	Jackson	Round Lake	83-5C	38			•			•	•		-	22.9	72.3	-	-	4.5
Rupp WMA	440	Murray	Currie	64-3A	83	•		•			•	•		-	2.8	44.0	-	46.9	-
View the wetland from the township road. This area has a small marsh and floodplain forest adjacent to the Des Moines River. Des Moines River floodplain has a riverbottom forest of box elder, cottonwood, and ash, as well as a wetland. Access to south portion of the area is difficult except in dry years.																			
Russ Blanford WMA	599	Rock	Luverne	80-3B	154	•					•		•	36.0	15.9	4.5	7.3	-	25.5
This recently acquired unit contains floodplain forest along the Rock River. Cropland being restored to native prairie, with some wildlife winter cover plantings and food plots.																			
Russell WMA For more information call 507-537-6250.	291	Lyon	Russell	48-1B	35	•		•			•	•		-	44.7	55.0	-	-	-
Rustic Retreat WMA	850	Mower	Taopi	92-3D	16						•			-	57.4	-	6.2	21.6	14.2
Some pheasant hunting, but be careful because of the proximity to the trail and to Hwy 56. WMA is a prairie/forest/wetland complex with the Upper Iowa River running through it. A 2-acre planted prairie is on the unit's east side. Mesic oak forest and other saturated deciduous cover types. Managed for pheasants. Root River Bike Trail borders unit on the south.																			
Ruthton WMA - Central Unit	364	Murray	Ruthton	47-5D	159	•		•			•	•		8.0	7.4	75.8	-	8.9	-
Roadside wildlife viewing. Floodplain wetland on the Redwood River with associated upland grassland, willow patches, and food plot.																			
Ruthton WMA - East Unit	372	Murray	Ruthton	47-5E	80	•		•			•	•		8.5	39.7	40.0	-	7.2	4.6
Roadside wildlife viewing. Small marsh with associated upland grassland, woody cover and food plots.																			
Ruthton WMA - West Unit	361	Pipestone, Murray	Ruthton	47-5D	55	•		•			•	•		-	17.1	83.3	-	-	-
Roadside wildlife viewing. Area has a marsh and associated upland grassland.																			
Rutstrum WMA	491	Washington	Scandia	16-1D	24	•		•				•	•	-	-	1.7	80.8	17.9	-
Accessible by water only; area offers unique boat-access hunting opportunities. Floodplain forest wildlife viewing. WMA is 24 acres along St. Croix River. WMA is primarily floodplain and subject to high water, so boundary posting is sparse; a GPS unit is recommended. Accessible by water on the St. Croix River only by traveling about a mile upstream from the carry-in access at Otisville or by floating about 4 miles downstream from the county access at Osceola.																			
Sacred Heart WMA For more information call 320-231-5163.	240	Renville	Renville	36-1B	141	•		•			•	•		7.0	27.8	30.2	18.1	11.2	5.2
Saiki WMA For more information call 507-225-3572. No wheelchair access.	703	Blue Earth	Good Thunder	70-1B	39	•		•	•		•	•	•	36.3	-	29.2	10.5	23.8	0.5
Sakatah WMA - Main Unit	714	Rice	Morristown	55-6D	48			•	•		•	•		-	11.9	52.4	-	18.9	17.3
Look for wood ducks, pheasants, squirrels, cottontail rabbits, mink, pelicans, red-winged blackbirds, sedge wrens, and savannah sparrows.																			
Salem Comm Prairie WMA	100	Stearns	Roscoe	10-1A	38						•	•		1.1	90.2	8.4	-	-	-
The larger of the two manmade wetlands in the unit's SE corner often hosts exceptional concentrations of migrating waterfowl in spring.																			
Salix WMA For more information call 507-537-6250.	230	Lincoln	Ivanhoe	33-4E	86	•		•			•			10.3	85.6	-	-	-	4.1
Salt and Pepper WMA	452	Murray	Chandler	63-5C	99	•		•			•			25.1	69.6	-	-	-	5.5
Creek valley grassland containing medium- to high-quality prairie, seeded native grass, and food plots. Unit managed for upland game habitat.																			
Salt Lake WMA - Main Unit For more information call 320-289-2493.	55	Lac Qui Parle	Marietta	18-2B	769	•		•			•	•		9.8	49.5	39.5	-	-	1.2
Salt Lake WMA - North Unit For more information call 320-289-2493. Observation deck.	53	Lac Qui Parle	Marietta	18-2B	11	•		•			•			-	30.9	69.1	-	-	-
Sandy Slough WMA For more information call 320-231-5163.	288	Redwood	Milroy	49-4A	79	•		•			•	•		-	50.5	39.6	5.1	-	5.0
Sangl WMA For more information call 507-831-2900.	730	Jackson	Lakefield	84-2D	260	•		•			•	•		11.3	64.7	18.7	-	-	5.3
Santiago WMA	208	Sherburne	Santiago	12-3A	83	•		•	•			•	•	-	-	32.3	14.6	-	53.0
Hunting, trapping, wildlife viewing, and hiking. Good habitat for waterfowl and other wetland wildlife, deer, turkeys and other associated species.																			
Sarah-Mason WMA - Central Unit	418	Murray	Slayton	48-2E	69	•		•			•	•		18.7	43.3	34.3	-	-	3.6
Scenic vista of the main sub-unit from the township road. WMA consists of three separate sub-units. Central sub-unit has small wetlands with associated upland grassland, woody cover, and food plots.																			
Sarah-Mason WMA - East Unit	419	Murray	Slayton	48-2E	40	•		•			•	•		-	67.7	13.4	-	8.7	10.2
East sub-unit has a small wetland with associated grassland upland and woody cover.																			
Sarah-Mason WMA - West Unit	414	Murray	Slayton	48-2E	12			•			•	•		-	31.1	68.1	-	-	-
West sub-unit is a small wetland with associated upland grassland.																			
Saum Memorial WMA For more information call 507-537-6250.	154	Yellow Medicine	Hendricks	32-2B	81	•		•			•	•		-	71.0	28.7	-	-	-
Sautter Marsh WMA	640	Le Sueur	Le Center	55-4B	51						•	•		-	-	100.2	-	-	-
For more information call 507-225-3572. Public access at WMA's south end, but no parking available. Parking by permission only.																			
Save the Wetlands WMA	792	Faribault	Alden	89-4C	100	•		•			•			-	68.5	22.3	2.6	6.6	-
For more information call 507-225-3572. Wheelchair access limited to adjacent cty/township roads.																			
Schendel WMA	363	Hennepin	Rockford	27-4B	14			•			•	•		-	-	100.7	-	-	-
WMA is all emergent vegetation marsh that may offer some late-season pheasant hunting after freeze-up. Bring hip boots.																			
Scheuring WMA - North Unit	525	Murray, Nobles	Iona	64-2D	22	•		•			•	•		-	48.9	50.7	-	-	-
Limited waterfowl hunting. WMA is two sub-units containing small prairie marshes with associated grasslands. North sub-unit is a small wetland with associated upland grassland.																			
Scheuring WMA - South Unit	527	Nobles	Wilmont	64-2D	37	•		•			•	•		-	51.0	41.7	-	-	7.1
Limited waterfowl hunting. WMA is two sub-units containing small prairie marshes with associated grasslands. South sub-unit contains small marshes with associated upland grassland, woody cover plantings and medium-quality native prairie.																			
Schindel WMA For more information call 507-537-6250.	289	Lincoln	Verdi	46-2C	156	•		•			•			1.5	89.7	4.3	-	-	4.4

Name	Number	County	Nearest Town	Pg / Coord	Acres	Deer	Bear	Small Game	Forest Birds	Sharptail	Pheasant	Waterfowl	Turkey	Cropland	Grassland	Emergent Wetland	Open Water	Lowland	Upland
						Game Species								% Cover Type					
Schletty WMA - Easement Unit For more information call 507-280-5066.	784	Dodge	Wasioja	74-1A	1	•		•						-	-	-	-	-	100.0
Schletty WMA - Main Unit For more information call 507-280-5066.	785	Dodge	Wasioja	74-1A	13	•		•						-	-	1.5	-	52.6	45.9
Schmalz WMA For more information call 320-231-5163.	328	Renville	Buffalo Lake	38-2A	120	•		•			•	•		13.4	30.8	47.7	-	7.0	1.2
Schmidt WMA	390	Hennepin	Champlin	14-1E	46	•		•	•				•	-	17.3	6.6	-	7.7	68.4
This area offers a unique opportunity to see a high-quality oak forest in an urban environment. WMA closed to waterfowl hunting.																			
Schneewind WMA	435	Carver	Waconia	40-3A	245	•		•	•		•	•	•	0.9	40.8	36.4	0.5	14.2	7.2
WMA is predominantly wetland with surrounding upland areas that have been planted to prairie. Managed for grassland and wetland species.																			
Schoeberl WMA	516	Murray	Iona	64-2D	150	•		•			•	•		-	41.5	56.6	-	-	1.9
Corabelle Lake is a good place to view migrating waterfowl in the spring. Access by a long cartway that may be impassible during wet periods.																			
Schrafel WMA	820	Mower	Austin	91-4B	33	•								-	41.6	9.2	-	16.2	33.0
WMA borders Turtle Creek to the north. Habitat managed for upland wildlife. Closed to trapping and firearms hunting. Open to archery deer hunting.																			
Schweigert WMA	566	Nobles	Fulda	65-4D	219	•		•			•	•		5.7	55.3	35.2	-	-	3.9
WMA contains a small marsh with associated upland grassland, woody cover plantings, and food plots.																			
Schwerin Creek WMA	837	Mower	Cannon Falls	92-1B	37	•		•			•			-	17.2	-	-	73.9	8.9
Hunting and trapping are the primary activities. Unit managed for pheasants and deer.																			
SE Clifton WMA For more information call 507-537-6250.	312	Lyon	Tracy	48-3B	371	•		•			•	•		9.0	17.4	63.7	-	-	10.0
Seha WMA	706	Le Sueur	Elysian	55-4D	131	•		•			•	•		2.1	11.6	70.3	-	-	15.9
For more information call 507-225-3572. Wheelchair access limited to primitive parking lot and adjacent cty road.																			
Sena WMA	124	Chippewa	Willmar	22-1A	184	•		•			•	•		3.3	52.1	29.0	7.2	-	6.1
Unit contains native prairie, seeded native-grass areas, woody cover plantings, a food plot, non-native grass, willow patches, and several small gravel piles/parking areas at the unit's NW corner.																			
Senn-Rich WMA	759	Waseca	Waseca	71-6B	102	•		•			•	•	•	-	-	94.6	-	2.6	2.8
For more information call 507-225-3572. Wheelchair access limited to adjacent cty/township roads.																			
Severance Lake WMA	431	Sibley	Arlington	39-6C	54	•		•			•	•		-	15.3	70.0	-	-	14.9
For more information call 507-225-3572. Wheelchair access limited to primitive parking lot.																			
Seymour Lake WMA For more information call 507-831-2900.	723	Martin	Sherburn	85-6B	160	•		•			•	•		6.7	55.7	29.0	-	-	7.8
Shakopee WMA	89	Chippewa	Maynard	7-5E	40	•		•	•			•		-	2.3	36.3	27.0	-	34.8
Unit contains the inlet of Shakopee Creek and its namesake lake. The rest of unit is primarily woods and bottomland flowage with reed canary grass and brush.																			
Sham Lake WMA For more information call 507-537-6250.	229	Lyon	Cottonwood	34-3C	84	•		•			•			-	38.1	61.9	-	-	-
Shanghai Lake WMA	646	Le Sueur	Le Center	54-3B	115	•		•	•		•	•		-	0.2	78.8	-	3.6	17.5
For more information call 507-225-3572. Wheelchair access limited to primitive parking area.																			
Shaokatan WMA	214	Lincoln	Ivanhoe	32-2E	447	•		•			•	•		12.3	30.4	56.6	-	-	0.7
WMA is a wetland/prairie complex in an agricultural landscape. Duck boat access.																			
Sheas Lake WMA	605	Le Sueur	Heidelberg	55-4A	295	•		•	•		•	•		-	-	62.2	-	12.7	25.2
For more information call 507-225-3572. Wheelchair access limited to two primitive access lanes and parking lots.																			
Shelburne WMA For more information call 507-537-6250.	355	Lyon, Murray	Balaton	47-6D	162	•		•			•			-	52.0	48.0	-	-	-
Sheridan WMA - Tract 4a Both tracts: For more information call 320-231-5163.	304	Redwood	Redwood Falls	36-1E	19	•		•			•			-	64.7	35.8	-	-	-
Sheridan WMA - Tract 4c	310	Redwood	Redwood Falls	36-1E	39	•		•	•		•		•	-	70.3	-	7.1	-	22.3
Sherwood WMA	638	Nobles	Ellsworth	81-5C	82	•		•			•			-	46.1	37.6	-	-	16.1
WMA contains a marshy creek with associated upland grassland and woody cover plantings.																			
Shetek WMA - East Unit	423	Murray	Tracy	48-3E	413	•		•			•	•		6.8	18.6	37.0	30.4	2.8	3.4
Cty Rd 38 offers good waterfowl viewing on this sub-unit. East sub-unit contains a large marsh with associated upland grassland, woody cover plantings, and food plots.																			
Shetek WMA - West Unit	421	Murray	Tracy	48-3E	206	•		•			•	•	•	8.9	23.8	54.5	-	-	12.8
West sub-unit contains small marshes with oak woods, upland grassland, food plots, and a native prairie remnant. Carry-in access to Clear Lake on this sub-unit.																			
Shible WMA For more information call 320-289-2493.	23	Swift	Appleton	5-6D	47	•			•		•	•		8.5	52.6	18.6	12.2	-	8.1
Shirley's Slough WMA	507	Murray	Iona	64-2C	51	•		•			•	•		-	49.1	44.4	-	-	6.3
WMA is a small marsh with associated upland grassland and a woody cover planting.																			
Shumann WMA	826	Olmsted	Stewartville	74-3E	92	•		•			•			6.8	13.0	40.2	-	28.4	11.5
Pheasant and deer hunting and trapping are the main activities for this unit.																			
Sibley WMA	498	Sibley	Gaylord	39-5E	31						•			-	18.2	31.6	-	34.9	15.6
For more information call 507-225-3572. Wheelchair access limited to primitive parking area and adjacent township road.																			
Sigler WMA	539	Sibley	Rush River	54-1A	74	•					•	•		-	22.8	72.3	-	-	4.9
For more information call 507-225-3572. Wheelchair access limited to primitive access lane and parking area.																			
Sioux Indian WMA For more information call 320-289-2493.	110	Lac Qui Parle	Dawson	20-1C	64	•		•			•	•		8.1	16.3	52.0	-	-	23.5
Sioux Lookout WMA	273	Lincoln	Lake Benton	46-3C	83	•		•			•			-	79.9	14.2	-	-	5.8
WMA is mainly grassland with some wetlands, woody cover, and prairie remnants.																			
Sioux Nation WMA For more information call 507-537-6250.	141	Yellow Medicine	Canby	32-2B	487	•		•			•	•		1.4	76.8	15.8	6.0	-	-
Sioux Prairie WMA	257	Lyon	Ivanhoe	47-5A	387	•		•			•	•		-	75.7	20.8	-	-	3.4
WMA consists of three separate tracts that are wetland/prairie complexes WMA contains prairie remnants.																			
Sioux Valley WMA For more information call 507-831-2900.	725	Jackson	Sioux Valley	83-6D	403	•		•			•	•		2.2	10.7	84.7	1.5	-	1.0
Siyo WMA For more information call 507-537-6250.	153	Yellow Medicine	Clarkfield	20-2E	78	•		•			•			1.3	84.3	-	-	-	14.5
Skandia WMA	394	Murray	Balaton	48-1E	40	•		•			•	•		-	7.5	92.5	-	-	-
WMA is an emergent marsh with irregular boundaries that provides a good wildlife wintering area. Carry-in water access to the marsh on this unit.																			
Skunk Lake WMA	727	Jackson	Sioux Valley	84-1D	238	•		•			•	•		8.9	16.3	67.9	3.4	0.6	2.9
Mostly emergent wetlands on the south shore of Skunk Lake.																			
Smith WMA	743	Faribault	Delavan	70-1E	337	•		•	•		•	•	•	5.6	7.2	71.9	3.7	8.8	2.8
For more information call 507-225-3572. Wheelchair access limited to adjacent cty/township roads.																			
Sodus WMA For more information call 507-537-6250.	337	Lyon	Balaton	48-1C	586	•		•			•	•		8.4	51.7	38.3	-	-	1.7
Sokota WMA For more information call 507-537-6250.	184	Lincoln	Hendricks	32-2D	144	•		•			•	•		-	38.3	61.8	-	-	-
Somerset WMA For more information call 507-280-5066.	770	Steele	Owatonna	72-2B	395	•		•			•	•	•	5.0	14.3	21.2	4.6	42.8	3.7
Somsen WMA WMA is a wildlife sanctuary and closed to hunting.	503	Brown	New Ulm	52-2C	49							•		-	20.5	19.9	55.6	-	4.1
South Fork Zumbro River WMA	807	Olmsted	Rock Dell	74-2D	11	•						•	•	-	-	-	-	100.0	-
Deer hunting. WMA is primarily riparian woodland. Mgmt. objective to provide habitat for deer and turkeys.																			
Southeast Hanska WMA For more information call 320-231-5163.	592	Brown	Hanska	52-1E	125	•		•			•	•		9.5	61.2	12.7	2.2	6.9	7.5
Spannaus WMA	513	Sibley	Henderson	40-1E	30	•		•	•				•	-	-	-	-	-	100.0
For more information call 507-225-3572. Wheelchair access limited to adjacent township road.																			
Spanton WMA For more information call 507-537-6250.	241	Lincoln	Ivanhoe	46-3A	48	•		•			•	•		-	34.2	65.8	-	-	-
Spartan WMA	166	Chippewa	Wegdahl	21-4E	231	•		•	•		•	•	•	-	7.1	36.1	-	-	56.9
Unit lies in a bend of the MN River on its north side. This unit is accessed by traveling across a private field.																			
Spartina WMA	632	Scott	Elko	42-2D	15	•		•			•	•	•	-	68.0	-	5.4	-	26.5
Unit is located entirely within a drained wetland basin and is managed for wetland and brushland species.																			
Spellman Lake WMA For more information call 507-537-6250.	203	Yellow Medicine	Hanley Falls	34-2B	60	•		•			•	•		18.2	57.3	-	0.8	-	23.7
Spiering WMA	410	McLeod	Brownton	39-4C	49						•	•		-	10.8	88.8	-	-	0.4
For more information call 507-225-3572. Wheelchair access limited to adjacent cty roads.																			
Spirit Prairie WMA	111	Stearns	Paynesville	10-1B	182	•		•			•			-	24.7	17.3	-	13.7	44.3
Hunting, trapping, wildlife viewing, and hiking. Important wintering area for resident wildlife including deer and pheasants.																			
Spring Valley WMA	847	Fillmore	Spring Valley	93-4A	80	•		•			•			3.9	81.4	-	-	-	14.6
Hunting, trapping, and wildlife viewing. Primarily upland gamebird habitat.																			
Springwater WMA	536	Rock	Luverne	80-2A	152	•		•			•			64.8	12.6	19.8	0.2	-	1.8
Cropland on this WMA being converted to native prairie. Some tree plantings for winter wildlife cover and some food plots.																			
St. Leo WMA For more information call 507-537-6250.	140	Yellow Medicine	St. Leo	19-5E	241	•		•			•	•		1.7	6.3	91.4	-	-	0.5
St. Patrick WMA	603	Scott	New Prague	41-6D	82			•			•	•		-	7.0	74.4	15.0	3.5	-
Waterfowl including tundra swans often seen in spring and fall. Unit managed for wetland species and has a fair amount of open water in central area.																			
St. Thomas Lake WMA	583	Le Sueur	Saint Thomas	40-3E	320	•		•	•		•	•	•	7.7	9.4	65.6	-	-	17.3
WMA is a wetland/prairie/forest complex. Emergent wetlands cover most of the unit with grassy and wooded uplands.																			
Stable Banks WMA	588	Nobles	Fulda	64-3E	48	•		•			•			-	93.8	6.2	-	-	-
WMA is a grassland creek valley with Jack Creek running through it.																			
Stearns Prairie Heritage WMA	78	Stearns	Regal	9-5A	470	•		•			•	•		2.6	41.2	23.5	-	6.3	26.4
Hunting, trapping, wildlife viewing, and hiking. Important wintering area for deer and pheasants.																			
Stokke WMA For more information call 507-537-6250.	173	Yellow Medicine	Clarkfield	34-2A	108	•		•			•	•		-	28.2	67.4	-	-	4.3
Stokman WMA	762	Blue Earth, Faribault	Minnesota Lake	70-3E	456	•		•			•	•	•	-	33.2	38.9	13.1	14.9	-
For more information call 507-225-3572. Wheelchair access limited to adjacent cty/township roads.																			
Stoney Run WMA For more information call 507-537-6250.	151	Yellow Medicine	Clarkfield	20-2E	268	•		•			•	•		6.1	63.6	24.3	-	-	5.9
Succonnix WMA	212	Wright	Clearwater	12-1C	1,019	•		•	•		•	•	•	0.1	40.9	14.0	7.8	14.0	23.1
Hunting, trapping, wildlife viewing, and hiking. WMA is home to a variety of wildlife because of its habitat components and large size. Good area to watch for spring migrants.																			
Suess WMA	817	Olmsted	Stewartville	74-2D	54	•					•			-	5.8	14.1	-	57.4	22.7
WMA is an excellent example of a SE MN shrub carr plant community. The road ditch on the west side contains many prairie plants. There is a calcareous fen on the unit. WMA managed for deer and pheasants. The tall blazing star is a sight in late July.																			
Suhr WMA For more information call 507-537-6250.	235	Lincoln	Arco	46-2A	7	•		•			•			-	59.5	-	-	-	39.2
Sulem Lake WMA For more information call 507-831-2900.	641	Watonwan	Butterfield	67-5C	55	•		•	•		•	•		26.4	17.6	29.1	1.8	-	22.0
Summers WMA For more information call 507-831-2900.	700	Jackson	Lakefield	84-1C	162	•		•			•	•		10.5	39.6	47.2	-	-	2.5
Sumter WMA	351	McLeod	Brownton	39-4A	80						•			2.6	50.1	36.6	-	-	6.6
This unit is a wetland/prairie complex managed as a pheasant production area. Wheelchair access limited to gravel parking lot at unit's south end and adjacent road and highway.																			
Sunburg WMA	68	Kandiyohi	Sunburg	8-2C	114	•		•			•	•		-	12.3	9.2	71.3	1.4	5.3
WMA contains abundant open water with a small amount of seeded upland grass and brush/lowland grass along the basin edges.																			
Swag WMA For more information call 507-831-2900.	773	Martin	Fairmont	86-3E	74	•		•			•	•		-	32.0	28.9	23.5	-	14.9
Swan Lake WMA - Courtland Bay Unit	535	Nicollet	Nicollet	53-4C	55	•					•	•		4.0	74.5	21.3	-	-	-
Unit can be hunted during early goose season because it is possible to hunt away from water. Look for pelicans and nesting trumpeter swans. Unit consists mostly of upland cover adjoining Swan Lake and is considered one of the best waterfowl nesting areas on the lake. Waterfowl hunters work hard to reach birds. Primitive public water access. Canoe to reach Courtland Bay. Be prepared for wet feet.																			
Swan Lake WMA - Courtland Central Unit	550	Nicollet	Courtland	53-4C	114	•		•			•	•		3.8	60.0	26.9	-	8.3	-
Hike to the wetlands to look for migrating waterfowl. Explore unit on skis. No improved trails. Look for a small rookery of colonial birds in a stand of dead trees on unit's west section.																			
Swan Lake WMA - Courtland East Unit	546	Nicollet	Nicollet	53-4C	113	•					•	•		1.2	37.8	56.4	-	-	4.6
Wildlife watching. Painted turtles very common. Migrating waterfowl, great blue herons, and egrets may be seen in the wetlands. Look for restored prairie flowers. Predator hunters may find foxes or coyotes. Waterfowl and upland birds thrive on the Courtland East Unit, which contains three open-water wetlands and extensive prairie grass. A prairie flower planting in unit's NW corner attracts grassland birds and butterflies.																			
Swan Lake WMA - Courtland West Unit	543	Nicollet	Courtland	52-3C	127	•					•	•		1.6	15.4	79.6	-	-	2.8
Hike to the wetlands to look for migrating waterfowl. Explore unit on skis. No improved trails. Highway divides the unit. Wetlands and parking areas on both sides of the road. Cover is a mix of upland prairie and wetlands. Mgmt. calls for future tree planting, prescribed burns, and conversion of ag fields to prairie grass. Plan on hiking to reach main part of unit. In the western unit, look for a small rookery of colonial birds in a stand of dead trees. Access to this portion is easier. Wheelchair access at two gravel parking lots, one on either side of CSAH 12. At the southern parking lot, a primitive trail leads back into the unit.																			
Swan Lake WMA - Duck Lake Unit	569	Nicollet	Nicollet	53-5B	294	•		•			•	•		7.2	28.5	61.5	-	-	2.8

Name	Number	County	Nearest Town	Pg / Coord	Acres	Deer	Bear	Small Game	Forest Birds	Sharptail	Pheasant	Waterfowl	Turkey	Cropland	Grassland	Emergent Wetland	Open Water	Lowland	Upland
Popular place to hike and see spring migrants. Drive around the area at dusk to see deer and other wildlife.																			
Swan Lake WMA - Hackberry Pt. Central Unit	568	Nicollet	Nicollet	53-4C	11	•		•			•	•	•	-	-	16.5	-	-	83.5
All Hackberry Pt. Units: If you can get there, hunting opportunities exist. Managed to provide habitat for a diverse array of woodland and wetland wildlife. Excellent stand of hardwoods. Water access only.																			
Swan Lake WMA - Hackberry Pt. Main Unit	565	Nicollet	Nicollet	53-4C	109	•		•			•	•	•	13.5	20.1	22.7	-	-	43.8
Swan Lake WMA - Hackberry Pt. South Unit	571	Nicollet	Nicollet	53-4C	9	•		•	•		•	•	•	-	-	57.6	-	-	41.2
Land access to the peninsula is private. Public and private holdings are mixed on the peninsula, so WMA users must be aware of land boundaries. There is no public access to this unit, except by water. The lake is too shallow for motor use. Wheelchair access along roads through the unit requires permission from adjacent landowner.																			
Swan Lake WMA - Hackberry Pt. West Unit	560	Nicollet	Nicollet	53-4C	2	•		•			•	•	•	-	-	100.0	-	-	-
Swan Lake WMA - Johnson Marsh Unit	635	Nicollet	Nicollet	53-6D	40						•			-	17.5	75.0	-	-	7.5
Some pheasant hunting opportunities. Predator hunting is possible.																			
Swan Lake WMA - Larson Unit	623	Nicollet, Le Sueur	St. Peter	54-1C	237	•		•			•	•	•	-	7.3	-	12.7	75.2	2.8
Anglers hike into the river. No nearby boat access. Unit contains former agricultural lands in the MN River bottoms that are naturally regenerating with willow and cottonwood. Bottomland ecosystem is flooded by the river every spring. Managed for deer and turkey habitat. E. MN River Refuge is across the river from this unit. There is a field approach off the highway, but no water access. A long, unimproved walking trail leads to a river sandbar that is popular with anglers. Wheelchair access limited to small gravel parking area and primitive trail running from parking area to the MN River.																			
Swan Lake WMA - Nicollet Bay Main Unit	586	Nicollet	Nicollet	53-5C	163	•		•			•	•		6.6	47.9	41.1	-	-	4.2
Use a canoe to explore the marsh. Be careful not to disturb nesting areas on floating mats of vegetation. This unit is managed as a prairie ecosystem. The lake has one of the state's largest concentrations of western grebes. There is a nesting colony of rare Forster's terns. Water access only. A 680-foot wheelchair-accessible dock leads to a duck blind on Swan Lake maintained for hunters with disabilities. The access road and gravel parking lots are also accessible to wheelchairs.																			
Swan Lake WMA - Nicollet Bay North Unit	579	Nicollet	Nicollet	53-4C	18	•		•				•		-	-	-	-	-	100.0
Use a canoe to explore the marsh. Be careful not to disturb nesting areas on floating mats of vegetation. WMA contains former farmland converted to warm-season native grasses. This unit is managed as a prairie ecosystem. The dock is an excellent place to see the stars and listen to the marsh. Lake has one of the state's largest concentrations of western grebes. There is a nesting colony of rare Forster's terns. Water access only. A 680-foot wheelchair-accessible dock leads to a duck blind on Swan Lake that is maintained for hunters with disabilities. Skiing and snowshoeing are possible. No improved trails.																			
Swan Lake WMA - Nicollet Bay South Unit	587	Nicollet	Nicollet	53-5C	26	•		•			•	•		-	56.4	43.6	-	-	-
Use a canoe to explore the marsh. Be careful not to disturb nesting areas on floating mats of vegetation. WMA contains former farmland converted to warm-season native grasses. Unit is managed as a prairie ecosystem. The lake has one of the state's largest concentrations of western grebes. There is a nesting colony of rare Forster's terns. Water access only. A 680-foot wheelchair-accessible dock leads to a duck blind on Swan Lake that is maintained for hunters with disabilities. Skiing and snowshoeing are possible. No improved trails.																			
Swan Lake WMA - Nicollet Creek Unit	597	Nicollet	Nicollet	53-5D	7									-	100.0	-	-	-	-
For more information call 507-225-3572. This sub-unit is accessible by water only.																			
Swan Lake WMA - North Star Unit	616	Nicollet	Nicollet	53-5D	441	•		•	•		•	•	•	5.1	9.2	3.7	-	0.3	30.9
Watch for migrating raptors along river bottoms. Excellent place to hike in solitude. Monarch and other butterflies and snakes are abundant. The unit contains a snake winter denning site. The topography is rolling and terraced, containing deep ravines and a reclaimed gravel pit. Unit managed for wildlife diversity. A high point in the former gravel pit offers an extraordinary view of the MN River Valley. Rock hounds will stay busy here. Indigo buntings and bluebirds are seen. Wheelchair access limited to gravel parking lot and adjacent cty/township roads.																			
Swan Lake WMA - Northeast Angle Unit	581	Nicollet	St. Peter	53-6B	40						•			-	41.8	58.2	-	-	-
Unit managed for pheasants. Look for rooster pheasants in their brilliant plumage. Finches may be seen here.																			
Swan Lake WMA - Oak Leaf Lake Unit	613	Nicollet	St. Peter	54-1C	52						•	•		-	84.1	14.5	-	-	1.1
Oak Leaf Lake is a migratory bird feeding and resting area. The unit is managed to provide nesting and migrational habitat for waterfowl. Look for migrating waterfowl on the lake. Restored prairie flowers bloom beside the highway. Waterfowl and pheasant hunting. Area is open and has little winter cover. Uplands have been seeded with prairie grasses. Good place to watch migrating waterfowl from a vehicle. No motors allowed during waterfowl season. Wheelchair access limited to gravel parking lot.																			
Swan Lake WMA - Oshawa Unit	594	Nicollet	St. Peter	53-6C	149	•					•	•		11.6	48.8	39.7	-	-	-
Hike the field road for a view of Middle Lake. Heavy cover in summer makes access difficult. Managed as year-round habitat for pheasants and deer and as nesting cover for ducks. There is a parking lot on Cty 13, but no water access. Unit is inaccessible in the winter. Wheelchair access limited to gravel parking lot at unit's north end and adjacent township road.																			
Swan Lake WMA - Pehling's Bay/South Bay Unit	573	Nicollet	Nicollet	53-4C	47	•		•			•	•		-	19.0	60.1	-	-	20.9
Access to WMA is through private property only. Please ask for permission to cross private property.																			
Swan Lake WMA - Peterson Lake Central Unit	538	Nicollet	Nicollet	53-4B	84	•		•			•	•	•	15.1	78.2	1.8	-	-	5.0
Late-season bow-hunting or muzzleloading. A full range of wildlife species. Managed to provide habitat for migratory birds and resident species. Wild turkeys are found here. Oaks provide mast for wildlife. An island on Swan Lake is tangled with wind-felled trees and provides excellent deer habitat.																			
Swan Lake WMA - Peterson Lake East Unit	540	Nicollet	Nicollet	53-4B	9	•		•			•	•	•	-	-	-	-	-	100.0
Parking lot on north side of Cty 5 offers a scenic view of the lake, where migrating waterfowl may be present. The area is difficult to enter during summer. Opportunities exist for late-season bow-hunting or muzzleloading. Managed to provide habitat for migratory birds and resident species. Wild turkeys are found here. Oaks provide mast for wildlife. An island on Swan Lake is tangled with wind-felled trees and provides excellent deer habitat.																			
Swan Lake WMA - Peterson Lake North Unit	534	Nicollet	Nicollet	53-4B	116	•		•	•		•	•	•	-	23.7	67.6	-	-	8.7
Parking lot on the north side of Cty 5 offers a scenic view of the lake where migrating waterfowl may be present. The area is difficult to enter during summer. Opportunities for late-season bow-hunting or muzzleloading. Managed to provide habitat for migratory birds and resident species. Wild turkeys are found here. Oaks provide mast for wildlife. An island on Swan Lake is tangled with wind-felled trees and provides excellent deer habitat. Wheelchair access limited to three gravel parking lots and adjacent cty/township roads. A primitive trail leads from the southern parking lot to a corn food plot.																			
Swan Lake WMA - Tri-Island Central Unit	557	Nicollet	Nicollet	53-4C	60									-	-	-	-	-	100.0
All Tri-Island units: This sub-unit is a wooded island on Swan Lake accessible by water only and within the Swan Lake Waterfowl and State Game Refuge. Consult MN hunting regulations for restrictions.																			
Swan Lake WMA - Tri-Island East Unit	558	Nicollet	Nicollet	53-4C	18									-	-	-	-	-	100.0
Swan Lake WMA - Tri-Island North Unit	556	Nicollet	Nicollet	53-4C	57									-	-	-	-	-	100.0
Swan Lake WMA - Tri-Island South Unit	570	Nicollet	Nicollet	53-4C	37									-	100.0	-	-	-	-
Swan Lake WMA - Tri-Island West Unit	552	Nicollet	Nicollet	53-4C	2									-	-	-	-	-	100.0
Swan Lake WMA - Wiwi Bay Unit	580	Nicollet	St. Peter	53-6C	165	•					•	•		-	29.2	70.6	-	-	-
Opportunities to jump-shoot, decoy, or pass-shoot waterfowl for hunters who are willing to walk. Pheasants found here. Predator hunting is possible, but cover is limited. Mostly a narrow strip of shoreline along the north side of Middle Lake. Cover consists of prairie grass, cattails, and reed canary grass. Area is often wet. Managed for waterfowl habitat. An 8-acre hard-bottomed prairie pothole is excellent duck habitat. Parking lot on Cty Rd 5, but no water access. Wheelchair access limited to gravel parking lot.																			
Swan WMA For more information call 507-280-5066.	752	Steele	Owatonna	72-1A	238			•			•	•	•	-	1.9	61.1	0.2	16.0	21.0
Swartout WMA	249	Wright	Maple Lake	12-1D	110	•		•			•	•		-	12.3	83.0	-	-	4.8
Hunting, trapping, wildlife viewing, and hiking. Access to unit is on the property's east and west sides.																			
Sween WMA	157	Chippewa	Wegdahl	21-4D	291	•		•	•		•	•		2.5	50.3	31.2	1.2	-	12.3
This is a long, fairly narrow unit with a flowage through its center. Contains seeded native-grass fields, woody cover plantings, a food plot, an old farmstead grove, a large wetland impoundment, and natural wetlands. Access from roads adjacent to to the unit.																			
Sweetman WMA	470	Murray	Avoca	64-3B	35	•		•			•	•		-	41.0	49.0	-	2.3	7.7
Wintering area for upland birds. There is a small, shallow marsh with associated upland grassland and a woody cover planting. The marsh only attracts occasional waterfowl.																			
Sweetwater WMA - Center Unit All units: For more information call 320-289-2493.	81	Lac Qui Parle	Madison	18-3D	79	•		•			•	•		2.7	73.9	23.5	-	-	-
Sweetwater WMA - Northeast Unit	80	Lac Qui Parle	Madison	18-3D	80	•		•			•	•		29.9	23.3	38.8	-	-	8.1
Sweetwater WMA - Southwest Unit	83	Lac Qui Parle	Madison	18-3D	132	•		•			•	•		1.4	39.5	59.0	-	-	-
Swessinger WMA	542	Nobles	Wilmont	64-2E	69	•		•			•	•		5.3	49.9	40.2	-	4.6	-
WMA contains a small marsh with associated upland grassland, a willow patch, and a food plot.																			
Talcot Lake WMA	554	Murray, Cottonwood	Dundee	65-5D	4,676	•		•			•	•		12.4	34.6	23.6	24.2	2.6	1.4
Historically important for migrating waterfowl. Controlled hunt zones, wildlife sanctuary, and waterfowl refuge boundaries are posted, however, visitors are strongly encouraged to obtain a map from headquarters. WMA closed from 10 p.m. - 5 a.m. Wildlife sanctuary – no trespassing anytime. Waterfowl refuge – no waterfowl hunting allowed. Motors permitted on the lake (except during waterfowl season) but prohibited on the river and marshes all year. Wheelchair-accessible blinds available for deer and goose hunting.																			
Tamarack WMA	45	Stearns	Brooten	8-3A	591	•		•	•		•	•	•	4.2	10.6	61.7	-	12.8	10.7
Good hunting, trapping, wildlife viewing, and hiking. Significant wintering area for deer, pheasants, and turkeys.																			
Tangential WMA	731	Goodhue	Cannon Falls	44-1E	26	•		•	•		•		•	-	2.3	-	-	-	97.7
Numerous forest bird species can be seen; scarlet tanagers migrate through in spring.																			
Teal Scurry WMA	145	Meeker	Manannah	10-1C	158	•		•	•		•	•		6.7	57.8	23.0	-	-	12.2
Brome/alfalfa nesting cover, several shallow wetland areas, a small section of woods, and a permanent food plot.																			
Teal WMA	775	Waseca	New Richland	72-1D	74	•		•			•	•		1.4	-	74.1	-	17.9	6.5
For more information call 507-225-3572. Wheelchair access limited to adjacent cty/township roads.																			
Teapail WMA For more information call 507-280-5066.	788	Dodge	Dodge Center	73-6A	15	•		•						-	-	2.0	1.3	21.6	74.5
Teardrop WMA For more information call 507-537-6250.	129	Lac Qui Parle, Yellow Medicine	Clarkfield	19-5E	42	•					•	•		-	19.8	78.1	-	-	-
Ten Sloughs WMA For more information call 507-537-6250.	202	Lincoln	Hendricks	32-3D	50	•		•			•	•		-	53.9	46.1	-	-	-
Ten-Well WMA For more information call 320-289-2493.	118	Lac Qui Parle	Boyd	19-6D	175	•		•			•	•		-	21.4	78.1	-	-	-
Tennessen WMA A tree planting provides good winter cover for pheasants.	488	Murray	Iona	64-1C	23	•		•			•	•		-	28.3	45.1	-	4.9	21.7
Terrace WMA	416	Pipestone	Woodstock	63-4A	446	•		•			•			7.7	81.8	3.4	-	-	7.1
WMA contains a large native prairie and restored prairie with some woody cover plantings and food plots.																			
Terri WMA For more information call 320-231-5163.	518	Brown	Comfrey	51-4E	74	•		•			•		•	12.9	27.0	45.0	-	8.7	6.2
Thielke Lake WMA For more information call 320-289-2493.	3	Big Stone	Clinton	4-3A	357	•					•	•		7.9	28.7	1.7	60.2	-	1.5
Thompson Slough WMA	745	Blue Earth	Minnesota Lake	70-3C	27	•		•			•	•	•	-	-	69.5	-	3.1	24.1
For more information call 507-225-3572. Wheelchair access limited to adjacent cty/township roads.																			
Thomson WMA For more information call 320-289-2493.	4	Big Stone	Clinton	4-3A	119	•					•	•		-	21.9	35.6	33.8	-	8.7
Thorpe WMA	838	Winona	Minneiska	61-4E	143	•		•				•	•	-	-	1.4	23.3	75.3	-
Recreation dominated by hunting, trapping, fishing and wildlife viewing.																			
Thostenson WMA For more information call 507-537-6250.	253	Lincoln	Arco	47-4A	161	•		•			•	•		16.8	32.8	41.9	-	-	8.6
Tiedemann WMA	774	Goodhue	Zumbrota	58-3C	136	•		•			•			4.5	90.4	-	-	2.0	3.1
Hunting for deer, small game, pheasants, and Hungarian partridge. Eastern kingbirds and palm warblers frequent open areas; American kestrels patrol edges.																			
Tierney WMA For more information call 507-831-2900.	668	Watonwan	Saint James	68-3B	55	•		•			•	•		-	31.7	60.9	-	-	7.5
Tiger Lake WMA - Dahlberg Tract	317	Redwood	North Redwood	36-3D	100	•		•	•		•	•	•	-	43.0	29.3	-	10.8	17.1
Look for migrating raptors on this sub-unit. This tract is a wetland/prairie complex with some forested areas.																			
Tiger Lake WMA - Hansen, Sperl and Stancer Tracts	333	Renville, Redwood	North Redwood	36-3D	527	•		•	•		•	•	•	6.9	15.0	0.5	19.9	43.2	14.1
Look for migrating raptors. This tract is composed of the Hansen, Sperl, and Stancer Tracts and is primarily lowland brush and contains Tiger Lake.																			
Tillemans WMA	224	Lyon	Minneota	33-5D	155	•		•			•			15.9	73.1	-	-	-	11.2
WMA is primarily open grasslands with some small forested areas throughout and some remnant prairie.																			
Timber Lake WMA	637	Jackson	Wilder	66-1E	916	•		•			•	•		11.5	56.6	22.2	0.6	1.6	7.1
WMA consists of three tracts of land. All are grassland/wetland complexes with some forested areas. The two largest tracts are along the north and SE shores of Timber Lake. The third tract lies SW of Wilder. This unit is part of a waterfowl refuge - check signs. A portion is closed to firearms deer hunting (as posted). The Timber Lake WPA is adjacent to the southern boundary of the south tract. Concrete ramp water access to Timber Lake on the south tract.																			
Timm's Lake WMA For more information call 507-537-6250.	266	Yellow Medicine, Redwood	Wood Lake	35-4D	203	•		•			•	•		-	17.7	31.6	49.4	-	1.2
Tjosaas WMA For more information call 320-289-2493.	58	Swift	Benson	6-3E	90	•		•	•		•		•	20.1	60.3	-	-	3.1	16.5
Toe WMA For more information call 507-831-2900.	693	Jackson	Lakefield	84-2B	343	•		•			•	•		13.9	50.5	31.9	-	1.4	2.4
Tom Cliff Jr. Memorial WMA	744	Waseca	Waseca	71-6A	32	•		•			•	•		-	1.9	96.5	-	1.6	-
This unit is a refuge — no hunting allowed. Wheelchair access limited to adjacent cty/township roads.																			
Tri-Cooperative WMA For more information call 507-280-5066.	800	Dodge	Oslo	74-2C	47	•					•			-	16.8	-	-	-	83.2
Tribute WMA	76	Stearns	Regal	9-5A	233	•		•			•	•		0.8	63.2	23.0	-	10.7	2.2
Good hunting, trapping, wildlife viewing, and hiking. Good numbers of wintering deer and pheasants. 40 acres of mesic-prairie remnants exist. Upland sandpipers and marbled godwits have been seen during nesting season.																			
Trongard WMA For more information call 320-231-5163.	218	Renville	Sacred Heart	35-6A	100	•		•			•			12.9	52.5	9.5	-	12.3	12.9
Troy WMA	360	Pipestone	Pipestone	46-2E	55	•		•			•			6.6	24.7	54.5	-	-	14.4
WMA contains a marshy drainage with associated upland grassland, a woody cover planting, and a food plot.																			
Tunsberg WMA	85	Chippewa	Montevideo	20-3B	81	•		•			•	•		12.7	45.6	12.0	13.8	-	13.3
Two wetlands, seeded native-grass fields, a food plot, and small woody cover planting.																			
Turtle WMA For more information call 507-831-2900.	664	Watonwan	Saint James	68-1D	13	•		•			•	•		-	-	60.3	-	38.9	-
Tutt WMA	392	Murray	Lake Wilson	47-6E	103	•		•			•	•		7.8	49.1	35.1	1.8	-	6.1
Scenic vista of the marsh from the hilltop on the south side. View wetland wildlife from the township road on the unit's west side.																			
Two Rivers WMA For more information call 320-231-5163.	403	Redwood	Revere	49-5C	724	•		•			•		•	6.2	79.4	1.1	-	10.0	3.1

Name	Number	County	Nearest Town	Pg / Coord	Acres	Game Species: Deer	Bear	Small Game	Forest Birds	Sharptail	Pheasant	Waterfowl	Turkey	% Cover Type: Cropland	Grassland	Emergent Wetland	Open Water	Lowland	Upland
Two Sloughs WMA For more information call 507-537-6250.	264	Lincoln	Lake Benton	46-3B	17	•		•			•	•		-	23.4	77.2	-	-	-
Tyler WMA For more information call 507-537-6250.	295	Lincoln	Tyler	47-4C	435	•		•			•	•		7.9	17.2	74.9	-	-	-
Typhoon WMA For more information call 507-831-2900.	457	Cottonwood	Storden	50-1E	83	•		•			•	•		17.7	25.9	35.0	8.0	-	13.3
Tyro WMA For more information call 507-537-6250.	162	Yellow Medicine	St. Leo	34-1A	302									3.1	38.1	51.8	-	-	7.0
Upper Antelope Valley WMA For more information call 507-537-6250.	161	Yellow Medicine	Canby	33-4B	162	•		•			•			-	33.0	67.0	-	-	-
Upper Iowa River WMA Hunting, trapping, and wildlife viewing.	855	Fillmore	Le Roy	93-4E	131	•		•	•		•	•	•	1.7	37.0	24.2	2.7	25.0	9.4
Upper Twin Lake WMA For more information call 507-280-5066.	801	Freeborn	Albert Lea	90-1C	14									-	11.8	-	-	27.8	47.9
Vale WMA	512	Sibley	Henderson	40-2D	299	•		•	•		•		•	1.0	7.4	9.3	-	-	82.3
WMA is primarily forest with some small wetlands and small grassy open areas. The north part of the unit is cut off by High Island Creek.																			
Valleau WMA For more information call 507-831-2900.	631	Jackson	Heron Lake	65-6E	309	•		•	•		•	•		5.6	28.6	57.4	0.9	-	7.5
Vallers WMA	228	Lyon	Marshall	34-2D	771	•		•			•	•		8.0	52.5	38.0	-	-	1.5
WMA is a prairie/wetland complex with some remnant prairie and some woody cover plantings.																			
Van Beek WMA	412	Pipestone	Woodstock	63-5A	23	•		•			•	•		-	41.2	50.4	-	-	7.9
WMA contains a small marsh with associated upland grassland and a woody cover planting.																			
Vaneck WMA	376	Murray	Ruthton	47-5E	77	•		•			•	•		-	10.2	76.4	-	13.7	-
Prairie wetland basins with associated uplands and dense willow cover.																			
Velishek WMA	677	Le Sueur, Rice	Kilkenny	55-5B	80	•		•			•	•	•	4.1	37.8	13.8	-	-	44.3
For more information call 507-225-3572. Wheelchair access limited to gravel parking lot and adjacent county road.																			
Vermilya WMA	848	Winona, Olmsted	Dover	76-2D	198	•		•	•		•		•	5.6	32.4	-	-	0.5	61.5
Good pheasant hunting; some small game and deer hunting. Turkeys also present. A food plot is provided for wintering wildlife. Small parking lot on unit's SW corner.																			
Vernon WMA For more information call 507-280-5066.	804	Dodge	Oslo	74-1D	85	•					•			-	45.2	12.1	-	39.8	2.0
Victory WMA For more information call 320-289-2493.	13	Big Stone	Ortonville	4-3B	682	•					•	•		1.9	63.1	12.4	20.0	-	2.3
Vogel WMA For more information call 320-231-5163.	476	Brown	Springfield	50-3D	82	•		•			•	•		15.4	46.3	29.7	2.7	2.3	3.5
Voit WMA	593	Cottonwood, Jackson	Windom	65-5D	49	•					•	•		18.1	57.5	13.2	3.0	-	7.2
This WMA, located on the south shore of Clear Lake, has grasslands, tree plantings, and food plots. Unit also provides access to an undeveloped water access for Clear Lake.																			
Vorce WMA For more information call 507-280-5066.	777	Dodge	Claremont	73-5A	40	•		•			•		•	-	10.0	0.3	-	0.3	88.5
Voss WMA For more information call 507-831-2900.	607	Watonwan	Darfur	68-1A	43	•		•			•	•		22.8	3.0	69.7	-	1.2	3.5
Wachter WMA	697	Nobles	Worthington	82-3D	86	•		•			•	•		-	5.6	93.2	-	-	1.2
WMA contains three small wetlands bordered by open grasslands. Carry-in water access to one of the wetlands.																			
Wajer WMA	490	Murray	Slayton	64-2C	81	•		•			•			-	29.9	60.1	-	-	10.1
Limited waterfowl hunting. The area is managed for upland birds.																			
Walnut Lake WMA	786	Faribault	Wells	88-3B	2,516	•		•	•		•	•	•	7.2	4.3	59.3	16.6	9.0	3.3
For more information call 507-225-3572. Wheelchair access limited to adjacent cty/township roads.																			
Walter WMA - Main Unit All units: For more information call 320-289-2493.	34	Lac Qui Parle	Nassau	18-3A	155	•		•			•			-	39.5	55.9	-	-	4.4
Walter WMA - North Unit	31	Lac Qui Parle	Nassau	18-2A	29	•		•			•			-	80.6	16.0	-	-	3.5
Walter WMA - Southeast Unit	37	Lac Qui Parle	Nassau	18-3A	163	•		•			•	•		10.1	55.9	30.7	-	-	3.4
Walter WMA - West Unit	35	Lac Qui Parle	Nassau	18-2A	114	•		•			•	•		-	41.8	55.4	-	-	2.8
Ward Lake WMA	401	McLeod, Sibley	Winthrop	38-3C	34						•	•		19.8	59.2	10.4	-	-	10.7
For more information call 507-225-3572. Wheelchair access limited to gravel parking lot and adjacent cty/township roads.																			
Warsaw WMA	729	Goodhue	Kenyon	57-4A	34			•			•			-	-	90.2	-	7.2	2.7
Some grassland bird species can be seen, however, due to its small size and lack of diverse habitats, wildlife viewing is limited.																			
Waseca WMA	755	Waseca	Waseca	72-1A	303	•		•	•		•	•	•	0.5	22.8	65.1	0.1	2.9	8.6
For more information call 507-225-3572. Wheelchair access limited to adjacent cty/township roads.																			
Wasioja WMA For more information call 507-280-5066.	787	Dodge	Dodge Center	73-5B	11			•			•			-	19.4	29.6	3.7	28.7	16.7
Waterbury WMA For more information call 320-231-5163.	379	Redwood	Wanda	49-6B	81	•		•			•	•		-	29.1	56.8	2.2	-	12.0
Watline WMA For more information call 507-831-2900.	673	Watonwan	Saint James	67-6D	107			•			•			2.2	91.6	-	0.5	-	5.7
Weeks Lake WMA For more information call 507-537-6250.	245	Lincoln	Ivanhoe	46-2A	103	•		•			•	•		-	27.6	72.4	-	-	-
Welfare WMA	404	Anoka	Thompson Heights	14-2E	16									-	18.7	81.9	-	-	-
Welfare WMA is along US Hwy 10 within the city of Coon Rapids. No firearms discharge allowed.																			
Wells WMA	778	Faribault	Wells	89-4A	27			•			•			-	-	94.1	-	-	6.3
For more information call 507-225-3572. Wheelchair access limited to adjacent cty/township roads.																			
West Graham WMA - North Unit	589	Nobles	Kinbrae	65-4E	205	•		•			•	•		4.2	64.3	26.0	-	-	5.4
North sub-unit contains several restored wetlands with associated upland grassland, woody cover, and food plots.																			
West Graham WMA - South Unit	601	Nobles	Kinbrae	65-4E	301	•		•			•	•		8.0	70.0	15.3	-	-	6.6
South sub-unit is a large grassland area along the west shore of West Graham Lake, containing small wetlands, woody cover, and food plots.																			
Westline WMA For more information call 320-231-5163.	315	Redwood	Lucan	49-5A	257			•			•	•		-	19.3	25.4	51.0	-	4.2
White Prairie WMA This small WMA is native prairie.	283	Lyon	Marshall	48-2A	18	•		•			•			-	100.0	-	-	-	-
Whitefield WMA	169	Kandiyohi	Willmar	22-3B	164	•		•			•			3.2	64.2	22.9	-	0.9	8.1
Wetlands on this unit usually are very shallow, with little or no standing or open water. Access via adjacent roadways.																			
Whitewater WMA - Callahan Unit	834	Winona	Elba	76-2B	305	•		•	•		•		•	18.8	1.9	-	-	-	79.3
All units: hunting and fishing. Wetlands, forest, and grassland communities grant wildlife watchers the chance to see sandhill cranes, ducks, geese, swans, black terns, eagles, and otters. Bluff prairies dot south-facing slopes, while trout streams bisect the valley floor. Seventeen manmade and natural wetlands dapple the valley. There is a 2,300-acre state game refuge inside Whitewater WMA. It is closed to deer and waterfowl hunting; open to small game hunting, wild turkey hunting, and trapping by permit from the area wildlife manager. A wheelchair-accessible duck blind is located on the dike of Dorer Pool Number One within the WMA.																			
Whitewater WMA - DeWitz Unit	821	Wabasha	Elba	76-1A	68	•		•	•			•	•	7.2	1.9	3.7	6.5	-	80.5
Whitewater WMA - Gengler Unit	825	Wabasha	Plainview	60-2E	58	•		•	•				•	13.5	-	-	-	-	86.5
Whitewater WMA - Heaser Unit	822	Wabasha	Elba	60-1E	49	•		•	•			•	•	-	-	-	-	2.5	97.5
Whitewater WMA - Jilk Unit	845	Winona	Elba	76-3B	8	•		•	•				•	-	-	-	-	-	100.0
Whitewater WMA - Main Branch Unit	831	Wabasha, Winona	Elba	76-2A	20,939	•		•	•		•	•	•	13.9	6.2	6.0	1.6	12.8	57.7
Whitewater WMA - McCarthy Ravine Unit	824	Winona	Plainview	60-2E	379	•		•	•				•	-	8.3	-	-	-	91.7
Whitewater WMA - North Branch Unit	830	Wabasha, Winona, Olmsted	Elba	76-1A	3,357	•		•	•		•	•	•	14.6	5.1	-	1.8	17.7	60.6
Whitewater WMA - Osprey Unit	827	Wabasha	Elba	60-3D	6	•		•	•			•		-	-	-	-	100.0	-
Whitewater WMA - Ploetz Unit	844	Winona	Elba	76-3B	9	•		•	•				•	100.0	-	-	-	-	-
Whitewater WMA - South Branch Unit	841	Winona	Elba	76-3B	1,631	•		•	•		•	•	•	13.2	6.9	0.6	1.1	9.0	69.2
Whitewater WMA - Tschumper Unit	835	Winona	Elba	76-2A	68	•		•	•		•	•	•	14.3	4.0	-	-	-	79.2
Whitewater WMA - Upper South Branch Unit	846	Winona	Elba	76-3B	438	•		•	•			•	•	-	6.9	-	2.4	-	90.7
Wieker WMA	199	Kandiyohi, Meeker	Grove City	23-6B	305	•		•			•	•		1.5	28.3	22.9	41.0	2.6	3.3
Contains a 104-acre deep marsh, several smaller wetlands, a large cover planting, a food plot, introduced-grass upland, and scattered deciduous trees.																			
Wig WMA	121	Kandiyohi	Willmar	8-3E	3			•	•			•		-	-	11.5	-	-	80.8
Wig WMA	122	Kandiyohi	Willmar	8-3E	10			•				•		-	-	15.5	1.9	-	76.7
Both units: Primarily used by colonial nesting birds and other woodland birds. Bird watching. Very limited hunting opportunities.																			
Wild Wings WMA For more information call 320-289-2493.	127	Lac Qui Parle	Boyd	19-6E	113	•		•			•	•		-	11.2	87.0	-	-	1.9
Wilder WMA	621	Jackson	Wilder	66-1D	4			•	•			•		-	5.6	-	-	-	91.7
The String Lake WPA is adjacent to the south. This WMA contains a concrete boat ramp access to String Lake.																			
William Pease WMA	849	Fillmore	Chatfield	75-6E	65	•		•	•		•		•	-	61.2	5.4	1.4	-	32.0
Hunting, trapping and wildlife viewing. Managed to develop and maintain mixed hardwoods and upland bird habitat.																			
Willmar WMA	138	Kandiyohi	Willmar	8-3E	127	•		•	•		•	•		-	48.7	39.9	-	1.8	9.5
Wildlife observation, hiking, and other non-consumptive uses only. Unit is a state game refuge and lies within the city limits of Willmar.																			
Willow Creek WMA For more information call 507-831-2900.	695	Watonwan, Martin	Ormsby	68-1E	69	•		•	•		•	•		11.6	40.2	27.2	1.2	-	19.5
Willow Lake WMA For more information call 320-231-5163.	409	Redwood	Wanda	50-2C	178						•	•		-	1.4	2.0	96.1	-	0.4
Windot WMA	460	Sibley	Winthrop	38-3E	11			•				•		-	-	79.5	-	-	20.5
For more information call 507-225-3572. Wheelchair access at primitive parking area along SH 15.																			
Winfield WMA For more information call 320-231-5163.	215	Renville	Danube	22-3E	108	•		•			•			9.7	7.4	70.7	-	4.3	7.8
Winkler WMA For more information call 507-831-2900.	606	Cottonwood, Jackson	Heron Lake	65-6D	78	•		•			•	•		13.7	28.5	46.0	3.3	-	8.7
Winnebago Creek WMA	862	Houston	New Albin, Iowa	96-3D	175	•		•	•				•	5.3	23.7	-	-	-	71.2
Hunting, trapping, fishing, and wildlife viewing. Bluff prairies dot south-facing slopes, while a trout stream (Winnebago Creek) bisects the valley floor.																			
Winter WMA - East Unit East sub-unit is a small grassland.	343	Pipestone	Pipestone	46-2E	13			•			•			-	100.0	-	-	-	-
Winter WMA - West Unit	341	Pipestone	Pipestone	46-2E	258	•		•			•			18.9	73.0	-	-	-	8.1
West sub-unit is a large grassland with some native prairie remnants, woody cover plantings, and food plots.																			
Wirock WMA	519	Murray	Slayton	64-2D	122	•		•			•	•		3.8	47.3	43.2	-	5.6	-
Shallow wetlands are excellent for wildlife observation during spring migration. Often dry during duck season. Restored prairie near parking area.																			
Wolf Lake WMA - Cottonwood County Unit	629	Cottonwood	Windom	66-2D	56	•		•			•	•		-	44.3	25.3	-	-	1.1
WMA is a wetland/grassland complex along the west shore of Wolf Lake just SE of Windom. A portion of unit is closed to hunting, with signs indicating the restricted area. The Wolf Lake WPA is adjacent along the WMA's south boundary.																			
Wood Lake WMA - Tract 1 All tracts: For more information call 320-231-5163.	541	Brown	Comfrey	51-5E	2	•		•			•	•		-	-	100.0	-	-	-
Wood Lake WMA - Tract 4	572	Watonwan	Comfrey	67-5A	5	•		•			•	•		-	50.0	-	-	-	52.0
Wood Lake WMA - Tracts 19, 27-28, 30, 32-35	548	Brown, Watonwan	Comfrey	67-5A	254	•		•			•	•		-	6.5	86.4	1.4	4.4	1.0
Wood Lake WMA - Tracts 6 and 9	577	Watonwan	Comfrey	67-6A	23	•		•			•	•		-	78.4	-	-	-	22.0
Woodbury WMA Pheasants and numerous other grassland bird species nest here.	771	Goodhue	Zumbrota	58-1C	76	•		•	•		•		•	7.3	63.4	9.2	-	10.5	9.6
Woodland WMA	336	Wright	Montrose	26-2B	701	•		•			•	•		-	3.6	88.0	-	-	8.4
Hunting, trapping, wildlife viewing, and hiking. An important spring and fall waterfowl area. Excellent area to view spring and fall bird migrations. Water access limited to a NE parking lot and an east parking lot where a longer boat carry/drag is necessary																			
Woodstock WMA - East Unit	388	Pipestone	Woodstock	47-5E	204	•		•			•	•		-	50.4	46.7	-	-	2.8
East sub-unit is a remnant prairie with several marshes and woody cover.																			
Woodstock WMA - West Unit West sub-unit is a medium-sized marsh.	387	Pipestone	Woodstock	47-5E	46			•			•	•		-	8.2	91.6	-	-	-
Yohi WMA	165	Kandiyohi	Kandiyohi	23-5A	85	•		•			•	•		-	22.0	57.5	11.7	-	7.2
Contains a large, open-water wetland and a smaller, shallower basin; woody cover plantings, grass covered fields of seeded natives and non-native grasses. Access strips and parking areas on unit's north and west ends.																			
Zion WMA	97	Stearns	Lake Henry	9-6A	217						•	•		-	82.1	16.8	-	-	0.9
WMA typifies prairie pothole country. Great area to watch spring and fall bird migrations.																			

Hunting -Small Game Mammals

Eastern Cottontail Rabbit *(Sylvilagus floridanus)*

Many a youngster has been introduced to hunting via the eastern cottontail rabbit. Known for their prolific reproduction, cottontail numbers are good most years and spectacular in others.

This common rabbit is found throughout Minnesota, and is locally abundant, except in the densest of forests. However, dense cover characterizes the best cottontail habitat – woodlots, thickets, willow and white cedar swamps, and brushpiles provide cover from predators.

Hunters should dress in thick, heavy clothes and prepare to bust the brush to find cottontails. Look for rabbits around fencerows, near deciduous saplings, in berry bushes, and around brushpiles and hedges. The presence of droppings (small, hard pellets) is the first clue to a cottontail's whereabouts. Look for clusters of pea-sized pellets on the ground. If the droppings are fresh, you're likely in good rabbit country. Finding tracks in snow is another indication that a cottontail may not be far away. Oftentimes, these tracks will lead straight to a rabbit's hideaway, where the animal can be flushed.

Cottontails are most active between late afternoon and dusk and can be hunted by walking grassy cover in and around brush and other nearby cover. Don't be in a hurry to cover ground. Walk slowly and stop every so often – many hunters choose to walk 50 or 100 yards, stopping for a couple of minutes. Rabbits can remain remarkably still, but often become nervous when hunters stop moving and will often betray their location by fleeing their hiding place. Hunters can either take a shot or remain still, as rabbits may stop running if they no longer feel threatened.

During rainy and snowy weather, cottontails will hold very tight to brush and other thick vegetation, or they may tuck under any structure offering a temporary roof. If frightened, rabbits will exit their lairs and run off; however, they usually return to the same location within about 30 minutes.

Because cottontails frequent such dense cover, they are often hunted with dogs. Beagles are the most popular sporting breed with rabbit hunters, and are commonly hunted in groups of three or more dogs. After a rabbit has been jumped from cover, the dogs will give chase. Rabbits rarely run far in a straight line, zigging and zagging across the land to thwart their pursuers. As the chase goes on, hunters need to pick a likely ambush spot to shoot from. Often, hunters remain at the site of the flush and wait for the rabbit to circle back around.

The most popular weapons for rabbit hunting are .410 and 12-gauge shotguns, or .22-caliber rifles.

White-Tailed Jackrabbit *(Lepus townsendii)*

The white-tailed jackrabbit is found in agricultural areas across southwest Minnesota. Despite the animal's name, it is technically classified as a hare because hares are born with hair and with their eyes open; rabbits are born blind and hairless.

The white-tailed jackrabbit is the largest rabbit or hare in the state and is characterized by its long ears. It can weigh up to 10 pounds and measures about two feet long. It has a brownish-gray coat with a white belly, feet and tail in summer. In northern areas, the coat changes to white in winter; in more southern regions, the coat stays brownish-gray year-round.

Jackrabbits inhabit grasslands, agricultural fields and brushy areas. They need open areas with few trees to outrun their predators. In winter they may burrow into the snow. They eat a variety of plants including dandelions, winter wheat and gramma grass.

At one time hunting jackrabbits was extremely popular. Jackrabbits numbers were higher, and pelts were in demand for use in the hatter's trade, while the meat was commonly used to feed ranched mink. Large groups of farmers frequently gathered to put on impressively large jackrabbit hunts. Hunters would surround a section of land and push toward the center. Dozens of jackrabbits could be killed in a day of hunting.

Today, however, those drives are things of the past. For one thing, rabbit populations are much lower, in part because of urban development, but also because farmers practice modern rowcropping and leave fewer brushy fence lines and sloughs undisturbed. Most jackrabbits today are killed incidentally when hunting for pheasants or other small game. However, jackrabbit meat is very good and tastes much like that of cotton-tailed rabbits.

White-tailed jackrabbits can be difficult targets when flushed. They can cover 10 feet in a single bound and reach speeds of 40 miles per hour. Hunters looking to target jackrabbits should concentrate on areas of farm fields mixed with grassy cover. Look for overgrown fence rows, dry sloughs and other available cover. A 12-gauge shotgun with No. 6 shot should do the trick.

Squirrels

Squirrels are one of the most commonly hunted species in the country. Many hunters start out hunting squirrels as youths, and some continue pursuing them for the rest of their lives. The small mammals can be challenging to hunt, and on top of that, they taste great when fried or made into stew.

In southern Minnesota, red squirrels are common. These small rodents are at home in the coniferous forests, where available, and hardwood forests. Gray and fox squirrels are more hardwood-oriented species. The red squirrel has a reddish-brown coat and a white belly. It is active all winter. It feeds on coniferous seeds, as well as acorns, nuts and other seeds. It often chatters when it sees people and is the scourge of deer hunters.

Gray squirrels *(Sciurus carolinensis)* are probably the most familiar species to most people. Their coloration is generally gray, but varies and can even be black. Gray squirrels are found throughout Minnesota, generally in hardwood forests where they eat acorns, nuts, maple seeds and other foods.

Fox squirrels *(Sciurus niger)* are the largest squirrels in Minnesota. They are similar in coloration to gray squirrels, but their underbelly is a yellow-orange tinge and their ears are light in color. They are most abundant in the western part of the state. Fox squirrels feed on nuts, acorns, maple seeds, conifer seeds and corn where available.

Hunting squirrels requires minimal equipment. Despite their seeming tameness around bird feeders, forest-dwelling squirrels unaccustomed to humans can be challenging to hunt. One of the best techniques to hunt squirrels is to quietly enter the woods and sit down in an area you know contains squirrels. Sit quietly and keep your eyes in the trees around you, and eventually the squirrels will come out of their dens and reveal themselves. This tactic takes patience, but is very effective.

Another way to hunt squirrels is to creep very quietly through the woods and try to spot squirrels before they see you. This is a good way to refine your stalking technique for deer hunting. Sneaking through the woods this way is best done after a rain, when wet vegetation allows you to walk silently.

Squirrels can also be called. Clicking two quarters together works. There are also commercially made squirrel calls available. Sit quietly and call to arouse a squirrel's curiosity.

Squirrel season runs from mid-September to the end of February. Hunters use either shotguns or small-caliber rifles for hunting squirrels. Any shotgun loaded with light game loads will work. Squirrels and .22 rifles go together like peanut butter and jelly. It takes a good shot to bag a squirrel with a .22.

Norma G Chambers

Muzzleloader Hunting

Muzzleloader hunters often march to the beat of their own drummers. Why would hunters handicap themselves by carrying primitive weapons and go hunting after a half-million hunters have trudged through the state's fields and forests and killed hundreds of thousands of deer? Well, you'd just have to ask a muzzleloader hunter to find out.

A muzzleloader, by definition, loads from the muzzle, or barrel, unlike normal rifles and shotguns. First black powder – a highly volatile propellant – is carefully measured and then poured down the muzzle. Traditional muzzleloader hunters next take a patch made of cotton or other fabric and lubricate it. (Modern muzzleloader bullets may not require a patch.) This will help the bullet slide down the barrel. Finally, a bullet is seated atop the patch and then started down the barrel with an instrument called a "starter" or "short starter." Once the bullet is in the barrel, a long "ramrod" is used to push the bullet down until it rests on the powder. The other requirement of a muzzleloading gun is some sort of charge to ignite the powder. Flintlocks are the same style of rifles used in the pioneer days. A flint – an actual piece of stone – produces sparks that (hopefully) ignite black powder when the trigger is pulled. Weather conditions such as rain or snow can wreak havoc on flintlocks, and there's no guarantee the gun will fire when the trigger is pulled. Caplocks are similar to flintlocks in that they have an exposed hammer. Caplocks are charged with "caps" which create a spark when the hammer hits them. They are a little more reliable than flintlocks. Modern in-line muzzleloaders vary in style, but they use a 209 primer, which is the most reliable ignition system. They also often have a breech plug on the closed end of the barrel that can be removed to make cleaning easier. Black powder is highly corrosive and will quickly rust a gun barrel when fired. Flintlocks and caplocks don't usually have breech plugs, which means they must be cleaned from the muzzle end of the barrel only, which makes cleaning significantly more difficult.

Many muzzleloader hunters, like archers, prefer the challenge of their sport. Although modern in-line muzzleloaders are nearly as accurate and have almost the same range as centerfire rifles, many go afield with caplocks or flintlocks. It takes an adventurous individual to carry a flintlock, but in Minnesota, even those who carry modern in-line muzzleloaders are handicapping themselves because the use of scopes is not allowed.

One benefit of muzzleloader season is there are far fewer hunters in the woods. By late November and early December, most hunters have called it a season. Deer may begin to return to their normal routines after the melee of the rifle season. Plus, there is frequently snow on the ground by muzzleloader season, and hunters can more easily spot deer and track them. Some hunters particularly like to hunt deer simply by tracking, and reduced hunting pressure and increased snow depth makes this more practical.

Even though muzzleloading may seem a bit intimidating and gear intensive, once you get the hang of it, it's fun and easy. A sport shop can outfit you with the right equipment and some basic shooting instructions to help you take up the muzzleloading challenge!

Bow-hunting

The bow season has several distinct time periods, each with advantages and disadvantages for hunters. Obviously, the more time you can spend in the woods, the better, but here's the pros and cons of hunting before, during and after the rut.

Believe it or not, the first week of bow season in mid-September is one of the best times to be in the woods. Bucks may still be in their predictable summertime patterns then. Those bucks you watched so predictably appear each night in soybean fields during the summer may still be following this routine when bow season opens. Deer will continue to utilize summer foods as they wait for acorns and other fall mast to ripen. Plus, you may get a crack at the ultimate trophy – a buck still in velvet – early in the season. Despite these fine reasons for hunting early, there are some equally good reasons for waiting. Mosquitoes will be out in force on opening day, and the often warm weather causes hunters to sweat and makes it hard to remain scent-free. Also, lush green leaves and grasses limit visibility and can reduce the size of shooting lanes.

From late September through mid-October is the period hunters refer to as the "October lull." At that time, bucks seemingly go underground and sightings are few. This is an excellent time to shoot a doe for the freezer. Dropping leaves increase visibility, and early rubs and scrapes can help hunters key in on those mysterious bucks. Doe-in-heat scents can attract bucks that are just itching to begin breeding.

Rutting activity begins in late October and runs into November. The seeking phase of the rut, when bucks actively look for estrous does, is the most anticipated time of the bow season. Mature bucks lose their wariness and can be seen running in the open at all times of the day. This is arguably the most exciting time to be hunting, and multiple buck sightings in the same day are not uncommon. The only drawback is the firearms season opens about this time, and hunter activity can throw off deer movements, and obviously a lot of deer are killed at this time by gun hunters. Bow season remains open, but bow-hunters must wear blaze orange.

From the end of the gun season to the end of bow season can be a surprisingly good time to hunt. Granted, many deer won't survive the gun season. However, with impending cold weather, deer – particularly bucks – are looking to pack on weight to survive the winter. Mature bucks, which may lose up to one-third of their body weight as they endlessly chase does during the rut, especially need to feed heavily before heavy snow covers up available food. Evening hunts near food sources can be very productive, particularly during cold weather when deer feed earlier. The drawbacks are reduced deer numbers and trying to hunt in what can be extremely cold, miserable weather.

Trapping

Minnesota has a long history of trapping. Native people have trapped here for thousands of years. When early European explorers arrived in the area, they were amazed by the large furbearer populations in this new land and quickly set up a fur trade in North America to make up for furbearer populations that had been decimated in Europe. Much of the early North American exploration was conducted in the name of finding new navigation routes for the fur trade.

Wild furbearer populations are still good throughout southern Minnesota. The area's open grasslands, agricultural regions, river bottoms and hardwood forests support a wide array of furbearers. Trappers can find abundant muskrats in cattail marshes, raccoons in bottomland forests, coyotes in open fields and agricultural areas, and many other furbearer species including foxes, mink, opossums, skunks, and more.

Whether you prefer placing water sets for muskrats in the area's pothole lakes region, dry-land trapping in the woods for raccoons, or just putting out a small line at home on the farm, you'll find something to suit you in southern Minnesota.

Non-Migratory Birds - Hunting

▶ Ruffed Grouse *(Bonasa umbellus)*

For many Minnesota hunters, ruffed grouse are the kings of upland game birds. Because the grouse population follows a pattern of boom and bust – typically a 10-year cycle – some years offer spectacular hunting, with more than 1,000,000 birds taken; in lean years, hunters may walk the woods all day and never flush a bird. But on a late-autumn afternoon, when the sun is streaming through the woods and a dog is working grouse cover, it doesn't get much better. And ruffed grouse hunting doesn't get much better than in Minnesota: The Department of Natural Resources reports that Minnesota is the top ruffed grouse-producing state in the country, with more grouse habitat than any other state.

Ruffed grouse live in forests, favoring areas of younger growth either from logging or wildfires. The best ruffed grouse territory exists where small blocks (10 to 40 acres) of aspens have been clear-cut, leaving a mix of young (6 to 10 years old) and mature aspens. The birds depend on the trees for food and cover, foraging on buds and leaves. Although ruffed grouse may also be found in coniferous forests, their numbers will be more limited because trees such as spruce and pines offer year-round cover for predators including great-horned owls and northern goshawks.

Ruffed grouse are solitary birds and spend most of their adult lives away from other grouse, except during the breeding season. The drumming of male ruffed grouse during the spring mating season is one of the quintessential sounds of the northwoods. Staking out a territory, male grouse perch on a log and rapidly beat their wings, compressing the air beneath, which results in a drumming-like sound.

Ruffed grouse are about the size of a small chicken, weighing from one to two pounds. Cryptically colored, their mottled gray and brown bodies blend well into the forest landscape. Males are usually larger than females and sport larger "ruffs" (feathers around the neck that are displayed during courting). In winter, temporary scales grow out from the bird's toes and serve as natural snowshoes. To stay warm, ruffed grouse burrow into snow. Hard, crusty snow or winters without suitable snow cover make it difficult for the birds to find shelter.

Many grouse hunters use a pointing or flushing dog to help locate birds in thick cover. Ruffed grouse can be very stubborn and will often sit still in heavy brush, not moving until a dog or hunter is very near. On rainy days, ruffed grouse are very difficult to flush. On windy days, by contrast, they often flush quickly because the wind makes it harder for birds to track the sound of a predator's movements. Hunters without dogs can do well by working areas of likely habitat, stopping every so often to anticipate a flushing bird. Sometimes grouse will become nervous in the stillness and go airborne. Fast reflexes and the ability to make a snap shot at close range are needed to put a bird or two in the game bag. The most popular guns for ruffed grouse are the 20-gauge over/under and a lightweight 12-gauge.

Although the Minnesota opener for ruffed grouse hunting is in mid-September, abundant forest foliage usually limits the shots hunters can take. Most hunting takes place after deciduous trees and shrubs have dropped their leaves and after a couple of frosts. The challenge of hunting these fidgety forest dwellers draws hunters back to the woods year after year, regardless of overall bird numbers.

Mourning Dove *(Zenaida macroura)*

Mourning doves are one of the most challenging of Minnesota's game animals – not because they are wary or because they have excellent senses – but rather, simply because they are hard to hit.

This common game bird is no stranger to most folks, whether they dwell in urban areas or in the country. The adaptable dove is at home around bird feeders as well as in grain fields. Mourning doves are a grayish-brown bird with black splotches on their wings and black markings on the head. They are roughly the same size as, or maybe a bit smaller than, their cousin, the pigeon. Doves also have more-pointed tails than pigeons. Mourning doves are named for their mournful, cooing call.

Mourning doves are swift fliers and regularly cruise at about 30 mph, but can reach speeds of more than 60 mph. This, in addition to their twisting and turning while in flight, makes them difficult targets for dove hunters.

Most dove hunting is done near agricultural fields, such as oats, wheat, rye, sunflower, canola, beans or other small grains. Doves also feed in weed fields that produce small seeds. In addition to food, water is an important consideration for dove hunters. The best hunting areas have good food sources in close proximity to water sources and roosting cover. Some hunters set up along water sources, where they wait for doves in the evening. Decoys are commonly used in trees, along fence lines or next to water. Pass shooting is also popular.

Some of the best dove hunting occurs on private lands. Be sure to get landowner permission before hunting on private lands. Some people even plant food plots for dove hunting or time their crop harvests in coordination with dove hunts. Check hunting regulations to learn what constitutes legal hunting over crop fields. The regulations also have information on wildlife management areas that have fields managed for dove hunting.

Any type of shotgun loaded with light loads, such as No. 8 shot, will be adequate for dove hunting. Dove hunters would be wise to practice regularly on a trap, skeet or sporting clays range prior to the dove season, which runs through September and October. Regular shooting practice improves hand-eye coordination and reminds you of the importance of swinging the gun while shooting. Should you fail to heed this lesson, the birds will remind you. If you don't keep swinging the gun as you fire, you're sure to shoot behind your target.

Equipment for dove hunting is minimal. All you really need is a gun and plenty of shells. However, you may wish to bring along a cooler to keep the birds cool in the warm weather of early autumn. The cooler can double as a seat. A dog is also a good idea. Doves are small and their cryptic coloration blends amazingly well with most environments. A dog's sense of smell will help you find downed birds. Be sure to bring plenty of water to keep Rover going in hot weather. If you don't have a dog, carefully mark where your bird falls and rush to the spot without taking your eyes off it. Pass on any shots that would drop birds in thick or tall cover.

In addition to being sporty gamebirds, doves are excellent on the table. The daily bag limit of 15 birds will allow you to have a good-sized meal of doves … if you're lucky to bag that many!

Hunting - Non-Migratory Birds

Ring-Necked Pheasant *(Phasianus colchicus)*

Pheasant hunters from Illinois or Wisconsin who are bent on heading for the famed pheasant grounds of the Dakotas often drive right through some mighty good pheasant country in southern Minnesota. After all, there's not much difference in landscape – or pheasant hunting – between western Minnesota and the eastern part of the Dakotas.

Although they are not native to this country, pheasants have become one of our most prized gamebirds. They are wily, strong-flying, beautifully colored and excellent on the table. A native of Asia, pheasants were first planted in Minnesota in 1905.

To effectively hunt pheasants, you should try to understand where they will be located at a given time of the day so you don't spend a lot of time walking aimlessly when the birds are somewhere else. At night, pheasants roost in thick grasses. At first light, birds often travel to road edges where they pick gravel, which goes to their gizzards and helps them digest their food. Soon after, pheasants begin to feed. By the 9 a.m. daily opener, birds are usually still feeding, so look for them in standing cornfields or other unharvested crop fields. When they are done feeding around midday, pheasants will travel to adjacent grassy cover to loaf. In late afternoon they hit the fields again to feed before returning to their roosting cover for the night.

Pheasants thrive on a mixture of agricultural areas interspersed with cover. However, in recent years, modern farming practices have increased the amount of acreage cultivated on a given farm (with the elimination of overgrown fencerows and the like) and the harvest of crops has become more efficient, leaving less waste grain. However, conservation groups have bought and improved habitat, and land set aside in the Conservation Reserve Program has created more places for pheasants to roost and loaf.

In areas where pheasant cover is limited, hunt ditches – both roadside and streamside. You can also find birds along railroad right-of-ways, in shelterbelts and in cattail marshes.

Early in the season, birds will use a variety of habitats. However, as hunting thins out the population, birds will avoid obvious cover and retreat to more inaccessible places and pieces of cover that are more difficult to walk through. Late in the season when the snow flies, look for birds in sheltered areas such as cattail marshes, shelterbelts and even small evergreen forests.

Pheasant hunters are required to wear at least one article of blaze-orange clothing above the waist in Minnesota. You'll also want a comfortable pair of hiking boots and perhaps some brush chaps for walking through thick, thorny cover. It's also a good idea to wear a vest with a game pouch. A 12-gauge shotgun with No. 4, 5, or 6 shot works well.

A good, close-working dog is also a huge benefit for hunters. A dog can help flush birds in range, which might otherwise hold tight and let dog-less hunters pass by. Plus, a dog can retrieve your bird once it's on the ground.

Hunters should be quiet when exiting their vehicles. Speak softly and close car doors quietly to avoid alerting wary pheasants. When pushing a section of cover, especially standing cornfields, it's a good idea to have one person serve as a blocker. That person swings wide around the cover to be pushed, then stands at the end of that cover to fire at birds that run or fly ahead of the rest of the group. Use common sense and wear generous amounts of blaze orange when using a blocker to avoid shooting accidents. Lone hunters without dogs can utilize a stop-and-go technique. By periodically stopping for a few moments, you can cause tight-holding birds to become nervous because they can no longer hear you walking. This often causes birds to flush.

Hungarian/Gray Partridge *(Perdix perdix)*

The Hungarian or gray partridge has long been a popular gamebird in Europe and Asia, but wasn't introduced into Minnesota until the early 20th century. These stocky birds stand about 12 to 14 inches high and have a body similar to a ruffed grouse, but lack the ruffed's outer tail feathers. "Huns" have gray breasts, orangish-brown faces and throats; brown barring on the flanks, and russet tail feathers (visible in flight). They are also heavily feathered and able to withstand the frequent high winds and cold temperatures of Minnesota's extreme western regions during winter. To conserve body heat during cold weather, partridges huddle in a circle, facing outward so they can escape quickly if necessary. Partridges also roost in winter by burrowing into small depressions in the snow.

Huns prefer cool, dry climates and open country such as farm fields and pastures, where they forage for weed seeds, leaves, and occasionally insects. The birds generally feed in the early morning and then rest until late afternoon when they resume foraging.

Partridges are social and non-territorial outside of the breeding season. They stick close together in groups called "coveys," usually composed of 15 birds or less. When pursued or frightened, the birds often voice a warning cry and flush together, attempting to confuse predators with a manic burst of flight. They rarely fly for more than 200 yards when flushed, however, so hunters can follow their movements and, with luck, flush them again. Partridges are fast flyers and make challenging targets for even experienced wingshooters.

Like pheasants and other flushing gamebirds, Huns are often hunted with dogs. Look for birds in grasslands, plowed corn and grain fields, and field edges. Hunters should prepare to cover lots of ground on foot, walking through standing vegetation during the day and targeting feeding areas in late afternoon. Partridges often cover long distances on foot before flushing, using crop rows as lanes of escape.

A 12-gauge shotgun with No. 6 or 7½ shot should do the trick for Huns.

Wild Turkey *(Meleagris gallopavo)*

The comeback of the wild turkey in America is one of the greatest conservation success stories. Turkeys were nearly eliminated from most of their native range by the early 1900s. A combination of overzealous market hunting and general habitat loss almost spelled the end for the birds. However, reintroduction efforts, habitat improvements, and the turkey's uncanny adaptability have contributed to the remarkable rebound of the wild turkey population today. In fact, turkeys are now found in every state except Alaska, and their numbers are in the millions. The Department of Natural Resources estimates the total Minnesota wild turkey population alone to be more than 30,000 birds, creating opportunities for hunters to match wits with these wily woodland denizens. Although turkeys are found in most counties in the southern half of Minnesota, the greatest harvests occur in the bluff country of the southeast.

The eastern wild turkey – the subspecies found in Minnesota – is a bird of the woodlands, making its home in mixed and hardwood forests. Turkeys are omnivorous, spending their days scratching along the ground to uncover buds, grapes, seeds, insects, acorns, and more. Unlike many birds, turkeys don't migrate south in winter. They are exceptionally hardy, limited only by their ability to find food during the coldest, snowiest Minnesota winters.

As the woods start to come alive in spring, adult male turkeys (called gobblers or toms) turn their attention to finding a mate. Attracting females (hens) requires a combination of bravado and just plain showing off. Turkeys are extremely vocal, eliciting many different calls, including "gobbles," "yelps," "putts," and "cutts" to communicate. Gobblers will, why yes, gobble to attract a hen(s) during the breeding season. After calling in a hen, a gobbler will strut around, puffing out his feathers, dragging his wings on the ground, and fanning out his tail feathers in a spectacular display. Such activity usually occurs in open fields bordering forests.

Competition for hens is fierce, and can often result in fighting between birds. Males sport (usually) a pair of razor-sharp "spurs" on the backs of their legs, and use them as weapons in combat to establish dominance. A single male may mate with several females during the breeding season.

Wild turkeys are among the most challenging animals to hunt. They are exceptionally wary and quick to detect anything out of the ordinary. Turkeys have excellent hearing and daytime vision, making them doubly difficult to fool. Fortunately, the birds have relatively predictable behavioral patterns that hunters can use to locate them.

Locating these food-holding areas is the first step to finding birds. Woodlands adjacent to farm fields offer access to shelter and food, making them very attractive to turkeys and great places to start searching for them. Look for birds feeding in fields during the day. They will often return to the same locations each day to forage. At night, turkey flocks will fly up and "roost" in trees to avoid predators. A dozen or more birds may use the same roosting area and will remain there through the night if undisturbed. Finding such an area is no guarantee of success, but it clearly ups

Brian Upton

Non-Migratory Birds - Hunting

the odds for finding birds the following morning. If you're lucky enough to find such a roosting area, make note of the exact location and look for a place(s) to set up nearby from which to hunt. Choose a well-concealed spot that affords a clear view of the surroundings and a clear shot. The most common tactic involves setting up against the base of a tree, sitting with one's back tight to the trunk with the gun propped up on one knee or a shooting stick. For safety, choose a tree whose base is slightly wider than your body.

Finding a place to hunt is the first step. Getting to the spot undetected before the birds awake and leave the roost is the next challenge. To avoid detection, hunters usually dress in head-to-toe camouflage, but it doesn't stop there. Several 12-gauge shotguns are now built specifically for turkey hunting and come in camouflage as well. Even so disguised, hunters must be extremely stealthy to get into place before the birds descend from the roost. Walk slowly and softly, making cat-like steps to avoid crunching fallen leaves and branches.

Early in the morning, usually before dawn, turkeys become active. It can begin with one gobble – once one bird becomes vocal, others soon follow, calling out in a chorus of gobbles and yelps. After a period of vocalization, the birds will descend from the roosting area and begin searching for food. This is a great time to separate a gobbler from the group. While the other birds forage, hunters can try calling gobbler in for a shot. The most common calls mimic the sounds of a hen. Box calls, slate calls, and mouth calls are three popular calls used by turkey hunters trying to lure a wily gobbler. Begin with a series of soft "clucks" or "yelps" and then call more aggressively if your first efforts fail to bring results.

One good calling technique is to try to engage another hen while you call. Hens quickly pick up the sound of an intruding "bird" and may call back or even investigate the source of the calling. This can essentially act as a live decoy and bring in a hesitant gobbler. On the downside, however, the hen may bust you and ruin your hunt.

Trying to call in a gobbler is next to impossible if it has already collected a harem of hens for the morning. In that situation, a hunter's best bet is to find a new location or wait until midmorning after breeding has occurred. At that time, hens go off to sit on their nests, and lonely gobblers are still looking for willing hens. Thus, they are susceptible to calling.

Minnesota also has a fall turkey hunting season. Although it's more exciting to call in actively gobbling spring birds, fall hunting can be productive as well.

In the fall, hunters may shoot any turkey, while only bearded birds (generally males) are legal game in spring. In fall, gobblers are much more silent, but hens communicate verbally with their poults (young turkeys).

A common fall hunting tactic is to locate a flock of turkeys, then, after putting your gun down, rushing into the flock and scattering birds in as many directions as possible. After breaking up a flock of birds, the hunter sits at the site of the bust, waits about a half-hour, then begins calling to reassemble the flock. This technique can be very effective and equally exciting.

If a turkey is beyond 40 yards, consider it out of range. Hunters should try to call the bird in closer or wait for it to come in on its own. Bringing a turkey to the gun is one of the great challenges in hunting and one sure to provide a lifetime of memories for turkey hunters.

Migratory Birds - Hunting

▶ Waterfowl

Southern Minnesota waterfowl hunters have a diverse array of hunting opportunities, from hunting divers on the Mississippi River to pursuing flights of dabblers on prairie pothole lakes.

One good way to prepare for duck season is to note where you see ducks on summer fishing trips or fall deer hunts. That tiny, out-of-the-way pond you skirt on the way to your deer stand may harbor early season ducks.

In southern Minnesota, mallards, pintails, gadwall and teal are common. These dabbling ducks use a variety of habitats, from small ponds and creeks to large marshes. In some areas, particularly in eastern Minnesota, wood ducks can be found. These tree nesters are often found in beaver ponds and small creeks. Some diving duck species can also be found in the south, particularly during the fall migration. Redheads, bluebills, canvasbacks and ring-necked ducks are common. Although these species will use prairie potholes, some of the best diver hunting occurs on the Mississippi river. In fact, a large percentage of the continent's canvasbacks migrate down the Old Man.

For the first week of waterfowl hunting season, shooting hours close at 4 p.m. in order to lessen harassment of local ducks and encourage fresh migrants to stay. However, the best duck hunting is usually very early in the morning and right before sunset, making hunting difficult during the early closure period. One good early season technique is to jump-shoot ducks. Simply walk up on a pothole or float down a small stream to roust loafing ducks during midday. Keep in mind, jump-shooting by boat is restricted to streams less than 100 yards in width. On lakes, your boat must be partially concealed by natural emergent vegetation as you move, and you must propel your boat by manual power (no motors allowed). Jump-shooting is also an excellent technique late in the season when lakes have frozen and only moving water remains open. Then, ducks – particularly mallards – will congregate in streams, rather than flying south. These birds are often freshly arrived from Canada and the Dakotas and are not particularly wary. Plus, by late season they are fully plumed and quite beautiful. Late-season mallards are true trophies on the table or on the wall.

Part of the mystique of waterfowling is the art of decoying. Watching a flock of ducks come fully committed to your fake renditions of birds is truly breathtaking. On small potholes a half-dozen decoys will usually suffice. Mallard decoys are the most common choice, and they will attract all varieties of puddle ducks. Early in the season, before birds have grown their brightly colored breeding plumage, use mostly hen mallard decoys to mimic the drab coloration of birds. Gradually add more drakes as the birds color up. After a few weeks of heavy hunting pressure, ducks may flare from decoy spreads. A time-honored trick is to put out a large spread of coot decoys and mix in just a few mallards. The coots act as confidence decoys and may convince ducks that your spread is safe.

Diving duck hunters live and die by their decoy spreads, or rather, their ducks do. You can't have too many diving duck decoys because these birds frequently fly very low to the water and navigate over large waters. Visibility is critical to success, so employ as many decoys as you can. Also, use mostly drakes in your spread, for their better visibility. Canvasback decoys are great choices because they have a large amount of high-visibility white. Bluebills are also great choices. Large lakes and rivers often attract diving ducks because they frequently migrate in large flocks and need room to take off. Diving ducks, like loons, have to run across the water to get airborne, although they lift off much quicker than loons. Although they are thought of as big-water birds, don't ignore smaller lakes with good supplies of coontail, wild celery, wild rice and other preferred aquatic plants. Divers also eat animal matter including snails and fish and are not as good on the table as puddle ducks like mallards, wood ducks and teal. Redheads, canvasbacks and ringnecks are probably the best-tasting divers. Mergansers, which eat mostly fish, are oily birds and taste somewhat fishy.

Goose hunting is also popular in Minnesota, and the state consistently ranks as one of the top goose-hunting states in the nation. Canada geese, snow geese, blue geese, white-fronted geese or Ross's geese can be found in the region. Field hunting is popular and effective in agricultural areas. Water hunting can also be effective. Special hunts in September and December have liberal bag limits. During the middle of the hunting season, geese are often a bonus for duck hunters. Throw out a few goose decoys when you're duck hunting for increased visibility and to attract passing geese. Geese are very social birds, and lone geese in particular can be easily called to decoys.

With any luck, waterfowl opportunities will improve in the coming decades because the Minnesota DNR has implemented an aggressive management plan to nearly double the state's waterfowl production from an estimated 636,000 ducks to 1 million ducks in 2054. The plan also calls to add 600,000 acres of waterfowl habitat by 2025 and increase management of wild rice lakes and shallow wetlands.

American Woodcock *(Scolopax minor)*

The woodcock is a small, stout, brownish-gray migratory bird that lives in forests. It stands about 8 inches tall and has big eyes and a long bill (nearly 3 inches) that it uses to probe the ground for worms and other invertebrates. Females are larger than males and have longer bills.

A woodcock's eyes are located on the side of its head, set back so far that the bird can see what is directly behind it. As such, a woodcock can detect predators from nearly all angles as it mines the soil for food.

Male woodcock are known for their aerial courtship acrobatics. During the mating season, each day, usually near dusk, a male will become vocal, producing a series of nasally calls known as "peents." The bird will then take flight in an upward spiral, ascending as high as 300 feet and making a whistling sound as air passes through its primary wing feathers. At the peak of his flight, the male will turn and descend steeply toward ground, landing very near where he took off. He will peent again before taking to the air once more. This behavior is repeated multiple times.

Woodcock prefer wooded areas with a thick overstory for protection, and plenty of openings at ground level, where they can easily search for food. Areas with moist, soft soil are ideal because they are easy to probe for earthworms. Thick stands of tag alders make classic habitat. Woodcock are also found in forests composed primarily of aspen and birch that have thick stands of shrubs adjacent to them. Because woodcock hunting requires walking through dense cover, hunters will need briar-proof pants and jackets, and protective eyewear is a must.

There are two signs hunters can look for when scouting woodcock – probe holes left by birds in the ground as they search for earthworms and white liquid droppings or splashings (referred to as "whitewash") on the ground and fallen leaves.

Woodcock, like ruffed grouse, tend to sit tight and still, even when in close proximity to a hunter. The bird's natural camouflage makes it very difficult to detect, and some birds can be virtually underfoot before they finally take flight to escape. Hunting with pointing, flushing, or even retrieving dogs can be very effective. Be prepared to make snap shots. Woodcock aren't particularly swift flyers, but they are small birds and move erratically when flushed. Couple this with the dense cover they favor and you have the recipe for difficult shooting. A lightweight, short-barreled shotgun can help hunters connect on the quick, short shots usually required to harvest these forest birds.

Most hunters try to time being in the woods with the "flight" of the woodcock – that time in the fall when groups of birds pass through on their way south.

How long birds remain in one area is weather dependent, as cold weather pushes them farther south. The best woodcock hunting usually occurs in October.

*Shotguns used to hunt woodcock must not be capable of holding more than three shells, unless plugged with a one-piece filler that cannot be removed without disassembling the gun, so its total capacity does not exceed three shells. A 12-gauge is plenty of gun, and many hunters instead opt for smaller 20- or 28-gauge shotguns. No. 8 shot will bring down woodcock, even in thick cover.

Waterfowl Production Areas

In the not too distant past – perhaps 150 years ago – the wetlands, grasslands, and prairie pothole lakes of western Minnesota would be positively electric with the sounds and activities of millions of ducks, geese, and other water birds returning to breeding grounds or resting before continuing their migrations. As the state's grasslands and wetlands were drained and tiled for agriculture, crucial habitat disappeared and waterfowl numbers likewise suffered.

In 1958, Congress amended the 1934 Duck Stamp Act, which gave the Federal Government authority to purchase wetlands for waterfowl production areas (WPAs). WPAs are wetlands and grasslands preserved and managed for waterfowl and migratory bird production and other wildlife. These public lands are part of the National Wildlife Refuge System and are funded by money earned from Federal Duck Stamp sales. Southern Minnesota is home to several hundred WPAs, that serve as critical habitat for breeding waterfowl and stopover points for birds migrating beyond the state's borders. In addition, WPAs are home to many rare plants, as well as animals associated with wetlands including beavers and muskrats. Since the first WPA was created in January 1959, more than 20,000 wetland easements have been acquired, with the majority located in the prairie pothole regions of the Dakotas, Minnesota, and Montana.

WPAs are also popular with wildlife and outdoor enthusiasts. These public lands are open to multiple forms of recreation, including hiking, cross-country skiing, hunting, bird watching, and berry picking and mushroom gathering.

For a complete list of WPAs in the southern region of Minnesota, see the index on p. 157.

Wilson's Snipe *(Gallinago delicata)*

Wilson's snipe (sometimes called jacksnipe) are long-legged, long-billed wading birds related to woodcock. They bear a superficial resemblance to the stocky woodcock, although snipe are grayish-brown and thinner-bodied, weighing only about half as much. They also issue a characteristic "winnowing" sound while in flight.

Unlike the woodland habitat favored by woodcock, snipe prefer damp meadows, shallow wetlands, and open marshes. Snipe are found throughout many wetland areas but are most common in the northern tier of Minnesota, where they return from their southern wintering grounds to nest in spring. Snipe use their long bills to probe wet ground for earthworms, grubs, and insect larvae. Like woodcock, snipe put on a daredevil diving display during the breeding season, most often seen early in the morning as they beat their wings while plummeting earthward before settling back to the marshes.

Few hunters pursue snipe, with only a few thousand birds being harvested annually in Minnesota. Hip waders and a good flushing dog are a snipe hunter's best friends. Walking through marshy and swampy areas and jump-shooting is a common hunting method. Snipe hold tenaciously tight to cover, often remaining motionless until nearly stepped upon. Once flushed, they fly low, zig-zagging through the landscape to confuse predators. They often sound a nasally "scaip" call when alarmed.

On windy days, snipe seem more eager to take wing. Because the birds often rise against the wind, heading into it before turning away, hunters can do well hunting downwind. With some patience and a bit of luck, it's possible to take one of these birds with a gun. Lightweight shotguns with an ounce of No. 8 or 9 shot are all the ammo a snipe hunter needs. Because they blend so well into their surroundings, however, it's imperative to follow birds and retrieve birds that have been hit immediately – making a dog all the more valuable.

Flocks of snipe generally head south in September or October, depending on the weather. They are urged along by the first frost or two.

Wild Fact: The term "sniper" comes from hunters who were adept enough to shoot this elusive bird.

Sora Rail *(Porzana carolina)*

Sora rails are small (8 to 10 inches long and weighing 2 to 3 ounces), stocky marsh birds with grayish-brown patterning, short yellow bills, black faces and throat patches, and greenish legs.

They are the most widely distributed rail in North America and can be found primarily in freshwater marshes with pockets of open water nearby. Their diet is composed mainly of plants and plant material such as the seeds of wild rice and sedges. They are strong swimmers and flyers, although they often run and hide if alarmed, rather than taking to the air. Soras are migratory birds, wintering in Central and South America as well as the southern United States. They return to Minnesota in spring and remain until early fall, and are found locally in southern Minnesota wherever favorable habitat exists.

Because these birds inhabit wet, difficult-to-access terrain and are reluctant to go airborne, they are infrequently hunted. The same methods used for snipe can work for soras. Hunt by walking slowly through marshy areas and jump-shooting at flushing birds, or try scattering birds by poling a small boat through the wet stuff.

Retrieving dogs are helpful for locating and securing downed rails.

Rail hunters must be HIP certified – a simple agreement to hunt and report migratory birds harvested. Light, nontoxic shot loads will be adequate for taking birds.

Virginia Rail *(Rallus limicola)*

Virginia rails are largely absent in the Arrowhead region, found primarily west of central St. Louis County and throughout the rest of Minnesota. Virginias have long, reddish-orange bills that curve down; gray heads, coppery breasts, and barred flanks. These small (8 to 11 inches long), secretive birds hang out in dense cattail and bulrush marshes, probing the wet ground for snails, earthworms, insect larvae, and other invertebrates. They are well adapted for the tight confines of marsh life, possessing flexible vertebrae for navigating constricted passages, long toes for purchase in the wet ground, and modified feathers that resist the wear and tear of rough wetland vegetation. Virginia rails migrate into Minnesota in April and May from wintering areas along the east coast all the way down to Mexico. They are ground nesters and may build several dummy nests as decoys.

The same hunting methods used for soras apply for these birds. Like sora rails, Virginia rails are loath to fly when frightened. Instead, they prefer to escape by sneaking through the surrounding vegetation.

Wild Fact: Rails have the highest ratio of leg muscles to flight muscles of any birds.

▶ Berry Picking

Outdoor enthusiasts with a flair for cooking should head out into the woods with a pail come summer and take advantage of the many opportunities for berry picking in Minnesota's woods. Some of the region's state forests, state parks and wildlife management areas are good places to begin. Contact area park or ranger offices for further recommendations.

RT Images

Blueberry *(Vaccinium angustifolium)*

Blueberries are typically ripe for picking and eating from late July through August. Plants are low, branching shrubs that can reach about two feet in height and bear oblong leaves and clusters of white or pinkish flowers. Berries may be found in clumps of one to eight. Plants are found in dry, sandy soil, often with jack pines. Look for blueberries in logged areas and wooded clearings, particularly around rock outcroppings. These tasty berries are at home in muffins, pies, pancakes, and cobblers.

Raspberry *(Rubus sp.)*

Wild raspberries are at their best in July and August and can perk up any jam, jelly, or sauce. Raspberry plants are broad, curved and very prickly (gloves are helpful to avoid scrapes and cuts). They have alternate, compound leaves with typically three to five leaflets per leaf. Look for raspberry bushes near wood edges, forest clearings, and along roads.

Wild strawberry *(Fragaria virginiana)*

In June and early July, look for these tiny berries in forest openings. Wild strawberries are smaller than their cultivated relatives and have leaves bearing three sharply toothed oval-shaped leaflets and white flowers with five petals.

Currant *(Ribes sp.)*

These low-growing (three- to five-feet tall) shrubs of the genus Ribes (also containing gooseberries) bear three- to five-lobed leaves resembling those of maples and are found in the cool, damp understory of forests. The fruits range in color from rosy to dark red and are usually cooked down for jams and jellies.

Gooseberry *(Ribes sp.)*

These relatives of the wild currant are low-growing vining plants found in a variety of damp woodlands. They have alternate, lobed leaves and prickly stems and fruits, although the berries are edible. Fruits range from green to dark purple and black and are ripe for picking in July and August. They are used in jams, jellies, and sauces.

In addition, other wild fruits including elderberry, wild plum, chokecherry, and sandcherry can be found across the region. Consult a field guide for more information.

Mushrooms

Of the some two dozen edible varieties of mushrooms found in Minnesota, it is the morel that is most coveted by mushroom hunters and eaters. The morel, in fact, is the state mushroom of Minnesota. The earthy flavor of these dimpled morsels beautifully complement wild game such as venison, pheasant, ruffed grouse, and woodcock.

In Minnesota, morels usually emerge from late April until early June, when air and soil temperatures have moderated. There is no consensus about the ideal conditions for mushrooms to push up from the ground, but all agree that just the right combination of temperature, humidity, and rainfall are needed for a bumper mushroom crop.

Look for morels in woodlands, near stream beds, decaying or dead trees, and recently burned areas. Be prepared to rummage through leaves and other duff on the forest floor to uncover mushrooms. Find one morel and you'll often find more nearby. Not to be confused with the poisonous false morel, true morels are hollow if sliced open, and are generally lighter in color – tannish rather than the reddish-brown of the false morel. False morels are usually wavy instead of pitted, and have irregular lobes that give them a brain-like appearance. Also, the cap of a true morel is fused to the stalk.

* Before harvesting any wild plant for consumption make certain you can positively identify it. Many edible plants resemble others that are poisonous (even potentially deadly) to humans. As mushroom hunters like to say, "When in doubt, throw it out!"

CAMPING

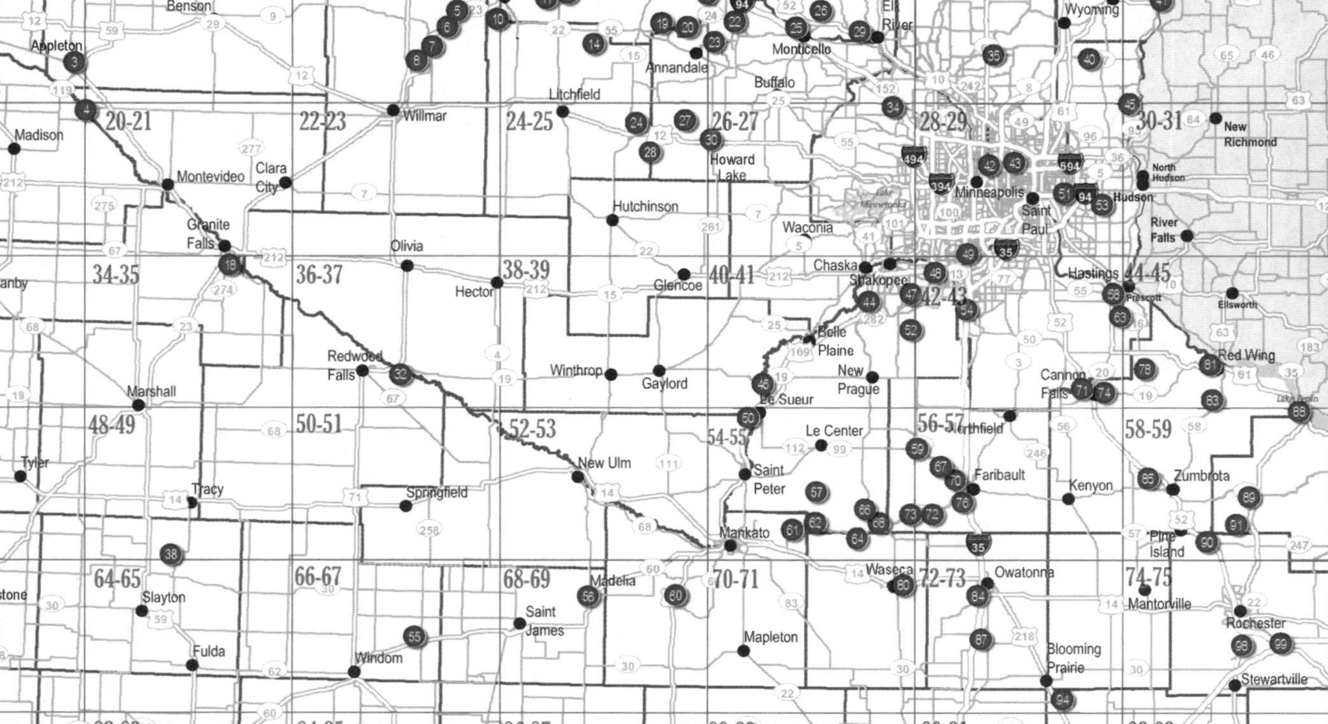

LEGEND

Private Campgrounds

For details, refer to table on following page

Psst. We're going to let you in on something private – private campgrounds, that is. Unlike private golf courses, which require a membership (with often very expensive fees), private campgrounds are simply privately owned and not part of the federal, state, or county park system, which administer the other campgrounds throughout the state. Private campgrounds are open to everyone, and are extremely popular with people who want to enjoy the outdoors without "roughing it." Private campgrounds often provide extensive services and facilities not found in even county and state parks, including long-term setup for recreational vehicles (RVs). Many offer dump stations, electric and water hook-ups, laundry facilities, showers, convenience stores, fuel, swimming pools, recreational equipment rental, tennis courts, mini-golf, and more.

PRIVATE CAMPGROUNDS

The table on the facing page provides additional information for all private campgrounds in the southern Minnesota region. Consult corresponding map pages for specific locations of individual campgrounds. For more details on other amenities, contact the campground operator directly at the phone numbers provided.

Deleon

PRIVATE CAMPGROUNDS

Number	Name	County	Nearest Town	Pg / Coord	Campsites	Electricity	Water	RV Dump	Recreation	Phone
1	Lakeshore RV Park	Big Stone	Ortonville	4-2B	43	•	•	•	•	(800) 9FO-RFUN
2	Hilltop Manor Mobile Home Park	Big Stone	Ortonville	4-2C	11	•	•	•	•	(320) 839-2533
3	Appleton Lion's Park Campground	Swift	Appleton	5-6D	-	•	•		•	(320) 289-1363
4	Milan Beach Resort	Chippewa	Milan	20-1A	20	•			•	(320) 734-4400
5	Old Wagon Campground	Kandiyohi	Hawick	9-5C	130	•	•	•	•	(320) 354-2165
6	Hideaway Campground	Kandiyohi	New London	9-5C	40	•	•	•	•	(320) 354-2148
7	Ye Olde Mill Inn Resort	Kandiyohi	Spicer	9-4D	4	•	•		•	(320) 796-2212
8	Island View Resort - Nest Lake	Kandiyohi	Spicer	9-4D	4	•	•	•	•	(800) 421-9708
9	Twilight Acres Resort	Stearns	Richmond	10-2B	10	•	•	•	•	(320) 597-2483
10	Koronis Regional Park	Stearns	Paynesville	9-6C	37	•	•	•	•	(320) 276-8843
11	Morning Star Resort and Campground	Stearns	Richmond	10-2B	142	•	•	•	•	(320) 453-7121
12	Your Haven Seasonal Campground	Stearns	Richmond	10-2B	117	•	•	•	•	(320) 597-2450
13	Grandview Resort	Stearns	Cold Spring	11-4A	1	•	•		•	(320) 654-1811
14	Clear Lake Campground	Meeker	Watkins	10-3D	49	•	•	•	•	(320) 764-2592
15	St. Cloud/Clearwater KOA	Stearns	Clearwater	12-1B	100	•	•	•	•	(320) 558-2876
16	A-J Acres Campgrounds	Stearns	Clearwater	12-1B	200	•	•	•	•	(320) 558-2847
17	Lake Hendricks Campground	Lincoln	Hendricks	32-2D	25	•	•	•	•	(507) 275-3192
18	Prairie View RV Park and Campground	Yellow Medicine	Granite Falls	35-4A	55	•	•	•	•	(320) 564-6029
19	Castaways Campground and BJ's Bait and Tackle	Wright	South Haven	11-5C	38	•	•	•	•	(320) 274-3730
20	Clearwater Forest Community	Stearns	South Haven	11-6C	90	•	•		•	(320) 274-8857
21	Rivers Edge RV Park	Sherburne	Becker	12-2A	70	•	•	•	•	(763) 261-3440
22	Olson's Campground	Wright	Maple Lake	12-1C	100	•	•	•	•	(320) 963-5173
23	Schroeder Park	Wright	Annandale	12-1D	50	•			•	(320) 274-8870
24	Lakedale Campground	Meeker	Dassel	25-4A	45	•	•	•	•	(320) 275-3334
25	River Terrace Park	Wright	Monticello	12-3C	87	•	•	•	•	(763) 295-2264
26	Shady River Campgrounds	Sherburne	Big Lake	13-4C	115	•	•	•	•	(612) 263-3705
27	Cokato Lake Camping and RV Resort	Wright	Cokato	25-5A	225	•	•	•	•	(320) 286-5779
28	Collinwood Regional Park	Wright	Cokato	25-5B	50	•		•	•	(320) 286-2801
29	Wapiti Park Campground	Sherburne	Elk River	13-5C	108	•	•	•	•	(763) 441-1396
30	Codger's Cove Campground	Wright	Howard Lake	26-1B	104	•	•	•	•	(320) 543-2218
31	Country Camping Tent and RV Park on the Rum River	Isanti	Isanti	14-2A	100	•	•	•	•	(763) 444-9626
32	Jackpot Junction Casino Hotel RV Park	Redwood	Morton	36-3D	40	•	•	•	•	(507) 644-7854
33	Kozy Oaks Kamp	Isanti	North Branch	15-4A	100	•	•	•	•	(651) 674-8471
34	Minneapolis NW/Maple Grove KOA Campground	Hennepin	Maple Grove	27-5A	150	•	•	•	•	(763) 420-2255
35	Ham Lake Campground	Anoka	Ham Lake	14-3D	143	•	•	•	•	(763) 434-5337
36	Pipestone RV Campground	Pipestone	Pipestone	62-3B	51	•	•	•	•	(507) 825-2455
37	Hillcrest RV Park	Chisago	Lindstrom	15-6B	60	•	•	•	•	(651) 257-5352
38	Schreiers On Shetek Campground	Murray	Currie	48-3E	115	•	•	•	•	(507) 763-3817
39	Camp Waub-o-Jeeg	Chisago	Taylors Falls	16-2A	50	•	•	•	•	(651) 465-3500
40	Timm's Marina and Seasonal RV Parks	Washington	Forest Lake	15-5D	30	•	•	•	•	(651) 464-3890
41	Wildwood RV Park and Campground	Chisago	Taylors Falls	16-2B	67	•	•	•	•	(651) 465-6315
42	Lowry Grove Community	Hennepin	St. Anthony	28-3C	81	•	•	•		(612) 781-3148
43	Roseville Estates MHP	Ramsey	Roseville	28-3C	4	•	•	•	•	(651) 483-5859
44	Minneapolis SW KOA/Shakopee/Jordan	Scott	Jordan	41-5B	120	•	•	•	•	(952) 492-6440
45	Golden Acres RV Park and Picnic Area	Washington	Stillwater	30-1A	54	•	•	•	•	(651) 439-1147
46	Allanson's Park	Sibley	Henderson	40-2E	15	•	•	•	•	(507) 248-3234
47	Dakotah Meadows Campground	Scott	Prior Lake	41-6B	122	•	•	•	•	(952) 445-8800
48	Town and Country Campground and RV Park	Scott	Savage	42-1A	78	•	•	•	•	(952) 445-1756
49	Krestwood RV and Mobile Home Park	Hennepin	Bloomington	42-2A	11	•	•	•		(952) 881-8218
50	Peaceful Valley Campsites	Nicollet	Le Sueur	54-2A	49	•	•	•	•	(507) 665-2297
51	Landfall Terrace	Washington	Landfall	29-5D	13	•	•	•	•	(651) 739-8284
52	Fish Lake Acres Campground	Scott	Prior Lake	41-6C	143	•	•	•	•	(952) 492-3393
53	St. Paul East RV Park	Washington	Woodbury	29-5D	76	•	•	•	•	(651) 436-6436
54	Queen Anne Courts	Dakota	Lakeville	42-2B	7	•	•	•	•	(952) 435-7979
55	Island View Campground	Cottonwood	Mountain Lake	67-4C	10	•	•	•	•	(507) 427-2999
56	Watona Park	Watonwan	Madelia	68-3B	32	•	•	•	•	(507) 642-3608
57	Beaver Dam Resort	Le Sueur	Cleveland	54-3C	48	•	•	•	•	(507) 931-5650
58	Hastings Terrace	Dakota	Hastings	43-6B	28	•	•	•		(651) 437-3060
59	Shields Lake Campground	Rice	Lonsdale	56-1B	45	•	•	•	•	(507) 334-8526
60	Shady Oaks Campground	Blue Earth	Garden City	69-5B	70	•	•	•	•	(507) 546-3986
61	Point Pleasant Campground	Blue Earth	Madison Lake	54-3E	80				•	(507) 243-3611
62	Sakatah Trail Resort	Le Sueur	Madison Lake	54-3D	115	•	•	•	•	(507) 267-4000
63	Greenwood Campground	Dakota	Hastings	43-6C	87	•	•	•	•	(651) 437-5269
64	Best Point Resort	Le Sueur	Waterville	55-5D	10	•	•	•	•	(507) 362-8526
65	Eastside Acres Campground	Jackson	Round Lake	83-5D	60	•	•	•	•	(507) 945-8900
66	Tetonka Lake Resort	Le Sueur	Waterville	55-5D	29	•	•	•	•	(507) 362-8206
67	Winjum's Shady Acres Resort of Faribault	Rice	Faribault	56-1C	86	•	•	•	•	(866) 334-6661
68	Kamp Dels	Le Sueur	Waterville	55-5D	300	•	•	•	•	(507) 362-8616
69	Jackson KOA Kampground	Jackson	Jackson	84-3B	60	•	•	•	•	(507) 847-3825
70	Roberds Lake Resort and Campground	Rice	Faribault	56-2C	50	•	•	•	•	(507) 332-8978
71	Lake Byllesby Reg'l Park Campground	Dakota	Cannon Falls	43-5E	57	•	•	•	•	(507) 263-4447
72	Camp Maiden Rock West	Rice	Morristown	55-6D	65	•	•	•	•	(507) 685-2240
73	Camp Maiden Rock	Rice	Morristown	55-6D	170	•	•	•	•	(507) 685-4430
74	Cannon Falls Campground	Goodhue	Cannon Falls	43-6E	198	•	•	•	•	(507) 263-3145
75	Caven's Landing	Martin	Sherburn	85-6B	10	•	•	•	•	(712) 580-6451
76	Camp Faribo	Rice	Faribault	56-2C	71	•	•	•	•	(507) 332-8453
77	Everett Park	Martin	Sherburn	85-6B	30	•	•	•	•	(507) 728-8294
78	Hidden Valley Campground	Goodhue	Welch	44-1D	200	•	•	•	•	(651) 258-4550
79	Checkers Welcome Campground	Martin	Welcome	86-1B	34	•	•	•	•	(507) 728-8811
80	Kiesler's Campground and RV Resort	Waseca	Waseca	71-6A	300	•	•	•	•	(800) 533-4642
81	Island Camping and Marina	Goodhue	Red Wing	44-3D	50	•	•	•	•	(715) 222-1808
82	Flying Goose Campground	Martin	Fairmont	86-3C	71	•	•	•	•	(507) 235-3458
83	Hay Creek Valley Campground	Goodhue	Red Wing	44-3E	150	•	•	•	•	(651) 388-3998
84	River View Campground	Steele	Owatonna	72-2B	185	•	•	•	•	(507) 451-8050
85	Shades of Sherwood	Goodhue	Zumbrota	58-1C	250	•	•	•	•	(507) 732-5100
86	RJ's Lakeside Campground	Martin	Fairmont	86-2D	140	•	•	•	•	(507) 235-5753
87	Hope Oak Knoll Campground	Steele	Owatonna	72-2C	90	•	•	•	•	(507) 451-2998
88	Lake Pepin Campground and MHP INC	Goodhue	Lake City	59-5A	40	•	•	•	•	(651) 345-2909
89	Bluff Valley RV Park and Campground	Wabasha	Zumbro Falls	59-4C	275	•	•	•	•	(507) 753-2955
90	Hidden Meadows RV Park Inc (was Waziona)	Olmsted	Pine Island	58-3E	100	•	•	•	•	(507) 356-8594
91	Ponderosa Campground	Wabasha	Mazeppa	59-4D	80	•	•	•	•	(507) 843-3611
92	Bailey Park/RV Community	Wabasha	Wabasha	60-2B	15	•	•	•		(651) 565-0174
93	Wabasha Motel and RV	Wabasha	Wabasha	60-2B	7	•	•	•	•	(651) 565-9932
94	Brookside Campground	Mower	Blooming Prairie	73-4E	90	•	•	•	•	(507) 583-2979
95	Hickory Hills Campground	Freeborn	Albert Lea	90-1D	99	•	•	•	•	(507) 852-4555
96	Albert Lea/Austin KOA Campground	Freeborn	Hayward	90-3B	110	•	•	•	•	(507) 373-5170
97	Pioneer Campsite	Wabasha	Wabasha	60-3C	240	•	•	•	•	(651) 565-5366
98	Willow Creek RV Park	Olmsted	Rochester	75-4C	34	•	•	•		(507) 282-1414
99	Rochester/Marion KOA	Olmsted	Rochester	75-5C	75	•	•	•	•	(800) 562-5232
100	Beaver Trails Campground and RV Park	Mower	Austin	92-1B	320	•	•	•	•	(800) 245-6281
101	Lazy 'D' Campground and Trail Rides	Winona	Altura	76-2A	112	•	•	•	•	(507) 932-3098
102	Bass Camp Resort	Winona	Minnesota City	61-4E	200	•		•	•	(507) 689-2856
103	Prairie Island Campground	Winona	Winona	77-5A	201	•	•	•	•	(507) 452-4501
104	Maple Springs Campground	Fillmore	Preston	93-6C	115	•	•		•	(507) 352-2056
105	Old Barn Resort and Rivers Bend Golf	Fillmore	Preston	94-2B	170	•	•	•	•	(507) 467-2512
106	Pla-Mor Campground and Marina	Winona	Winona	78-1B	111	•	•	•	•	(507) 454-2851
107	Eagle Cliff Campground	Fillmore	Lanesboro	94-3A	100	•	•	•	•	(507) 467-2598
108	Money Creek Haven Inc.	Houston	Houston	77-6E	200	•	•	•	•	(507) 896-3544
109	Cushon's Peak Campground	Houston	Houston	95-6A	44	•	•	•	•	(507) 896-7325
110	Hidden Bluffs Resort	Houston	Spring Grove	95-5C	106	•	•	•	•	(507) 498-5880
111	Dunromin' Park Campground	Houston	Caledonia	96-1D	106	•	•	•	•	(507) 724-2514
112	Wildcat Landing Campground	Houston	Brownsville	96-3B	68	•		•	•	(507) 894-4253

SEE INDEX ON PAGE 160 FOR ALPHABETICAL LISTING OF PRIVATE CAMPGROUNDS

CAMP COOKING

One of the joys of wilderness travel is cooking in the great outdoors. There's nothing quite like a steaming cup of campfire coffee on a cool morning or freshly baked biscuits from a reflector oven. Preparing meals far from the convenience of a home kitchen can seem daunting, but cooking in the wild has come a long way. Camp stoves are lightweight, efficient, and easy to use. A tremendous variety of foods specifically formulated for camp cooking are available in lightweight, dehydrated or freeze-dried pouches. All that's needed is water to rehydrate them. Using such items, it's a snap to whip up lasagna, beef stroganoff, chicken teriyaki, cherry cheesecake and much more. Many "instant" or quick-cooking foods such as potatoes and rice can be adapted for camp cooking. Or why not try dehydrating your own food? The only limitation to camp cooking is one's imagination.

Galyna Andrushko

COUNTY PARKS

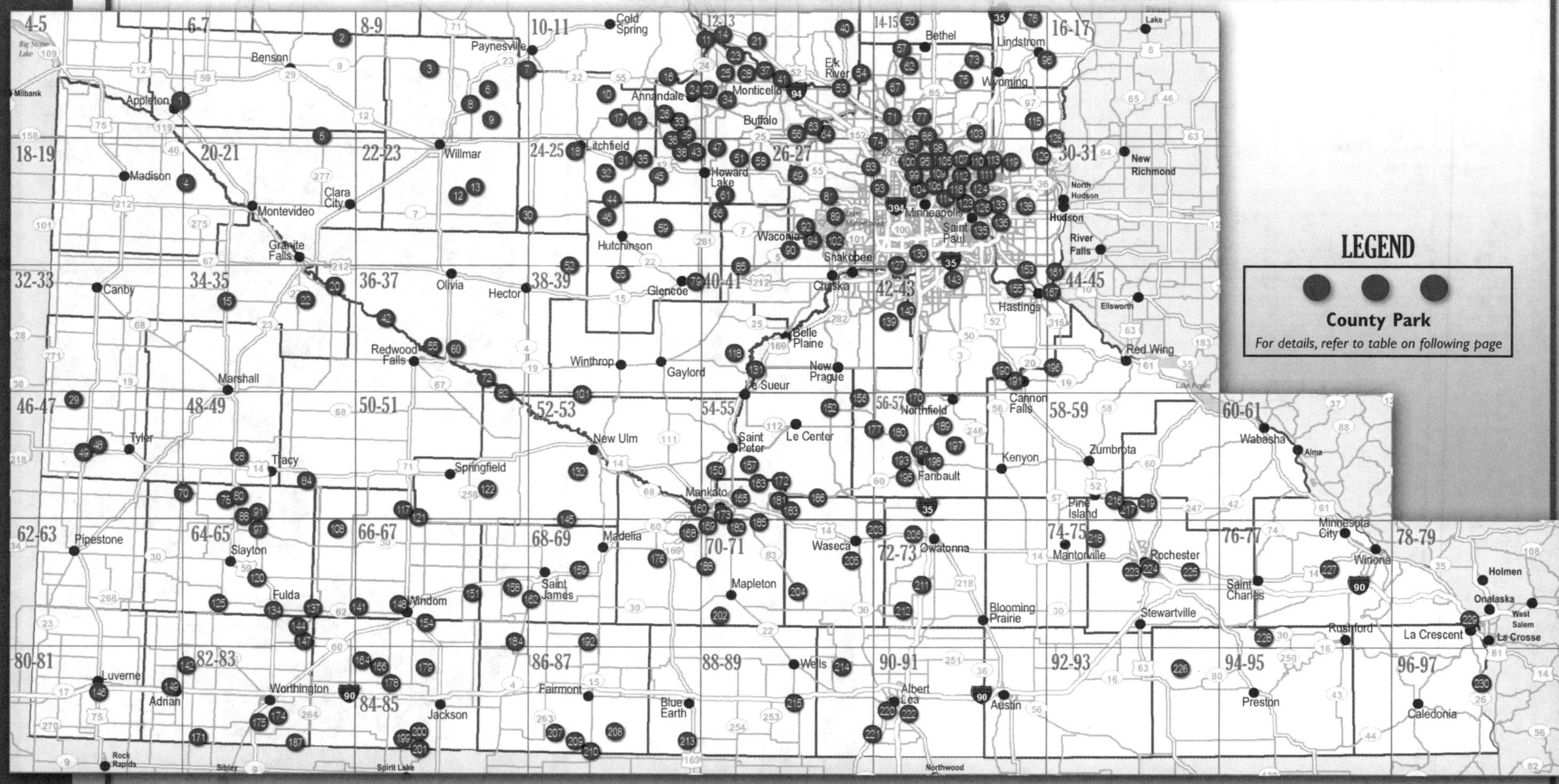

The many county and city parks spread out across southern Minnesota serve locals and visitors alike with their easy access, facilities, and amenities. Although county parks exist to provide recreational opportunities for county residents, they are open to everyone. They make a perfect afternoon getaway or an alternative when traveling longer distances is impractical. Many parks are family-friendly destinations, often providing amenities including boat ramps, cooking grills, hiking trails, picnic tables, play areas, potable water, swimming pools or beaches, volleyball, basketball, and horseshoe courts. Many parks also have campsites for tent camping and/or recreational vehicle sites. Also, several are open year-round, providing four-season fun for young and old alike. Every park is a new experience. Get out and enjoy!

COUNTY/CITY PARKS

The table on the facing page has recreational information for all county parks in the southern Minnesota region. Consult corresponding map pages for specific locations of individual parks. Additionally, a detailed recreational table for regional parks and park reserves located within the Minneapolis/St.Paul metropolitan region can be found on page 17.

COUNTY PARKS

Number	Name	County	Nearest Town	Pg / Coord	Electricity	Water	RV Camping	RV Dump	Tent Camping	Toilet	Fee	Picnic	Boat Ramp	Boat-In	Beach	Hiking Trails	Recreation	All Year	Phone
193	Ackman Park	Rice	Faribault	56-1C															(507) 332-6105
149	Adrian Spring County Park	Nobles	Adrian	81-6B								•						•	(507) 468-2224
170	Albers Park	Rice	Faribault	56-2A						•		•	•			•	•		(507) 332-6105
43	Albright's Mill County River Park	Wright	Buffalo	25-6A					•	•		•	•						(763) 682-7693
217	Allis Park	Olmsted	Rochester	58-3E									•					•	(507) 285-8231
199	Anderson County Park	Jackson	Jackson	84-2D	•	•	•	•	•	•	•	•	•				•		(507) 847-2240
72	Anderson Lake County Park	Renville	Olivia	37-5E						•								•	(320) 523-3798
100	Anoka County Riverfront Regional Park	Anoka	Anoka	28-2B	•					•	•	•	•			•	•	•	(763) 757-3920
229	Apple Blossom Overlook Park	Winona	Winona	78-3D														•	(507) 457-6335
1	Appleton Area ORV Park	Swift	Appleton	5-6D								•				•			(320) 843-5341
214	Arrowhead Point County Park	Freeborn	Albert Lea	89-5A	•	•				•		•	•			•	•		(507) 377-5188
81	Baker Park Reserve	Hennepin	Plymouth	27-5C	•	•	•	•	•	•	•	•	•		•	•	•	•	(763) 559-9000
113	Bald Eagle-Otter Lakes Regional Park	Ramsey	St. Paul	29-4A						•		•	•			•	•	•	(651) 748-2500
136	Battle Creek Regional Park	Ramsey	St. Paul	29-4D												•		•	(651) 748-2500
85	Baylor Regional Park	Carver	Norwood Young America	40-2A	•	•	•	•	•	•	•	•	•		•	•	•		(952) 466-5250
55	Beaver Falls County Park	Renville	Olivia	36-3D					•		•					•		•	(320) 523-3798
133	Beaver Lake County Park	Ramsey	St. Paul	29-4C						•		•					•		(651) 748-2500
212	Beaver Lake County Park	Steele	Owatonna	72-1D						•		•	•		•	•	•	•	(507) 451-1093
56	Beebe Lake Regional Park	Wright	Buffalo	13-4E		•				•	•	•	•		•	•	•		(763) 682-7693
179	Belmont County Park	Jackson	Jackson	84-3A	•	•				•		•				•		•	(507) 847-2240
36	Betty Mason County River Park	Wright	Buffalo	25-5A									•						(763) 682-7693
115	Big Marine Park Reserve	Washington	Stillwater	15-6E						•	•		•					•	(651) 430-8368
47	Bill Anderson Memorial County River Park	Wright	Buffalo	26-1A					•	•		•	•		•			•	(763) 682-7693
60	Birch Coulee County Park	Renville	Olivia	37-4D		•			•	•	•	•						•	(320) 523-3798
203	Blowers Park	Waseca	Waseca	72-1A						•		•	•			•	•	•	(507) 835-0590
181	Bray Park	Blue Earth	Mankato	54-3E		•	•	•	•	•	•	•	•		•	•	•		(507) 625-3282
41	Bridgeview Park Reserve	Sherburne	Elk River	12-3C												•		•	(763) 241-2939
207	Bright Lake County Park	Martin	Fairmont	86-1D								•	•			•		•	(507) 238-3126
200	Brown County Park	Jackson	Jackson	84-2D	•	•	•		•	•	•	•	•				•		(507) 847-2240
130	Bryant Lake Park	Hennepin	Eden Prairie	28-2E		•				•	•	•	•		•	•	•	•	(763) 559-9000
228	Bucksnort Park	Fillmore	Preston	76-2E					•			•						•	(507) 765-4566
79	Buffalo Creek County Park	McLeod	Hutchinson	39-6A						•		•				•	•		(320) 587-0770
5	Buffalo Lake County Park	Chippewa	Montevideo	7-5E						•		•	•				•		(320) 269-7447
77	Bunker Hills Regional Park	Anoka	Anoka	14-2E	•	•	•	•	•	•	•	•			•	•	•	•	(763) 757-3920
189	Cannon River Wilderness Area	Rice	Faribault	56-3B		•			•	•		•	•			•		•	(507) 332-6105
33	Carl Johnson County Forest	Wright	Buffalo	11-5E								•				•		•	(763) 682-7693
197	Caron Park	Rice	Faribault	56-3B		•				•		•				•			(507) 332-6105
94	Carver Park Reserve	Carver	Plymouth	27-4E		•	•	•	•	•	•	•	•		•	•	•	•	(763) 559-9000
184	Cedar-Hanson County Park	Martin	Fairmont	67-6E		•	•		•	•	•	•	•		•	•	•		(507) 238-3126
225	Chester Woods Park	Olmsted	Rochester	75-5C	•	•	•	•	•	•	•	•	•		•	•	•	•	(507) 285-8231
10	Clear Lake County Park	Meeker	Litchfield	10-3D						•		•	•					•	(320) 693-5450
101	Clear Lake County Park	Sibley	Gaylord	52-2A		•	•		•	•		•	•		•		•		(507) 237-4092
14	Clearwater Wayside	Wright	St. Cloud	12-1B						•		•						•	(763) 682-7693
24	Clearwater-Pleasant Regional Park	Wright	Annadale	11-6D						•		•	•		•	•	•		(763) 682-7693
139	Cleary Lake Regional Park	Scott	Plymouth	42-1C		•			•	•	•	•	•		•	•	•	•	(763) 559-9000
93	Clifton French Regional Park	Hennepin	Plymouth	28-1B		•				•	•	•	•		•	•	•	•	(763) 559-9000
45	Collinwood Regional Park	Wright	Cokato	25-5B	•	•	•		•	•	•	•	•		•	•	•	•	(763) 682-7693
166	Community Point County Park	Jackson	Jackson	84-1A	•	•				•		•	•		•		•	•	(507) 847-2240
75	Coon Lake County Park	Anoka	Anoka	14-3C	•					•		•	•		•	•	•	•	(763) 757-3920
87	Coon Rapids Dam Regional Park	Hennepin	Brooklyn Park	28-2A		•				•	•	•				•		•	(763) 559-9000
86	Coon Rapids Dam Regional Park	Anoka	Anoka	28-2A						•	•	•	•			•	•	•	(763) 757-3920
125	Corabelle Park	Murray	Slayton	64-2D						•		•	•					•	(507) 836-6148
30	Cosmos County Park	Meeker	Litchfield	23-6D						•		•					•		(320) 693-5450
153	Cottage Grove Ravine Regional Park	Washington	St. Paul	43-5A						•		•				•	•	•	(651) 430-8368
12	County Park 1	Kandiyohi	Willmar	23-4C	•	•	•		•	•	•	•	•		•		•		(320) 231-6202
13	County Park 2	Kandiyohi	Willmar	23-4B	•	•	•	•	•	•	•	•	•		•		•		(320) 231-6202
9	County Park 3	Kandiyohi	Willmar	9-5E	•	•	•	•	•	•	•	•	•		•		•		(320) 231-6202
8	County Park 4	Kandiyohi	Spicer	9-4D						•		•	•		•				(320) 231-6202
6	County Park 5	Kandiyohi	Willmar	9-5D	•	•	•	•	•	•	•	•	•		•	•	•		(320) 231-6202
3	County Park 7	Kandiyohi	Willmar	8-3C	•	•	•	•	•	•	•	•	•		•		•		(320) 231-6202
205	Courthouse Park	Waseca	Waseca	71-5B		•			•	•	•	•				•	•	•	(507) 835-0590
206	Crane Creek County Park	Steele	Owatonna	72-2A	•					•		•							(507) 451-1093
64	Crow Hassan Park Reserve	Hennepin	Rogers	13-4E		•				•	•	•				•		•	(763) 559-9000
58	Crow Springs County River Park	Wright	Buffalo	26-2A					•	•		•	•						(763) 682-7693
202	Daly Park	Blue Earth	Mapleton	70-1D		•	•	•	•	•	•	•	•		•	•	•		(507) 625-3282
31	Dassel-Darwin County Park	Meeker	Litchfield	25-4A						•		•				•		•	(320) 693-5450
172	Duck Lake Park	Blue Earth	Mankato	54-3D						•		•	•		•		•		(507) 625-3282
148	Dynamite Park	Cottonwood	Windom	66-2D								•					•	•	(507) 831-2060
165	Eagles Lake Wayside	Blue Earth	Mankato	54-2D									•					•	(507) 625-3282
159	Eagles Nest County Park	Watonwan	St. James	68-2B	•	•	•		•	•	•	•				•		•	(507) 375-3393
54	East Twin Lake County Park	Anoka	Anoka	13-6C						•		•	•		•	•	•	•	(763) 757-3920
74	Elm Creek Park Reserve	Hennepin	Plymouth	28-1A		•				•	•	•			•	•	•	•	(763) 559-9000
97	End-O-Line Railroad Park	Murray	Slayton	64-3A		•				•		•				•	•		(507) 836-6148
204	Eustice Park	Waseca	Waseca	71-4C		•				•		•				•	•	•	(507) 835-0590
16	Fairhaven Mill Historic Wayside	Wright	South Haven	11-5C						•		•	•					•	(763) 682-7693
198	Falls Creek Park	Rice	Faribault	56-2C		•				•		•				•			(507) 332-6105
227	Farmers Community Park	Winona	Winona	77-4B		•				•		•					•		(507) 457-6335
83	Fish Lake Regional Park	Hennepin	Plymouth	27-6B		•				•	•	•	•		•	•		•	(763) 559-9000
17	Forest City County Park	Meeker	Litchfield	10-3E						•		•					•		(320) 693-5450
91	Forman Acres	Murray	Slayton	64-3A						•		•	•					•	(507) 836-6148
147	Fury Island County Park	Nobles	Worthington	65-4E		•	•		•	•	•	•	•				•		(507) 468-2224
68	Garvin Park	Lyon	Marshall	48-2C	•	•	•	•	•	•	•	•				•	•	•	(507) 629-4081
224	Graham Park	Olmsted	Rochester	75-4B															(507) 285-8231
40	Grams Regional Park	Sherburne	Elk River	13-5A												•		•	(763) 241-2939
28	Harry Larson County Forest	Wright	Buffalo	12-2C						•		•				•		•	(763) 682-7693
187	Hawkeye County Park	Nobles	Worthington	83-4D								•	•					•	(507) 468-2224
177	Heron Island	Rice	Faribault	55-6B															(507) 332-6105
118	High Island Creek County Park	Sibley	Gaylord	40-2D		•				•		•							(507) 237-4092
180	Hirdler Park	Rice	Faribault	56-1B						•		•	•				•		(507) 332-6105
49	Hole in the Mountain County Park	Lincoln	Lake Benton	46-3C	•	•	•	•	•	•	•	•				•	•	•	(507) 368-9350
211	Hope School County Park	Steele	Owatonna	72-2C						•		•					•	•	(507) 451-1093
51	Humphrey Arends County River Park	Wright	Buffalo	26-2A					•	•		•	•						(763) 682-7693
182	Hungry Hollow Stop	Blue Earth	Mankato	70-2A								•	•						(507) 625-3282
127	Hyland-Bush Lakes Park	Hennepin	Plymouth	28-1E		•				•	•	•	•		•	•	•	•	(763) 559-9000
173	Indian Lake Conservation Area	Blue Earth	Mankato	70-1A												•		•	(507) 625-3282
112	Island Lake County Park	Ramsey	St. Paul	28-3B						•		•	•			•	•		(651) 748-2500
99	Islands of Peace County Park	Anoka	Anoka	28-2B								•	•			•		•	(763) 757-3920
156	Kalina Park	Rice	Faribault	55-6A															(507) 332-6105
158	Kansas Lake Park	Watonwan	St. James	67-6C								•	•					•	(507) 375-3393
126	Keller Regional Park	Ramsey	Maplewood	29-4C								•	•			•	•		(651) 748-2500
96	Ki-Chi-Saga Park	Chisago	North Branch	15-6B								•				•	•	•	(651) 213-6271
194	King Mill Park	Rice	Faribault	56-2C						•		•							(507) 332-6105
19	Kingston County Park	Meeker	Litchfield	11-4E						•		•	•				•	•	(320) 693-5450
210	Klessig Park	Martin	Fairmont	86-2E								•	•					•	(507) 238-3126
106	Kordiak County Park	Anoka	Anoka	28-2B						•		•				•	•	•	(763) 757-3920
76	Kost Dam Park	Chisago	North Branch	15-6A						•		•	•				•	•	(651) 213-6271
4	Lac Qui Parle County Park	Lac Qui Parle	Madison	20-1B								•	•			•		•	(320) 598-7444
52	Lake Allie County Park	Renville	Olivia	38-2A			•	•	•	•	•	•	•						(320) 523-3798
191	Lake Byllesby County Park	Goodhue	Cannon Falls	43-5E		•				•		•	•		•		•		(651) 385-3000
190	Lake Byllesby Regional Park	Dakota	Cannon Falls	43-5E	•	•	•	•	•	•	•	•	•		•	•	•		(952) 891-7000
138	Lake Elmo Park Reserve	Washington	Lake Elmo	29-5C	•	•	•	•	•	•	•	•	•		•	•	•	•	(651) 430-8368
163	Lake George Park	Blue Earth	Mankato	54-2D								•	•		•		•		(507) 625-3282
62	Lake George Regional Park	Anoka	Anoka	14-2B						•	•	•	•		•	•	•	•	(763) 757-3920
124	Lake Gervais County Park	Ramsey	Little Canada	29-4C						•		•			•		•		(651) 748-2500
145	Lake Hanska County Park	Brown	New Ulm	68-2A	•	•	•	•	•	•	•	•	•		•	•	•		(507) 233-6640
114	Lake Josephine County Park	Ramsey	St. Paul	28-3B						•		•	•		•		•		(651) 748-2500
7	Lake Koronis Regional Park	Meeker	Litchfield	9-6C	•	•	•		•	•	•	•	•		•	•	•		(320) 693-5450
32	Lake Manuella County Park	Meeker	Litchfield	24-3B						•		•	•		•			•	(320) 693-5450
65	Lake Marion Park	McLeod	Hutchinson	38-3A		•	•	•	•	•	•	•	•		•	•	•		(320) 587-0770
123	Lake McCarrons County Park	Ramsey	Roseville	29-4C						•		•	•		•	•	•		(651) 748-2500
92	Lake Minnetonka Regional Park	Hennepin	Plymouth	27-4D		•				•	•	•	•		•	•	•	•	(763) 559-9000
102	Lake Minnewashta Regional Park	Carver	Norwood Young America	27-5E	•					•	•	•	•		•	•	•	•	(952) 466-5250
116	Lake Owasso County Park	Ramsey	St. Paul	28-3B						•		•	•		•		•		(651) 748-2500
69	Lake Rebecca Park Reserve	Hennepin	Plymouth	27-4B		•				•	•	•	•		•	•	•	•	(763) 559-9000
80	Lake Sarah East	Murray	Slayton	48-2E						•		•	•				•	•	(507) 836-6148
78	Lake Sarah West	Murray	Slayton	48-2E	•	•	•	•	•	•	•	•	•				•		(507) 836-6148
90	Lake Waconia Regional Park	Carver	Norwood Young America	26-3E						•		•			•		•		(952) 466-5250
157	Lake Washington County Park	Le Sueur	Kasota	54-2D	•	•	•	•	•	•	•	•	•						(507) 725-5822
143	Lebanon Hills Regional Park	Dakota	Eagan	42-3A	•	•	•	•	•	•	•	•	•		•	•	•	•	(952) 891-7000
120	Lime Lake Park	Murray	Avoca	64-3C						•		•	•					•	(507) 836-6148
98	Locke County Park	Anoka	Anoka	28-2A						•		•				•	•	•	(763) 757-3920
183	Lone Pine Rest Area	Blue Earth	Mankato	54-3E									•					•	(507) 625-3282
162	Long Lake Park	Watonwan	St. James	68-1D						•		•	•		•				(507) 375-3393
105	Long Lake Regional Park	Ramsey	St. Paul	28-3B						•		•	•		•	•	•	•	(651) 748-2500
132	Lost Dog and Fox Hunter's County Park	Brown	New Ulm	52-2D	•	•				•		•	•				•		(507) 233-6640
82	Mack County Park	Renville	Olivia	51-5A					•	•		•	•					•	(320) 523-3798
144	Maka-Oicu County Park	Nobles	Worthington	65-4E		•	•		•	•	•	•	•		•	•			(507) 468-2224
95	Manomin County Park	Anoka	Anoka	28-2A						•		•	•			•		•	(763) 757-3920
23	Marcus Zumbrunnen County Park	Wright	St. Cloud	12-2B								•				•		•	(763) 682-7693
88	Marsh's Landing	Murray	Slayton	48-2E						•		•	•					•	(507) 836-6148
73	Martin-Island-Linwood Lakes Regional Park	Anoka	Anoka	15-4B		•				•	•	•	•		•	•	•	•	(763) 757-3920
226	Masonic Park	Fillmore	Preston	93-5A					•			•						•	(507) 765-4566
223	Mayowood Corridor	Olmsted	Rochester	74-3C												•		•	(507) 285-8231
142	Midway County Park	Nobles	Worthington	82-1A														•	(507) 468-2224
196	Miesville Ravine Park Reserve	Dakota	Hampton	44-1E						•		•				•		•	(952) 891-7000
37	Montissippi Regional Park	Wright	Monticello	12-3C						•		•	•			•	•	•	(763) 682-7693
121	Mound Creek County Park	Brown	New Ulm	50-2E						•		•	•		•	•	•		(507) 233-6640
151	Mountain County Park	Cottonwood	Windom	67-4C														•	(507) 831-2060
39	Mud Lake County Park	Wright	Buffalo	25-6A						•		•	•						(763) 682-7693
140	Murphy-Hanrehan Park	Scott	Plymouth	42-1B							•		•			•		•	(763) 559-9000
131	Ney Center Park	Le Sueur	Le Center	40-2E						•		•				•		•	(507) 357-2251
89	Noerenberg Garden Park	Hennepin	Plymouth	27-5C															(763) 559-9000
104	North Mississippi Park	Hennepin	Minneapolis	28-2B		•				•		•				•	•	•	(763) 559-9000
48	Norwegian Creek County Park	Lincoln	Ivanhoe	46-3C	•	•	•	•	•	•	•	•	•		•	•			(507) 368-9350
21	Oak Savanna Land Preserve	Sherburne	Becker	12-2B												•		•	(763) 241-2939
154	Obie Knutson County Park	Jackson	Jackson	66-3E						•		•	•				•	•	(507) 847-2240
186	Okaman Park	Waseca	Waseca	55-4E						•		•	•					•	(507) 835-0590
15	Oraas County Park	Yellow Medicine	Hanley Falls	34-2B					•	•		•				•		•	(320) 564-3331
216	Oronoco Park	Olmsted	Rochester	58-3E		•			•	•		•					•		(507) 285-8231
61	Oscar and Anna Johnson County Park	Wright	Buffalo	26-1C						•		•	•		•				(763) 682-7693
53	Otsego Regional Park	Wright	Elk River	13-5D						•		•	•			•	•		(763) 682-7693
218	Oxbow Park	Olmsted	Byron	74-2A		•	•		•	•	•	•				•	•		(507) 285-8231
141	Pat's Grove	Cottonwood	Windom	66-1D								•							(507) 831-2060
192	Perch Lake County Park	Martin	Fairmont	68-2E		•	•		•	•	•	•	•			•	•		(507) 238-3126
220	Pickerel Lake County Park	Freeborn	Albert Lea	90-1C		•				•		•	•						(507) 377-5188
29	Picnic Point County Park	Lincoln	Ivanhoe	46-3A	•	•	•	•	•	•	•	•	•		•		•		(507) 368-9350
44	Piepenburg Park	McLeod	Hutchinson	24-3C	•	•	•		•	•	•	•	•		•		•		(320) 587-0770
215	Pihls Park	Faribault	Blue Earth	88-3C	•	•	•	•	•	•	•	•	•			•	•		(507) 526-3291
129	Pine Point Park	Washington	Stillwater	29-6A						•		•				•		•	(651) 430-8368
84	Plum Creek Park	Redwood	Walnut Grove	49-4D	•	•	•		•	•	•	•			•	•	•		(507) 859-2491
167	Point Douglas Park	Washington	St. Paul	44-1A						•		•			•	•		•	(651) 430-8368
168	Rapidan Dam Park	Blue Earth	Mankato	69-6A		•			•	•	•	•	•		•	•	•		(507) 625-3282
169	Red Jacket Park	Blue Earth	Mankato	70-1A						•		•	•			•		•	(507) 625-3282
117	Red Rock Falls Park	Cottonwood	Windom	50-2E												•		•	(507) 831-2060
103	Rice Creek Chain of Lakes Regional Park Reserve	Anoka	Anoka	15-4E	•	•	•	•	•	•	•	•	•		•	•	•	•	(763) 757-3920
152	Richter's Woods Park	Le Sueur	Le Center	55-5A						•		•				•		•	(507) 357-2251
63	Riverside County River Park	Wright	Hanover	13-4E					•	•		•	•						(763) 682-7693
34	Robert Ney Memorial Park Reserve	Wright	Maple Lake	12-1D						•		•	•			•		•	(763) 682-7693
201	Robertson County Park	Jackson	Jackson	84-2D	•	•	•	•	•	•	•	•	•			•	•		(507) 847-2240
67	Rum River Central Regional Park	Anoka	Anoka	14-1C	•					•	•	•	•			•	•	•	(763) 757-3920
57	Rum River North County Park	Anoka	Anoka	14-1B						•		•	•			•	•	•	(763) 757-3920
71	Rum River South County Park	Anoka	Anoka	14-1E	•					•		•	•			•	•	•	(763) 757-3920
161	Saint Croix Bluffs Regional Park	Washington	St. Paul	44-1A	•	•	•	•	•	•	•	•	•			•	•	•	(651) 430-8368
222	Saint Nicholas Park	Freeborn	Albert Lea	90-2C								•				•		•	(507) 377-5188
164	Sandy Point County Park	Jackson	Jackson	84-1A	•		•			•	•	•	•				•		(507) 847-2240
188	Schimek Park	Blue Earth	Mankato	70-1B								•				•		•	(507) 625-3282
146	Schoneman County Park	Rock	Luverne	80-3B						•		•				•	•		(507) 283-5010
27	Schroeder Regional Park	Wright	Buffalo	12-1D	•	•	•		•	•	•	•	•		•	•	•		(763) 682-7693
150	Seven Mile Creek Park	Nicollet	St. Peter	54-1D						•		•	•			•	•	•	(507) 931-1760
134	Seven Mile Lake Park	Murray	Fulda	64-3D	•	•	•	•	•	•	•	•	•		•		•		(507) 836-6148
195	Shager Park	Rice	Faribault	56-1D						•		•	•		•	•	•		(507) 332-6105
20	Skalbekken County Park	Renville	Olivia	35-5A			•		•	•	•	•	•			•		•	(320) 523-3798
108	South Dutch Charlie Park	Cottonwood	Windom	65-5A	•		•		•	•		•							(507) 831-2060
178	Sparks Environmental County Park	Jackson	Jackson	84-2B														•	(507) 847-2240
174	Sportsman County Park East	Nobles	Worthington	83-4C									•					•	(507) 468-2224
35	Spring Lake County Park	Meeker	Litchfield	25-4A						•		•	•				•		(320) 693-5450
155	Spring Lake Park Reserve	Dakota	Hastings	43-5A						•		•				•	•	•	(952) 891-7000
128	Square Lake County Park	Washington	Stillwater	30-1A						•		•	•		•			•	(651) 430-8368
46	Stahl's Lake County Park	McLeod	Hutchinson	24-3C						•		•	•			•		•	(320) 587-0770
26	Stanley Eddy Memorial Park Reserve	Wright	Cokato	11-5E						•		•				•		•	(763) 682-7693
25	Stirewalt Memorial County Park	Wright	Maple Lake	12-1C								•							(763) 682-7693
171	Sunrise Prairie County Park	Nobles	Worthington	82-1D														•	(507) 468-2224
175	Sunrise Prairie County Park	Nobles	Worthington	82-3D														•	(507) 468-2224
59	Swan Lake County Park	McLeod	Hutchinson	25-5D						•		•	•						(320) 587-0770
70	Swensen Park	Murray	Slayton	47-6D	•	•	•	•	•	•	•	•	•				•		(507) 836-6148
2	Swift Falls Park	Swift	Benson	7-6B		•	•		•	•	•	•				•	•		(320) 843-5341
137	Talcot Lake County Park	Cottonwood	Windom	65-5D	•	•	•	•	•	•	•	•	•		•		•		(507) 831-2060
135	Thompson County Park	Dakota	St. Paul	29-4D						•		•				•	•	•	(952) 891-7000
209	Timberlane County Park	Martin	Fairmont	86-2E									•			•		•	(507) 238-3126
22	Timm County Park	Yellow Medicine	Granite Falls	35-4B			•		•	•		•	•						(320) 564-3331
109	Tony Schmidt County Park	Ramsey	St. Paul	28-3B						•		•	•		•		•		(651) 748-2500
122	Treml County Park	Brown	New Ulm	51-5D	•					•		•				•			(507) 233-6640
107	Turtle Lake County Park	Ramsey	St. Paul	28-3A						•		•	•		•		•		(651) 748-2500
110	Vadnais-Snail Lakes Regional Park	Ramsey	St. Paul	28-3B						•		•	•		•	•	•	•	(651) 748-2500
111	Vadnais-Snail Lakes Regional Park	Ramsey	St. Paul	29-4B						•		•	•		•	•	•	•	(651) 748-2500
42	Vicksburg County Park	Renville	Olivia	36-1C					•	•	•	•	•					•	(320) 523-3798
11	Warner Lake County Park	Stearns	St. Cloud	12-1B						•		•	•		•	•			(320) 255-6172
176	Watonwan Stop	Blue Earth	Mankato	69-5B								•	•						(507) 625-3282
50	Wayside Prairie	Isanti	Cambridge	14-2A						•		•				•		•	(763) 689-8220
18	West Ripley Park	Meeker	Litchfield	24-2A						•		•	•				•		(320) 693-5450
119	White Bear Lake County Park	Ramsey	St. Paul	29-4A						•		•	•		•	•	•	•	(651) 748-2500
219	White Bridge Fishing Access	Olmsted	Rochester	59-4E						•		•						•	(507) 285-8231
221	White Woods County Park	Freeborn	Twin Lakes	89-6D		•				•		•				•			(507) 377-5188
230	Wildcat Park	Houston	Caledonia	96-3B	•	•	•	•	•	•	•	•	•						(507) 725-5822
38	Wildlife County River Park	Wright	Buffalo	25-5A					•	•		•	•						(763) 682-7693
185	Wildwood Park	Blue Earth	Mankato	70-2A												•		•	(507) 625-3282
66	William May County Park	McLeod	Hutchinson	26-1C						•		•							(320) 587-0770
160	Williams Nature Center	Blue Earth	Mankato	53-6E						•		•			•	•		•	(507) 625-3282
208	Wolter Park	Martin	Fairmont	86-3D						•		•	•				•		(507) 238-3126
213	Woods Lake Park	Faribault	Blue Earth	87-6D	•	•	•	•	•	•	•	•			•		•		(507) 526-3291

County Parks Camping & Amenities

STATE PARKS

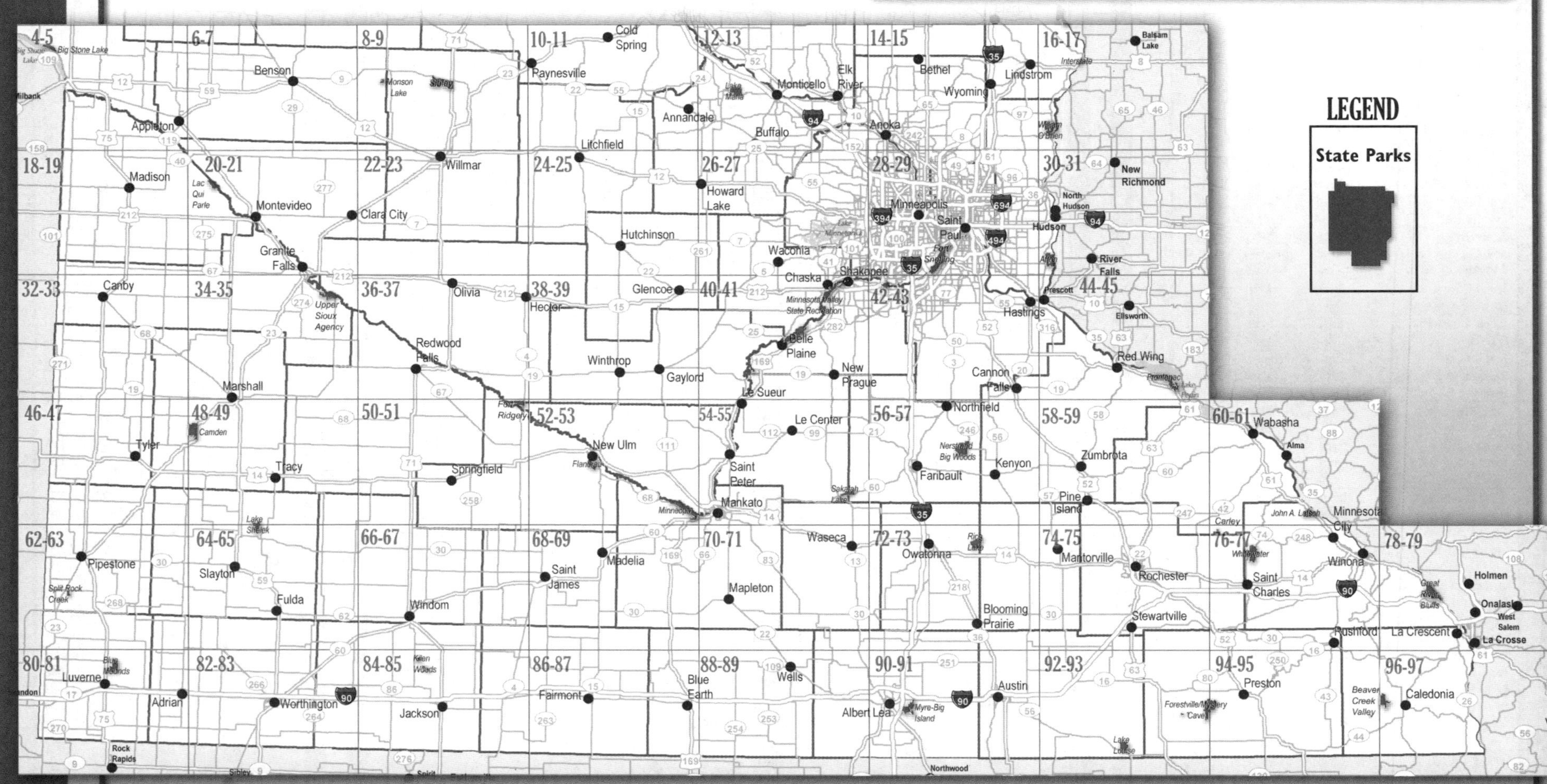

Name	Pg / Coord	County	Nearest Town	Acres	Phone	Drive-In Sites (# Pull Thrus)	Elec Sites	RV Length Limit (ft)	Backpack Sites	Other Site Types	HCA Sites	Horse Camp Sites (Max)	Group Camp (# sites)	Group Center	Camper Cabins	Lodging	Self-Guided	Hiking	Surfaced Bike	Mountain Bike	Horse Trail	Handicapped Accessible
						Camping / Lodging / Restroom Facilities											Miles of Trail					
Afton State Park	30-1E	Washington	Hastings	1,695	(651) 436-5391				24	1-CI			2				1	20	4		5	0.6
Beaver Creek Valley State Park	96-1B	Houston	Caledonia	1,187	(507) 724-2107	42	16	55		6-CT	1		1(3)		1(S)			8				
Big Stone Lake State Park	4-2A	Big Stone	Ortonville	986	(320) 839-3663	37	10	48					1					3				
Blue Mounds State Park	81-4A	Rock	Luverne	1,826	(507) 283-1307	73	40	50		14-WI	2		1				1	13	2.2			
Camden State Park	48-1B	Lyon	Lynd	2,245	(507) 865-4530	80 (7)	29	50			2	12(50)	1				2	15		4	10	
Carley State Park	76-1A	Wabasha	Altura	209	(507) 932-3007	20		30					3				1	5				
Flandrau State Park	52-3C	Nicollet	New Ulm	1,006	(507) 233-9800	89 (1)	34	66		3-WI				HCA				8				
Forestville / Mystery Cave State Park	93-6C	Fillmore	Preston	3,170	(507) 937-3251	73	23	50				24 (360)	1(2)					17			15	
Fort Ridgely State Park	51-6A	Redwood	Fairfax	1,040	(507) 46-7840	31 (1)	15	60		3-WI		20 (80)	1					11	0.5		10	
Fort Snelling State Park	28-3E	Dakota	St. Paul	2,931	(612) 725-2389												1	18	5	10		
Frontenac State Park	45-5E	Goodhue	Frontenac	2,237	(651) 345-3401	58	19	53		6-CT			1				3	13	1			1
Great River Bluffs State Park	78-2C	Winona	Winona	3,067	(507) 643-6849	31		60		5-BK	2		1(4)				3	7				
Interstate State Park	16-2B	Chisago	Taylors Falls	298	(651) 465-5711	37	22	45			4		1(4)				3	4				0.5
John A. Latsch State Park	61-4E	Winona	Winona	1,871	(507) 932-3007					7-WI								1				
Kilen Woods State Park	84-3A	Jackson	Lakefield	548	(507) 662-6258	33-(3)	11	50		4-CT	1							5				
Lac Qui Parle State Park	20-1B	Lac Qui Parle	Montevideo	1,055	(320) 734-4450	85 (8)	58	60		3-CT	2		1(6)					6			5	
Lake Louise State Park	92-3D	Mower	Leroy	1,147	(507) 324-5249	20	11	60				6 (36)	1(2)					12	10		9.7	
Lake Maria State Park	12-2C	Wright	Monticello	1,614	(763) 878-2325				17				2		3(Y)		2	14			6	
Lake Shetek State Park	64-3A	Murray	Currie	1,108	(507) 763-3256	97 (3)	66	60		10-WI	2		2	1	1(Y)		1	14	6			7.5
Minneopa State Park	53-6E	Blue Earth	Mankato	2,691	(507) 389-5464	61	6	60					1(4)		1(Y)			4	0.2			
Minnesota Valley State Recreation Area	41-4C	Hennepin	Jordan	5,501	(952) 492-6400	25		60		8-WI		8-(40)					5	41	6	29	29	1
Monson Lake State Park	8-1C	Swift	Sunburg	187	(320) 354-2055	20												1				
Myre-Big Island State Park	90-2C	Freeborn	Albert Lea	2,028	(507) 379-3403	93	32	60	4		1		1	1	1(S)		8	16	1	7		0.5
Nerstrand Big Woods State Park	56-3B	Rice	Nerstrand	2,882	(507) 333-4840	51-(1)	27	60		4-WI	1		3(9)				13					
Rice Lake State Park	73-4A	Steele	Owatonna	1,071	(507) 455-5871	42	16	50		5CI/5WI/4CT	1		2					5				0.5
Sakatah Lake State Park	55-5D	Rice	Waterville	842	(507) 362-4438	62	14	55		4-BK			2		1(S)			5	3			0.4
Sibley State Park	8-3C	Kandiyohi	New London	2,509	(320) 354-2055	132	53	35-70			2	9(54)	1(3)	1			2	18	5		9	2
Split Rock Creek State Park	62-2C	Pipestone	Jasper	1,303	(507) 348-7908	28	19	52		6-WI	1		1				5	5				0.5
Upper Sioux Agency State Park	35-5A	Yellow Medicine	Granite Falls	1,281	(320) 564-4777	34	14	60		3-WI		33				2 Tipi	2	18			16	
Whitewater State Park	76-2B	Winona	Altura	2,745	(507) 932-3007	106 (5)	47	50		4-WI	2		1(3)	1	1(S)		3	10				2
William O'Brien State Park	16-1E	Washington	Marine on St. Croix	1,620	(651) 433-0500	124	60	60		2-WI	7		2(4)		1(S)		2	12	1			2

Wild, wonderful, and wow are just three words that can be used to describe Minnesota's state park system. The state's incredible wealth of natural resources is displayed dramatically within this extensive system of 72 parks, covering more than 260,000 acres, and providing a wealth of recreational opportunities. Boating, camping, canoeing, fishing, hiking, cross-country skiing, mountain biking, and wildlife viewing are just some of the activities that draw visitors to state parks. The detailed chart below shows the staggering variety of recreational choices awaiting visitors.

State parks have a storied history in Minnesota, being just the second state to introduce a state park system. Minnesota's first state park – Itasca State Park – was created in 1891, after a law was enacted "to maintain intact, forever, a limited quantity of the domain of this commonwealth, seven miles long and five in width, in a state of nature." The law passed by only one vote in the Minnesota legislature. In 1905, the rustic Douglas Lodge was constructed – the first rustic-style building and the oldest in the state park system. By 1930, another dozen such buildings had been added to Itasca. This form of construction has since been adopted by 21 other Minnesota state parks.

Your southern Minnesota state park experience varies from natural oases within urban areas to vast forests covering hilly landscapes to underground caves waiting to be explored. At Fort Snelling State Park you can step back in time and learn about frontier life of the 1820s while listening to the background noise of Twin Cities traffic. Visitors to Minneopa State Park will thrill to a pair of waterfalls that spill a total of 45 feet. At Myre-Big Island State Park, you can witness dozens of wildflower species that dot the landscape. Ever explored a cave? If not, or even if you have, it's worth a trip to Forestville State Park to explore Mystery Cave – Minnesota's largest cave. The South Branch of the Root River "disappears" inside the cave, only to resurface above ground 1.5 miles away. Visitors to Lac Qui Parle State Park in spring and fall will hear the deafening calls of the thousands of migratory waterfowl that stop over here on their biannual migrations. Some years more than 200,000 geese stage here on their journey. These parks are but a sampling of what southern Minnesota has to offer. To really get a feel for them, you'll just have to plan a visit!

Many parks have special programs and events running throughout the year. Visitors can enjoy interpretive hikes, make a pair of snowshoes, build birdhouses, stargaze, tap trees for maple syrup, learn about wetlands, and much more. Whatever your interest and whenever the season, state parks are year-round treasures for Minnesota residents and visitors.

RULES

Park hours

8 a.m.-10 p.m., 365 days a year. Office hours vary by season.

State Park Permit

All vehicles entering a state park must display a valid Minnesota State Park vehicle permit, which must be affixed to the lower right hand corner of the windshield. Annual and day permits can be purchased at a park. Funds from state park vehicle permits and fees are used to help manage park resources and facilities.

Biking

Biking is permitted only on designated trails or park roads where motor vehicles are allowed, unless otherwise posted.

Camping

Campers must register at the office or self-registration station. Only registered campers are allowed in the park after 10 p.m. Quiet hours are from 10 p.m. to 8 a.m.

Firewood

Gathering firewood disrupts the forest and soil cycle and is not permitted. Firewood may be purchased at the park office.

Check in / check out

Overnight guests must check out by 4 p.m. If you choose to stay another day in the campground or park lodging, you must re-register by 11 a.m.

Fishing

When fishing in waters entirely within state parks, anglers must comply with Minnesota fishing laws and rules.

Flotation devices

In a state park, while in the water, use of air mattresses, inner tubes or other flotation devices that are not approved by the Coast Guard is prohibited except when used in an area specifically designated for that use.

Hunting

Hunting is prohibited in state parks unless authorized by the Commissioner of the Department of Natural Resources.

Parking

Parking on the grass is not allowed. Park in designated areas only and on the parking spaces provided in the campground.

Pets

Pets are welcome in state parks but must be kept on a leash of not more than six feet and must be personally attended at all times. No pets other than hearing or seeing-eye dogs or other service animals are allowed in state park buildings, lodging, cabins, camper cabins, on tours or in beach areas.

Rock climbing

Rock climbing in state parks is allowed only in designated areas and only by permit. Permits are available at the park office.

Skiing

When using groomed trails in parks, skiers 16 years of age and older must have in their possession a valid Minnesota ski pass.

Snowmobiles

Snowmobiles in state parks can be operated only on designated trails or posted areas.

Snowshoes

Snowshoeing is allowed anywhere is state parks except on groomed trails or where posted.

Chandler Hall

Summer Recreation										Winter Recreation				Park Facilities / Services										
Picnic Area	Open Picnic Shelter	Enclosed Picnic Shelter	Swimming Beach	Fishing	Fishing Pier	Access	Boating Restrictions	(V)olleyball / (H)orseshoes / (R)ock Climbing	Playground	X-Country Ski (trail miles)	Skate-Ski (trail miles)	Snowshoeing	Snowmobile (trail miles)	Warming House	Visitor Center	Naturalist Programs	Interpretive Exhibits	Historic Site	Tours (fee)	Gift Shop	Rentals	(F)irewood /(I)ce Sales	Public Phone	All Year
HCA	HCA	HCA	•	R		+	I	V/H		18		•		•	HCA		•			•		F/I	HCA	•
HCA		HCA		ST				V	•			•		•			•			•		F/I	HCA	•
HCA			•	L		Ramp / CD		H	•			•			HCA						C	F/I	HCA	•
HCA		HCA	•	L		CD	N	V/H/R	•			•	3					•		•	C	F/I	HCA	•
HCA	HCA	HCA	•	L/R	HCA	Ramp	EM	H	•	5	1.4	•	8	•				•		•	C	F/I	HCA	•
HCA	HCA			ST					HCA	5		•										F/I	•	•
HCA		HCA	HCA	R		CD		V/H	•	8		•		•			•			•	SK/SS	F/I	HCA	•
HCA	HCA	HCA		ST						11		•	6	•	HCA	S	•	•	HCA	•		F/I	HCA	•
•	HCA	HCA		ST				V/H	•	5		•	8	•	•		•	•		•	Golf/T	F/I	•	•
HCA	HCA	HCA	HCA	L/R	HCA	Ramp / CD	EM	V	•	12	6	•		•	HCA	I	•	•	•	•	Golf/C/CH		HCA	•
HCA	HCA	HCA		L/R						5		•	5	•				•		•		F/I	HCA	•
HCA									HCA	9	1	•								•	SS	F/I	HCA	•
HCA	•	HCA		R		Ramp	SP/W	V/R							HCA		•	•		•	C	F/I	•	•
HCA												•												
•		HCA		R				V/H		2		•	4	•								F/I	•	•
•	HCA	HCA	•	L/R		Ramp	I	H		5		•		•	HCA	I	•	•		•		F/I	HCA	•
HCA	HCA		•	L/ST		CD	EM			3		•	10									F/I	HCA	•
HCA		HCA		L	•	Ramp / CD	I			14	2	•		•	HCA	I	•			•	B/C/SS	F/I	HCA	•
HCA	HCA	HCA	•	L		Ramp / CD		V/H	HCA	3		•	5	•	HCA		•	•		•	B/C	F/I	HCA	•
•	HCA			R/ST		CD		V/H		4		•			•		•	•		•		F/I	•	•
•	HCA	HCA		R		Ramp / CD				5		•	39					•				F		•
•	HCA			L	•	Ramp						•						•			C	F		•
•	HCA	•		L		Ramp	I			8		•	7	•						•	C	F/I	HCA	•
HCA	HCA							V/H	•	7		•	5	•	HCA		•			•	SS	F/I	HCA	•
HCA	HCA	HCA		I		Ramp	I		•	3		•	3	•		I	•			•	C	F/I	HCA	•
HCA				L	HCA	Ramp		H		5		•	3							•	B/C	F/I	HCA	•
HCA	•		•	L/ST	HCA	Ramp		V/H		10	2	•	6	•	HCA	•	•	•		•	B/C	F/I	HCA	•
HCA		HCA	•	L	HCA	Ramp	SP/W	V/H	•			•		•	•		•	•		•	B/C/PB	F/I	•	•
•	•			R		Ramp / CD	I	V/H	•	2		•	14	•	•		•	•		•	C/SS	F/I	•	•
HCA	HCA		•	ST	HCA			V/H		8		•		•	HCA	•	•	•		•	SS	F/I	HCA	•
HCA	HCA		•	L/R	HCA	Ramp		V/H		12	12	•		•	HCA	•	•			•	C	F/I	HCA	•

KEY

Camping/Lodging/ Restroom Facilities

- **BI** - Boat In
- **CB** - Cabin
- **CI** - Canoe In
- **CT** - Cart In
- **GH** - Guest House
- **HCA** - Handicapped Accessible
- **K** - Kayak
- **LO** - Lodge
- **ML** - Motel
- **WI** - Walk In

Trails/Recreation/ Park Facilities Services

- **B** - Boat
- **BK** - Bike
- **C** - Canoe
- **CD** - Carry Down
- **EM** - Electric Motors Only
- **HCA** - Handicapped Accessible
- **I** - Inquire at Park
- **K** - Kayak
- **L** - Lake
- **M** - Motor Rental
- **N** - No Motors
- **P** - Pontoon
- **PB** - Paddle Boat
- **R** - River
- **SK** - Skis
- **SS** - Snowshoe
- **SP** - Speed Limit
- **ST** - Stream

STATE FORESTS

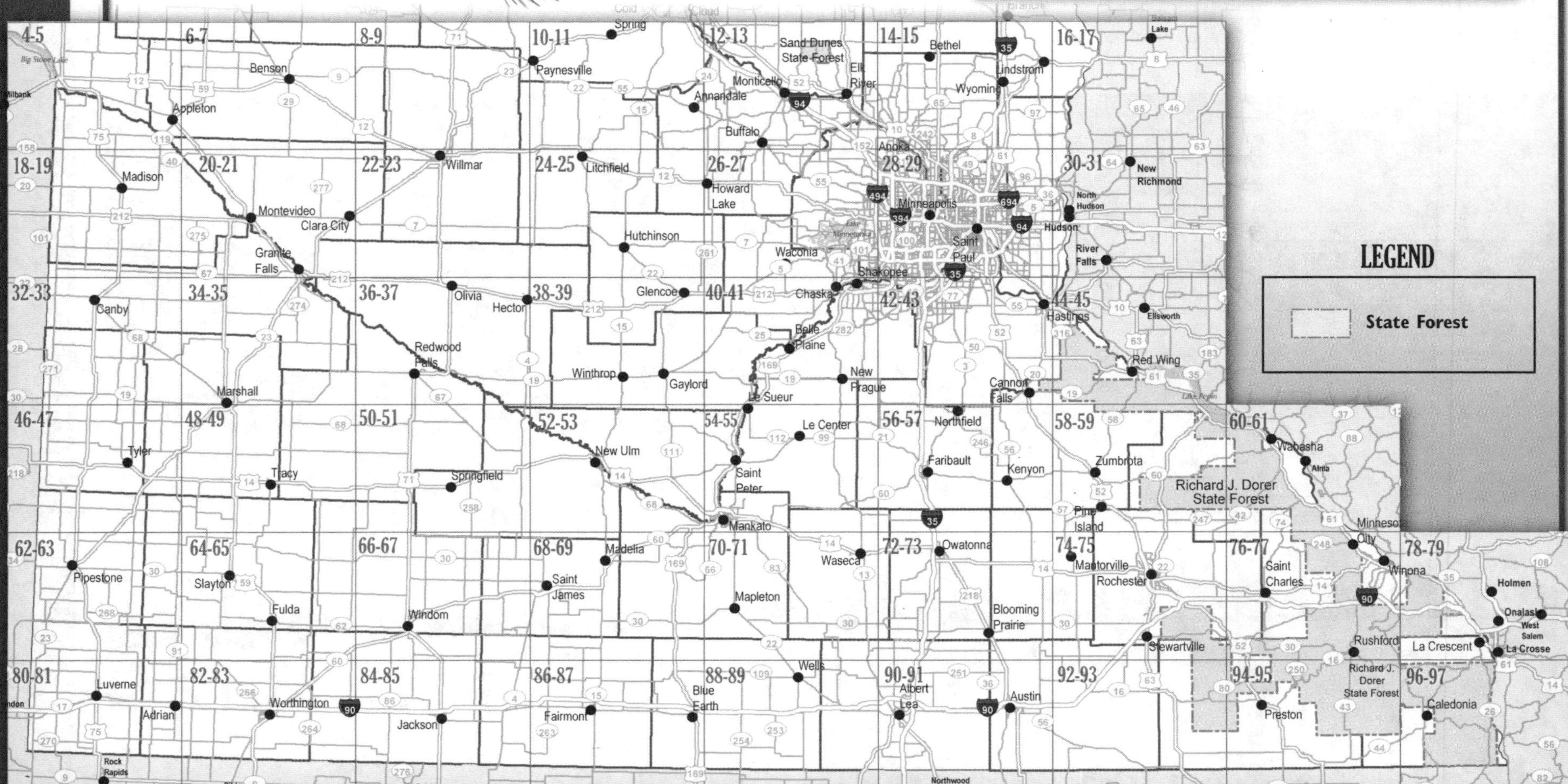

> **Minnesota's woods are nearly as famous as its waters. A network of 58 state forests encompasses nearly 4 million acres. Some forests are less than 1,000 acres in extent, while others are several hundred thousand acres in size. Although they are actively managed for timber production, state forests are also important areas for outdoor recreation. Most forests are open to a variety of activities, including camping, hiking, mountain biking, fishing, hunting, skiing, bird watching, mushroom and berry picking, and more. Activities such as photography and wildlife viewing are strongly encouraged.**

State forest campgrounds are generally less developed than state park facilities, lacking amenities such as showers and flush toilets. Visitors instead find a more self-directed experience awaiting them.

State forests provide miles of trails for hiking, skiing, biking, snowmobiling, and riding off-highway vehicles. More than 2,000 miles of forest roads and numerous logging roads are open to many of these activities unless otherwise posted. In addition, there are more than 150 miles of hiking and ski trails that are closed to motor vehicles. You'll also find some roads (and campgrounds) specifically suited to horseback riding. Mountain bikes are allowed on most public and state forest roads, while OHVs are allowed on forest roads and trails not closed to motor vehicles. Many state forest snowmobile trails receive regular grooming and link up to state trails.

The pride and joy of southern Minnesota state forests is undoubtedly the massive Richard J. Dorer Memorial Hardwood State Forest. This expanse of woods spreads through seven counties, encompassing some 1 million acres. Much of the land runs along the bluffs framing the Mississippi River and many of the big river's watersheds. The region is rich in wetlands and sloughs and features abundant bird, mammal, and plant life; blue-ribbon trout fisheries; steep cliffs; hiking, biking, and cross-country ski trails; several state parks; and some of the most jaw-dropping scenery in the state.

STATE FORESTS

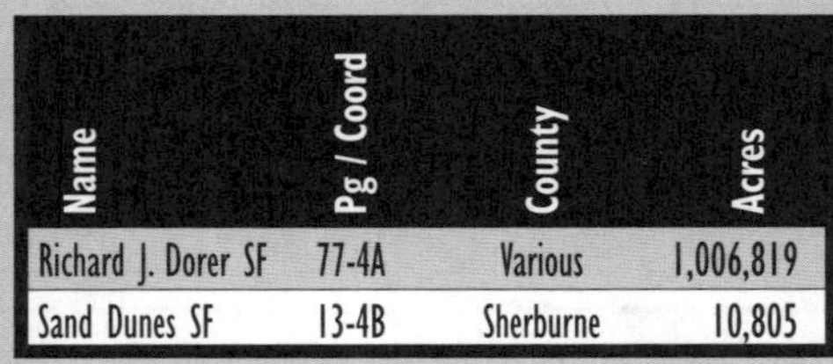

Name	Pg / Coord	County	Acres
Richard J. Dorer SF	77-4A	Various	1,006,819
Sand Dunes SF	13-4B	Sherburne	10,805

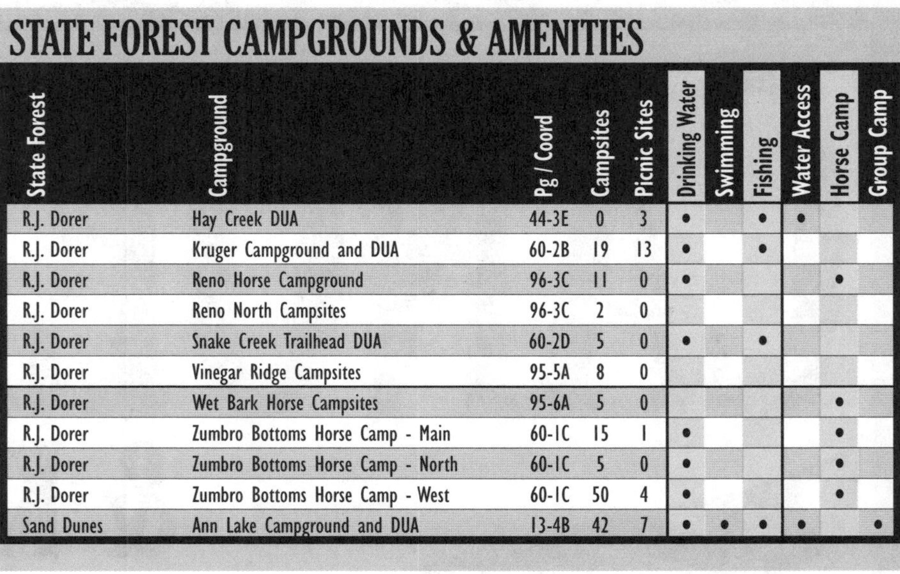

STATE FOREST CAMPGROUNDS & AMENITIES

State Forest	Campground	Pg / Coord	Campsites	Picnic Sites	Drinking Water	Swimming	Fishing	Water Access	Horse Camp	Group Camp
R.J. Dorer	Hay Creek DUA	44-3E	0	3	•		•	•		
R.J. Dorer	Kruger Campground and DUA	60-2B	19	13	•		•			
R.J. Dorer	Reno Horse Campground	96-3C	11	0	•				•	
R.J. Dorer	Reno North Campsites	96-3C	2	0						
R.J. Dorer	Snake Creek Trailhead DUA	60-2D	5	0	•		•			
R.J. Dorer	Vinegar Ridge Campsites	95-5A	8	0						
R.J. Dorer	Wet Bark Horse Campsites	95-6A	5	0					•	
R.J. Dorer	Zumbro Bottoms Horse Camp - Main	60-1C	15	1	•				•	
R.J. Dorer	Zumbro Bottoms Horse Camp - North	60-1C	5	0	•				•	
R.J. Dorer	Zumbro Bottoms Horse Camp - West	60-1C	50	4	•				•	
Sand Dunes	Ann Lake Campground and DUA	13-4B	42	7	•	•	•	•		•

STATE FOREST TRAILS

Name	Segment	Pg / Coord	MILES OF TRAIL: Total Summer Trails	Forest Roads	Walking-Hunting-Hiking	Cross-Country Ski	Forestry-Snowmobile	Horseback Riding	Mountain Bike	ATV	Off-Road Motorcycle	Off-Road Vehicle
R.J. Dorer	Vinegar Ridge	95-6A	6.2		6.2		6.2					
R.J. Dorer	Isinours	94-2B	3.2	0.2	3.2	3.2						
R.J. Dorer	Snake Creek	60-2D	22.1		3.7	3.7		13.5		14.4	14.4	
R.J. Dorer	Bronk	76-3A	6.5			6.5		6.5	6.5			
R.J. Dorer	Oak Ridge	95-5C	10.8	4.8		6		6				
R.J. Dorer	Zumbro Bottoms	59-5C	46	10.2				46				
R.J. Dorer	Kruger	60-1C	11	1				11				
R.J. Dorer	Trout Valley	60-3E	7				7	7		7	7	
R.J. Dorer	Hay Creek	44-3E	32.9	0.2		5.6	10.6	16.7				
R.J. Dorer	Reno	96-3C	29.8				15		14.8			
R.J. Dorer	Brightsdale	94-2B	5.7	0.6	5.7	5.7						
R.J. Dorer	Money Creek	77-6E	0					6.2				
Sand Dunes		13-4B	53	12	4	4	23	26				

CANOEING & KAYAKING

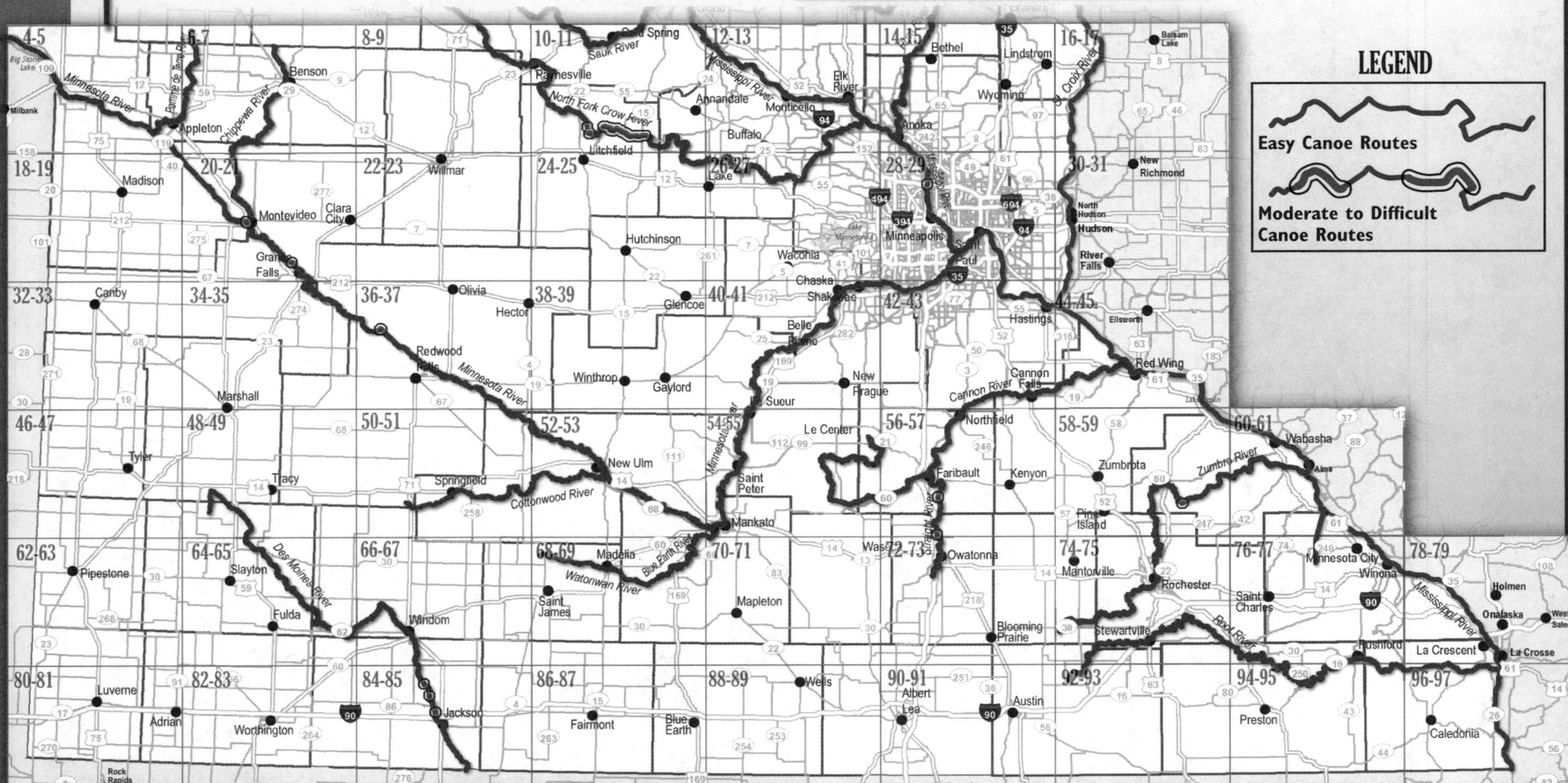

Canoeing in Minnesota is a popular activity. One obvious reason is because the state is home to the Minnesota icon: the Boundary Waters Canoe Area Wilderness. At 1.3 million acres with more than 1,200 miles of canoe routes, it's a paddler's delight. Motors are not allowed in most areas of the BWCA, so canoes are the only game in town. Loading a canoe with a week's worth of gear and sleeping under the stars is a Minnesota tradition.

But the BWCA isn't the only place to dip a paddle. Thousands of small pothole lakes and numerous rivers in the southern part of the state are just begging to be explored, and on small, out-of-the-way gems, canoes are the way to go. A canoe can be carried relatively easily into small lakes and ponds, offering adventurous souls untapped fishing, hunting and wildlife watching opportunities. Canoes are quiet, which will help you see more wildlife, including deer, eagles, ducks, geese and loons. And despite their tippy reputation, a wide, stable canoe will allow you to fish all day without worrying about taking an unexpected swim.

River	Segment	Pg / Coord	Miles	Camping	Rental/Shuttle	State Park Access	Notes
Cannon		56-3A	80	•	•	•	Wooded valley, bluffs, nice river towns
Chippewa		6-2E	50				Bluffs, heavily wooded banks, farmland scenery
Cottonwood		51-5D	65	•		•	Narrow tributary of the Minnesota River. Forested, farmland
Des Moines		65-5D	70	•	•	•	Farmland with areas of hills, woods, and bluffs
Minnesota	Ortonville to Granite Falls	20-1A	81	•	•	•	Broad, bottomland forest, bluffs, and farmland
Minnesota	Granite Falls to Highway 4	36-2C	91	•	•	•	Bottomland forest, ancient rock outcroppings
Minnesota	Highway 4 to Le Sueur	53-4D	109	•	•	•	Broad bottomland forest
Minnesota	Le Sueur to Fort Snelling State Park	41-5B	87	•		•	Broad, sandy banks, bottomland forest, power boats
Mississippi	Anoka to Fort Snelling State Park	28-2B	35	•	•	•	Wooded to urban, bluffs, Lock and Dam #1, power boats
Mississippi	Fort Snelling State Park to Hastings	29-4E	35	•	•		Dramatic bluffs, forest, Lock and Dam #2, power boats
Mississippi	Hastings to Red Wing	44-2C	27	•			Extensive backwaters, Lock and Dam #3, power boats
Mississippi	La Crescent to Iowa border	96-3B	31	•			Bluffs, forests, islands, Lock and Dam #8, power boats
Mississippi	Red Wing to Wabasha	45-5E	34	•		•	Through Lake Pepin, islands, power boats
Mississippi	St. Cloud to Anoka	12-3C	57	•	•		Mixed hardwood forest, sandbars, good fishing
Mississippi	Wabasha to Winona	60-3D	38	•	•		Bluffs, forests, islands, Lock and Dam #4 and #5, power boats
Mississippi	Winona to La Crescent	78-2C	31	•	•		Bluffs, forests, islands, Lock and Dam #6 and #7, power boats
North Fork Crow		10-3E	126	•	•		Shallow, passes through prairie, farmland and lowlands
Pomme de Terre		6-1C	25	•			Bottomland forest, wooded banks, farmland
Root		76-2E	111	•	•		Limestone bluffs, hardwood forest, Root River Trail
Rum		14-3B	145	•	•	•	Easy rapids, good fishing, dense hardwood forest
Sauk		10-2A	90	•	•		Prairie grasslands, hardwood forests, abundant waterfowl.
St. Croix	Wild River State Park to William O'Brien State Park	16-2C	32	•	•	•	Potholes, rapids, towering cliffs at Taylor's Falls
St. Croix	William O'Brien State Park to Mississippi River	30-1C	48	•	•	•	Broad and placid, islands, sandbars, power boats
Straight		56-2E	34				Narrow through wooded farm land, good day trip
Watonwan / Blue Earth		69-4B	35	•			Tributary of the Minnesota River. Forested, farmland
Whitewater		60-3E	18				Deep valley, high limestone bluffs, dense forest
Zumbro		75-4A	115	•	•		Deep valley, high limestone bluffs, dense forest

Canoeing & Kayaking

If it's pure recreation you're seeking, canoes are hard to beat. A paddle down a river you've never been to makes a great adventure. It's also fun just to tool around in your craft, or go for an evening paddle as the sun sets on your favorite lake.

Vast prairies once covered most of southern Minnesota. Today, most of the prairies have been converted to fertile farmland. Many of the region's rivers flow through this type of landscape, including the Des Moines, Cottonwood, Cannon, Minnesota, Watonwan, Straight, and others.

However, the southeastern corner of the state bears stark contrast to the rest of the state. The crushing force of glaciers missed this region during the last ice age, and the area is characterized by scenic limestone bluffs and rich, almost jungle-like growth. Some of the most scenic waters in the state are found here, including the Root, Mississippi, St. Croix, and other rivers.

Where you paddle can dictate what you should paddle. Canoes are made of various materials to suit your paddling intentions. Aluminum is a great all-around choice because it is inexpensive and relatively light and durable. If you feel the need for speed or want to put on the miles, consider a Kevlar canoe. They are extremely light and you can really move in a Kevlar canoe, but they are expensive and can puncture easily if you hit a rock. Royalex canoes are a good middle-of-the-road choice. They are fairly light and durable, and moderately expensive. They are made with layers of lightweight foam sandwiched inside plastic. Rotomolded canoes are made of solid plastic. They are durable and can withstand rocky waters, but are relatively heavy. They are fairly inexpensive.

In recent years, kayaking has significantly grown in popularity. The basic difference between canoes and kayaks is kayaks are closed on top, and a paddler sits inside the closed cockpit (with the exception of sit-on-top kayaks, which are quite similar to canoes). Kayakers also use special paddles with blades on each end.

A variety of kayaks are available (with one- or two-person models in some cases), but most people use touring kayaks. This style is a good all-around choice for recreational paddlers. Touring kayaks are a compromise in style between sea kayaks and whitewater kayaks. Sea kayaks are long and slender and are designed for long-distance paddling. They track straight, but are not very maneuverable. Whitewater kayaks are made for navigating raging rivers. They are short and easy to maneuver, in order to avoid obstacles.

Kayakers enjoy their sport because their crafts take them into scenic territory and provide tranquility. A kayak, due to its snug-fitting nature, almost seems a part of you, and people who try kayaking often fall in love with the sport.

WILDLIFE VIEWING

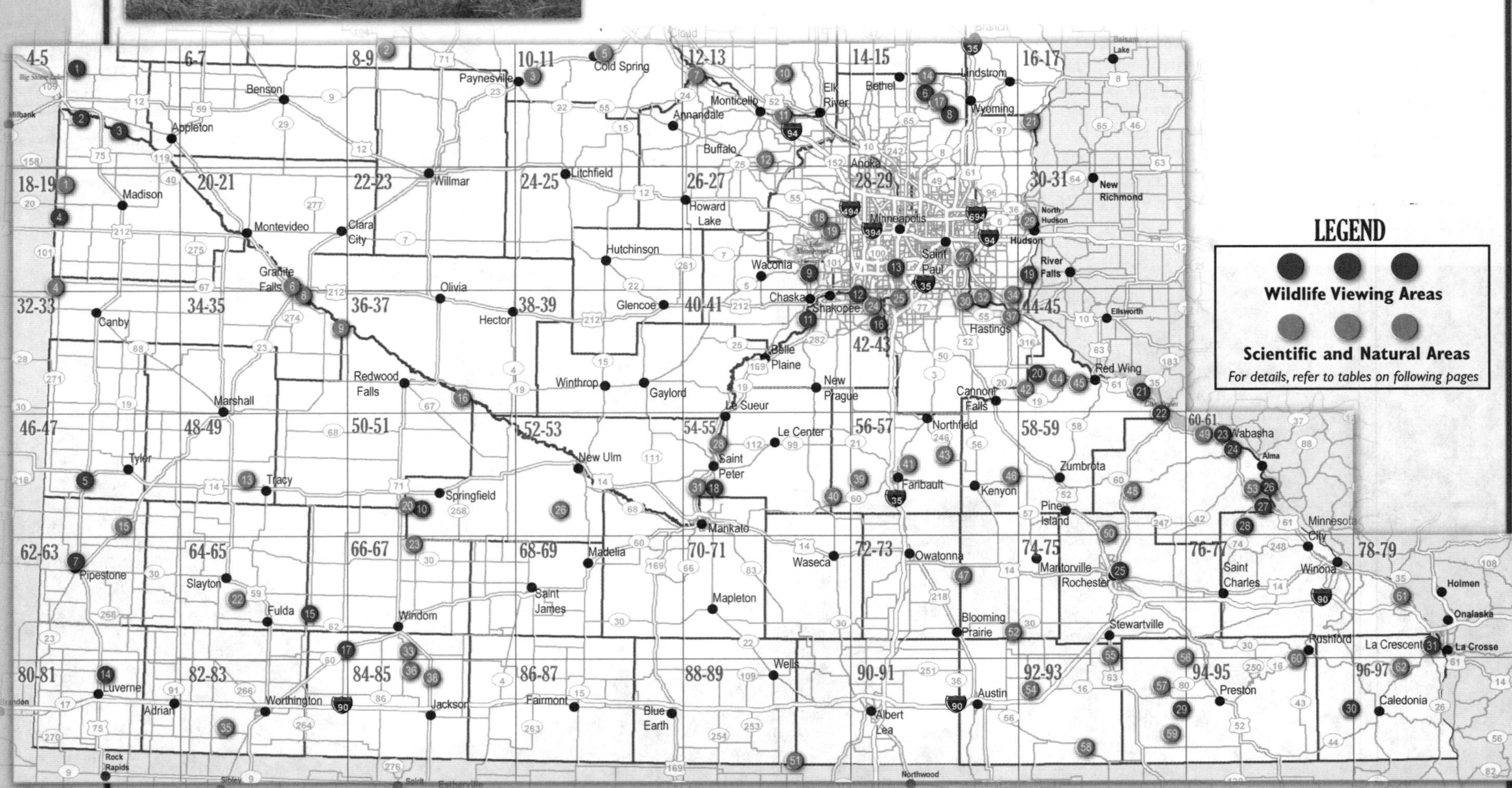

Wildlife watching, and bird watching in particular, has become one of the fastest-growing and most popular outdoor activities during the past two decades. It's a hobby that nearly anyone can participate in and requires little more equipment than binoculars and a field guide. Minnesota offers many superb wildlife-watching opportunities for common and uncommon species alike.

Surprises and delights await wildlife watchers across southern Minnesota. From its wooded eastern ridges to the fields and prairies of the west, wildlife enthusiasts will find an astonishingly diverse group of plants and animals. Southeastern Minnesota's bluffs attract many warblers and other songbirds in spring - drawn to the hardwood forests and river and stream valleys that make up this picturesque section of the state. The Mississippi River and its labyrinth of backwaters, in turn, are great places to see bald eagles, waterfowl, shorebirds, and other animals throughout the year. Surprisingly, some of the best bird watching can be had within the metropolitan sprawl of Minneapolis and St. Paul. These twin cities are home to numerous wooded parks that are visited by many migrant birds on their way north in spring and on their return journey south in fall. Plus, the Minnesota Valley National Wildlife Refuge runs for many miles within this urban corridor. Often overlooked are Minnesota's southwestern counties, where agriculture is heavy, but opportunities to see shorebirds, waterfowl, and grassland species are numerous. And extreme southwest Minnesota is unlike any other part of the state. With wide-open prairie, prickly-pear cactus, bison, and other plant and animals usually found farther west, visiting this region is like taking a giant step into the Great Plains of the central United States. The suggested wildlife-viewing areas listed on Page 141 are only starting points. Wildlife can be seen and enjoyed across much of southern Minnesota. Nature enthusiasts will find much more to explore in one of the region's more than 60 Scientific and Natural Areas, which host rare and endangered plants, animals, and other features in their natural communities. SNAs are open to public use, with some exceptions reserved for research/educational use.

In fact, the state boasts:

- The largest wolf population in the lower 48 states. An estimated 3,020 timber wolves live in Minnesota.
- More than 1 million white-tailed deer
- 428 recorded bird species
- 80 species of mammals
- More than 700 pairs of bald eagles
- 12,000 common loons - more than any other state in the Lower 48
- More than 20,000 black bears
- More than 4,000 moose
- 30 known breeding pairs of peregrine falcons
- More than 1,500 trumpeter swans

American bison *(Bison bison)*

James E. Knopf

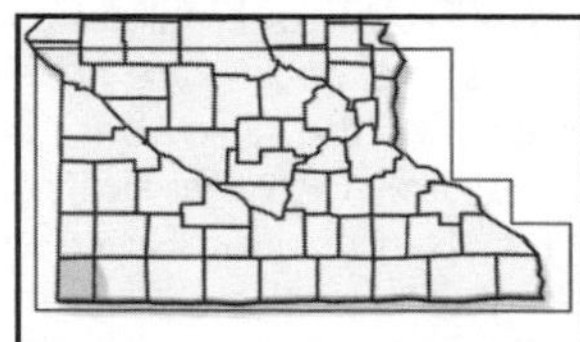

American bison are the largest mammals found in Minnesota, with mature bulls reaching one ton in weight and standing six feet high at the shoulder and spanning nine feet in length. These massive animals were once abundant on Minnesota's prairies and far beyond. By the beginning of the 20th century, however, American bison numbers had dwindled to a fraction of their original population due to market hunting and wholesale slaughter. Minnesota's wild bison population is now confined to Blue Mounds State Park in the state's southwest corner. Approximately 100 bison comprise the herd. Bison are grazing animals, eating mostly grasses and sedges.

Wild Fact: Bison are often called "buffalo," but they are actually a separate species from the "true" buffalo native to Africa and Asia only. The large shoulder hump of the American bison is one distinguishing feature. Buffalo don't have large humps on their backs.

Fisher *(Martes pennanti*

Dudley Edmondson

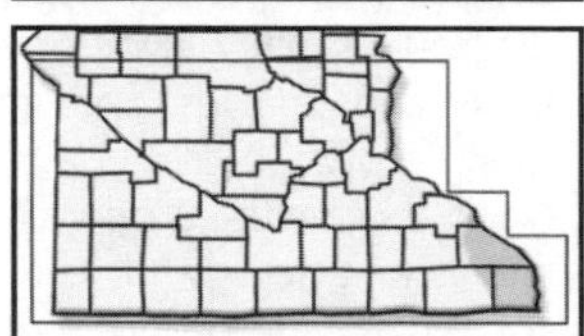

Fishers are large (males are much larger than females and can weigh more than 15 pounds) members of the weasel family. Fishers thrive in old stands of coniferous forests, particularly those near stands of deciduous woods. They are agile tree climbers and feed on chipmunks, squirrels, mice and even porcupines, along with nuts, berries and carrion. Contrary to its name, the fisher doesn't eat or catch fish. Minnesota is home to more than 10,000 of these animals.

Wild Fact: Fishers readily prey on porcupines. To avoid getting a face full of quills, fishers roll porcupines over onto their backs and then bite the porkie's soft throat and belly areas.

Mink *(Mustela vison)*

Richard C. Bennett

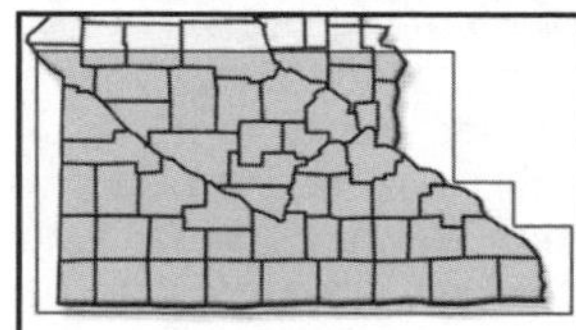

One of Minnesota's most widespread weasels, mink, nevertheless, are not often seen because of their nocturnal and solitary habits. Minks are rarely found far from lakes, rivers, or creeks, where they skillfully pluck fish from the water or dive to catch a meal. Additionally, mink eat ducks, frogs, mice, lizards, and muskrats. Mink tracks can often be seen in wet soil and sand along stream banks. Adult mink range from 14 to 20 inches long and can weigh up to 4 pounds. They nest in hollow logs, dig burrows into river banks or use muskrat dens to rear their young. Best known for their prized fur, mink wear a soft and silky dark-brown coat with long guard hairs that help repel water. A white patch is usually present on the throat or chest.

Wild Fact: Mink are expert swimmers, able to dive down 15 feet and swim for 100 feet underwater.

River Otter *(Lutra Canadensis)*

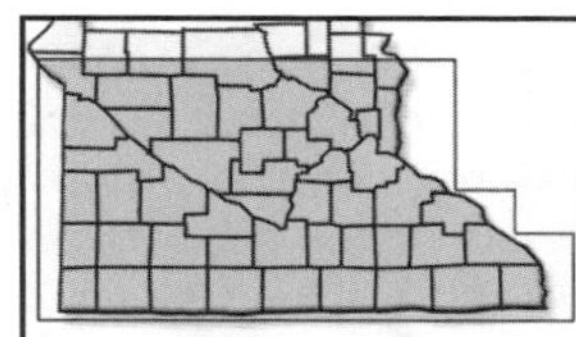

River otters are Minnesota's largest aquatic carnivore – a male adult can weigh upward of 30 pounds and measure four feet in length. River otters have webbed feet, long tails, and are strong, agile swimmers. They are found in rivers, streams, lakes, and ponds, primarily in northern Minnesota as well as along the Mississippi River. The DNR estimates the statewide population at 12,000.

Porcupine *(Erethizon dorsatum)*

Dan Bannister

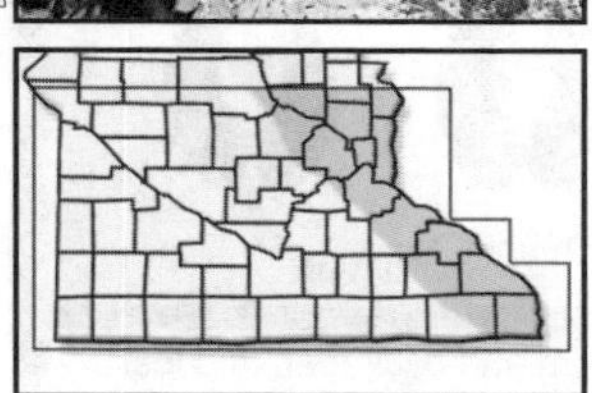

With an upper body armed with thousands of long, sharp quills, the porcupine is unlike any other animal found in Minnesota. These dark-gray forest dwellers can weigh upward of 35 pounds and be more than three feet long with a six-inch tail. Porcupines are primarily vegetarians, foraging on berries, nuts, tree bark, and conifer needles. Female porcupines give birth to one "porcupet" in the spring. Babies are born with open eyes and a full set of quills. Although porkies are lumbering, slow-movers, they are well protected from predators – few of which care to tangle with the quill-laden critter – and can live 20 years in the wild. The only predator of significance is the fisher, which is adept at rolling porcupines over onto their backs to attack the soft belly area.

Beaver *(Castor Canadensis)*

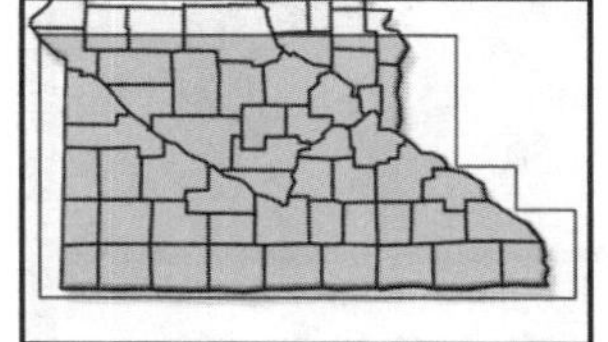

Beavers are the largest members of the rodent family, and can weigh more than 70 pounds. With a flat, paddle-like tail and huge front teeth, beavers are unlikely to be mistaken for another animal. They can be found throughout Minnesota, living near lakes and rivers with nearby trees. Beavers are vegetarians, consuming buds, leaves, twigs, fruits, stems, and roots. They are expert builders, creating dams and lodges from logs, sticks, brush, and mud.

Wild Fact: Beavers can chew through a six-inch tree in 15 minutes and can remain underwater for 20 minutes.

Wildlife Viewing Areas

Number	Name	County	Pg / Coord	Look For
1	Thielke Lake Wildlife Management Area	Big Stone	4-3A	Western grebes, American white pelicans, black and Forster's terns, great blue herons, great egrets, ring-billed gulls
2	Big Stone National Wildlife Refuge	Big Stone/Lac Qui Parle	4-3C	Migratory waterfowl; least, stilt, and pectoral sandpipers; loggerhead shrikes; short-eared owls; bobolinks; Swainson's hawks; orchard orioles, greater prairie-chickens
3	Lac Qui Parle Wildlife Management Area/State Park	Lac Qui Parle	5-4D	American white pelicans, double-crested cormorants, ring-billed gulls, Canada geese, cattle egrets, eastern grebes, Forster's terns, marbled godwits, river otters, white-tailed deer
4	Salt Lake Wildlife Management Area	Lac Qui Parle	18-2B	Minnesota's only alkaline wetland. Willets, piping plovers, sandpipers, eared grebes, Hudsonian and marbled godwits
5	Hole-In-The-Mountain Prairie	Lincoln	46-3C	Dakota skippers and other prairie butterflies; Richardson's ground squirrels; clay-colored, savannah, and vesper sparrows; bobolinks; dickcissels
6	Helen Allison Savanna Scientific and Natural Area	Anoka	14-3B	Lark sparrows, wood frogs, bull snakes
7	Pipestone National Monument	Pipestone	62-3A	Upland sandpipers, American woodcock, horned larks, bobolinks, western meadowlarks, orchard orioles, clay-colored sparrows, prairie falcons, painted turtles
8	Carlos Avery Wildlife Management Area	Anoka	15-4C	Bald eagles, trumpeter swans, sandhill cranes, belted kingfishers, green herons
9	Minnesota Landscape Arboretum	Hennepin	27-5E	Blue-gray gnatcatchers, swamp sparrows, great crested flycatchers, red-eyed vireos, sedge wrens, butterflies, ruby-throated hummingbirds, eastern wood-pewees
10	Cottonwood River Prairie Scientific and Natural Area	Brown	50-3D	Blue grosbeaks
11	Carver Park Reserve	Hennepin	27-4E	Ospreys, migrating/nesting waterfowl, ruby-throated hummingbirds, eastern bluebirds, bobolinks, white-tailed deer, raccoons
12	Minnesota Valley National Wildlife Refuge	Hennepin	42-1A	Spring warblers, American bitterns, Bell's vireos, willow flycatchers, beavers, wild turkeys, coyotes, white-tailed deer, bald eagles
13	Wood Lake Nature Center	Hennepin	28-2E	Yellow-headed blackbirds, Forster's terns, common yellowthroats
14	Blue Mounds State Park	Rock	81-4A	Bison; white-tailed jackrabbits; gray partridges; eastern screech-owls; sedge wrens; dickcissels; willow flycatchers; white-tailed deer; savannah, swamp, clay-colored and grasshopper sparrows
15	Talcot Lake Wildlife Management Area	Cottonwood	65-5D	American bitterns, Virginia and sora rails, indigo buntings, gray partridges, northern harriers, beavers, red fox, mink, white-tailed deer
16	Murphy-Hanrehan Park Reserve	Scott	42-1B	Yellow-bellied sapsuckers; Acadian flycatchers; American redstarts; ovenbirds; cerulean, yellow, hooded, golden-winged, blue-winged, chestnut-sided, prothonotary, Kentucky, and mourning warblers
17	Lindgren-Traeger Bird Sanctuary	Jackson	65-6E	Black-crowned night herons, Forster's terns, American bitterns, American avocets, Franklin's gulls
18	Kasota Prairie Scientific and Natural Area	Le Sueur	54-1C	Horned larks, loggerhead shrikes, upland sandpipers, ring-necked pheasants, white-tailed deer
19	Afton State Park	Washington	30-1E	Pileated woodpeckers, eastern bluebirds, spring warblers, white-tailed deer
20	Cannon River Turtle Preserve Scientific and Natural Area	Goodhue	44-2D	Wood turtles
21	Frontenac State Park	Goodhue	45-5E	Bald eagles, turkey vultures, spring warblers (early May), bobolinks, Louisiana waterthrushes, eastern meadowlarks, Bell's vireos, white-tailed deer, raccoons, opossums, red foxes, coyotes, woodchucks, various ground squirrels, beavers, and wild turkeys
22	Hok-Si-La Park	Goodhue	59-5A	Spring warblers; least, solitary, and spotted sandpipers; ruddy turnstones
23	Read's Landing	Wabasha	60-2B	Bald eagles
24	National Eagle Center	Wabasha	60-2B	Wintering bald eagles
25	Silver Lake	Olmsted	75-4B	Giant Canada geese
26	Kellogg-Weaver Dunes Scientific and Natural Area	Wabasha	60-3D	Blanding's turtles, ottoe skippers, regal fritillaries, bull snakes, Bell's vireos
27	Weaver Bottoms (Upper Mississippi National Wildlife Refuge)	Wabasha	60-3D	Tundra swans during fall migration (late Oct.-Nov)
28	Whitewater Wildlife Management Area/State Park	Winona	60-2E	Ospreys, belted kingfishers, red-shouldered hawks, wild turkeys, Karner blue butterflies, great egrets
29	Forestville/Mystery Cave State Park	Fillmore	93-6C	Wild turkeys, coyotes, timber rattlesnakes, little brown bats, red-shouldered hawks, house wrens, Blanding's turtles
30	Beaver Creek Valley State Park	Houston	96-1C	Acadian flycatchers, Louisiana waterthrushes, cerulean warblers, wild turkeys, timber rattlesnakes
31	Shepherd's Marsh	Houston	78-3E	Bald eagles, Bell's vireos, black terns, wood ducks, Virginia and sora rails, river otters, great blue herons, map and painted turtles

Wildlife Viewing -Mammals

Bison and white-tailed deer have two toes on each foot and leave heart-shaped prints. Dew claw (small hind toes) tracks may or may not be present. Bison tracks are wider and more squared off than a deer's. The pad at the back edge of the hoof is much wider than it is at the front edge.

Weasels have five toes on their front and back feet, and leave claw marks when they walk. They are bounders and bring their back feet together toward their front feet before lifting their front legs to run. Mink tracks resemble a fisher's, but are only about half the size.

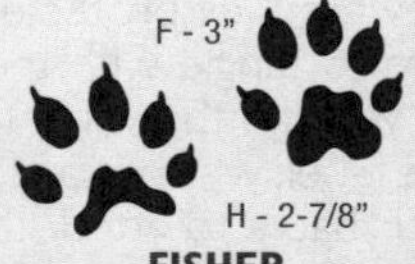

Otters have webbed front and rear feet with five toes and claws on each foot. Otters leave football-shaped toe prints and round pad prints. Beavers have hand-like front prints and larger, webbed rear prints. A beaver's back track lands on and often obscures part of the front print. Beavers and otters often leave an additional track as they drag their tails. Muskrats have four-toed front feet and five-toed hind feet. Their tracks show front and hind feet overlapping.

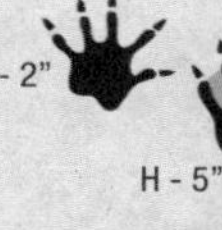

Porcupines have long hind feet with five toes and shorter front feet with just four toes. Claw marks are usually visible. A tail mark is sometimes visible.

F - 2-3/4"
H - 3-1/4"
PORCUPINE

Red foxes, gray foxes, coyotes, and other members of the dog family all have four toes and center pads. Unlike cats, dogs leave claw marks when they travel. A coyote's track is larger than a fox's.

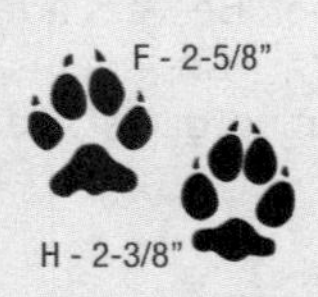

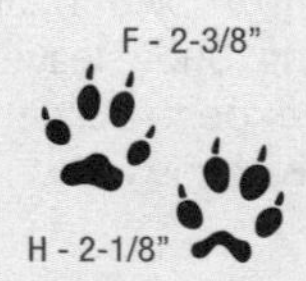

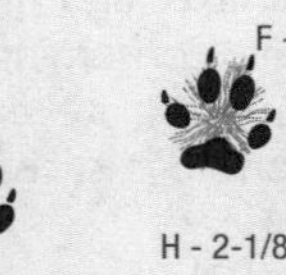

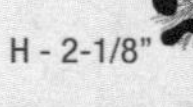

Raccoons have hand-like front feet, with five evenly spaced toes. Hind feet are longer. Tracks are paired, with a front foot appearing next to a hind foot. Claw marks are usually visible

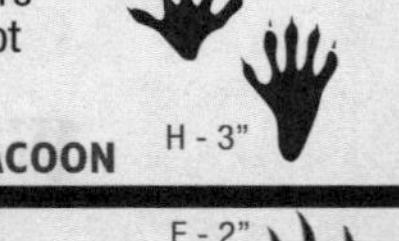

Badgers are pigeon-toed with long claws and large toe pads on the front feet; the hind feet have smaller pads and shorter claws.

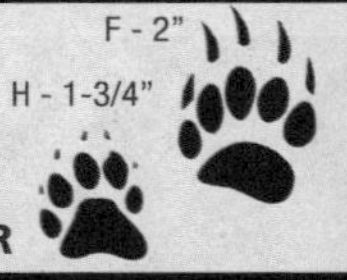

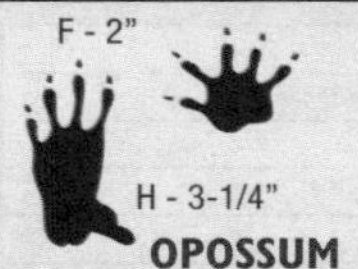

Opossums have five toes on all feet. The hind foot has an opposable "thumb," which makes a distinct track. The front and hind feet often overlap when walking.

Muskrat *(Ondatra zibethicus)*

Michael West

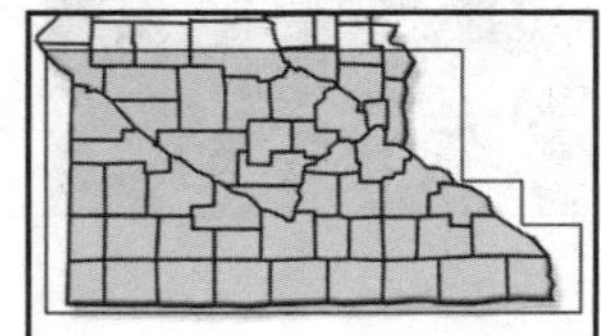

Muskrats are brownish-red rodents, weighing from two to five pounds and averaging about 20 inches in length. They make their homes in creeks, marshes, lakes, and similar wetland environments. Along with its cousin, the beaver, the muskrat is the only other mammal in Minnesota that builds its home on the water – often constructing a domed house of mud and plant materials. Not only do these structures provide shelter for the muskrat, ducks and geese often use them as nesting platforms. Muskrats are primarily plant eaters, with a particular fondness for cattails and other aquatic plants, although clams and fish also comprise their diet. They are prolific breeders, with a single female giving birth to three litters each summer.

Coyote *(Canis latrans)*

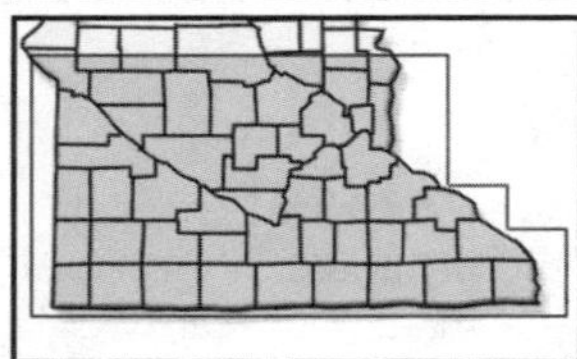

If you see an animal in the wild that resembles a small German Shepherd Dog (adult coyotes generally weigh between 20 and 30 pounds) it is likely a coyote. Like German Shepherds, coyotes have long, heavy fur and thick, bushy tails. These abundant and adaptable animals are found throughout Minnesota, but they are most at home in areas offering a combination of agricultural land and woodlands. Coyotes are often heard howling and/or barking at night, particularly in the fall.

Wild Fact: A male coyote's range can be more than 30 miles.

Gray fox *(Urocyon cinereoargentus)*

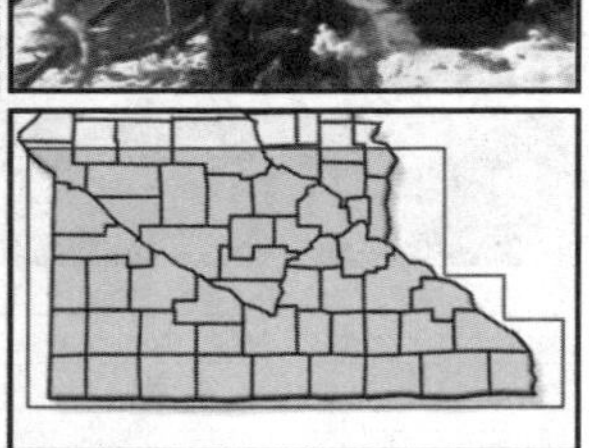

The gray fox is distinguished from the red fox by its gray fur and its largely nocturnal habits. However, parts of the neck, ears, chest, legs, feet, and tail are reddish-brown, which can lead to confusion when identifying the species. Gray foxes feed on cottontail rabbits, mice, birds, insects, corn, nuts, and fruits. They are at home in woodlands and brushy areas, and will seek hollow logs and trees, small caves, rock piles and other openings to den in. Grey foxes occasionally will modify a woodchuck's burrow, enlarging it to use as a den.

Wild Fact: Gray foxes are able to climb trees, and can readily hop from branch to branch while hunting or seeking refuge.

Red fox *(Vulpes vulpes)*

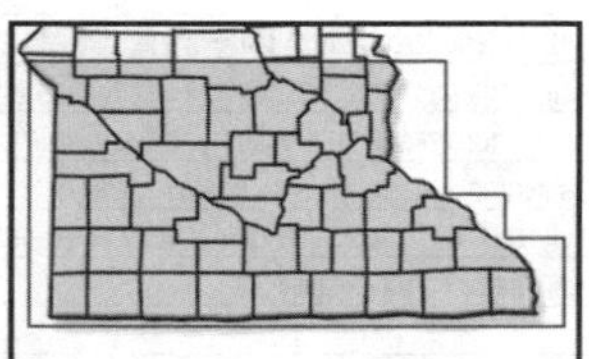

The red fox wears a thick coat of reddish-orange fur on its head, back, and sides. In contrast, its neck, chest, and tip of the tail are dressed in white, while its ears, legs and feet are black. Adult red foxes are medium-dog-sized and inhabit farmlands, prairies, and woodlands where they feed on acorns, apples, birds, corn, crickets, grasses, grasshoppers, and mice. Red foxes have very keen hearing, being particularly sensitive to low-frequency sounds, and can detect small animals underground and under snow cover.

Raccoon *(Procyon lotor)*

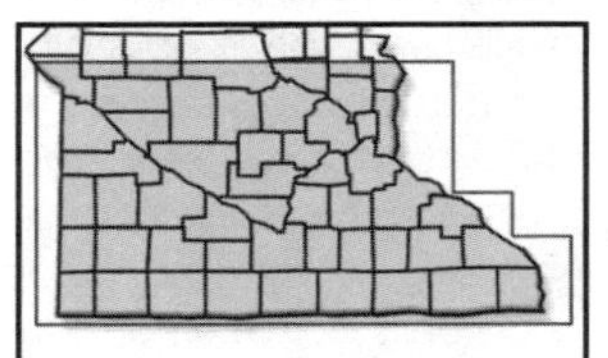

Raccoons are widespread in Minnesota, common in all but three counties (St. Louis, Lake, and Cook). Despite their abundance (state population estimate is 800,000 to 1 million animals), raccoons are rarely seen in the wild, because they are nocturnal and solitary in behavior. Raccoons are agile climbers – able to climb down trees forward and backward by rotating their back feet 180 degrees. They are also good swimmers and have excellent dexterity in their toes, enabling them to grasp and manipulate objects (including door knobs). Raccoons are omnivorous, eating everything from berries and nuts to insects, bird eggs, and mice. A raccoon's preferred habitat is near streams, where it hunts and uses water to enhance its sense of feel, rinsing to separate edible portions of food and discarding other foreign matter. Raccoons sleep most of the day; in winter, they may sleep for several weeks in a den, with many animals sharing the same shelter. In mid-winter, males and females mate, and after about two months a litter of three to six young (called "kits") is born. Adult raccoons average between 15 and 25 pounds, and measure about three feet in length.

Wild Fact: Though not known for their speed, raccoons can run up to 15 mph.

Badger *(Taxidea taxus)*

Gary M Stolz

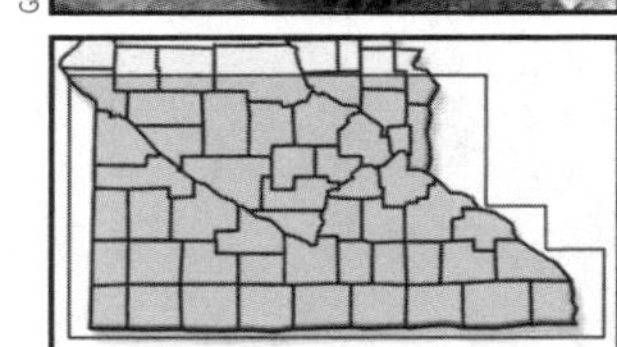

Badgers are stocky, muscular members of the weasel family capable of growing to 30 pounds. They favor open fields and prairies. Sporting long, brownish-gray hair, a black-and-white striped face, and short legs and tail, a badger has a broad, stout appearance. Nocturnal and secretive, they are rarely seen in the wild, partly because much of the day is spent below ground. The feisty badger uses its powerful legs and long claws to burrow into the ground, creating tunnels leading to a den. Badgers eat insects including bumblebees, small mammals, ground-nesting birds and their eggs, and carrion. If cornered, badgers will attack tenaciously. They are also capable of releasing a skunk-like scent to ward off predators.

Virginia opossum *(Didelphis virginiana)*

Michael West

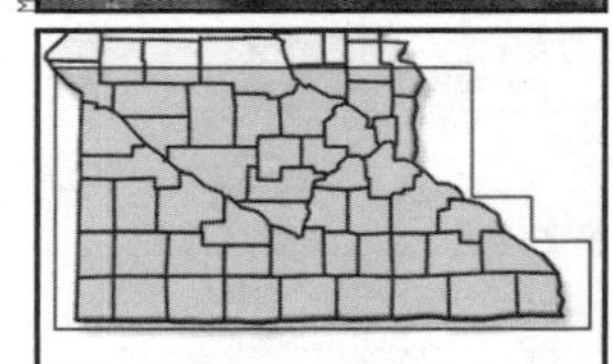

The Virginia opossum is North America's only marsupial – related to kangaroos and other pouched mammals found a hemisphere away in Australia. Opossums weigh from four to 10 pounds and can measure three feet long from nose to tail. Opossums are excellent tree climbers, and use the opposable toe on each hind foot to aid in grasping. They also have a prehensile tail that can wrap around tree limbs. Opossums are found in woodlands in central and southern Minnesota. Their hairless ears, nose, and tail don't offer adequate protection from extreme cold, and these parts are susceptible to frostbite. Opossums are nocturnal omnivores, consuming bird eggs, fruits, insects, seeds, and carrion. They give birth to very small, partially developed young. Newborns must crawl up the mother's chest, into her pouch and find a teat to suckle. They'll remain in the pouch for about two months, and then spend another month climbing in and out of the pouch, feeding on their mother's milk. When the young are about two inches long, they climb onto their mother's back, staying close to her until they are capable of more independent activity.

Wild Fact: Opossums have a natural resistance to snake venom and sometimes eat rattlesnakes. They are also the only furbearers with an opposable toe.

Birds of Prey - Bird Watching

USFWS / Dave Menke

Bald eagle

(Haliaeetus leucocephalus)

There are few sights in nature as thrilling as a soaring bald eagle. The majestic bird, with its wide, brown wings, white head, yellow bill, penetrating eyes, and hook-like talons, is always a welcome addition to any bird watcher's day. Bald eagles are most often found near lakes and rivers, where they use their excellent vision to locate fish, water birds, or small mammals from the air. Eagles generally mate for life and build massive nests out of large sticks in trees, often using the same nest for several years.

Wild Fact: A bald eagle's nest can weigh 2,000 pounds.

Osprey *(Pandion haliaetus)*

Ospreys are large, powerful birds and master fish catchers (live fish comprise nearly all of their diet). Sporting a curved bill, intense yellow eyes, white head with dark eye stripe, white crown and forehead, dark brown back and wings, and white breast, the osprey is a most imposing-looking predator. At home near lakes, rivers, and marshes, ospreys will dive feet-first into the water to seize prey, sometimes descending below the surface. Sharp spines on the toes and recurved talons prevent fish from escaping an osprey's grasp. Ospreys nest in treetops, building large stick nests that may be used for several years.

Wild Fact: Ospreys can close their nostrils while underwater.

Scientific and Natural Areas

Number	SNA Name	Pg / Coord	Acres	Ecological Interest
49	Bald Eagle Bluff	60-1A	22	Roosting site for wintering bald eagles
25	Black Dog	42-2A	126	Mesic prairie and calcareous fen communities (very rare in MN); spring/summer wildflowers
6	Blue Devil Valley	21-4E	30	Large population of rare lizard: five-lined skink; spring/summer/fall wildflowers
17	Boot Lake	14-3C	592	SNA within ice-block lake chain; rare plants; Blanding's turtles, Louisiana waterthrushes, white-tailed deer
2	Bruce Hitman Heron Rookery	8-2A	6	Water bird rookery (herons, egrets, cormorants); closed to public April 1-July 15
44	Cannon River Turtle Preserve	44-2D	836	Floodplain forest; wood turtles; sand bars
41	Cannon River Trout Lily	56-2C	95	Maple-basswood community containing dwarf trout lily
16	Cedar Mountain	37-4E	317	SNA lies on bedrock more than 3 billion years old; rare plants include prairie bush clover, prickly pear cactus, and water hyssop
28	Chamberlain Woods	54-2A	254	Large basswoods, cottonwoods, and elms; oak savanna in uplands
59	Cherry Grove Blind Valley	93-6D	40	Large cave system; sinkholes; streams; rare speleothem formations; calcite formations
7	Clear Lake	12-1A	62	Oak forest, floodplain forest, and sumac thicket; rare plant: Hill's thistle
5	Cold Spring Heron Colony	10-3A	62	Former heron rookery; open floodplain meadow and floodplain forest; visitation by permit only
35	Compass Prairie	82-2C	20	Largest remaining prairie in Nobles County; compass plants, powesheik skippers
20	Cottonwood River Prairie	50-3D	181	Prairie wildflowers; rare prairie bush clover
33	Des Moines River	66-2E	210	Large population of rare prairie bush clover
21	Falls Creek	16-1D	136	Virgin hardwood and white pine forest; rare plants; spring wildflowers
13	Glynn Prairie	48-3C	80	Mesic blacksoil prairie; many prairie grasses and wildflowers
8	Gneiss Outcrops	35-5A	241	Ancient gneiss outcrops more than 3 billion years old; Great Plains prickly pear and brittle cactus
32	Grey Cloud Dunes	43-5A	220	Sand terraces and dunes along Mississippi River; sea-beach needlegrass; blue racers (snake uncommon in MN)
37	Hastings	43-6B	69	Upland hardwood and floodplain forests; spring wildflowers
14	Helen Allison Savanna	14-3B	86	Illustrative of sand dune plant succession; oak sand savanna, dry prairie, sedge marsh; spring wildflowers
36	Holthe Prairie	34-3A	148	Calcareous seepage fen; numerous native forbs and grasses
47	Hythecker Prairie	73-4B	40	Mesic tallgrass prairie; spring/summer wildflowers
52	Iron Horse Prairie	73-6D	35	Mesic tallgrass prairie; spring/summer wildflowers
26	Joseph A. Tauer Prairie	52-2D	80	Undisturbed mesic/wet mesic prairies contain two rare plants: tuberous Indian plantain and rattlesnake master
31	Kasota Prairie	54-1D	42	High rock terrace; prairie, wet meadow, oak, woodland, and lowland hardwood plant communities; horned larks, loggerhead shrikes
53	Kellogg-Weaver Dunes	60-3D	1,004	Rolling sand dunes; large population of Blanding's turtles; rough-seeded fameflower blooms midsummer in late afternoon
61	King's and Queen's Bluff	78-2C	178	Varied plant communities and types with many rare plants; summer wildflowers
34	Lost Valley Prairie	43-6A	200	Bluff prairie; contains rock sandwort, rare in rest of MN; summer wildflowers
22	Lundblad	64-2C	80	Mesic prairie containing many prairie plants such as big bluestem, goldenrod, and prairie rose
12	Mary Schmidt Crawford Woods	12-3E	120	Maple-basswood forest; wetlands; spring wildflowers
11	Mississippi River Islands	13-4C	73	Five-island complex formed by river outwash
62	Mound Prairie	96-2A	257	Three goat prairies containing rare plants including goat's rue, jeweled shooting star, and Ohio spiderwort
4	Mound Springs Prairie	32-2A	465	Large, dry prairie; calcareous seepage fen; varied grasses and wildflowers
46	North Fork Zumbro Woods	57-6C	65	Maple-basswood forest; floodplain forest; lowland hardwood forest; dwarf trout lily, snow trillium, glade mallow
50	Oronoco Prairie	58-3E	80	80-acre kame; dry gravel and bedrock bluff prairie; rare plants include white wild indigo, tuberous Indian paintain, and Hill's thistle
51	Osmundson Prairie	89-4E	6	Mesic blacksoil prairie remnant; spring/summer wildflowers
27	Pig's Eye Island Heron Rookery	29-4D	100	Rookery for herons and cormorants; one of few areas in MN where yellow-crowned night herons nest
56	Pin Oak Prairie	75-6E	184	Wet meadow community - rare in bluffland environment; dry, barrens prairie; oak forest
30	Pine Bend Bluffs	43-4A	185	Relatively undisturbed site along lower Mississippi River; mesic oak forest; 200-foot bluffs
38	Prairie Bush Clover	84-3A	25	Large population of prairie bush clover; small calcareous fen; summer wildflowers
15	Prairie Coteau	47-4E	329	Southwestern dry hill and dry sand-gravel prairie; sheer slopes; rare butterflies; numerous wildflower species
43	Prairie Creek Woods	57-4B	87	Contains rare dwarf trout lily - blooms in April
55	Racine Prairie	75-4E	6	Small mesic prairie contains four rare plants: wild quinine, white wild indigo, rattlesnake master, and compass plant
42	River Terrace Prairie	44-1E	84	Gravel prairie community; large population of the rare kitten tail
23	Rock Ridge Prairie	66-3A	200	Blacksoil prairie lying along Sioux quartzite outcrops
3	Roscoe Prairie	10-1A	57	Undisturbed blacksoil prairie; Dakota skippers, marbled godwits, American woodcock; spring/summer wildflowers
60	Rushford Sand Barrens	95-4A	230	Dry-sand oak and jack pine savannas; rare plants include rough-seeded fameflower, clasping milkweed, and witch hazel
24	Savage Fen	42-1A	45	Rare wetland plant community includes valerian and marsh arrow grass
58	Shooting Star Prairie	92-3D	8	Mesic tallgrass prairie remnant; spring/summer wildflowers
45	Spring Creek Prairie	44-2D	145	Maple-basswood community; bedrock bluff prairie contains two rare plants: silvery bladderpod and long-bearded hawkweed
29	St. Croix Savanna	30-1C	112	Hill prairie and oak savanna; varied grass species; rare plants include kitten tail, James' polanisia, and Illinois tick-trefoil
9	Swedes Forest	35-6B	202	Granite outcrop community home to rare five-lined skink; undisturbed wetlands
40	Townsend Woods	55-5D	73	Virgin forest of sugar maple, red oak, and basswood; spring wildflowers
10	Uncas Dunes	13-4B	745	Relic dune field associated with Glacial Lake Grantsburg; rare Uncas skipper found here; summer wildflowers
39	Whitney Island	56-1C	40	Upland and floodplain forests; good bird watching for warblers
54	Wild Indigo Prairie	91-5B	150	Mesic tallgrass prairie; more than 300 native plant species
18	Wolsfeld Woods	27-5C	221	Remnant of the "Big Woods," with mature hardwoods; spring wildflowers
19	Wood-Rill	27-5C	150	Undisturbed old-growth forest with some trees 400 years old; spring wildflowers
57	Wykoff Balsam Fir	93-5B	62	Contains plants usually found further north including balsam fir, white pine, and sugar maple; rare plants and snails
1	Yellow Bank Hills	18-2A	80	Sand-gravel prairie; plants rare to MN: Missouri milkvetch, Nuttall's violet, soft goldenrod; prairie vole; summer wildflowers
48	Zumbro Falls Woods	59-4D	300	Steep bluffs; dolomite outcrops; jeweled shooting stars; spring wildflowers

National Wildlife Refuges

Name	Acres	Pg / Coord	Location	Season	Visitor Center	Visitor Center Open Weekends	Walk-In Only Areas	Day Use Only	Food/Lodging Near	Literature	Educational Programs	Auto Tour Route	Hiking Trails	Viewing Sites	Archaeological Sites	Wilderness Areas	Non-Motorized Water	Motorized Water	Hunting	Fishing
Big Stone NWR	11,521	4-3C	3 miles south of Ortonville, on Highway 7	Spring/Fall			●	●	●	●		●	●	●	●		●		●	●
Minnesota Valley NWR	12,000	42-1A	Visitor center is located in Bloomington, across from the Airport Hilton Hotel. From I-494, exit on 34th Ave. and drive south. Turn left on American Blvd. East and drive 1/4 mile to the entrance.	Spring/Summer/Fall	●	●	●	●	●	●	●		●	●	●				●	●
Northern Tallgrass Prairie NWR	77,000	4-3C	In scattered tracts across Minnesota and Iowa. The refuge is administered from the Big Stone NWR headquarters.	Spring/Summer																
Sherburne NWR	30,700	13-4A	5 miles west of Zimmerman	Spring/Summer/Fall	●		●	●	●	●		●	●	●			●		●	●
Upper Mississippi NWR	32,000	97-4B	50 river miles, from north of Nelson, WI south to Trempealeau, WI	Spring/Summer/Fall/Winter																

Northern harrier *(Circus cyaneus)*

Dudley Edmondson

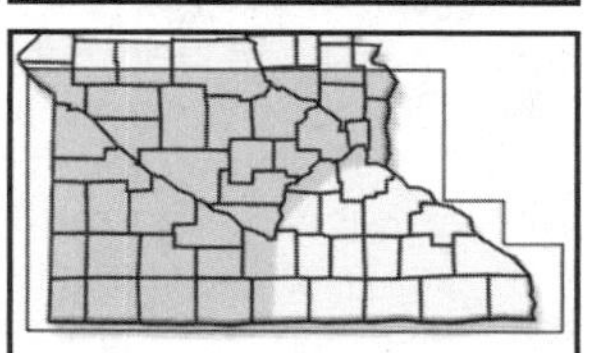

Because it often patrols marshes and wet meadows, flying low over emergent vegetation as it hunts small animals, the northern harrier was once called "marsh hawk." Harriers build nests in cattails and other tall vegetation from sticks and grasses. Females incubate a clutch of three to six eggs for about one month. Harriers can be difficult to identify, as immature birds, adult females, and adult males are all dissimilar in appearance. Juveniles have rich, brown plumage on their wings and backs, with reddish-brown breasts. Adult males have blueish-gray upper parts and grayish-white underparts. Adult females are larger than males (up to 24 inches long with four-foot wingspans), but sport the same colorations as immature birds and have copious streaking on the underparts. To make a positive ID, look for the harrier's long tail, black wing tips, and white rump, which are visible during flight. Like all birds of prey, harriers have excellent eyesight; they also have facial discs similar to owls, which allow them to hunt by sound as well.

Peregrine falcon *(Falco peregrinus)*

Karl R. Martin

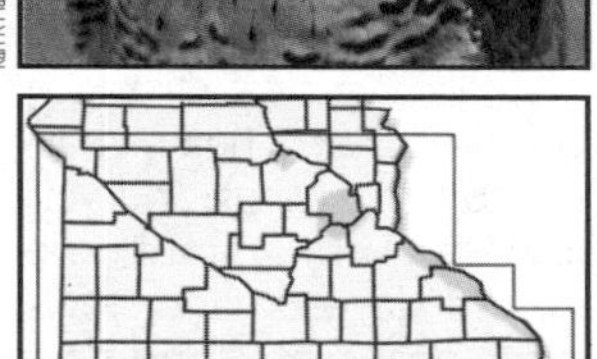

Capable of achieving speeds greater than 200 mph, the peregrine falcon is acknowledged as the fastest flyer in the bird world. These acrobatic aerialists hunt from the sky, swooping down on other birds and hitting them in midair with closed feet. Peregrines are generally smaller than gyrfalcons (14 to 20 inches), with a wingspan measuring 36 to 42 inches. Adult peregrines have dark heads with black marks under the eyes. The under parts are white with black spotting and barring.

Wild Fact: Peregrines may travel 15,000 miles in one year, journeying between their South American wintering grounds and their breeding grounds on the Canadian and Alaskan tundra.

Long-eared owl *(Asio otus)*

Dudley Edmondson

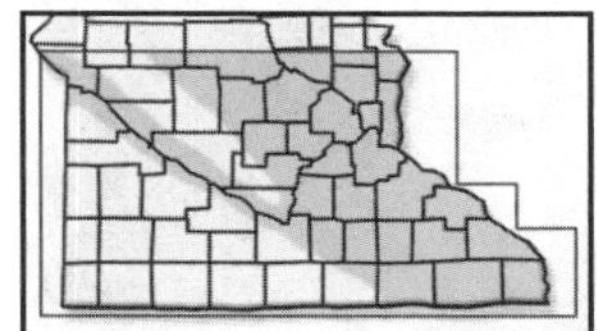

Like many nocturnal animals, long-eared owls are more common than sightings would indicate. With its preference for thick forests, secretive habits, and plumage that matches its surroundings, it's not surprising that this owl is often overlooked. Long-eared owls are medium-sized birds, measuring 14 to 16 inches with three-foot wingspans. They have markedly long ear tufts, thin bodies, mottled brown plumage, heavily streaked chests, yellow eyes, copper-colored facial discs, and white feathers between their eyes that form an X. They are master night hunters, capable of locating and capturing mice and other small mammals in total darkness as they fly low over open ground before dispatching prey with a bite to the back of the skull. Long-eared owls are opportunistic nesters, often using an abandoned crow or hawk nest to lay their eggs in and rear young.

Bird Watching -Birds of Prey

Eastern screech-owl *(Otus asio)*

Brian McEntire

Eastern screech-owls are year-round residents of southern Minnesota, occupying mature deciduous woodlands, suburban parks, and other treed areas where natural nesting cavities exist. These small owls (8 to 9 inches long, 20-inch wingspan) are cryptically colored, with heavily streaked reddish or grayish plumage that blends almost perfectly with the bark of trees where they perch and nest. They have visible ear tufts, yellow eyes, and large feet with feathered toes. Screech-owls spend most of the day sleeping, tucked into a tree cavity, and hunt at night, catching moths on the fly as well as eating fish and small birds. They mate in late winter in Minnesota, with females incubating a clutch of two to six white eggs for a month. Owlets are born with a layer of white down with eyes closed and are tended by their parents for about two months.

Wild Fact: Eastern screech-owls are polychromatic, exhibiting one of two color morphs: red or gray. The red morph is less common in Minnesota, as birds in this plumage are not as winter-hardy.

Barred owl *(Strix varia)*

Peter Darcy

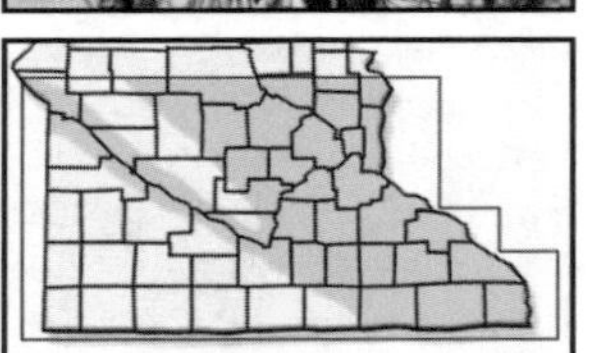

Barred owls lack ear tufts. These hunters of the night prey on mice, rabbits, squirrels, birds, and other small animals. Barred owls have dark eyes, brownish-gray plumage, vertical streaking on the chest, heavy barring on the wings, and yellow feet. They are at home in old forests and lowlands near water and nest in large tree cavities or deserted stick nest. Males are responsible for feeding females during incubation.

Wild Fact: A barred owl's eyesight in darkness is 100 times keener than a human's.

Great horned owl *(Bubo virginianus)*

Brad Thompson

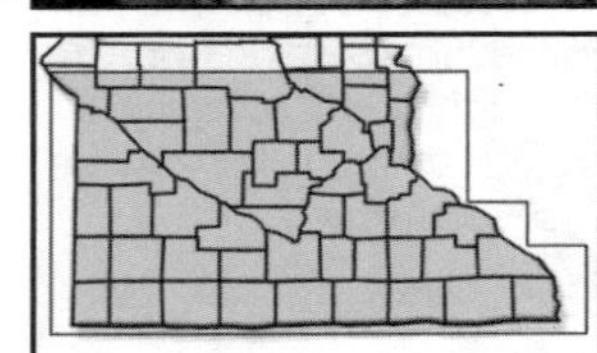

Great horned owls are incredibly skilled hunters, surveying the woods at night for unsuspecting birds, rabbits, mice, snakes, and fish. These large owls can stand two feet high and sport a wingspan longer than four feet. The "who-who-whooo" call of this owl is perhaps the quintessential owl vocalization, and can be heard in the early evening wherever these birds of prey are found – deciduous woodlands, meadows, bogs, and forests are all suitable habitats for great horneds. They often use abandoned bird nests or usurp one in use.

Wild Fact: Great horned owls have poorly developed senses of smell, and are one of the few animals that actively hunt skunks.

American kestrel *(Falco sparverius)*

USFWS / Dave Menke

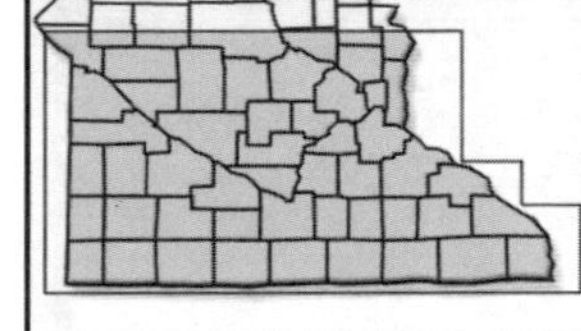

This small falcon (8 inches tall) is readily observed near fields, perched upon power lines and gaining vantage before swooping down on its prey: mice, grasshoppers, small birds, and other small animals. These handsome birds have two black face stripes (one below the eye and another slightly behind it) and copper-colored backs. Males have blue-gray wings and crowns; females have rust-colored wings and breast spots and barred tails. Kestrel pairs form strong bonds and often nest in old woodpecker holes or nest boxes.

Swainson's hawk *(Buteo swainsoni)*

Dudley Edmonson

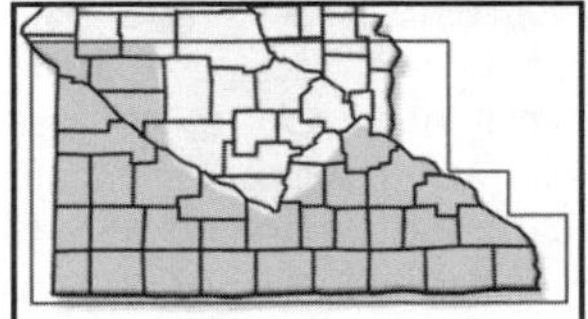

Swainson's hawks are medium-sized (20 to 22 inches tall, 54-inch wingspan) hawks of open fields, grasslands, and farmlands. Though not abundant in Minnesota, they can be seen locally in the west-central and southwest part of the state. Swainson's hawks are great travelers, with some individuals migrating 12,000 miles in one year from South America to northern Canada and Alaska and back again. Swainson's hawks appear in two color phases: light morph or dark morph. Birds of both phases have brown heads, backs, upper wings, and tails. Light morphs (more common) have reddish-brown "chins," light-colored chests, and white wing linings. The less-common dark-morph birds are brown all over, save for a light tail patch. During flight, wings are held in a "V." On the open fields of Minnesota, these raptors hunt ground squirrels, mice, snakes, and small birds.

Red-tailed hawk *(Buteo jamaicensis)*

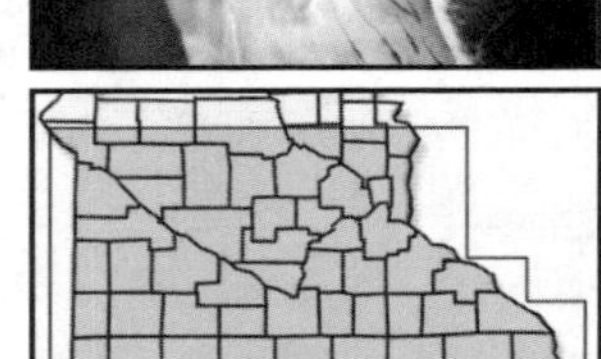

The piercing cry of a red-tailed hawk is not soon forgotten. These majestic birds are most often seen soaring above fields and farmlands scanning the underworld for prey. They have white chests bordered by dark belly streaking, and reddish-orange fan-shaped tails. Females are slightly larger than males (up to 25 inches tall); their wingspan approaches five feet.

Bird Watching

USFWS / Dave Menke

Indigo bunting *(Passerina cyanea)*

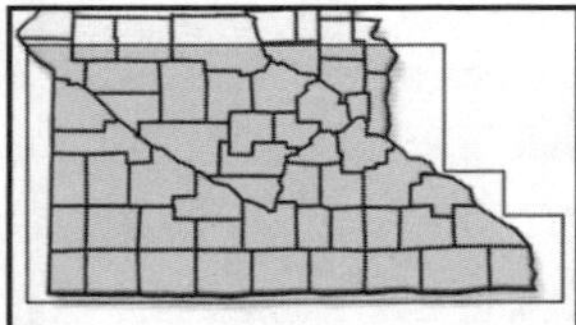

The breeding male indigo bunting, dressed in blue with black wing stripes, can appear black at first. It's not until the bird is seen backlit by the sun that its resplendent coloration can be appreciated. These lovely birds are spring and summer visitors to Minnesota, where they nest in woodlands, old fields, pastures, and brushy areas. Females are drab by comparison, primarily brownish. Males lose their blue feathers in fall, and then more closely resemble females, however, they usually retain some blue in their feathers. Indigo buntings are primarily ground feeders, foraging for insects, seeds, and berries.

Bobolink *(Dolichonyx oryzivorus)*

David Watkins

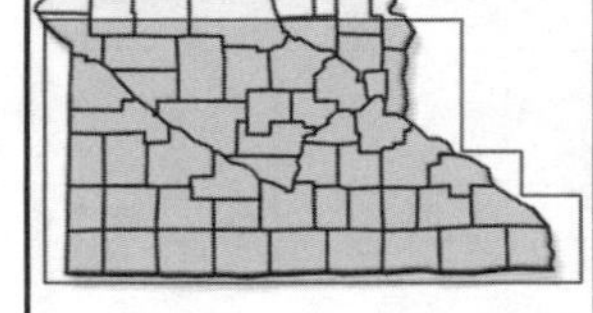

Bobolinks frequent grasslands, meadows, and prairie environments, where they forage for insects and seeds. Breeding males have distinctive plumage, with black faces and sides, white-and-black backs, and a tannish cap. After breeding, females and nonbreeding males are similar in appearance – brownish-yellow overall with dark streaks on the upper parts. Bobolinks are ground nesters, with females stitching grass and stems into a cup where she deposits four to six eggs.

Wild Fact: Unlike most songbirds, bobolinks molt on both their breeding and wintering grounds (Central and South America).

Tufted titmouse *(Baelophus bicolor)*

James Hornig

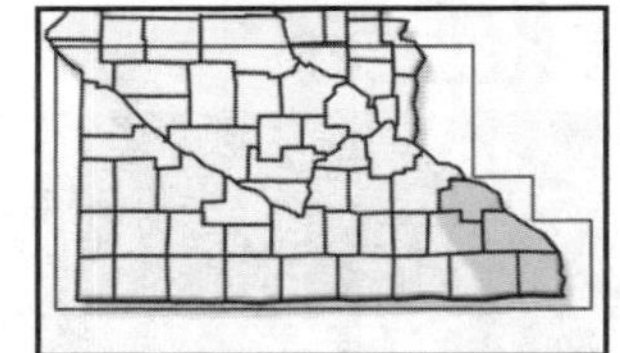

The tufted titmouse is a favorite at backyard bird feeders, being naturally curious and very comfortable near humans. In addition to wooded residential settings, titmice can be found in deciduous woods and parks where mature trees are present. Insects, seeds, and fruits make up the bulk of their diet. Titmice often hang upside down to forage. These perky birds sport cool, bluish-gray upper parts, a tufted crown, a black patch above the bill, a white chest, and chestnut flanks. Adults are about six inches tall with 10-inch wingspans. Titmice form strong bonds between mating pairs and with their young, of which one sometimes stays with the parents long enough to assist with nesting and feeding the following year. Titmice nest in tree cavities, with females laying a half-dozen speckled, white eggs and incubating them for two weeks.

Dickcissel *(Spiza Americana)*

USFWS / Steve Maslowski

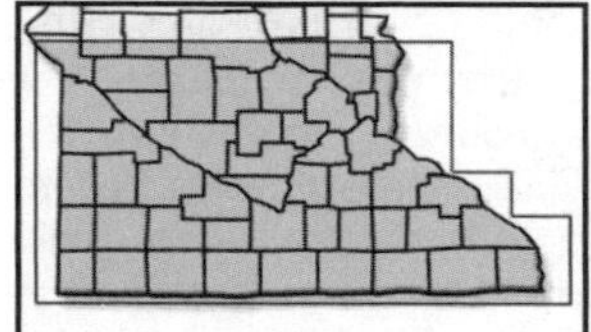

If you see a bird that looks like a small meadowlark, it's likely a dickcissel. These sparrow-sized (6 to 7 inches) birds share the meadowlark's preferred habitats of grasslands, farm fields, and meadows. Dickcissels have gray heads and underparts, yellow "eyebrows," and reddish-orange shoulder patches. Additionally, males sport white chins and black triangular bibs. Females have white throats, also, but lack the black bib. Dickcissels are primarily insect eaters in summer, while their diet on Central and South American wintering grounds consists mostly of seeds. They build nests of grass and leaves near or on the ground, where the female lays up to a half-dozen pale-blue eggs.

Rose-breasted grosbeak *(Pheucticus ludovicianus)*

USFWS / Steve Maslowski

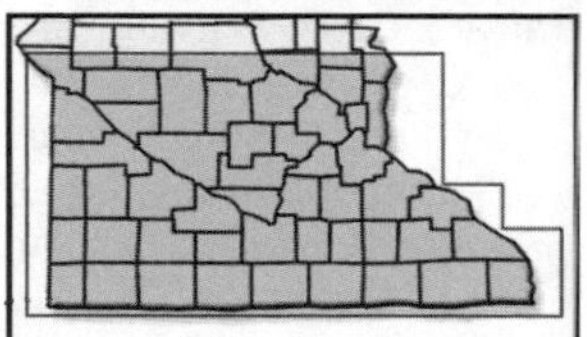

One look at a male rose-breasted grosbeak is about all it takes to identify it. The combination of rosy, triangular-shaped breast patch, black head and back, and white chest are unlike any other bird. Females are largely brown and white, with a white eye stripe. Rose-breasteds generally arrive in Minnesota in May and may still until mid-October or later depending on weather. Open woodlands, and deciduous and mixed forests attract breeding birds. Females build a delicate nest of plant materials in a tree or shrub. Insects, seeds, and berries comprise the bulk of a grosbeak's diet. These birds winter in Mexico, northern South America, and the Caribbean.

White-breasted nuthatch *(Sitta carolinensis)*

Cathy Keifer

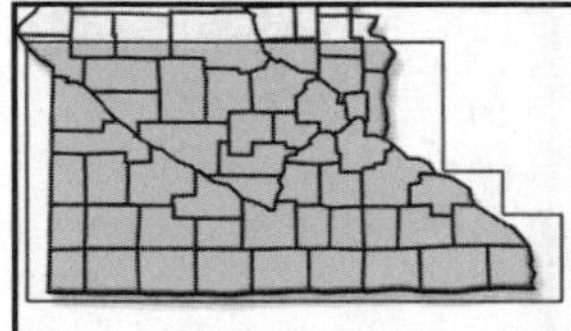

Nuthatches have the remarkable ability to walk vertically up and down trees, and can hold their heads parallel to the ground as they descend a trunk. They can even walk upside down! White-breasted nuthatches are stout-bodied, with short tails, grayish-blue backs, black eyes, and white under parts. Males have black caps, while females have gray heads. These year-round residents can be seen in mixed forests, parks, and at backyard bird feeders. Suet is a favorite nuthatch treat.

American robin *(Turdus migratorius)*

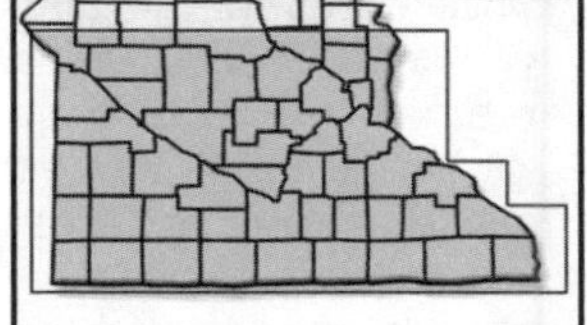

One of our most common birds and the one most often associated with the coming of spring, the American robin is a familiar visitor to those residing in the city and country alike, where the bird plies patches of ground in search of earthworms. Robins often locate earthworms by running across the ground and then stopping to listen and watch for them slithering in the soil. Not all robins migrate, some birds will winter in Minnesota if there are berries or other foods available. Males and females are similarly patterned, however, males have darker heads and backs and richer reddish-orange breasts.

Eastern towhee *(Pipilo erythrophthalmus)*

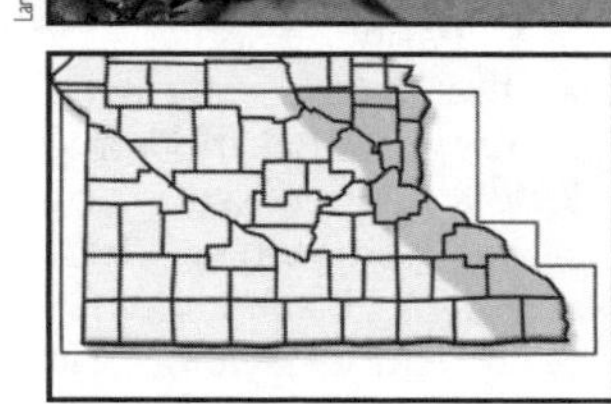

These large (8-inch-tall), colorful members of the sparrow family are known for their double-footed foraging method, scavenging through leaves and other ground debris for insects, seeds, fruits, and spiders. Eastern towhees show up in Minnesota's woodlands and fields in April and may remain through October before venturing south. Male towhees sport a black hood, throat, wings, and tail (with white spot); chestnut sides; and white breasts. Females are similarly patterned, however, they wear brown where the male wears black. Towhees nest on the ground in a cup-like nest of small twigs, bark, grass, and animal hair. Males are at their most demonstrative in spring, when they perch on shrubs and trees to sing to prospective mates. Females typically lay three to six eggs, which are incubated for about two weeks. Both parents feed the nestlings.

Cedar waxwing *(Bombycilla cedrorum)*

Andreas Nilsson

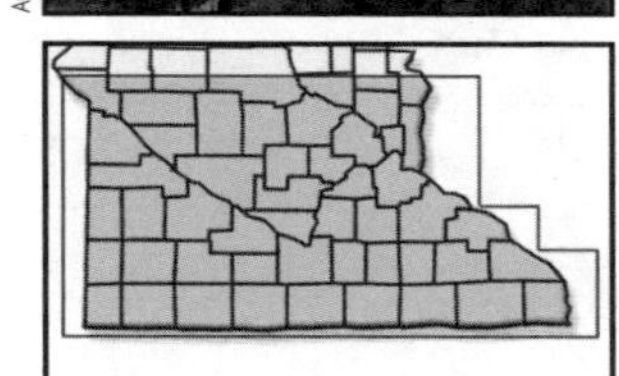

Cedar waxwings are beautiful birds with distinguished markings: buff upper parts, black "masks" that extend all the way to the back of the head, cinnamon-yellow chests, yellow-tipped tails, and red spotting on the wings. They inhabit woodlands and parks – places with abundant trees and shrubs. Waxwings often feed on insects, but have a particular penchant for berries. These communal birds forage together, eating as much as their crops will hold. Once full, they may continue foraging, passing along surplus berries to still-hungry birds. This sharing of food is taken a step further during courtship, when males and females exchange berries back and forth, strengthening pair bonds. Because much of their diet is fruit, waxwings are not territorial and migrate frequently to locate new food sources.

Wild Fact: Waxwings sometimes consume berries that have fermented, resulting in inebriation. Birds may be seen staggering about on the ground, waiting for the effect to subside.

Eastern bluebird *(Sialia sialis)*

USFWS

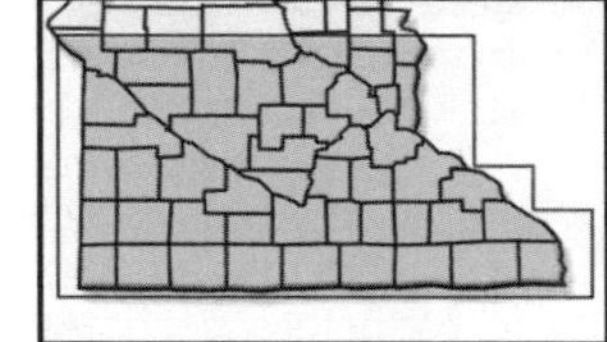

The beautiful eastern bluebird is often seen perched in and around fields, woodland edges, and meadows, where it searches for insects. Bluebirds are cavity-nesting birds, and will make use of old woodpecker holes or natural cavities in trees. Human-built bluebird nest boxes are often erected to provide additional sites for nesting birds. These nest boxes should feature a 1½-inch entrance hole – too small for European starlings, which often compete with bluebirds for nesting locations.

Wild Fact: The eastern bluebird is a member of the thrush family, which includes the American robin.

Ruby-throated hummingbird *(Archilochus colubris)*

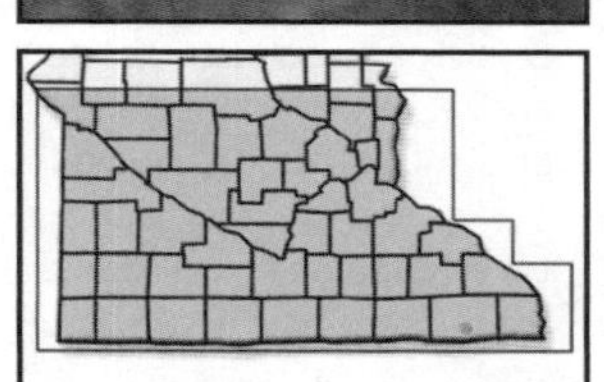

If you see a hummingbird in Minnesota, it is most likely a ruby-throated. It is the only hummingbird species that breeds east of the Mississippi River, and is found throughout the state in spring, summer, and early fall. Ruby-throateds can be found in open and mixed woodlands, wetlands, flower gardens, and visiting feeders. They winter in Central America.

Wild Fact: A ruby-throated hummingbird's heart may beat up to 1,200 times per minute.

Northern cardinal *(Cardinalis cardinalis)*

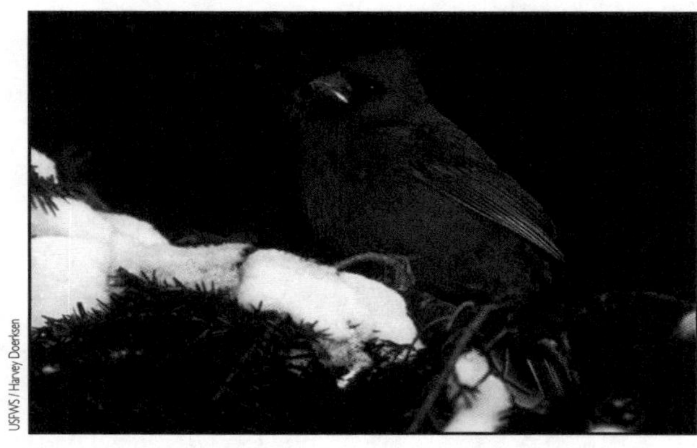
USFWS / Harvey Doerksen

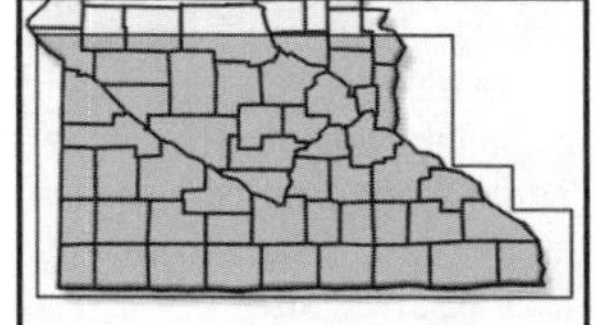

The northern cardinal is one of the most popular birds in the eastern United States. These cheer-inducing redbirds prefer woodlands adjacent to open spaces, but can be easily attracted to residences offering food, especially sunflower seeds. Males and females can be seen together year-round, but it's during spring and summer that mating pairs remain in closest contact. Male cardinals – with their tufted crests, deep-red bodies, and black faces – are easily identified, while females are more modestly dressed in subdued shades of brown. Cardinals are often the last birds to visit feeders during the day, preferring to feed at dusk when other birds have retreated to their evening shelters.

Wild Fact: A male cardinal will feed bits of food to a female to win her affection.

Western meadowlark *(Sturnella neglecta)* & Eastern meadowlark *(Sturnella magna)*

Bryan Eastham

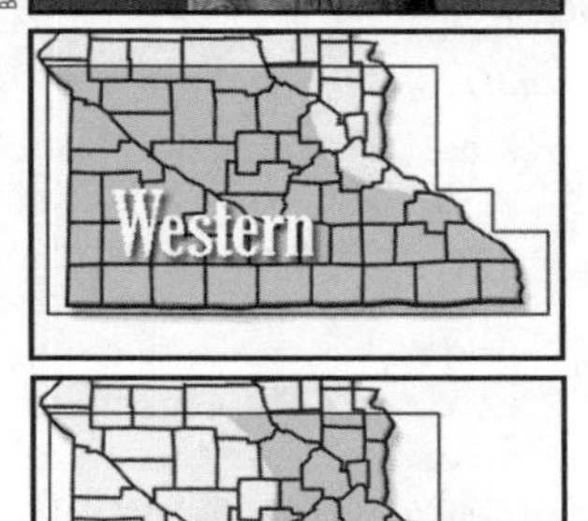

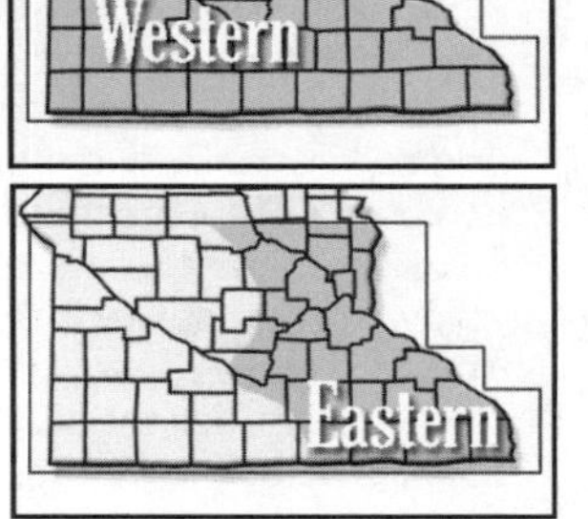

The warbling of a meadowlark on an early summer morning in the country is music to many a bird watcher's ears. Meadowlarks are found near meadows, farm fields, pastures, and grassy roadsides. Often, they are seen perched on a power line or fence post. Meadowlarks are ground feeders, consuming grasshoppers, spiders, crickets, and caterpillars. The birds stand about 10 inches high and are stout in appearance. Males and females alike have bright-yellow chins and chests interrupted by a black "V" mark. Meadowlarks nest on the ground, under the cover of thick grass, where the female lays a clutch of tan-colored eggs with purple spots. Eastern and western meadowlarks are nearly identical: easterns have darker upper parts and more yellow on the throat.

Wild Fact: Meadowlarks are actually members of the blackbird family.

Bird Watching

Black-capped chickadee *(Poecile atricapilla)*

USFWS / Donna Dewhurst

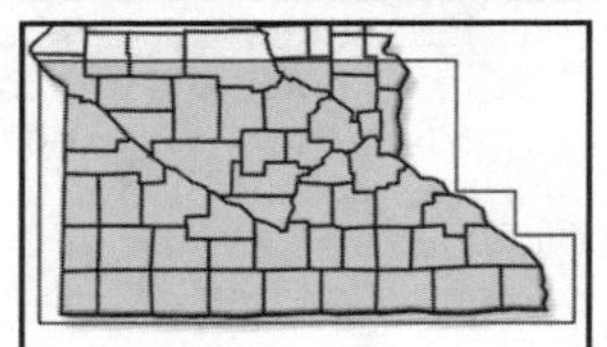

The black-capped chickadee is a favorite of bird watchers everywhere. They seem too delicate to survive a Minnesota winter, but these hardy little birds are able to regulate their body temperatures.

Black-capped chickadees are at home in deciduous and mixed forests, wooded parks, and are reliable visitors to backyard bird feeders (black-oil sunflower seeds are a favorite). Their natural diet includes insects, spiders, small fruits, and seeds. Chickadees are cavity nesters and will line holes with plant materials and feathers. Males and females are alike in appearance, with black caps and chins, white cheeks, chestnut sides, and white under parts.

Barn swallow *(Hirundo rustica)*

USFWS / Dave Menke

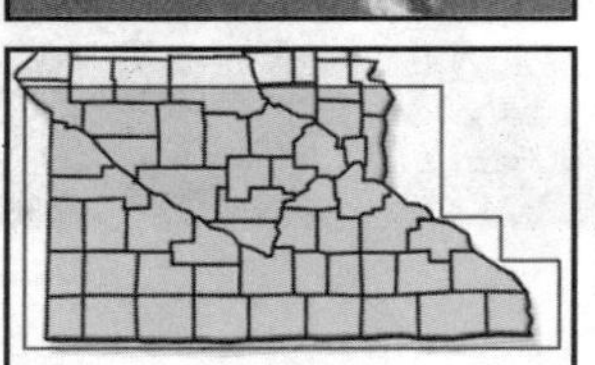

Watching a barn swallow navigate effortlessly through the air, swooping and diving, turning and veering, can be humbling for us ground dwellers. These gifted flyers ride upon long, pointed wings balanced by elongated, forked tail feathers. Barn swallows have dark, glossy-blue upper parts and sandy-orange under parts. They inhabit roadside edges near open fields and lakes and rivers, where they hunt and snatch flying insects from the air. The birds build nests of mud and lined with grass, straw, and feathers, beneath eaves, bridges, culverts, and rafters. The birds depart Minnesota in the fall for their wintering grounds in Mexico and Central and South America.

American redstart *(Setophaga ruticilla)*

USFWS / Steve Maslowski

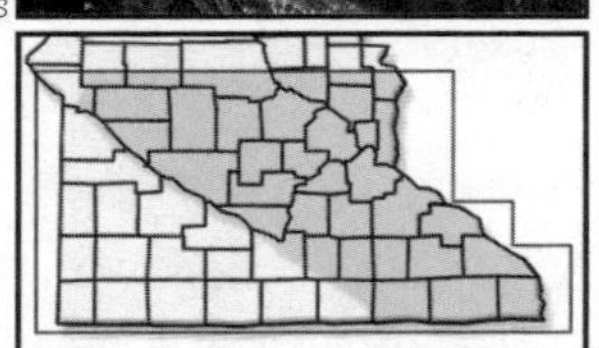

The male American redstart is really an "orangestart," carrying as it does orange wing, fore-shoulder and tail patches set against a black upper body and white under side. In contrast, females sport yellow patches and are olive brown where the male is black. These wood warblers return to Minnesota's deciduous and mixed woodlands to nest in young trees. Redstarts feed on a variety of insects and spiders, often flushing prey by flashing their showy wings or hovering over their prey.

Yellow-headed blackbird
(Xanthocephalus xanthocephalus)

Wolfgang Zintl

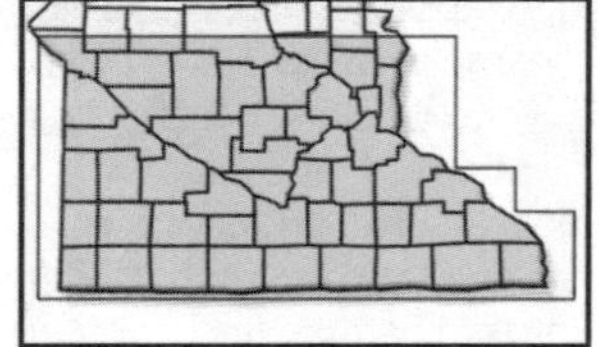

Male yellow-headed blackbirds, with their bold yellow heads and breasts set off against their black bodies, are unlikely to be confused with other birds. Females share the male's yellow throat, but lack the vibrant yellow head and black bodies. Yellow-headeds are at home in cattail marshes, where they nest in small colonies, building nests in vegetation directly over water. They will take over the most favored locations from red-winged blackbirds in areas where their ranges overlap.

Downy woodpecker *(Picoides pubescens)*

USFWS / Donna Dewhurst

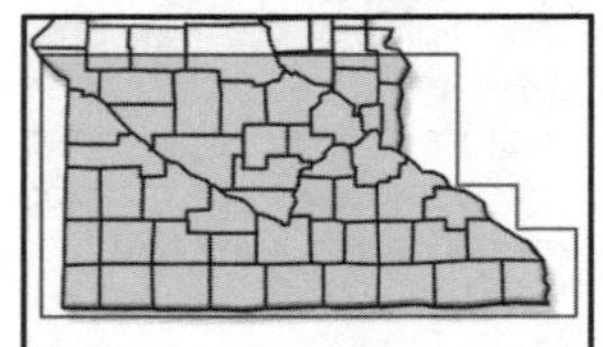

The tiny downy woodpecker (6 to 7 inches) along with its larger look-alike (the hairy woodpecker), is a common sight in deciduous and mixed forests and at suet feeders. The males and females are easily distinguished, as the male sports a red head patch that the female lacks. Otherwise, both sexes have white chests and backs, black-and white wing feathers, and black eye lines. Downies probe and chip tree trunks and branches for insects, insect eggs, and spiders. They nest in spring, excavating a hole in a dying or dead tree and then lining it with wood chips. They are year-round residents throughout Minnesota.

Wild Fact: Woodpeckers have reinforced skulls to absorb the shock of pecking on trees.

Pileated woodpecker *(Drycopus pileatus)*

Bruce Amos

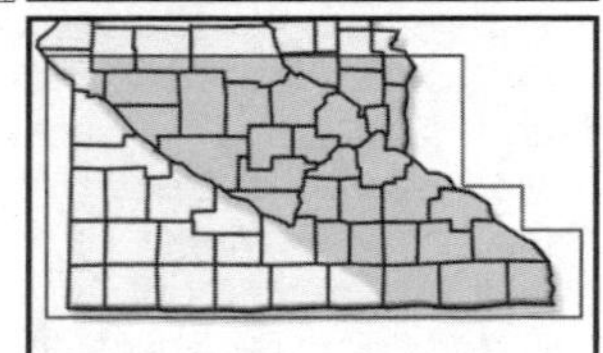

Pileated woodpeckers are very large forest dwellers (16 to 20 inches long) sporting a bold red crest, yellow eyes, black body, and white stripes on the wings and from the bill to the shoulders. Additionally, males have an extra swash of red running parallel from the base of the bill to behind the eye. Pileated woodpeckers are often the first to excavate nest cavities in decaying or dead trees, creating future nesting spots for other birds (including owls) and mammals. Pileateds require large tracts of mature forest, thus, they are not commonly seen even in their home ranges.

Northern flicker *(Colaptes auratus)*

USFWS / Dave Menke

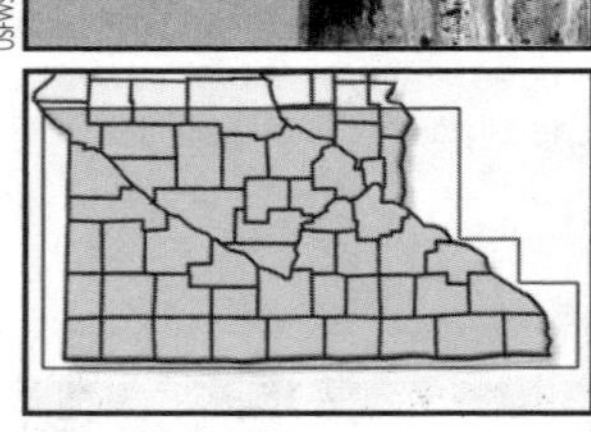

These common year-round resident woodpeckers seem to "flick" their tails as they glide through the air. The flicker is distinguished by its barred wings and back, yellow underwings, white rump, gray head, red nape crescent, black bib, spotted breast, and long bill. Males carry a black patch on the cheek that females lack. They are at home in most wooded environments and will readily come to suet feeders. Unlike most other woodpeckers, flickers commonly forage on the ground for insects – ants are a favorite food.

Red-headed woodpecker *(Melanerpes erythrocephalus)*

Tony Campbell

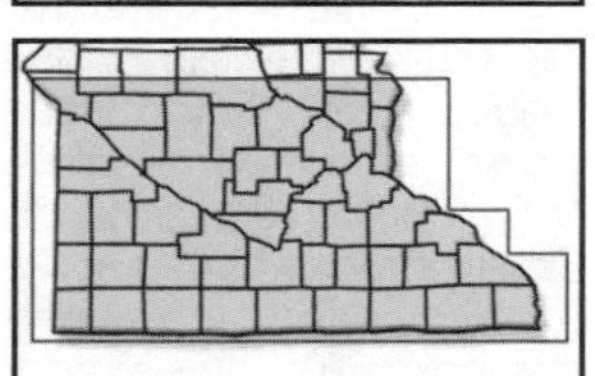

As the only woodpecker in the region with a completely red head (the red actually extends to the neck), the red-headed woodpecker is difficult to mistake for another bird. The eye-catching red head is strikingly contrasted by the bird's snowy white chest, black back, and black wings highlighted by white patches. Before the introduction of the European starling in the 1890s, red-headed woodpeckers were in greater abundance and common throughout most of the eastern United States. Today, they are confined primarily to oak woodlands and woods bordering rivers, where the birds feed on acorns, insects, spiders, and even mice and young birds.

Killdeer *(Charadrius vociferous)*

USFWS / Gary Kramer

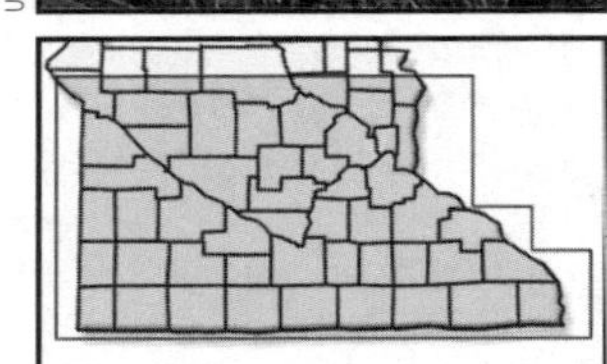

Killdeer are shorebirds (members of the plover family) that are commonly seen in open fields, sod farms, golf courses, mudflats, and lakeshores. They feed using a jerky "start-and-stop" motion, gleaning insects, earthworms, snails, crayfish, and other invertebrates from the ground. Killdeer have two black breast bands, brownish backs and wings, white under parts, and a white face patch. Their signature "killdeer" call is a final clue to ID-ing this bird. Killdeer are well known for their "acting" ability – if a predator gets too close to a killdeer nest, one of the parents will sound an alarm call and drag a wing against the ground to simulate a broken wing. Once a predator is led far enough from the nest, the killdeer will take flight and escape.

Trumpeter swan *(Cygnus buccinator)*

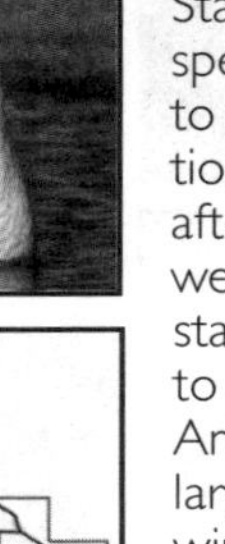

Dudley Edmondson

Minnesotans can rightly take pride when flocks of trumpeter swans descend onto the Mississippi River in winter. It was the North Star State, after all, that spearheaded early efforts to resuscitate ailing populations in the 1960s, decades after these regal birds were extirpated from the state and hunted nearly to extinction across North America. Trumpeters are large birds, with 7-foot wingspans and weighing up to 35 pounds. They look similar to tundra swans, but trumpeters are larger, with black bills and black feet, and most tundra swans have some yellow in front of their eyes. Trumpeters are birds of lakes and wetlands, and nest near shore. Nesting pairs are very territorial, defending more than 100 acres against other swans. Young swans are born in summer after eggs are incubated for about one month. They migrate south with their parents in winter and return north with them in the spring.

Wild Fact: Trumpeter swans are the largest waterfowl species in the world.

Scarlet tanager *(Piranga olivacea)*

USFWS / Steve Maslowski

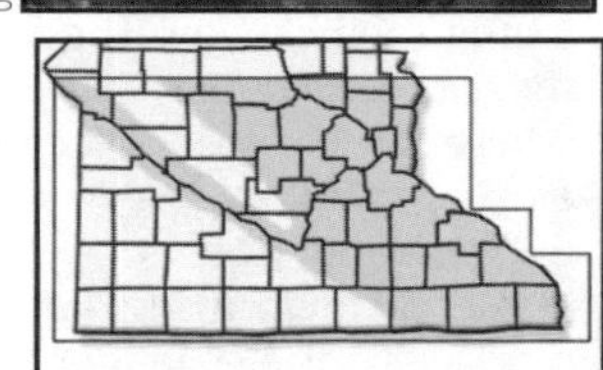

Coming upon a male scarlet tanager in the woods during spring is a bit like stepping into the tropics. In full breeding plumage and sporting an almost impossibly brilliant red body and ebony wings and tail, the tanager resembles a small fire engine among the green hues of fresh foliage. They generally arrive in Minnesota in late spring and will depart by mid-October for its wintering grounds in Central and South America. Scarlet tanagers feed primarily on insects, and forage among the top branches of deciduous trees for prey. Once captured, the birds will beat insects against tree branches to kill them. Scarlet tanagers also eat berries, including those from poison ivy plants. Like most songbirds, female tanagers lack the showy colors of the male, and are olive-yellow, with grayish wings.

Bird Watching

Great blue heron *(Ardea herodias)*

USFWS / Lee Karney

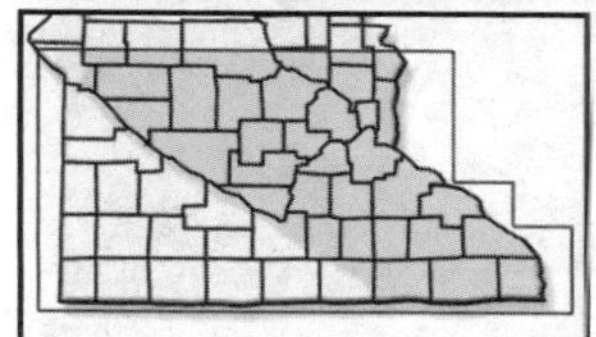

Great blue herons are the largest herons found in North America – adults stand four feet tall with a wingspan of six feet. These graceful birds of marshes, rivers, and lakes are equipped with nimble legs, long beaks, and a neck that is usually held in an S-shape when at rest. Great blue herons are expert waders and fishers of the shallows, where they pick their finny prey along with frogs, snakes, crayfish, rodents, insects, and small mammals. Herons nest in colonies called rookeries. They typically build large nesting platforms in tall trees – males gather sticks which the females place onto the nests. In flight, great blue herons fold their necks back compared to sandhill cranes, which hold their necks straight while flying.

Common loon *(Gavia immer)*

USFWS / NWF

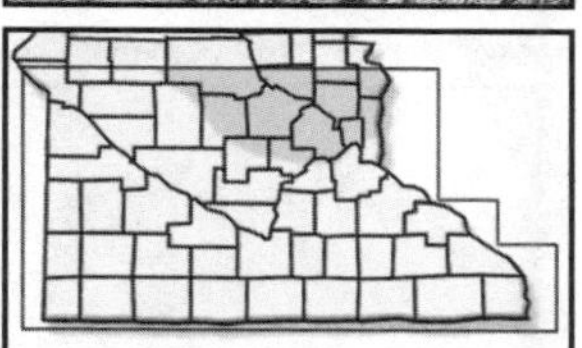

The haunting song of the loon is one of the most indelible sounds of the Minnesota wilderness. These ancient diving birds return to Minnesota in spring to breed and rear their young. Males and females have a hand in building nests, as well as incubating eggs. Young loons are born with the ability to swim and dive and can take flight after about 10 weeks, at which time they leave their parents. After breeding, loons are generally solitary and can often be found swimming and diving in many of the large lakes present in Minnesota.

Wild Fact: Common loons can fly 75 mph.

Wood duck *(Aix sponsa)*

USFWS / Dave Menke

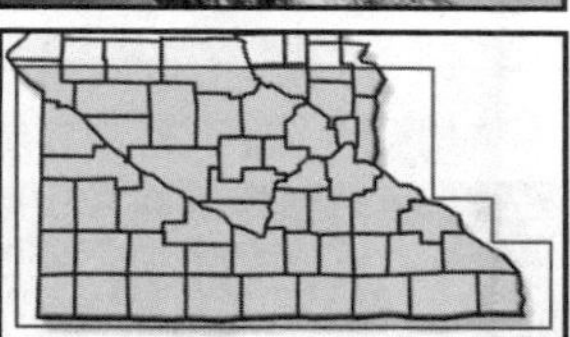

There may be no more beautiful bird than a male (drake) wood duck in breeding plumage. With their green and black heads, white chins, red eyes, reddish-orange bill, leathery brown chests and tan wings, drake woodies look as if they've been painted on wood. However, their name stems from their habit of nesting high up in trees, sometimes a mile or more away from water. As soon as one day after being hatched, wood duck chicks will tumble out of the nest and jump to the ground to follow the female to water. Wood ducks prefer settings where water and woods meet, including marshes, swamps, and ponds.

Mallard *(Anas platyrhynchos)*

USFWS / Erwin & Peggy Bauer

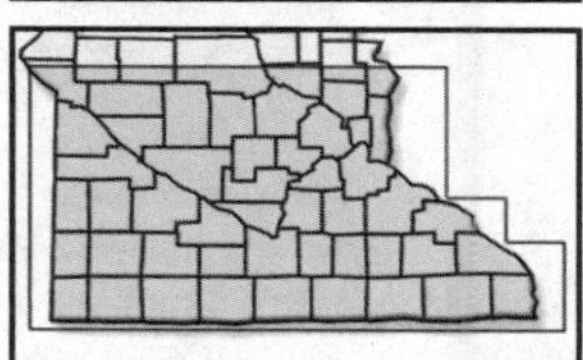

Along with the northern cardinal, the ubiquitous mallard is often one of the first birds new bird watchers come to know. The green head and broad, yellow bill of the male mallard make it easy to identify. Females wear no such finery – being brownish overall with an orange bill – but are often seen near males. Mallards are found in a variety of wetland habitats, from large lakes to small rivers and ponds. They are dabbling ducks, dipping their heads underwater with their back ends held skyward while searching for seeds, insects, small fish, and other small animals.

Wild Fact: Mallards often interbreed with other duck species including domesticated ducks.

USFWS / C. Schlawe

Belted kingfisher *(Ceryle alcyon)*

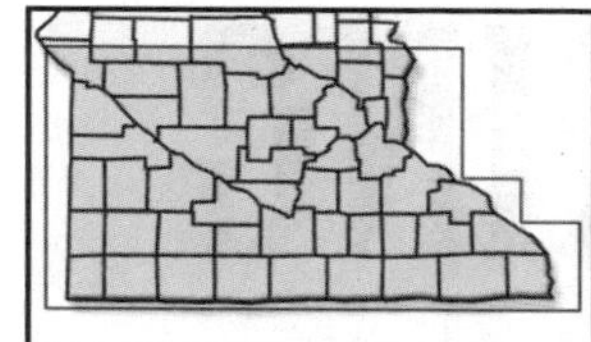

Within its home range, the belted kingfisher will never be far from water, staying close to streams, rivers, lakes, and marshes. This strange-looking bird, with its large, blue-gray crested head, white neck, blue-gray back and wings, and massive bill, appears almost cartoonish. But these birds are expert fishers, locating their prey by sight and then diving head first into water for the capture. Once a fish is caught, kingfishers take their quarry to a perch and subdue it by whacking it against the perch with its bill. Kingfishers prefer to nest in a dry soil bank, excavating a tunnel that can be six feet long.

Wild Fact: Unlike most bird species, it is the female kingfisher that is the more colorful of the two sexes. She sports a copper-colored belt on the chest that males lack.

Red-winged blackbird *(Agelaius phoeniceus)*

USFWS / Kent Olsen

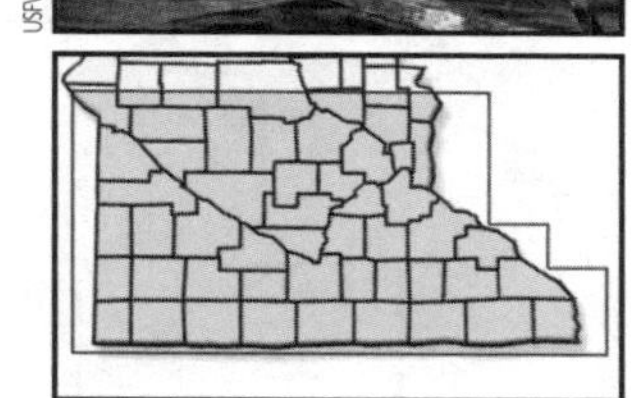

In early spring, Minnesota's cattail marshes and wetlands come alive with the song of red-winged blackbirds. The males are first to arrive, spending a week or so staking out territories before the females join them. After males have attracted one or more females, she begins weaving a cup-shaped nest among the existing vegetation. Compared to males – with their black bodies and reddish-orange shoulder patches – females are more difficult to identify. They are dressed in a wash of brown and white streaking, such coloration helps them remain concealed while on nests. Red-winged blackbirds feed mostly on seeds.

Baltimore oriole *(Icterus galbula)*

Daniel E. Johnson

The male Baltimore oriole is one of the most strikingly patterned birds visiting Minnesota. Adorned in black and deep orange, these woodland birds are also one of nature's greatest singers. Underappreciated are the females of the species, richly colored as well, with yellow-orange under parts but sans the black head. Baltimore orioles inhabit deciduous woodlands, parklands, and waterways, among other settings. Baltimores feed on insects during the spring and summer but will also come to backyard feeders offering grape jelly or slices of orange or other fruits tacked onto a board. They also are attracted to hummingbird feeders and will try valiantly to sip nectar from the tiny feeder holes. Orioles construct nests that hang high from the limbs of deciduous trees.

Purple martin *(Progne subis)*

Vladimir Ivanov

Purple martins are famous for their large colonies and for nesting communal-style in martin houses and other manmade nesting structures. Martins often compete with the non-native house sparrow and European starling for nesting rights. These birds are the largest North American swallows, standing about 8 inches tall, with wingspans up to 18 inches. They are deep, dark blue, with large heads and pointed wings. Females and sub-adult males have mottled, grayish underparts. Martins favor semi-open country, especially near water. They are remarkably agile fliers, and spend the day taking flying insects on the wing. Martins winter across much of South America.

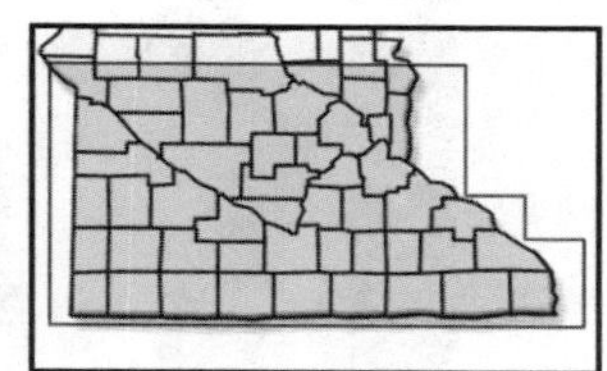

Yellow warbler *(Dendroica petechia)*

Tim Zurowski

Because yellow warblers – males and females alike – are covered in yellow plumage, they are one of the easiest warblers to identify. Breeding males also sport rusty-red breast streaks, an additional identifying mark of these lovely birds. Yellow warblers return to Minnesota in May from their wintering grounds in Central and South America. They'll seek out deciduous woodlands and thickets as well as shrubby fields to nest in. Females build cup-like nests of grass and bark, lining them with fur. Yellow warbler nests are often parasitized by brown-headed cowbirds – female cowbirds will lay eggs into an existing warbler nest. To counter, female warblers may build a new nest on top of the foreign eggs, sometimes creating elaborate multi-tiered structures.

American goldfinch *(Carduelis tristis)*

USFWS / Lee Karney

The American goldfinch seems at home under the bright summer sun. Male goldfinches, particularly – adorned in bright yellow breeding plumage, black caps, and black-and-white wings – seem to paint the sky as they swoop through the air. Females are a more subdued olive-gold and lack the black cap of the males. In fall and winter, males lose their brilliant color, more closely resembling females. Goldfinches feed hungrily on seeds from a variety of plants including thistle, alder, and birch. They are fond of unkempt farm fields, woodland edges, and weedy pockets near open areas. Goldfinches nest later than many songbirds, waiting until their food sources are ripe with seed. Nests are built in shrubs or deciduous trees and lined with thistle down. Goldfinches will readily visit feeders offering thistle seed. They typically feed in pairs and groups, and may feed while hanging upside down.

Blue jay *(Cyanocitta cristata)*

USFWS / Dave Menke

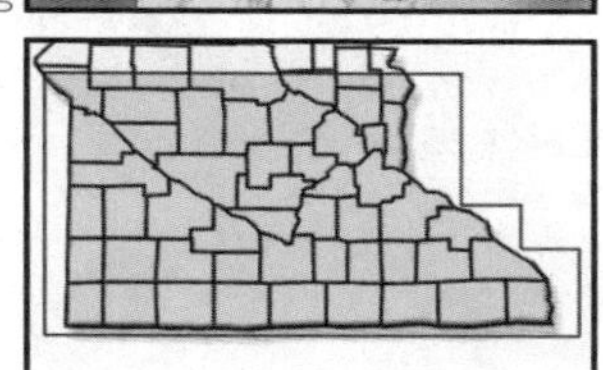

Find a wooded area with oak trees and you'll likely find blue jays nearby. These large (11-12 inches long; 16-inch wingspan) members of the corvid family (which includes ravens and crows) are particularly fond of acorns, and often bury the protein-rich nuts by the hundreds for later feeding. Only a portion of these cached nuts are ever recovered, so in effect, the blue jay plays a role in planting new oaks. Blue jays are also common visitors to backyard bird feeders, where they will muscle in on other birds to take the lion's share of sunflower seeds. Males and females are similarly colored and patterned, each adorned with a striking blue crest and back, black-and-white barred wings, a blue tail with black barring, and white under parts.

Wild Fact: Blue jays frequently mimic the call of a red-tailed hawk as they descend into an area with bird feeders. Such a call often frightens smaller songbirds and causes them to flee.

TRAILS

HIKING & BIKING

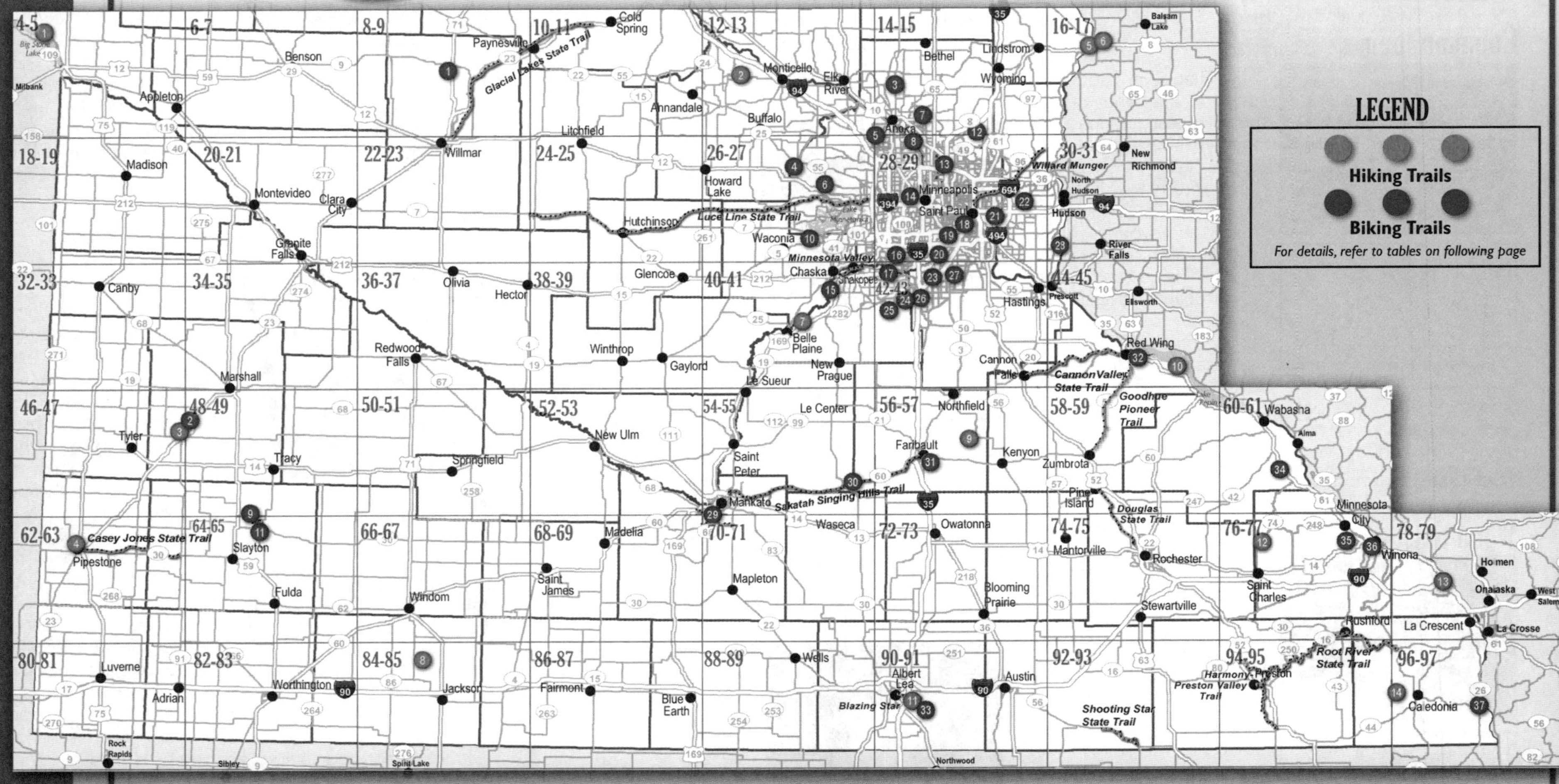

HIKING

If the best things in life are free, then hiking surely must be one of them. Sometimes the best way to really experience an area is to slow down and walk through it. The rewards of trekking in the outdoors are endless, and southern Minnesota's hiking trails give hikers a snapshot at the diverse topography that makes up the region. Woods, waters, wide-open prairies, and wildlife are present in great variety and often in great abundance. Hikers may encounter wildflower-dotted prairies, steep bluffs, river valleys, uncommon plants and animals, quiet lakes, unusual geologic features, and much more on the area's trails.

Hiking can be as simple as a short walk to a picturesque overlook or a series of walks to really sample what the region has to offer. It's a great activity for families, getting outdoors with friends or even going solo. And it doesn't require mountains of gear – a trail map, comfortable pair of boots and socks, clothing to suit the current weather conditions, a bottle of water and a snack for quick energy are all that's needed.

There are literally thousands of miles of "trails" open to hikers in Minnesota. Because the majority of trails in the state are designated as "multi-use," hikers are able (in most cases) to enjoy the same trails used by mountain bikers and horseback riders in summer as well as those used by cross-country skiers and snowmobilers in winter. Along with the trails noted in other sections of this atlas – state parks, state forests, off-road, cross-country skiing, and snowmobiling – there are others that may not fit neatly into any one category. In addition, some trails are significant for their history, scenery, etc., and merit additional discussion within these pages.

As a starting point, we recommend the following trails/spurs as watermarks of what southern Minnesota has to offer – a "best of" list if you will. We hope experiencing these routes will inspire hikers to get out and explore the other trails in the region and come up with their own list of favorites.

BIKING

Bicycling is an activity that can be enjoyed by nearly anyone. Not only is biking an excellent form of exercise, it can also take one places where automobiles can't be driven. In addition to the more than 1,000 miles of trails open to biking across Minnesota, the numerous secondary and rustic back roads crisscrossing the region can be treated like trails as well. Most roadways – highways excepted – can be enjoyed by pedal.

HIKING TRAILS

Number	Name	Pg / Coord	Miles	Difficulty	Highlights
1	Bluebird Trail	4-2A	2	Moderate	Big Stone Lake State Park. Wooded lakeshore. Waterfall.
2	Kettle and Kame Trail	12-2C	2	Moderate	Lake Maria State Park. Glacial geology including kettles and kames along with lakes and old-growth forest.
3	Dakota Valley Trail	48-1B	2.2	Moderate	Camden State Park. Bluffs, woodland valley, prairie. Fall foliage. Moderate climb to overlook.
4	Circle Trail	62-3B	0.8	Easy	Pipestone National Monument. Quartzite ridge. Large granite boulders. Tallgrass prairie. Waterfall.
5	Pothole Trail	16-2B	0.3	Easy	Interstate State Park. Glacial potholes, basalt cliffs.
6	Sandstone Bluffs Trail	16-2B	1	Moderate	Interstate State Park. Sandstone cliffs overlooking St. Croix River.
7	Lawrence Headquarters Loop	41-4C	3.5	Easy	Minnesota Valley State Recreation Area. River valley marshes and abundant waterfowl.
8	Dinosaur Ridge Overlook	84-3A	1.5	Easy	Kilen Woods State Park. Views of Des Moines River Valley.
9	Hidden Falls	57-4C	1.2	Easy	Nerstrand Big Woods State Park. Oak and maple forest, wildflowers, ferns. Exposed limestone deposits.
10	Bluffside Trail	45-5E	1.5	Moderate	Frontenac State Park. Bluffs overlooking Mississippi River.
11	Bur Oak Esker Trail	90-2C	4	Moderate	Myre-Big Island State Park. Part of trail follows esker. Lakeside camping.
12	Chimney Rock Trail	76-2B	1	Moderate	Whitewater State Park. Overlooks of the Whitewater River Valley. Good spot to view hawks.
13	King's Bluff Nature Trail	78-2C	1.3	Moderate	Great River Bluffs State Park. Overlooks of Mississippi River Valley.
14	Steep Rock	96-1C	1.2	Moderate To Difficult	Beaver Creek Valley State Park. Bluffs, spring wildflowers, overlooks.

BIKING TRAILS

Number	Name	Pg / Coord	Paved	Miles	Notes
1	Sibley State Park	8-3C	•	5	Trails connect Lakeview Campground and the interpretive center.
2	Camden State Park	48-1B		4	Redwood River, Dakota Valley Lookout, and Brawner Lake attractions.
3	Rum River Park	14-1D		15	Fast and level single track. Views of the Rum River.
4	Lake Rebecca Park Reserve	26-3B	•	11	7 mi. paved. 4 mi. single track. Wide range of scenery.
5	Elm Creek Park Reserve	14-1E	•	20	Abundant wildlife. Enjoy the visitor center and Eastman Nature Center.
6	Baker Park Reserve	27-4B	•	12	8 mi. paved. 4 mi. for mtn biking in winter only.
7	Bunker Hills Regional Park	14-2E	•	6	Paved and limestone trails. No biking on natural-surface trails.
8	Hennepin Trail Corridor	28-2A	•	6	Connector trail along wetlands, farmland, forests.
9	Lake Shetek State Park	48-3E	•	6	Historic and informational sites.
10	Carver Park Reserve	27-4E	•	9	Abundant wildlife. Trails surround Lowry Nature Center.
11	End-O-Line Railroad Park	64-3A	•	6	Extends from historic rail station museum.
12	Rice Creek West Regional Park	15-4E	•	4	Significant native wildlife habitat. Many activities within the park.
13	Long Lake Regional Park	28-3B	•	3	Trails connect all areas of the park.
14	Theodore Wirth Park	28-2C		6	Very technical single track.
15	Minnesota Valley State Rec. Area	41-4C	•	35	6 mi. paved. Wide double track along Minnesota River.
16	Hyland Lake Park Reserve	28-1E	•	6	Relaxing ride over rolling hills, meadows, and woods.
17	Minnesota River Bottoms Trail	42-1A		10	Variety of terrain. Mostly single track. Suitable for beginners.
18	Lilydale Park Trail	28-3D	•	14	Well maintained. Runs along Minnesota and Mississippi rivers.
19	Fort Snelling State Park	28-3E	•	15	5 mi. paved. Intersection of Minnesota and Mississippi Rivers.
20	Bass Ponds Loop	28-2E		3	Easy ride. Wide, smooth gravel. No hills.
21	Battle Creek City Park	29-4D	•	7	Single track through thick woods. Moderate to advanced level.
22	Lake Elmo Park Reserve	29-5C		8	Eagle Point Lake views. Share trail with horses.
23	Terrace Oaks	42-2A		3	Technical single track. Surrounded by forest.
24	Murphy-Hanrehan Park Reserve	42-1B		20	6-mile mtn bike portion only open during the fall.
25	Cleary Lake Regional Park	42-1B	•	4	Fairly flat loop around Cleary Lake.
26	Buck Hill Trails	42-2B		4	Small ski area. Up and down single track.
27	Lebanon Hills Regional Park	42-3A		7	Winding single track through woods. Several climbs and descents.
28	Afton State Park	30-1E	•	4	St. Croix River overlooks. Rugged and rolling terrain.
29	Mount Kato Mountain Bike Park	54-1E		9	Mostly wooded single track. All skill levels represented.
30	Sakatah Lake	55-5D	•	3	Paved rail bed through hardwood forest.
31	River Bend Nature Center	56-2C		10	Trails intertwine woods, prarie, river, ponds.
32	Memorial Park Trail	44-3D		7	Intermediate level. Single and double track. Rolling and wooded.
33	Myre Big Island State Park	90-2C		7	Grass trails. Limited accessibility during wet periods.
34	Snake Creek Trail	60-2D		10	Intermediate skill level. Rocky hills. Mostly double track.
35	Bronk Unit (R.J. Dorer State Forest)	77-5B		7	Overlooks on all sides of a plateau. Watch out for hikers.
36	Holzinger Lodge Trail	77-5B		10	Technical single track. Climbs, tight turns, and drops.
37	Reno Unit (R.J. Dorer State Forest)	96-3C		15	Scenic views. Watch out for horses and hikers.

STATE TRAILS

Name	Segment	Pg / Coord	Miles	Bike / Inline Skate / Asphalt	Bike / Limestone	MTN Bike	Hike-Walk	Horseback	Snowmobile	Groomed Ski	Rest Area	Access to Camping	Access to Fishing	Designated Swimming	State Park Access
Blazing Star	Albert Lea - Big Island State Park	90-2C	6	6			6				•	•	•		•
Casey Jones	Pipestone - Pipestone/Murray Co. Line	63-4B	12			12	12	12	12						
Douglas	Rochester - Pine Island	74-3A	13	13			13	13	13	13	•				
Glacial Lakes	Hawick - Richmond	10-1B	22						4						
Glacial Lakes	Willmar - New London - Hawick	9-4D	18	13			18	18	18		•	•	•	•	•
Goodhue-Pioneer	Red Wing - Hay Creek Unit	58-1D	4				4	4	4		•		•		
Goodhue-Pioneer	Zumbrota - 4 miles north	58-3B	4			4	4	4	4		•	•			
Harmony-Preston Valley	Root River Trail - Harmony	94-2C	18	18			18			18	•		•		
Luce Line	Cedar Mills - Cosmos	24-1D	10			10	10	10	10		•	•			
Luce Line	Plymouth - Stubbs Bay Rd.	27-5C	7		7		7	7		7	•		•		
Luce Line	Stubbs Bay Rd. - Winsted	26-3C	23		23		23	23	23		•		•		
Luce Line	Winsted - Cedar Mills	25-4D	23			23	23	23	23		•	•	•		
Minnesota Valley	Chaska - Belle Plaine	41-4B	20			20	20	20	20						
Minnesota Valley	Ft. Snelling - Shakopee	42-2A	19	6		19	19		19	5	•	•	•		•
Minnesota Valley	Shakopee - Chaska	41-5A	5	5		5	5		5		•	•			
Root River	Fountain - Houston	94-3A	42	42			42			42	•	•	•		
Sakatah Singing Hills	Mankato - Faribault	55-4D	39	39			39	39	39	6	•	•	•	•	•
Shooting Star	LeRoy - Taopi	92-3D	8	8			8				•	•	•	•	•
Willard Munger	Gateway Segment	29-5B	18	18			18	10		10	•		•	•	

Southern Minnesota has a number of bike trails, many of which are in and around the Twin Cities metropolitan area. You'll also find bike trails at city and state parks, nature reserves and other areas. These trails take bikers through diverse landscapes and natural features.

Mountain Biking

The term "mountain biking" has evolved in a more general sense to simply mean "off-road biking" or riding on dirt trails and other unpaved surfaces. Unlike road bikes, which usually employ a frame and curved handlebars similar to the classic 10-speed bike, mountain bikes sport stouter frames, straight handlebars, and wide, knobby tires for extra traction to navigate through mud and streams, and over rocks, wood and other natural obstacles. Many mountain bikes now also have some form of suspension – front or front and rear – to reduce the shock and strain to a rider's arms and body.

Beyond the designated mountain bike and multi-use state trails included in the accompanying table, mountain biking is permitted on all public and state forest roads unless posted as closed. In addition, many if not most trails designated for winter use as cross-country skiing (p. 153) and snowmobiling (p. 151) are potential mountain biking options, as well as many of the trail systems within the state parks (p. 134), state forests (p. 137), county parks (p. 133), and city parks.

Many cities and towns also have bike paths that can be enjoyed by mountain and road bikers alike, but they may not necessarily be represented within these map pages, due to restrictions of scale. Pedalers desiring more information on these trails are advised to contact the cities/towns or local chambers of commerce directly.

Rules of the Road

Bicycles are defined as vehicles by Minnesota law; therefore, bicyclists must follow the same laws as motorists. The Minnesota Department of Transportation has posted these general guidelines for road biking:

- Bicyclists may ride on all Minnesota roads, except where restricted
- Bicyclists should ride on the road, and must ride in the same direction as traffic
- Motorists must maintain a three-foot clearance when passing a bicyclist
- Bicyclists must obey all traffic-control signs and signals, just as motorists
- Motorists and bicyclists must yield the right-of-way to each other
- Bicyclists should signal their turns and should ride in a predictable manner
- Lights and reflectors are required at night
- Bicyclists should always wear helmets

TRAILS

SNOWMOBILING & OFF-ROADING

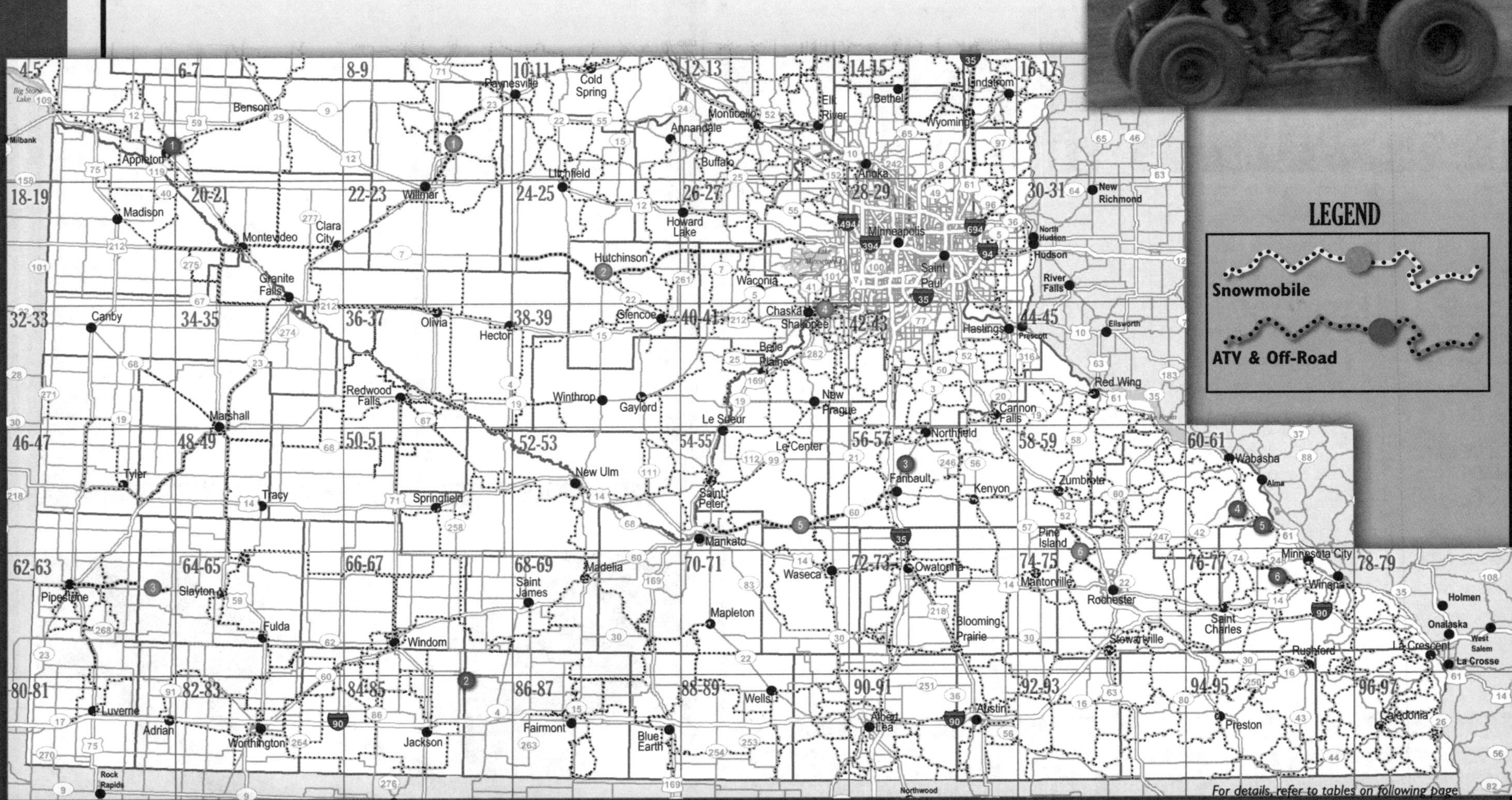

Minnesota has one of the most extensive and developed networks of snowmobile trails in the United States. Some 20,000 miles of trails cross through its forests and fields, passing lakes, rivers and streams, and showcasing the natural diversity of the state. As well, many towns and cities are connected by trails, making it possible for riders to find services and facilities including food, gas, restrooms, and lodging along their travels. With generally reliable snowfall and a riding season that can last four months or longer, Minnesota is a snowmobiler's delight.

In addition to the longer state trails, numerous spur trails and feeder trails maintained by local snowmobile clubs offer many more riding options. The accompanying overview map, displaying the vast trail system across southern Minnesota, should whet the taste of any snowmobile enthusiast. For a more detailed view of trails, see corresponding individual map pages throughout the Atlas.

A Snowmobile State Trail Sticker is required for all snowmobiles operating on state or grant-in-aid trails. The annual trail sticker is valid from Nov. 1 - April 30 and costs $16 ($15 permit fee plus $1 filing fee). A $31 three-year sticker is also available, but can be purchased in conjunction with a registration only. Anyone stopped by enforcement and found operating on a state or grant-in-aid trail without a sticker will be required to purchase a $31 annual sticker. ($30 permit fee plus $1 filing fee.)

State law bans snowmobiles with studs from paved trails. Some state trails have paved surfaces. Wherever possible, parallel trails adjacent to the paved surface have been developed to accommodate snowmobiles with studs and in some cases, all snowmobiles. In many cases, nearby grant-in-aid trails connect the same communities as the state trails. Refer to a snowmobile map of the area for more detailed information or call the DNR Information Center for the most up-to-date information at 888-MINNDNR (888-646-6367).

Adult snowmobile safety certification is for snowmobile operators age 16 and older. Anyone born after Dec. 31, 1976, is required by law to hold snowmobile certification. The course is designed to show students the most common causes for snowmobile accidents in Minnesota, and how to avoid becoming an accident statistic. To obtain the Snowmobile Safety Training CD, or for complete snowmobile safety laws, rules, and regulations, please call (888) 646-6367, (651) 296-6157, or (800) 366-8917, or email at info@dnr.state.mn.us.

ATV and off-highway vehicle (OHV and ORV [off-road vehicle]) enthusiasts also have a variety of trail-riding opportunities in southern Minnesota. Trails include state forest roads and forest trails and abandoned railroad beds. Some trails permit the dual-use of ATVs and OHVs, while others are designated for ATV use only. See the corresponding table for more information and any restrictions.

SNOWMOBILE TRAILS

Number	Name	Counties	Pg / Coord	Miles	Phone
	Major Trails				
3	Casey Jones State Trail	Pipestone	63-4B	13	(507) 831-2900
6	Douglas State Trail	Goodhue/Olmsted	74-3A	12.74	(507) 285-7176
1	Glacial Lakes State Trail	Kandiyohi	9-4D	17.19	(320) 354-4940
2	Luce Line State Trail	Meeker/Hennepin/McLeod/Carver	25-5D	59.26	(952) 826-6750
4	Minnesota Valley State Trail	Carver/Scott	41-5A	25	(612) 492-6400
5	Sakatah Singing Hills State Trail	Blue Earth/Le Sueur/Rice	55-4D	38.83	(507) 359-6067
	Other Trails				
	Beaver Creek Trail	Lyon/Murray/Cottonwood	64-2B	108.03	(507) 763-3746
	Big Island State Park Trails	Freeborn	90-2C	13	(507) 379-3403
	Big Stone Lake Sno-Riders Trail	Traverse/Stevens/Big Stone	4-3C	114.56	(320) 325-5309
	Blue Earth River Trail	Blue Earth/Faribault	70-1D	86.82	(507) 524-4766
	Bluff Valley Trail	Fillmore	94-2C	56.14	(507) 765-2413
	Brown County Trails	Redwood/Brown/Cottonwood	51-6C	98.54	(507) 217-7429
	Buffalo Ridge Trail	Pipestone/Rock	80-3A	58.14	(507) 283-4606
	Cambridge/Weber/Stark/Isanti Trail	Isanti/Chisago	14-3A	33.29	(763) 444-9033
	Camden State Park Trails	Lyon	48-1B	7.67	(507) 865-4530
	Corridor 30 - Quad Link	Winona/Fillmore	77-4C	72.06	(507) 454-2673
	Corridor 60/Ridgeway Trail	Winona	77-6C	52.21	(507) 452-1018
	Corridor 70	Wabasha/Winona	77-4A	41.05	(507) 767-4790
	Cottonwood County Snowmobile Trail	Cottonwood/Watonwan/Jackson	66-2B	133.2	(507) 831-1489
	Cross Country Trail Blazers	Kandiyohi/Chippewa/Renville	21-6C	40.48	(320) 894-3200
	Crow River Snowmobile Trails	McLeod/Carver/Sibley	25-5E	110.93	(507) 359-6067
	Dakota County Trails	Dakota	43-4C	119.34	(651) 772-7937
	Dodge County Trails	Steele/Dodge/Olmsted/Mower	73-6B	69.19	(507) 458-5165
	Driftskippers Trail	Olmsted/Mower	74-3D	40.26	(507) 285-7176
	Faribo-Sno-go Trail	Steele/Rice	56-2C	57.4	(507) 334-3083
	Forestville State Park Trails	Fillmore	93-6C	5.79	(507) 352-5111
	Freeborn County Trails	Steele/Faribault/Freeborn/Mower/Waseca	90-1B	215.73	(507) 256-7596
	Frontenac State Park Trails	Goodhue	45-5E	8.54	(651) 345-3401
	Glacial Lakes Trail	Kandiyohi/Meeker	9-4D	150.25	(320) 235-4650
	Goodhue Bellechester Rail Riders Trail	Goodhue	58-1A	11.53	(651) 764-1554
	Goodhue County Trails	Dakota/Goodhue/Wabasha/Dodge/Rice	58-2A	244.29	(651) 345-2218
	Gopherland Trail	Houston	96-2C	150.67	(507) 725-7669
	Heartland Sno-Goers	Olmsted/Fillmore/Mower	92-3B	69.77	(507) 280-5061
	Hiawatha II Trail	Olmsted/Fillmore	76-2E	17.89	(507) 867-2994
	Hiawatha Sno Blazers Trail	Pipestone/Murray/Rock	62-3B	91.33	(507) 348-4086
	Hiawatha Trail	Wabasha/Olmsted	75-6C	80.67	(507) 867-2994
	Inver Grove Hts Connection Trail	Dakota	43-4A	6.7	(651) 772-7937
	Jackson County Snowdrifters Trail	Cottonwood/Nobles/Jackson	84-2B	265.63	(507) 831-5079
	Kasson-Mantorville Trails	Dodge/Olmsted	74-1B	16.5	(507) 633-2942
	Kilen Woods State Park Trails	Jackson	84-3A	1.38	(507) 662-6258
	Kiwi Krossing	Isanti/Chisago/Anoka	15-4B	63.76	(651) 462-6806
	La Crescent Trail	Winona/Houston	78-2E	55.42	(507) 895-8364
	Lake Louise State Park Trails	Mower	92-3D	10.54	(507) 324-5429
	Lake Shetek State Park Trails	Murray	64-3A	5.28	(507) 763-3256
	Lakeville Sno-Trackers Trail	Dakota/Scott/Rice	42-2C	43.87	(507) 645-0524
	Le Sueur County Snow Trails	Blue Earth/Scott/Le Sueur/Rice	55-4B	112.81	(507) 357-4969
	Lincoln County Drift Clippers Trail	Lincoln/Lyon	46-3A	59.87	(507) 275-3900
	Lonsdale Snowmobile Trail	Rice	56-1A	19.93	(507) 744-2881
	Lyon County Trail	Lyon	48-1A	160.44	(507) 532-3613
	Mabel Trail Busters	Houston/Fillmore	95-4D	47.75	(507) 493-5784
	Meeker County Trails	Stearns/Meeker/McLeod	10-2E	114.22	(320) 693-8773
	Mn River Valley Trails	Brown/Nicollet/Le Sueur	53-5C	77.62	(507) 327-8200
	Money Creek Trail	Houston/Fillmore	96-1A	74.56	(507) 896-3544
	Mower County Mgmt CommitteeTrails	Dodge/Fillmore/Freeborn/Mower	92-2B	172.68	(507) 433-1972
	Mystic Trails	Kanabec/Isanti/Sherburne/Mille Lacs	14-1A	134.44	(763) 389-4397
	Nerstrand-Big Woods State Park Trails	Rice	57-4C	4.24	(507) 334-8848
	Nobles County Snowmobile Trails	Murray/Nobles/Jackson	82-2B	157.51	(507) 372-4034
	North Branch Sno Drifters	Isanti/Chisago	15-4A	40.83	(651) 674-5887
	Northern Lights Trails	Stevens/Pope/Swift	7-4C	72.28	(320) 567-2155
	Northwest Trails	Hennepin	27-5A	88.78	(763) 497-1811
	Orrock Trail, Sand Dunes State Forest	Sherburne	13-4A	0.34	(320) 255-4279
	Prairieland Trail	Martin/Faribault	86-3B	135.19	(507) 238-2190
	Randolph Trail	Dakota/Goodhue/Rice	57-4A	23.4	(651) 772-7937
	Redwood County Trails	Redwood	50-2A	311.85	(507) 828-2265
	Renville County Drift Runners Trail	Kandiyohi/McLeod/Renville/Sibley/ Redwood/Nicollet	37-4B	217.57	(320) 848-2306
	Rice Creek	Anoka/Washington	15-4E	69.63	(763) 783-1694
	Rice Lake State Park Trails	Steele	73-4A	4.71	(507) 455-4870
	Ridge Runners Trail	Big Stone/Swift/Lac Qui Parle/Chippewa	5-6E	161.24	(320) 289-1069
	Riverside Trail	Brown/Blue Earth/Cottonwood/ Watonwan/Martin	68-2C	106.39	(507) 642-8981
	RJD SF-Hay Creek Unit Trail	Goodhue	44-3E	6.16	(651) 345-3216
	RJD SF-Reno Unit Trail	Houston	96-3C	9.19	(507) 285-7176
	RJD SF-Snake Creek Unit Trail	Wabasha	60-2D	7.25	(651) 345-3216
	RJD SF-Trout Valley Unit Trail	Renville/Nicollet	51-6A	1.4	(651) 345-3216
	Rum River Trail	Isanti/Anoka	14-1B	63.83	(651) 772-7937
	Scott County Trails	Carver/Dakota/Sibley/Scott/Le Sueur	41-4C	227.31	(612) 366-4938
	Sherburne County Trails	Benton/Sherburne	13-4B	150.96	(320) 255-4279
	Sibley County Seat Trails	Sibley/Nicollet	39-6D	33.2	(507) 964-5247
	Sibley State Park Trails	Kandiyohi	8-3C	4.97	(320) 354-2055
	Snow Rovers/Stateliners	Blue Earth/Martin/Faribault/Freeborn	88-2B	164.45	(507) 526-3844
	Snow-Drifters Of Montevideo Trails	Swift/Lac Qui Parle/Chippewa/ Yellow Medicine/Lyon	20-3D	202.94	(320) 269-5084
	Southwest Trails	Hennepin/McLeod/Carver	27-4E	100.73	(952) 826-6750
	Star Trail	Washington	29-6C	139.71	(651) 439-8974
	Stearns County Trails	Todd/Douglas/Stearns/Pope/Kandiyohi/Wright/ Meeker/Morrison	10-2C	444.9	(320) 255-4279
	Steele County Trails	Steele/Dodge/Freeborn/Waseca	72-3B	195.27	(507) 446-0587
	Sunrise Snow Eagles	Chisago	16-1A	11.04	(651) 674-4382
	Tiger Bear I Trail	Olmsted	74-2B	27.19	(507) 951-0570
	Tri-County Trail	Olmsted/Fillmore/Mower	93-5B	58.49	(507) 273-8560
	Upper Sioux Agency State Park Trail	Yellow Medicine	35-5A	13.52	(320) 564-4777
	Valley Crest Trail	Houston/Fillmore	94-3A	66.23	(507) 285-7176
	Viking Ridge Riders	Houston	95-6C	43.64	(507) 498-3455
	Waseca County Trails	Blue Earth/Steele/Le Sueur/Waseca	71-5B	101.9	(507) 835-3848
	Waterford Warriors Trail	Dakota/Rice	42-3E	51.1	(507) 645-5224
	Whitewater Trail Blazers	Winona/Olmsted/Fillmore	76-2C	64.08	(507) 796-5231
	Wild River	Chisago/Washington	16-1B	95.99	(651) 257-5305
	William O'Brien State Park Trails	Washington	16-1E	1.08	(651) 433-0500
	Wright County Trails	Wright/Meeker/Hennepin/McLeod/Carver	12-2E	237.54	(763) 787-1617
	Zumbrowatha - Wabasha Trail	Goodhue/Wabasha/Winona/Olmsted	59-5D	273.11	(651) 345-3249

ORV General Operations

Effective Jan. 1, 2006, anyone who operates an ATV and is born after July 1, 1987, must complete the ATV CD Training Course before operating an ATV. Contact the DNR Information Center to receive a copy at (888) 646-6367 or (651) 296-6157.

- All ORV passengers and operators must wear seat belts.
- A person younger than 16 years of age may not operate an ORV.
- A valid driver's license is required to cross roads. The only exception would be for those portions of a designated trail that specifically include a road right-of-way.
- ORVs are required to have lights on while crossing public roads one-half hour after sunset to one-half hour before sunrise and during periods of reduced visibility.
- An ORV environmental and safety training course is available on CD for persons 16 or older. The course covers ORV familiarization, operation procedures, laws, towing procedures, ethics, safety hazards and environmental considerations. Contact the DNR Information Center at (888) 646-6367 or (651) 296-6157 to request a copy of the CD.

OFF-ROAD TRAILS

FACILITIES KEY: F-Food, G-Gas, L-Lodging, R-Restrooms

Number	Name	County	Pg / Coord	Season	Facilities	Miles	Phone	Info
1	Appleton Recreation ORV Park	Swift	5-6D	All Year	R	6	(320) 760-0889	From Appleton, 1 mi E on Hwy 59.
2	Elm Creek	Martin	85-5A	Dec. 22 - Sept. 30	FGR	7	(507) 831-2900	From Trimont W on CR 38, 1 mi to CR 44, 7 mi L on twp Rd and 0.5 mi to trail parking entrance.
4	Richard J. Dorer State Forest: Snake Creek OHV Trails	Wabasha	60-2D	May 1 - Nov. 1	LR	13.5	(507) 285-7176	From Kellogg, 3 mi S on Hwy 61 in the Richard J. Dorer State Forest.
5	Richard J. Dorer State Forest: Trout Valley OHV Trails	Wabasha, Winona	60-3E	May 1 - Nov. 1	R, Water	7.4	(507) 285-7176	From Winona, 15 mi NW on Hwy 61, then 1.7 mi SW on CR 29, within the Richard J. Dorer State Forest.
6	Southeast Minnesota	Winona	77-4B	May 15 - Oct. 31	FGL	12.7	(507) 689-2639	Access off Hwy 14, W side of Stockton at trailer court.
3	Tri County ATV Park	Rice	56-2B	All Year	R	6	(507) 332-8901	From Faribault, 4 mi north on Hwy 3 to Landfill Rd (CR 75) then 0.25 mi east to Cabot Ave, 0.25 mi on right.

SKIING

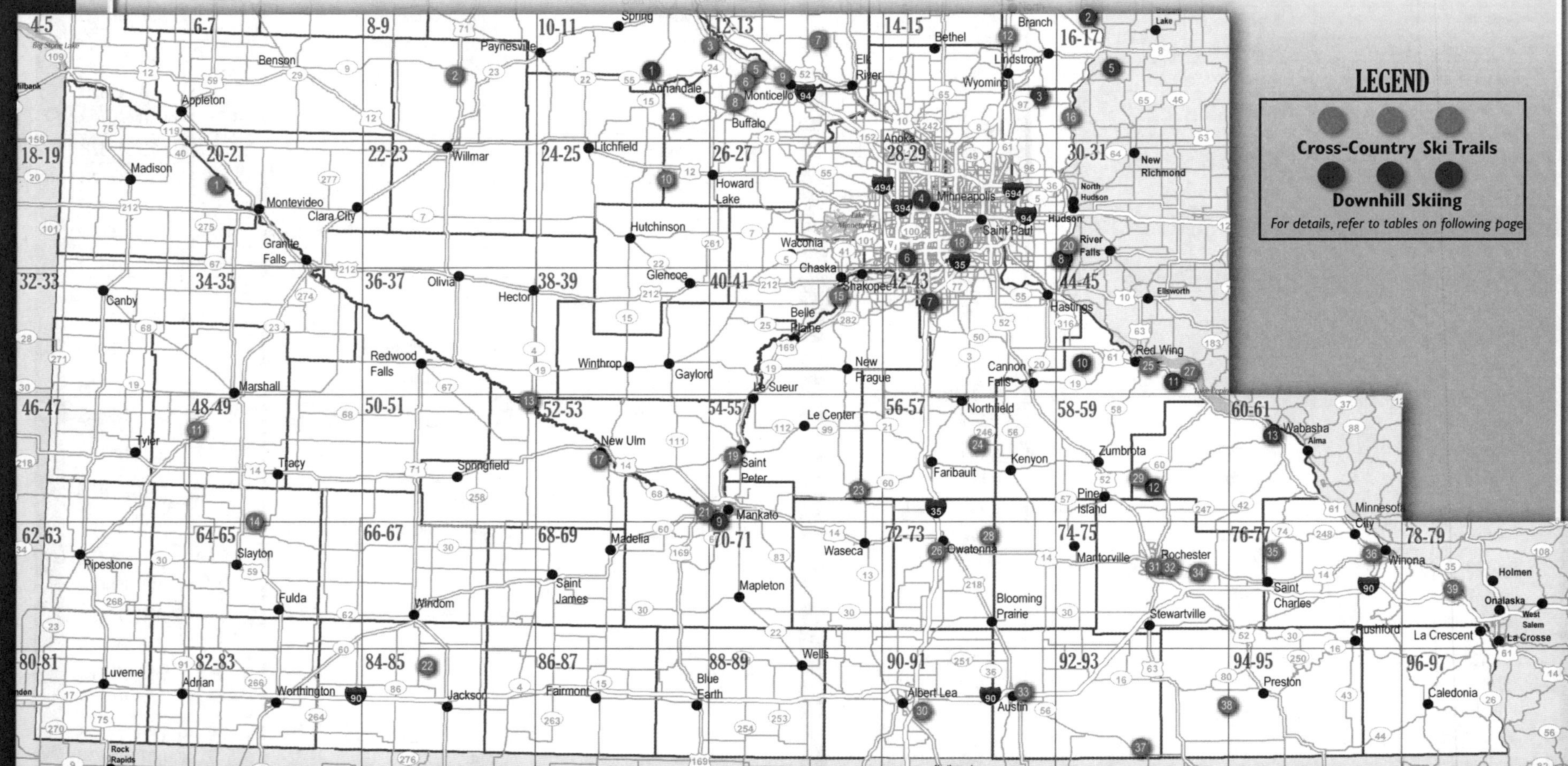

Downhill

Every year, more Minnesotans and visitors to the North Star State are discovering that some very good downhill skiing exists close to home. Although Minnesota will likely never supplant downhill skiing meccas such as Colorado and Utah, it does offer surprisingly challenging and varied downhill skiing. In all, 23 downhill ski areas are found in Minnesota, with several located in the southern region. Southeast Minnesota's bluff country is particularly popular with skiers, offering some of the state's finest downhill runs amid beautifully rugged wooded terrain. In addition to skiing, several operators have runs dedicated or shared by snowboarders and tubers. Most ski hills begin operating in November and may remain open until early April. See the accompanying table for more information on individual slopes.

Cross-country

Spend a day gliding quietly over smooth snow beneath a graceful canopy of conifers and you'll probably be hooked on cross-country skiing for life. Many state parks, state forests, county parks, and downhill ski areas maintain groomed cross-country trails, catering to traditional and skate skiers alike. The metropolitan parks in the twin cities of Minneapolis/St. Paul have many miles of cross-country ski trails as well as lakes that the adventurous can ski on after safe ice has formed.

All cross-country skiers on public ski trails who are age 16 and older must have a Minnesota Ski Pass. The ski pass must be signed and carried when skiing.

DOWNHILL SKI AREAS

Number	Name	County	Nearest Town	Pg / Coord	Runs	Longest (ft)	Vert Drop (ft)	Chair Lifts	Other Lifts	Rentals	Lessons	Lodging	Freestyle	Tubing	Phone	Web
1	Powder Ridge Winter Recreation Area	Stearns	Kimball	11-4C	15	2,500	300	3	3	●	●		●	●	(800) 348-7734	powderridge.com
2	Wild Mountain Ski Area	Chisago	Taylors Falls	16-2A	25	5,280	300	4	3	●	●		●	●	(651) 465-6315	wildmountain.com
3	Echo Backen Snow Tubing	Washington	Forest Lake	15-5D	3	700	50	-	1					●	(651) 433-2422	
4	Theodore Wirth Winter Recreation Area	Hennepin	Golden Valley	28-2C	2	250	65	-	2	●	●		●	●	(763) 522-4584	theodorewirth.org
5	Trollhaugen Ski and Snowboard Area	Chisago	Taylors Falls	16-2C	22	2,500	260	3	7	●	●		●	●	(651) 433-5141	
6	Hyland Ski and Snowboard Area	Hennepin	Bloomington	28-1E	14	2,200	174	3	4	●	●		●		(763) 694-7800	hylandski.com
7	Buck Hill Ski Area	Dakota	Burnsville	42-2B	13	2,500	316	4	7	●	●		●	●	(952) 435-7174	buckhill.com
8	Afton Alps	Washington	Afton	30-1E	45	3,000	350	18	3	●	●		●		(651) 436-5245	aftonalps.com
9	Mount Kato Ski Area	Blue Earth	Skyline	54-1E	19	2,800	240	8	3	●	●		●	●	(507) 625-3363	mountkato.com
10	Welch Village Ski and Snowboard	Goodhue	Red Wing	44-1D	50	4,800	360	8	2	●	●	●	●		(651) 258-4567	welchvillage.com
11	Mount Frontenac Ski and Golf	Goodhue	Lake City	45-4E	11	5,000	420	3	2	●	●		●	●	(651) 388-5826	
12	Steeplechase Ski and Snowboard Area	Wabasha	Mazeppa	58-3D	19	2,000	240	4	1	●	●		●	●	(507) 843-3000	skisteeplechase.com
13	Coffee Mill Ski Area	Wabasha	Wabasha	60-2B	11	4,300	425	2	1	●	●				(651) 565-2777	coffeemillski.com

Cross-Country Skiing Information

Ski Pass Rates
Daily ski pass: $5
One-season ski pass: $15
Three-season ski pass: $40

Electronic Licensing System

Get your daily, one-season and three-season ski passes using Minnesota's electronic licensing system. There are 1,750 locations around the state where you can use ELS. For a list of these, go to the ELS page (www.dnr.state.mn.us) or call the DNR Information Center at (651) 296-6157 or (888) 646-6367.

Minnesota State Parks

A daily pass can be purchased in person at all parks except Carley, George H. Crosby Manitou, Monson, or Schoolcraft state parks.

Self-registration for daily, annual and three-year ski passes are available in parks with ski trails in winter. A mail-in envelope and an application are provided for the purchaser. Payment or credit card information, along with a signature and personal information, are required from the purchaser. The purchaser will retain a receipt until the ski pass arrives in the mail.

DNR License Center

Get daily, one-season and three-season passes on site at the DNR central office License Center, 500 Lafayette Road, St. Paul, MN 55155-4026.

Buy your daily, one-season and three-season ski passes through the DNR online licensing system at www.dnr.state.mn.us

By Phone

Call 1-888-MNLICENse (1-888-665-4236) to buy a daily, one-season or three-season ski pass. It's instant and easy. Have your date of birth, driver's license and credit card (Discover, MasterCard, or Visa) ready when you call. (There is a $3.50 processing fee for this convenience.)

By Mail

Purchase a one-season or three-season ski pass by mail (daily pass not available by mail). Print out a ski pass order form and send it with a check (payable to "MN DNR") or money order to:

MN DNR License Center

500 Lafayette Road, Box 26

St. Paul, MN 55155-4026

The pass should arrive within two weeks.

CROSS-COUNTRY SKI TRAILS

Number	Name	County	Nearest Town	Pg / Coord	Length (km)	Facilities	Skate	Lights	Phone
1	Lac qui Parle State Park	Lac qui Parle	Watson	20-1B	8	●			(320) 734-4450
2	Sibley State Park	Kandiyohi	New London	8-3C	17	●	●		(320) 354-2055
3	Warner Lake Park	Stearns	Clearwater	12-1B	6	●	●		(320) 255-6172
4	Stanley Eddy Park Reserve	Wright	Kingston	11-5E	12		●		(763) 682-7693
5	Harry Larson County Forest	Wright	Becker	12-2C	3				(763) 682-7693
6	Lake Maria State Park	Wright	Becker	12-2C	26	●	●		(763) 878-2325
7	Sand Dunes State Forest	Sherburne	Zimmerman	13-4B	150	●			(763) 878-2325
8	Robert Ney Regional Park	Wright	Maple Lake	12-1D	6				(763) 682-7693
9	Montissippi Park	Wright	Monticello	12-3C	4	●			(763) 682-7693
10	Collinwood Park	Wright	Cokato	25-5B	6	●			(763) 682-7693
11	Camden State Park	Lyon	Lynd	48-1B	10	●	●		(507) 865-4530
12	Falcon Ridge Nordic Trails	Chisago	North Branch	15-4A	230	●	●		(651) 462-5797
13	Fort Ridgley State Park	Nicollet	Fairfax	51-6A	8	●			(507) 426-7840
14	Lake Shetek State Park	Murray	Currie	48-3E	4	●			(507) 763-3256
15	Minnesota Valley State Recreation Area	Scott	Carver	41-5B	5	●			(612) 725-2389
16	William O'Brien State Park	Washington	Marine on Saint Croix	16-1E	19	●	●		(651) 433-0500
17	Flandrau State Park	Brown	New Ulm	52-3C	14	●	●		(507) 233-9800
18	Fort Snelling State Park	Dakota	Mendota Heights	28-3E	19	●	●		(612) 725-2389
19	Glueck Park	Nicollet	Saint Peter	54-1C	5		●		(507) 934-0667
20	Afton State Park	Washington	Afton	30-1E	29	●			(651) 436-5391
21	Minneopa State Park	Blue Earth	North Mankato	53-6E	6	●			(507) 389-5464
22	Kilen Woods State Park	Jackson	Lakefield	84-3A	2	●			(507) 662-6258
23	Sakatah Lake State Park	Le Sueur	Waterville	55-5D	8	●			(507) 362-4438
24	Nerstrand-Big Woods State Park	Rice	Nerstrand	57-4B	13	●	●		(507) 334-8848
25	Mississippi National Ski Trails	Goodhue	Red Wing	44-3D	16	●	●		(651) 388-4724
26	Kaplan's Woods	Steele	Owatonna	72-2B	10		●	●	(507) 444-4321
27	Frontenac State Park	Goodhue	Lake City	45-5E	10	●	●		(651) 345-3401
28	Rice Lake State Park	Steele	Claremont	73-4A	4	●			(507) 455-5871
29	Steeplechase	Wabasha	Mazeppa	58-3D	2	●	●		(507) 843-3000
30	Myre-Big Island State Park	Freeborn	Albert Lea	90-2C	13	●			(507) 379-3403
31	Soldier's Field	Olmsted	Rochester	75-4B	6		●		(507) 281-6160
32	Eastwood Golf Course	Olmsted	Rochester	75-4B	13		●		(507) 281-6160
33	Hormel Nature Center	Mower	Austin	91-5B	15		●		(507) 437-7519
34	Chesterwoods Park	Olmsted	Eyota	75-5C	20		●		(507) 285-7050
35	Whitewater State Park	Winona	Elba	76-2B	13	●			(507) 932-3007
36	Saint Mary's University	Winona	Winona	77-5B	14		●		(507) 452-4430
37	Lake Louise State Park	Mower	Le Roy	92-3D	5	●			(507) 352-5111
38	Forestville / Mystery Cave State Park	Fillmore	Wykoff	93-6C	14	●	●		(507) 352-5111
39	Great River Bluffs State Park	Winona	Dakota	78-2C	15	●	●		(507) 352-5111

SEE INDEX ON PAGE 160 FOR ALPHABETICAL LISTING OF CROSS-COUNTRY SKI TRAILS

GOLF COURSES

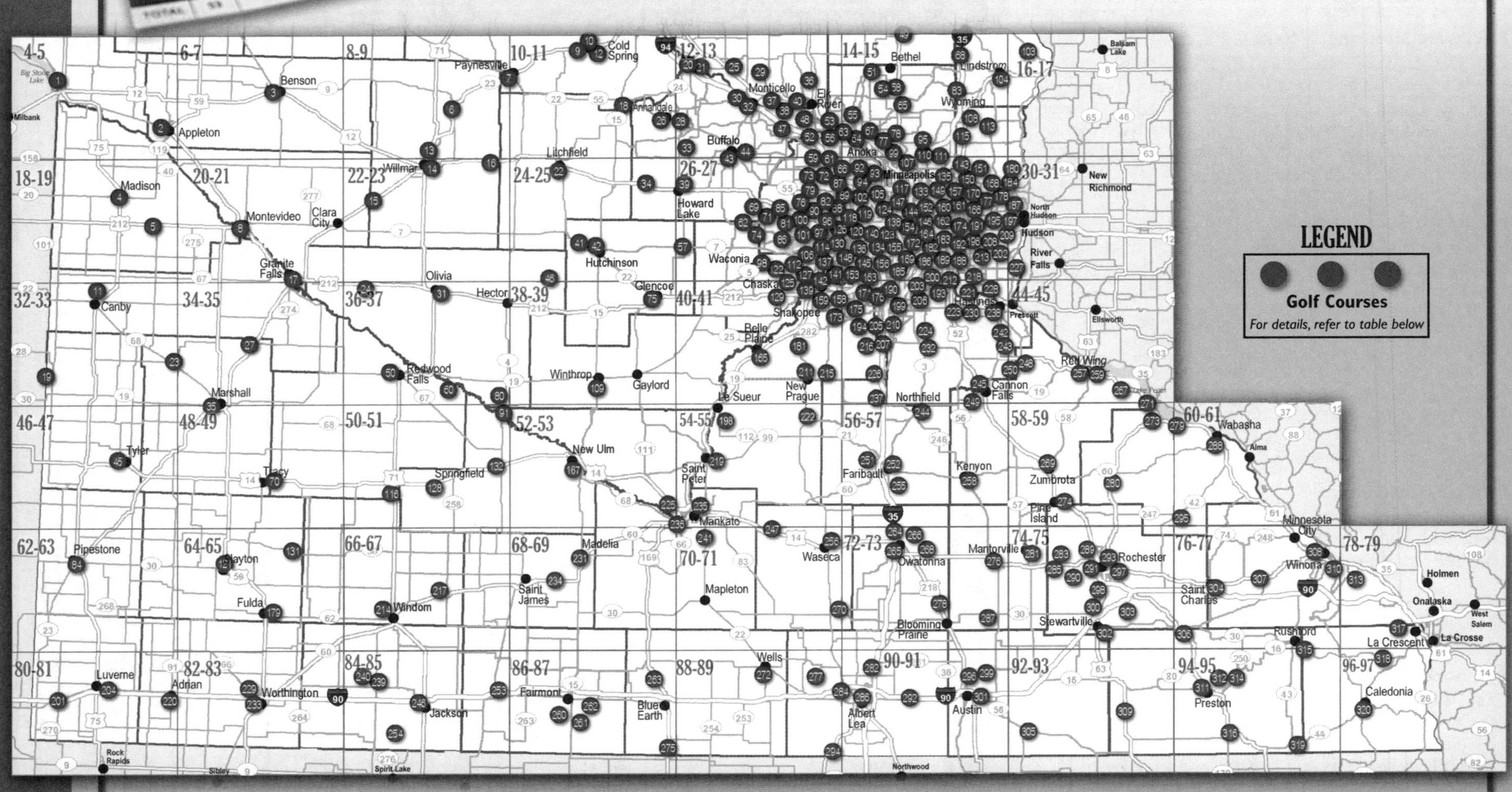

PB	- Public	SP	- Semi-private
PV	- Private	R	- Resort

Though Minnesota is justly known as a land of lakes, it's also a land of links, bunkers, and sand traps. Sporting more golfers per capita than any other state and more than 500 courses statewide, golf enthusiasts will find plenty of places to tee it up. Minnesota is also the only state to have hosted all 13 USGA Championships. From expert-level to 9-hole par-3 courses, golfers are sure to find the perfect fairways and greens to swing and putt their way to contentment.

Number	Name	Nearest Town	Pg/Coord	Holes	Pub/Private	Phone
1	Ortonville Municipal Golf Course	Ortonville	4-2B	18	PB	(320) 839-3606
2	Appleton Golf Club	Appleton	5-6D	9	SP	(320) 289-2511
3	Benson Golf Club	Benson	7-4C	18	PB	(320) 842-7901
4	Madison Country Club	Madison	19-4B	9	SP	(320) 598-7587
5	Dawson Golf Club	Dawson	19-5C	9	SP	(320) 769-2212
6	Little Crow Country Club	Spicer	9-4C	27	SP	(877) 659-5023
7	Koronis Hills Golf Course	Paynesville	9-6B	18	SP	(320) 243-4111
8	The Crossings	Montevideo	20-3C	18	PB	(320) 269-6828
9	Rich Spring Golf Club	Cold Spring	10-3A	18	SP	(320) 685-8810
10	River Oaks Golf Course	Cold Spring	10-3A	18	PB	(320) 685-4138
11	Canby Golf Club	Canby	32-3A	9	SP	(507) 233-5607
12	City View Golf Club	Cold Spring	10-3A	9	PB	(320) 685-7000
13	Eagle Creek Golf Club	Wilmar	8-3E	18	SP	(320) 235-1166
14	Valley Golf Course (Willmar)	Willmar	22-3A	9	PB	(320) 235-6790
15	Hawk Creek Country Club	Raymond	22-2B	9	PB	(320) 967-4653
16	Pine Island Golf Club	Pine Island	23-5A	18	SP	(320) 974-8600
17	Granite Falls Golf Club	Granite Falls	21-4E	9	SP	(320) 564-4755
18	Kimball Golf Club	Kimball	11-4C	18	SP	(320) 398-2285
19	Hendricks Golf Club	Hendricks	32-2D	9	PB	(507) 275-3852
20	Eagle Trace Golfers Club at Clearwater Estates	Clearwater	12-1B	18	SP	(320) 558-4653
21	Travelers Country Club on the Mississippi	Clear Lake	12-1B	9	PV	(320) 743-3133
22	Litchfield Golf Club	Litchfield	24-2A	18	PB	(320) 693-6059

Number	Name	Nearest Town	Pg/Coord	Holes	Pub/Private	Phone
23	Countryside Golf Club	Minneota	33-6D	9	SP	(507) 872-6335
24	Stoney Creek Golf Course	Renville	36-1A	9	PB	(320) 329-8400
25	Pebble Creek Golf Club	Becker	12-2B	27	PB	(763) 263-4653
26	Southbrook Golf Club	Annandale	11-6D	18	PB	(877) 292-9630
27	Cottonwood Country Club	Cottonwood	34-3C	9	SP	(507) 423-6335
28	Whispering Pines Golf Club	Annandale	12-1D	18	PB	(320) 274-8721
29	Carefree Country Club	Big Lake	12-3B	18	PV	(763) 263-6050
30	Silver Springs Golf Course	Monticello	12-3C	36	PB	(763) 295-2951
31	Olivia Golf Course	Olivia	37-4A	9	SP	(320) 523-2313
32	Monticello Country Club	Monticello	12-3C	18	SP	(763) 295-4653
33	Albion Ridges Golf Course	Annandale	12-1E	27	PB	(320) 963-5500
34	Cokato Town and Country Club	Cokato	25-5B	9	SP	(320) 286-2007
35	Marshall Golf Club	Marshall	48-2A	18	SP	(507) 537-1622
36	Elk River Country Club	Elk River	13-5C	18	SP	(763) 441-4111
37	The Vintage Golf Course	Otsego	13-4D	18	PB	(763) 271-5000
38	Riverwood National	Monticello	13-4D	18	PB	(763) 271-5000
39	The Greens at Howard Lake	Howard Lake	26-1B	9	PB	(320) 543-3330
40	Pinewood Golf Course	Elk River	13-5C	9	PB	(763) 441-3451
41	Crow River Country Club	Hutchinson	24-3D	18	SP	(320) 587-2709
42	Meadow Links Golf Course	Hutchinson	24-3D	9	PB	(320) 234-9533
43	Wild Marsh	Buffalo	26-2A	18	PB	(763) 682-4476
44	Buffalo Heights Golf Course	Buffalo	12-2E	9	PB	(763) 682-2854
45	Tyler Community Golf Club	Tyler	47-4C	9	SP	(507) 247-3242
46	Oakdale Country Club	Buffalo Lake	24-2E	18	SP	(888) 462-5325

Golf Courses

Number	Name	Nearest Town	Pg/Coord	Holes	Pub/Private	Phone
47	Cedar Creek Golf Course	Albertville	13-4D	18	PB	(763) 497-8245
48	Stone Bridge Golf Course	Otsego	13-5D	9	PB	(763) 441-0900
49	Sanbrook Golf Course	Isanti	14-3A	18	PB	(763) 444-9904
50	Redwood Falls Golf Club	Redwood Falls	36-2D	18	SP	(507) 627-8901
51	The Ponds Golf Course	St. Francis	14-2B	36	PB	(763) 753-1100
52	Fox Hollow Golf Club	Rogers	13-5E	18	SP	(763) 428-4468
53	The Links at Northfork	Ramsey	13-6D	18	PB	(763) 241-0506
54	Refuge Golf Club	Oak Grove	14-2C	18	PB	(763) 753-8383
55	Rum River Hills Golf Course	Ramsey	14-1D	18	PB	(763) 753-3339
56	Daytona Country Club	Dayton	13-6E	18	PB	(763) 427-6110
57	Shadowbrooke Golf Course	Lester Prairie	26-1D	18	PB	(320) 395-4250
58	Hidden Haven Country Club	Cedar	14-2C	18	PB	(763) 434-6867
59	Pheasant Acres Golf Club	Rogers	27-5A	18	PB	(763) 428-8244
60	Dacotah Ridge Golf Club	Morton	37-4E	18	PB	(507) 644-4653
61	French Lake Open Golf Club	Maple Grove	13-6E	9	PB	(763) 428-4544
62	River's Edge Country Club	Watertown	26-3C	9	PB	(952) 955-2223
63	Hayden Hills Executive Golf	Dayton	14-1E	18	PB	(763) 421-0060
64	Greenhaven Golf Club	Anoka	14-1E	18	PB	(763) 422-8161
65	Viking Meadows Golf Club	Cedar	14-3C	18	PB	(763) 434-4205
66	Sundance Golf Club	Maple Grove	13-6E	18	PB	(763) 420-4700
67	Woodland Creek Golf Club	Andover	14-1D	9	PB	(763) 323-0517
68	Falcon Ridge Golf Course	Stacy	15-4A	18	PB	(651) 462-5797
69	Pioneer Creek Golf Course	Maple Plain	26-3C	18	PB	(952) 955-3982
70	Tracy Country Club	Tracy	49-4D	9	SP	(507) 629-4666
71	Windsong Farms Golf Club	Maple Plain	27-4C	18	PV	(763) 479-3535
72	Rush Creek Golf Club	Maple Grove	27-6A	18	PB	(763) 494-8844
73	Shamrock Golf Club	Corcoran	27-5B	18	PB	(763) 478-9977
74	Timber Creek Golf Course	Watertown	26-3C	18	SP	(952) 955-3600
75	Glencoe Country Club	Glencoe	39-5A	18	SP	(320) 864-3023
76	Baker National Golf Course	Medina	27-5B	18	PB	(763) 694-7670
77	Bunker Hills Golf Club	Coon Rapids	14-2E	27	PB	(763) 755-4141
78	Majestic Oaks Golf Club	Ham Lake	14-2E	18	PB	(763) 755-2142
79	Rolling Green Country Club	Hamel	27-5B	18	PB	(763) 478-6020
80	Mayflower Country Club	Fairfax	37-6E	9	PB	(507) 426-9964
81	Burl Oaks Golf Club	Minnetrista	27-4C	18	PV	(952) 472-1326
82	Elm Creek Golf Course	Plymouth	27-5B	18	PB	(763) 478-6716
83	Greenwood Golf Links, Inc.	Wyoming	15-4C	18	PB	(651) 462-4653
84	Pipestone Country Club	Pipestone	62-3B	9	SP	(507) 825-2592
85	Lakeview Golf Course	Mound	27-4C	18	PB	(952) 472-3459
86	Red Oak Golf Club	Mound	27-4C	9	PB	(952) 472-3999
87	Hollydale Golf Club	Plymouth	27-6B	18	PB	(763) 559-9847
88	Hampton Hills Golf Club	Plymouth	27-6B	18	PB	(763) 559-9800
89	Begin Oaks Golf	Plymouth	27-6B	9	PB	(763) 559-7574
90	Spring Hill Golf Club	Wayzata	27-5C	18	PV	(952) 473-2815
91	Fort Ridgley Golf Course	Fairfax	51-6A	9	PB	(507) 426-7840
92	Brookland Executive Nine Golf Course	Brooklyn Park	28-1A	9	PB	(763) 561-3850
93	Edinburgh USA	Brooklyn Park	28-2A	18	PB	(763) 493-8098
94	Eagle Lake Golf Center	Plymouth	28-1B	9	PB	(763) 694-7695
95	TPC of the Twin Cities	Blaine	14-3E	18	PV	(763) 785-0800
96	Orono Golf Course	Crystal Bay	27-5C	9	PB	(952) 473-9904
97	Woodhill Country Club	Wayzata	27-5C	18	PV	(952) 473-024
98	Island View Golf Club	Waconia	26-3E	18	SP	(952) 442-6116
99	National Youth Golf Center at Victory Links	Blaine	14-3E	18	PB	(763) 717-3240
100	Wayzata Country Club	Wayzata	27-5C	18	PV	(952) 473-7900
101	Lafayette Club	Minnetonka Beach	27-5D	9	PV	(952) 471-8493
102	New Hope Village Golf Course	New Hope	28-1B	9	PB	(763) 531-5178
103	Countryside Golf Course	Schafer	16-1A	9	PB	(651) 257-6387
104	Chisago Lakes Golf Course	Lindstrom	15-6B	18	SP	(651) 257-1484
105	Centerbrook Golf Course	Brooklyn Center	28-2B	9	PB	(763) 561-3239
106	Minnetonka Country Club	Shorewood	27-5D	18	PV	(952) 474-9571
107	The Bridges of Mounds View	Mounds View	28-3A	9	PB	(763) 785-9063
108	Castlewood Golf Course	Forest Lake	15-5D	9	PB	(651) 464-6233
109	Winthrop Golf Club	Winthrop	38-3E	9	SP	(507) 647-5828
110	KateHaven Golf Course	Circle Pines	28-3A	9	PB	(763) 786-2945
111	Chomonix Golf Club	Lino Lakes	15-4E	18	PB	(651) 482-7528
112	Deer Run Golf Club	Victoria	27-4E	18	SP	(952) 443-2351
113	Forest Hills Golf Club	Forest Lake	15-5D	18	PV	(651) 464-3097
114	Meadowwoods Golf Course	Minnetonka	27-6D	9	PB	(952) 470-4000
115	Tanners Brook Golf Club	Forest Lake	15-5D	18	PB	(651) 464-2300
116	Farmers Golf and Health Club	Sanborn	50-2D	9	PB	(507) 648-3629
117	Brightwood Hills Golf Course	New Brighton	28-3B	9	PB	(651) 638-2150
118	Brookview Golf Course	Golden Valley	28-1C	18	PB	(763) 512-2330
119	Golden Valley Country Club	Golden Valley	28-1C	18	PV	(763) 545-2511
120	Minneapolis Golf Club	Minneapolis	28-1C	18	PV	(612) 544-0021
121	Slayton Country Club	Slayton	64-2B	9	SP	(507) 836-8154
122	Chaska Town Course	Chaska	27-4E	18	PB	(952) 443-3748
123	Theodore Wirth Golf Club	Golden Valley	28-2C	18	PB	(763) 522-4584
124	Columbia Golf Club	Minneapolis	28-2B	18	PB	(612) 789-2627
125	Chaska Par 30	Chaska	27-5E	9	PB	(952) 448-7454
126	Oak Ridge Country Club	Hopkins	28-1D	18	PV	(952) 935-7721
127	Hazeltine National Golf Club	Chaska	27-5E	18	PV	(952) 448-4500
128	Springfield Golf Club	Springfield	51-4D	9	SP	(507) 723-5888
129	Dahlgreen Golf Club	Chaska	41-4A	18	SP	(952) 448-7463
130	Glen Lake Golf and Practice Center	Minnetonka	27-6D	9	PB	(952) 934-8644
131	Rolling Hills Golf Club	Westbrook	65-4A	9	PB	(507) 274-5166
132	Sleepy Eye Golf Club	Sleepy Eye	51-6C	9	PB	(507) 794-5249
133	Island Lake Golf Training Center	Shoreview	28-3B	9	PB	(651) 787-0383
134	Meadowbrook Golf Club	Hopkins	28-1D	18	PB	(952) 929-2077
135	North Oaks Golf Club	North Oaks	29-4B	18	PV	(651) 484-1635
136	Interlachen Country Club	Edina	28-1D	18	PV	(952) 924-7444
137	Bent Creek Golf Club	Eden Prairie	27-6E	18	PV	(952) 937-9347
138	Francis A. Gross Golf Course	Minneapolis	28-3C	18	PB	(612) 789-2542
139	Bluff Creek Golf Course	Chaska	27-5E	18	PB	(952) 445-5685
140	The Minikahda Club	Minneapolis	28-2D	18	PV	(612) 924-1666
141	Bearpath Golf and Country Club	Eden Prairie	27-6E	18	PV	(952) 975-5255
142	Halla Greens Chanhassen Executive Golf Course	Chanhassen	27-5E	9	PB	(952) 941-8422
143	Oneka Ridge Golf Course	White Bear Lake	29-5A	18	PB	(651) 429-2390
144	Midland Hills Country Club	St. Paul	28-3C	18	PV	(651) 631-2017
145	Edina Country Club	Edina	28-1D	18	PV	(952) 927-5775
146	University of Minnesota Golf Course	St. Paul	28-3C	18	PB	(621) 627-4000
147	Roseville Cedarholm Golf Course	Roseville	28-3C	9	PB	(651) 415-2166
148	Braemar Golf Course	Edina	28-1E	27	PB	(952) 826-6799
149	Gem Lake Hills Golf Course	White Bear Lake	29-4B	18	PB	(651) 429-8715
150	Dellwood Hills Golf Club	Dellwood	29-5A	18	PV	(651) 426-3218
151	White Bear Yacht Club	Dellwood	29-5A	18	PV	(651) 429-5002
152	Como Golf Club	St. Paul	28-3C	18	PB	(651) 488-9673
153	Olympic Hills Golf Club	Eden Prairie	28-1E	18	PV	(952) 941-6265
154	Town and Country Club	St. Paul	28-3D	18	PV	(651) 659-2549
155	Hiawatha Golf Club	Minneapolis	28-2D	18	PB	(612) 724-7715
156	Braemar Executive Golf Course	Edina	28-2E	9	PB	(612) 915-6606
157	Country View	Maplewood	29-4B	9	PB	(651) 484-9809
158	Stonebrooke Golf Club	Shakopee	41-5A	18	PB	(952) 496-3171
159	Stonebrooke Golf Club: Water's Edge	Shakopee	41-5A	9	PB	(952) 496-3171
160	Keller Golf Club	St. Paul	29-4C	18	PB	(651) 484-3011
161	Manitou Ridge Golf Club	White Bear Lake	29-4B	18	PB	(651) 777-2987
162	Phalen Park Golf Course	St. Paul	29-4C	18	PB	(651) 778-0413
163	Hyland Greens	Bloomington	28-1E	9	PB	(952) 948-8868
164	Highland National Golf Course	St. Paul	28-3D	18	PB	(651) 695-3774
165	Valley View Golf Club	Belle Plaine	40-3D	18	PB	(952) 873-4653
166	Goodrich Golf Club	Maplewood	29-4C	18	PB	(651) 777-7355
167	New Ulm Country Club	New Ulm	52-3C	18	SP	(507) 359-4410
168	Sawmill Golf Club	Stillwater	29-6B	18	SP	(651) 439-7862
169	Highland Nine Golf Course	St. Paul	28-3D	9	PB	(651) 695-3708
170	Oakdale Greens	Oakdale	29-5B	9	PB	(651) 777-4653
171	Minnesota Valley Country Club	Bloomington	42-1A	18	PV	(952) 884-2409
172	Fort Snelling Public Golf Course	Fort Snelling	28-3D	9	PB	(612) 726-6222
173	The Meadows at Mystic Lake	Prior Lake	41-6B	18	SP	(612) 207-3575
174	Hillcrest Golf Club	St. Paul	29-4C	18	PV	(651) 771-1515
175	The Wilds Golf Club	Prior Lake	41-6B	18	PB	(952) 445-3500
176	Dwan Golf Club	Bloomington	42-2A	18	PB	(952) 948-8702
177	Indian Hills Golf Club	Stillwater	29-5B	18	PV	(651) 770-2366
178	Loggers Trail Golf Course	Stillwater	29-6B	18	SP	(651) 439-7862
179	Town and Country Golf Club	Fulda	64-3D	9	PB	(507) 425-3328
180	Oak Glen	Stillwater	29-6B	18	PB	(651) 439-6963
181	Ridges at Sand Creek	Jordan	41-5C	18	PB	(952) 492-2644
182	Somerset Country Club	Mendota Heights	28-3D	18	PV	(651) 457-1224
183	Mendota Heights Par 3	Mendota Heights	28-3D	9	PB	(651) 454-9822
184	Stillwater Country Club	Stillwater	30-1B	18	PV	(651) 439-7979
185	Lost Spur Country Club	Eagan	28-3E	9	PB	(651) 454-5681
186	Mendakota Country Club	Mendota Heights	28-3E	18	PV	(651) 454-4200
187	Applewood Hills Public Golf Course	Stillwater	29-6B	18	PB	(651) 439-7276
188	Thompson Oaks Golf Course	West Saint Paul	29-4D	9	PB	(651) 457-6064
189	Southview Country Club	West Saint Paul	29-4E	18	PV	(651) 451-1169
190	Birnamwood Public Golf Course	Burnsville	42-2A	9	PB	(952) 707-6393
191	Oak Marsh Golf Club	Oakdale	29-5C	18	PB	(651) 730-8886
192	The Ponds at Battle Creek	Maplewood	29-5D	9	PB	(651) 501-6321
193	Carriage Hills Country Club	Eagan	28-3E	18	PB	(651) 452-7211
194	Cleary Lake Park Golf Course	Prior Lake	42-1B	9	PB	(952) 447-2171
195	Tartan Park Golf Course	Lake Elmo	29-6C	27	PV	(651) 733-3480
196	Mulligan Masters Golf Learning Facility	Lake Elmo	29-5C	9	PB	(651) 777-4653
197	Cimarron Golf Course	Lake Elmo	29-6C	9	PB	(651) 436-6188
198	Le Sueur Country Club	Le Sueur	54-2A	18	SP	(507) 665-6292
199	Apple Valley Golf Course	Apple Valley	42-2A	9	PB	(952) 432-4647
200	Inver Wood Golf Club	Inver Grove Heights	29-4E	18	PB	(651) 457-3667
201	Beaver Creek Golf Course	Beaver Creek	80-2B	9	PB	(507) 673-0011
202	Country Air Golf Park	Lake Elmo	29-5C	18	PB	(651) 436-6549
203	Parkview Golf Club	Eagan	42-3A	18	PB	(651) 454-9884
204	Luverne Country Club	Luverne	81-4B	9	SP	(507) 283-4383
205	Brackett's Crossing Country Club	Lakeville	42-2B	18	PV	(952) 435-7700
206	Valleywood Golf Course	Apple Valley	42-3A	18	PB	(952) 953-2323
207	Legends Golf Club	Prior Lake	42-1C	18	PB	(952) 226-4777
208	Eagle Valley Golf Course	Woodbury	29-5D	18	PB	(651) 714-3750
209	Stone Ridge Golf Club	Stillwater	29-6D	18	SP	(651) 436-4653
210	Crystal Lake Golf Club	Lakeville	42-2B	18	PB	(952) 432-6566
211	New Prague Golf Club	New Prague	41-5E	18	PB	(952) 758-5326
212	Arbor Pointe Golf Club	Inver Grove Heights	29-4E	9	PB	(651) 451-9678
213	Prestwick Golf Club	Woodbury	29-5D	18	PB	(651) 731-4779
214	Windom Country Club	Windom	66-2D	9	SP	(507) 831-3489
215	Creeksbend Gold Course	New Prague	41-6D	18	PB	(952) 758-7200
216	Heritage Links Golf Club	Lakeville	42-1C	18	PB	(952) 440-4653
217	Mountain Lake Golf Course	Mountain Lake	67-4C	9	SP	(507) 427-3869
218	All Seasons Golf Course	Cottage Grove	29-5E	9	PB	(651) 459-2135
219	Shoreland Country Club	St. Peter	54-2C	18	SP	(507) 931-3470
220	Adrian Golf Course	Mahtowa	81-6B	9	SP	(507) 483-2722
221	Mississippi Dunes Golf Links	Cottage Grove	43-5A	18	SP	(651) 768-7611
222	Montgomery Golf Course	Montgomery	55-5A	18	SP	(507) 364-5602
223	Rich Valley Golf Club	Rosemount	43-4B	27	PB	(651) 437-4653
224	Southern Hills Golf Club	Farmington	42-3C	18	PB	(651) 463-4653
225	North Links Golf Course	North Mankato	53-6E	18	PB	(507) 947-3355
226	Boulder Pointe Golf Club	Elko	42-2D	18	PB	(952) 461-4900
227	Afton Alps Golf Course	Hastings	30-1E	18	PB	(651) 436-320
228	River Oaks Municipal Golf Course	Cottage Grove	43-5A	18	PB	(612) 438-2121
229	Prairie View Golf Links	Worthington	82-3B	18	PB	(507) 372-8670
230	Emerald Greens Golf Course	Hastings	43-5B	18	PB	(651) 480-8558
231	Madelia Golf Course	Madelia	68-3B	9	PB	(877) 302-1875
232	Fountain Valley Golf Club	Farmington	42-3C	18	SP	(651) 463-2121
233	Worthington Country Club	Worthington	82-3B	18	SP	(507) 376-4281
234	St. James Country Club	St. James	68-2C	18	SP	(507) 375-7484
235	Mankato Golf Club	Mankato	54-1E	18	PV	(507) 387-5636
236	Minneopa Golf Club	Mankato	54-1E	9	PB	(507) 625-5777
237	Willingers Golf Club	Northfield	42-2E	18	PB	(952) 440-7000
238	Hastings Country Club	Hastings	43-6B	18	PV	(651) 437-4612
239	Vallebrook Golf Club	Lakefield	84-2B	9	PB	(507) 662-5755
240	Emerald Valley Country Club	Lakefield	84-2B	9	PB	(507) 662-5755
241	Terrace View Golf Club	Mankato	70-1A	18	PB	(507) 625-7665
242	Hidden Greens Golf Course	Hastings	43-6C	18	PB	(651) 437-3085
243	Bellwood Oaks Golf Course	Hastings	43-6C	18	PB	(651) 437-4141
244	Northfield Golf Course	Northfield	56-3A	18	SP	(507) 645-4026
245	Cannon Golf Club	Cannon Falls	43-5E	18	SP	(507) 263-3126
246	Jackson Golf Club	Jackson	84-3C	9	SP	(507) 847-2660
247	Prairie Ridge Golf Course	Janesville	71-4A	9	PB	(507) 234-5505
248	Gopher Hills Golf Course	Cannon Falls	44-1D	18	PB	(507) 263-2507
249	Summit Golf Club	Cannon Falls	43-5E	18	PB	(507) 263-4648
250	Elmdale Hills Golf Course	Cannon Falls	44-1D	9	PB	(888) 487-6634
251	Faribault Golf and Country Club	Faribault	56-2C	18	SP	(507) 334-3810
252	Legacy Golf	Faribault	56-2C	18	PB	(507) 332-7177
253	Fox Lake Golf Club	Sherburn	85-6B	9	SP	(507) 764-8381
254	Loon Lake Golf Club	Jackson	84-2D	9	PB	(507) 847-4036
255	Straight River Golf Course	Faribault	56-2D	18	PB	(507) 334-5108
256	Waseca Lakeside Club	Waseca	71-6A	18	SP	(507) 835-2574
257	Red Wing Country Club	Red Wing	44-3D	18	SP	(651) 388-9562
258	Kenyon Country Club	Kenyon	57-5C	9	SP	(507) 789-6307
259	Mississippi National Golf Links	Red Wing	44-3D	18	PB	(651) 388-1874
260	Rolling Green Fairways	Fairmont	86-2C	9	PB	(507) 235-9533
261	Interlaken Golf Club	Fairmont	86-2C	18	SP	(507) 235-5145
262	Rose Lake Golf Club	Fairmont	86-3C	18	SP	(507) 235-5274
263	Riverside Town and Country Club	Blue Earth	87-5B	9	SP	(507) 526-2764
264	Brooktree Golf Course	Owatonna	72-3A	18	PB	(507) 444-2467
265	Owatonna Country Club	Owatonna	72-2A	18	PV	(507) 451-1363
266	Havana Hills Golf	Owatonna	72-3A	9	PB	(888) 667-4653
267	Mount Frontenac Golf Course	Frontenac	45-4E	18	PB	(800) 488-5826
268	Hidden Creek Golf Club	Owatonna	72-3A	18	PB	(888) 667-4653
269	Zumbrota Golf Club	Zumbrota	58-2C	9	SP	(507) 732-5817
270	Riverview Golf Course	New Richland	71-6D	9	PB	(507) 465-3516
271	Lake City Country Club	Lake City	59-5A	18	PB	(651) 345-3221
272	Wells Golf Club	Wells	88-3A	9	PB	(507) 553-3313
273	The Jewel Golf Club	Lake City	59-5A	18	SP	(651) 345-5999
274	Pine Island Golf Course	Pine Island	58-2E	18	SP	(320) 974-8600
275	Minn-Iowa Golf Club	Elmore	87-6D	9	PB	(507) 943-3149
276	Dodge Country Club	Dodge Center	73-6B	9	SP	(507) 374-2374
277	Oak View Golf Course	Freeborn	89-5B	9	PB	(507) 863-2288
278	Blooming Prairie Country Club	Blooming Prairie	73-4D	9	SP	(507) 583-2887
279	Lake Pepin Golf Course	Lake City	60-1A	18	SP	(651) 345-5768
280	Zumbro Falls Golf Club	Zumbro Falls	59-4D	9	PB	(507) 753-3131
281	Zumbro Valley Golf Club	Mantorville	74-1B	9	SP	(507) 635-2821
282	Clarks Grove Golf Course	Clarks Grove	90-1A	9	PB	(507) 256-7737
283	Somerby Golf Club	Byron	74-2B	18	PV	(507) 775-6006
284	Albert Lea Country Club	Albert Lea	90-1B	18	PV	(507) 377-1683
285	Links of Byron	Byron	74-2B	9	PB	(507) 775-2004
286	Green Lea Golf Course	Albert Lea	90-1B	18	PB	(507) 373-1061
287	Oaks Golf Club	Hayfield	73-5D	18	SP	(507) 477-3233
288	Coffee Mill Golf and Country Club	Wabasha	60-2B	9	SP	(651) 565-4332
289	Northern Hills Golf Club	Rochester	74-3A	18	PB	(507) 281-6170
290	Meadow Lakes Golf Club	Rochester	74-3B	18	PB	(507) 285-1190
291	Rochester Golf and Country Club	Rochester	74-3B	18	PV	(507) 282-3170
292	Holiday Park Golf Course	Hayward	90-3B	9	PB	(507) 373-3886
293	Soldiers Memorial Field Golf Course	Rochester	75-4B	18	PB	(507) 281-6176
294	Arrowhead Country Club	Emmons	89-6E	9	PB	(507) 297-5767
295	Piper Hills Golf Course	Plainview	60-1E	9	PB	(507) 534-2613
296	Meadow Greens Golf Course	Austin	91-5B	9	PB	(507) 433-4878
297	Eastwood Golf Club	Rochester	75-4B	18	PB	(507) 281-6173
298	Willow Creek Golf Course	Rochester	75-4C	18	PB	(507) 285-0305
299	Ramsey Golf Club	Austin	91-5B	18	PB	(507) 433-9098
300	Oak Summitt Golf Course	Rochester	74-3D	18	PB	(507) 252-1808
301	Austin Country Club	Austin	91-5B	18	PV	(507) 433-7736
302	Riverview Greens	Stewartville	75-4D	18	PB	(507) 533-9393
303	Maple Valley Golf and Country Club	Rochester	75-4D	18	PB	(507) 285-1255
304	St. Charles Golf Course	St. Charles	76-2C	18	SP	(507) 932-5444
305	Cedar River Country Club	Adams	92-1D	18	SP	(507) 582-3595
306	Chosen Valley Golf Club	Chatfield	76-1E	9	SP	(507) 867-4305
307	Lewiston Country Club	Lewiston	76-3C	9	SP	(507) 523-2060
308	Westfield Golf Club	Winona	77-5B	9	PB	(507) 452-6901
309	Root River Country Club	Spring Valley	93-4C	9	PB	(507) 346-2501
310	Winona Country Club	Winona	77-6B	18	PV	(507) 452-3535
311	Preston Golf and Country Club	Preston	94-1B	9	PB	(507) 765-4485
312	River's Bend at the Old Barn Resort	Preston	94-2B	9	PB	(507) 467-2512
313	Cedar Valley Golf Course	Winona	78-1C	27	SP	(507) 457-3241
314	Lanesboro Golf Club	Lanesboro	94-3B	9	SP	(507) 467-3742
315	Ferndale Country Club	Rushford	95-5A	9	SP	(507) 864-7626
316	Harmony Golf Club	Harmony	94-2D	9	SP	(507) 886-5622
317	Pine Creek Golf Course	La Crescent	78-2E	9	PB	(507) 895-2410
318	Valley High Golf Club	Houston	96-2A	18	PB	(507) 894-4444
319	Meadowbrook Country Club	Mabel	95-5D	9	PB	(507) 493-5708
320	Ma-Cal-Grove Country Club	Caledonia	96-1C	9	SP	(507) 724-2733

SEE INDEX ON PAGE 160 FOR ALPHABETICAL LISTING OF GOLF COURSES

SCENIC DRIVES & BYWAYS

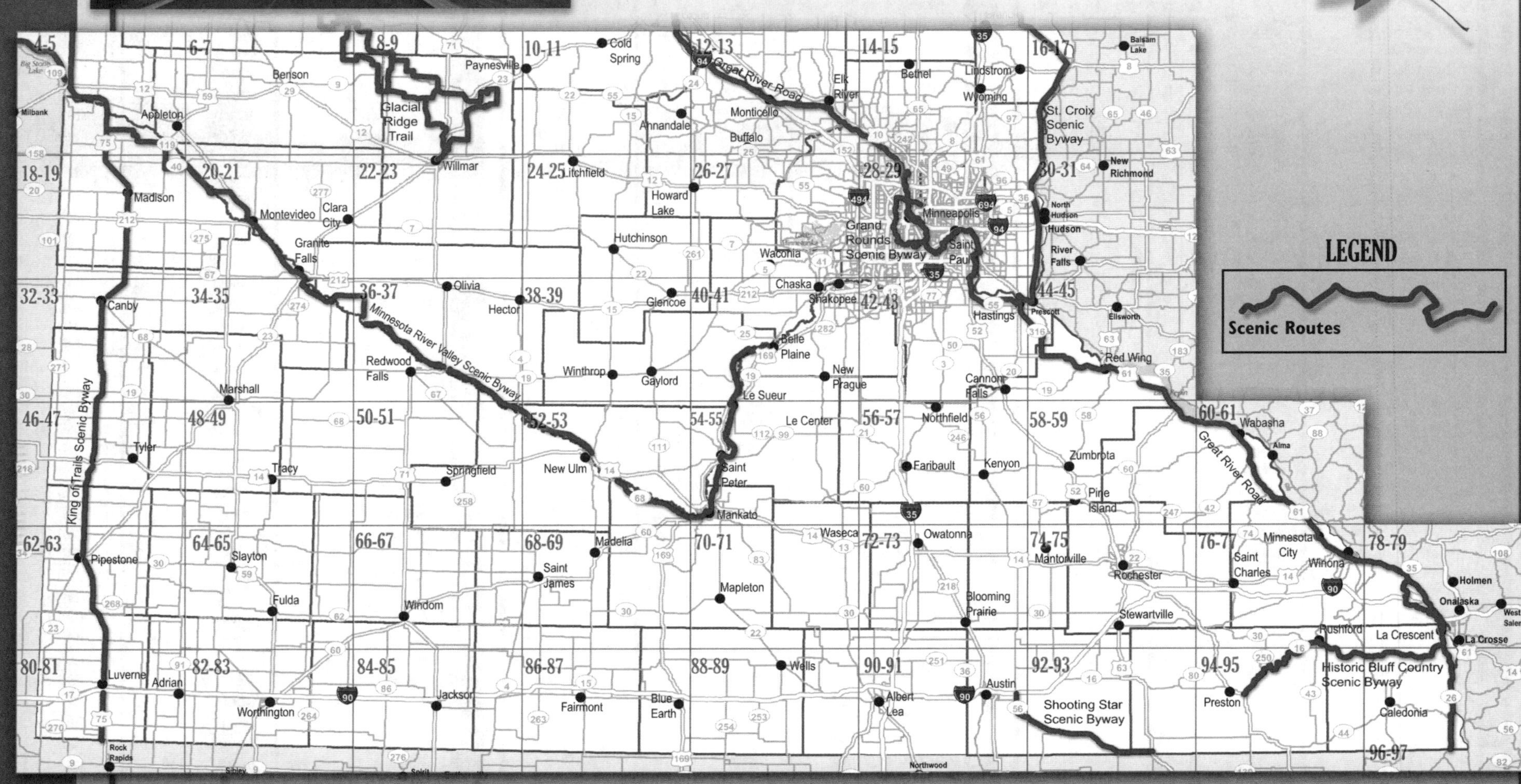

There are 22 designated scenic byways located throughout Minnesota. Together, these drives encompass more than 2,500 miles of back roads winding through forests, farmlands, bluffs, quaint towns and villages, past lakes and rivers, waterfalls, state parks and much more. The beauty and diversity of southern Minnesota is readily apparent when touring the region by automobile. Expect the unexpected in a region where big cities and quiet towns, big rivers and tiny trout streams, and high bluffs and flat prairies, can all be found in a day's drive. Rich in history and culture and long on charm, touring the area's scenic roads makes for an unforgettable day's (or more) outing. See the accompanying table and overview map for more information and the location of each byway.

Name	Pg / Coord	Miles	Route	Attractions	Phone	Web
Apple Blossom Drive	78-2D	19	On county roads from La Crescent north to Highway 61	Mississippi River Valley overlooks/Orchards/Bluffs/Farms	800-926-9480	bluffcountry.com
Glacial Ridge Trail	8-3C	245	Several loops in the countryside between Willmar and Glenwood, with extensions to Alexandria and Sauk Centre	Rolling terrain of lakes, woods, prairie, and farmland	800-845-8747	
Grand Rounds Scenic Byway	28-2C	53	Follows a loop of city and parkway roads in Minneapolis	Chain of lakes/Mississippi River/City skyline	612-370-4969	minneapolisparks.org
Great River Road	44-2D	575	A series of roads following the Mississippi River from Itasca State Park in northwest Minnesota, down through the Twin Cities, and along the state's southeast border	Mississippi River	763-212-2560	mnmississippiriver.com
Historic Bluff Country Scenic Byway	95-5A	88	Highway 16 between La Crescent and Dexter	Bluffs/Root River/Farmland	800-428-2030	bluffcountry.com
King of Trails Scenic Byway	32-3E	414	Highway 75 near the western border of the state, running the entire length of Minnesota	Rural landscapes/Farms/Towns	800-336-6125	highway75.com
Minnesota River Valley Scenic Byway	36-2C	300	A series of roads following the Minnesota River between Browns Valley on the state's western border and Belle Plaine, southwest of Minneapolis	Minnesota River/Farmland/Woods/River towns and cities	888-463-9856	mnrivervalley.com
Shooting Star Scenic Byway	92-2D	31	Highway 56 between I-90 and Highway 63 near the Iowa border, about 10 miles east of Austin	Rural countryside/Prairie grasses and wildflowers	800-428-2030	bluffcountry.com
St. Croix Scenic Byway	30-1A	123	Follows several roads near the St. Croix River east of the Twin Cities and parallels I-35 north of the Twin Cities	St. Croix River/River towns/Forest/Farmlands		stcroixscenicbyway.org

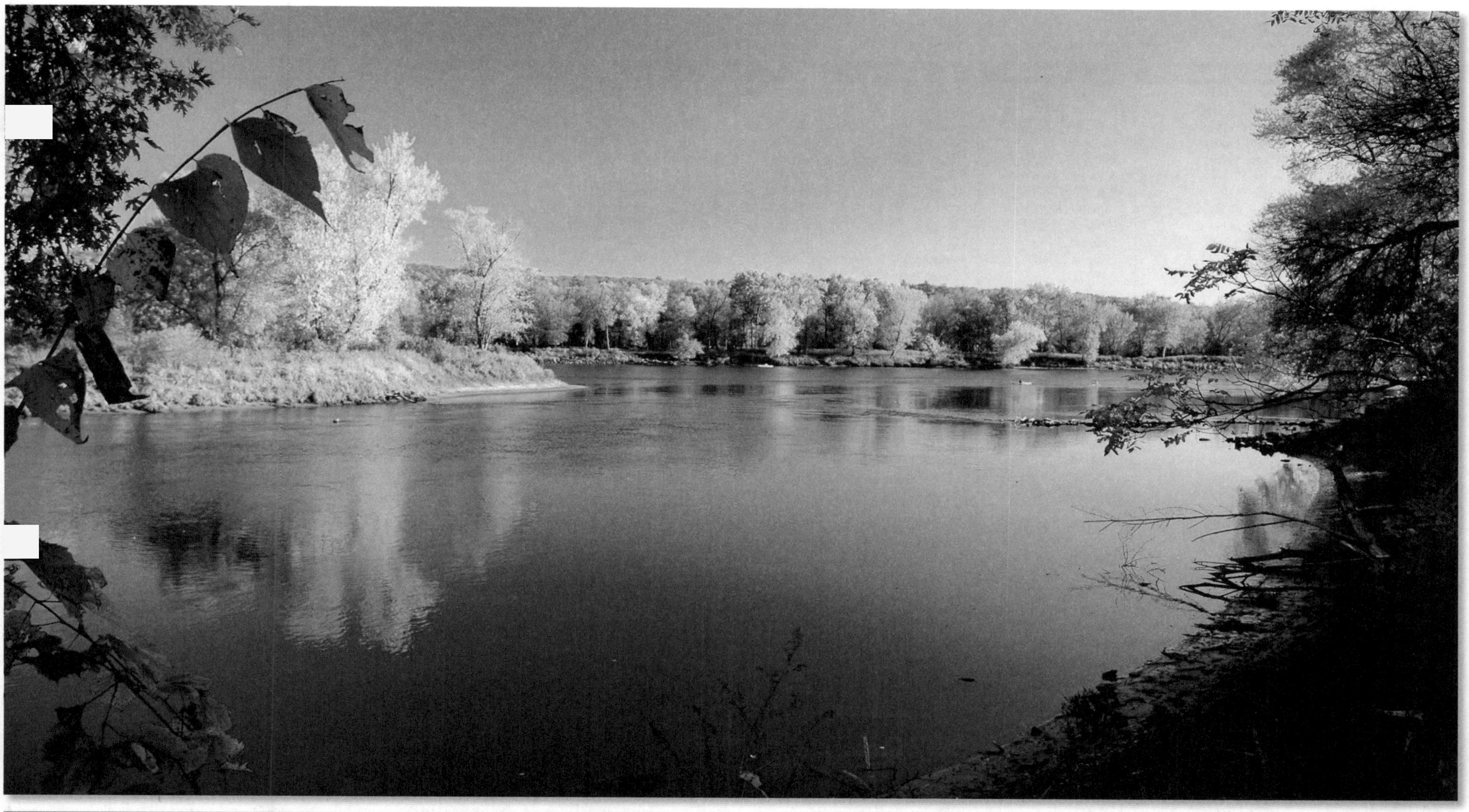

INDEX OF WATERFOWL PRODUCTION AREAS

WPA, pg, coordinates

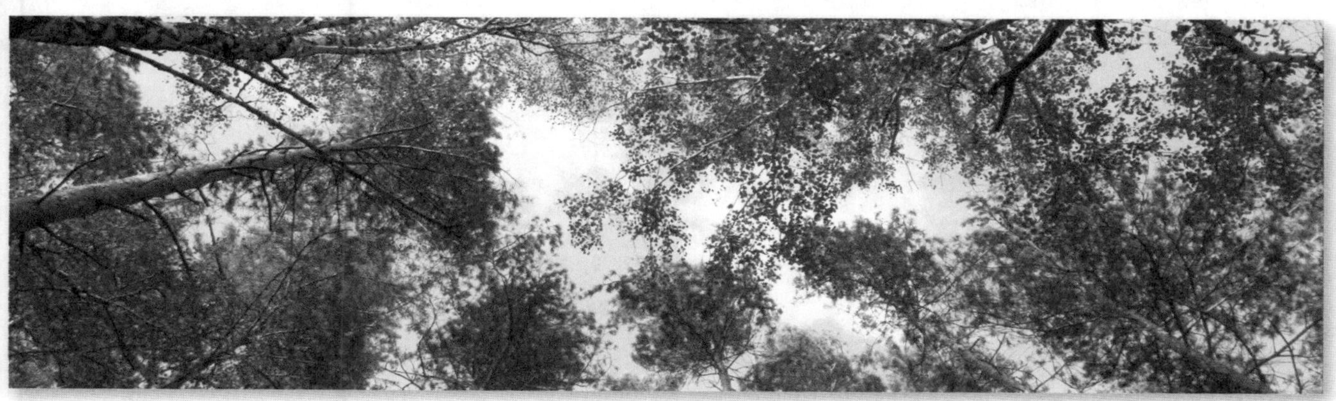

GUIDE TO ALPHABETICAL INDEXES

INDEX OF LAKES

Lakes highlighted in blue are featured in Sportsman's Connection Fishing Map Guide Books www.scmaps.com

Lakes, pg, coordinates

Lakes highlighted in blue are featured in Sportsman's Connection Fishing Map Guide Books **www.scmaps.com**

INDEX OF LAKES

Lakes, pg, coordinates

INDEX OF LAKES

INDEX OF PRIVATE CAMPGROUNDS

INDEX OF CROSS-COUNTRY SKI TRAILS

INDEX OF GOLF COURSES